LIBRARY OF HEBREW BIBLE/
OLD TESTAMENT STUDIES

393

Formerly Journal for the Study of the Old Testament Supplement Series

Editors
Claudia V. Camp, Texas Christian University
Andrew Mein, Westcott House, Cambridge

Founding Editors
David J. A. Clines, Philip R. Davies and David M. Gunn

Editorial Board
Richard J. Coggins, Alan Cooper, John Goldingay,
Robert P. Gordon, Norman K. Gottwald, John Jarick,
Andrew D. H. Mayes, Carol Meyers, Patrick D. Miller

EUROPEAN SEMINAR IN
HISTORICAL METHODOLOGY

5

Editor
Lester L. Grabbe

GOOD KINGS AND BAD KINGS

EDITED BY
LESTER L. GRABBE

t & t clark

Copyright © 2005 T&T Clark International
A Continuum imprint

Published by T&T Clark International
The Tower Building, 11 York Road, London SE1 7NX
15 East 26th Street, Suite 1703, New York, NY 10010

www.tandtclark.com

All rights reserved. No part of this publication may be reproduced or transmitted in any form or by any means, electronic or mechanical, including photocopying, recording or any information storage or retrieval system, without permission in writing from the publishers.

British Library Cataloguing-in-Publication Data
A catalogue record for this book is available from the British Library

Typeset and edited for Continuum by Forthcoming Publications Ltd
www.forthcomingpublications.com

Printed on acid-free paper in Great Britain by Antony Rowe Ltd, Chippenham, Wiltshire

ISBN 0826469760 (hardback)
     0567082725 (paperback)

Contents

Abbreviations   vii
List of Contributors   xi

Part I
Introduction

Lester L. Grabbe
     INTRODUCTION   3

Part II
Articles

Rainer Albertz
     WHY A REFORM LIKE JOSIAH'S MUST HAVE HAPPENED   27

Ehud Ben Zvi
     JOSIAH AND THE PROPHETIC BOOKS: SOME OBSERVATIONS   47

Philip R. Davies
     JOSIAH AND THE LAW BOOK   65

Lester L. Grabbe
     THE KINGDOM OF JUDAH FROM SENNACHERIB'S INVASION
     TO THE FALL OF JERUSALEM: IF WE HAD ONLY THE BIBLE...   78

Christof Hardmeier
     KING JOSIAH IN THE CLIMAX OF THE DEUTERONOMIC HISTORY
     (2 KINGS 22–23) AND THE PRE-DEUTERONOMIC DOCUMENT OF A
     CULT REFORM AT THE PLACE OF RESIDENCE (23.4-15): CRITICISM OF
     SOURCES, RECONSTRUCTION OF LITERARY PRE-STAGES AND THE
     THEOLOGY OF HISTORY IN 2 KINGS 22–23   123

Ernst Axel Knauf
     THE GLORIOUS DAYS OF MANASSEH   164

Nadav Na'aman
     JOSIAH AND THE KINGDOM OF JUDAH   189

Francesca Stavrakopoulou
     THE BLACKBALLING OF MANASSEH   248

Marvin A. Sweeney
KING MANASSEH OF JUDAH AND THE PROBLEM OF THEODICY
IN THE DEUTERONOMISTIC HISTORY   264

Christoph Uehlinger
WAS THERE A CULT REFORM UNDER KING JOSIAH?
THE CASE FOR A WELL-GROUNDED MINIMUM   279

David A. Warburton
THE IMPORTANCE OF THE ARCHAEOLOGY
OF THE SEVENTH CENTURY   317

Part III
Conclusions

Lester L. Grabbe
REFLECTIONS ON THE DISCUSSION   339

Index of References   351
Index of Authors   365

Abbreviations

AASOR	Annual of the American Schools of Oriental Research
AB	Anchor Bible
ABC	A.K. Grayson, *Assyrian and Babylonian Chronicles* (Texts from Cuneiform Sources 5; Locust Valley, NY: J.J. Augustin, 1975)
ABD	David Noel Freedman (ed.), *The Anchor Bible Dictionary* (New York: Doubleday, 1992)
ADPV	Abhandlungen des Deutschen Palästina-Vereins
AfO	*Archiv für Orientforschung*
AGAJU	Arbeiten zur Geschichte des antiken Judentums und des Urchristentums
AHI	Graham I. Davies, *Ancient Hebrew Inscriptions: Corpus and Concordance* (Cambridge University Press, 1991)
AJA	*American Journal of Archaeology*
ALGHJ	Arbeiten zur Literatur und Geschichte des hellenistischen Judentums
AnBib	Analecta biblica
ANET	James B. Pritchard (ed.), *Ancient Near Eastern Texts Relating to the Old Testament* (Princeton, NJ: Princeton University Press, 1950)
ARAB	Daniel David Luckenbill, *Ancient Records of Assyria and Babylonia* (4 vols; 1926–27; repr. London: Histories and Mysteries of Man, 1989)
ASOR	American Schools of Oriental Research
ATANT	Abhandlungen zur Theologie des Alten und Neuen Testaments
ATD	Das Alte Testament Deutsch
ATSAT	Arbeiten zu Text und Sprache im Alten Testament
AUSS	*Andrews University Seminary Studies*
BA	*Biblical Archaeologist*
BAR	*Biblical Archaeology Review*
BASOR	*Bulletin of the American Schools of Oriental Research*
BBB	Bonner biblische Beiträge
BCE	Before the Common Era (= BC)
BeO	*Bibbia e oriente*
BETL	Bibliotheca ephemeridum theologicarum lovaniensium
BEvT	Beiträge zur evangelischen Theologie
BHS	*Biblia hebraica stuttgartensia*
Bib	*Biblica*

BibOr	Biblica et orientalia
BJRL	*Bulletin of the John Rylands University Library of Manchester*
BN	*Biblische Notizen*
BO	*Bibliotheca orientalis*
BWANT	Beiträge zur Wissenschaft vom Alten und Neuen Testament
BZ	*Biblische Zeitschrift*
BZAW	Beihefte zur *ZAW*
CBC	Century Bible Commentary
CBET	Contribution to Biblical Exegesis and Theology
CBQ	*Catholic Biblical Quarterly*
CBQMS	*Catholic Biblical Quarterly*, Monograph Series
ConBOT	Coniectanea biblica, Old Testament
CR:BS	*Currents in Research: Biblical Studies*
CRAIBL	*Comptes rendus de l'Académie des inscriptions et belles-lettres*
CWS	Nahman Avigad and Benjamin Sass, *Corpus of West Semitic Seals* (Jerusalem: Israel Academy of Sciences and Humanities, 1997)
DOTT	D. Winton Thomas (ed.), *Documents from Old Testament Times* (London: Nelson, 1958)
DtrH	Deuteronomistic History
EsIs	*Eretz-Israel*
ESHM	European Seminar in Historical Methodology
ET	English translation
EvT	*Evangelische Theologie*
FAT	Forschungen zum Alten Testament
FOTL	The Forms of the Old Testament Literature
FRLANT	Forschungen zur Religion und Literatur des Alten und Neuen Testaments
FS	Festschrift
GGG	Othmar Keel and Christoph Uehlinger, *Gods, Goddesses, and Images of God in Ancient Israel* (trans. Thomas H. Trapp; Minneapolis: Fortress Press; Edinburgh: T. & T. Clark, 1998); ET of *Göttinnen, Götter und Gottessymbole: Neue Erkenntnisse zur Religionsgeschichte Kanaans und Israels aufgrund bislang unerschlossener ikonographischer Quellen* (Quaestiones Disputatae, 134; Freiburg: Herder, 4th expanded edn, 1998)
GGIG	Othmar Keel and Christoph Uehlinger, *Gods, Goddesses, and Images of God in Ancient Israel* (trans. Th.T. Trapp; Minneapolis: Fortress Press; Edinburgh: T. & T. Clark, 1998 [translation of German 3rd edn])
HAT	Handbuch zum Alten Testament
HdA	Handbuch der Archäologie
HSM	Harvard Semitic Monographs
HSS	Harvard Semitic Studies
HTR	*Harvard Theological Review*

HUCA	Hebrew Union College Annual
ICC	International Critical Commentary
IDB	George Arthur Buttrick (ed.), *The Interpreter's Dictionary of the Bible* (4 vols.; Nashville: Abingdon Press, 1962)
IDBSup	*IDB*, Supplementary Volume
IEJ	Israel Exploration Journal
JANES	Journal of the Ancient Near Eastern Society of Columbia University
JAOS	Journal of the American Oriental Society
JARCE	Journal of the American Research Center in Egypt
JBL	Journal of Biblical Literature
JCS	Journal of Cuneiform Studies
JEA	Journal of Egyptian Archaeology
JNES	Journal of Near Eastern Studies
JNSL	Journal of Northwest Semitic Languages
JPSTC	Jewish Publication Society Torah Commentary
JQR	Jewish Quarterly Review
JSOT	Journal for the Study of the Old Testament
JSOTSup	*Journal for the Study of the Old Testament*, Supplement Series
JSPSup	*Journal for the Study of the Pseudepigrapha*, Supplement Series
JSS	Journal of Semitic Studies
JTS	Journal of Theological Studies
KAI	H. Donner and W. Röllig, *Kanaanäische und aramäische Inschriften* (3 vols.; Wiesbaden: Otto Harrassowitz, 1962–64)
KAT	Kommentar zum Alten Testament
LSTS	Library of Second Temple Studies (formerly JSPSup)
LXX	Septuagint version of the Old Testament
MNDPV	*Mitteilungen Und Nachrichten des deutschen Palästina-Vereins; Palastina-Jahrbuch*
MT	Masoretic text
NEAEHL	Ephraim Stern (ed.), *New Encyclopedia of Archaeological Excavations in the Holy Land* (4 vols.; New York: Simon & Schuster; Jerusalem: Israel Exploration Society, 1992)
NEB	*New English Bible*
NJPS	New Jewish Publication Society translation of the Hebrew Bible
OBO	Orbis biblicus et orientalis
Or	*Orientalia*
OT	Old Testament/Hebrew Bible
OTL	Old Testament Library
OTS	*Oudtestamentische Studiën*
PAPS	Proceedings of the American Philosophical Society
PEQ	*Palestine Exploration Quarterly*
PJb	*Palästina-Jahrbuch*
QD	Quaestiones disputatae
RA	*Revue d'assyriologie et d'archéologie orientale*

RB	*Revue biblique*
RGG[4]	Hans Dieter Betz, Don S. Browning, Bernd Janowski, and Eberhard Jüngel (eds.), *Religion in Geschichte und Gegenwart: Handwörterbuch für Theologie und Religionswissenschaft*, Band 1– (Tübingen: J.C.B. Mohr [Paul Siebeck], 4th rev. edn, 1998–)
SAAS	State Archives of Assyria Studies
SANE	Studies on the Ancient Near East
SBL	Society of Biblical Literature
SBLASP	SBL Abstracts and Seminar Papers
SBLDS	SBL Dissertation Series
SBLMS	SBL Monograph Series
SBLSBS	SBL Sources for Biblical Study
SBLSBL	Studies in Biblical Literature (Society of Biblical Literature)
SBLSCS	SBL Septuagint and Cognate Studies
SBLSymS	SBL Symposium Series
SBLTT	SBL Texts and Translations
SBT	Studies in Biblical Theology
SEL	*Studi epigrafici e linguistici*
SHANE	Studies in the History of the Ancient Near East
SHCANE	Studies in the History and Culture of the Ancient Near East
SJOT	*Scandinavian Journal of the Old Testament*
STW	Suhrkamp Taschenbuch Wissenschaft
SWBA	Social World of Biblical Antiquity
TA	*Tel Aviv*
TRu	*Theologische Rundshau*
TZ	*Theologische Zeitschrift*
UF	*Ugarit-Forschungen*
VWGTh	Veröffentlichungen der Wissenschaftlichen Gesellschaft für Theologie
VT	*Vetus Testamentum*
VTSup	*Vetus Testamentum*, Supplements
WBC	Word Biblical Commentary
WMANT	Wissenschaftliche Monographien zum Alten und Neuen Testament
WSS	Nahman Avigad and Benjamin Sass, *Corpus of West Semitic Stamp Seals* (Jerusalem: Israel Exploration Society, 1997)
ZA	*Zeitschrift für Assyriologie*
ZAH	*Zeitschrift für Althebraistik*
ZAW	*Zeitschrift für die alttestamentliche Wissenschaft*
ZDPV	*Zeitschrift des deutschen Palästina-Vereins*
ZTK	*Zeitschrift für Theologie und Kirche*

List of Contributors

Rainer Albertz is Professor of Old Testament at the Westfälische Wilhelms-Universität in Münster.

Ehud Ben Zvi is Professor of History and Religious Studies at the University of Alberta.

Philip R. Davies is Research Professor of Biblical Studies at the University of Sheffield.

Lester L. Grabbe is Professor of Hebrew Bible and Early Judaism at the University of Hull.

Christof Hardmeier is Professor of Old Testament at the University of Greifswald.

Ernst Axel Knauf is Professor of Hebrew Bible and Biblical Archaeology at the University of Bern.

Nadav Na'aman is Professor of Biblical History in the Department of Jewish History at the University of Tel Aviv.

Francesca Stavrakopoulou is Career Development Fellow in Theology at the University of Oxford.

Marvin A. Sweeney is Professor of Hebrew Bible at the Claremont School of Theology and Professor of Religion at Claremont Graduate University.

Christoph Uehlinger is Professor of the History of Religions at the University of Zürich.

David A. Warburton is Research Fellow at the University of Aarhus.

Part I

INTRODUCTION

INTRODUCTION

Lester L. Grabbe

The seventh meeting of the European Seminar on Methodology in Israel's History met in Berlin, 21 July 2002. It was part of the European Association of Biblical Studies which met in conjunction with the Society of Biblical Literature International Meeting that year. The theme was the history of Judah in the seventh century BCE, with a focus on the Josiah tradition. A number of members and guests had contributed preliminary papers for discussion at the meeting, and others were produced subsequently.

As always, the aim of that meeting and the present volume is to address questions of historical methodology. Contributors were free to come up with their own ideas for papers, and the volume was not pre-planned to give a comprehensive treatment of either the seventh century or the age of Josiah. Nevertheless, the variety of papers has meant that a comprehensive treatment of most of the sources and historical issues is to be found in this volume. The paper by Na'aman looks at the main issues and questions relating to the reign of Josiah specifically. Grabbe's paper surveys the sources and historical issues from about 700 to the fall of Jerusalem in 587/586. The archaeology is surveyed in Warburton and Grabbe, while Uehlinger is especially rich in discussion of the iconographic sources. A number of the papers analyze the biblical traditions. In addition, the first section of this Introduction looks at some other recent studies of the seventh century or particular issues within it.

Some Recent Studies of the Seventh Century and Josiah's Reign

There has been no lack of interest in the reign of Josiah in particular nor even more broadly in the seventh century BCE. One recent example is the lengthy monograph by M. Sweeney (2001) on *King Josiah of Judah: The Lost Messiah of Israel*. Much of this wide-ranging study is literary analysis, devoted to a detailed exegesis of biblical passages, but it also attempts to draw some historical conclusions as well. Sweeney argues that Josiah sought to be anointed king (messiah) of a restored united kingdom of Israel with Jerusalem and the temple at its centre. Josiah's experiment failed with his death at Megiddo; nevertheless, his dream was remembered and left its mark on a variety of books and passages in the Bible, including Zephaniah, Nahum, Jeremiah, First Isaiah, Hosea, Amos, Micah, Habakkuk, and especially the Deuteronomistic History (DtrH). Josiah is presented as the ideal ruler but was unable to prevent the divine punishment brought on by the sins of Manasseh; however, he became the model for a restored Davidic monarchy. Yet his failure meant that some were already abandoning the idea of a restored monarchy even before the time of Zerubbabel, and the final form of DtrH (exilic period) calls the role of the Davidic house into question. Sweeney argues that Jeremiah 2–4 and 30–31 refer to Josiah's reforms, and that earlier editions of Deuteronomy and DtrH prepared the way for both Josiah's reforms and his subsequent image.

Sweeney has presented a particular theory that needs further debate (cf. also his article below [pp. 264-78]), but a number of recent publications have discussed the question of the biblical text and historicity of the period in a more general way, thus relating to the aims of the Seminar. Before actually discussing the subject in the essays that follow, a consideration of some of the positions taken will help to illustrate the difficulties and possibilities of reconstructing the history of this period. Three examples will be given here to show the range of positions on the subject. One could say that they represent the two extremes and the middle.

The first of these positions is found in *A Biblical History of Israel* by I. Provan, V.P. Long and T. Longman III (2003; see the review of Grabbe 2004). The term 'maximalist'—one that takes the biblical text more or less at face value unless it can be disproved—has often been misused. Very few scholars working in history are in fact true maximalists. Nevertheless, the history of Provan/Long/Longman seems to represent a genuine maximalist position. In the 200 pages of text that cover the history of Israel, the period of about 135 years from the fall of Samaria to the fall of Jerusalem (c. 722–586 BCE) receives only about ten pages (pp. 271-81).

Hezekiah is said to have become king in 727 BCE but not as sole ruler, this interpretation serving to salvage the biblical text which has Hezekiah beginning his reign before the fall of Samaria but the invasion of Sennacherib in his 'fourteenth year'.[1] He began his reforms in his 'first year' (2 Chron. 29.3): the question of whether this should be taken literally is deferred (it 'requires some discussion'), though it 'is not inconceivable'. Nevertheless, many of his activities in the former Northern Kingdom—normally associated with Hezekiah's reforms—'are perhaps best located in the years following 705 B.C., even if we allow that he was "from the beginning" a reforming king' (p. 273). Sennacherib sent an army from Lachish to Jerusalem, and the three biblical accounts 'and Sennacherib's own account all agree that Jerusalem ended up being besieged by an Assyrian army'—a statement patently wrong.[2]

---

1. Unfortunately, as so often in this book, the serious problems of interpretation or chronology occasioned by this statement are not dealt with.

2. As discussed in Grabbe 2003—a book not available to Provan, Longman, and Long, but the ideas summarized there are not new—there is no evidence for a siege of Jerusalem in the normal sense of an army investing it and casting up a siege mound around it. Rather, the communication routes to the city were evidently cut. As for 2 Kgs 18.17–19.9 and the episode of the Rabshakeh, the authors do not discuss the historicity of this event. Readers should note, however, that it has been widely questioned, though some have defended it (cf. Grabbe [ed.] 2003: 28-29).

Introduction 5

Manasseh 'appears for much of his reign to have been a loyal Assyrian vassal' (the references to him in the inscriptions of Esarhaddon and Ashurbanipal are cited); nevertheless, it is 'quite conceivable' that he did something to occasion the events described in 2 Chron. 33.11-13 in which he is said to have been taken to Babylon [*sic*]. The background for this is speculated to be the rebellion of Shamash-shuma-ukin's in 652–648 BCE: 'A trip to Babylon during the siege or after the fall of this city (648 BCE) to answer charges would then be quite comprehensible' (p. 275). Manasseh's successor Amon receives one sentence, the narrative quickly moving to Josiah.

It is noted that 'Chronicles has him beginning his reforms even before the finding of the law book...while Kings mentions reforms only afterwards', but the apparent contradiction is immediately eased with the statement, 'The precise connection between discovery and reform therefore remains unclear'. With the death of Ashurbanipal about 630 BCE, the opportunity to expand north existed by Josiah's twelfth year, since the Assyrians had little interest or capability of exercising control. Egypt increasingly became the major power in Syria–Palestine, but for the earlier part of Josiah's reign no 'evidence survives from this period that the Egyptians...exercised direct control over Judah' (p. 276). Only at the end of Josiah's reign, when he moved to confront the Egyptians directly, 'was direct Egyptian "interest" in the Judaean king kindled'. In 609 BCE Necho II marched north, and Josiah opposed him at Megiddo, though the 'circumstances in which this conflict was initiated are not explained in the biblical texts, and we are left to wonder whether Josiah was attempting early in the reign of the new pharaoh...to establish his independence from an increasingly powerful Egypt'.

Jehoahaz who succeeded to the throne was immediately removed by Necho and replaced by Jehoiakim. The latter changed his allegiance to Nebuchadnezzar when the Babylonians conquered the area in 604 BCE, but then rebelled. This brought the Babylonian army to Jerusalem in March 597 BCE when the new king Jehoiachin was deported. For a 'biblical history', however, certain biblical statements are strangely left unaddressed. Jeremiah's prediction that Jehoiakim's body would be cast out of Jerusalem and left unburied (Jer. 22.18-19; 36.30), which evidently did not happen, does not seem to be mentioned. The erroneous chronology of Dan. 1.1 is basically ignored except for a comment in a footnote: 'Where 2 Chr. 36.6-7 and Dan. 1.1-7 fit into such a scenario is not entirely clear... The "siege" of Dan. 1.1 is the same as the one we read about in 2 Kgs. 24.10' (p. 381 n. 112). Based on 2 Chron. 36.6-7 and Dan. 1.1-2, it is suggested that Jehoiakim was deported to Babylonia (p. 381 n. 113)—an event that seems to go contrary to 2 Kings 24.

The fall of Jerusalem in 587/586 is treated in a discussion of the exile and post-exilic period (pp. 278–303). The biblical texts are briefly summarized (and harmonized), and brief reference is made to the archaeological indications of widespread Neo-Babylonian destruction. Uncharacteristically, the authors suggest that the different numbers of deportees in 2 Kings 24 and Jeremiah 52 cannot be reconciled by suggesting that they have different referents; however, the tension is still relieved by suggesting that the numbers in 2 Kings are 'not intended literally'.

In sum, it appears that Provan, Long, and Longman have indeed given us a 'maximalist' history. Their 'biblical history of Israel' brings in archaeology and Near Eastern sources to widen the context for understanding Israel and Judah. Yet this extra-biblical information is not normally allowed to challenge the biblical picture. Discussion often takes the form of resolving tensions, explaining away contradictions between sources, and generally supporting the biblical outline. Yet data—including biblical data—are often ignored when they cause difficulties with the general scenario in the biblical text.

For what might be characterized as a 'medialist' position, we should consider M. Liverani's recent history of Israel in Italian (2003), *Oltre la Bibbia*. Ironically, in contrast with the Provan/Long/Longman 'biblical history', Liverani's has the title of 'beyond the Bible'. An interesting innovation is his division of the book into two parts, 'normal history' and 'invented history'. By 'normal history' is meant history as reconstructed by the historian from all available sources, whereas 'invented history' is the past that the biblical writers/editors created for Israel for theological or ideological reasons. This includes the patriarchs, the conquest, the judges, the united monarchy, the temple of Solomon, and the law. However, this distinction does not seem to affect Liverani's account of the seventh century which uses the biblical text as an major source.

As a noted historian of the ancient Near East, Liverani puts particular emphasis on situating the Judah of the seventh century in the wider history of the Near East. Manasseh was a faithful vassal of the Assyrians and furnished assistance to the Egyptian campaigns of both Esarhaddon and Ashurbanipal (2003: 165). But he also benefited from the *pax Assyriaca* in the middle of the century. Liverani makes no reference to Manasseh's being taken captive to Babylon (so 2 Chron. 33.10-17), which suggests that he regards that account as unhistorical.

The main account of the seventh and early part of the sixth century is found in chs. 8–9 (pp. 183-220). Manasseh's reign was followed by the progressive collapse of Assyrian imperial power from about 640 BCE which gave a measure of freedom to the vassal states, exemplified in new developments in Tyre, the Transjordanian provinces, Judah, and elsewhere. Josiah inherited the long favourable situation under Manasseh—indeed, archaeologically it is difficult to distinguish the activities of the two kings. Particularly interesting is the establishment of outposts into the arid zones to the east and south. There was also expansion to the west and north. Toward the west, Josiah took Lachish and Gezer; more dubious is whether he reached as far as Meṣad Ḥashavyahu. As for expansion to the north, the biblical sources are elusive. The more normal indications from the material culture are as far as Bethel but not throughout the north nor as far as the Mediterranean coast.

Liverani broadly accepts the account of the finding of the law; that is, he does not reject the story as completely a later invention, but he notes the expediency of the discovery of an 'ancient' manuscript that provides authority for a new reform. This 'pretended' discovery corresponds to Deuteronomy 4–28 (perhaps composed by Shaphan, Josiah's scribe? [p. 202]). The fundamental (and new) commandment was the first, the others being routine socio-juridical rules of probable antiquity. The real innovation was one god, one cult, one cult site. Important construction work was done on the (undoubtedly 'ancient') temple. The old pastoral festival of Passover was made into a pilgrimage festival and connected with the exodus from Egypt. But the greatest emphasis was devoted to the non-Yahwistic cult places, both in Jerusalem and throughout Judah. These included cults of Baal and Asherah, the Sun and Moon, and other astral divinities in the Jerusalem temple. This reform reached as far north as Bethel; however, the extension to all Israel—to all the cities of Samaria—was apparently a later rereading of events and supplement to the text.

Archaeological and epigraphical confirmation of the Josiah's reform is not easy to give because it is difficult to date ostraca precisely. The Kuntillet 'Ajrud inscription shows Yahweh associated with his consort Asherah, whereas the ostraca of Tel Arad are strongly Yahwistic. An ostracon of Meṣad Ḥashavyahu is interesting from a legal point of view (cf. Deut. 24.12-17). Finally, an ostracon from an unknown site makes provision for a sum of three shekels of 'silver of Tarshish' for the temple of Yhwh, 'as Josiah [*'šyhw*] the king ordained' [on this ostracon, see below, p. 10].

The biblical account of the death of Josiah in Megiddo in 609 is brief and ambiguous (2 Kgs 23.29 vs. 2 Chron. 35.20-24), though it clearly makes Josiah wanting to oppose Necho militarily. This decision would have been coherent with his ideology: 'Israel' had turned to serving Yhwh according to the covenant, and the exclusive loyalty to Yhwh required opposition to Necho's actions, despite the latter's superior numbers (cf. Deut. 20.1). The tragic result of his actions had immediate negative consequences: the heir to the throne Jehoahaz was deported to Egypt and another son of Josiah, Jehoiakim, was made to reign as Necho's tributary. But shortly afterward Nebuchadnezzar defeated Necho at Carchemish and succeeded to the Babylonian throne. In the space of a few years Judah briefly recovered its independence.

The death of Josiah left unfulfilled his project: the unification of Israel became a dead letter and the rigorous reform was abandoned (except by a few elite, including some in the royal family). This is attested in the writings of Jeremiah who had, before the reform of the king, manifested his explicit support for the principles of the reform. He refers to the new covenant of Josiah in several passages (e.g. Jer. 11.3-8) and is concerned about practical aspects of the reform (such as the destruction of the *tophet* in the Valley of Hinnom). But the reform quickly lost its momentum. Josiah's political project set up a model of unity that was not realized, but his scheme of faithfulness to a covenant with the deity provided a key for reading the tragic events that soon engulfed Judah. In particular the historiographical scheme that the 'Proto-Deuteronomist' elaborated under him furnished the structure for the retroactive reconstruction of the history of Israel that would be affirmed in successive centuries.

After defeating the Egyptians in 609 BCE Nebuchadnezzar led the Neo-Babylonian campaigns to bring all the areas of Syro-Palestine into subjection. He was the new 'scourge of God' (cf. Hab. 1.6-10). In contrast to the Assyrian 'strategy of terror', the Babylonians attempted to emphasize the freedom of the peoples and the cultural use of resources. But beyond this, in actual warfare the Babylonians were as violent as ever, as evidenced by the two most famous sieges (from kingdoms who had profited from this vacuum of power): Judah and Tyre. Thus, when Jehoiakim sought to rebel, Jerusalem was quickly besieged. As this was about to take place, the king died and his son Jehoiachin capitulated.

The local kingdoms exhibited disunity in the face of the Babylonians who exploited old rivalries among the Palestinian populations. The main source of these local conflicts is the collections of 'Oracles against the Nations'. These indeed inveigh against Babylonia (and Assyria) as the source of divine punishment, but the majority are against the other victims (alongside Judah) of the imperial conquest, in particular the cities of Philistia and the Transjordanian states. Ezekiel is notable for its oracles against Tyre (probably because of using the power vacuum of 640–600 BCE to increase its competitiveness to Judah at the level of commerce and the economy) and Egypt.

An internal debate within Jerusalem can be followed (especially within the books of Jeremiah and Ezekiel) which can be grossly characterized as 'pro-Chaldean' and 'anti-Chaldean'. Jeremiah was consulted by Zedekiah but advised against trusting in the efficacy of Egyptian intervention, maintaining that Chaldean intervention was inevitable. He was against any anti-Babylonian grand coalition of Judah, Tyre and Sidon, Moab, and Edom (Jer. 27.1-6). Jeremiah's was not a lone voice. Ezekiel was similar in the major theological principles, though differing on the political fall. The fact that Yhwh had abandoned his temple and city did not authorize trust in the Babylonians or indulging in their idolatry: salvation could come only from Yhwh.

With regard to political events, Liverani follows largely the biblical text, supplemented by archaeology. The latter includes the 'house of bullae' and other residences excavated in the Ophel that show the flourishing of this Jerusalem quarter in its final days. When Zedekiah rebelled, Nebuchadnezzar quickly responded by taking the fortresses in the Shephelah (data being provided by the Lachish ostraca) and setting siege to Jerusalem. Zedekiah tried to escape and was captured, punished, and taken to Babylonia. The city capitulated soon afterward and was systematically destroyed and the population deported. Other towns destroyed were Ramat Raḥel, Lachish and Azekah, Timnah, Beth-Zur, Tell Beit Mirsim and Gezer, Debir and Hebron. Sites in the Judaean Desert and the Arabah escaped, but the destruction of sites in the Negev (in the Beersheba Valley and Kadesh Barnea) are attributed to the Edomites. On the other hand, in the territory of Benjamin there was continuity: Mizpah, Gibeon, Bethel, and the fortress of Khirbet Abu et-Twein. At Megiddo the fortress built by either Josiah or the Egyptians came to be used by the Babylonians, but the city no longer existed.

Gedaliah, who had been prefect of the palace and the senior member of the Shaphan family, was made 'governor' of Judah. He was killed by a group of conspirators who had not been deported because they were in a peripheral area not conquered by the Chaldeans. The remaining population elected to take refuge in Egypt, though Jeremiah counselled against it. Judah remained in total chaos, without upper class and with a population decimated by war, disease, famine, and emigration.

The difference between the Assyrian and Babylonian deportations is that the Assyrians made the conquered area into an Assyrian province, partly by creating a uniform population by the mixing of native population and deportees. On the other hand, the Babylonians seem to abandon the conquered land to a rather degraded socio-political and cultural state, but the deported elite did not lose its identity. The Assyrian deportees lost their identity, but the Babylonian exiles maintained their political–ethnic and religious individualities. The sack of Jerusalem created a demographic and cultural crisis: the archaeology indicates a total collapse. The number of inhabited sites fell two-thirds in the seventh and sixth centuries (from 116 to 41), the average size of sites also fell by about two-thirds (from 4.4 hectares to 1.4), with a sudden collapse of the population by 85–90 per cent. Inhabited sites tended to be without walls or public buildings, production of high-status handicrafts ceased, and the use of writing was rare. Only the central region of Benjamin escaped. With the fall of Jerusalem and other large sites in the Shephelah, a region of impoverished villages was left, with a population of 10,000 to 20,000 persons.

The empty space was occupied in part by neighbours better able to provide a revival. Well documented is the case of the Negev where the Edomites progressively infiltrated: Ḥorvat 'Uza, Tel Masos, and 'Aro'er. The old Philistine city-states expanded into the Shephelah, and the coastal strip was dominated by Phoenician and Greek commerce. We do not have concrete data on the administration of Judah under the Babylonians, but it was possibly attached to Samaria, with the Shephelah under the province of Ashdod, and the Gilead occupied by the Ammonites.

A good example of the 'minimalist' position is found in the German article on 'The Reform of Josiah: Methodological, Historical, and History of Religions Aspects' by H. Niehr (1995). His study formed part of a debate about Josiah's reform with C. Uehlinger (1995; a revised version of Uehlinger's article, in English, is found in this volume [pp. 279-316]). Niehr finds a double problem in 2 Kings 22–23, a problem of context (especially the historical and religious history aspects) and a problem of text (especially relating to the literary critical analysis and to the dating of sources). What will be given is more in the nature of pinpointing problems than finished conclusions. The distinction between primary and secondary sources is important. The Old Testament text is only a secondary source, though the secondary source often serves to organize and systematize the primary. There are no primary sources for Josiah's reign (the evidence once adduced through the Arad 'sanctuary' and the horned altars from Beersheba, is no longer valid). Following E.A. Knauf, the 'minimalist approach' ('everything which is not corroborated by evidence contemporary with the events to be reconstructed is dismissed') commends itself to the historian as a means of avoiding wide-ranging, uncontrolled speculation (as opposed to 'the maximalist approach which implies that everything in the sources that could not be proved wrong has to be accepted as historical'). Naturally, the results of the minimalist approach are modified when new primary evidence becomes available. The two sorts of history of the 'annales school' are both to be considered (the *histoire des événements* and the *histoire de la longue durée*).

The primary evidence shows that the religious history of Judah and Israel does not agree with what is in the Old Testament. We must treat the Josian reform just as one does the Hezekian reform and the 'Assyrian crisis' under Manasseh. The Hezekian reform is a Deuteronomistic fiction. Neither primary nor secondary evidence supports the idea of an 'Assyrian crisis', which means that this particular motive for a Josian reform disappears. The most convincing analysis of 2 Kings 22–23 is that of C. Levin who sees the original narrative only in 2 Kgs 22.1-2; 23.8a, 25a, 25b, 28-30. In view of the two basic views concerning the origin of the DtrH, it is doubtful that one can ascribe the original narrative to Dtr I and a source for the Josianic reform rather than to DtrH from the early exilic period. The problem of sources and dating can only be noted but not resolved.

In the historical context Assyrian domination of Syro-Palestine was replaced by Egyptian after the death of Ashurbanipal (c. 630 BCE). The proposed massive expansion of Josiah's kingdom can no longer be supported (though it is possible that he annexed Bethel). The events around the death of Josiah are matters of speculation, but most likely he was executed for one or more reasons. With regard to internal events, Judah could be called a state only in the second half of the eighth century. The primary evidence of seals and seal impressions shows the increase in officialdom, as the royal administration was put in place and developed. Another area was the creation of a system of state jurisprudence, with the appointment of professional judges who stepped into the local sphere previously the preserve of the elders (e.g. the Meṣad Ḥeshavyahu ostracon). The lists in Joshua indicate the division of the state into administrative districts. Jerusalem became a capital city as shown by its massive expansion. Epigraphic witnesses are found only in towns connected militarily or economically with Jerusalem. The development of the nation state is shown by the lack of city cultic shrines (which are characteristic of city states).

The oldest piece of information on Josiah's actions is 2 Kgs 23.8a, but this bald statement says only that Josiah profaned the altars. One can explain the measures as part of the centralization of administration going on since the late eighth century. What he did was also part of the judicial reform. One cannot say more than that, except that there is no indication of religious motives. That there was no religious reform is shown by our knowledge of the succeeding kings where no evidence for such is found. The prophets also give no indication. Even when Zephaniah and Jeremiah have been scrutinized for any possible hint, they are silent. There is also nothing in the small finds or forms of artistic expression to provide evidence of a reform under Josiah. The fiction of a reform in 2 Kings 22–23 mirrors the situation of the priesthood in the Second Temple period who had no royal support and could not tolerate other sanctuaries, such as the temple at Elephantine. There were also the dangers of Phoenician 'infiltration', which led to an attempt at this time to create a religion distanced from the Canaanites.

Summaries of Contributions

Rainer Albertz ('Why a Reform Like Josiah's Must Have Happened') gives a critique of Philip Davies's paper (see pp. 65-77) and responds to his specific arguments. The first argument concerns the dating of Deuteronomy 12–26 which Davies places in the fifth century BCE. It is incorrect to assert that Judah being called 'Israel' is only a late development. Passages that call Judah 'Israel' also refer to 'Israel and Judah', showing that one cannot distinguish between them traditio-historically. The trauma of the split in the kingdom is still obvious in 1 Kings 12 and Isa. 7.17. The Persian period is not the most likely setting for 'Israel' to be used of Judaeans since Nehemiah does not have this usage but wants to exclude the Northern Kingdom from God's people. The citation of Deut. 23.4 in Neh. 13.1-2 suggests that the latter was composed long after the former. Contrary to Davies the shape of the covenant in Deuteronomy is quite different from that in Ezra–Nehemiah. Deuteronomy 17.14-20 is not very applicable to the Persian period since there was no restoration of the monarchy in the post-exilic period; neither is all authority conferred on the priests, but a constitutional monarchy is envisaged. The second argument relates to the dating of the Deuteronomistic History (DtrH). If the earliest parts of Deuteronomy are dated to the fifth century, the DtrH cannot be earlier than the beginning of the fourth century BCE. Yet the dating of DtrH to the exilic period is indicated by a number of arguments. Recent studies have argued that 2 Kings 22–23 arose in the exilic period (see C. Hardmeier's contribution to this volume, pp. 123-63).

The release of Jehoiachin by Amel-Marduk makes the DtrH post-562; on the other hand, none of the significant Persian-period events is reflected in it nor is there any knowledge of the end of the exile or the fall of Babylon. It most likely preceded Cyrus's conquest of Lydia in 547–546 BCE. Only two passages in the DtrH move beyond this date: Deut. 4.25-32 and 30.1-10. Both are part of a hopeful frame around Deuteronomy and thus a part of a deliberate redaction of DtrH. This means that the account of the Josianic reform was only 50–75 years after the event. Yet that reform does not fit DtrH's ideology since it should have averted the captivity. Thus, DtrH has to invent a horrible apostasy under Manasseh to account for the exile. The third argument concerns the historical evidence. Following H. Niehr (cf. p. 9, above) and N. Na'aman (pp. 189-247, below) Davies argues that there was no time when Judah was free, since the Assyrian hegemony was replaced by the Egyptian without a break. But this is less than certain, being a general reconstruction rather than testimony of a specific source. Isaiah 8.23–9.6 suggests that the Assyrian withdrawal was seen as a great victory. In any case, Egyptian hegemony would not necessarily prevent a cultic, social, and even national reform. There might even have been limited expansion into the northern hill country. There are few sources for Josiah's reform, apart from 2 Kings 22–23. Archaeology really gives nothing decisive. On the other hand, Jeremiah does know of the reform (cf. Jer. 3.22–4.2; 5.4-6; 8.7-8; 31.2-6), in spite of frequent statements to the contrary, and his preaching against syncretism was only against the North (2.4–4.2) but not the Judaeans (4.3–6.30). Ideally, the evidence would have been better, but on balance the arguments for the traditional hypothesis of Josiah's reform seem to outweigh those of Philip Davies.

Ehud Ben Zvi ('Josiah and the Prophetic Books: Some Observations') stresses how remarkable it is that only two prophetic books are associated with Josiah, and he is no central character in any. Other kings—before and after Josiah—play a central role in the prophetic books, but not Josiah. This is especially noticeable in the book Jeremiah which has (a) parallels with 2 Kings, (b) a 'Deuteronomic' flavour, (c) a good deal of narrative that could have included Josiah. Yet where Josiah's name appears it is only in passing. Further he asks how do prophetic books that mention Josiah construct his period? The impression is that the time of Josiah was one of social and cultic sin and refusal to listen to Yhwh. Harmonizers have attempted to resolve this problem in relation to the book of Zephaniah by proposing two phases to Josiah's reign, but they introduce into the book what is not there at all. As for Jeremiah, how would ancient readers have understood it? The overall tone of Jeremiah is negative toward the Judaean kings. Once the text is carefully examined on its own, there is no real reason to think ancient readers would have seen things differently for the reign of Josiah. Only one possible exception to this overwhelmingly negative impression occurs: Jer. 22.13-17, 19. The text includes a typical comparison between the evildoer son and his pious father. At first it looks as if the evil son/king is Shallum, but at v. 18 Jehoiakim seems to be the subject. But who is the 'father'? The 'wicked king' in this passage is said not to do 'justice and righteousness', characteristics associated in the DtrH with David and Solomon. The contrast David/Solomon vs. Jehoiakim fits the theme of Jeremiah (i.e. the fall of Jerualem and the end of the Davidic dynasty) better than Josiah vs. Jehoiakim. In any case, the most one can say is that any praise of Josiah here is muted and not clearly communicated to the reader. If the writer wanted to praise Josiah, surely he would have been more explicit.

What, then, do we make of the fact that the prophetic texts contradict the other texts' claim of a Josianic reform and depict his reign in such negative tones? Texts that contradicted the DtrH, and conveyed divergent images of the past were tolerated. (This has implications for questions of ancient understanding/s of constructions of the past/historicity.) The failure of editors to lionize Josiah or even make him a major figure was probably due to the enormous significance of the fall of Jerusalem—which Josiah's reform had failed to stop. Instead, the Josiah story is chipped away in favour of Hezekiah under whom Jerusalem was delivered. This said, eventually harmonization won over.

Can we learn about the 'historical' Josiah from prophetic books written during or in close temporal proximity to his reign even if they fail to mention his name at all? There is no lack of literature assigned to Josiah's reign by modern scholars, but the criteria used are problematic. The big question continues to be: If the texts were produced at that time and even under that king's patronage, why are they so self-effacing? Except for Nahum and Zephaniah—two books whose writing some scholars date to the Josianic era—the texts assigned to the period are all scholarly reconstructions, with the supposed historical background influencing the reconstruction in many cases. Moreover, Zephaniah is a postmonarchic book and even if one were to accept the highly debatable dating of Nahum to the period, one would not learn much from it about Josianic Judah. The result is that the prophetic books in their present form are not particularly helpful for the purpose of reconstructing Josiah's reign. We must reconstruct his reign on the basis of other sources. Prophetic books, however, tell us much about the variety of images of the Josianic past that existed in ancient Israel.

Philip Davies ('Josiah and the Lawbook') engages with two colleagues in the Seminar, Nadav Na'aman and Rainer Albertz. After an appreciative summary of Na'aman's paper, he asks whether the latter goes far enough in criticism of the biblical text. Even the most critical can easily fall into the trap of a 'rationalistic midrash' of the text rather than treating its data in a fully critical way. If we start from the picture well demonstrated by Na'aman—that Josiah is an idealized figure—we have to ask whether the text is any more reliable about internal events than the external. Why should we accept the picture of a religious reform? One might reply with the question: Why would a writer invent such a story? Yet a reason has already been given for why Josiah was not pictured by the sources as subservient to the Assyrians. Was he righteous because he initiated a reform, or was he pictured as carrying a purge of the cult because that is what 'righteous' kings do? This ideological creation has already been argued for Hezekiah. The key to resolving the question seems to be the law book (which is where interaction with Albertz comes in). It (or its core) needs to be dated, but since there is no hint of it in Jeremiah or Zephaniah or any independent sources, we are forced back on internal criteria. Since almost all accept that parts of Deuteronomy date from different periods, the focus will be on Deuteronomy 12–26. A number of important features can be isolated and questions asked about the social situation presupposed by them: (1) The nature of 'Israel'. There was no Israel in the time of Josiah, only Judah. It is difficult to find a time when both Judah and Samaria were called Israel, though possibly Elephantine letter 30-32 might be an example. (2) 'The nations'. Deuteronomy does not refer to the Canaanites but 'the nations' is used in two senses, as all nations other than Israel and as nations dispossessed from the land. This usage does not fit the age of Josiah, but it fits usage found in Nehemiah. (3) 'The covenant'. Garbini points out that the notion of a covenant of a people with the deity is unusual: normal ancient Near Eastern practice was a covenant between the deity and the king. It is in Nehemiah that a public covenant ceremony with the people is enacted. The Torah as an organ of personal religion (rather than a body of social teaching upheld by the state) belongs to the post-exilic age rather than the time of the monarchy. (4) Role and function of the king. Deuteronomy 17.14-15 refers to a foreign king ruling over Israel, which was not true while Judah had a monarchy but was true in the Persian period. Deuteronomy 17.16-20 abolishes the main roles of the king, which are to provide security and justice. These functions were taken over by the high priest no later than the Ptolemaic period. Deuteronomy 28.36 has the king go into exile. (5) Centralization of the cult. The temple played a prominent role in the Persian period, whereas we don't know its status in the exilic period.

The important point being made is that there is no compelling reason to put Deuteronomy in Josiah's time. We cannot show a Josianic date for Deuteronomy on the basis of its contents, so we do not know that any reform took place. What we cannot show, we do not know. No special claim is being made for the fifth century BCE at this point, though that does seem to fit well for all the features. Deuteronomy fits the context of an immigrant population, based around a temple, in conflict with some of the indigenous population as well as with Samaria, and encouraged to live and exercise their control by means of a written law.

Lester Grabbe ('The Kingdom of Judah from Sennacherib's Invasion to the Fall of Jerusalem: If We Had only the Bible...') uses a format already developed earlier (for an article in a forthcoming volume on the Omride dynasty). The aim is to try to test out the question of the extent to which one can use the biblical text when it is uncontrolled by primary evidence. The various primary sources for the period from 701 to 587/586 BCE are quoted or summarized: archaeological, Assyrian, Babylonian, Egyptian, epigraphic. A brief resumé is given of the reigns of each king, as reconstructed from a consideration of the various sources. The first set of conclusions seeks to indicate the relative state of our knowledge by observing (1) where the biblical text is confirmed, (2) where it is not confirmed by primary evidence but may be correct, (3) where it is demonstrably or likely incorrect, and (4) where there are significant gaps.

Finally, suggestions about general historical methodology are made: (1) The fruitfulness of a multiple-source approach is clear, at least for the seventh century. (2) The biblical text can and should be used in historical reconstruction, but the data must be controlled where possible by primary data. (3) What is or is not likely to be reliable in the biblical text: (a) A comparison of 2 Kings and 2 Chronicles shows that the former is much more likely to be credible where the two texts differ. (b) The book of Jeremiah is shown to have some reliable statements about external events. (c) Other books present a less credible picture: namely, Ezekiel and Daniel. (4) Where the biblical material seems to have some reliable material, some statements are more likely to be usable than others: straightforward descriptions of events or actions where the biblical author is unlikely to have had a particular motive for mentioning them (names, dates, the 'political' actions of kings). Those relating to 'theological' or 'religious' issues, on the other hand, are more likely to be invented or distorted. (5) The compiler of 2 Kings is likely to have had a documentary source of some sort, perhaps a chronicle similar to the *Babylonian Chronicles*. (6) The compiler of Jeremiah probably also had a source, but something more like a diary or 'biography'.

Christof Hardmeier ('King Josiah in the Climax of DtrH [2 Kings 22–23] and the Pre-Dtr Document of a Cult Reform at the Place of Residence [23.4-15*]: Criticism of Sources, Reconstruction of Earlier Texts and the History of Theology of 2 Kings 22–23') notes that his literary study complements C. Uehlinger's archaeology treatment (pp. 279-316, below). The account of Josiah's reforms in 2 Kgs 22.2–23.27 is marked off as a unit by the pre-Dtr frame of 22.1 and 23.28-30. Evaluative notes at 22.2 and 23.25-27 express the aim and function of the narrative. They themselves frame the account of Josiah's work which begins and ends with the same temporal marker at 22.3 and 23.23. This account depicts Josiah's unique example of rule and kingship, his *res gestae*. The framing notes at 22.2 and 23.25 embed the king's uniqueness into the general horizon of DtrH. This uniqueness consists of the changing of his ways which was carried through according to the whole of Moses's Torah. After Moses and Joshua he was the only Israelite ruler who understood and put into practice the Torah, as indicated by the 'formula of perfection' in 2 Kgs 22.2. 2 Kings 22.1-23, 25 is the climax of the whole of the DtrH. In it Josiah is the model of changing his ways. It will lead to Israel changing its ways and Yhwh turning against his people. But since the 'best king in history' did not avert Yhwh's wrath, the exiles who hear the story should seize the opportunity to put the Torah into practice. The whole of the first temple is pictured as a period of Torah oblivion; therefore, the temple is not an inevitable means of salvation. The temple is subject to the Torah; moreover, the only physical continuation from pre-exilic times is the Davidic dynasty, for whom the model is Josiah.

The *res gestae* of Josiah is made up of two reports: 'the discovery report' (2 Kgs 22.3-20) followed by the 'reform report' (23.1-24). Only the first is narrative in the proper sense with a dramatic internal structure. The first part of the 'discovery report' (22.3-10) makes Josiah analogous to the child-king Joash in the time of Athaliah and also emphasizes the remarkable coincidence which let the Torah become known. The second part (22.11-20) emphasizes 'listening', to avert Yhwh's wrath. Using the language of the Deuteronomistic stratum of Jeremiah (JerD), Huldah's oracle (22.16-20) stresses the catastrophe that will fall on the nation for past and present disobedience. Because Josiah listens to the Torah, Yhwh will listen to him. Elaborate structuring of various layers is evident in the passage. Thus, this first narrative (22.3-10) has the function of (1) documenting the ideal obedience of the king and (2) of clarifying his personal fate in the face of the curses leading to immanent catastrophe. Yhwh's personal listening results in the oracle of salvation in v. 20a. Yet Josiah's initiative was not able to avert Yhwh's wrath because the curses operated above the level of the individual and weighed too heavily for even Josiah's exemplary faithfulness to break them. In sum, this first narrative (22.3-20) is a Dtr exilic construct and not based on the events of 622 BCE. There is no historical primary document in 22.3-20. The 'reform report' (23.1-24) has a clear structure, with framing material in 23.1-3 (covenant renewal) and 23.21-23 + 24b (Passover celebrations). There are no documentary pre-stages to these Dtr-shaped measures of Passover and covenant renewal and no evidence of historically reliable memory. 2 Kings 23.4-20 + 24a is diachronically more complex, suggesting a primary source at its base. 2 Kings 23.16-20 + 24a depends on vv. 4-15 and thus seems to be a Dtr reshaping of the latter. The tensions within the text show that 23.4-15 is a Dtr reshaping of an old catalogue of reform measures. The 'minor' cult reform of the old catalogue has been transformed into a 'major' reform that removes Jeroboam's and Manasseh's sins once and for all. The changes include the following:

The plain enumeration style of the original catalogue was assimilated to a narrative style. The documentary pre-stage spoke only of dismissing the כמרים of the Assyrian cults, whereas the Dtr editing changes the interest to high places and their priests countrywide. The exilic criticism of the cult in Jeremiah 44 has been extended back to Josiah by the editorial reshaping. On the other hand, Hilkiah and his fellow priests are exempted from the verdict of 23.5, 8. The tendency of geographical extension can be seen in the move from Jerusalem to the towns of Judah to the former northern kingdom of Israel. The abolished cultic installations are ascribed to early kings of Israel and Judah: Solomon, Jeroboam I, and Manasseh. Specific measures associated with Manasseh are part of this reshaping. The geography of Jerusalem is explained to an exilic audience. The closeness of 2 Kgs 23.4-15 to Jeremiah 44 leads to the conclusion that JerD tradents bore the DtrH tradition. Jeremiah 2–6 provides a large-scale model of forgetting Yhwh—confronted by an ideal covenant relationship and an exhortation to return—that shaped 2 Kgs 23.4-15.

The original catalogue of measures, constituting a minor cult reform, had a threefold structure: (1) 23.4-5: all cults of foreign gods and their staff and instruments, in the Jerusalem surroundings; (2) 23.6-12: the central cults of Asherah and Baal and of astral gods, with the immobile installations in Jerusalem removed or profaned and the mobile cult symbols burnt; (3) 23.13-15: immobile cult installations outside Jerusalem. A homogeneous terminology and style are used and an intimate knowledge of Jerusalem topography demonstrated. This catalogue was thus pre-587. With the exception of the altar at Bethel the geographical horizon is limited to Jerusalem. There is hardly any doubt that an annalistic document forms the pre-stage of the Dtr account in 2 Kgs 23.4-15. The measures catalogued in this literary source coincide with the results gleaned from archaeology and religious history. These include opposition to the Assyrian astral cult established in the royal residence in Jerusalem; Canaanite installations strongly criticized as Baalism since Elijah and Hosea (Asherahs, stone pillars, cult prostitutes, the Tophet cult). All measures were limited to the king's residence (and temple) in Jerusalem except for the destruction of the altar and Asherah in Bethel. Against the scepticism of the 'minimal approach' it has been possible to construct a primary source even from the traditional literature of the Hebrew Bible.

Axel Knauf ('The Glorious Days of Manasseh') points out that historical study requires us to pay attention both (a) to what actually happened and (b) how the memory of what happened is preserved. The data have to be taken from wherever they can be found, but we should distinguish between 'facteme' (the minimum information that is true or false in the real world) and 'factoid' (information created in the mental process of formulating and transmitting the narrative, which may be wrong in time and space). The macrohistorical structure of the seventh century is a remake of the tenth. The ordinary people of Judah were actually better off, but they would have perceived a great inequality of wealth. In a non-money economy the formula for finding the amount of inequality (q) is found by dividing the largest settlement type by the smallest, or the greatest amount of wealth by the least. In the tenth century BCE the inequality factor was $q = f(10)$, but in the seventh it was $q = f(100)$. This was not caused by decadence or moral corruption but by the simple fact of population growth.

Manasseh was a loyal vassal, contributing not only tribute but also corvée labour and even troops to the Assyrians. Because of the rivalry between the Egypt and Assyria in the period 701–670 BCE, the Assyrians would have integrated Judah into the Assyrian economy, which was the key to its survival. The Siloam tunnel is best explained as a project of prestige under Manasseh, a royal park project never brought to full completion. Similarly, Knauf would see the seventh century revival at Ramat Raḥel as a royal park, an example of 'conspicuous consumption' (rather than as a residence for an Assyrian official). Increased trade and the production of olives and cattle made up for the loss of the Shephelah. If a good king is one who brings peace, security, and prosperity to his people, Manasseh was one of the best. Some biblical literature probably derives from Manasseh's age. Deuteronomy 32.8-9 in its original form pre-dates Josiah's reform. Certainly, in Manasseh's day 'sons of El' would have been interpreted as 'sons of Ashur' or at least as sons of Sin of Harran who was regarded as 'lord of the west'. The first version of Isaiah 6–8 contained pro-Assyrian prophecies (with reference to the events of 734 BCE) which were probably interpreted by the government of Manasseh as supporting his policies, but these seem to have been edited by the Manasseh opponents to turn them into their opposite. Psalm 48 (Appendix II) could also have be written—or at least lent itself to a pro-Assyrian interpretation—in Manasseh's day.

This leads to a historical evaluation of the picture of Manasseh in the Bible. The one undoubtedly true statement is that Manasseh succeeded Hezekiah as king. A number of other statements are probably true (names of his father and mother, age at accession, length of reign, his burial, his son who succeeded him). Some of the statements about religious practice under his rule are not completely untrue (though given a distorted interpretation). Whether he sacrificed a son, restored high places destroyed by Hezekiah, or built altars for 'Baal' cannot be evaluated. Ideological nonsense are statements that he did not keep the Torah of Moses (it didn't exist) or that Jerusalem was destroyed in 586 because of his sins. 2 Chronicles 33.1-20 is mostly a rewriting of 2 Kings 21, the Chronicler acting as a historical interpreter (a king who reigned 55 years cannot have been all bad) by 'reconstructing' a deportation to Babylon and repentance on the part of Manasseh. But he may have had additional data in one area: Manasseh's building activities in the Kidron Valley. It is thus completely impossible to write a biography of Manasseh, but it is becoming increasingly possible to write a history of Judah in the days of Manasseh.

Appendix III examines the question of cult centralization, which surprisingly began under Manasseh (under Assyrian influence). The altars of Arad were not violently destroyed in a religious purge but in the early years of Manasseh (end of stratum IX) were dismantled and reverently buried to make way for building a commercial district. The centralization in Jerusalem and the Assyrian practice of having only one temple for Ashur seems to have let to the abandonment of some local sanctuaries. Yet this was only partial because Deuteronomy 12 was likely to have been interpreted as a law of cultic legitimacy, not cultic centralization, as evidenced by a variety of Jewish temples into the fourth century.

In a long article that is almost a monograph ('The Kingdom of Judah under Josiah') *Nadav Na'aman* attempts to present a review of Josiah's kingdom and contemporary history by making use of new historical data, especially from archaeology (religious and cultic issues are mainly omitted). As a platform on which to set out a number of the issues, the first part of the article examines Alt's theory that the town lists of Joshua (15.21-62; 18.21-28; 19.2-8, 40-46) actually belong to Josiah's kingdom. Na'aman asks several questions, the main ones being whether the lists reflect the administrative system of the kingdom of Judah and to what period they should be dated. The key seems to be Jerusalem. Its status cannot be reconciled with the idea that the lists show the Judahite administrative districts. The lists were probably based on an administrative document that listed settlements only by major geographical–administrative territories, a division initiated shortly after the emergence of the kingdom of Judah (but also attested in Jeremiah). As for the dating, the details of the lists do not fit the situation of the tenth or ninth: the choice is between the late eighth and late seventh centuries. When a number of factors are considered about the content of the lists (including the correspondence between the town lists and the settlements of the eighth and seventh centuries, the topographical names in inscriptions, and the finds of rosette seal impressions), the eighth century is ruled out but the time of Josiah fits.

The limited borders of Judah in the seventh century, as shown by these town lists and archaeology, are important for evaluating the widespread idea of Josiah as a strong and independent ruler. It is often believed that Josiah operated in a virtual power vacuum because of the collapse of the Assyrian empire after 640. Part of the argument for such a collapse is the supposed Scythian invasion mentioned by Herodotus, but his invasion has little support in the archaeological record or contemporary inscriptions. The real crisis in the Assyrian empire did not begin until after the death of Ashurbanipal (631 BCE) and the Babylonian revolt of 626 which reached a peak in 623, just before Josiah's reform began in 622 (the statement of 2 Chron. 34.3-7 that the reform began in Josiah's twelfth year is based on creative theology, not historical data). Neither the Egyptian nor the classical sources show a rivalry between Egypt and Assyria after Egypt gained independence under Psammetichus I; rather all the evidence available shows them as allies. Egypt became the successor state to Assyria, moving in by agreement as Assyria withdrew, in return for providing military support to Assyria against Babylon. Nevertheless, with all its preoccupations Egypt was probably not very concerned with Judah, and Josiah seems to have had considerable freedom of action which he exploited.

Contrary to historical reality, 2 Kings gives the impression that Hezekiah threw off the Assyrian yoke and that no foreign rulers oppressed Judah until Egypt took control in the time of Jehoahaz after Josiah's death—a Deuteronomistically invented picture to fit its model of the righteous king. Some have suggested that Josiah sought to restore a greater kingdom of David by expanding his territory to include Transjordan and even Galilee; most think he occupied at least as far as the Samarian hill country and the northern Shephelah as far Meṣad Ḥashavyahu on the coast. For the support of an expanded territory under Josiah, archaeology does suggest he moved as far north as Bethel. How much further he extended into Samaria is difficult to say, but any movements too far north or east would have met opposition from the Egyptians who now controlled this territory. The Egyptians were not primarily interested in the hill country, which would have given Josiah some limited scope for expansion and perhaps aroused a new nationalist consciousness that encouraged him to begin his religious reforms. But other evidence adduced for expansion is questionable. The fortress at Meṣad Ḥashavyahu was probably not Judahite but Egyptian, though it included some Judahite vassal soldiers. The 'Kittim' in the Arad ostraca were probably Greek mercenaries in the pay of Egypt or Babylonia, not Judah (also at Kadesh-barnea). The rise of Ekron in the early seventh century was also a barrier to the west.

As for Josiah's death, scholars have depended on 2 Chron. 35.20-24 to assume a pitched battle between Josiah and Necho II. Yet it is unlikely that Necho marched his army overland to support the Assyrians at Carchemish; they would have gone by sea. The account in 2 Kgs 23.28-30 does not suggest a battle but is oddly reticent about how Josiah met his death. Egypt was still very much in control of this area, and it would have been madness for Josiah to attack his overlord. On the other hand, it was normal for the new Egyptian ruler to require an oath from his vassals. It is more likely that Necho II sailed to Megiddo (rather than marched) and received the regional vassals. For whatever reason, Josiah had displeased him, and he had him executed. Yet even if Josiah had survived, he would have been constrained by the political realities of the time; any nationalistic hopes of major expansion and independence were unlikely to have succeeded. His kingdom was weaker than that of Judah in the eighth century. There was no 'conspiracy of silence': Josiah's political impact was probably not that great.

Francesca Stavrakopoulou ('The Blackballing of Manasseh'), building on a recently published study (Stavrakopoulou 2004), begins by pointing out that Manasseh's vilification is a theological means of accounting for the fall of Judah. That is, he is a scapegoat serving to distance Judah from direct responsibility for the exile. This blackballing of Manasseh is constructed on two ideological premises: (1) cultic mispractice as characteristic of foreigners and bringing on divine punishment; (2) the appraisal of the Northern Kingdom as theologically negative. Manasseh is seen as tolerating or even promoting foreign cultic practices and also as following the northern kings: he becomes 'Judah's Ahab', indeed is even worse than Ahab. He is even compared with Jeroboam son of Nebat, the only Judaean king with whom such a comparison is made. However, the common view that Manasseh serves as a negative foil to Josiah is unpersuasive. A more convincing reason for his vilification may be that he bears a northern name. Surprisingly, Manasseh's is mentioned only in Kings and Chronicles, except for one reference in Jer. 15.4. This last is curious because it goes against the rest of Jeremiah by blaming Manasseh for the exile instead of the nation as a whole.

The lack of reference to Manasseh elsewhere might be due to censorship, but some passages referring to a (different) person named Manasseh may be coloured by polemical undertones against King Manasseh. The occasional placing of Ephraim before Manasseh in the tribal lists (in spite of archaeological indications that the Manasseh region was dominant) might be an example. More blatant is the change of the name Moses in Judg. 18.30 to Manasseh, associating a Levitical priest of a pagan cult with the king who supposedly introduced pagan cults. There are also remarkable parallels in Josephus' story of Manasseh, the son of the Jerusalem high priest, who is pictured as marrying a daughter of Sanballat governor of Samaria just before the coming of Alexander. Manasseh has continued to be vilified in modern times. Following the biblical ideological bias, many commentators continue to blame him for promoting 'foreign elements' in the Jerusalem cult. Some have gone further and accused Manasseh of cult crimes beyond those listed in the Bible or even assumes a personal and intentional villainy on his part.

Marvin Sweeney ('King Manasseh of Judah and the Problem of Theodicy in the Deuteronomistic History') notes that a crucial debate is taking place with regard to the interpretation of the Old Testament historical narratives. There has been a modern preoccupation with history, and a preference for the DtrH over the more theological writings of Chronicles and Ezra–Nehemiah. Yet the theological nature of DtrH has also been recognized, which has led a group of revisionist scholars to propose that it is all but impossible to reconstruct history on the basis of the biblical narratives. They have opened an old—and necessary—methodological debate about the relationship of history and literature. In order to re-examine the question, the focus will be on the figure of King Manasseh. First, the DtrH account of Manasseh in 2 Kgs 21.1-18: he is presented as the worst king in the Davidic line, and is directly compared with Ahab. The narrative is remarkable because (1) it applies the standards of judgment for the fall of the Northern Kingdom to the impending destruction of Judah and Jerusalem, and (2) it holds Manasseh singularly responsible for the destruction of the nation. As it stands, the DtrH narrative does not prepare the reader for the destruction of the kingdom. Some Judaean kings did wrong, but the emphasis is on God's faithfulness to the house of David. For the destruction of the Northern Kingdom, it is the sins of the entire nation, not just of one or even a few men, that bring it down. So ascribing Jerusalem's fall solely to Manasseh creates great tensions in the narrative.

The Chronicler's account (2 Chron. 33.1-20) has some striking differences from DtrH. The sins are the same, except for the shedding of innocent blood, but then Manasseh is taken captive to Babylon and subsequently repents of his evil. Manasseh's repentance has long been interpreted as a theological creation of the Chronicler to explain Manasseh's length of reign. But this story helps to make sense of the historical data. Shamash-shuma-ukin's revolt of 652–648 BCE necessitated Ashurbanipal's intervention. Hezekiah had attempted to revolt against Assyria by allying himself with Merodach-baladan. Ashurbanipal may have wondered about Manasseh's loyalty and called him to Babylon to account. The expansion of Judaean settlements into various areas of the Negev might have aroused suspicion, if they were not done with Assyrian connivance or approval. As a result of appearing before Ashurbanipal, Manasseh may have won greater freedom of action. The story is still stamped with the Chronicler's theological concerns. It also leads to Josiah's being presented as partly responsible for his own death and the subsequent fate of the nation.

The tension involved in DtrH's having Yhwh renege on his promises to David is often overlooked. The release of Jehoiachin by Evil-merodach would be read, not as hope for the restoration of the Davidic monarchy, but as evidence that it would not be restored (just as David took Mephibosheth to his table without suggesting the restoration of the Saulide dynasty). Thus, the issue of divine culpability must be taken seriously—it lies at the centre of DtrH's presentation of Israelite and Judaean history. So how does the reader respond to the DtrH presentation? Perhaps it was designed to raise questions rather than provide answers. Exilic and post-exilic Judah would have had to face such questions. Wolff's understanding of the DtrH agenda as a call for repentance would fit with this interpretation. If it points to a reality in which Yhwh failed, it may be an early example of theodicy literature. In conclusion, the point to be stressed is the role that both historical and theological considerations must play in the reading of the historical literature of the Hebrew Bible. Both the narratives in DtrH and Chronicles appear to have their basis in history but both also display a theological perspective. We cannot go back to the days in which we uncritically and naively read biblical literature as a witness to history precisely as it is presented in the narrative, but neither can we naively and uncritically dismiss it as historical literature simply because it presents history according to its own theological and historiographical viewpoint.

Christoph Uehlinger ('Was There a Cult Reform under Josiah? The Case for a Well-Grounded Minimum') argues that historical reconstruction must depend fundamentally on primary sources; we cannot allow our picture to be dominated by secondary sources such as the Bible: the 'sub-Deuteronomism' that M. Weippert warns about. In this Uehlinger is a 'minimalist', though there is more than one way to practise minimalism. The historian of Israel and Judah's religion should focus on F. Braudel's *histoire conjoncturelle* or social time. Granted, there are at present no direct primary sources for Josiah's reform, but that is not justification for simply dismissing it. It is important not to be too narrow: a complete picture of the religious world in the Iron IIC period from the primary sources is needed. Two pieces of primary evidence once thought to support Josiah's reform are no longer valid as evidence: the Tell es-Seba' II horned altars and the removal of a holy place and burial of altars between Arad VIII and VI. On the other hand, the fact that the shrine of Arad was not rebuilt together with the fortress in stratum VII requires an explanation. Uehlinger takes it as one aspect of an on-going process, contributing as much as being subject to Jerusalem's growing centrality. Glyptic imagery and epigraphy can provide additional context and background information. The astral imagery of the late eighth and seventh centuries has disappeared from seals and seal impressions of the Jerusalem elite by the early sixth. Also, the blessing and salvation functions of Yhwh's 'Asherah', known from several inscriptions, have been absorbed by Yhwh by the time of the Lachish and Arad ostraca. Similarly, Yhwh seems to have taken over functions of the sungod and the underworld, as indicated by amulets from Ketef Hinnom in Jerusalem.

As for 2 Kings 22–23, two sorts of measures are mentioned—cult centralization and cult purification—but most scholarly attention has gone toward the former. Measures for cult purification are more plausible than programmatic centralization. The 'reform notes' of 23.4-20 have been thought to be relatively independent of 2 Kings 22 which recounts the discovery of the law book. They make no reference to the finding of the law book and do not use Deuteronomistic language (except for a few passages which are probably late additions). Are there measures in the 'reform notes' that are probable in Josiah's time? At least two measures seem to be against cult practices and institutions that began with the Assyrian expansion and are tied to the Assyro-Aramaic astral cults of the late eighth and early seventh centuries: the removal of the horses and chariots of the sun(god) and the $k^e m\bar{a}r\hat{\imath}m$. The sungod became the chief deity of divination in the Sargonid period; only under Sennacherib were these rituals carried out before a chariot. The Jerusalem temple was the residence of the sungod (Ezek. 8.16), though it is not clear whether the initiative for this came from the Judaean or the Assyrian side. But they would have lost meaning by the time of Josiah and would have been removed as a new orientation of the cult (not as an anti-Assyrian measure). The $k^e m\bar{a}r\hat{\imath}m$ were not just those priests outside Jerusalem but a specific class of priests functioning exclusively for astral deities. They are present in Jerusalem (not outside it) because of Aramaic influence. The altars on the roof (23.12, with pre-Deuteronomic information) are poorly attested in the primary sources, representing neither Assyrian nor Aramaic practice, but their removal would go along with the other two measures of cult removal. All three measures would most plausibly have the 'axial age' of the seventh century for their background. Whether they all fell at the same time cannot be stated, but they form a coherent group: all three eliminate practices that had lost significance in the changed political orientation after the withdrawal of the Assyrians, and all three are concentrated on Jerusalem and do not affect cults outside the capital. There was no real programme of reform but a more limited removal of obsolete rituals from the Jerusalem state cult.

The correlation of primary and secondary sources is notoriously difficult. Nevertheless, our picture of the religion is incomplete if we use exclusively the archaeological primary sources. No serious historian can renounce the secondary sources when the primary are inadequate. For example, if we put forward a hypothesis that the horses and chariots of the sun were removed by Josiah, what is the probability of confirming this through primary sources? We know relatively little about the past and should take the trouble to interpret adequately that little. On the other hand, historical reconstruction should only be based on secondary sources whose plausibility has been established by the primary sources. An example of the correlation of primary and secondary evidence is the removal of the Asherah in 2 Kgs 23.6. The seal owners of the early sixth century seem to give no value to Asherah symbols. Asherah has disappeared from the traditional greeting formulae. Neither primary nor secondary sources indicate the further existence of an Asherah in the Jerusalem temple after Josiah.

David Warburton ('The Importance of the Archaeology of the Seventh Century') draws a contrast between the actual archaeological material and the discussions of that material by the archaeologists. At various points the archaeology can be interpreted in a different fashion than has generally been done. A look at some of the key sites shows that there is no evidence of construction at Ramat Raḥel before the eighth century; the main fortification and water work construction is after the demise of Samaria; evidence for ninth-century construction is lacking at Tell en-Nasbeh and at Lachish. Archaeologists have admitted apparently slow pottery change in Iron Age Judah, making isolating pottery assemblages difficult, yet considerable change is known elsewhere (e.g. Philistia). The absence of imports before the seventh century makes the dating more speculative. Thus, the timeframe for pottery assemblages has been based on the assumption of a Jewish state in the ninth century, that is, on the Bible rather than the archaeology. The royal stamped jar handles previously assigned to different eras are now all dated to the late eighth century. Archaeological evidence would allow dating of Lachish IV and V to the eighth century; there is nothing to show that Lachish was certainly fortified before the fall of the Northern Kingdom. The four-room house at Tell en-Nasbeh post-dates the wall that was abandoned in Neo-Babylonian times, while the seal impressions are parallel with Ramat Raḥel. The palace and fortifications of Ramat Raḥel were built after the fall of Samaria, its earliest level not being much before the destruction of Samaria. There is no compelling earlier date for Arad. There is almost no trace of royal construction in Judah before the conquest of Israel.

The archaeology therefore indicates that Judah was not urban or politically organized before the eighth century. It looks as if the Northern Kingdom, for which there is archaeological evidence for the ninth and eighth centuries, was then replaced by the Southern Kingdom in the late eighth and seventh. The seventh century was not the 'high point' of the Kingdom of Judah but its entire history. It was brought to an end in the Neo-Babylonian period, and the archaeology again indicates a hiatus of occupation until the Achaemenid period. The land may not have been empty in the sixth century, but it was not organized as a state, and there is no evidence of an elite nor any significant construction. It is interesting that the archaeology, the Near Eastern sources, and the biblical text come together for the late eighth and seventh centuries (and also the sixth) but not before. We are left with the picture of a Northern Kingdom which began in the Iron Age and looks very much like its neighbours: worshipping a plethora of gods, a language more like those to the north, the presence of pig bones. When it was destroyed, Judah was created as an insignificant entity by Assyria on the inhospitable margin of the major Philistine cities which dominated the region in the seventh century. But the Kingdom of Judah adopted the Northern Kingdom as its ancestor to secure a historical background. Memory of the Assyrians was fresh, but not of the Northern Kingdom. This is why the seventh century marks a break with the past, and the biblical account prior to the late eighth century does not match the archaeology.

BIBLIOGRAPHY

Grabbe, Lester L.
    2004   Review of I. Provan, V.P. Long and T. Longman, *A Biblical History of Israel*, *Review of Biblical Literature* (08/2004); available to subscribers at <http://www.bookreviews.org> (including information on becoming a subscriber).

Grabbe, Lester L. (ed.)
    2003   *'Like a Bird in a Cage': The Invasion of Sennacherib in 701 BCE* (JSOTSup, 363; ESHM, 4; London and New York: Sheffield Academic Press).

Gross, Walter (ed.)
    1995   *Jeremia und die 'deuteronomistische Bewegung'* (BBB, 98; Beltz: Athenäum).

Liverani, Mario
    2003   *Oltre la Bibbia: Storia antica di Israele* (Storia e Società; Roma: Editori Laterza).

Niehr, Herbert
    1995   'Die Reform des Joschija: Methodische, historische und religionsgeschichtliche Aspekte', in Gross (ed.) 1995: 33-55.

Provan, Iain, V. Philips Long and Tremper Longman III
    2003   *A Biblical History of Israel* (Louisville, KY/London: Westminster/John Knox Press).

Stavrakopoulou, Francesca
    2004   *King Manasseh and Child Sacrifice: Biblical Distortions of Historical Realities* (BZAW, 338; Berlin and New York: W. de Gruyter).

Sweeney, Marvin
    2001   *King Josiah of Judah: The Lost Messiah of Israel* (Oxford: Oxford University Press).

Uehlinger, Christoph
    1995   'Gab es eine joschijanische Kultreform? Plädoyer für ein begründetes Minimum', in Gross (ed.) 1995: 57-89.

Part II

ARTICLES

WHY A REFORM LIKE JOSIAH'S MUST HAVE HAPPENED

Rainer Albertz

1. *The Role of the Josianic Period for Israel's Religious and Political History*

In his contribution to the present volume (pp. 65-77), Philip R. Davies cited a statement that I made about ten years ago: 'The most important decision in the history of Israelite religion is made with a dating of an essential part of Deuteronomy in the time of Josiah' (Albertz 1994: I, 199). I had become aware that any reconstruction of Israel's religion decisively depends on whether you— in accordance with W.M.L. de Wette—equate the core of Deuteronomy with Josiah's law book (2 Kgs 22.8, 11), dating it in the last third of the seventh century, or whether you dissolve this connection and—in company with Hölscher (1922) and Kaiser (1984: 132-34)—shift the date of Deuteronomy to the postexilic period. Since the date or even the existence of the Pentateuchal sources J and E have been heavily questioned, the dating of the Deuteronomy constitutes the last fixed point in Old Testament literary history. So, giving up the seventh-century dating of the Deuteronomy would have far-reaching consequences: not only important features of Israel's religion like monotheism, exclusivism, and brotherhood would have to be dated much later, but also most of the Deuteronomic reform ideas like the centralisation of cult or the subordination of all the state to the law would lose any connection to societal reality. In the Persian province of Yehud there was only one temple and there existed no king, thus there were no need for centralisation and subordination any longer. As a result of this, an important turning point in the development of Israel's religious history would disappear.

Recently it was shown that Josiah's reform became the decisive fixed point for the reconstruction of Israel's political history as well. In their recent book, Finkelstein and Silberman (2001)[1] developed their new view of the history of Israel and Judah, which they claimed to be based mainly on archaeological findings and not on the biblical text, whose historicity in their opinion is largely to be doubted. According to their view there was no United Monarchy under David and Solomon, and the Davidic empire never existed. The two states Israel and Judah came into existence independently, the state of Israel during the ninth, the state of Judah not before the eighth century. Nevertheless, in spite of this

---

1. The title of the German edition (2002) is more aggressive: *No Trumpets before Jericho: The Archaeological Truth about the Bible.*

rather minimalistic view Finkelstein and Silberman do believe in the historicity of Josiah's reform. Moreover, they title their chapter on it 'A Great Reformation' and even call it a 'revolution' (Finkelstein and Silberman 2001: 275, 285, 288). The authors praise Josiah's reign as 'the climax of Israel's monarchic history' (Finkelstein and Silberman 2001: 275). And they add: 'During his thirty-one-year reign over the kingdom of Judah, Josiah was recognized by many as the greatest hope for national redemption, a genuine messiah who was destined to reform the fallen glories of the house of Israel' (Finkelstein and Silberman 2001: 275-76). According to the authors Josiah was not only the key figure of a 'new religious movement', but also created a new Israelite identity by attempting to unify the Judaeans with the people of the former northern state. In their view, vast parts of the biblical literature, not only Deuteronomy and the first edition of the Deuteronomistic History (DtrH) but also the stories of the Patriarchs, the Exodus, the Conquest, and the Judges were written during this great religious and national upheaval.[2] Even the stories about David and Solomon and their empire must be understood as reflections of the national hopes raised under Josiah and projected back into the past (cf. Finkelstein and Silberman 2001: 144). In 'Appendix F' of the book, which curiously enough was not included in the German edition, Finkelstein and Silberman admit on the grounds of archaeological considerations, however, that Josiah was possibly not able to realize his plans of a united monarchy to any large extent (cf. Finkelstein and Silberman 2001: 347-53).

One may ask what caused two scholars, who are inclined towards a minimal position, to reconstruct a vast religious and national movement under king Josiah that goes even beyond a scenario which 'conservative maximalists' like me would venture to draw? All methodical restrictions they made seemed to be forgotten: there are no, or no unambiguous, archaeological data which could verify Josiah's reform. The biblical text, which includes the report given by the DtrH in 2 Kings 22–23, is suddenly taken to be reliable. If we ask in amazement how that could happen, in my opinion the answer will be easy: Finkelstein and Silberman feel obliged to create a substitute for the United Monarchy that they denied. If it is right that pre-state Israel emerged from different populations and was organized in separate tribes, if it is right that the states of Israel and Judah 'represent two sides of ancient Israel's experience, two quite different societies with different attitudes and national identities' (Finkelstein and Silberman 2001: 24), then it must be explained how the unifying concept of 'Israel' was born, which included all tribes and all the people from both states. Since the unifying concept is spread throughout all the exilic Prophets[3] and is present throughout the book of Deuteronomy,[4] the reform of Josiah—accepting the traditional dating—is the latest

---

2. Cf. Finkelstein and Silberman 2001: 45-46, 68-71, 95, 120-22; in their early dating of the DtrH Finkelstein and Silberman are still following F.M. Cross. That they date awkwardly many of the sources of DtrH in the same years as the DtrH itself, which levels all distinctions of literary analysis, does not seem to trouble them.

3. Isa. 11.11-16; Jer. 30.3; 31.2-6, 15-22; Ezek. 37.15-22, etc.

4. As also stated by Philip R. Davies in his contribution to the present volume (pp. 65-77), but with different consequences.

opportunity that would explain such a development to some extent. Therefore it was taken up by Finkelstein and Silberman and stressed so heavily. In their view the 'great reformation' of Josiah in the late seventh century not only gave birth to Israel's unique religion, but also to Israel's new identity as a united nation under Judaean leadership. From this example we learn that we cannot just deal with the historicity of one period, but we are forced to observe the interdependency between the assessments of different periods and must somehow bring them into balance.

Compared with Finkelstein and Silberman Philip Davies is more radical. In his article he is questioning the historicity of Josiah's reform,[5] even though he has denied the existence of the Davidic and Solomonic empire as well (cf. Davies 1992: 67-70). For the former, his main arguments are the following: first, at the time of Josiah there existed no political vacuum after the decline of the Assyrian empire. Davies shares the suggestion of Na'aman (1991: 39-41),[6] that the Assyrians ceded control over Palestine 'in a more or less orderly way' to Egypt in return for its military assistance against the Medes and Babylonians. Therefore 'the Judaean king had little or no opportunity for the exercise of political independence' (see p. 65, below). Second, since the report of 2 Kings 18–23 does not mention any Assyrian dominance over Judah after Hezekiah's revolt in 701 BCE, which contrasts sharply with the historical evidence drawn from the extrabiblical sources, there is no reason to believe that it is more reliable on what it tells about the internal political conditions of Judah, including also Josiah's cultic measures. Third, since the book of Deuteronomy, even in its core, does not belong to the late seventh century but is better dated to the fifth century, there is no legislation that could serve as a base for Josiah's reform. Davies is not quite sure about the fifth-century date; however his negative result is clear: 'Once the 2 Kings account of a Josianic reform is put into question rather than assumed, there seem to be no compelling, even cogent reasons, for thinking that a text such as Deuteronomy (specifically the legal material) comes from this time. On the contrary, for every single topic discussed there are more plausible contexts. I have not set out here to argue in detail for a fifth-century date, but I have noted that all of the features discussed fit well with such a period' (see p. 75, below). In contrast to Finkelstein and Silberman the question of how the unifying concept of the 'biblical Israel' could emerge does not bother Philip Davies. In his opinion, it was just an idealized myth of the past, invented by the post-exilic Golah-society of Yehud (1992: 87-93).[7]

Thus, Davies' argument has to do with the historical assessment of the international political situation during the reign of Josiah, the reliability of the DtrH, especially in the book of Kings, and the chronological setting of the Deuteronomic legislation in Deuteronomy 12–26. I would like to respond to that in the opposite sequence.

    5. Cf. already Davies 1992: 40-41.
    6. See also Na'aman's contribution to the present volume (pp. 189-247, below).
    7. The fact that the concept occurs already in the books of the exilic prophets (Ezekiel, Deutero-Isaiah, see above) conflicts with this solution and forces us to date these later likewise.

2. Dating Deuteronomy 12–26

I think Philip Davies is absolutely right when he states that any dating of Deuteronomy 12–26 must be done without the use of de Wette's hypothesis that the law book found by Josiah (2 Kgs 22–23) can be identified with it (see pp. 69-70, below). Even if it is probable, that the Deuteronomistic Historian wanted his readers to believe that the law book was nothing else than the Deuteronomic law, which he had then included in his work,[8] this identification could be a misleading invention. Methodologically, inner-Deuteronomic observations have to decide whether a Josianic dating of the Deuteronomic law can be accepted or not.

2.1. Davies rightly notes that the name given to the society for which the Deuteronomy legislates is 'Israel' (see p. 71, below). One can add: the Deuteronomic legislation even stresses the concept that Israel constitutes a unity, where all members are brothers. It does not know any divisions concerning north or south; even a division into tribes is not mentioned in the core of Deuteronomy, where Israel is conceptualized as 'the people of God'.[9] The alternative concept of Israel as a nation composed of twelve tribes, which is so prominent in the Patriarchal Narratives and the Priestly Source, occurs only on the fringe of the book of Deuteronomy, in Deuteronomy 33, and has there only peripheral importance.

However, Davies' argument that this Deuteronomic concept of Israel would be historically problematic in the late seventh century and excludes such a dating is not convincing. It would be convincing only if one shares the historical and terminological reconstruction of Philip Davies: that there was no United Monarchy, that there existed only two different kingdoms, Judah and Israel, and that the meaning of the term 'Israel' in its historical sense must be restricted to the Northern Kingdom. If one takes those presuppositions for granted, the outcome that at the end of the seventh century Deuteronomy 12–26 should use only the name of the Northern Kingdom, which had perished a century before, for Judaean society would indeed be astonishing. But the presuppositions are questionable.

My first point is that already on the level of semantics the strict division that Davies made between the historical 'Israel', restricted to the Northern Kingdom, and the so-called 'biblical Israel', envisaging the ideal concept of a unified nation, is not true. I investigated the term 'Israel' in detail many years ago (Albertz 1987) and found that the name has an exclusive and an inclusive meaning. In its exclusive meaning it denotes the territory of Eshbaal (2 Sam. 2.9-10; 3.12, 21), the ten tribes of the middle and northern Palestinian hill country (2 Sam. 19.42-44), and later the Northern Kingdom (1 Kgs 12–2 Kgs 17). In its inclusive meaning it denotes all the tribes including Judah, so the 'men of Israel' (2 Sam. 15.13; 16.15, 18; 17.14, 24, etc.) and the 'elders of Israel' (2 Sam. 17.4, 15, etc.) during the Absalom revolt, when the northern and the southern tribes formed an alliance, or

---

8. Cf. the identical expression ספר התורה in 2 Kgs 22.8, 11 and Deut. 28.61; 29.20; 31.26 (cf. 31.24) and the scene, where Moses writes down the Deuteronomic law in Deut. 31.9-13.

9. The assumptions Philip R. Davies made in this context are not fully correct, see pp. 71-72, below.

the united kingdom of David and Solomon (2 Sam. 5.12; 6.20-21; 8.15; 19.23; 1 Kgs 1.34; 4.1; 11.42), that could also be called 'Israel and Judah' (2 Sam. 5.5; 11.11; 1 Kgs 1.35; 4.20). Since the exclusive and inclusive meaning are often alternating confusingly in one and the same literary unit (e.g. 2 Sam. 5.5, 12; 1 Kgs 1.34, 35), it seems to me extremely difficult to divide them diachronically and to assign them to an old historical or a late ideological level. If Davies' thesis was right, all narratives and reports on David and Solomon would have to be dated into the post-exilic period, when according to him the inclusive concept of 'biblical Israel' was invented (cf. 1992: 87-93). But even though the dating of the David narratives varies in the recent discussion,[10] there still remains one passage that clearly contradicts Davies' hypothesis: in Isa. 8.17 the prophet Isaiah could call the Southern and Northern Kingdom 'both houses of Israel'. Here the term 'Israel' explicitly embraces the two states (בתים). This means that unless one wants to question Isaiah's preaching during the Syro-Ephraimite crisis 734–732 BCE, the inclusive meaning of the name 'Israel' is already common during the eighth century. Therefore, it is still likely that the expansion of the term took place much earlier. In my view, 'Israel' denoted in the pre-state period a coalition of tribes in the middle and northern Palestinian hill country and was expanded in order to include the southern tribes during the late pre-state and the early monarchic period.[11] Accordingly, the fact that the Deuteronomy uses the name 'Israel' in a definitely inclusive sense is in no way astonishing and does not rule out a seventh-century date. On the contrary, the course of history in which the Northern Kingdom was destroyed and many refugees from the north joined the Judaean society in the late eighth century makes it comprehensible that the Deuteronomic legislators could easily appropriate the name 'Israel' for the Judaean society and stress—admittedly in archaic diction—the unity of the people without any tribal subdivisions.

Philip Davies suggested that the Persian period would be the most likely setting for the usage of the name 'Israel' in Deuteronomy. I have my serious doubts about this suggestion. The Nehemiah Memoir,[12] which we can date with a high degree of probability in the second part of the fifth century, does not lay any emphasis on the term 'Israel'. It uses 'Israel' only four times, two times for the people of the past (Neh. 1.6; 13.26) and just two times for those of the present (2.10; 13.18). Much more prominent is the usage of the term 'Jews', mostly with

10. The date of the Succession Narrative (2 Sam. 9–1 Kgs 2*) varies from the time of Solomon (L. Rost) to the post-exilic period (J. van Seters), but even very critical scholars such as D.M. Gunn ('several centuries after the events') and O. Kaiser ('between Hezekiah and Jehoiakim') defended a pre-exilic dating; see the discussion in Dietrich and Naumann 1995: 213-16.

11. Since not only 1 Kgs 12 but also Isa. 7.17 testify to the separation of the northern tribes from Judah, there must have existed some kind of United Monarchy under David and Solomon. Two independent and trustworthy sources cannot so easily be denied, not even by possible negative archaeological evidence. It must be taken into account that for the prophet Isaiah in the eighth century the separation of the north is still the most traumatic event in the history of Judah.

12. Neh. 1.1–7.5a; 12.21-32, 37-40; 13.4-31; probably without 7.1b; 13.24a, 30a. Cf. Mowinckel 1923: 278-322; Kellermann 1967: 4-56; Rudolph 1949: XXIV; Williamson 1985: XXIV-XXVIII; Gunneweg 1987: 176-80; Blenkinsopp 1988: 46-47; Karrer 2001: 128-213; Reinmuth 2002.

the article 'the Jews' (ה/יהודים), which appears ten times (1.2; 2.16; 3.33, 34; 4.6; 5.1, 8, 17; 6.6; 13.23) and denotes all descendants of the inhabitants of the former kingdom of Judah wherever they live, whether in the province Yehud, in other territories of Palestine or in Babylonia or Persia. This new linguistic usage accords with Nehemiah's policy to strengthen the independence of Yehud by excluding all the non-Jewish from the community, especially the descendants of the former northern tribes in the province Samaria. For such a policy the term 'Israel', which originally had denoted and always had included the northern tribes, would be counter-productive. In the rest of the books Ezra and Nehemiah the term 'Israel' is more prominent, but it does not include the whole people, but is mostly restricted to the emigrants of the Babylonian Golah.[13] Thus it seems to me extremely difficult to explain the inclusive usage of the term 'Israel' in Deuteronomy from a fifth-century background.

Progressing from the terminology to the cultural background, it must be stated that the inclusive use of the name 'Israel' was not a pure fiction but mirrors a social reality. In spite of all political differences, the members of the northern and southern tribes had the feeling that they shared common moral and religious values. 'No such thing ought to be done in Israel', said the Judaean princess Tamar to Amnon who wanted to rape her in Jerusalem. The God YHWH is always named the 'God of Israel',[14] never the God of Judah,[15] even when he was venerated in Jerusalem.[16] Therefore the authors of Deuteronomy could combine religious and legal traditions from the north and the south when they stressed the ethnic, moral and religious unity of 'Israel'.

2.2. Philip Davies thinks that the sharp distinction between Israel and the foreign nations presented by the Deuteronomy would make no sense in a reform under a king whose subjects include a plurality of cultures or population elements (see p. 72, below). Interpreted as a contrast between the immigrants and the indigenous population it would fit much better in the conflict between the returnees and the 'people of the land' in the Persian period. It can be admitted that there are material parallels between the concepts of Deuteronomy and Ezra/Nehemiah. Nevertheless, there is the problem that the terminology in Deuteronomy and in Ezra/Nehemiah is completely different: the foreign nations, who would seduce Israel and whom Israel should expel, are called in Deuteronomy 12–26 generally (eighteen times) גוים, 'nations' or 'many nations', 'big nations', 'strong nations', and so on,[17] but only four times is עמים used.[18] But in Ezra/Nehemiah the term

---

13. Cf. Ezra 2.2, 5, 59, 70; 3.1; 6.21; Neh. 9.2; the expression עם/ה ישראל in Ezra 2.2; 9.1; Neh. 7.7 does not appear in the Deuteronomy.

14. Altogether 202 times in the Hebrew Bible from Judg. 5.3, 5 to Mal. 2.16.

15. This result is statistically significant; the expression אלהי ירושלם occurs in the Hebrew Bible only in 2 Chron. 32.19 and probably in the inscription A of Khirbet Bet Lei. Here it is stated, that the hills of Judah belong to YHWH, who is also called אלהי כל ארץ; see Renz and Röllig 1995: 245.

16. Cf. the expression 'The Holy One of Israel' coined by Isaiah, Isa. 5.19, 24; 30.11, 12, 15; 31.1.

17. Deut. 7.1, 17, 22; 8.20; 9.1, 4, 5; 11.23; 12.2, 29, 30; 15.6; 17.14; 18.9, 14; 19.1; 20.15; 26.19.

18. Deut. 6.14; 17.14, 19; 20.16.

גוים is used hardly at all; it occurs only once in the expression גוי הארץ ('people of the land', Ezra 6.21) and several times in the older Nehemiah Memoir for non-Jewish people elsewhere in the world.[19] In Ezra/Nehemiah the groups, from which the Golah-community should separate itself, are called עמי הארץ/הארצות ('people of the land' or 'people of the lands').[20] The same expression עמי הארץ is used in Deut. 28.10 and in the DtrH (Josh. 4.24; 1 Kgs 8.43, 53, 60) with the total different meaning 'the nations of the world', like simple עמים in Deuteronomy 12–26 and its admonitory frame.[21] Thus it is not possible to bring Deuteronomy and Ezra–Nehemiah into a literary coherence. In contrast, to date Deuteronomy to a similar time as Ezra/Nehemiah, one must suppose that both literary works emerge in two totally separated groups whose terminologies had no mutual influence. Such a suggestion would not be totally impossible, though a little bit difficult, if we take the small size of the province Yehud into account. But if we become aware that the editors of Ezra/Nehemiah cited explicitly the law of Deut. 23.4 from 'the book of Moses' as authoritative (Neh. 13.1-2), it will be more likely that the Deuteronomic legislation preceded the writing of Ezra/Nehemiah by a long time. That would not completely exclude a Persian date but would limit it to the early Persian period.

Davies' doubts that the sharp distinction between Israel and the former inhabitants of the land would not be useful for a reform in the seventh century can perhaps be dispelled. Whatever different people had formed the people of Israel and Judah during a long historical process, their differences had fused for the most part in the late seventh century. Under those conditions, the Deuteronomic demand to expel the indigenous population from the land and keep apart from their horrible customs can be understood as an attempt to denounce specific Judaean and Israelite beliefs and practices as dangerous foreign influences that must be radically removed. The Deuteronomic reformers wanted to implant a new feeling of being a particular, a 'holy people'[22] in Judaean society. Such a target would fit well the conditions of the seventh century, after Judah had suffered a century of Assyrian domination.

2.3. In his analysis, Philip Davies followed S.A. Geller (2000: 273-319) who stated that Deuteronomic legislators support an individual concept of covenant that would constitute a close parallel to the book of Nehemiah. Geller thinks that a new examination of Deuteronomy would conclude 'that the collectivity of the covenant community barely masks the fact that it is a radically new type of association of individuals' (2000: 300). Geller and Davies have rightly pointed out that many laws of Deuteronomy stress the responsibility of the individual, like Deut. 13.7-12. But their assessment that it 'negates the doctrine of collective responsibility for sin' can be questioned in this generality, because the rule of Deut. 24.16 that a son should not be punished for the sins of his father and vice

19. Neh. 5.8, 9, 17; 6.6, 16; 13.26.
20. Ezra 3.3; 9.1, 2; 10.2, 11; Neh. 9.24, 30; 10.29, 31; cf. גוי הארץ, Ezra 6.21.
21. Deut. 4.6, 9; 6.14; 7.6, 7, 14, 16; 10.15; 13.8; 14.2; 28.10, 37, 64; 30.3; 32.8.
22. Deut. 7.6; 14.2, 21; 26.19.

versa is only valid for human jurisdiction. If God's jurisdiction is involved, then Deuteronomic legislators know a collective responsibility for appeasing God's anger (e.g. Deut. 21.1-9). And the same is valid for the Deuteronomic concept of covenant: in all passages where it is unfolded in some detail (Deut. 26.16-19; 28.69–29.28) it is always a collective 'you' who enters into the covenant with YHWH.[23] This collective shape of the Deuteronomic concept is a heritage of the Assyrian vassal-treaties, which gave the model. A closer comparison between the shapes of covenant in Deuteronomy and Ezra/Nehemiah reveals a decisive difference: what had been a collective covenant in accordance with the vassal-treaties in Deuteronomy became in Ezra 10 and Nehemiah 10 an individual commitment according to private contracts; no longer God but only the community made the agreement, and all leaders of the families of the different groups of society signed personally that they were going to commit themselves to specific moral and religious duties.[24] Not by chance does a different terminology for such a self-commitment (אמנה instead of ברית) occur in Neh. 10.1. These differences in the covenant concepts are so fundamental that it is unlikely that both could come from the same post-exilic period. In my view, the parallels between the Deuteronomic concept of covenant and the Assyrian vassal-treaties make a dating in the seventh or at latest in the sixth century more probable.[25]

2.4. Philip Davies reflects the somewhat utopian character of the law of kings (Deut. 17.14-20) in order to undermine the traditional seventh-century dating. Here he is in good company with G. Hölscher, who argued likewise that 'the ideological character of the Deuteronomic legislation' demonstrates 'that it could not have emerged in the pre-exilic Judah, but belongs to the period after the destruction' (1922: 228). Davies mainly pointed out that the radical limitations of monarchical power made in 17.16-20 were completely unrealistic: 'There are no plausible explanations why a king should accept a reform that deprives him of the essential powers of monarchy, justice and warfare' (see p. 74, below). Admittedly, the law of kings sounds unrealistic to us; the question remains whether a later date would make its utopian concept more realistic. Moreover, there is no hint in the text that its author was looking forward to the restoration of an idealized kingship (cf. Nelson 2002: 223), in contrast to many exilic and post-exilic prophetic texts.[26] Every attempt to date Deut. 17.14-20 in the Persian period is confronted with the problem that this law still held on to the divine election of the king according to the Davidic theology (Ps. 89.4, 20), whereas the Davidides disappeared from the political stage after the failure of Zerubbabel 519/518 BCE. After him, Nehemiah would be in accordance with that law in some

---

23. The same is true for the covenant of Josiah in 2 Kgs 23.1-3. It was the king as the representative of the people who made the covenant, the people only entered into it collectively, of course.

24. I owe this insight to Dr Ralf Rothenbusch, with whom I co-operated in the 'Sonderforschungsbereich 493' in Münster.

25. Cf. also the close material parallels between Deut. 28.20-44 and the vassal treaties of Esarhaddon pointed out by Steymans 1995.

26. Cf. Isa. 11.1-5; Jer. 23.1-7; Ezek. 34.23-24; 37.24-25; Mic. 5.1-5; Zech. 9.9-10, etc.

way: a pious, selfless ruler, one who was obedient to God's law, as he presented himself (Neh. 5). And there were some people who wanted to make this Persian governor a king (6.6-7). Anyhow, he was no Davidide; therefore he and persons like him possibly did not influence the concept of Deut. 17.14-20.[27] So there are good reasons for dating the Deuteronomic law of kings during a period when Davidic kings were still on the throne.

Philip Davies overstates a little the radicalism of that law. As Nelson rightly points out, 'it does not forbid characteristic royal activities, but rather thoroughly limits them' (Nelson 2002: 222). That the king, who traditionally had been the supreme judge and legislator in the ancient Near East, is subjected to that law must be seen as the intended consequence of all Deuteronomic legislation: Moses as mediator of the divine law is promoted in order to replace the king as legislator (cf. Albertz 1997: 124-30). In reality that does not mean that 'authority is conferred exclusively on the priests', as Davies suggested (see p. 74, below). According to Deut. 17.8-13 the supreme legal authority is conferred on a kind of upper court in Jerusalem, which consists of priests and laymen (v. 9). In the matters of warfare again priests and lay officials are provided with authority (20.1-9), but the functions of the king as military leader are not excluded (17.16).[28] What the Deuteronomic legislators intended with their radical law was nothing else than the creation of what was called later a 'constitutional monarchy'. The measures may have been impractical to some degree and somewhat utopian like other archaic reform models of the ancient world,[29] but the goal was very concrete and—as we can see in the later history of humankind—with other measures definitely realizable. But why should such a far reaching constitutional reform be conceptualized at a time when the legal limitation of monarchic power was completely irrelevant for Judah? In my view, the most probable period for dating the Deuteronomic law of kings are the reigns of Jehoiakim and Zedekiah, when the alliances with Egypt became a new threat for Judah (17.16) and when the Shaphanide scribes, who are the best candidates for having written the Deuteronomic law, resisted the ruling kings (Jer. 26.24; 36.9-26).[30]

---

27. The same would be true for Gedaliah, who otherwise would be also a good candidate for the ideal of a ruler with limited power.

28. Thus Davies' criticism of my thesis that the עם הארץ was the promoter of the Josianic reform falls short twice. First, his statement 'that these people would hardly have transferred authority over warfare or justice to the *priesthood*' (see p. 75, below) does describe the intention of the Deuteronomic legislation correctly. Second, in my opinion a broad coalition promoted the Josianic reform, consisting not only of the עם הארץ but also of scribal circles like the Shaphanides, priestly circles like the Hilkiades, and prophets like Huldah and Jeremiah, cf. Albertz 1994: 201-203.

29. Cf. Rüterswörden 1987: 102-105, who pointed out that the deprivation of the king's power as seen in Deut. 17 has some similarities in the Greek history of polity.

30. The strange prohibition of bringing back the people to Egypt in order to multiply horses motivated by an oracle of YHWH (Deut. 17.16aβb), which seems to be inserted into its context, can easily have reference to the military alliance between Zedekiah and Psammetichus II in the years between 594 and 591 BCE. That alliance probably included the supply of Judaean mercenaries for Egypt, cf. Albertz 2002: 27. If this reference is accepted, we would have a *terminus ad quem* for the Deuteronomic law of kings.

2.5. Finally Philip Davies suggested that the centralization of the cult was a problem of the early Persian period, when after the reconstruction of the Jerusalem temple its claim to be the only authorized temple of YHWH had to be carried through against the claim of other cult places like that in the former capital Mizpeh. These suggestions are highly speculative. Whether there existed any YHWH-temple in Mizpeh during the period of exile is totally uncertain. The בית יהוה of Jer. 41.5, sometimes taken as a piece of evidence (cf. Veijola 1982: 190-210), probably refers to the temple in Jerusalem.[31] No archaeological evidence has been found. It seems that the sanctuary in Bethel played a role during the exilic and early post-exilic period (cf. 2 Kgs 17.24-34a; cf. Albertz 1994: II, 525), but its legitimacy was heavily questioned. Again no temple has been found, so it is difficult to assess what really happened. We can only state, that in none of the post-exilic books of the Hebrew Bible—neither in Haggai and Zechariah nor in Ezra and Trito-Isaiah—is there any hint of a dispute on the question of whether any other sanctuary than Jerusalem should be reconstructed or put into operation. On the contrary, the prophet Haggai presupposed that no other sanctuary existed apart from the Jerusalem temple that could bring about the blessing over the land (Hag. 1.7-11). Thus, we cannot rule out that there were again rivalries between different YHWH sanctuaries in the post-exilic time,[32] but we can say that cult centralization was no serious problem of that period.

Thus we can conclude: None of Davies' arguments that Deuteronomy 12–26 should be better dated into the fifth century is convincing. There might be some doubts on a seventh century dating, but the Deuteronomic legislation fits rather less well the socio-political conditions and the literature of the Persian period.

3. *Dating the Deuteronomistic History*

Since 2 Kings does not know any Assyrian hegemony during the seventh century, Philip Davies questioned the historicity of the DtrH altogether. That seems to be appropriate in so far as Davies assigns a very late date to the DtrH. He has not dealt with it explicitly in the present article, but if he thinks of a fifth-century date for the earliest pieces of Deuteronomy, then the DtrH, which also included most of its later parts, cannot have emerged before the beginning of the fourth century. A History that is separated from Josiah's reform by more than 200 years can be of doubtful reliability. But the question must be raised: Is such a late dating of the DtrH possible at all?

---

31. Not only in the tale of Jeremiah's woe (Jer. 38.14), but always in the book of Jeremiah the expression denotes the Jerusalem temple.

32. The temple of YHW in Elephantine seems to be simply disregarded by the officials of Jerusalem, cf. Cowley 1923: 31.18-19. According to Lemaire 2002: 149-56, there existed a temple or shrine of YHW (יהו בית) in Idumaea during the fourth century. But the idea that somewhere in remote southern Palestine should have existed a proper cult centre where not only YHWH, but also the Babylonian God Nabû, and the Arabic Goddess 'Uzza were venerated, sounds to me very unlikely. Since the *Gattung* of text 283 is a cadaster, perhaps the names should be better interpreted as personal names of the land owners.

The suggestion that the report of Josiah's reform was contemporary with the events, which is advocated by most scholars of the Cross school, has led I. Finkelstein and N.A. Silberman, among others, to believe that the DtrH is completely reliable on this point. But recently Th. Römer, who sympathizes with the Cross school, has shown convincingly that 2 Kings 22–23 'should be dated from the exilic period' (Römer 1997: 10).[33] What is true for this report is also true for the whole DtrH, whose climax it constitutes. Other evidence comes from 1 Kgs 8.46-53, where Solomon's prayer refers explicitly to the exile. Since it can be shown that this passage is no later addition but belongs to the Deuteronomistic edition of the chapter (8.1, 9, 14-30, 44-53, 55-61), which includes an older prayer in 8.31-43,[34] the exilic dating of DtrH becomes unavoidable. The last piece of evidence comes from the end of the DtrH (2 Kgs 25.27-30), which reports the release of Jehoiachin by Amel-Marduk in the year 562 BCE. Leaving apart the question to what extent the Deuteronomistic Historians used older material, it becomes likely that the years after 562 are the first possible date for the DtrH, as M. Noth (1957: 91) has already proposed. If one is not tied to the model of the Cross-school, the *terminus a quo* 562 BCE will be relatively certain.

The uncertainty concerns the *terminus ad quem*. Since several scholars are inclined to date the DtrH partly or completely into the Persian period (cf., among others, Würthwein 1994: 1-11; Römer 1997: 10-11), the question arises whether it is possible to define a latest possible date. Taking into consideration some older text- and literary-critical studies of A. Rofé (1985, 1987) and E. Tov (1985, 1986), R.F. Person (2002: 31-63) recently pleaded for a longer genesis of the DtrH, starting during the period of exile and coming to an end not before the time of Ezra. Person draw a vivid picture of what he called the 'Deuteronomic School' that he imagined as a scribal guild: after it had come home from Babylonia it supported Zerubbabel, but disillusioned with his failure and a later Persian supported administration, it developed an increasingly eschatological critique. Finally, Ezra's mission and the introduction of a new law led to its demise (Person 2002: 121-22, 135, 152). Whether that all happened, we do not know, but if we ask more concretely what passages would derive from the year 520 onwards, Person can name only a small number and mostly no others than those which have often been seen to be the latest.[35] Sometimes the historical setting

---

33. Römer points to the Huldah oracle, which presupposes the exile (cf. 2 Kgs 22.16-17), and other features (1997: 6). As Hardmeier (2000: 81-145) has shown, the report must be seen as a mostly coherent literary unit, which included in 2 Kgs 23.4-15 an older arrangement of cultic reform measures (*waw-perfect* sentences). Only a few verses are probably later additions: 23.15*, 16-18, 19-20, 24a.

34. 1 Kgs 8.46-53 belongs to the same literary layer as 8.44-45 (cf. השמים תעמשו in vv. 45, 49 in distinction from the expressions used in the *Vorlage*, cf. vv. 32, 34, 36, 39, 43; and the use of דרך in the sense 'towards' in vv. 44, 48, etc.); both passages are bound to the Deuteronomistic introduction (cf. v. 44 and 18.19; vv. 48 and 16). The Deuteronomistic reworking can be seen by the fact that vv. 44-45 is a doublet of vv. 33-34. Moreover, the passage 8.46-53 contains many parallels to other Deuteronomistic texts, especially to Deut. 4 and 30.1-11.

35. So Deut. 4.29-31; 30.1-14; 1 Kgs 8; 2 Kgs 17; 25.27-30 and some others: Josh. 1.1-11; Judg. 3.1-6; 17.6; 21.25; 1 Sam. 16–18; 2 Sam. 7.1-17; 23.1-7; 1 Kgs 21.1-20.

given by Person remains obscure; for example, Person dates Deut. 30.1-14 during both the time of Zerubbabel and the period after him. Moreover, it remains strange that in none of the passages can we find an allusion to any event that we know from the period between Zerubbabel and Ezra: neither the reconstruction of the temple, nor the reconstruction of the Jerusalem wall is mentioned. So Person's results are not really convincing. There might have been smaller additions and limited alterations as the differences between the text traditions (MT, LXX, Samaritanus) show, but they are less substantial and may be even later than Person thinks. Rather, his investigation demonstrates that the Persian period, apart from its very beginning (539–520 BCE), did not leave any clear footprint in the DtrH.[36] The substantial redactions of DtrH seem to have happened earlier.

In this connection, it is of crucial importance that, apart from a few exceptions that will be discussed below, DtrH reveals no knowledge that the exile would ever come to an end. That can be demonstrated by 1 Kgs 8.46-50, one of the passages that clearly reflect the experience of the exilic period. According to vv. 49-50 God is asked to hear the prayers of the exiles in order to forgive them 'and grant them mercy before those who have taken them captive so that they may show them mercy'. In this passage, there is no hint of knowledge that the mighty Babylonian empire could ever collapse, there are no expectations that God would liberate the exiles and bring them home. The only hope is the wish to find mercy in the eyes of the Babylonian officials, to whose despotism they are hopelessly subjected.[37] What is meant more concretely can be demonstrated by the parallel passage in Jer. 42.12: the wish that the Babylonian king would not also punish all Judaeans for the murder of Gedaliah but would spare those who were loyal to him. The Deuteronomistic Historians describe a similar event at the very end of their work (2 Kgs 25.27-30): the Babylonian king Amel-Marduk released Jehoiachin from prison and restored his position of an honoured vassal. Probably Nebuchadnezzar had sentenced him to be his hostage because of the murder of Gedaliah by a member of the royal family.[38] When after his accession Amel-Marduk reprieved Jehoiachin, he actually 'showed him mercy' in accordance with the prayer of 2 Kgs 8.49-50.

Thus, 1 Kgs 8.46-50 and 2 Kgs 25.27-30 share the same horizon of hope and probably belong to the same literary layer. Both do not expect the downfall of the Babylonian empire, but a better treatment under the Babylonian government. Thus, these texts cannot have been written after 539 BCE, when the Babylonian empire was destroyed. Since there is no hint of a major political change, it is very probable that these passages emerged before Cyrus' impressive victory over

---

36. Römer (1997: 11) admitted this fact, when he wrote: 'We may still ask why are there no direct allusions to the Persian period in DH?' But his answer, that the Deuteronomistic Historians—like modern ones—avoided including their own present, is not convincing. The present can be excluded or not, but in every historical work, whether ancient or modern, the reader can find out from what temporal perspective it was written.

37. Cf. the same expression נתן רחמים לפני in Gen. 43.14; Jer. 42.12; Neh. 1.11; Ps. 106.46; Dan. 1.9.

38. For the historical reconstruction of this event and its far reaching consequences, see Albertz 2001: 63-64, 89-91.

Lydia in 547/46 BCE. As 2 Kgs 25.27-30 constitutes the compositional ending of the DtrH, therefore most of that history can be dated between 562 and 547 BCE.

There are only two passages in the present DtrH that move beyond this glimmer of hope. The first is Deut. 4.25-32, the second Deut. 30.1-10. All of the long sermon of Deut. 4.1-40 is an addition to its context, which presupposes the introduction to DtrH (Deut. 1–3),[39] but is still not known by it. Nevertheless, its shape is Deuteronomistic in style and theology. Within 4.25-32, which bends the listener's eyes to the future, vv. 29-31 seem to be again a later addition (cf. Nelson 2002: 62, 68). After giving a grim portrayal of the exile in vv. 25-28, the text turns abruptly to a positive viewpoint:

> You will seek YHWH your God from there and you will find him, if only you search for him with all your heart and all your being. In your distress when all these things have happened to you, in the days to come[40] you will return to YHWH your God and obey him. For a merciful God is YHWH your God. He will not desert or destroy you. He will not forget the covenant with your ancestors that he swore them.[41] (Deut. 4.29-31)

In this passage there is still no hope for a return to the homeland, though its author expects a drastic change between God and his people. YHWH will become attainable again for his people, and the people will return to its God. Israel will no longer be confronted with YHWH's jealous anger, but will experience his mercy again. The same kind of hope expressed by a very similar wording can be found in Jer. 29.10-14a.[42] As I could show elsewhere, this passage belongs to the second edition of the Deuteronomistic book of Jeremiah (JerD²).[43] This edition can probably be dated during the years 545–540, just before the downfall of the Babylonian empire.[44] During the same years the anonymous prophetical group whom we call Deutero-Isaiah proclaimed that the period of God's wrath was over and a new period of God's mercy would begin (Isa. 40.1-2). So it is highly probable that a Deuteronomistic Historian—by adding Deut. 4.29-31—actualized the DtrH during those years when a drastic change in the Near Eastern history could be foreseen.

The second passage, Deut. 30.1-10, has so many significant features in common that it may have been written by the same author.[45] However, R.D. Nelson

---

39. Cf. Deut. 4.3-4 and 3.29; 4.21-22 and 3.23-28. The chs. 1–3 of Deuteronomy do not prepare for the sermon. With regard to the content, Deut. 4 interprets Deut. 5.

40. The term באחרית הימים has nothing to do with eschatology as Person (2002: 125-26) suggests, but means a just and fairer future like in Gen. 49.1; Num. 24.14; Deut. 31.29; Jer. 30.24.

41. The translation is taken from Nelson 2002: 58-59.

42. Jer. 29.14bβ does not occur in LXX and is a later addition.

43. Albertz 2001: 326-55; in my opinion the second edition consists of Jer. 1–45* without the book of consolation (Jer. 30–31) and its narrative transition (Jer. 32–35).

44. Jer. 29.10 reckons a 70-year duration of the Babylonian dominion. The most probable solution to identify the beginning of that period can be seen in Nebuchadnezzar's accession to the throne in 605 or his first regnal year 604 BCE (cf. Schmid 1996: 224-25). Then the 70-years period would end in the years 535 or 534. Since the collapse of the Babylonian empire happened some years earlier, the passage must have been written before the year 539.

45. So Nelson 2002: 348. The phrase שוב עד־יהוה—with the preposition עד instead of normal אל—occurs within the DtrH only in Deut. 4.30 and 30.2, and is extremely infrequent in the Hebrew

(2002: 348) is right to state that '30.1-11 goes a step further than 4.29-31 to envision the return home from the exile'. Along with that, God promised to multiply his people and make them prosperous again (v. 5). The wide horizon of hope reminds one of the promises of salvation made in the 'Book of Consolation' (Jer. 30–31), although it is still less detailed. In my view, those belong to the third edition of the Deuteronomistic book of Jeremiah (JerD^3).[46] Likewise the hope that God would circumcise the heart of his people (Deut. 30.6) and by this would restore the broken relationship from his side has its closest parallels in JerD^3 (Jer. 31.31-33; 32.37-41; cf. Jer. 4.4 and Deut. 10.16). JerD^3 can be dated with some probability in the years between 525 and 521/0 BCE, after Cambyses' campaign against Egypt focused the Persian interest on the southwest of the empire, including Palestine, and before Darius conquered Babylon, which rebelled against him.[47] Thus, it is very probable that Deut. 30.1-10 also has to be dated in these dramatic years when, after the Gaumata rebellion and the usurpation of Darius, the Judaean minority got the first chance of repatriation. Both passages, Deut. 4.29-31 and 30.1-10, constitute a hopeful frame around the book of Deuteronomy. Thus, their insertion is part of a deliberate redaction of the DtrH. The time when that took place cannot be determined exactly, but it is improbable that it happened much later than the year 520 BCE, when after the return of Zerubbabel and Joshua the restoration in Judah was started. Since the discernible latest passages of the DtrH belong still in the late sixth and not in the fifth century as R.F. Person suggested, its *terminus ad quem* can probably be fixed around the year 520 BCE. However, the concept and most of the text of that history was largely drafted before the rise of Cyrus in 547 BCE.

In the event that the DtrH emerged largely between 562 and 547 and its later parts followed until the year 520, then several conclusions can be drawn which are of some importance for the assessment of the Josianic reform. First, we get another important confirmation that the book of Deuteronomy could not have emerged in the later Persian period but must have been written earlier. Since Deuteronomy 4 presupposes not only the Deuteronomic core in chs. 12–26, but also includes its admonitory frame in Deut. 4.44–30.20, the book of Deuteronomy must have been largely finished by 540. Second, since most of the DtrH was composed during the 15 years following the release of Jehoiachin (562), their authors were not too far away from the period when Josiah's reform was carried through (622–609 BCE). The time covers just the range of 47 to 75 years.[48] This

---

Bible (Hos. 14.2; Isa. 19.22; Lam. 3.40); the parallelism of returning to YHWH and hearing his voice occurs in 4.30 and 30.2; cf. 30.8, 10, the phrase 'with all your heart and all your being' in 4.29 and 30.2, 6, 10, etc.

46. Cf. Jer. 30.18-22; 31.10-14, 21-22, 23-26; 32.37-44; 50.17-20, 33-34; 51.34-37. In my view, JerD^3 consists of Jer. 1–51*, including the book of consolation and the oracles against foreign nations, cf. Albertz 2001: 255-60.

47. Cf. the last oracle of the book of Jeremiah (51.58), which expects the occupation of Babylon.

48. Handy (1995: 252-75) rightly points out that the report of Josiah's reform is not contemporary, but 'cannot have been written prior to the sixth century' (p. 259). But when he concludes that the report cannot be reliable, because it would have been written 'a century or more' after the events

would mean that the Deuteronomistic Historians had to be aware that there were still some eye-witnesses alive and that there were a lot of people among their audience whose fathers or grandfathers had participated in Josiah's government. So they could not invent fabulous fairy tales, whatever religious ideology they wanted to promote. They could overstate some measures and they could ignore others—and they did both: they generalized the cult reform, but they ignored the social and national reform attempts—nevertheless, they could not lie. This means that the reliability of the DtrH for the events of the late seventh and early sixth century can be assessed as good, if we take its ideology into account. For example, as it is obvious that the Deuteronomistic Historians shared a nationalistic view and therefore praised revolts against the Assyrian dominance (2 Kgs 17.2-4; 18.5-6), there is no wonder that they ignored the re-establishment of the Assyrian domination under Manasseh.[49] As far as reliability is concerned, we cannot extrapolate conclusions from their treatment of foreign policy to that of domestic policy, as Philip Davies did.[50]

Apart from the temporal proximity, there is another strong argument that excludes the suggestion of a pure invention. The Josianic reform does not really fit the DtrH. According to the theological concept of the Deuteronomistic Historians, Josiah's exceptional cult reform that met YHWH's demands as never before should have opened Judah to a wonderful future. At least, it should have averted the catastrophe, the destruction of Judah and the deportations of major parts of its inhabitants. The historians had a great deal of trouble, to bring the course of history in line with the Josianic reform: they actually invented(!) a period of horrible apostasy under Manasseh, claimed that this provoked YHWH to decide on destruction (2 Kgs 21.10-15), and explained that this decision could not be removed by Josiah's reform, but only delayed (23.25-27). The concept of such an unchangeable destiny contradicts their effort to show God's morality in history. Their will to keep the Josianic reform and to defend its correctness forced the Deuteronomistic Historians to distort their own theology in some way. So it must have been such an important event for them that they could not deny it.

4. *The Historical Evidence*

Finally, Philip Davies argued that the basic historical conditions during the late seventh century did not admit any significant reform movement. In his view, after the decline of the Assyrian power in Palestine, Egypt took over the hegemony directly. After having been a vassal of Assyria, Josiah became immediately an Egyptian vassal and did not have the scope of action for any bigger changes. In

of Josiah's reign (p. 275), then it becomes apparent, that he has no clear idea about the *terminus ad quem* of the DtrH.

49. They were also forced to do so by incorporating the nationalistic Isaiah narrative (2 Kgs 18.9-10; 18.13–19.37*) into their history, which asserted the departure of the Assyrians; cf. Hardmeier 1989. The Deuteronomistic Historians also ignored that Jehu became a vassal of Assyria as can be seen and read on the 'Black Obelisk' of Shalmanesar III.

50. See pp. 65-77, below.

this assessment, Davies agrees with H. Niehr, who stated: 'All of these statements result in a picture of Josiah as an Egyptian vassal, unable to establish an enlarged kingdom or to pursue independent politics'.[51]

However, it must be remembered that such a historical reconstruction, which has now become more popular,[52] is not attested by any source but is a conclusion of more general considerations. Neither the archaeological results of Meṣad Ḥashavyahu nor the mysterious death of Josiah at Megiddo convey a clear picture.[53] How Assyrian rule collapsed in Judah, Samaria, and the other Palestinian provinces, and when and to what degree it was replaced by Egyptian rule, we do not know exactly. Biblical sources rather suggest a break and a certain vacuum of power until the Egyptians established their hegemony over Palestine in the year 609 BCE. In Isa. 8.23b–9.6 the withdrawal of the Assyrian armies could be compared with a great victory and is experienced as liberation.[54] And according to Jer. 2.36-37 influential groups of the population of the former Northern Kingdom obviously believed that the Egyptians could help them to restore their political independence, possibly against Josiah's national ambitions (cf. Albertz 2003: 228-30). Perhaps Josiah's strange interference in Megiddo has to do with such competing political interest. There seemed to be unsettled political conditions in Judah and Israel for some years, which could raise very different expectations and options.

Whatever concrete scenario one might imagine, however, it is interesting to notice that even most of those scholars who think that the domination over Palestine passed uninterrupted from the Assyrians to the Egyptians do not want to deny the possibility of the Josianic reform. According to N. Na'aman the emphasis of the Egyptian rule 'was placed on control of the valley districts and the coast, whereas the mountain areas were considered of secondary importance' (1991: 40). So, in his view the Egyptian vassalage of Josiah was of a more nominal kind. The same is true for Finkelstein and Silberman who restricted the

---

51. 'Aus allen diesen Angaben ergibt sich das Bild eines ägyptischen Vasallen Joschija, der keineswegs ein Großreich etablieren und eine eigenständige Politik verfolgen konnte' (Niehr 1995: 44).

52. Cf. Miller and Hayes 1986: 383-91; Na'aman 1991: 40-41, 52-53; Ahlström 1993: 763-67, 778-79.

53. See the interpretation of Na'aman, referred to by Davies (pp. 65-67, below). Miller and Hayes 1986: 388, draw from Jer. 2.16-18, 36-37 the conclusion that in Palestine 'there was a hegemony shared between the Nile and Mesopotamian superpowers'. But this interpretation is very doubtful. Jer. 2.4–4.2 is addressed to Israel, the people of the former Northern Kingdom (2.4). The first passage, Jer. 2.14-18, does not deal with the present but with the past (cf. *waw* consecutive imperfect in v. 15), when the Northern Kingdom pursued its ruinous seesaw politics between Assyria and Egypt (cf. Hos. 5.12-14). On the contrary, Jer. 2.36-37 (and also the actualizing verse, 2.16) deals with present dangers and warns the northern brethren to place their hope in Egypt because they will fail, as their hope of Assyria had failed in the past. It can be suggested that—after becoming free from Assyrian rule—the population in the North hoped to win the restoration of their state with the help of Egypt. Thus, during the late-seventh century Egypt clearly succeeded Assyria in Palestine; cf. Albertz 2003.

54. That Isa. 8.23b–9.6 is to be dated in the late seventh century and refers to the young king Josiah was convincingly shown by Barth 1977: 141-77.

Egyptian interest 'mainly to the coast' and saw the path 'open for a final fulfilment of Judahite ambitions' (2001: 283). Thus, in any case the change of hegemony in Palestine during the last third of the seventh century opened a space where a cultic, social, and national reform could take place in Judah. Even a limited expansion of Judah to the north on the hill country is conceivable under such international conditions.[55]

Admittedly, apart from the report in 2 Kings 22–23, other sources for the Josianic reform are rather scarce. The archaeologists could not provide anything essential for it.[56] Only a little bit more did the biblical scholars! The often repeated argument that contemporary texts like the book of Jeremiah[57] do not know anything of the reform is not correct. The passages of Jer. 5.4-6 and 8.7-8 refer explicitly to a law of YHWH that should give advice to the people, especially to the learned and wealthy upper class, but was neglected after Josiah's death. In Jer. 3.22–4.2; 31.2-6 the Israelites of the former Northern Kingdom are invited to come to Jerusalem and worship YHWH there, in accordance with Josiah's national policy. And a closer reading of Jeremiah 2–6 reveals that the accusation against syncretism, which played a prominent role in Jeremiah's preaching to the brethren in the north (2.4–4.2), does not appear in his preaching to the Judaeans at all (4.3–6.30), which could testify to the results of Josiah's reform indirectly. Sometimes it is said that the different kinds of syncretism and foreign cult practices in the accusation in Ezek. 8.7-18 contradicted any Josianic reform; but this event belongs to a much later period (593/2 BCE), 29 years after the cult reform (622 BCE). Moreover, it must be taken into account that Ezekiel could easily misunderstand or overstate a rumour from Jerusalem that he heard in Babylonia.[58]

Thus, the body of evidence that the Josianic reform happened during the late seventh century could have been much better. Often we possess only clues, not hard facts. Philip Davies is to be commended for not only denying the Josianic reform and pushing the book of Deuteronomy into any later period but also trying to give reasons for a fifth-century dating. But in my view, the evidence given by him is rather less convincing than that of the traditional hypothesis.

---

55. Heltzer (2000) thinks that the seventh-century bulla of the Shlomo Moussaieff Collection would testify that Josiah annexed even such a northern place like 'Arubboth in the vicinity of Taanach as early as 630/629 BCE from the Assyrians. But the evidence remains doubtful.

56. Cf. Finkelstein and Silberman 2001: 287-88. The little that was found was partly made unusable by improper excavation; cf. the unclear closure or abandonment of the temple in Arad. The only possible evidence is provided by the seal impressions of the late seventh century, which include only names, sometimes decorated with some floral ornaments, but are lacking the religious, often astral icons, in contrast to the seals before, cf. Uehlinger 1995: 67-70, as well as his contribution to the present volume (pp. 279-316). But they also can mean just a higher level of literate persons or simply a new fashion.

57. So again Kaiser 1984: 134.

58. Why Ezekiel personally charged with apostasy a member of the Shaphan family (Ezek. 8.12) who had been one of the promoters of the reform remains obscure.

Bibliography

Ahlström, G.W.
    1993   *The History of Ancient Palestine from the Palaeolithic Period to Alexander's Conquest* (JSOTSup, 146; Sheffield: Sheffield Academic Press).

Albertz, R.
    1987   'Israel I: Altes Testament', in *Theologische Realenzyklopädie* XVI: 368-79.
    1994   *A History of Israelite Religion in the Old Testament Period* (OTL; 2 vols.; Louisville, KY: Westminster/John Knox Press).
    1997   'Die Theologisierung des Rechts im Alten Israel', in *idem* (ed.), *Religion und Gesellschaft. Studien zu ihrer Wechselbeziehung in den Kulturen des Antiken Vorderen Orients* (Alter Orient und Altes Testament, 248; Münster: Ugarit-Verlag): 115-32.
    2001   *Die Exilszeit, Das 6. Jahrhundert v. Chr.* (Biblische Enzyklopädie, 7; Stuttgart: Kohlhammer).
    2002   'Die Zerstörung des Jerusalemer Tempels 587 v. Chr.: Historische Einordnung und religionspolitische Bedeutung', in J. Hahn (ed.), *Zerstörungen des Jerusalemer Tempels: Geschehen—Wahrnehmung—Bewältigung* (Wissenschaftliche Untersuchungen zum Neuen Testament, 147; Tübingen: Mohr Siebeck): 23-39.
    2003   'Jer 2–6 und die Frühzeitverkündigung Jeremias', in *idem*, *Geschichte und Theologie: Studien zur Exegese des Alten Testaments und zur Religionsgeschichte Israels* (ed. I. Kottsieper and J. Wöhrle; BZAW, 326; Berlin: W. de Gruyter): 209-38 (orig. *ZAW* 94 [1982]: 20-27).

Barth, H.
    1977   *Die Jesaja-Worte in der Josiazeit: Israel und Assur als Thema einer produktiven Neuinterpretation der Jesajaüberlieferung* (WMANT, 48; Neukirchen–Vluyn: Neukirchener Verlag).

Blenkinsopp, J.
    1988   *Ezra–Nehemiah: A Commentary* (OTL; Philadelphia: Westminster Press).

Cowley, A.
    1923   *Aramaic Papyri of the Fifth Century B.C.* (Oxford: Clarendon Press).

Davies, P.R.
    1992   *In Search of 'Ancient Israel'* (JSOTSup, 148; Sheffield: Sheffield Academic Press).

Dietrich, W., and Th. Naumann
    1995   *Die Samuelbücher* (Erträge der Forschung, 287; Darmstadt: Wissenschaftliche Buchgesellschaft).

Finkelstein, I., and N.A. Silberman
    2001   *The Bible Unearthed: Archaeology's New View of Ancient Israel and the Origin of Its Sacred Texts* (New York: Free Press).
    2002   *Keine Posaunen vor Jericho. Die archäologische Wahrheit über die Bibel* (Munich: Beck).

Geller, S.A.
    2000   'The God of the Covenant', in B.N. Porter (ed.), *One God or the Many: Concepts of Divinity in the Ancient World* (Transactions of the Casco Bay Assyriological Institute, 1; New York: The New Yorker Collection): 273-319.

Gross, W. (ed.)
    1995   *Jeremia und die 'deuteronomistische Bewegung'* (BBB, 98; Weinheim: Beltz Athenäum).

Gunneweg, A.H.J.
    1987   *Nehemia* (KAT, XIX, 2; Gütersloh: Gütersloher Verlagshaus).

Handy, L.K.
 1995 'Historical Probability and the Narrative of Josiah's Reform in 2 Kings', in S.W. Holloway and L.K. Handy (eds.), *The Pitcher is Broken: Memorial Essays for Gösta W. Ahlström* (JSOTSup, 190; Sheffield: Sheffield Academic Press): 252-75.
Hardmeier, Chr.
 1989 *Prophetie im Streit vor dem Untergang Judas. Erzählkommunikative Studien zur Entstehungssituation der Jesaja- und Jeremiaerzählungen in II Reg 18–20 und Jer 37–40* (BZAW, 187; Berlin: W. de Gruyter).
 2000 'König Joschia in der Klimax des DtrG (2Reg 22f.) und das vordtr Dokument einer Kultreform am Residenzort (23,4-15*)', in R. Lux (ed.), *Erzählte Geschichte: Beiträge zur narrativen Kultur im Alten Israel* (Biblisch-Theologische Studien, 40; Neukirchen–Vluyn: Neukirchener Verlag): 81-145.
Heltzer, M.
 2000 'Some Questions Concerning the Economic Policy of Josiah, King of Judah', *IEJ* 50: 105-108.
Hölscher, G.
 1922 'Komposition und Ursprung des Deuteronomiums', *ZAW* 40: 161-255.
Kaiser, O.
 1984 *Einleitung in das Alte Testament: Eine Einführung in Ergebnisse und Probleme* (Gütersloh: Gütersloher Verlagshaus, 5th edn): 132-34.
Karrer, Chr.
 2001 *Das Ringen um die Verfassung Judas. Eine Studie zu den theologisch-politischen Vorstellungen im Esra–Nehemia–Buch* (BZAW, 308; Berlin: W. de Gruyter).
Kellermann, U.
 1967 *Nehemia. Quellen, Überlieferung, Geschichte* (BZAW, 102; Berlin: W. de Gruyter).
Lemaire, A.
 2002 *Nouvelle inscriptions araméennes d'Idumée*, II (Transeuphratène, Supplement, 9; Paris: J. Gabalda).
Miller, J.M., and J.H. Hayes
 1986 *A History of Ancient Israel and Judah* (Philadelphia: Westminster Press).
Mowinckel, S.
 1923 'Die vorderasiatischen Königs- und Fürsteninschriften. Eine stilistische Studie', in H. Schmidt (ed.), *Eucharisterion* (Festschrift H. Gunkel; FRLANT, 36; Göttingen: Vandenhoeck & Ruprecht): 278-322.
Na'aman, N.
 1991 'The Kingdom of Judah under Josiah', *TA* 18: 3-71.
Nelson, R.D.
 2002 *Deuteronomy: A Commentary* (OTL; Louisville, KY: Westminster/John Knox Press).
Niehr, H.
 1995 'Die Reform des Joschija: Methodische, historische und religionsgeschichtliche Aspekte', in Gross (ed.) 1995: 33-52.
Noth, M.
 1957 [1943] *Überlieferungsgeschichtliche Studien* (Tübingen: Max Niemeyer, 2nd edn).
Person, Jr, R.F.
 2002 *The Deuteronomic School: History, Social Setting, and Literature* (Studies in Biblical Literature, 2; Atlanta: Society of Biblical Literature).

Reinmuth, T.
    2002   *Der Bericht Nehemias. Zur literarischen Eigenart, traditionsgeschichtlichen Prägung und innerbiblischen Rezeption des Ich-Berichts Nehemias* (OBO, 183; Fribourg: Universitätsverlag).

Renz, J., and W. Röllig
    1995   *Handbuch der althebräischen Epigraphik*, I,1 (Darmstadt: Wissenschaftliche Buchgesellschaft).

Rofé, A.
    1985   'The Monotheistic Argumentation in Deuteronomy 4.32-40: Content, Composition, and Text', *VT* 35: 434-45.
    1987   'The Battle of David and Goliath: Folklore, Theology, Eschatology', in J. Neusner, A. Levine and E.S. Frerichs (eds.), *Judaic Perspectives on Ancient Israel* (Philadelphia: Fortress Press): 117-51.

Römer, Th.C.
    1997   'Transformations in Deuteronomistic and Biblical Historiography: On the "Book-Finding" and Other Literary Strategies', *ZAW* 109: 1-11.

Rudolph, W.
    1949   *Esra und Nehemia* (HAT, I, 20; Tübingen: J.C.B. Mohr).

Rüterswörden, U.
    1987   *Von der politischen Gemeinschaft zur Gemeinde. Studien zu Dt 16,18–18,22* (BBB, 65; Frankfurt/Bonn: Peter Hanstein Verlag).

Schmid, K.
    1996   *Buchgestalten des Jeremiabuches: Untersuchungen zur Redaktions- und Rezeptionsgeschichte von Jer 30–33 im Kontext des Buches* (WMANT, 72; Neukirchen–Vluyn: Neukirchener Verlag).

Steymans, H.U.
    1995   *Deuteronomium 28 und die Adê zur Thronbesteigung Asarhaddons: Segen und Fluch im Alten Orient und Israel* (OBO, 145; Fribourg: Universitätsverlag).

Tov, E.
    1985   'The Composition of I Samuel 16–18 in the Light of the Septuagint Version', in J. Tigay (ed.), *Empirical Models for Biblical Criticism* (Philadelphia: University of Pennsylvania Press): 97-130.
    1986   'The Nature of Differences between MT and LXX', in D. Barthélemy *et al.* (eds.), *The Story of David and Goliath: Textual and Literary Criticism* (OBO, 73; Fribourg: Universitätsverlag): 19-46.

Uehlinger, Chr.
    1995   'Gab es eine joschijanische Kultreform? Plädoyer für ein begründetes Minimum', in Gross (ed.) 1995: 57-89.

Veijola, T.
    1982   *Verheißung in der Krise. Studien zur Literatur und Theologie der Exilszeit anhand des 89. Psalms* (Annales Academiae Scientiarum Fennicae, Series B, 220; Helsinki: Suomalainen Tiedeakatemia).

Williamson, H.G.M.
    1985   *Ezra, Nehemiah* (WBC, 16; Waco, TX: Word Books).

Würthwein, E.
    1994   'Erwägungen zum sog. deuteronomistischen Geschichtswerk: Eine Skizze', in *idem*, *Studien zum Deuteronomistischen Geschichtswerk* (BZAW, 277; Berlin: W. de Gruyter): 1-11.

Josiah and the Prophetic Books: Some Observations

Ehud Ben Zvi

1. *The Josiah of the Prophetic Books*

1.1. *Introduction*

In stark contrast to the abundance of reconstructed texts and redactional activity within the prophetic books[1] that have often, though controversially, been associated with the Josianic period (see §2, below), the ancient readers of the prophetic books were asked to associate only two of them with Josiah's reign, namely the book of Zephaniah and that of Jeremiah, but the latter only in a very partial way.

This fact by itself is already remarkable and demands some further consideration, and in particular a study of its possible implications, given (a) the strong lionization of Josiah in the book of Kings, and (b) the close relationship between deuteronomic/deuteronomistic ideas, and according to some social movements,[2] with the king's initiatives as reported in Kings. This fact, however, does not stand by itself; rather it is only one piece of information within a larger set whose cumulative weight cannot be simply explained away.

1.2. *Additional Data*

1.2.1. First, whereas the 'other great king of the tradition', that is, Hezekiah is a central character in some narratives included in the prophetic books (see Isa. 36–39), and whereas kings later than Josiah and other Judahite personages play

---

1. By 'prophetic books' I refer here to books that were eventually included under the rubric of 'Latter Prophets'. I discuss the genre of prophetic book in a forthcoming work, E. Ben Zvi, 'The Prophetic Book: A Key Form of Prophetic Literature', in M.A. Sweeney and E. Ben Zvi (eds.), *The Changing Face of Form Criticism for the Twenty-First Century* (Grand Rapids: Eerdmans, 2003), pp. 276-97.

2. According to many scholars, the deuteronomistic movement/s strongly influenced prophetic literature. Even if one were not to accept such a position, many of the ideas associated with proposed deuteronomic or deuteronomistic movements became central to post-monarchic discourses and strongly influenced prophetic literature. For my own 'skeptic' position on the matter of the historical existence of 'deuteronomistic *movements*' in general, and particularly on their purported influence on the books that eventually became 'The Twelve', see E. Ben Zvi, 'A Deuteronomistic Redaction in/among "The Twelve": A Contribution from the Standpoint of the Books of Micah, Zephaniah and Obadiah', in L.S. Schearing and S.L. McKenzie (eds.), *Those Elusive Deuteronomists: The Phenomenon of Pan-Deuteronomism* (JSOTSup, 268; Sheffield: Sheffield Academic Press, 1999), pp. 232-61; cf., in the same volume, R.A. Kluger, 'The Deuteronomists and the Latter Prophets', pp. 127-44, and S.L. Cook, 'Micah's Deuteronomistic Redaction and the Deuteronomists' Identity', pp. 216-31. Of course, there is no denial that there is deuteronomistic language in the book of Jeremiah.

central roles in narratives that are integral to the book of Jeremiah (e.g. Jer. 26; 28; 35; 37; 40–43), nothing similar can be said about Josiah.

This is particularly salient in a book such as Jeremiah that includes a text that (a) parallels another present in the book of Kings,[3] and as such evokes in the mind of its readers the memory of the other text; (b) shows a 'deuteronomistic flavor', and (c) contains a considerable amount of narrative and therefore, could have easily included stories about Josiah.

1.2.2. Even in the only two prophetic books in which Josiah's name is mentioned, it appears in the most conventional, non-salient way. In fact, his name appears there only as required by common use, that is, as the name of the reigning king in temporal clauses[4] or as a patronym, in references to other kings who do stand at the center of the story.[5]

1.2.3. The readers of the prophetic books would have never learned about the reform/purge[6] that Josiah carried out according to the book of Kings, a reform which supposedly represented a major departure from the traditional ways of monarchic Judah. There is no clear, concrete reference to that reform in any prophetic book, even those that are set in that period and even those that include quotations from the book of Kings.[7]

1.2.4. The book of Kings does associate a prophetic figure with Josiah and his reform, namely Hulda (see 2 Kgs 22.14-20). Significantly, his figure is not mentioned at all in prophetic literature.

1.2.5. The overwhelming impression of Josianic times in the prophetic books that are set in these days is that this was an appalling period characterized by social and cultic sin and by a refusal to listen to YHWH's way. Josianic times are therefore deeply intertwined with the general description and evaluation of the late monarchic period as one that directly led to the (ideologically just) destruction of Jerusalem and the Judahite polity.

---

3. See Jer. 52 and cf. 2 Kgs 24.18–25.30.
4. Jer. 1.2; 3.6; 25.3; 36.2; Zeph 1.1.
5. Jer. 1.3 (twice); 22.11, 18; 25.1; 26.1; 27.1; 35.1; 36.1, 9; 37.1; 45.1; 46.2. The possible exception is the reference to 'Shallum, son of Josiah, who reigns in place of Josiah, his father' in Jer. 22.11. But this is probably a literary development of the patronymic name formula. In any case, Shallum, not Josiah, is the main character in the literary unit. On this text see §1.2.6.
6. It is debatable whether Josiah's actions should be referred to as 'reform' or as 'purge'. For the sake of simplicity and following a long tradition, I use hereafter the term 'reform'.
7. Some scholars have considered Jer. 11.1-17 as proof that Jeremiah advocated Josiah's reform during Josiah's days. See, for instance, H.H. Rowley, 'The Early Prophecies of Jeremiah in their Setting', in L.G. Perdue and B.W. Kovacs (eds.), *A Prophet to the Nations: Essays in Jeremiah Studies* (Winona Lake, IN: Eisenbrauns, 1984), pp. 33-61; and cf., in the same volume, L.G. Perdue, 'Jeremiah in Modern Research: Approaches and Issues', pp. 1-32 (esp. pp. 4-6). But the text in Jer. 11.1-17 certainly did not inform its intended and primary readers of the reform, nor ask them to set the text in Josiah's days; in fact, the text does not even mention Josiah or any of his actions.

This is so notoriously evident in the book of Zephaniah that attempts to harmonize its depiction of Josiah's times with the glorious picture of the book of Kings often involved either a complete removal of Josiah from the book,[8] or a partition of the Josianic period in two: (a) a first phase in which Josiah was lad and not actually in control and so the historical circumstances were as described in the book, and (b) a second phase in which he was an adult, carried out his reform, and thus overturned the previous appalling state.[9] In either case, the harmonizer is introducing into the book of Zephaniah something that is not there at all. The book is clearly set in the time of Josiah, and nowhere tells its readers that the world it describes reflects only the first years of Josiah's reign, or the period when he was a minor. The readers of the book are told nowhere that Josiah actually changed the reported circumstances in his own days. Moreover, the text shows no expectation that this particular king, or any human king for that matter, will ever lead the people out of its abysmal situation and behavior. Significantly, this observation—along with others, see below—undermines also the position that the book was written during the time of Josiah, and for the purpose of supporting his reform and his supposed attempt at royal revival and political expansion.[10]

In fact it is most likely that an authorship and readership that among others, (a) 'was influenced by other prophetic traditions, wisdom literature, the *'anawim*

---

8. See, e.g., J.P. Hyatt, 'The Date and Background of Zephaniah', *JNES* 7 (1948), pp. 25-29; D. Williams, 'The Date of Zephaniah', *JBL* 82 (1963), pp. 77-88.

9. See already Radak, and among contemporary scholars, for instance, J.J. Roberts, *Nahum, Habakkuk and Zephaniah* (OTL; Philadelphia: Westminster Press, 1991), p. 163. In addition to the tension between the depiction of Josianic Judah in Zephaniah (and Jer. 3.6-11; see below) and in 2 Kgs 23, the attempt to associate the book or, alternatively, its hypothetical forerunners or reconstructed sources to the pre-reform period, and particularly to the time when Josiah was a minor is often based on (a) the assertion in the book of Kings that Josiah became king when he was eight years old (2 Kgs 22.1), and (b) the lack of reference to the king in Zephaniah. None of these observations requires that the book of Zephaniah or any of its hypothetical textual forerunners be composed when Josiah was a minor. Incidentally, according to the narrative in Kings, a substantial number of years separate the time in which Josiah ceased to be a minor and his decision to begin the reform. It was only when he was 26 years old that he did the latter (see 2 Kgs 22.1-3). The ideological tension created by this substantial period and the glorious evaluations of Josiah in Kings is resolved in Chronicles by changing the date of the reform (see 2 Chron. 34.1-3). Moreover, Chronicles reflects and communicates a set of standards of age for a maturing boy: (a) when he is eight years old, he is a minor; (b) when he reaches sixteen, he is a kind of 'mature minor', who can or perhaps should show initiative (though he remains a minor and, therefore, is not able to exercise fully power nor to take upon himself the responsibilities associated with an adult of his status); (c) when he is of twenty years of age, he is a full adult and then he assumes his responsibilities (cf. the case of the Levites, and see 1 Chron. 23.24-27 and cf. Ezra 3.8). Josiah, a pious king, of course, does not delay and begins his reform when he is twenty years old (see 2 Chron. 34.3).

10. For this position, see, for instance, M.A. Sweeney, *King Josiah of Judah: The Lost Messiah of Israel* (Oxford: Oxford University Press, 2001), pp. 185-97, 317; idem, *The Twelve Prophetic Books* (Berit Olam; 2 vols.; Collegeville, MN: Liturgical Press, 2000), II, pp. 493-526. For the position that the words of Zephaniah belong to the Josianic period, but that they point to school of thought other than the one that drove the reform of Josiah, see J. Vlaardingerbroek, *Zephaniah* (HCOT; Leuven: Peeters, 1999), pp. 17-24.

psalms, the *malak* psalms, and congregations psalms', (b) thought of an ideal community as one of 'poor humble people without a king or a royal elite, oppressed by wealthy, proud impious enemies', and (c) 'waits for salvation from God alone—no king or national leader is expected to raise' belongs to the post-monarchic rather than the monarchic period.[11] This being so the book of Zephaniah belongs in all likelihood to that period and the absence of references to Josiah's reform and to him at all is to be explained in a different manner (see below).

Turning to the book of Jeremiah, the precise extent of literary readings or units within the book that the intended readership was supposed to set in Josiah's time is unclear. In any case, whereas these readers were explicitly asked to associate a large number of these reports about prophetic activities and related matters with the times of kings later than Josiah, only *one* report clearly asks them to anchor the ensuing text to the Josianic period, namely the one that begins in Jer. 3.6. The temporal reference there could have been understood from the perspective of the ancient readership as pointing only to Jer. 3.6-11, but could also have been grasped as somewhat more open-ended and could have left these readers wondering whether they were supposed to read some of the undated prophetic words reported in literary units following 3.6-11 (e.g. 3.12-13, 14-18, 19-25) as set in Josianic times. In either case, (a) given the explicit and extremely negative tone of 3.6-11, which is singled out as the only unequivocal text that they should associate with the time of Josiah, and (b) the overall contents of the other units or readings as well, it is obvious that the readers were asked to imagine the period in very negative terms.

In addition, although Josiah is a very minor royal character in the book of Jeremiah, and particularly so when compared to Jehoiakim or Zedakiah,[12] both the temporal introduction (see Jer. 1.1-3) and the inclusion of numerous reports

---

11. The quotations are from A. Berlin's summary of my own position on the matter. For her position, see A. Berlin, *Zephaniah* (AB, 25A; New York: Doubleday, 1994), pp. 31-43. For the quotations, see p. 36. For my own position, see also E. Ben Zvi, *A Historical-Critical Study of the Book of Zephaniah* (BZAW, 198; Berlin: W. de Gruyter, 1991); and *idem*, 'History and Prophetic Texts', in M.P. Graham, J. Kuan and W.P. Brown (eds.), *History and Interpretation: Essays in Honor of John H. Hayes* (JSOTSup, 173; Sheffield: JSOT Press, 1993), pp. 106-20. My position may be contrasted with that of M.A. Sweeney. For bibliography, see above. It bears note, however, that at times M.A. Sweeney uses a very cautious and open language. For instance, he enunciates four issues that according to him are central to the argument for the late dating of Zephaniah and then remarks, 'there are various problems with these views that *hold open the possibility* that the present form of the book of Zephaniah can and should *be read* in relation to Josiah's reign' (Sweeney, *Josiah*, p. 186 [emphasis mine]; on this matter see also §2.3.2, below). To be sure, the ancient readers were asked to read it in relation to Josiah's reign, but the question is one of dating and of the historical background of the authorship and the readership for which the book in its present form was composed. For the detailed arguments advanced by M.A. Sweeney and myself, see the bibliographic references above, and cf. both of our positions with that of A. Berlin. It may be mentioned that on this matter M.A. Sweeney follows and develops further positions advanced in C.F. Christensen, 'Zephaniah 2.4-15: A Theological Basis for Josiah's Program of Political Expansion', *CBQ* 46 (1984), pp. 669-82.

12. This fact is by itself worth noting, and particularly so given the 'deuteronomistic' flavor that characterizes the book of Jeremiah. See §1.3.3.

that are not explicitly anchored to the reign of a particular Judahite king[13] created a connoted message of temporal openness and continuity within the late monarchic period (Josiah–Zedekiah).[14] The connoted general continuity in Jeremiah's words and, by necessity, in the basic, general circumstances that he was condemning during his reported period of activity could not but contribute to the shaping of a negative image of Josiah's period. It is worth stressing that this connoted meaning becomes quite explicit in, and is supported by texts in which the words of Jeremiah of different regnal periods are treated basically as one (see Jer. 25.2-3; 36.2-3).

From the viewpoint of the basic ideological question of whether the people followed YHWH's ways or rejected them, and on the basis of the book of Jeremiah, the ancient readers of this book could have only imagined the circumstances that existed in Josianic Judah as not too different from those prevalent during the reigns of the last four kings of Judah. In sum, even if one allows for the fact that the Josianic period is not at the center of the book, there is no doubt that the overall construction of the Josianic period that the book of Jeremiah suggested to its intended readers was very negative. It was an integral part of an appalling era that led directly to the (ideologically just) destruction of Jerusalem, its temple and the Judahite polity.[15]

1.2.6. The mentioned overwhelming negative impression of Josiah's time that is conveyed by the only two prophetic books that are set fully or partially in his days is not substantially undermined by any explicit reference to Josiah's reign in the entire corpus of prophetic books. Nothing similar to the note in Jer. 26.18-19 concerning Hezekiah's times is present in the corpus.

The only possible exception is Jer. 22.13-17/19. This text is often quoted to show how much Jeremiah, the prophet, appreciated Josiah.[16] Leaving aside (a) the problematic association of Jeremiah the historical prophet and the words attributed to the literary (and ideological) character Jeremiah in the text, (b) questions about the date of the text and any examination of scholarly hypotheses of its possible redactional history,[17] and (c) the presence of basic elements of royal

---

13. Provided, of course, that he is included in the set of later monarchic kings comprising Josiah, Jeohahaz, Jehoiakim, Jeohiachin and Zedekiah.

14. The presence of these texts and the message referred to here created a balance between dated and undated reports. The former were deeply associated with particular times and events and therefore tended to shape an image of the conditions in Judah at a very particular point in time during the late monarchic period; the latter contributed to the image of the period as a whole. This image is, of course, a very negative one.

15. On Jer. 22.13-19, see §1.2.6.

16. See, e.g., A.A. Wieder, 'Josiah and Jeremiah: Their Relationship According to Aggadic Sources', in M.A. Fishbane and P.R. Flohr (eds.), *Texts and Responses: Studies Presented to Nahum N. Glatzer on the Occasion of his Seventieth Birthday by his Students* (Leiden: E.J. Brill, 1975), pp. 60-72 (60); Sweeney, *Josiah*, p. 211.

17. See R.P. Carroll, *Jeremiah: A Commentary* (OTL; Philadelphia: Westminster Press, 1986), esp. pp. 422-29; W. McKane, *A Critical and Exegetical Commentary on Jeremiah*. I. *Introduction and Commentary on Jeremiah 1–XXV* (ICC; Edinburgh: T. & T. Clark, 1986), pp. 526-34;

ideology that were common in the ancient Near East, the central question for the present purposes is whether this reference required the ancient readers for whom the book of Jeremiah was composed to change substantially the characterization of Josianic times conveyed by the book as a whole. A brief analysis of some aspects of the unit is required to answer this question.

First, the unit is marked from the outset by the initial formula 'participle+הוי'. The interjection הוי introduces the ensuing text, informs its readers of what it is about and suggests to them that ill-fate will befall the evildoer/s referred to by the attached participle. Moreover, the participle already contributes to the characterization of that evildoer/s. But who is the evildoer? If or when the ancient readers of Jer. 22.13 approached the text from a perspective informed by the preceding verses, they were likely to consider him to be Shallum. But such a reading falters in v. 18. As the text is read from a perspective governed by Jer. 22.18-19, the referent becomes obvious; he is Jehoiakim. Although the latter is the main personage characterized as the evildoer king in the unit, it bears notice that within its literary context, the text is presented to the readers in such a way that elicits them to contemplate whether Shallum may be such a king. In other words, the text works at more than one level. It directly focuses on a certain personage of the past, but also hints at, and indirectly contributes to the association of its negative characterizations with another personage from the past.

Keeping this in mind, let us turn to another and, for the present purposes, crucial observation. The text includes a comparison between the evildoer son and his pious father. This is a common literary topos that serves the rhetorical and ideological purpose of emphasizing the sinful character of the son within a discourse that assumes that sons 'naturally' tend to follow the traits of their fathers or forefathers (i.e. the male ancestral line). One who did not follow the positive traits of his male ancestor is thus characterized as not only wicked but 'unnaturally' wicked. The use of such a common literary topos carries by necessity a positive characterization of the father/male ancestor of the wrongdoer, even if the focus of the text is clearly on the latter. The wording of the text here and particularly the characterization of Jehoiakim in this unit seem to recall the wording present in book of Kings,[18] and this being so, it is likely that the intended readers of this portion of Jeremiah were asked to evoke their own readings of Kings. Against this background, it is particularly interesting that the contrast between the father and the son here is not that present between Josiah and Jehoiakim in the book of Kings. 'Jehoiakim is not condemned for his cultic sins (cf. 2 Kgs 23.37) and Josiah is not praised by his Yahwistic piety (cf. 2 Kgs 23.25).'[19] The evil king in Jer. 22.13-17 is described as one who built his own magnificent palace but failed to 'do' משפט וצדקה. Significantly, there are only two kings that

---

W.L. Holladay, *Jeremiah*. I. *A Commentary on the Book of the Prophet Jeremiah Chapters 1–25* (Hermeneia; Philadelphia: Fortress Press, 1986), pp. 591-99.

18. See על דם נקי לשפוך in v. 17 and cf. 2 Kgs 21.16; 24.4. The latter verse attributes this action to Jehoiakim.

19. McKane, *Jeremiah*, I, p. 527.

are explicitly and precisely described as 'doing' משפט וצדקה in the so-called deuteronomistic history. The two are David and Solomon (see 2 Sam. 8.15 and 1 Kgs 10.9). Both built their own magnificent palaces (2 Sam. 5.11; 1 Kgs 3.1; 7.1), and were certainly considered the archetypal builders of Judah. Thus the figure of the father with whom the readers were supposed to contrast the sinful, builder king included that of Josiah, but also that of fathers David and Solomon.[20] One might claim that the text associated Josiah with David/Solomon, but it also bears note that among the reasons for which a sinful king may be compared with pious David in Kings is that his biological father was not so pious (see 1 Kgs 15.3, but cf. 2 Kgs 16.2). Moreover, if the text of Kings is kept in the background of the readers, then how strong is the rhetorical argument that good befalls the pious kings if the latter are exemplified by Josiah[21]? In addition, the contrast between David–Solomon and Jehoiakim suits better than that of Josiah–Jehoiakim, given the main theme of the book of Jeremiah of explaining the destruction of the Temple and the fall of the Davidic monarchic, and reversal topos such as the builder who is in fact a demolisher. In sum, for rhetorical purposes the text shapes here a composite image of the 'father' that includes Josiah but goes much beyond him, and, as such, dilutes the praise associated with him.

In any event, even if one grants that the text likely conveyed, or at least connoted to its intended readership an implied praise of Josiah, this praise is not clearly communicated, and in any case it does not call particular attention to itself, but stands as a background to the salient theme. It serves a secondary role as a device to shape the text's negative characterization of Jehoiakim (and at a contextual, connoted level possibly that of Shallum). Such a faint, secondary and only implicit praise is no rhetorical match to the overly negative texts explicitly presented to the readers as representing the Josianic society (see above). Had the authorship of the book of Jeremiah wished to communicate an explicit praise of Josiah that could have countered the negative impression created by the other units in the book, it would have included in the book a literary unit very different from Jer. 22.13-17/19.

1.3. *Implications and Conclusions*

1.3.1. Despite all their differences, the books of Jeremiah and Zephaniah, that is, the *only* two prophetic books that ask their readers to anchor prophetic texts to the Josianic period, agree in their explicit request from their readers to imagine the period in the most negative, ideological terms. In both cases, Josiah is not referred to as a major character and his religious reform is nowhere mentioned.[22] In fact, the situation described in these texts seems to contradict any claim that such a reform ever took place. What can be learned from this conclusion?

---

20. It is worth mentioning that the image of David as the 'father' of all the kings of Judah is well established in Kings (cf. 1 Kgs 15.3; 22.51; 2 Kgs 16.2; 18.3; 22.2) and particularly for the purpose of comparisons.
21. See 2 Kgs 23.29-30.
22. On this matter, see also below, §2.

1.3.2. The presence of texts whose stories or claims are at odds with those advanced in the collection of books usually called the deuteronomistic history is attested elsewhere in post-monarchic Judah/Yehud. In fact, the stories they constructed about their past had to agree only on certain core issues, but evidently could diverge on others.[23] For instance, the book of Ruth asked its readers to imagine a period in which 'there was no king' and in which a couple of women —without any man to 'guard' them—could and did walk freely from Moab to Judah,[24] and as a period in which people did not do what 'was right in their own eyes'. The contrast with Judges 19 is obvious.[25] Tensions between the historical narratives of Kings and Chronicles and within the book of Judges itself are well known. Moreover, even when books by their choice of language and through the presence of shared ideological viewpoints were set in relation to each other within the repertoire of authoritative books accepted by the readership/s, clear and meaningful contradictions were still allowed to stand. For instance, the ideological and 'constitutional' role of the king in Deuteronomy, which leaves him with very restricted powers (see Deut. 17.14-20 and cf. Deut. 16.18–18.22) stands at odds with the description and evaluation of his office in the narrative in Kings. In fact, it is difficult to find in the former any legal support or authority for many of the actions taken by Josiah as king and for which he is praised in the book of Kings.[26]

---

23. I wrote elsewhere on the degree of malleability in ancient Israelite historical reconstructions. See E. Ben Zvi, 'Shifting the Gaze: Looking at the Lack of Change in Chronicles. Historiographic Constraints and Their Implications', in M. Patrick Graham and J. Andrew Dearman (eds.), *The Land that I Will Show You: Essays on the History and Archaeology of the Ancient Near East in Honor of J. Maxwell Miller* (JSOTSup, 343; Sheffield: Sheffield Academic Press, 2001), pp. 38-60; idem, 'Malleability and its Limits: Sennacherib's Campaign Against Judah', in L.L. Grabbe (ed.), *'Like a Bird in a Cage': The Invasion of Sennacherib in 701 BCE* (JSOTSup, 363; ESHM, 4; London and New York: Sheffield Academic Press), pp. 73-105; idem, 'The Secession of the Northern Kingdom in Chronicles: Accepted "Facts" and New Meanings', in M.P. Graham, S.L. McKenzie and G.N. Knoppers (eds.), *The Chronicler as Theologian: Essays in Honor of Ralph W. Klein* (JSOTSup, 371: London: T&T Clark International, 2003), pp. 61-88.

24. The image of women traveling alone was a common, transcultural, rhetorical topos used to gauge and describe the degree of safety and security in a country. If women could travel alone—that is, without any man to guard them—then the land enjoyed a great degree of safety; conversely, if women were attacked even when a man guarded them, the land was full of lawlessness. Similar images are used even today, although usually to describe the degree of safety in parks and neighborhoods at particular times of the day rather than nations as a whole.

25. The period of Judges, that is, the period in which there was no king over Israel, was imagined in positive terms in some postmonarchic books. It bears note that ideal futures in which no (human) king is envisaged appear in the book of Zephaniah and in another post-monarchic prophetic book, Obadiah. Moreover, the language of Obad. 21 is evocative of language associated with Judges and connotes a positive evaluation of the period. These issues stand, however, beyond the scope of this paper.

26. On the tension between the narrative in Kings and the prescriptive 'legislation' of Deuteronomy regarding the position, status and responsibilities of the king, see G.N. Knoppers, 'Rethinking the Relationship between Deuteronomy and the Deuteronomistic History: The Case of Kings', *CBQ* 63 (2001), pp. 393-415. This tension may have implications for the dating and social location of the book of Deuteronomy and of its conception of the desired organization of the state. It may have also

However, at times or among some groups, tensions among constructions of the past that are authoritative within the community tend to be 'resolved' rather than maintained. Whereas the book of Kings, which does not mention Jeremiah in relation to Josiah (cf. the prophetic books) or at all, Chronicles adds a note to inform its readership that Jeremiah and Josiah—two main pious figures of the past who were contemporary to each other—were on the same side, and that Jeremiah lamented the death of the king (see 2 Chron. 35.25).[27] Thus the different constructions of the Josianic past discussed here allow us to study shifts in that which is included among core 'historical' facts and evaluations agreed upon by different ancient Israelite communities. It seems, for instance, that the overwhelming weight of the positive description of the Josianic period in Kings was a major determinant in the way in which the period was constructed through generations. Against this background, the construction of that past within the corpus of prophetic books in general, and the books of Zephaniah and Jeremiah in particular is all the more remarkable.

1.3.3. Within the discourse/s of post-monarchic literati for whom and among whom the books later included in the Hebrew Bible were written, read, reread, maintained and the like, the main issue facing a community holding constructions of the past that stood at odds with each other was not the issue of 'historicity' as understood today, but that of the ideological messages conveyed by these constructions of the past.

The consistent and explicit failure of prophetic literature to ask its intended and primary readership to reconstruct a lionized Josiah, or even to consider this king as a major character in late monarchic Judah is probably related to a general tendency in post-monarchic discourse/s to chip away from the figure of Josiah in favor of that of Hezekiah. This process is clearly reflected in Chronicles.[28] The reasons underpinning such a development within the mentioned constructions of the past is clear: the Josianic reform reported in Kings could not and did not save Judah and Jerusalem, Hezekiah's actions just did so. In fact, the beginning of the

---

implications for the question of the interrelation between the book of Kings and Deuteronomy. These implications are particularly interesting since the text of the former suggests to its readers that the book that was found (2 Kgs 22–23) is likely to be Deuteronomy, though it is never explicit about its contents—except that it states that disaster will come because the people have not followed YHWH—and never quotes from it (ct. 2 Kgs 14.6). In other words, the book suggests that the book found is in many regards very similar to Deuteronomy, but not necessarily that book. Thus Kings leaves a degree of openness that is consistent with a position of both (a) acceptance of much of Deuteronomy's ideology but also (b) reluctance concerning some of its elements (e.g. the constitutional role of the king, the required punishment of a sinful city in Deut. 13). These considerations are the more remarkable if one takes into account that both books, at least in their present forms, are post-monarchic. Needless to say, they deserve a separate study and any analysis of them is far beyond the scope of this particular chapter.

27. Many centuries later, rabbinic literature addressed and 'solved' the problem. See Wieder, 'Josiah and Jeremiah'.

28. P.R. Ackroyd, 'The Biblical Interpretation of the Reigns of Ahaz and Hezekiah', in W.B. Barrick and J.R. Spencer (eds.), *In the Shelter of Elyon: Essays on Ancient Palestinian Life and Literature in Honor of G. W. Ahlström* (JSOTSup, 31; Sheffield: JSOT Press, 1984), pp. 247-59.

process of the ideologically necessary marginalization of the importance of the reform is already present in Kings itself (see 2 Kgs 23.26-27[29]).

In addition, the consistent and explicit failure of prophetic literature to ask its intended and primary readership to reconstruct a lionized Josiah, or even to consider this king as a major character in late monarchic Judah is also related to, and consistent with the tendency in these books to construct a general picture of late monarchic Judah shaped around an ideologically necessary correspondence between the magnitude of the divine punishment inflicted on Judah in 586 BCE and the behavior that caused it.

1.3.4. These observations about the Josiah of the prophetic books are particularly helpful for the purpose of developing historical reconstructions of the discourses of postmonarchic communities and the ways in which they shaped the past. The overt lack of centrality of Josiah and his reform communicated by these texts is of great importance for that task, and its implications deserve further study.

These observations, however, are not particularly helpful for the purpose of using the prophetic books, in their present form, to develop historical reconstructions of the most likely Josiah of the sixth century and his times. To state the obvious, the lack of references to Josiah's reform or territorial expansion in the prophetic corpus cannot be used to support scholarly claims that such developments actually happened. But by itself, such a lack cannot rule out them out either, and particularly so, given the ideological tendencies that shaped these books.

Moreover, any attempt to identify the historical Josiah with the Josiah of the prophetic books would be mistaken and methodologically faulty, since such attempts would involve blurring the differences between literary/ideological characters and historical figures. The reconstruction of the historical Josiah and his actions must be carried out on the basis of other sources. Are the prophetic books particularly helpful in this regard?

2. Josiah or the Josianic Period in the Prophetic Books

2.1. Introduction

Although aside of the texts discussed above Josiah is not mentioned in prophetic literature nor his reform ever mentioned, it is certainly reasonable to attempt to learn about his times by analyzing prophetic literature written or read and reread during his reign. Lack of direct references to Josiah's times should not be an impediment for that purpose.[30] As mentioned above, there is a plethora of hypothetical forerunners of the prophetic books, redactional levels in different prophetic books, or even independent literary subunits later attached to prophetic books that have often, though controversially, been related to the Josianic period

---

29. Cf. 2 Kgs 22.15-20, though within the narrative his actions did not even merit him to die in peace, only to die before the destruction of Jerusalem.

30. Incidentally, I, for one, have followed this methodological approach time and again in my studies of Persian period Yehud.

in modern research.³¹ The crux of the matter is, of course, one of dating. To be relevant to this discussion the texts must have been composed within and for a readership/s who lived in the Josianic period and its immediate aftermath.³²

2.2. Basic Criteria Governing Dating

Although it is impossible to deal separately and at length with each and every case of proposed Josianic dates in a paper—or perhaps even in a monograph—it is not only possible but essential for the goal of this paper to discuss the basic criteria according to which texts have been associated with this period. These criteria are thematic. They can be grouped around four related themes: (a) Josiah's territorial expansion—either achieved or only planned; (b) anti-Assyrian spirit and propaganda; (c) the idea of the re-unification of the 'twelve tribes' under a Davidide who thus becomes a great 'new David'—or even a quasi-Messianic David, or in its more general version, the exaltation of Israel under its Davidic king;³³ and (d) Josiah's reform and the ideology of Deuteronomy.

Thus if a scholar relates a text such as Zeph. 2.4-15 to Judahite territorial expansion towards Philistia, the Transjordan region or the territories of the former kingdom of Israel, then the text is associated with the Josianic period.³⁴

Similarly, texts such as Isa. 30.27-33 that show much animosity or hatred of Assyria and refer to YHWH's actions to bring about the fall of Assyria become associated with the Josianic period, and so are texts such as Isa. 10.15/16-19 in which an interpretative tradition has identified YHWH's foe with Assyria.³⁵

Criterion (c) is at work in the attribution of the composition, reading or rereading of texts such as Isa. 8.23–9.6,³⁶ the reconstructed *Urtext* of Jeremiah 30–31 (namely a text close to Jer. 30.5–31.26+31.35-37),³⁷ and proposed redactional

---

31. These texts include, among others, the so-called Josianic (or Assyrian) redaction of Isaiah, the book of Nahum, many texts in Jeremiah, the whole or much of Zephaniah, and redactional levels in Hosea, Amos and Micah. See, for instance, R.E. Clements, *Isaiah 1–39* (NCB; Grand Rapids: Eerdmans; London: Marshall, Morgan & Scott, 1982), pp. 5-6; Sweeney, *Josiah*, pp. 179-313; and idem, *Twelve Prophets*, passim. See also the discussion below.

32. For example, the book of Habakkuk, as often claimed.

33. In many cases when this thematic criterion is used, there is a debate whether the text belongs to the Hezekianic period and was later reread in terms of the Josianic era. See below.

34. See, for instance, Christensen, 'Zephaniah 2.4-15'.

35. See, for instance, Clements, *Isaiah 1–39*, pp. 252-54 and 113-14, respectively; and see his general considerations on pp. 5-6.

36. See, for instance, J. Vermeylen, *Du prophète Isaïe à l'apocalyptique: Isaïe, I–XXXV, miroir d'un demi-millénaire d'expérience religieuse en Israël* (Paris: J. Gabalda, 1977–78), I, pp. 232-49.

37. See M.A. Sweeney, 'Jeremiah 30–31 and King Josiah's Program', *ZAW* 108 (1996), pp. 569-83. There he concludes: '...the *Urtext* of Jeremiah 30–31 supports Josiah's efforts to return territory and people of the former northern kingdom of Israel to Davidic rule and thereby unite Israel and Judah. Such reconstruction has significant implications for the study of Jeremiah. It demonstrates that the prophet was active during the reign of King Josiah, and that he supported Josiah's reform. It further points to a redactional process that produced the present form of the book of Jeremiah, in that an earlier text concerned with the restoration of Israel and its reunification with Judah under Davidic rule was modified and updated to address the restoration of both Israel and Judah in the light of the Babylonian catastrophe' (p. 382). Here a redaction-critical method not only brought Josiah to a text in which he was not, but even blurred the border between a character in the book and a historical figure

levels in the books of Hosea and Micah to Josianic times, though an Hezekianic original background is often discussed. For instance, M.A. Sweeney writes,

> The interest in calling for Israel's return to YHWH and in the reunification of Israel and Judah under a single Davidic monarch is the key factor in establishing the setting for the composition of the book of Hosea. Given such an interest, it would appear that the period of Hosea's composition could extend any time from the lifetime of the prophet in the mid-eighth century B.C.E. through the reign of King Josiah in the late-seventh century. Certainly, the reunification of Israel and Judah under a Davidic monarch is central to Josiah's concerns, but the concern to show mercy to Judah and the interest in reuniting Israel and Judah under one king is hardly exclusive to the period of King Josiah. As indicated elsewhere, there is extensive interest in such issues during the time of King Hezekiah and perhaps before that time as well. Nevertheless, such considerations point to the fact that the book of Hosea would have been read in the late-seventh century B.C.E. as a prophetic justification for the reform program of King Josiah. In such a scenario, Hosea's critique of the northern kingdom, including its faithlessness, the failure of its religious leaders and kings, and its alliance with Assyria, would all be read as fulfilled prophecy in the time of Josiah. Only the last element of the prophet's message would need to be realized at such a time, viz., the reunification of the people of Israel with Judah and the return of Israel to YHWH and to the house of David.[38]

Criterion (d) has been used, for instance, in relation to texts such as Jeremiah 2, Jer. 1.4-10 and Zeph. 1.4-6. Concerning Jeremiah 2, J. Milgrom once wrote,

> ...If in each of many instances where Jeremiah castigates the prophets, he does so solely on the grounds of immorality and never for idolatry, we must conclude that the time setting for chapter 2 is separated from the rest of the book by some great action which purged the prophetic class of its idolatrous practices. We have now to ask what momentous event in the lifetime of Jeremiah and reflected in his writings could have been responsible for the complete and irrevocable purge of all idolatrous elements? Happily the answer is obvious to all students of biblical literature and history: the great reform of 622.[39]

(Jeremiah). Further, the study goes on to reconstruct the relations between the (reconstructed) historical Jeremiah with a historical Josiah, who is understood as a king who attempted to expand the Davidic rule over the north—on that matter, see §2.3.5. Of course, Sweeney is certainly not alone. His methodology is used by many other scholars and, in fact, here he develops further a position advanced first in N. Lohfink, 'Der junge Jeremia als Propagandist und Poet, Zum Grundstock von Jer. 30–31', in P.-M. Bogaert (ed.), *Le Livre de Jérémie. Le prophète et son milieu. Les oracles et leur transmission* (BETL, 54; Leuven: Leuven University Press, 1981), pp. 351-68.

38. M.A. Sweeney, 'A Form-Critical Rereading of Hosea', *JHS* 2 (1998/99) §3.9; <http://purl.org/jhs> and cf. *idem*, *Josiah*, pp. 256-72 (272). Note also Sweeney's comment: 'The book would thereby present prophetic legitimation to Hezekiah's attempts to revolt against the Assyrians who had subjugated Judah during this period. This earlier form of Micah would be quite pertinent in the late seventh century, when Josiah attempted to restore the Davidic state in the aftermath of Assyria's collapse, and would likewise present prophetic legitimation to Josiah's restoration program as the anticipated outcome of YHWH's purposes in the aftermath of Assyria's collapse... Josiah is the anticipated monarch of the book of Micah, who enables the scenario of reunification and restoration in Jerusalem to take place. The concluding chapters of Micah, which call for justice on the part of Israel (Micah 6) and express the prophet's confidence that YHWH will act to restore Israel, thereby point to Josiah's reign as the time when the restoration will take place' (Sweeney, *Josiah*, p. 300).

39. J. Milgrom, 'The Date of Jeremiah, Chapter 2', *JNES* 14 (1955), pp. 65-69.

According to J. Vlaardingerbroek, 'the spiritual abuses of idolatry and syncretism, pictured in [Zeph.] 1.4-6, 8f., 12 fit this dating [i.e. the time of Josiah]'.[40] W.L. Holladay stated,

> ...If the proclamation of Deuteronomy was initially in 622 [Josiah's reform], then subsequent readings would have taken place in the autumn of 615, 608, 601, 594, and 587... As I have already indicated, Deuteronomy would have been recited again in the autumn of 615; by our reckoning Jrm would have been twelve years old. With hesitation I suggest the possibility that this was the occasion of his call (1.4-10): vv. 7 and 9 are very similar to Deut 18.18, the word of Moses about a prophet like Moses in time to come. Is this not a likely occasion? Jrm himself protests that he is 'only a youth [נער]' (v. 6)...[41]

Examples in which the mentioned criteria for dating, separately or in any possible combination, have played a decisive role in associating prophetic texts to the Josianic times can be easily multiplied. The crux of the matter is, however, not this particular detail here or there, but how sound are these criteria for the purpose that they are used for, that is, to associate a text, or an aspect of the text with the time of Josiah rather than with any other possible period in ancient Judahite (including Yehudite) history.

2.3. An Assessment of the Criteria
2.3.1. Four sets of somewhat interrelated concerns can be raised about the mentioned criteria. Whereas one may take issue with the way a particular question is dealt with here, it is their cumulative weight on the question of what can be learned from the prophetic books about the actual historical conditions in the times of Josiah that seems to undermine the entire enterprise.

2.3.2. Thematic criteria such as those expressed above can at the very best point to a possible date, and at times to the earliest possible date of a text. Certainly not every text that may seem consistent with wishful thinking concerning a program of, or an actual territorial expansion encompassing northern Israel and neighboring countries must be Josianic, as the book of Obadiah clearly shows.

There is no reason to assume that texts expressing animosity against Assyria could have been written *only* during the narrow window between, let's say 625 BCE—the year of Nabopolassar's accession—and 609 BCE—the year of Josiah's death.[42] There is clear attestation for Assyria standing as a powerful symbol in literature from periods far later than the Josianic (see Jonah; Neh. 9.32). In addition, not only did the term 'Assyria' clearly point to other empires in some cases (see Ezra 6.22), but also there cannot be much doubt that, for instance, the rereaders of the book of Isaiah—as a whole—understood and were asked to understand 'Assyria' as pointing to the 'imperial successors of Assyria'.[43] If they

---

40. Vlaardingerbroek, *Zephaniah*, p. 13.
41. Holladay, *Jeremiah 1*, pp. 1-2.
42. Cf. J. Blenkinsopp, *Isaiah 1–39* (AB, 19; New York: Doubleday, 2000), p. 92. On this matter, see also §2.3.5.
43. Cf. Blenkinsopp, *Isaiah 1–39*, pp. 256, 423-24.

understood Assyria in these terms, why couldn't a later-than-Josianic writer have done so, at any time, including the postmonarchic era?

Ezekiel 37.24-28, certainly a post-Josianic text, expresses the idea of the reunification of the tribes under a Davidic king. Hopes for a new David and for a gathering of exiles are often expressed in much later literature (e.g. the Jewish prayer, the Shemoneh Esreh, which no one, to my knowledge, ever dated as a whole or in part to Josianic times).

Similarly, knowledge of Deuteronomy and a negative attitude towards the type of cultic practices that the Josianic reform aimed at uprooting according to Kings are very common, in fact, one may say ubiquitous, in clearly post-Josianic literature (e.g. Chronicles) and were representative of the ideological discourse of the Achaemenid Yehud.

In sum, arguments based on the thematic criteria mentioned above may at best hold the *possibility* that the relevant texts were written in, or were read during the Josianic period in direct relation to his assumed policies and programs. A study of how likely this possibility is compared to other possibilities cannot be carried out on the basis of these criteria, or for that matter simply on the basis of historical references to Assyria, because its fate and basic facts about its history were known also at times later than the Josianic period.[44]

2.3.3. If one were to grant that a very substantial number of prophetic texts do come from the Josianic period and reflect the position, deeds or even plans of the king and his court and supports them, then the obvious question is why none of them clearly pointed at the actions of the king reported in the book of Kings, and why the name of the king is missing in almost every text including those that were or could have been explicitly set in his times (e.g. the books of Zephaniah, Jeremiah, Nahum). Is it likely that texts written during the time of a Near Eastern king, and produced directly or indirectly through the resources of the local center of power and for its consumption, and purportedly aimed at supporting the king and his policies would have carried and communicated an image of a self-effacing king? Is it likely that such texts would have advanced an ideology in which there is no need for a human king, as the book of Zephaniah—in its present form—does?

If the answer to the previous questions is negative, as the balance of the evidence suggests, then to maintain the likelihood that many texts from the period remained in prophetic literature one would have to assume a process of selection and reinterpretation of those references whose result was that the expected references were consistently dropped out. But if so an additional hypothesis has to be entertained. Following Ockham's razor—the principle that states that things not known to exist should not be postulated as existing unless it is absolutely necessary—one must raise the question of whether this is actually a case of 'absolute necessity'.

---

44. Therefore references to Assyria were somewhat expected in books whose world is set in the relevant period.

2.3.4. With the exception of the books of Nahum and Zephaniah whose present form some scholars date to Josianic times,[45] the rest of the texts relevant to the present discussion that are often associated with the Josianic era are scholarly reconstructions based on redaction-critical methods. This observation raises general and particular concerns.

Turning to the former, even if the prophetic books were the result of a long redactional process, the ability of scholars today to reconstruct precise original texts and redactional layers is much in doubt. Since I have written on this matter on several occasions,[46] it would suffice here to say that if texts evolved through the addition and omission of reports about prophecies, of notes, and interpretations and reinterpretations of older material, as this model requires, then do we have accurate enough tools to distinguish them? This question is particularly poignant since prophetic books, in part because they are texts to be read and reread and studied, tend to show multiple meanings that at times stand in tension with, and balance each other. They tend to show multiple voices and multivocal perspectives, abrupt changes of addressees, speakers and settings in the world of the book, and do tend to defamiliarize social interactions (and literary genre). And, of course, there is no possible way to reconstruct textual omissions. Further, the prophetic books do not include textually inscribed markers that require their intended readership to read the books in ways informed by its redactional process; in other words, the presumed authors of these changes did not call attention to their own actions of textual addition, reconfiguration and omission and asked the readers of the books to recognize their own works and separate them from those of the author/s of the 'original' text. It is not by chance that scholars who use very similar methodological approaches and accept similar assumptions still tend to diverge on their precise reconstructions. Even within their methodological approaches it is difficult to identify the precise textual subunits that belong to this or that redactional level or actually to reconstruct the wording of an *Urtext*.[47] Finally, these reconstructions often involve more than one reconstructed redactional action. Mathematics shows that two independent sequential decisions in

---

45. On the dating of Zephaniah, see above. Even if one were to grant that the book of Nahum in its present form was written during Josianic times—which is highly debatable—the book would not shed much light on the historical period in Judah, except for the ability to 'publish' at least one prophetic book that carries a strong anti-Assyrian sentiment. But the book of Nahum may be later than Josiah's times. For instance, it, or most of it, may have been written during the period of Babylonian hegemony. On the matter of strong negative characterizations of Assyria and of joy over his fall, see below.

46. See, for instance, E. Ben Zvi, *Micah* (FOTL, 21b; Grand Rapids: Eerdmans, 2000); and *idem*, *A Historical-Critical Study*.

47. For instance, and related to our present task, Clement's Josianic redaction is different from Barth's Assyrian redaction. Cf. J. Blenkinsopp's comments on the matter in his *Isaiah 1–39*, pp. 91-92. Note also his treatment of texts often associated with the Assyrian/Josianic redaction of Isaiah such as Isa. 8.9-10; 10.16-19; 11.1–12.6; 14.24-27; 17.12-14; 28.23-29; 29.8 (or 5-8); 30.27-33; 31.5, 8-9; and 32.1-5, 15-20 on pp. 239-41, 254-56, 262-70, 289-90, 306-7, 396-98, 398-402, 422-24, 425-28, 425-38 respectively. (For Sweeney's position regarding Josianic elements in Isaiah, see his *Josiah*, pp. 234-55 and bibliography.)

which one has as high as twice the chance of being correct than not lead to a conclusion that by itself has more chances of being wrong than correct.[48]

In addition to these general issues, there are particular concerns regarding these proposals. The reconstruction of redactional levels or original texts to be associated with or dated to the Josianic era is most often influenced by a historical reconstruction of the period that is assumed by the scholar beforehand. For instance, some of these scholars obviously assume that Josiah's court was or became strongly anti-Assyrian, rather than being a partner of Assyria and of its successor empire, Egypt. They often assume that Josiah's court either led to a territorial expansion or planned it, that Josiah wished and perhaps even attempted to reunite the Northern tribes with Judah under his and Jerusalem's rule, or the full historicity and success of his reform. But if these historical reconstructions are assumed beforehand then the proposed Josianic texts constructed on the grounds of their acceptance cannot be used to prove the very same historical reconstructions that serve as starting point for the scholars' analysis. The best possible argument that may be advanced under these circumstances, without falling into circular thinking, is that *if* the mentioned historical reconstructions are correct, then it would be possible to reconstruct texts that, if they existed at that time, would be consistent with the mentioned historical reconstructions. But if this is the best possible scenario, then the mentioned reconstructed prophetic texts cannot be taken as independent sources for the study of the Josianic period.[49] This being so, they cannot be used for the critical reconstruction of the most likely historical circumstances in Josianic Judah.

2.3.5. The preceding discussion leads to another central concern: What if the historical reconstructions that underlie the proposed dating of the mentioned prophetic texts—or reconstructed prophetic texts—to the Josianic period turn out to be groundless? For instance, what if there was no substantial Josiah's territorial expansion—either achieved or planned? Or, what if there is no evidence that the court was involved in anti-Assyrian actions or propaganda or that even attempted to free itself from Assyria—or its friendly, allied and successor state in the area, Egypt? Or, what if there is no evidence that there was ever a plan for, never mind a real attempt to achieve the re-unification of the 'twelve tribes' under a Davide in Josiah's times? Or, what if there are questions about the extent of Josiah's reform and its relation to Deuteronomy?

These questions are not hypothetical. They stand at the center of the present debate on the historical circumstances of Josianic Judah.[50] Other contributions to this seminar will deal with them, and I myself have addressed some of them and

---

48. Two-thirds multiplied by two-thirds results in four-ninths—that is, the conclusion will be wrong five times out of nine.
49. On circular thinking as related to the dating of prophetic texts, see Ben Zvi, 'History and Prophetic Texts'.
50. Cf. N. Na'aman, 'The Kingdom of Judah under Josiah', *TA* 18 (1991), pp. 3-71 (a modified version of which appears in the present volume).

their implications in a previous work.⁵¹ There is no point in repeating the arguments advanced in that contribution. It would suffice here to restate that there was no 'Josianic empire'; instead, there was only a minimal territorial expansion (the Bethel area)⁵² that did not involve any kind of rebellion against Assyria or Egypt. In fact, I am convinced that there is *no* evidence that the Josianic court developed an anti-Assyrian or anti-Egyptian policy at all.⁵³ Nor is there any evidence that Josiah carried out the reunification of the twelve tribes under his throne.⁵⁴

Of course, it is possible to advance the position that although Josiah and his court did not extend the Judahite territory except for a few miles, they planned a large expansion; that although they did not rebel against Assyria or Egypt, they planned to do so and rejoiced at their failures; and that although they did not 'reunite the tribes' (i.e. they did not annex the territories of the former kingdom of Israel to that of Judah), they planned and hoped to do so. And if so, since they planned to do all these things, the (reconstructed) prophetic literature mentioned above was or could have been created to promote these goals. But this position suffers from critical weaknesses. Not only is there no independent evidence to support it,⁵⁵ but also the position itself is essentially unverifiable. Moreover, things not known to exist should not be postulated as existing unless it is absolutely necessary, and there is no 'absolute necessity' here. To be sure, the assumption

51. Ben Zvi, 'History and Prophetic Texts'.
52. There is no evidence suggesting that there existed tensions between Josiah and the Transjordanian kingdoms, and certainly not any pointing at Judahite territorial conquests in that area. Similarly, there is no evidence that Josiah conquered Philistine territories. For the extent of the Josianic kingdom, see Na'aman, 'Kingdom of Josiah', and bibliography; R. Kletter, 'Pots and Polities: Material Remains of Late Iron Age Judah in Relation to its Political Borders', *BASOR* 314 (1999), pp. 19-54 and bibliography; I. Finkelstein and N.A. Silberman, *The Bible Unearthed* (New York: Free Press, 2001), pp. 347-53, and cf. and partially contrast with G. Galil, 'Geba'-Ephraim and the Northern Boundary of Judah in the Days of Josiah', *RB* 100 (1993), pp. 358-67.
53. It bears note his kingdom and certainly its elite benefited much from *Pax Assyriaca*. The fact that the transition from Assyrian to Egyptian hegemony did not involve a grave upheaval of the regional system, and particularly so from the perspective of vassal states, in other words that *Pax Assyriaca* turned into *Pax Egytiaca* without serious turmoil, is consistent with the idea that the local elites that benefited from their participation in the regional system had a vested interest in maintaining it. Significantly, by and large, local powers tended to oppose the Babylonian takeover of the area.

It bears note also that (a) since Egypt never rebelled against Assyria during Josiah's days, any Judahite rebellion becomes very unlikely, and (b) since Judah was most likely a loyal Egyptian vassal at the time the latter was an ally of Assyria and fought on its side against the 'neo-Babylonian' alliance, it is unlikely that the official position of the Jerusalemite court was anti-Assyrian and that it rejoiced at the latter's defeats, that is, at the victories of the enemies of its own great king, the Egyptian king.

54. Despite all its lionization of Josiah, even the book of Kings does not claim so. 2 Kgs 23.19-20 suggests a raid on Samarian territory, not its annexation. The difference from a text such as 2 Sam. 5.1-3 is obvious.

55. Any sources abstracted or reconstructed from the prophetic books that were associated with the time of Josiah and its historical circumstances on the basis of the assumption that Josiah and his court did plan any of the above cannot be taken as evidence without engaging in circular thinking. See §2.3.4.

that there existed unfulfilled and unverifiable plans could be used to maintain the validity of the first three criteria mentioned, once the historical reconstruction that supported them fell apart, and so to allow these criteria to reconstruct or to assign prophetic texts to the Josianic period[56]—but this cannot be considered a 'critical necessity'.

In the preceding paragraph I have left the question of the historicity of the reform of Josiah and its likely extent and influence.[57] For the purposes of the discussion advanced here it suffices to restate emphatically that knowledge of Deuteronomy and a negative attitude towards the type of cultic practices that the Josianic reform aimed at uprooting, according to Kings, were very common in clearly post-Josianic literature and cannot be a reliable consideration for assigning a text to Josiah's times. In fact, this criterion is the least commonly used among the four mentioned above.

3. *Conclusions*

Although it is possible that some material in the prophetic books, or their precursors, may go back to Josianic Judah, and that this material was composed or read at that time, there are no solid, non-circular criteria to identify them. Thus, the prophetic books do not provide identifiable, independent sources for the reconstruction of the historical circumstances in Josianic Judah. Other sources are required for this task.

The images of Josianic Judah and of Josiah reflected and shaped in the prophetic books, however, are particularly helpful for the purpose of historical reconstructions of the discourses of post-monarchic communities—both in terms of how they dealt with accepted images of the past that stood at odds with each other, and in term of the way in which they constructed what they considered to be their own past.

---

56. Perhaps they also serve to preserve, even if as a wisp, or as much as possible of the old glorious, quasi-messianic image of Josiah's days, which existed not only till recent times in modern research, but that goes back centuries and is clearly present in, for instance, rabbinic literature. There it is claimed that Jeremiah 'brought back' the ten tribes during the reign of Josiah and the latter reigned over them (*b. Meg.* 14b).

57. These matters are dealt with in other contributions to this volume and were seriously addressed in the seminar that spawned it. A summary of the discussion appears in the introduction of the volume. These matters, however, go beyond the scope and goal of this particular chapter.

Josiah and the Law Book

Philip R. Davies

> The most important decision in the history of Israelite religion is made with a dating of an essential part of Deuteronomy to the time of Josiah.
> —Rainer Albertz, *History of Israelite Religion*: I, 199

> The remarkable narrative about Josiah in the DtrH has proved to be a pivotal text in biblical scholarship and has shaped the entire discipline of Hebrew Bible. It provides the fundamental linchpin by which modern critical scholarship reconstructs the development of Israelite/Judean religion and the compositional history of much of the biblical literature.
> —Marvin Sweeney, *King Josiah of Judah: The Lost Messiah of Israel*: 5

> Über Alter und Herkunft des Dt sind die Akten jedenfalls nicht geschlossen.
> —Otto Kaiser, *Einleitung, in das Alte Testament*: 124

> What we can't show, we don't know.
> —Jacob Neusner, *passim*

Josiah's Ambitions

The various historical questions surrounding Josiah have been very thoroughly covered elsewhere in this volume, and my own contribution is conceived largely as a methodological one, in which I shall engage with two of my colleagues in the Seminar. My starting point is Nadav Na'aman's study on the politics of the kingdom of Judah under Josiah (Na'aman 1992), which offers a very fine critique of scholarship on the reign of Josiah, summarized as follows.

The first part of Na'aman's study argues that the town lists of Judah and Benjamin in Joshua 15 and 18 reflect, despite some editorial enhancement, the situation in seventh-century Judah. The second part deals with the chronology of the decline of Assyrian power, often thought to have occurred suddenly in the early part of Josiah's reign, prompting a policy of Judaean expansion over adjacent territory. Na'aman shows this proposed scenario to be unlikely; on the contrary, the Assyrians seem to have ceded control over Palestine in a more or less orderly way to Egypt, so that the Judaean king had little or no opportunity for the exercise of political independence; in short, there was no 'power vacuum'. In connection with the death of Josiah, Na'aman argues that Necho marched through Palestine (rather than sailing his army to a Phoenician port, the more usual procedure) not to do battle with Babylonia but in order to receive the pledge of loyalty from the local kings that required to be renewed on the accession of a new sovereign pharaoh. Noting that nothing is said in 2 Kings of a battle with

Josiah, Na'aman deduces that Josiah died not in battle but by assassination or execution for some reason, possibly a suspicion of disloyalty on Necho's part; thus Josiah's visit to Megiddo may have been in response to a summons to pledge his loyalty personally before the new pharaoh.

What might have provoked Josiah's execution? Although Na'aman allows that effective control of Palestine passed to Egypt as Assyrian power declined, Josiah might nevertheless have enjoyed (or felt he had) some freedom to 'unify' and 'crystallise' (1992: 41) his kingdom, while the efforts of the Egyptians were, as usual, concentrated on the coastal and valley districts. Only a limited expansion of borders, however, could have been even contemplated, let alone achieved; no grand design for extensive territorial gains.

This reconstruction makes sense of a death that otherwise, as Miller and Hayes (1986: 402) remark, 'remains a mystery'. While 2 Kgs 23.29 possibly hints at military confrontation in its use of לקראתו and its comment וירכבה ועבדיו (chariot and, perhaps 'soldiers'), military confrontation is not explicitly mentioned; and קרא does not necessarily mean 'meet in battle', nor are עבדים necessarily 'soldiers'. Nor is the chariot an inappropriate way to transport a royal corpse even in peacetime. The account of Josiah's death is tantalizingly vague, even mysterious—and perhaps deliberately so. At any rate, the hint of a military defeat allows 2 Chron. 35.20-24 to show the pious king dying of battle-wounds in Jerusalem, in turn encouraging most modern scholars to conclude that Josiah went into battle, even though it leaves them puzzled over the motives for such a suicidal venture.[1]

Even if Na'aman is not correct over Josiah's manner of death, his analysis of the political situation is well-grounded in the evidence. The often-asserted expansion of Judah under Josiah did not, and could not, take place. Statements such as 'He [Josiah] attempted to restore the kingdom or empire of David in all detail' (Cross 1973: 283) Na'aman dismisses as 'built on shaky foundations'; there are, he says (1992: 44), 'no grounds for the assumption that Josiah attempted to conquer the entire north and to impose his reforms throughout the territory of Palestine'—a conclusion already anticipated by a few earlier historians.[2]

There remains, however, some apparent epigraphic evidence to the contrary in letters from Arad and Meṣad Ḥashavyahu. Arad ostraca 1–18, dated to the reign of Josiah or his successor, belong to a collection sent to Eliashib, a military commander, and most give instructions for the provisioning of troops. However, these instructions are not necessarily evidence of Judaean military resurgence or of Judaean refortification of Arad. Under Egyptian jurisdiction Josiah would have

---

1. Two motives that have been suggested are obedience to a treaty or understanding with Babylonia, against which Necho was marching; and a defence of Josiah's newly won territories. The biblical reports, perhaps significantly, state no motive for such an engagement.

2. Cf. Miller and Hayes 1986: 401: 'It is highly doubtful, however, that Josiah extended Judean borders...except in the case of Bethel'; Ahlström 1993: 764: '[I]t is unrealistic to think that Josiah could have extended his kingdom in this period to include the Assyrian province of Samerina, perhaps also Magidu and Gal'aza, territories of the former kingdom of Israel, as well as part of the coast, as if often maintained'.

been permitted or required to take responsibility for providing garrisons (Greeks, 'Kittim', are especially mentioned) and agricultural workers in adjacent areas, following the practice reflected much earlier in the Amarna correspondence. From Meṣad Ḥashavyahu the complaint from a worker (possibly from the time of Josiah or his successor) points rather to Judaeans obliged to work in the vicinity of the fortress (see Davies 1991: 76-77 [Meṣad Ḥashavyahu]; 11-16 [Arad]; for a convenient discussion, Smelik 1991: 93-115) The evidence of these ostraca is entirely consistent with known Egyptian practice during its periods of rule over Palestine and does not contradict Na'aman's reconstruction.

The conclusion of Na'aman's arguments is that 'The picture of Josiah's reign, as reflected in this discussion, is far removed from the description of those years as reflected in the book of Kings, and no less distant from the sketch of his period presented in modern historiography' (Na'aman 1992: 55). This points to a not unfamiliar state of affairs; a misleading biblical portrait further distorted by the speculations of biblical scholarship; in this case the thesis of a golden period of Josian *Wiederaufbau*. That portrait has to be redrawn—but not just in respect of territorial ambition or achievement, but also for other aspects of his reign.

The presentation of Josiah in 2 Kings is, then, misleading, and modern scholars have often magnified the distortion. But let us not be too arrogant about this; it can be extremely easy to fall back on seemingly innocent biblical details as historical data. Thus, Na'aman himself reports at the beginning of his essay what he says we *know* about Josiah: that he succeeded Amon, 'who had been murdered by his courtiers; the rebellion was quashed and the conspirators executed; Josiah was crowned at the age of 8 and was supported by his mother and by those circles which had ensured his accession'; Josiah then 'assumed full authority only upon reaching maturity' (Na'aman 1992: 3). But compare the text of 2 Kings, where the support of Josiah's mother is not mentioned: merely her name is given. And as for when Josiah assumed 'full authority'—we are told only that he issued an order at the age of 18. So here too Na'aman is drawn into saying things about Josiah that we do not really know, however minor these details may be! The value of a regular seminar of historians is that we can alert each other to our lapses, 'keep each other honest', as far as we can. More, rather than less, skepticism is needed if we are interested in historical knowledge, as distinct from scriptural testimony.

Josiah's 'Reform'

I now wish to pick up Na'aman's baton and run a little further with it. Does the account of Josiah's reform also belong to the idealization evident in respect of his territorial ambition? In modern scholarship, Josiah's assumed policy of expanding a newly independent Judah into territory formerly of the kingdom of Israel is founded, after all, in the report of his religious reform; or, the other way round, the reform is commonly explained as part of his measures to signal, or consolidate, his political independence. But if that independence could never have been achieved, only at best a modest acquisition of territory beyond the Judaean border, then the modern explanation given for Josiah's reform does not hold. Indeed, we are left unclear as to what it *was* intended to achieve. Religious reforms at the beginning of a king's reign are not uncommon: they serve to commend the new monarch to his subjects and deity. But this reform was not undertaken until well into his reign.

The account in 2 Kings does not in fact portray Josiah as expanding his territory; it takes his control over the erstwhile kingdom of Israel for granted, conveniently erasing (from the time of Hezekiah onwards) any hint of Assyrian domination. Na'aman has suggested that Josiah could not have been portrayed as subservient to Assyria because he was a just king, as Hezekiah before him. This is plausible, and both Hezekiah (2 Kgs 18) and Josiah are credited with a religious reform; but, according to the scheme of 2 Kings, any good king following a bad king would *have* to undertake religious reform and freedom from Assyrian influence is required to make this plausible. Given this theo-logic, whether either king actually did perform the Deuteronomistic requirement is really not easy to affirm. The historical reality of Hezekiah's resistance—as debated in an earlier seminar (Grabbe [ed.] 2003)—is that he lost most of his territory and paid off Sennacherib with a large fortune. The mere fact that Jerusalem was not taken and that the Assyrian king departed has permitted Hezekiah to be accorded the rank of a righteous king. The case of Josiah is more interesting. What qualified *him* for the same status? Was it his 'heroic' death? Or was it, indeed, some seemingly pious act? Was Josiah credited with a reform because his status required it, or was his status prompted by some Deuteronomistically approved deed that he accomplished? I shall try and arrive at an answer, if only provisionally.

The reform story falls into three episodes: the discovery and verification of the law book, followed by the covenant (22.3–23.3); and the destruction of religious objects and places (23.4-20). A third episode (23.21-24), comprising the celebration of the Passover and removal of certain religious practitioners, refers again to the law book. Whether the second episode is intrinsically connected to the first is unclear; the literary structure of 2 Kings 22–23 remains disputed and there is a possibility either that the law book motif was inserted into a reform narrative or a reform narrative developed after a story of the discovery of a law book (see Lohfink 1985). It should also be noted that Josiah's reforming activities are confined to Judah and its immediate environs, notably Bethel—with the exception of a single brief notice about the territory of Samaria (2 Kgs 23.19). What other evidence have we for either? We should begin (as have many previous scholars) by seeking allusions to a reform or echoes of it (or lack of either), in other biblical texts. Then the nature of the law book itself requires analysis.

The Impact of Josiah's Reform

There seems little or no hint of any reform in other biblical literature that might be assigned to the period, for instance the books of Jeremiah or Zephaniah. Albertz (1994: 200) points to Jer. 8.7-8, suggesting a written law in the hands of priests. But this text does not mention any *reform*. He also mentions Jer. 22.15, 31.2-6 and 44.18 as offering some support for the idea of a 'climate of reform'.

But there is no clear or direct indication in the book—whose hero is a contemporary of Josiah and which has received substantial Deuteronomic editing—that a major religious reform has taken place. Sweeney (2001: 129-313) has more recently analyzed a wider range of prophetic texts (Zephaniah, Nahum, Jeremiah, Isaiah, Hosea, Amos, Micah and Habakkuk), concluding that 'Prophets who were contemporary with Josiah actively addressed aspects of his reform program and frequently point to aspects that are not evident in the DtrH account of his reign' (p. 310). Space does not, unfortunately, permit a detailed appraisal of Sweeney's lengthy discussion. But those texts that he cites in support pointing to the centrality of Jerusalem hardly indicate unambiguously the time of Josiah rather than a later period; several texts are said to refer to aspects of the reform not mentioned in 2 Kings (and so cannot in fact corroborate it!); and several other texts are said to have provided legitimation for the reforms, including the re-unification of the divided kingdoms, but do not necessarily presuppose it. Having assessed Sweeney's evidence and arguments, I have not found any convincing reference to a reform as described in 2 Kings 22–23, and very little that suggests any religious reform at all at this time, with one important exception, to which I shall return presently—and which does not involve a law book. I maintain, then, that we do not have any text that, in the absence of 2 Kings 22–23, would lead us to suggest a religious reform. This must be required of any independent corroboration. A few texts *might* refer to such a thing, *if it had happened*, but do not entail it having happened). In short, Sweeney's arguments (the fullest panoply yet assembled) depend on the assumption that there was a reform, and do not provide adequate evidence that there was one. Such absence is significant if not conclusive.[3]

This conclusion brings us, then, to the question of the law book. As is well-known, de Wette can be credited with having bequeathed to us the realization that Josiah's law book was the book of Deuteronomy, or some form of it. This identification provided him with a vital key to detaching the law from the Mosaic origins of Judaism, and thus to developing a critical reconstruction of the history of Israel's and Judah's religion. (It is, however, worth recalling that de Wette regarded D as the *latest* of the Pentateuchal sources, and that his identification of the law book as Deuteronomy has not been universally accepted to the present.[4]) Yet it takes no genius to see that the identification of Deuteronomy with the Josianic law book is precisely what the author of 2 Kings 22 intends. The language and ideology of the framework of 2 Kings is Deuteronomistic, and even before Noth's theory of the 'Deuteronomistic History' it could have been realized

---

3. I cannot refrain from commenting here on the oft-quoted dictum that 'absence of evidence is not evidence of absence'. True, but as a principle it cannot cope with cases of extra-terrestrial abduction, charges of wife-beating or fairies in my garden. It allows anything to be true that is not contradicted. Not surprisingly, those who invoke this principle seem to confine it to the Bible and keep it well away from real life!

4. This opinion has from time to time been challenged, though usually in terms of an *exilic* date (e.g. Hölscher 1922; Würthwein 1976). For a review of the history of scholarship on Deuteronomy, see Kaiser 1978: 113-20.

that any *Deuteronomistic* account of the finding of a law book would present that law book as *Deuteronomy* (rather than, say, Leviticus or the 'Covenant Code' of Exodus). The writer of the law book story wishes to make it clear that in the days of the kings of Judah, the scroll of Deuteronomy, which had been lost temporarily, was recovered and used as the basis of a religious reform, and with the full authority of a Davidic king, no less. Albertz's comment that 'it is only possible to assess Josiah's cultic reform more precisely when the identity of the law book which provided its basis has been established' (1994: 198-99) misses the point. We *know* what the law book of the story was: but we do *not* know if the story of its 'discovery' (or some modern rationalization, like a deliberate planting of the scroll soon after composition) is true! Our question now is: Is a seventh-century origin (or perhaps earlier) for Deuteronomy likely? Is it a plausible Josian law book?

Dating the Law Book

The method of dating Deuteronomy has to proceed entirely on internal evidence, interpreted in the light of what little we know of the history of Judah, its society and its religion, during the entire period in which Deuteronomy may have been written, which includes the monarchic period, the exilic period and the Second Temple period. For simplicity I will assume ben Sira's early second-century reference to the 'scroll of the covenant of El Elyon, the law that Moses commanded us' (24.23) as the *terminus ad quem*. In asking about the date of Deuteronomy, I am not trying to reopen a debate: that debate has never stopped—as the quotation from Kaiser at the top of this essay shows (for an excellent account of the history of discussion, see Lohfink 1985).

Obviously a brief discussion paper cannot cover the range of themes and topics in Deuteronomy that would need to be addressed in order to arrive at a sound theory. The following represent a small selection of the most significant topics. Before commencing, it is important to accept that many parts of the book may have originated at a time different from the law collection itself. The first introduction (1.1–4.40) and the final chapters (chs. 27–34) are widely understood as arising from a subsequent editing process; we must therefore not seek to date the presumed 'law-book' on the basis of any material in these chapters. I shall also exclude the second introduction in 4.44–11.32 and concentrate only on the legal material, chs. 12–26.

In this core legal material (for convenience I shall treat it as a 'document') we find a sketch of a society that reflects some historical circumstances but is essentially utopian, and in some parts impractical. Its utopian character is expressed through a fictional past setting in which the utopia remains a future possibility: when 'Israel' comes into 'the land Yahweh your god is giving you as a possession' (12.1; 15.4, etc.). The key question for its dating is: What purpose does such a document serve, and in what kind of historical and social context would its definition of 'Israel' have any meaning or impact? These questions will be considered (very briefly) with respect to the definition of 'Israel', the 'nations', the 'covenant', the role and function of the king, and the centralization of the cult.

The Definition of 'Israel'

In the legal core of Deuteronomy, 'Israel' designates a society, and its members are called בני־ישראל. What this 'Israel' consists of is not specified in much detail. The double mention of the 'tribe' of Levi might indicate a tribal structure for the whole, but no other 'tribe', or set of tribes, is mentioned, nor does a tribal structure have any organizational role. The repeated mention of 'the land' implies a territorial dimension to 'Israel', and the acquisition of this land is by military conquest (19.1; 20.16). The laws concerning the king (ch. 17) also imply a territorial state. Yet (see below), the role of the monarch is in fact virtually ceremonial.

Deuteronomy's 'Israel' is scarcely historical. In the monarchic period, there existed two kingdoms, one called 'Judah' and the other sometimes known as 'Israel'. The results of recent Iron Age archaeology in central Palestine strongly suggest that the areas later represented by the two kingdoms underwent separate settlement. The biblical claim that they were united under David and Solomon (and a few years under Rehoboam) is equally without any archaeological support, and indeed, there are strong indications to the contrary (see Finkelstein and Silberman 2001 for an overview and archaeological reconstruction).

The notion of this 'Israel' acquiring the land through conquest and annihilation of the previous occupants is also utopian; indeed, the presentation of 'Israel' as coming from outside the land contradicts the archaeological evidence, which can reveal no non-indigenous population element in central Palestine in the centuries prior to the establishment of the two kingdoms (the Philistines did not settle in the highlands).

But utopias have a function; it is no good dismissing them as 'fiction', as if that resolved the most important question. In what historical context does such a utopian 'Israel' (something larger than Judah) have a role? The notion that Josiah wished to reunite Judah and the erstwhile kingdom of Israel has been discussed already; it is highly improbable, but a previously united 'Israel' is also improbable. In the kingdom of Israel itself, before 722 BCE, such an ambition might be entertained—and indeed many scholars have considered Deuteronomy to be an originally Israelite document, perhaps brought south in the wake of Samaria's destruction. But, apart from other considerations that exclude this (see below), such a theory does not explain the discovery and adoption of this document in late seventh-century Judah. How and to what effect could Josiah's Judah be represented in this 'Israel'? Indeed, even if Deuteronomy's origin lay in the kingdom of Israel, on what basis would Judah call itself by that name?

The 'Nations'

The legal section of Deuteronomy refers to 'Canaanites' once, in 20.17 ('Canaan' occurs only once in the whole book, in 32.49). But there are many references to 'the nations', which fall into two categories. In 14.2, 15.6, 17.4, 18.9, 14 and 26.19 the phrase refers to all other nations, undifferentiated. 'Israel' is to be quite distinct from these, creating the dichotomy Israel/nations that still persists in our modern use of the term 'gentiles'. The second category is 'the nations that you will dispossess': these are characterized as (a) occupying the land that 'Israel' has been promised and will take over, and (b) practising religious customs that are abhorrent to Yahweh and that 'Israel' is not to imitate.

Let us concentrate on the nations dispossessed. These are specified as seven in Deut. 7.1 and 20.17 ('Girgashites' is missing, probably accidentally, from 20.17) and are to be destroyed, along with their culture. What kind of social and political background gives rise to this notion of two nations of entirely different cultures in the same space, one indigenous, the other immigrant? Is this a historical reality or, again, a utopian one? That nation and culture are synonymous is an important principle in Deuteronomy, for 'Israel' itself is defined by its culture—specifically its covenant-determined religion. 'Canaanite is as Canaanite does' we might say; and the same for 'Israel'.

While it can be argued that some cultural difference existed between population elements in early Iron Age Palestine—for instance, between highland farmers and those living under a city-state regime—the stark animosity towards the Canaanite 'nations' that Deuteronomy betrays probably does not belong to Iron Age history, because the kingdom of Israel (if not Judah) was evidently composed of several population elements, among whom there was a widely shared set of religious practices. Religious persecution, let alone genocide, as ordained by Deuteronomy, thus translates into civil war, which monarchs and ruling elites on the whole do not seek to provoke. Certainly, religion can be used to promote chauvinistic sentiments and practices, which can aid a monarch; but Deuteronomy's remedy would be disastrous for a monarchic state. Even if we translate 'nations of Canaan' into 'enemies of the royal cult', Deuteronomy's ideology appears over-enthusiastic. What, precisely, would a call to wage war on 'Canaanites' achieve—even supposing one could identify a 'Canaanite' in the first place?

Deuteronomy's 'war' is, of course, not physical or even military but ideological: the framers of the document do not intend that 'Canaanites' shall be wiped out. But the issue might well be of rightful ownership of the land, of membership of 'Israel', of proper worship of the deity; and it might involve conflict between indigenous and immigrant populations. Such a context *can* be postulated in the history of Judah. But not for the seventh century.

The 'Covenant'

Garbini (2003: 65) makes the point that the notion of a covenant between deity and people is quite startling. He claims that:

> For all Near Eastern peoples a 'covenant' between a god and his people simply made no sense: the covenant concerned only the king and his dynastic god and the king was legitimate just because of this direct relationship with the god. It was through it that the king could grant the prosperity of his people and legitimated his own function. This is clear even from the Biblical text, where it is written, just about Josiah: 'And the king stood by a pillar and made a covenant (*wayyikrot 'et ha-b^{e}rit*) before Yahweh' (2 Kgs 23,3). The question was never posed why this book, which supposedly guided the steps of the pious Josiah, does not contain any mention of covenant rites or pillars of this kind. The same ceremony, besides, was said to have been celebrated at the time of Solomon,

as it is clear from the narrative of 1 Kings 8, in spite of all Deuteronomistic amplifications. Consecrating the temple, Solomon made a covenant (8,23) with Yahweh, god of the dynasty (8,25), invoking his protection on the people, especially in the hard moments of war and famine.

This point can, however, be put more positively, as it has been by Geller in an essay on the role of Deuteronomy in the history of monotheism (Geller 2000: 300). He describes Deuteronomy as a 'radically new type of association of individuals... Israel is, in the deuteronomic formulation of covenant, ultimately each Israelite'. (This phenomenon, of the direct bond between the god and every individual, is of course strengthened rhetorically by the use of the singular 'you' in large sections of the book.) Geller further notes the denial of collective responsibility for sins in Deuteronomy 34. Deuteronomy marks the beginning of a personal definition of 'Israelite' religion—one might even say the fount of Judaism. In short, we have here, as Geller implies, a stage on the development of 'torah' into an organ of personal religiosity and not a body of social teaching upheld by a state institution (be that the monarchy or the priesthood).

How such a notion arose in the first place is an intriguing question. What sort of conditions prompted the emergence of a religion that was both social and individual? But again, the key question is: How does this personal character of Deuteronomy's covenant make sense in a small monarchic state? What is the goal and effect of such a redefinition of religion? And again, one does not have to reply that Deuteronomy is simply 'utopian'; it is necessary to suggest a context in which this vision makes sense, among a community that had formed itself, or wished to, into a community of such a kind that membership entailed individual responsibilities, especially religious ones.

Weinfeld (1972: 59-157), among others, has argued, in defence of a Josianic date for Deuteronomy, that the Assyrian vassal-treaty form (exemplified by those of Esarhaddon) supplies a model for Deuteronomy. But to be valid, this argument has to show that knowledge of such literary forms vanished at a certain point. However, the influence of Assyria on the diplomatic rhetoric and literature (as well as the imagination) of the ancient Near East persisted for several centuries. A seventh-century *terminus a quo* for Deuteronomy is not particularly indicative. More pertinent, again, is the question: Under what circumstances would a suzerainty treaty inspire a new theory of religion as a covenant between a deity and a nation, both corporately and individually conceived? And under what circumstances would such a concept acquire currency?

The Role and Function of the King

The king of 'Israel' appears in only two texts in the legal material of Deuteronomy. The first (17.14-15) runs:

> When you come to the land which Yahweh your God is giving you, and possess it, and inhabit it, and say, 'I will set a king over me, like all the nations that are about me', you shall in any case make king over you one whom Yahweh your God will choose: one from among yourselves you shall make king over you, and not put a foreigner over you, one who is not your own kin.

> He shall not multiply horses to himself, nor cause the people to return to Egypt, in order to multiply horses: for Yahweh has said unto you, 'You shall from now on return no more that way'. Nor shall he take many wives, or else his heart will turn away: nor shall he accumulate silver and gold. And when he sits on the throne of his kingdom, he shall write for himself a copy of this law in the presence of the levitical priests. It shall remain with him, and he shall read it all the days of his life: that he may learn to fear Yahweh his god, observing all the words of this law and these statutes. Thus he will not exalt himself above his fellows, nor turn not aside from the commandment, either to right or left, so that he may prolong his days in his kingdom, he, and his descendants, in the midst of Israel.

It is unlikely that the threat of a foreign king was substantial in the monarchic period (the canonized texts do not relate that this ever happened or was even threatened); even under the Assyrians and Babylonians, there was a native king on the throne—but this is a trivial matter. The major issue is this: two of main functions of a king (according to both modern sociology and also ancient monarchs themselves) are security and justice; the former protects the people from external threats and the latter from internal exploitation. Both contribute to social order. Without these functions, the role of a king is redundant. The passage quoted proposes to abolish the role of monarch; to replace his right to be the fount of justice and to have a cavalry force. Elsewhere, Deuteronomy prescribes the rules for war (ch. 20) from which the king is entirely absent. There, as here, authority is conferred exclusively on the priests. The king is subject to the law that they hold and they, not he, dictate its contents. The king becomes a constitutional monarch.

The same question returns, but with rather more force: at what point in the history of Judah does such a political revolution make sense, even as a utopian ideal? When might the rule of a Judaean monarch be replaced by a book of laws? There is no parallel at all in the monarchic period for any such notion, and indeed it is an absurd idea for such a time. The ancient law codes of Mesopotamia have, like the Assyrian suzerainty treaty, undoubtedly served as one model for the book of Deuteronomy, but in a complete reversal from the ancient tradition whereby the king issues his law code, as representative of the god.

There are no plausible explanations why a king should accept a reform that deprives him of the essential powers of monarchy, justice and warfare. To suggest that Josiah was very young at the time and that the document is an attempt on the part of priests to control royal power is naive. Would the priests have the power to do this, against the opposition of all those retainers whose privilege depended precisely on the preservation of the power of the monarchy? The notion that such reform was instigated by the *'am ha-'aretz*, as Albertz also suggests (Albertz 1994: 201), is contradicted by the fact that these people would hardly have transferred authority over warfare or justice to the *priesthood*.

In short, the belief of most biblical scholars that a scroll depriving the monarch of all real powers (and in effect destroying the institution of monarchy) is a plausible product of seventh-century Judah is astonishing and can only be explained by assuming that such scholarship is taking the fact for granted and thus either ignoring the absurdity or fabricating an implausible rationalization for it.

Centralization of the Cult

Albertz rightly dismisses the idea of Würthwein (1976) that the centralization of the cult in Deuteronomy indicates the exilic period, asserting that 'there was no longer any conflict over the centralization of the cult in the early post-exilic period' (1994: 199-200), on the grounds that it is presupposed by Deutero-Isaiah and Ezekiel. But he cannot be thinking of the realties of life in Judah during the neo-Babylonian period, when the capital was at Mizpeh. We do not know whether Jerusalem had any kind of sanctuary at this time, but evidence does suggest that several sanctuaries in the vicinity of Mizpah functioned: Gibeon, Mizpah itself, and especially Bethel. How, and when, Jerusalem was reinstated as capital is not clear; the process of building the Persian period temple is itself unclear, and it is unthinkable that the change of capital from Mizpeh to Jerusalem was achieved without some resentment, nor the reinstatement of Jerusalem as the central sanctuary. Indeed, the replacement of Bethel by Jerusalem as the chief sanctuary of Judah in the mid-fifth century explains a great deal about the Josiah tradition, as I shall now suggest.

What did Josiah do?

Once the 2 Kings account of a Josianic reform is put into question rather than assumed, there seem to be no compelling, even cogent reasons, for thinking that a text such as Deuteronomy (specifically the legal material) comes from this time. On the contrary, for every single topic discussed there are more plausible contexts. I have not set out here to argue in detail for a fifth-century date, but I have noted that all of the features discussed fit well with such a period. Deuteronomy fits the context of an immigrant population, based around a temple, in conflict with some of the indigenous population as well as with Samaria, and encouraged to live and exercise their control by means of a written law, controlled by the priesthood.

But if such a date provides a better context for the core of Deuteronomy, we still need to account for the story of Josiah's reform as a later legend; but this follows fairly easily. Those population elements claiming to be the true 'Israel' (against the indigenous 'dispossessed nations') would require that the document on which their position depended was not ancient. Even better: that its imputed origin replicated the present situation: 'Israel' seeing itself threatened by the 'people of the land'. But the document requires further authentication: it must have been known, as a written source, and been authorized by a legitimate Judaean king. Why Josiah? This brings us back to another question already raised: Was Josiah commemorated for having done anything to earn the reputation?

The core element of the story of Josiah's reform (2 Kgs 23) concerns his destruction of Bethel, and this act is echoed in 1 Kgs 12.25–13.34 (cf. 2 Kgs 10.29) as well as in Exodus 32 (see Blenkinsopp 1998, 2003). If Josiah were executed for some offence against the pharaoh, the destruction of Bethel, signalling Judaean control over an area adjacent to Jerusalem itself, might have constituted such an act. Over a century later, when Jerusalem was being reinstated as the major sanctuary of the Persian province of Judah, perhaps at the expense of Bethel (see Blenkinsopp 2003), such an act would easily have identified Josiah as a righteous figure, and provided the context for the retrospective introduction of Deuteronomy into the earlier history of Judah. Indeed, the 'Deuteronomic reform' of 2 Kings 22–23 should then be seen, not as a historical event, but as a disguise for a new Jerusalem-centred community to seek to impose its definition of 'Israel', its god and its religion, and specifically its written law, on an 'idolatrous' indigenous population.

In short, the fifth century BCE provides a plausible context for both the law book of Deuteronomy and the story of Josiah's reform—in a number of ways. That case will, of course, have to be argued in more detail, but I suggest that even in the brief outline given here, it offers a better account of things than the idea of a 'Deuteronomic reform' under Josiah. The king's assault on Bethel earned him a reputation as a Deuteronomic champion, but the real 'reform' took place nearly two centuries later, and, as often happens, history was rewritten to give that reform the necessary authentication.

BIBLIOGRAPHY

Ahlström, G.
    1993   *The History of Ancient Palestine from the Palaeolithic Period to Alexander's Conquest* (JSOTSup, 146; Sheffield: Sheffield Academic Press).

Albertz, R.
    1994   *A History of Israelite Religion in the Old Testament Period* (trans. John Bowden; OTL; Louisville, KY: Westminster/John Knox Press; London: SCM Press [German edn Göttingen, 1992]).

Blenkinsopp, J.
    1998   'The Judean Priesthood during the Neo-Babylonian and Achaemenid Periods: A Hypothetical Reconstruction', *CBQ* 60: 25-43.
    2003   'Bethel in the Neo-Babylonian Period', in O. Lipschits and J. Blenkinsopp (eds.), *Judah and the Judean in the Neo-Babylonian Period* (Winona Lake, IN: Eisenbrauns): 93-107.

Cross, F.M., Jr
    1973   *Canaanite Myth and Hebrew Epic: Essays in the History of the Religion of Israel* (Cambridge, MA: Harvard University Press).

Davies, G.
    1991   *Ancient Hebrew Inscriptions* (Cambridge: Cambridge University Press).

Finkelstein, I., and N.A. Silberman
    2001   *The Bible Unearthed: Archaeology's New Vision of Ancient Israel and the Origin of its Sacred Texts* (New York and London: Simon & Schuster).

Garbini, G.
    2003   *Myth and History in the Bible* (JSOTSup, 362; Sheffield: Sheffield Academic Press).

Geller, S.A.
    2000   'The God of the Covenant', in B.N. Porter (ed.), *One God or Many? Concepts of Divinity in the Ancient World* (Transactions of the Casco Bay Assyriological Institute, 1; Chebeague, ME: Casco Bay Assyriological Institute): 273-319.

Grabbe, L.L. (ed.)
    2003   *'Like a Bird in a Cage': The Invasion of Sennacherib in 701 BCE* (JSOTSup, 363; ESHM, 4; London and New York: Sheffield Academic Press).

Hölscher, G.
    1922   'Komposition und Ursprung des Deuteronomiums', *ZAW* 40: 161-255.

Kaiser, O.
    1978   *Einleitung in das Alte Testament* (Gütersloh: Gerd Mohn, 4th edn).

Lohfink, N. (ed.)
    1985   'Zur neueren Diskussion über 2 Kön 22–23', in *idem* (ed.), *Das Deuteronomium. Entstehung, Gestalt und Botschaft* (BETL, 68; Leuven: Peeters): 24-48.

Miller, J.M., and J.H. Hayes
    1986   *A History and Ancient Israel and Judah* (Philadelphia: Westminster Press).

Na'aman, N.
    1992   *The Kingdom of Judah Under Josiah* (Tel Aviv Reprint Series, 9: Tel Aviv: Institute of Archaeology).

Smelik, K.A.D.
    1991   *Writings from Ancient Israel: A Handbook of Historical and Religious Documents* (Edinburgh: T. & T. Clark).

Sweeney, M.
    2001   *King Josiah of Judah: The Lost Messiah of Israel* (Oxford: Oxford University Press).

Weinfeld, M.
    1972   *Deuteronomy and the Deuteronomic School* (Oxford: Clarendon Press).

Würthwein, E.
    1976   'Die Josianische Reform und das Deuteronomium', *ZTK* 73: 365-423.

THE KINGDOM OF JUDAH FROM SENNACHERIB'S INVASION TO THE FALL OF JERUSALEM: IF WE HAD ONLY THE BIBLE...*

Lester L. Grabbe

In the current debate about the place of the biblical text in reconstructing the history of ancient Israel, a good deal of the discussion has taken place in a vacuum. As long as we have no control on the text from other sources, we are groping in the dark. We can create a scenario in which the text is mainly invention, or one in which a great deal of historical information is present. But these are theoretical exercises—useful in themselves but hardly definitive. One way of trying to get at the question is to work on examples where the text can be checked against external information.

Therefore, my purpose in this article is (1) to ascertain as far as possible what the text says in its own right, as a modern historian might read it without the benefit of any external checks, (2) to assemble as much of the non-biblical data as possible, and (3) compare and contrast them to determine how far the textual picture matches with that which a historian might reconstruct based on all the data. The ultimate aim is (4) to try to find a way of assessing the biblical stories which cannot be checked by means of external information.

The Biblical Story: 2 Kings 21–25 and Parallels[1]

Outline of the Contents

2 Kings	2 Chronicles	(a dash marks omissions in the parallel writing)
21.1-18	*33.1-20*	*reign of Manasseh.*
21.1	33.1	Manasseh begins reign at age 12 and reigns 55 years.
21.2-9	33.2-9	he does what is evil by building altars to Baal and an Asherah, worshiping the host of heaven, making his son to pass through the fire, practising divination.
—	33.10-13	Manasseh taken captive to Babylon, where he repents and turns to Yhwh.
—	33.14-17	Manasseh builds Jerusalem's wall and removes the religious abominations.

* I wish to thank Professors Nadav Na'aman and E. Axel Knauf for kindly reading and commenting on an earlier draft of this article. Naturally, I bear the responsibility for any of the views or interpretations found here, except where credited in formal references.

1. Only passages specifically mentioning the period are considered here. Other passages may well be from this time (e.g. the town lists of Josh. 15, 18, and 19) but are omitted here.

21.10-15	—	Yhwh speaks against Manasseh through prophets, promising disaster on Jerusalem and to deliver the remnant of the people to their enemies.
21.16	—	Manasseh puts the innocent to death and fills Jerusalem with blood.
21.17	33.18	the other events of Manasseh's reign are found in the annals of the kings of Judah.
—	33.19	words of Hozai recording Manasseh's sins and his prayer of repentance.
21.18	33.20	Manasseh dies and is buried.
21.19-26	*33.21-25*	*reign of Amon.*
21.19	33.21	begins reign at age 22 and reigns 2 years.
21.20-22	33.22-23	wicked like his father.
21.23-26	33.24-25	assassinated in a conspiracy.
22.1–23.30	*34.1–35.27*	*reign of Josiah.*
22.1	34.1	begins reign at age 8 and reigns 22 years.
22.2	34.2	is righteous like David.
—	34.3-7	begins purge of shrines and cults in his twelfth year.
22.3-7	34.8-13	Josiah orders the cleansing of the temple in his eighteenth year.
22.8-10	34.14-18	finding of scroll and reading of it to Josiah.
22.11-20	34.19-28	prophetess Huldah is consulted about the contents of the scroll.
23.1-3	34.29-32	Josiah makes a covenant with the people to keep the laws of the scroll.
23.4-7	—	cleansing of the temple and the removal of the *kemarim* from the shrines.
23.8-9	—	priests of the high places brought to Jerusalem.
23.10-14	—	other cults and objects removed from the temple and city.
23.15-18	—	Bethel purified, including destruction of Jeroboam's altar.
23.19-20	—	rest of Samaria purified of its cult places and priests.
—	34.33	summary of Josiah's reign.
23.21-23	35.1-19	Passover kept.
23.24	—	divination eliminated.
23.25-27	—	prophecy of Judah's destruction postponed because of Josiah's righteousness.
23.28-30	35.20-27	Josiah's death at the hands of Necho.
23.31-34	*36.1-3*	*reign of Jehoahaz.*
23.31	36.1-2	begins reign at age 23 and reigns 3 months.
23.32	—	is wicked like his fathers.
23.33-34	36.3	removed by Pharaoh Necho and taken to Egypt, and tribute imposed.
23.35–24.7	*36.4-8*	*reign of Jehoiakim.*
23.35	—	Jehoiakim collects money for tribute.
23.36	36.4	begins reign at age 25 and reigns 11 years.
23.37	36.5	wicked like his fathers.
24.1-2	—	vassal of Nebuchadnezzar 3 years and then rebels; raids against Judah.
24.3-4	—	happens because Jehoiakim sheds innocent blood.

	36.6-7	Nebuchadnezzar takes Jehoiakim captive to Babylon.
24.5-6	36.8	death of Jehoiakim.
24.7	—	king of Babylon had taken all land to borders of Egypt.
24.8-17	*36.9-10*	*reign of Jehoiachin.*
24.8	36.9	begins to reign at age 18 and reigns 3 months.
24.9	36.9	wicked like his father.
24.10-17	36.10	Nebuchadnezzar takes the city and deports Jehoiachin and family to Babylon.
24.18–25.21	*36.11-21*	*reign of Zekekiah.*
24.18	36.11	begins reign at age 21 and rules for 11 years.
24.19-20	36.12	wicked like Jehoiakim.
25.1-21	36.13-21	rebels and Jerusalem taken by Nebuchadnezzar; king and people exiled.

Jeremiah

22.18-19	prophecy that Jehoiakim would have the 'burial of an ass'.
25.1	first year of Nebuchadnezzar is the fourth of Jehoiakim.
32.1-2	Babylonian army besieging Jerusalem in the tenth year of Zedekiah, which is the eighteenth of Nebuchadnezzar.
34.7	only Lachish and Azekah of the fortified cities holding out against besieging Babylonians.
37.11	the Chaldean army lifts the siege of Jerusalem because of the Egyptian army.
39.1	Nebuchadnezzar besieges Jerusalem in the ninth year of Zedekiah, the tenth month.
39.2	Jerusalem falls in the eleventh year of Zedekiah, ninth day of fourth month.
39.3	Babylonian officers set up quarters.
39.4-7	Zedekiah taken prisoner.
39.8-10	exile of those left in the city.
43.8-13	prediction that Nebuchadnezzar would conquer Egypt.
44.30	prediction that Pharaoh Hophrah would be delivered into the hands of his enemies (Nebuchadnezzar?).
46–47	prophecy of Nebuchadnezzar's destruction of Egypt.
46.2	Egyptian army of Necho defeated at Carchemish by the Babylonians in the fourth year of Jehoiakim.
52.1	Zedekiah aged 21 when he became king and reigned 11 years.
52.3-4	Jerusalem besieged in the ninth year, the tenth day of the tenth month, by Nebuchadnezzar.
52.5-7	city falls in the eleventh year, the ninth day of the fourth month.
52.8-11	Zedekiah taken prisoner to Babylon.
52.12-14	Jerusalem razed by Nebuzaradan in Nebuchadnezzar's nineteenth year, tenth day of the fifth month.
52.15-16	those left in the city exiled.
52.28-30	captivities in seventh, eighteenth, twenty-third year of Nebuchadnezzar.

Ezekiel

26–27	prophecy against Tyre.
26.7	Nebuchadnezzar will come against Tyre and destroy it.
29–30	prophecy against Egypt.
29.8-16	Egypt to be ruined and desolate 40 years, then to become the lowest of the kingdoms.

GRABBE *The Kingdom of Judah* 81

    29.17-20   having failed to take Tyre, Nebuchadnezzar will be given Egypt as a reward.
    30.20-26   the king of Babylon will break the arms of the king of Egypt.

Ezra

    4.1-4   the enemies of Judah and Benjamin—'the people of the land'—were brought to the region by Esarhaddon.
    4.9-10   men of Erech, Babylon, Susa, and others had been settled in Samaria and elsewhere in Ebir-Nari by Osnappar (Ashurbanipal?).

Daniel

    1.1-2   Nebuchadnezzar besieges and takes Jerusalem in the third year of Jehoiakim.
    4   Nebuchadnezzar's 'madness'.

Analysis of the Text
The account of the seventh century in 2 Kings is generally regarded as a part of the Deuteronomistic History. My purpose is not to debate the question or nature of the Deuteronomistic History or its possible sources but only to ask about the final form of the text before us. The most part of the text of 2 Chronicles and some parts of Jeremiah parallel the narrative of 2 Kings. The relationship of Jeremiah to 2 Kings is not immediately apparent, but it seems plain that 2 Chronicles is mainly derived from 2 Kings; however, here and there are significant deviations. The main ones are the following:

- Manasseh's alleged captivity in Babylon and subsequent repentance is given in 2 Chron. 33.10-17 but completely absent from 2 Kings.
- 2 Chronicles 33.14, but not 2 Kings, states that Manasseh built the outer wall around part of Jerusalem.
- According to 2 Chron. 34.3-7 Josiah began the purge of 'foreign' cults in his twelfth year, an assertion absent from 2 Kings.
- Whereas 2 Kgs 22.21-23 mentions briefly Josiah's Passover, 2 Chron. 35.1-19 goes into great detail about how it was celebrated.
- According to 2 Chron. 35.20-27 Josiah was killed in a battle with Pharaoh Necho, but 2 Kgs 23.28-30 is unspecific and does not at all imply a battle.
- According to 2 Chron. 36.6-7 Jehoiakim was taken captive to Babylon, along with the temple vessels. On the other hand, according to Jeremiah he was to have 'the burial of an ass', cast outside Jerusalem unburied (Jer. 22.18-19).
- In spite of Josiah's far-reaching reform programme described in 2 Kings and 2 Chronicles, Jeremiah seems strangely silent about it.

Archaeology

The invasion of Sennacherib left Judah devastated, with only Jerusalem and a few other sites having escaped the Assyrian wrath. Of 354 Judaean settlements in existence in the late eighth century and destroyed, only 39 are presently known to have been rebuilt in the seventh (Stern 2001: 142; cf. Finkelstein 1994). The seventh century saw great changes, yet some were positive. Stern (2001: 163) sums up things in this way:

> The overall picture emerging from the excavations at the sites along the Judaean Hill ridge appears to corroborate that in other parts of the Judaean monarchy: a severe destruction followed Sennacherib's 701 BCE campaign at almost all sites, excluding Jerusalem. Between that date and the arrival of the Babylonians, the country enjoyed a period of rebuilding and relative prosperity.

According to Stern (2001: 130-31), despite the widespread destruction of Sennacherib, the rebuilding process was quite rapid. A number of archaeologists put specific times on developments in the seventh century; however, such a precise dating of events from archaeology can be disputed: 'Archaeologically, it is not easy to distinguish the finds of the early seventh century from those of the second half of that century' (Finkelstein and Silberman 2001: 265; cf. also 345-46). Being able to distinguish the archaeology from Manasseh's reign, as opposed to Josiah's, is not easy, though a number of finds go together to suggest that the main recovery of prosperity occurred early in the century (Finkelstein and Silberman 2001: 265-69; Stern 2001: 130-31).

Throughout the seventh century Jerusalem had no rivals, because most of those urban areas that approached it in size and importance in the eighth century had been destroyed by the Assyrians and had not been rebuilt (Tatum 1991: 141-42; Steiner 2001: 285; 2003a: 76-77). Even Lachish, which had its fortifications repaired, was only sparsely inhabited. There seems to be general agreement that in the Judaean heartland the settlement area in general increased in the seventh century, though it was mainly in rural areas (including the desert fringe) or new towns or fortresses (Tatum 1991: 142; Finkelstein 1994: 174-80). The increase in settlement area has been explained as the accommodation of those who were forced to leave the Shephelah when the Assyrians took it from Judaean control. The situation varied somewhat in different parts of the country, as did the situation in the eighth century in comparison with that in the seventh. Not all of the country was devastated by the Assyrian army. The old area of Benjamin (now a part of Judah north of Jerusalem) had prospered in the late eighth century and continued to do so in the seventh, apparently having escaped (at least to some extent) the ravages of Sennacherib (Ofer 2001: 29).

The result was that Jerusalem was left as the only real urban centre in Judah in the seventh century (on the archaeology of Jerusalem, see in particular the essays in Vaughn and Killebrew [eds.] 2003). Yet there is little evidence of the city's being an administrative centre: no public buildings were built in the seventh century, and the city seems mainly residential (Steiner 2001: 284). It may be that the city functioned primarily as a commercial and trading centre. This period also saw a huge expansion of Jerusalem, though exactly how early that began is disputed. Since the excavations in the Jewish Quarter in the 1970s, it is now widely accepted that this growth took in the western hill (Geva 2003). The expansion is thought by some to be a result of Sennacherib's invasion, but many now think that it began earlier, in the late eighth century BCE (Finkelstein 1994: 175;

Geva 2003: 203-207; Reich and Shukron 2003). One explanation for this unprecedented growth is that it was at least in part due to immigration from the Northern Kingdom after the conquest of Samaria and from the Shephelah after 701 BCE when a large part of it was removed from Judaean control (Broshi 1974). The Broad Wall was built about this time, apparently to protect this new western quarter. This growth is also evidenced by a new quarter on the eastern slope, in which a number of luxurious houses were constructed together with a new section of the city wall to the east to enclose this section within the fortifications. About this time there was also apparently expansion of settlement to the north, into an unfortified section of the city.

Conventional estimates put the size of all Jerusalem about 600 BCE at 600 dunams or a minimum of 6000–7000 inhabitants (Geva 2003: 206), but G. Barkay (as cited in Lipschits 2003: 327) thinks it was 900–1000 dunams in size, which could mean a population of up to a maximum of 25,000 persons; however, such an estimate would take in even farms on the edge of the built-up area (Lipschits 2003: 327 n. 14). It has been argued that residential parts of the city to the north were damaged in Sennacherib's siege and remained deserted (Geva 2003: 207), but it seems unlikely that the Assyrian army actually encamped at Jerusalem or laid siege to the city in traditional fashion (cf. Grabbe [ed.] 2003: 8-10). Nevertheless, both the eastern extension and the northern expansion seem to have been abandoned before the fall of Jerusalem to the Babylonians, while the settlement on the western hill appears to have withdrawn to within the wall (Geva 2003: 207; Reich and Shukron 2003: 217).

One site has become controversial in recent years. 2 Kings 20.20 states that Hezekiah made the 'pool' (הברכה) and the 'conduit' (התעלה) and brought water into the city. The Siloam tunnel has long been thought to provide the evidence for the truth of this verse. J. Rogerson and P.R. Davies (1996) challenged this consensus and sought to redate the tunnel and its inscription to the time of the Maccabees. This identification has been widely rejected (e.g. Hendel 1996; Norin 1998); however, E.A. Knauf (2001b) has now argued for the reign of Manasseh as the time of its building. Thus, the question of whether the Siloam tunnel belongs to Hezekiah's time is far from settled, but it well fits other trends in the seventh century and would fall logically in the reign of Manasseh.

In the Judaean hills south of Jerusalem, Ramat Raḥel was a major centre. The site, with its citadel, was probably destroyed at the time of Sennacherib's invasion. A new citadel was built in the seventh century (stratum VA) and shows some Assyrian influence. It has often been interpreted as a royal place, but why would the Judaean kings build a palace so close to Jerusalem? N. Na'aman (2001) argues that it was Assyrian policy to construct emporia and centres of government near the capitals of vassal kingdoms. Ramat Raḥel would be much better explained as an Assyrian building used as an administrative centre (though Judaeans would have been conscripted to do the actual work). As supporting evidence, the presence of Assyrian officials can be proposed for a number of vassal kingdoms at this time, including Byblos, Tyre, Ashdod, and Gaza.

According to this interpretation, economic considerations were a major factor, with Assyria actually competing with its vassals for revenues. No wonder anti-Assyrian rebellions broke out periodically! Assyria's relentless imperialism was severely damaging its subjects. No exact dating for the destruction of the fortress is possible, and 587 is only one possibility. It may have been abandoned by the withdrawing Assyrians, or even destroyed by them as they left. Yet, other interpretations are possible. A.E. Knauf (pp. 164-88, below) argues that such building projects were often undertaken as propaganda for the ruling dynasty. It was not as if a royal palace so close to Jerusalem was *needed* but simply that it proclaimed the splendour of the king.

The Judaean Hills cover the general area from just south of Jerusalem on the north to Beersheba Valley in the south, and from the Judaean Desert on the east to the descent to the Coastal Plain on the west, an area of approximately 900 km^2. The question of the population in the seventh century compared to the eighth is controversial (cf. Finkelstein 1994: 174-75). The Judaean Hills survey (by A. Ofer; cf. Ofer 2001) found that from the mid-eleventh to the eighth century the population nearly doubled in each century, but the seventh century showed a decline compared to the eighth. Although the number of settlements was similar (86 in the seventh, compared to 88 in the eighth), the settled area was much less (70 hectares in the seventh, vs. 90 in the eighth). This meant a decline in population from about 23,000 to about 17,000. Even if one slightly reinterprets the data for less of a contrast (from 84 to 74 hectares, or 21,000 to 18,500 inhabitants), there was still a marked fall off. This could be due to a variety of causes, but one obvious possibility is Sennacherib's invasion of 701 BCE.

I. Finkelstein, however, is not convinced of the contrast between the density of population in the Judaean highlands between the eighth and seventh centuries (Finkelstein 1994: 174-75). He notes that 'all major excavated sites in the Judaean highlands were occupied in both the eighth and seventh centuries BCE' (1994: 174). He makes several points (in addition to the one about the occupation of all major excavated sites in both the eighth and seventh centuries): that in the seventh century possibly Tell en-Nasbeh and Gibeon, and certainly Ramat Raḥel reached their peak; that a group of forts was established around Jerusalem; that a system of farmhouses was established around Jerusalem and Bethlehem; and that the Judahite population spread to nearby arid zones (Judaean Desert and Negev). Finkelstein argues that there may be reasons why the survey shows some differences between the two centuries, but he assumes that the Judaean hills south of Jerusalem were as densely populated in the seventh as the eighth.

Sennacherib's invasion was hard on the Shephelah: the city of Lachish was one of the major cities besieged by the Assyrians (Uehlinger 2003), but others destroyed were Tell Beit Mirsim and Beth-Shemesh. Afterwards, the Assyrians appear to have removed a good portion of the Shephelah from Judaean control. The late seventh and early sixth century saw a decrease of 70 per cent in built-up areas, mostly in unwalled villages and farmsteads and mostly in the eastern part of the region (Finkelstein 1994: 172-74). About 85 per cent of the eighth-century sites were not resettled in the seventh. Archaeologists disagree about the case of Tell Beit Mirsim. E. Stern (2001: 149) states that the town was certainly rebuilt in the seventh century, before being destroyed by the Babylonians. However, R. Greenberg (1993: I, 180) notes, 'There is slight ceramic and stratigraphic evidence for a partial reoccupation of the site in the seventh or early sixth century BCE'. The only site that grew was Tell Miqne (usually identified with ancient Ekron), but this area had generally been outside Judah. Tell Batash (Timnah) was also apparently outside Judah but likely under the control of Ekron (the pottery is mixed but Philistine predominates).

One of the interesting phenomena of the seventh century was the growth in settlement in the arid regions: the Negev and the eastern deserts. En-gedi may have been settled in the eighth. In any event, both it and Jericho grew considerably in the second half of the seventh century, with an unprecedented amount of settlement (59 sites) between the two sites (Lipschits 2003: 338-39). Beersheba was abandoned at this time, but new sites were also established at Tel Masos, Ḥorvat 'Uza, Ḥorvat Radom, Tel 'Ira, and 'Aro'er (Finkelstein 1994: 175-76).

Arad has often been discussed in connection with the reign of Josiah, but it is a site about which prominent archaeologists have come to some significantly different conclusions, mainly because the excavator Y. Aharoni was not able to publish a full report before his death (see especially the summary in Manor and Heron 1992). The original interpretation was that a shrine persisted through layers XI–IX, consisting of a courtyard with a large altar, a broadroom, and a small inner room apparently with a stela (מצבה) and two incense altars. Some alterations were made over time, but in stratum VIII some significant changes were made in the temple area: it was dismantled and much of it covered in a metre-thick layer of earth. This activity has been associated with the cult reforms of Hezekiah. Nevertheless, the stratigraphy, the dating of the strata, and the possible historical events with which they are to be associated are all disputed. D. Ussishkin (1988), for example, interpreted matters rather differently (though depending on the preliminary publications and interviews with some of the excavators). He noted (with others) that the homogeneity of the pottery from strata X–VIII suggests a relatively short period of time, and these layers may represent only different stages of a single building phase. The shrine, which some had dated even as early as stratum XI, was in fact not built until stratum VII.

Now, a new complete stratigraphical examination conducted in 1995–96 has led to a re-evaluation, with differences from that of the original excavator and the many studies built on it (Herzog 2001: 156-78; cf. Uehlinger's contribution to this volume [pp. 279-316, below]). There were particular problems in relating the temple complex to the stratigraphy by the earlier excavators, partly because of the 'biblical archaeology' paradigm embraced by the excavation team (among whom Herzog includes himself). Stratum VII elsewhere in the site was 2.5 m above the temple floor, showing that the temple was earlier than that (*contra* Ussishkin). The temple began in stratum X (not XI, as widely believed) or the eighth century, with a second phase of construction in stratum IX. The temple was not destroyed by fire but was dismantled in stratum VIII (late eighth century), which Herzog attributes to Hezekiah. The question is, though, whether the dismantling was done to destroy the temple or, on the contrary, to protect the pillars, etc., for future use (cf. Knauf [pp. 164-88, below]; Uehlinger [pp. 279-316, below]; Niehr 1995: 35; Ussishkin 1988).

This settlement in the eastern and southern arid regions was short lived for the most part, however, collapsing at the end of the Iron Age (Lipschits 2003: 334-37). In the eastern desert sites, there is no evidence of physical destruction but gradual abandonment. In the Negev, a number of the fortresses show signs of destruction (including Ḥorvat ʿUza and Arad and the settlement sites of Tel ʿIra and Tel Malḥata). Other sites appear to have been abandoned (e.g. Ḥorvat Radum). It seems that the decline came about primarily because the areas of Judah which the arid regions depended on for military and economic support had themselves been destroyed by the Babylonians. The inhabitants of the settlements gradually withdrew because they had no other choice.

The archaeology also provides data about aspects of the economy, though this often has to be put together with other data. The Edomite plateau gained a significant population at this time, and there are indications of contact with Arabia (Finkelstein 1994: 177-80; Finkelstein and Silberman 2001: 267-69). This could suggest the place of Judah in a trade route from Arabia. We know from Assyrian sources that Gaza was an important trading centre for the Assyrians. The seventh-century forts at Qadesh-barnea and Ḥaṣeva (both probably outside Judah; see below) may have been built with the protection of this trade in mind. There is also evidence of a major olive oil production centre at Tel Miqne (Ekron). This was an old Philistine city and not part of Judah; however, the olives could not be grown locally, which leads to the inference that they would most likely have been imported from the Samarian and Judaean highlands.

One feature of the archaeological data that particularly stands out is the sudden increase in the quantity of written objects preserved from the seventh century: seals/bullae, ostraca, and inscribed weights (Finkelstein and Silberman 2001: 270, 281, 284; Stern 2001: 169-200). This phenomenon is apparently not found in the neighbouring Assyrian provinces or vassal states. It thus appears to be a genuine increase in the production of written objects in Judah at the time and not just an impression created by the accidence of discovery. A number of conclusions have been drawn from this fact, not all of them justified (see below, pp. 106-107).

Attempts have been made to determine the borders of Judah from archaeological data. Several sites have been put forward as an indication of an expansion of the territory of Judah during the reign of Josiah. The arguments are only in part based on archaeology, but the archaeology of the sites is important: Megiddo, Meṣad Ḥashavyahu, Ḥaṣeva and Qadesh-barnea. With regard to Megiddo, no Judaean artifacts have been found from the seventh century (stratum II). A consideration of the historical situation suggests that it was more likely under Egyptian control (cf. Naʾaman 1991: 51-52), but no Egyptian artifacts have been found, either (Finkelstein and Silberman 2001: 350). This might be the case if the occupation was brief, whether by Josiah or the Egyptians, but the fact is that nothing in the archaeology connects Megiddo with Josiah. With regard to the fortresses at Ḥaṣeva and Qadesh-barnea (cf. Cohen and Yisrael 1995; Cohen 1981; 1997), the archaeology is ambiguous. They seem to be of Assyrian construction

(Na'aman 1991: 48). Although Judaean artifacts have been found at Qadeshbarnea (Judaean inscribed weights, pottery vessels, Hebrew ostraca), the material culture is mixed (Kletter 1999: 42). A number of ostraca were found at Qadeshbarnea, including two with Hebrew writing, some written in Egyptian hieratic, and at least two with a mixture of Hebrew and Egyptian. Once again, the connection with Josiah comes primarily from considerations other than the archaeology. Na'aman (1991: 48-49), on the other hand, suggests that the best way to explain the archaeology is that as the Assyrians withdrew, the Egyptians took over.

Based on an ostracon, as well as the pottery, Meṣad Ḥashavyahu has been a prime part of the argument for Josiah's expansion, since it is not only well outside the traditional territory of Judah but also on the coast, which could suggest an effort by Judah to obtain its own sea outlet. The excavations of this settlement on the coast have only recently been published (Fantalkin 2001). The settlement was very short lived, only a couple of decades or so. From archaeological evidence alone, it was either late seventh century or early sixth. There is actually no direct evidence for supposing it to be linked with Josiah. A large amount of East Greek pottery has suggested that a large portion of the population was Greek, but the names in the published ostracon (quoted on pp. 90-91, below) are Hebrew, three with the name Yahu and one with Baal (Gogel 1998: 423-24). One theory suggests that it was a Greek trading colony, but the location and the finds do not support this. More likely is that it was a settlement of Greek mercenaries, though also with some Judaeans in various capacities (Na'aman 1991: 44-46; Fantalkin 2001: 139-47; Finkelstein and Silberman 2001: 350-51). If so, they were probably in Egyptian service (Psammetichus I or possibly even Necho II). The Egyptians controlled this area between the withdrawal of the Assyrians and the coming of the Babylonians. For it to be settled by mercenaries in the service of Judah is not very credible. Judaean control is even less likely if the date of Meṣad Ḥashavyahu is lowered to 600 BCE (Kletter 1999: 42). Stern (2001: 140-42) objects, pointing to the lack of Egyptian remains; however, the site also lacks characteristic Judaean remains (e.g. rosette seal impressions), and the short time of occupation might have left no characteristic Egyptian remains (though one cooking pot lid is possibly Egyptian). The site could have been destroyed by the Babylonians in 604 BCE, along with Ashkelon and other areas on the coast.

Also as an indication of borders, a number of artifacts have been considered as of potential help (Kletter 1999). These include the following: (1) 'Judaean pillar figurines'. Most of these are from the eighth and seventh centuries. They show differences from pillar figurines of other areas (such as Israel and Transjordan). It has been suggested that these represent Asherah, though any direct proof is lacking, and little evidence exists of a relation to the cult. But none was apparently broken deliberately. (2) Inscribed scale weights. The main period of use was the seventh, though some are as early as the eighth. They are thus not an invention of Josiah. Most likely common weights rather than royal, they may represent private trade relations rather than public administration. (3) Horse and rider figurines. Most of these are from the eighth century, but some are dated to the seventh. Of the five types, the first type is definitely Judaean, while types 3 and 4 are Phoenicia and Transjordan, which means that the Judaean type is easily distinguishable from neighbouring areas.

A fourth category of artifact is the rosette stamps. They need to be considered in relation to the *lmlk* seal impressions. The *lmlk* seals have been an important part of the discussion about this general period of time. It is now widely accepted that the *lmlk* seals were adopted for use under Hezekiah's administration and are an important indication for the dating of the archaeological layer in which they are found. The question is whether they continued in use after that king's reign. The old view was that they continued to be used to the fall of the kingdom of Judah, but more recently interpreters have seen them as confined to the reign of Hezekiah. A. Mazar (1993: 455-58) and more recently E. Stern (2001: 174-78) have argued, however, that a few continued to be used for some decades after Hezekiah's death. Mazar seems to be suggesting not that more jars were manufactured but that jars already in use continued to be around and utilized until their working life came to an end; Stern, however, puts forward the view that the jars continued to be manufactured, with only the seal types changing (to the rosette and concentric circle), though at least one *lmlk* seal was used as late as Josiah's reign. The idea that *lmlk* jars continued to be produced has been strongly challenged by Vaughn (1999a: 106-109). He accepts that because Jerusalem would have had many such jars but was not conquered, it is inevitable that some would have been used after Hezekiah's time. But of the other sites adduced (including Arad) only Khirbet Shilḥah has a *lmlk* jar handle from a clear seventh-century context (and the jar itself was not restorable).

It seems to be generally accepted that the rosette seal and the concentric circles are developed stylized forms of the four-winged and two-winged seal impressions (Na'aman 1991: 31-33; Stern 2001: 176-78). The presence of these are indications of a seventh-century archaeological layer, much as the *lmlk* seals are of the late eighth. Some want to date the rosette seal impressions specifically to the reign of Josiah or Jehoiakim, but as Kletter (1999: 34-38) argues, there is no reason for such a narrow dating. It often seems to be taken for granted that they are royal, but the rosette motif was widespread in the ancient Near East, and there are many examples of non-royal use. Unlike the *lmlk* seal, which is dominant in the eighth, the rosette is only one of a number of types in the seventh century. Their distribution leaves no doubt of their Judaean identification, but since hardly any are found in the central hill country of Negev, it makes it hard to use them for political borders.

Kletter (1999: 40-43) comes to several conclusions about the artifacts in relation to Judah's possible borders. He notes that the overwhelming majority of artifacts are found in the Judaean heartland: 96 per cent of Judaean pillar figures, 98 per cent of the horse and rider figures, 96 per cent of the rosette seal impressions, and 75 per cent of the Judaean inscribed weights. Various explanations have been given for those outside the heartland, such as trade, but only the western Shephelah shows a meaningful concentration of Judaean artifacts. Archaeology cannot pinpoint accurate borders nor establish the political affiliation of single sites. But the finds fit more or less with the Judaean heartland and do not indicate large-scale expansion. They cannot prove or refute the possibility that Josiah or another king lost or gained small areas for short durations. Nevertheless, artifacts are varied and also of general value for political borders: some relate to trade, some to religious beliefs.

Conclusions with Regard to the Archaeology
If one assumed that archaeology was a straightforward putting together of 'facts', this survey should have dispelled such illusions. There are differences of opinion among respected archaeologists for a number of points in this survey. Archaeology requires interpretation, just as do texts and inscriptions. We cannot claim a complete consensus, though there is perhaps more of one now than was the case thirty years ago. On the other hand, the archaeology is vital for a proper understanding of any history of ancient Palestine.[2]

1. Two important horizons in the stratigraphy of this time are the destructions of Sennacherib and Nebuchadnezzar. They are helpful in defining the layers relating to the seventh and early sixth century. The stratigraphy and dating at Lachish is extremely important, and much of the interpretation of other sites depends on their relation to the finds at Lachish.

2. It is difficult, however, to distinguish between the early seventh century and the second half of the century. Very specific dating by archaeology alone is not necessarily possible. This means that assertions about developments in the reign of Manasseh vs. that of Josiah or later kings (some quoted in the discussion above) need to be looked at carefully.

3. The borders of Judah do not appear to have enlarged under Josiah's rule as is sometimes alleged. On the contrary, at the beginning of the seventh century, there was an immediate loss of territory in that much of the Shephelah was taken away. Perhaps to make up for this loss, evidence exists that settlements extended into some of the arid zones of the east and the south. There is some indication of a boundary as far north as Bethel, but the areas of Samaria, the Galilee, the coastal plain, or Transjordan do not show any signs of Judaean expansion (Na'aman 1991). Allegations that the borders of Judah took in areas as far as Meṣad Ḥashavyahu and even Megiddo do not appear to have much support in the archaeological record and would have been brief, if at all. Despite claims to the contrary, there seems little archaeological evidence of either political or religious centralization in the seventh century. The evidence of cult suppression claimed for Arad is ambiguous.

4. Jerusalem's position was considerably enhanced in the seventh century. Although the question of whether some of the main eighth-century sites were settled seems to be answered differently by different interpreters, the size and dominance of Jerusalem appears to have been many times greater than any other cities. The expansion had already begun in the eighth century, but because Sennacherib destroyed most other towns in Judah, Jerusalem was left without a rival.

---

2. See the recent evaluation of the relationship between archaeology and the history of ancient Israel by Knauf 2001a.

This dominance does not appear to have come about because of greater centralization of the administration, however, since the character of Jerusalem is that of a residential city. The Siloam tunnel, usually assumed to have been built during the time of Hezekiah, may well belong to the time of Manasseh.

5. The archaeology provides some evidence of economic developments. Population growth in the Negev area, objects allegedly inscribed with Old South Arabian inscriptions,[3] and forts in the south of the country (such as Qadesh-barnea) may be evidence of trade through the region of Judah. There is also evidence of olive oil production on a major scale at Ekron (Tel Miqre), though the olives themselves would have had to come from elsewhere, including the Judaean highlands.

6. The much greater number of ostraca, inscribed seals, and other written objects seems to be evidence of the development of the bureaucracy. Whether it indicates anything else, such as an increase in literacy is a matter of debate (see below).

Palestinian Inscriptions

The Adon Papyrus

The date and the sender of this document have not been preserved; however, a Demotic notation on the back of the document as been interpreted as a reference to Ekron (*CoS* III, 132-33). The papyrus is generally dated to the late seventh century, but this is only an educated guess. The translation is from *TSSI* 2 (text #21):

> To lord of kings, Pharaoh, your servant Adon, king of [... The welfare of lord of kings, Pharaoh, may...and all the gods] of heaven and earth and Baalshamayn, the [great] god, [seek at all times; and may they make the throne of lord of kings,] Pharaoh, enduring like the days of heaven. What... [the forces] of the king of Babylon have come; they have reached Aphek and (encamped)... [5] ...they have taken... For lord of kings, Pharaoh, knows that your servant...to send an army to deliver me. Let him not abandon me...and your servant has kept in mind his kindness. But this territory...a governor in the land, and as a border they have replaced it with the border...

Meṣad Ḥashavyahu

The following translation of ostracon 1 is from Gogel (1998: 423-24):

> 1   May the official, my lord, hear
> 2   the plea of his servant. Your servant
> 3   is working at the harvest...
> 6   When your [se]rvant had finished his reaping and had stored
> 7   it a few days ago, Hoshayahu ben Shabay came
> 8   and took your servant's garment. When I had finished
> 9   my reaping, at that time,
> 10 All my companions will testify for me, all who were reaping with me in the heat of
> 11 the sun—they will testify for me that this is true. I am guiltless of an

---

3. Professor Knauf has pointed out to me that the South Arabian connection is uncertain.

12 in[fraction. (So) please return] my garment. If the official does
   (= you do) not consider it an obligation to retur[n]
13 [your] ser[vant's garment, then hav]e pi[ty] upon him
14 [and re]turn your [se]rvant's [garment]. You must not remain silent...

Arad Ostraca

The Arad archive is associated with a man named Eliashib who seems to have been commander of the fortress. Ten of the ostraca speak about the 'Kittim', often with regard to distributing rations to them (##1, 2, 4, 5, 7, 8, 10, 11, 14, 17). These are usually interpreted as Greek mercenaries, but which king they served is still a moot point. The following quotation from Arad 18 is from Gogel (1998: 390-91):

1 To my lord Elyashib.
2 May YHWH concern
3 himself with your well-being. And now,
4 give Shemaryahu
5 one *letek*-measure, and to the Qerosite
6 give one *homer*-measure. Regarding
7 the matter about which you
8 gave me orders: everything is fine:
9 he is staying in
10 the house (temple) of YHWH.

Lachish Letters

The following translation from Lachish 4 is from Gogel (1998: 417):

1 May YHW[H] cause my [lord] to hear
2 good tidings at this time! ...
9 For if he [co]me[s around] during the morning tour
10 he will know that we
11 are watching the Lachish (fire-)signals, according to all the signs which my lord
12 gave us, for we cannot see
13 Azeqah.

The Ashyahu Ostracon

An ostracon published in 1996 has been associated with the reign of Josiah (Bordreuil, Israel and Pardee 1996, 1998). It reads as follows (translation from Eph'al and Naveh 1998: 269):

1 As Ashyahu the king has
2 ordered you to give by the hand of
3 [Ze]charyahu silver of Tarshish
4 to the House of YHWH
5 three shekels.

The ostracon was obtained on the antiquities market and is of unknown provenance. More recently I. Eph'al and J. Naveh (1998) have outlined their reasons for 'hesitations regarding the authenticity' of this document (plus another ostracon published at the same time).

Seals and Bullae

One of the valuable sources of information for the seventh century is the seal impressions (and occasionally the actual seals themselves) from both public officials and private individuals. A number of these have been found in proper archaeological contexts, but many were obtained on the antiquities market. This always leaves open the possibility that some of the seals and impressions cited in scholarly literature are counterfeits (cf. Rollston 2003).

Fortunately, we have a number of provenanced seal impressions. Extremely valuable are the bullae found in Y. Shiloh's excavations in Jerusalem and now published.[4] One reason for their value is that they were found in stratum 10B which appears to cover the last few decades of the kingdom of Judah and end with the destruction of Jerusalem by the Babyonians in 587/586. One of the seal impressions is that of 'Gemaryahu son of Shaphan' (לגמריהו בן שפן),[5] which the stratigraphy would date to about 630–586 BCE, a dating not contradicted by the epigraphy. This is the same name as Gemariah son of Shaphan the scribe who has a chamber in the temple precincts (Jer. 36.10) and is an official in the palace (Jer. 36.12). The name Gemariah occurs in six other provenanced inscriptions but Shaphan in only one (Mykytiuk 2004: 142 n. 133). The one missing ingredient in the seal inscription is the title 'scribe' or something similar. Nevertheless, the possibility of identification of the individual in this seal with one in Jeremiah is relatively high (Mykytiuk 2004: 146):

> In this instance, it is the *combination* of the following that creates specificity: the PN Gemaryahu, the infrequent PN Shaphan, the findspot very near the locations specified in the biblical narrative, and the indication that the seal owner was most likely a government official, as the biblical Shaphan's son Gemariah was.

Another provenanced seal impression from Lachish names 'Gedalyahu who is over the house' (לגדליהו [א]שר על הבי[ת]).[6] This has been widely identified with the Gedaliah who was made governor (king?) of Judah after the destruction of Jerusalem in 587/586; however, this identification has been labelled as 'disqualified' because if the script is dated to the mid-seventh century (as some do), it would be too early for the individual in Jeremiah 40–41 (Mykytiuk 2004: 235). Whether the alleged palaeographical dating is so accurate as to rule out the early sixth century is a question (cf. Vaughn 1999b), but the existence of another official called Gedaliah son of Pashhur (Jer. 38.61) shows that the name was a relatively common one. Another seal with a similar inscription (לגדליהו עבד המלך, 'Gedalyahu the servant of the king') is in identical script but was obtained as part of the 'Burnt Archive' published by Avigad (1986: 24-25). The lack of a proper provenance is a major difficulty. Thus, one has to conclude with B. Becking (1997: 78) that the possibility that this is from a seal belonging to the Gedaliah of Jeremiah 40–41 is relatively low.

---

4. Shiloh 1986; Shiloh and Tarler 1986; Shoham 1994, 2000; Avigad and Sass 1997; Mykytiuk 2004: 139-47.
5. See the discussion in Mykytiuk 2004: 139-47.
6. Gogel 1998: 487 (Lachish seal 6); *AHI*: 100.149; Becking 1997: 75-78.

Another seal impression found at Tell el-'Umeiri in Jordan gives the name 'Milkomor the servant of Baalisha' (למלכמער עבד בעלישע).⁷ The name 'Baalis' (בעלים) was unique to Jer. 40.14 until this seal impression was found. The names are not precisely the same, which might seem to rule out any identification. What must be kept in mind, though, is that the writer of Jeremiah is trying to render a foreign name. Even though the Ammonites spoke a language quite similar to Hebrew (judging from the Ammonite inscriptions), the pronunciation may have been rather different. The name used in Jeremiah could have come from an oral source rather than a written one, which could explain the *samek* instead of *shin* and the missing *ayin* in Jer. 40.14. Since a king of Ammonites with a name of this sort is so rare, I agree with Becking (1997: 82) that the possibility of an identification is high, despite the differences between the names.

The name 'Jaazaniah the servant of the king' (יאזניה עבד המלך) was found on a seal excavated in stratum 3 (IA II) at Tell en-Nasbeh.⁸ As well as the inscription, it contains the image of a fighting cockerel. A Jaazaniah son of the Maachite (יאזניהו בן־המעכתי) was associated with Gedaliah at Mizpah after the fall of Jerusalem (2 Kgs 25.23). The chances are that he was some sort of royal official before the Babylonian siege. In the parallel passage in Jer. 40.8, the name is spelled slightly differently as Jezaniah (יזניהו). Since there is no patronymic we cannot be certain that there is an identity, but the connection is plausible. I would consider the identification as of moderate probability. Finally, a seal found in the Shiloh excavations in Jerusalem has the name 'Azariah son of Hilkiah' (לעזריהו בן חלקיהו).⁹ The high priest Hilkiah (2 Kgs 22.4-14; 23.4) had a son named Azariah (1 Chron. 6.13; 9.11; Ezra 7.1). The stratigraphical and palaeographic dating of the seal (c. 630–586 BCE) is a good argument for identifying the persons of the seal with the biblical ones. The names Hilkiah and Azariah are fairly common through this general period, but the combination of names is unique. I would put the identification as moderately high.

The following bulla, once dated to the time of Jeremiah, should now be placed in the late eighth century: 'Belonging to Eliaqim servant of Yochan' (לאליקם נער יוכן).¹⁰ Impressions of this seal on jar handles were found at Tell Beit Mirsim and Beth-Shemesh, and eventually at Ramat Raḥel. When impressions of this seal were first found, the name Yochan or Yochin was thought to be a version of king Jehoiachin's name. Based on the interpretation of W.F. Albright, scholars long took this as the seal of Jehoiachin's steward, which resulted in the misdating of the strata where they were originally found and those strata elsewhere thought to be parallel. In Garfinkel's words this caused 'sixty years of confusion' in Palestinian archaeology. Although this interpretation is still widespread, especially in more general works, it has now been completely reassessed by specialists.¹¹ Even

---

7. Herr 1985; Becking 1993, 1997.
8. *AHI*: 100.069; Avigad and Sass 1997: no. 8
9. Gogel 1998: 485 (Jerusalem Bulla 27); *AHI*: 100.827; Mykytiuk 2004: 149-52.
10. Gogel 1998: 467 (Beth-Shemesh seal 2), 492 (Ramat Raḥel seal 8), 494 (Tell Beit Mirsim seal 1); *AHI*: 100.108; 100.277; 100.486; Garfinkel 1990.
11. Ussishkin 1976, 1977; Garfinkel 1990.

if some aspects of the seals and their owners have still not been clarified, they have now been dated to the period before 701 BCE.

We now come to the unprovenanced bullae. One set is that published by N. Avigad as 'remnants of a Burnt Archive from the time of Jeremiah'. Unfortunately, they were obtained on the antiquities market and are of unknown provenance. Avigad asserted that there 'was no reason to suspect their authenticity, and I seriously doubt whether it would be possible to forge such burnt and damaged bullae' (1986: 13). The question of forgery cannot be so lightly dismissed: no scientific tests appear to have been applied to these bullae. If they are authentic, the biblical parallels are striking—which is precisely why their authenticity needs to be scrutinized.

In some ways, these seal impressions in the 'Burnt Archive' are superficially more interesting than those excavated by Shiloh and other archaeologists because of their biblical parallels; however, this greater incidence of biblical names in itself might arouse some suspicions. By itself, this could be coincidence and would need much more evidence to label them forgeries, but it illustrates the problems of working with material bought on the antiquities market. The most famous seal impression from this archive has the name 'Berekyahu son of Neriah the scribe' (לברכיהו בן נריהו הספר).[12] The name differs slightly from Jeremiah's scribe Baruch in having the divine element Yhw. The difference is usually explained by saying that the name in the biblical text (Baruch) is a hypercoristicon of the real name. The difference is not a major obstacle. One might ask: Would a forger use this form of the name rather than the biblical version? The answer is that a clever forger might do precisely this. If the seal impression is authentic, the parallel to the biblical Baruch would be impressive.

Another bulla from the 'burnt house' names 'Jerahmeel son of the king' (לירחמאל בן המלך).[13] According to Jer. 36.26 an individual with this name and title was one of the officials sent by Jehoiakim to arrest Jeremiah and Baruch. Another individual named on a seal impression from Avigad's collection is 'Elishama servant of the king' (לאלשמע ע[ב]ד המלך). Elishama the scribe is one of the king's officials giving a hearing to Jeremiah's prophecies (Jer. 36.12); he could also be designated as 'servant of the king' because of his office.

Finally, there is 'Ishmael son of the king' (לישמעאל בן המלך; Barkay 1993; Becking 1997: 78-80). The dating to about 600 BCE is said to be consistent with the palaeography, but there is no confirmation from an archaeological context. As A.G. Vaughn's detailed investigation has shown, the palaeographic dating of seals is far from precise, with only half a dozen letters being diagnostic (1999b). The title 'son of the king' is found on a number of seals and impressions. Whether it is a literal son of the king or only a 'title of an official' is not certain,[14] Ishmael was apparently in some way a member of the royal family (2 Kgs 25.25; Jer. 41.1). Becking's estimation is that this had a moderate probability of being

---

12. Avigad 1978; 1986: 28-29; Avigad and Sass 1997: #417; Mykytiuk 2004: 188-90.
13. Avigad 1978; 1986: 27-28; Avigad and Sass 1997: #414; Mykytiuk 2004: 191-96.
14. See Mykytiuk (2004: 194 n. 109) for a bibliography of discussion on the subject.

authentically identified with the figure of Jeremiah 40;[15] I might put it a bit lower because the name was not infrequent, but I think this evaluation is reasonable (though the question of authenticity has not been seriously investigated, as far as I know).

An important question is the relationship of the iconic to the aniconic seals. It was observed several decades ago that there seems to have been a move from iconic to aniconic seals (or seals with only a small amount of ornamental decoration) in Judah between the eighth and seventh centuries.[16] This trend toward aniconic seals does seem to be genuine, as far as extant seals are concerned, though Uehlinger (1993: 287-88) has shown that the matter is more complicated than sometimes represented. Even though there are other possible factors (e.g. increasing literacy), the influence of a growing 'Deuteronomistic movement' is plausible. Perhaps more significant is the loss of astral images. The coming of the Assyrians in the eighth and seventh centuries saw a major increase in the use of Aramaean-influenced astral imagery on seals.[17] The change on Judaean seals is not so apparent, but when they are seen in the context of other seals in the region, the astralization of the iconography is readily identified. This imagery disappears from Judahite seals by the late seventh century.

Assyrian Sources[18]

Esarhaddon (680–669 BCE)[19]
Sennacherib was assassinated in 681 BCE and was succeeded by the crown prince Esarhaddon. During Esarhaddon's reign most areas of Syro-Palestine were submissive, but there were troubles with Phoenicia. Sidon rebelled about 680; it was recaptured in 677, though king Abdi-milkutti escaped. The next year the king was captured and executed, the population deported, and a new city (Kar-Esarhaddon) was created with an imported population. This city was put under the control of Tyre; however, Tyre then rebelled and allied with Taharqa of Egypt. The Assyrians besieged the city, but it was apparently not forced to submit. Esarhaddon's major military achievement was the conquest of Egypt in 671. The Egyptian king Taharqa fled, though his family was captured; however, this expedition was insufficient to bring Egypt into Assyrian empire. A new expedition in 669 was launched, but Esarhaddon died on the way.

---

15. On a scale of 1 to 10, he puts it at 5. Similarly, Mykytiuk rates it a 2 on a scale of 1–3 or 'reasonable but uncertain' (2004: 235).

16. Uehlinger (1993: 278-81) conveniently catalogues some of the past discussion. See also Keel and Uehlinger 1998: Chapter 8, especially 354-60.

17. See Uehlinger 1995: 65-67; also pp. 279-316, below; Keel and Uehlinger 1998: Chapter 8.

18. For convenience, the relevant Assyrian sources are cited mainly from *ANET*; another source for many of them is *CoS*. Other sources will be given for individual writings or passages. Background information on Assyrian and Babylonian rulers is based to a large extent on Grayson 1991a, 1991b and Oates 1991.

19. Most of the royal inscriptions for this ruler have been collected in Borger 1967, in transliteration and German translation.

Prism A i (*ANET* 290-91):

(I am Esarhaddon), the conqueror of Sidon, which lies (on an island) amidst the sea, (he) who has leveled all its urban buildings. I even tore up and cast into the sea its wall and its foundation, destroying (thus) completely the (very) place it (i.e. Sidon) was built (upon). I caught out of the open sea, like a fish, Abdimildutte, its king, who had fled before my attack into the high sea, and I cut off his head... I (then) called together and made all the kings of the country Hatti and of the seashore (do corvée-work for me) by making them erect the walls of another [residence] and I called its name Kar-Esarhaddon. I settled therein people from the mountain regions and the sea(shore) of the East, (those) who belonged to me as my share of the booty. I set over them officers of mine as governors. As for Sanduarri, king of Kundi and Sizu, an inveterate enemy... I caught him like a bird in his mountains and (likewise) cut off his head. (Then) I hung the heads of Sanduarri and of Abdimilkutte around the neck of their nobles/chief-officials to demonstrate to the population the power of Ashur, my lord, and paraded (thus) through the wide main street of Nineveh with singers (playing on) *sammû*-harps.

Prism B v (*ANET* 291):

I called up the kings of the country Hatti and (of the region) on the other side of the river (Euphrates) (to wit): Ba'lu, king of Tyre, Manasseh (*Me-na-si-i*), king of Judah (*Ia-ú-di*) Qaushgabri, king of Edom, Musuri, king of Moab, Sil-Bel, king of Gaza, Metinti, king of Ashekelon, Ikausu, king of Ekron, Milkiashapa, king of Byblos, Matanba'al, king of Arvad, Abiba'al, king of Samsimuruna, Puduil, king of Beth-Ammon, Ahimilki, king of Ashdod—12 kings from the seacoast...10 kings from Cyprus (*Iadnana*) amidst the sea, together 22 kings of Hatti, the seashore and the islands; all these I sent out and made them transport under terrible difficulties, to Nineveh, the town (where I exercise) my rulership, as building material for my palace: big logs, long beams (and) thin boards from cedar and pine trees, products of the Sirara and Lebanon (*Lab-na-na*) mountains, which had grown for a long time into tall and strong timber, (also) from their quarries (lit.: place of creation) in the mountains, statues of protective deities (lit.: of Lamassû and Shêdu)...

Prism B iv (*ANET* 291-92):

(From) Adumatu, the stronghold of the Arabs which Sennacherib, king of Assyria, my own father, had conquered and (from where) he has taken as booty its possessions, its images as well as Iskalatu, the queen of the Arabs, and brought (all these) to Assyria, Hazail, the king of the Arabs, came with heavy gifts to Nineveh, the town (where I exercise) my rulership, and kissed my feet. He implored me to return his images and I had mercy upon him; I repaired the damages of the images of Atarsamain, Dai, Nuhai, Ruldaiu, Abirillu (and of) Atarquruma, the gods of the Arabs, and returned them to him after having written upon them an inscription (proclaiming) the (superior) might of Ashur, my lord, and my own name. I made Tarbua who had grown up in the palace of my father their queen and returned her to her (native) country together with her gods.

Ashurbanipal (668–627 BCE)

Ashurbanipal's reign was in many ways the height of the Assyrian empire, but it had come to the edge of a precipice. The internal chronology of his reign is one of the most uncertain in Assyrian history: the last of the annals cease about 639, which leaves a gap in information until the *Nabopolassor Chronicle* takes up about 626 BCE. He had trouble holding Egypt. Taharqa rebelled and made a secret alliance with other Egyptian princes such as Necho I who were supposedly

Assyrian allies. The plot was discovered and most of the rebels were punished except for Necho. Thebes was taken, and Egypt submitted the rest of Ashurbanipal's reign. Syro-Palestine was generally acquiescent. The Assyrians besieged Tyre about 662: although Tyre was not taken, it submitted. A campaign against the Arabians occurred in 645. When Tyre rebelled again about 644, the Assyrians plundered the mainland city. Asshurbanipal's brother Shamash-shuma-ukin rebelled in Babylon, encouraged by Elam. The Babylonian revolt was put down, after which Elam was invaded with great ferocity and its capital Susa was destroyed. One of Ashurbanipal's lasting achievements was his collection of a famous library containing much of Mesopotamian literature.

Rassam Cylinder i-ii (*ANET* 294):

> In my first campaign I marched against Egypt (Magan) and Ethiopia (Meluhha). Tirhakah (*Tarqû*), king of Egypt (*Muṣur*) and Nubia (*Kûsu*), whom Esarhaddon, king of Assyria, my own father, had defeated and in whose country he (Esarhaddon) had ruled, this (same) Tirhakah forgot the might of Ashur, Ishtar and the (other) great gods, my lords, and put his trust upon his own power. He turned against the kings (and) regents whom my own father had appointed in Egypt… (Then) I called up my mighty armed forces which Ashur and Ishtar have entrusted to me and took the shortest (lit.: straight) road to Egypt (*Muṣur*) and Nubia. During my march (to Egypt) 22 kings from the seashore, the islands and the mainland…

Cylinder C i-ii (*ANET* 294-95):

> Ba'al, king of Tyre, Manasseh (*Mi-in-si-e*), king of Judah (*Ia-ú-di*), Qaushgabri, king of Edom…together 12 kings from the seashore, the islands and the mainland; servants who belong to me, brought heavy gifts (*tâmartu*) to me and kissed my feet. I made these kings accompany my army over the land—as well as (over) the sea-route with their armed forces and their ships (respectively)… Upon a trust(-inspiring) oracle (given) by Ashur, Bel, Nebo, the great gods, my lords, who (always) march at my side, I defeated the battle(-experienced) soldiers of his army in a great open battle…these kings, governors and regents whom my own father had appointed in Egypt and who had left their offices in the face of the uprising of Tirhakah and had scattered into the open country, I reinstalled in their offices and in their (former) seats of office… Afterwards, (however), all the kings whom I had appointed broke the oaths (sworn to) me, did not keep the agreements sworn by the great gods, forgot that I had treated them mildly and conceived an evil (plot). They talked about rebellion… They continued to scheme against the Assyrian army, the forces (upon which) my rule (was based), (and) which I had stationed (in Egypt) for their own support. (But) my officers heard about these matters, seized their mounted messengers with their messages and (thus) learned about their rebellious doings. They arrested these kings and put their hands and feet in iron cuffs and fetters. The (consequences of the broken) oaths (sworn) by Ashur, the king of the gods, befell them. I called to account those who had sinned against the oath (sworn by) the great gods (and those) whom I had treated (before) with clemency. And they (the officers) put to the sword the inhabitants, young and old, of the towns of Sais, Pindidi, Tanis and of all the other towns which had associated with them to plot, they did not spare anybody among (them). They hung their corpses from stakes, flayed their skins and covered (with them) the wall of the town(s). Those kings who had repeatedly schemed, they brought alive to me to Nineveh. From all of them, I had only mercy upon Necho and granted him life. I made (a treaty) with him (protected by) oaths which greatly surpassed (those of the former treaty)… I returned to him Sais as residence (the place) where my own father had appointed him king…

> In my third campaign I marched against Ba'il, king of Tyre, who lives (on an island) amidst the sea, because he did not heed my royal order... I (thus) intercepted (lit.: strangled) and made scarce their food supply and forced them to submit to my yoke. He brought his own daughter and the daughters of his brothers before me to do menial services. At the same time, he brought his son Iahimilki who had not (yet) crossed the sea to greet me as (my) slave.

British Museum Text K 1295 (*ANET* 301):

> Two minas of gold from the inhabitants of Bit-Ammon ($^{mat}Bît$-Am-man-na-a-a); one mina of gold from the inhabitants of Moab (^{mat}Mu-'-ba-a-a); ten minas of silver from the inhabitants of Judah (^{mat}Ia-$ú$-da-a-a); [...mi]nas of silver from the inhabitants of [Edom] ($^{mat}[U$-du-$ma]$-a-a)...

Babylonian Sources

Final Days of Assyrian Empire (627–609 BCE)

The fall of Assyria happened quickly and for unknown reasons since the data are missing at important points. Sin-sharra-ishkun was king for much of the time from 627–612 when Nineveh succumbed to a coalition of Babylonians and Medes under Nabopolassar. A remnant of the empire continued in the west for a few more years under Ashur-uballit II who ruled in Harran.

Nabopolassar (626–605 BCE)

He was the ruler of Babylon who allied with the Medes to bring down the Assyrian empire and was founder of the short-lived Neo-Babylonian empire. We know a good deal about him because of the *Nabopolassar Chronicle*.

> [Grayson 1975: 88 = Chronicle 2: 7] The [army of] Assyria went to Nippur and Nabopolassar retreated before them. [The army of As]syria and the Nippureans followed him to Uruk, they did battle against Nabopolassar in Uruk, and retreated before Nabopolassar. [10] In the month Iyyar the army of Assyria went down to Akkad. On the twelfth day of the month Tishri when the army of Assyria had marched against Babylon (and) the Babylonians had come out of Babylon; on that day, they did battle against the army of Assyria, inflicted a major defeat upon the army of Assyria, and plundered them. For one year there was no king in the land (Babylonia). On the twenty-sixth day of the month Marchesvan Nabopolassar [15] ascended the throne in Babylon.

> [Grayson 1975: 93 = Chronicle 3: 24] The twelfth year: In the month Ab the Medes, after they *had marched* against Nineveh... [28 The king of A]kkad and his army, who had gone to help the Medes, did not reach the battle (in time)... [29 The king of Akka]d and C[yax]ares (the king of the Medes) met one another by the city (and) together they made an entente cordiale...

> [Grayson 1975: 94-95 = Chronicle 3: 38] [The fourteenth year]: The king of Akkad mustered his army [and marched to...] The king of Umman-manda [*marched*] towards the king of Akkad [...]...they met one another. [40] [The k]ing of Akkad... [...Cy]axares...brought across and they marched along the bank of the Tigris. [...they encamp]ed against Nineveh. From the month Sivan until the month Ab—for three [months—...]...they subjected the city to a heavy siege. [On the Nth day] of the month Ab [...] they inflicted a major [defeat upon a g]reat [*people*]. At that time Sin-sharra-ishkun, king of Assyria, [*died*]...[...]... [45] They carried off the vast booty of the city and the temple (and) [turned] the city into a ruin heap... [On the Nth day of the] month [...*Ashur-uballit (II)*] [50] ascended the throne in Harran to rule Assyria.

Nebuchadnezzar II (604–562 BCE)

This was one of the great kings in history, even if the biblical portrait has made him notorious. Unfortunately, we have little information after 594 BCE when *Babylonian Chronicle 2* (*Nabopolasser Chronicle*) comes to an end and royal inscriptions become undatable.

Babylonian Chronicles

[Grayson 1975: 99-100 = Chronicle 5 Obverse: 1] [The twenty-first year]: The king of Akkad stayed home (while) Nebuchadnezzar (II), his eldest son (and) the crown prince, mustered [the army of Akkad]. He took his army's lead and marched to Carchemish which is on the bank of the Euphrates. He crossed the river [*to encounter the army of Egypt*] which was encamped at Carchemish. [...] They did battle together. The army of Egypt retreated before him. [5] He inflicted a [defeat] upon them (and) finished them off completely... For twenty-one years Nabopolassar ruled Babylon. [10] On the eighth day of the month Ab he died. In the month Elul Nebuchadnezzar (II) returned to Babylon and on the first day of the month Elul he ascended the royal throne in Babylon. In (his) accession year Nebuchadnezzar (II) returned to Hattu. Until the month Shebat he marched about victoriously in Hattu. In the month Shebat he took the vast booty of Hattu to Babylon. In the month Nisan he he took the hand of Bel and the son of Bel (and) celebrated the Akitu festival. [15] The first year of Nebuchadnezzar (II): In the month Sivan he mustered his army and marched to Hattu. Until the month Kislev he marched about victoriously in Hattu. All the kings of Hattu came into his presence and he received their vast tribute. He marched to *Ashkelon* and in the month Kislev he captured it, he seized its king, plundered [and sac]ked it. [20] He turned the city into a ruin heap. In the month Shebat he marched away and [returned] to Bab[ylon].

[Grayson 1975: 101-102 = Chronicle 5 Reverse: 5] The fourth year: The king of Akkad mustered his army and marched to Hattu. [He marched about victoriously] in Hattu. In the month Kislev he took his army's lead and marched to Egypt. (When) the king of Egypt heard (the news) he m[*ustered*] his army. They fought one another in the battle-field and both sides suffered severe losses (lit. they inflicted a major defeat upon one another). The king of Akkad and his army turned and [went back] to Babylon. The fifth year: The king of Akkad stayed home (and) refitted his numerous horses and chariotry. The sixth year: In the month Kislev the king of Akkad mustered his army and marched to Hattu. He despatched his army from Hattu and [10] they went off to the desert. They plundered extensively the possessions, animals, and gods of the numerous Arabs. In the month Adar the king went home. The seventh year: In the month Kislev the king of Akkad mustered his army and marched to Hattu. He encamped against the city of Judah and on the second day of the month Adar he captured the city (and) seized (its) king. A king of his own choice he appointed in the city (and) taking the vast tribute he brought it into Babylon.

Berossus, *History of Chaldaea* 3 (*apud* Josephus, *Ant.* 10.11.1 §§220-26).

When his father Nabopalasoros heard that the satrap appointed over Egypt and the districts of Coele-Syria and Phoenicia had revolted from him, being no longer himself able to endure hardships, he placed a part of his force at the disposal of his son Nebuchadnezzar, who was in his prime, and sent him out against this satrap. Then Nebuchadnezzar engaged the rebel, defeated him in a pitched battle and brought the country which was under the other's rule into his own realm. As it happened, his father Nabopalasoros fell ill at about this time in the city of Babylon and departed this life after reigning twenty-one years. Being informed, not long after, of his father's death, Nebuchadnezzar settled the affairs of Egypt and the other countries and also gave orders to some of his friends to conduct to Babylon the captives taken among the Jews, Phoenicians, Syrians and peoples of Egypt with the bulk of his force and the rest of the booty, while he himself set out with a few men and reached Babylon through the desert. There he found the government administered by the Chaldaeans and the throne preserved for him by the ablest man among them; and, on becoming master of his father's entire realm, he gave orders to allot to the captives, when they came, settlements in the most suitable places in Babylonia...

Jehoiachin Documents

Tablets from Babylon are generally believed to mention Jehoiachin who was in captivity (see Weidner 1939 for text, German translation, and discussion, and *DOTT*: 84-86 for translation and discussion; the following English translation is from *DOTT*: 86):

(a) To Ya'u-kīn, king [of the land of Yaudu].
(b) ½ (PI) for Ya'u kīnu, king of the land of Ya[hu-du]
2½ *sila* for the fi[ve]sons of the king of the land of Yahudu
4 *sila* for eight men, Judaeans [each] ½ [sila]
(c) ½ (PI) for Ya'u [-kīnu]
2½ *sila* for the five sons...
½ (PI) for Yakū-kinu, son of the king of the land of Yakudu
2½ *sila* for the five sons of the king of Yakundu by the hand of Kanama.
(d) ....Ya]'u-kīnu, king of he land of Yahudu
[...the five sons of the king] of the land of Yahudu by the hand of Kanama.

Egyptian Sources

Psammetichus Inscription

[Inscription of Psammetichus II = Griffith 1909: II, 95-96] In the fourth regnal year of Pharaoh Psamtek Neferibre they sent to the great temples of Upper and Lower Egypt, saying, 'Pharaoh (Life, Prosperity, Health) is going to the Land of Palestine. Let the priests come with the bouquets of the gods of Egypt to take them to the Land of Palestine'. And they sent to Teudjoy saying: 'Let a priest come with the bouquet of Amun, in order to go to the Land of Palestine with Pharaoh'. And the priests agreed and said to Pediese, the son of Essamtowy, 'you are the one who, it is agreed, ought to go the Land of Palestine with Pharaoh. There is no one here in the town who is able to go to the Land of Palestine except you. Behold, you must do it, you, a scribe of the House of Life; there is nothing they can ask you and you not be able to answer it, for you are a priest of Amun. It is only the priests of the great gods of Egypt that are going to the Land of Palestine with Pharaoh'. And they persuaded Pediese to go to the Land of Palestine with Pharaoh and he made his preparations. So Pediese, son of Essamtowy, went to the Land of Palestine, and no one was with him save his servant and an hour-priest of Isis named Osirmose.

Comparison of Biblical and Extra-Biblical Material

The following section is in part organized around the name of Judaean kings. The reason is that this particular study is asking specifically about the bibical data: what could we regard as reliable if we had only the Bible? Therefore, it makes sense to shape the question broadly around the Judaean kings.

Hezekiah

The firmest datum we have at the end of the eighth century is the invasion of Sennacherib. It can be precisely calculated to 701 BCE. We have detailed descriptions in the Assyrian sources, including mention of local Palestinian rulers by name (e.g. Hezekiah), and the widespread destruction left a distinct mark in the archaeological record. There is substantial agreement that reliable memory of this is found in 2 Kgs 18.13-16, and rather less reliable memory in various other parts of 2 Kings 18–20.[20] How much longer Hezekiah ruled after 701 and what events took place in his reign are not matters of agreement. Our only information is from the biblical text, and even the sequence of events of the original story is thought to be disturbed, making it that much more difficult to ask questions about their basis in historical reality. However, if Manasseh's reign was anything like as long as portrayed in the biblical text, Hezekiah could not have lived much past 701 BCE.

Manasseh

What emerges from recent study is the importance of the reign of Manasseh. Far from being a time of depravity and fear, many think it represents a remarkable recovery from the devastations of Sennacherib. It must have given many Judaeans a return to some sort of prosperity and hope for the future. Of course, the name of Manasseh is one of the blackest in the biblical text. He is perhaps equaled—but not surpassed—only by Ahab and Jezebel. This suggests that the long reign ascribed to him is likely to be a firm part of the tradition and thus to have some basis in fact. Manasseh's existence is well attested in the Assyrian inscriptions. He is named as an apparently loyal subject paying the required tribute to both Esarhaddon and Ashurbanipal (though it has been pointed out that Manasseh's tribute is smaller than that of his neighbours [Finkelstein and Silberman 2001: 265]). He also supplied military assistance for Ashurbanipal's attack on Egypt.

What the archaeology suggests is that Judah made a significant recovery from the disaster of 701 (Finkelstein 1994; Finkelstein and Silberman 2001: 264-74). The important agricultural region of the Shephelah remained sparsely populated, probably the larger part of it having been removed from Judahite control. Elsewhere, though, settlements were re-established in destroyed southern areas, possibly with even a population increase. Settlements were also pushed into the marginal desert areas to make use of all possible land for agricultural purposes. Although dating is not easy, the suggestion is that this happened under Manasseh's leadership. Manasseh seems to have been responsible for building a city wall (2 Chron. 33.15), which could be the one dating from the seventh century discovered on the eastern slope of Jerusalem's southeastern hill (Tatum 2003: 300). It has also been proposed by E.A. Knauf that Manasseh built some prestige projects, including the Siloam tunnel (Knauf 2001b) and a palace at Ramat Raḥel (p. 170, below).

20. See the discussion in Grabbe (ed.) 2003.

There is also some evidence of the part played by Judah in the economy of the Assyrian empire, a role that would have benefited the inhabitants of Judah. The territory of Judah formed a significant link in the caravan trade from Arabia, which the Assyrians would have controlled. The Idumaean plateau gained a substantial population at this time, with the trade route leading through the valley of Beersheba and the southern coastal plain to Gaza. There are possible indications of contact with South Arabia, and the seventh-century forts at Qadeshbarnea and Haseva might have been built with the protection of this trade in mind. There is evidence of a major olive oil production centre at Tel Miqne (usually identified with ancient Ekron); however, the olives were not grown locally but would most likely have been imported from the Samarian and Judaean highlands.

Of particular interest is the apparent increase in written material. The finds indicate a greater quantity of written objects preserved from the seventh century: seals/bullae, ostraca, and inscribed weights (Finkelstein and Silberman 2001: 270, 280-81; Stern 2001: 169-200). This 'explosion of writing' has been explained as evidence of an increase in the bureaucracy (Finkelstein and Silberman 2001: 270; Stern 2001: 169) and even that Judah had become a fully developed state by this time (Finkelstein and Silberman 2001: 281, 284). These conclusions seem quite reasonable ones. The sorts of written objects catalogued here do look like the type of written material that would be the product of the bureaucracy and state administration. Whether they are evidence of greater general literacy, however, is another issue (see under 'Josiah', below).

The question of an imposed Assyrian cult has been much debated in recent years. From the early days of cuneiform study it was argued that the Assyrians imposed their god Ashur on conquered peoples.[21] This consensus was challenged by two works that appeared about the same time. First, J. McKay (1973) argued that there are no indications of Assyrian cults in any of the accounts of the kings under Assyrian rule: Ahaz, Hezekiah, Manasseh, Josiah.[22] McKay also pointed out the importance of astral cults in the biblical account, which he ascribed to Canaanite practices rather than Assyrian. A telling point made by McKay is that the description of the cults set up under Manasseh and removed by Josiah indicates they were Syro-Phoenician, not Assyrian. Independently of McKay, M. Cogan (1974) also argued against an imposed Assyrian cult, his focus being on the cuneiform texts to try to determine Assyrian practice. He noted that the Assyrians made good use of the concept of divine abandonment by the gods. Although the Assyrians occasionally destroyed images and temples of recalcitrant peoples, their normal practice was to take the images of native gods to Assyrian territories. The treaties with conquered peoples invoked Ashur, and the Assyrians

---

21. This was apparently first proposed by George Rawlinson (McKay 1973: 1-4). It was given classic expression in 1908 by A.T. Olmstead (*Western Asia in the Days of Sargon of Asyria*). In 1923 T. Oestreicher proposed that Josiah's reform was in reality political, with his purge of the cult the removal of Assyrian impositions and thus a declaration of independence. More recently it was a view expressed in John Bright's *History of Israel* (1st edn, 1959).

22. Ahaz is said to have built an altar modeled on an Assyrian one, yet nowhere is it said that this was commanded by the Assyrians or was done to please them. Likewise, the Rabshakeh in his speech before Jerusalem does not mention the Assyrian cult in his diatribe on Hezekiah's rebellion.

certainly understood submission to Assyria as submission to Ashur, yet this does not imply cultic obligations. Regions which were turned into Assyrian provinces, however, were considered Assyrian and their peoples Assyrian citizens; in such cases an Assyrian cult was established (before 'Ashur's weapon', the symbol of Assyrian rule) though native cults were not prohibited. On the other hand, we are given few details on what part the native peoples had in the imposed Assyrian cult. The situation with vassals was different in any case, and there is no evidence that they were ever required to take on cultic obligations. Both books were well received and made an impact.[23] Then H. Spieckermann (1982) replied to both monographs, though most of his arguments related more to Cogan's work since he was looking mainly at cuneiform sources.[24] Although several years went by, Cogan eventually replied to Spieckermann (Cogan 1993) and, not surprisingly, reaffirmed the view that there was no evidence for imposed cults and that those described in the Bible seem to be indigenous ones. This is unlikely to be the last word on the subject, but although Manasseh seems to have been a loyal vassal, the cults in existence under his rule were more likely to be old indigenous ones rather than those imposed from the outside.[25] This does not, though, rule out foreign influence, such as from Assyro-Aramaic astral cults (see below).

One of the most curious episodes related in the Bible is about Manasseh's deportation to and imprisonment in Babylon, followed by a return to Jerusalem and his throne and by repentance from his wicked deeds. This story is found in only one passage, significantly in Chronicles (2 Chron. 33.10-17), but not a hint is found in 2 Kgs 21.1-18. Furthermore, other biblical passages know nothing of Manasseh's repentance: Jer. 15.4 speaks of Manasseh's wickedness; 2 Kgs 23.12 says that Josiah—not Manasseh—removed the abominations; and even 2 Chron. 33.22 says that Amon was wicked like Manasseh. If Manasseh actually did all this, why would the Deuteronomist omit it? He was either ignorant of the information or he deliberately suppressed it. It is difficult to believe that if such an incident took place he had no information, so we must assume that he knew of Manasseh's repentance but purposefully ignored it. Is this likely? Yes, perhaps if the idea of an act of repentance on Manasseh's part created problems with his underlying pattern of presentation, but this would be a serious reflection on the claim made by some that the Deuteronomist was writing history.

23. John Bright is an exception. He dismissed both books in a footnote whose wording suggested he did not appreciate their implications—and possibly even that he had not read them (Bright 1980: 276 n. 22).

24. Most of the inscriptions he looks at are the same as those considered by Cogan, yet he gives a different interpretation to a number of them. He especially disputes Cogan's conclusion that cultic imposts affected only provinces and argues that several inscriptions mentioning Assyrian cultic requirements include vassal states. He also considers references to the Assyrian gods in the vassal treaties as evidence of cultic duties.

25. Finkelstein and Silberman (2001: 265) think that there was a return to popular religion by the people of the countryside after Hezekiah's failed cultic reform. This assumes, of course, that Hezekiah attempted such a reform, which many are not willing to accept (e.g. Na'aman 1995). Others would argue that nothing innovative from a religious point of view happened under Manasseh; rather, he was just blamed for what had been the traditional religion among the people for many centuries.

Yet there is an interesting parallel which suggests that what is alleged to have happened to Manasseh was not unlikely in and of itself. During Ashurbanipal's invasion of Egypt, some of his allies plotted to rebel. When he discovered the plot, he removed them all from office except Necho II who was allowed to remain on the throne (*ANET*: 294-95). It is possible that Manasseh was also plotting to rebel (Elat 1975: 67). If so, he might have been allowed to regain his throne after appropriate punishment, just as Necho was. However, it must be admitted that this is entirely speculation—there is no evidence that Manasseh plotted to rebel or that he was punished by either of the Assyrian kings under whom he was vassal.

As has been pointed out, having Manasseh repent would fit the Chronicler's purpose very well: because Manasseh lived so long, he could have done so only if he repented of his evil deeds. To the Chronicler's way of thinking, length of life was a reward for obedience. Yet is it likely that the Chronicler invented the story out of whole cloth? It is always possible, but it seems more likely that he had knowledge—however tenuous—of some incident involving Manasseh, which is indeed indicated by his citation of the 'words of Hozai'. The events under Ashurbanipal, in which Manasseh and others had to accompany the Assyrian king in his invasion of Egypt, might well be such a pretext. In sum, though, the story of Manasseh's having been arrested and taken 'with hooks and bound in bronze fetters' to Babylon is unlikely.

Amon
We have no data on him other than what is in the Bible. He is unlikely to have been invented. It was unusual for a king to be assassinated, and there is nothing about Amon to give this a literary significance. Thus, it is likely to have happened. However, the figures given for his age look suspect: although it is theoretically possible that he had a child at age 16, this seems highly improbable. Possibly the problem is with the age of Josiah (see next section), though in cases of the sudden death of a king a minor child might well take the throne.

Josiah
Despite the importance given to him in the biblical tradition, Josiah is known only from the biblical text. Neither the surviving Babylonian nor Egyptian records contain any reference to him. We are left with archaeology and the biblical text with which to make sense of his reign, though the Egyptian material and the Babylonian chronicles provide useful background and contextual information. Many past reconstructions have depended on the picture in 2 Chronicles, even in those aspects which differ at significant points from those in 2 Kings.

One theory that has held considerable sway for a number of decades is that Josiah was attempting to create a 'greater Israel', perhaps on the model of the Davidic kingdom. There are many obvious parallels between Josiah and David, though one could put these down to literary creation rather than actual activity of the ruler. The 'righteousness' of both kings is the most obvious contact, but the conquest of territory is another that many scholars have managed to glean from the biblical material: the attempt to return to a 'greater Israel' and a recovery of former glory. It has been argued that, although Josiah's reform was indeed religious, the basis of it was economic (Claburn 1973).

Na'aman (1991: 33-41; cf. his contribution to the present volume, pp. 189-247) has argued, however, that there was no political vacuum which gave Josiah room to try to found a new Davidic 'empire'. Rather, the declining Assyrian power in the west was matched by the growing power of Egypt; indeed, there may have been an orderly transfer of territorial control by mutual agreement (Na'aman 1991: 40). Miller and Hayes (1986: 383-90) had already argued that Josiah was an Egyptian vassal his entire reign. Na'aman has gone on to create a picture of Judah as a vassal state during the entirety of Josiah's reign, first under the Assyrians and then under the Egyptians. This gave only very limited scope for expansion of territory. There is some evidence of shifting the border as far north as Bethel. However, the expansion further north into the Galilee or west into the area of Philistia is unjustified from either archaeology or the text.

A further potential source of information about Judah's boundaries are the town lists of Joshua (15.21-62; 18.21-28; 19.2-8, 40-46). It was argued by A. Alt that the lists of the southern tribes actually reflected Josiah's kingdom, and the question has now been investigated at length by Na'aman (1991; pp. 189-247, below). It is impossible to summarize the detailed textual analysis here, but the lists of Judah and Benjamin are the main ones in question. The northern border should be set along the Bethel–Ophrah line, which was north of the traditional border of the Kingdom of Judah (Josh. 18.21-28); Jericho is also included, though it had previously been an Israelite town. If Josh. 21.45-47 is deleted as an addition of the editor, the list includes the eastern Shephelah. 2 Kings 23.8 makes reference to the territory 'from Geba to Beersheba', which is likely to be an indication of Judah's actual extent under Josiah. Therefore, the reference to Qadesh-barnea (if this is indeed the site indicated in Josh. 15.23) is probably to be seen as an addition to the list, but most of the sites are no further south than Beersheba. The main point made by Na'aman is the extent to which archaeology (e.g. the rosette seal impressions) and other sources of data fit with these lists in Joshua.

The ostraca from Meṣad Ḥashavyahu do not seem to show a Judaean outpost, as often alleged, but probably an Egyptian one with some Judaean soldiers (Fantalkin 2001: 139-47; Na'aman 1991: 44-46; pp. 189-247, below). Other names in the texts are Phoenician, for example. Neither does the text of Ostracon 1 provide evidence of Josiah's religious reform. The sender of the ostracon appeals to the humanity of the recipient, not to the law of the king or the Torah. Similarly, the Arad ostraca indicate a contingent of Greek mercenaries in that area, which were probably in the employ of the Egyptians.

With regard to borders, R. Kletter (1999: 40-43) considers the question in the light of several types of artifacts. He argues that archaeology cannot pinpoint accurate borders nor establish the political affiliation of single sites. The overwhelming majority of the artifacts considered by him fit more or less with the Judaean heartland and do not indicate large-scale expansion. Various explanations have been given for those finds of artifacts outside the heartland; however, only the western Shephelah shows much of a concentration. Although Judaean artifacts have been found at Qadesh-barnea and Meṣad Ḥashavyahu (Judaean inscribed weights, pottery vessels, Hebrew ostraca), the material culture of both sites is mixed, as is that of the area bounded by Ekron–Gezer–Tel Batash; perhaps a similar phenomenon occurred in the Negev. According to Kletter, they could show a mixed population or a temporary Judaean domination; in any case, they cannot help in defining Judah's borders because they are isolated sites outside any sequence of Judaean settlements. They thus cannot prove or refute the possibility that Josiah expanded his territory for a short duration, though the few finds outside Judah are best explained by trade or exchange.

The significant increase in written artifacts (seals, seal impressions, ostraca, inscribed weights) have been interpreted as demonstrating a greater degree of literacy in Judah at this time. Indeed, it has been associated with the rise of the Deuteronomic movement and the promulgation of Deuteronomy under Josiah (Finkelstein and Silberman 2001: 280-81, 284):

> The very fact that a written law code suddenly appeared at this time meshes well with the archaeological record of the spread of literarcy in Judah...the report of the appearance of a definitive written text and its public reading by the king accords with the evidence for the sudden, dramatic spread of literacy in seventh-century Judah... Writing joined preaching as a medium for advancing a set of quite revolutionary political, religious, and social ideas.

I am not so sure that the inferences drawn here are justified. The increase in written material of the sort mentioned here would not necessarily indicate an increase of general literacy in the population, since the objects of the administration would have been produced by and for scribal bureaucrats, not the average Judaean. There are also levels of literacy: the ability to read the short inscription on a seal impression or even an administrative document does not demonstrate the reading of long religious documents. If Deuteronomy was really produced at this time—a view widely held but also disputed (see below)—the writers were naturally literate. But it does not follow that there was greater literacy in the general population. There is no evidence of multiple copies of the document or that people were reading it for themselves; on the contrary, it was by public reading and teaching that it would have been promulgated.

The archaeological finds of seals, seal impressions, and ostraca give no support to the view that 'writing joined preaching for advancing a set of quite revolutionary political, religious, and social ideas'. Where are such ideas promulgated in the seal impressions and ostraca? Granted, the apparent move to aniconic inscriptions on seals may be a datum giving evidence of the spread of Josiah's reform. But the mere presence of aniconic seals is not an overt means of propagating the revolutionary ideals that accompanied such a reform. The move away from iconography would be a consequence of such a reform, not the vehicle for advancing it. The changes in seal impressions would probably have been noted consciously only by a very few.

It was once conventional to accept Josiah's reform at face value, but the question is currently much debated.[26] We have no direct evidence outside the biblical text, which makes us at least ask whether it is an invention of the Deuteronomist. The alleged absence of any reference to this reform in Jeremiah has always been a major puzzle. Some have found allusions here and there, but one has to admit that they are surprisingly obscure. Considering Jeremiah's overall message and position, he should have embraced such a reform and made copious comments about it. Some have seen evidence in the material remains (e.g. Uehlinger 1995; pp. 279-316, below), but others have argued against it (e.g. Niehr 1995). The central passage is 2 Kings 22–23, however. It is widely agreed that this passage has been the subject of Deuteronomistic editing, leaving the question of how much might be Deuteronomistic invention. Two essays in this volume (Hardmeier and Uehlinger) argue that at the heart of 2 Kings 22–23 is a simple list of reform measures affecting mainly Jerusalem and perhaps Bethel, to which the Deuteronomistic editors have added an extensive superstructure that makes the reform much more extensive in scope and geography than the original list. Uehlinger argues that the original list—but not the much-expanded present text—is supported by the archaeology and iconography. Knauf, however, argues against any 'core' from the time of Josiah (pp. 166-68, below).

A related issue is the statement in 2 Chron. 34.3-7 that Josiah began to purge the country of the various shrines and cults in his twelfth year (i.e. at age 20). This does not accord with 2 Kgs 22.3-7 which has the reform follow the discovery of the law book in the temple. This is not an easy issue to address because the description in 2 Kings 22–23 is an idealized one: the only question is how idealized. This is perhaps why a significant opinion of scholarship has accepted the statement in 2 Chron. 34.3-7 that Josiah began his reform six years before the finding of the law book. Yet as Na'aman (1991: 38), among others, has pointed out, the theological motives of the writer of Chronicles have had their way here as elsewhere. He notes that when Josiah reached the age of majority at 20, it would have been 'unthinkable' in the theological world of the Chronicler that he would have done nothing about the 'pagan' shrines for another six years. Thus, it was theologically desirable that Josiah begin his reform in his twelfth year rather than wait until his eighteenth. Na'aman has also connected the dating of the reform (which he puts in 622 BCE) with the height of the crisis in Assyria during the revolt of Babylon in 626–623 BCE. It may be that the Assyrian ruler Sin-sharra-ishkun's problems were sufficient to give Josiah confidence to initiate his reforms without being in danger of attracting Assyrian disapproval, while the Egyptians who replaced them may not have been particularly concerned.

Many have followed the narrative of 2 Chronicles which has Josiah die in a pitched battle. This seems unlikely, however, since Judah as an Egyptian vassal

---

26. For a good summary of the arguments and references for the composition of Deuteronomy in the period between Hezekiah and Josiah, see Albertz (1994: 198-201) as well as the essays by Albertz and Hardmeier in this volume. For doubts about the dating and other aspects of the traditional theory of Deuteronomy, see Lohfink (1995), and the essays by P.R. Davies and E.A. Knauf in the present volume.

state is not likely to have been in a military position to challenge the Egyptian army. On the other hand, a vassal king would have been expected to appear before the new ruler (Necho II [610–595 BCE] in this case) to pay homage and swear allegiance. Doubts have been expressed about the fate of Josiah for some considerable period of time (Na'aman 1991: 51-55, with earlier literature). 2 Kings is clearly reticent to tell what happened, but Na'aman's argument that Necho had Josiah executed for suspected disloyalty of some sort makes the most sense, not only from the general historical situation but also from a close reading of the text in 2 Kings.

Jehoahaz
Nothing is known of him, though he has only the brief reign of three months. What does fit is that he would have been removed from the throne by the Egyptians who were probably in control of the region at this time (as discussed under 'Josiah' above).

Jehoiakim
Jehoiakim is known only from the biblical text, yet his reign illustrates the external politics of the ancient Near East at this time and fits in well with them. Judah was clearly an Egyptian vassal, since it was the Egyptians who put Jehoiakim on the throne. But in Jehoiakim's fourth year Nebuchadnezzar gained control of the region after the battle of Carchemish, and Judah became the vassal of the Babylonians. He then rebelled after three years. Why? The answer is that in 601 BCE Nebuchadnezzar fought a costly battle with Necho II which inflicted considerable damage on both armies; indeed, it took the Babylonians several years to recover, as indicated by *Babylonian Chronicle* 5. It was after this battle that Jehoiakim rebelled. It was not until two years later that Nebuchadnezzar retaliated by fostering raids against Judah, and it was not until late in 598 that he sent an army against Jerusalem. 2 Chronicles 36.6 states that Nebuchadnezzar besieged Jerusalem and took Jehoiakim captive to Babylon, while Jeremiah 22.18-19 predicts that he would have the 'burial of an ass' (i.e. his carcass would be dragged outside Jerusalem and left exposed and unburied). Neither appears to be what happened; from 2 Kings 24 it looks as if Jehoiakim died a natural death only a couple of months or so before Nebuchadnezzar set siege to Jerusalem, and it was his son who paid the price for his rebellion.

Jehoiachin
Although he reigned only very briefly, Jehoiachin is well attested. In the biblical writings his name is mentioned not only in 2 Kings and 2 Chronicles but also in Jeremiah (22.24, 28; 27.20; 28.4; 29.2; 37.1; 52.31), Ezekiel (1.2), and Esther (2.6). Jehoiachin is known (though not by name) from the *Babylonian Chronicles* which tell of Nebuchadnezzar's taking of Jerusalem and his carrying of the Judaean king into captivity. Jehoiachin's name has also been preserved in the Jehoiachin tablets from Babylon. Thus, this young ephemeral ruler is better known from extra-biblical sources than the famous Josiah.

Zedekiah

The last king of Judah is known from the *Babylonian Chronicles* as the king placed on the throne by Nebuchadnezzar after his conquest of Jerusalem in early 597 BCE. Zedekiah's name is known only from the biblical text, however. We have no Mesopotamia historical sources after 594 when the *Babylonian Chronicles* come to an end. Yet the inscription of Psammetichus II (595–589 BCE) describing a tour of Palestine fits a situation in which the king of Judah was constantly looking for ways to free himself from the overlordship of Nebuchadnezzar. The book of Jeremiah describes a number of episodes involving the king or courtiers (see below). The rebellion and final siege and capture of Jerusalem are, unfortunately, not known from any Mesopotamian source. Yet in view of the detailed information confirmed for 2 Kings in the period before this, the reasonableness (for the most part) of the picture in 2 Kings, and the general background situation in the ancient Near East, it does not take much of a leap of faith to accept the general picture and the approximate date for the destruction of Jerusalem.

The Case of Jeremiah

The late lamented Robert Carroll wrote some classic works on Jeremiah, in particular his large commentary (Carroll 1986). He makes sceptical but cogent observations on almost every page, yet despite the problems of reading the text of Jeremiah as a contemporary, dispassionate biography (as he points out), there are a number of statements in Jeremiah about external events that could be based only on contemporary knowledge. These involve the activities of Nebuchadnezzar and their dating. The writer knows about the battle of Carchemish and its correct dating (Jer. 26.2). He is aware of the siege of Lachish and Azekah (Jer. 34.6-7), a situation which has appeared in a remarkable way in Lachish Letter #4. Only some of the statements about Nebuchadnezzar can be checked with Mesopotamian sources, but the exact recital of events in particular years of the king have the look of authenticity.[27]

In addition, Jeremiah describes the prophet's interaction with the Judaean kings (especially Zedekiah) and various members of the court and temple. A whole network of supporters, opponents, and relatives appears in the book. We are unlikely to find confirmation of this information outside the Bible. However, data from other texts—which do not seem to be the author's sources—may give some independent support to the reliability of this information for the most part (cf. Long 1982). Yet the find of a seal of 'Baruch son of Neriah the scribe' does not prove that Jeremiah had a scribe named Baruch (cf. Carroll 1997: 96-100), even if the seal is authentic. An authentic seal could help to confirm the existence of Baruch the scribe, but the question would still remain as to whether a high government official—as this Baruch would seem to be—would have had the interest and leisure to serve as Jeremiah's private scribe.[28] As for the prophecies

---

27. For a further discussion of the question, see Grabbe forthcoming.
28. In a private communication, Axel Knauf has suggested that Baruch might have been deliberately assigned to Jeremiah to help keep an eye on this potentially dangerous prophet. This is an

about Jehoiakim's having the 'burial of an ass' and Nebuchadnezzar's conquest of Egypt, these seem to be mistaken.[29] Perhaps they were genuine prophecies—that failed!

The book of Jeremiah contains a variety of material; I think most would admit to that even if they did not subscribe to the specific analysis of S. Mowinckel (1914) or others. Carroll's sharp observations have called into question the amount of personal material from Jeremiah himself (Carroll 1981), yet he did not explain adequately some of the material in the book. It seems likely that some of the data there can be explained best as coming from a contemporary writer. Unlike 2 Kings, however, the information is not likely to come from a chronicle. Although it refers to international events on occasion, a lot of it is highly individual to Jeremiah or those around him. The best explanation seems to be that a contemporary of Jeremiah's did write some sort of 'biography' of the prophet. If this suggestion does not commend itself, any alternative theory has to take account of how the book has some statements that match what we know of the wider history of the ancient Near East at the time.

The Case of Nebuchadnezzar

One of the most interesting points that has arisen out of this study are the number of statements about Nebuchadnezzar in 2 Kings and Jeremiah that accord with the contemporary sources. The rule of Jehoiakim, Jehoiachin, and Zedekiah are tied closely to Nebuchadnezzar's reign. The battle of Carchemish is known and given the correct chronological position. Although Jehoiakim's rebellion is not explained in the biblical text, both the reason for it and the timing make sense in the light of Nebuchadnezzar's standoff with Egypt in 601 BCE. The biblical account of the Babylonian king's taking of Jerusalem in 597 BCE fits with everything we know from Mesopotamian sources. The Jehoiachin tablets confirm the presence of Jehoiachin in Babylon, along with his sons and other Judahites. Not every reference to contemporary history is accurate (e.g. whether Nebuchadnezzar ever conquered Egypt[30]), but the amount of specific information is remarkable.

When it comes to Ezekiel, however, the information is much more doubtful. It may be that Nebuchadnezzar besieged Tyre, since Ezekiel's original prophecy is 'corrected' later on. But there is no evidence for a 40-year period of desolation for Egypt, as predicted. 2 Chronicles seem to be dependent on 2 Kings, and none

interesting idea, but I tend to doubt that royal resources would have been used in such a fashion. Knauf is right that the royal court wanted to keep Jeremiah under observation; I just do not find convincing that the way to have done so was to assign him a valuable state scribe to take down his prophecies at dictation.

29. Our knowledge of Egypt during the Neo-Babylonian period often has gaps. Yet although there were apparently battles between Nebuchadnezzar and the Egyptians, no *conquest* in the conventional sense of the word took place. Apparently Pharaoh Hophrah (Apries) was removed by his successor Amasis, not Nebuchadnezzar (cf. James 1991: 718-20; Carroll 1986: 727). The clash between Egypt and the Babylonians in 568 did not result in a Babylonian takeover. One suggestion is that these prophecies relate to the conquest of Cambyses (McKane 1996: 1066-67).

30. See previous note.

of the additional passages is proved to have reliable information, with the possible exception of the city wall. The one specifically relating to Nebuchadnezzar is Jehoiakim's Babylonian captivity, and this goes contrary not only to 2 Kings but also the *Babylonian Chronicles*. As for Daniel, the writer seems to know of Nebuchadnezzar only through the biblical text. The siege of Jerusalem in Jehoiakim's third year is based on a partial misunderstanding of 2 Chronicles. The other stories in Daniel about Nebuchadnezzar seem at least in part based on legends rising out of the reign of Nabonidus (see the discussion and earlier literature in Grabbe 1987).

Conclusions

Conclusions with Regard to History
We can now summarize the results of the foregoing study. In doing so, it is difficult to indicate graphically the relative importance of the points listed below. Obviously, some agreements and disagreements are more significant than others. However, an attempt will be made to take account of this in the next section which discusses methodological implications.

Biblical data confirmed:
- In broad terms, Hezekiah's existence and revolt and Sennacherib's destructive invasion of Judah are supported by the Assyrian records and by archaeology, especially relative to the city of Lachish.
- Manasseh's existence and name are attested by the inscriptions of both Esarhaddon and Ashurbanipal.
- The one datum about Manasseh's reign found in the Chronicler, but not in Kings, that is likely to be correct concerns his building of a city wall (2 Chron. 33.14): something very like this was found down the eastern slope of the southeastern hill by K. Kenyon.
- Although some of the data from seals are problematic, because of either problems of interpretation or questions of authenticity, some are supportive of the biblical data, to a lesser or greater extent. Perhaps one of the most likely is the one reading 'Gemaryahu son of Shaphan' (cf. Jer. 36.10, 12); another is the reference to an official of 'Baalisha', king of Ammon (cf. Jer. 40.14). Moderately high in probability is 'Azariah son of Hilkiah' (cf. 2 Kgs 22–23; 1 Chron. 6.13; 9.11; Ezra 7.1). Of more moderate probability is the one reading 'Jaazaniah the servant of the king' (cf. 2 Kgs 25.23).
- Josiah's religious reforms—the aspect of his reign, and of the seventh century, of most interest to many modern scholars—are difficult to establish in any direct way. (There are some cogent arguments from textual analysis that a modest list of cult measures lies at the heart of 2 Kgs 22–23,[31] but my concern here is not primarily with inner-biblical analysis.) But the disappearance of Yhwh's consort and astral symbols from the

---

31. See in particular the essays of Hardmeier and Uehlinger in this volume.

iconography suggest a significant religious change. This does not by itself establish Josiah's reforms but combines with other considerations to make the general biblical account (not necessarily the details) plausible.
- Pharaoh Necho (II) and his support of the Assyrians against the Babylonians are confirmed by Egyptian sources and especially the *Babylonian Chronicles*.
- Jeremiah's references to the battle of Carchemish and other activities of Nebuchadnezzar (II) are remarkably accurate, suggesting they would have been based on contemporary or near contemporary information.
- Jehoiakim's rebellion in Nebuchadnezzar's fourth year fits the events described in the *Babylonian Chronicles*, even though Judah is not specifically mentioned in the entry for that year.
- Nebuchadnezzar's attack on Jerusalem of 597, and the deposition of one king and the replacement with another, is given substance by the *Babylonian Chronicles*. Although the name of Jehoiachin is not found in the *Babylonian Chronicles*, it seems confirmed by the reference in the Jehoiachin tablets.
- One of the Lachish ostraca mentions the siege of Lachish and Azekah (cf. Jer. 34.6-7).

Biblical data not confirmed, though they may be correct:
- Amon's assassination is not likely to have been made up, especially since he seems to have made so little impact in the history of Judah.
- Surprisingly, nothing of Josiah's reign can be directly confirmed from extra-biblical sources, not only his cultic reform but even his existence, since he is not mentioned in any Assyrian or Egyptian sources so far discovered.
- The statement of 2 Chron. 34.3-7 that Josiah began his religious purge already in his twelfth year may be true, and many scholars have accepted it. However, it seems unlikely; otherwise, why was there such a reaction to finding the law book in the temple? (This consideration is apart from the arguments of those who maintain that the cultic reform was not a part of Josiah's reign.)
- Ezra 4.2 refers to a deportation to Palestine under Esarhaddon, but the exact place is not specified. Ezra 4.9-10 mentions various peoples brought to Samaria by 'Osnappar', a name unknown in Assyrian history, though some think it is a corruption of Ashurbanipal or possibly Esarhaddon. In addition to the problems with the two passages just noted, no such deportation is known under either Esarhaddon or Ashurbanipal. One can only say that it is possible in the present state of our knowledge.
- The names and actions of the various palace and temple officials with whom Jeremiah interacts may be correctly recorded. As noted above, there are internal data that suggest the plausibility of some of them. There are no external data except possibly some seal inscriptions in a few cases.

- The destruction of Jerusalem by Nebuchadnezzar in 587/586 is likely to be correct, given the general accuracy of such data in this section of 2 Kings.
- Nebuchadnezzar may have besieged Tyre. The fact that Ezekiel first says he would conquer it and then admits that he did not is an indication of prophecies contemporary with the events.

Biblical picture is most likely incorrect:
- 2 Kings has Judah throw off the Assyrian yoke under Hezekiah, and no hint of an imposition until after the death of Josiah. This is an omission, but it goes further: it seems to be a deliberate attempt by the compiler to mask the fact that Josiah was a vassal, probably first of the Assyrians and then of the Egyptians.
- 2 Chronicles 33.10-17 has Manasseh being taken captive to Babylon. Although some event might lie behind this (see above, pp. 103-104), it is contradicted by the silence in 2 Kings, the general image of Manasseh in the Assyrian inscriptions (such as the lack of any indication of rebellion), and the unlikelihood that he would have been taken to Babylon if he had been taken captive.
- Although it is not impossible, Amon is unlikely to have had a child at age 16.
- The picture in 2 Chron. 35.20-27 that Josiah fought a pitched battle with Pharaoh Necho and was mortally wounded by an arrow is contradicted by 2 Kgs 23.28-30 and looks like a literary topos.
- The 2 Chron. 36.6-7 statement that Jehoiakim was taken captive to Babylon fits neither the picture in 2 Kings nor that in the *Babylonian Chronicles*.
- The statement in Jer. 22.18-19 that Jehoiakim would have 'the burial of an ass' by being thrown out without a proper burial is contradicted by the statements in 2 Kgs 24.6 that Jehoiakim simply 'slept with his fathers'—which usually means a peaceful death and burial.
- The prophecies of Jeremiah and Ezekiel that Nebuchadnezzar would conquer Egypt and that it would remain desolate for 40 years are contradicted by what we know of both Nebuchadnezzar's reign and of Egyptian history.
- Daniel seems to have known little or nothing about this period except what the author read in the biblical text or had received in the form of very legendary material. Jerusalem was not besieged by Nebuchadnezzar in Jehoiakim's third year. Nebuchadnezzar was not mad (or whatever word one wishes to use) for seven years.

Biblical picture omits/has gaps:
- The truly devastating effects of Hezekiah's rebellion on the cities and villages of Judah are only hinted at; the text is at pains to establish Hezekiah's faithfulness to Yhwh in his rebellion against Assyria rather than the suffering he caused to his country and people. Also, as noted above,

Judah remained an Assyrian vassal throughout the reign of Hezekiah, Manasseh, Amon, and the first part of Josiah's reign.
- The real achievements of Manasseh's reign from a political, economic, and social point of view (as attested especially in the archaeology) are completely ignored.
- The text is coy about giving the real reason for Josiah's death. The thesis that he was executed by Necho is plausible, though not certain, but it is unlikely he was killed in battle.

Conclusions with Regard to Methodology

Although this study has ranged over more than a century of history and has made suggestions about the historical interpretation and reconstruction of the period, the ultimate purpose has been to ask about methodology. Methodological questions involve all aspects of historical study, but one of the questions I have been addressing in several studies[32] is this: To what extent can we use the biblical text as a historical source? This has been the main focus of the present article, but other issues have also arisen that will be summarized here.

1. One of the points that emerges is the fruitfulness of a multiple-source approach. For the history of Judah, in the seventh century at least, the use of a variety of data—archaeological, inscriptional, contemporary textual, biblical—has turned out to give us a reasonable grasp of the history of large portions of this century. We have seen how important it is to study each source independently in the initial stages of the investigation, lest one 'contaminate' the evidence by circular interpretation of one against the other. Nevertheless, once the groundwork has been done and the nature of the different sources has been understood, then they can and should be synthesized in a rigorous way to work toward an understanding of the history of this period.

2. We can make an immediate assertion in answer to our main question—the biblical text can and should be used in historical reconstruction—but this statement must also be immediately qualified: 'the biblical text' is not a single entity but is made up of a variety of material (narrative, poetry, prophecy, theology, rewriting, early material, late material), often with a complex history of transmission. The minimalist argument is correct here: the biblical material must be controlled where possible and treated critically. However, where it cannot be controlled by external data, we have seen that for the late seventh century, at least, we can still sometimes have confidence in its data. Here some minimalist approaches are too rigid, I would argue.

3. One point emerging from this present study is the pattern of what is and is not likely to be reliable in the biblical text.

32. Grabbe 1997, 1998, 2001, forthcoming.

(a) First, a comparison of 2 Kings and 2 Chronicles shows that the former is much more likely to be credible where the two texts differ. In one example from the present study 2 Chronicles has a datum not in 2 Kings that may be authentic (Manasseh's building of a city wall), but otherwise it was found to be less reliable where it differed from 2 Kings (the captivity of Manasseh in Babylon, the beginning of Josiah's religious reform in his twelfth year, the death of Josiah, the captivity of Jehoiakim). In some cases where additional information is provided, it is possible that 2 Chronicles has reliable information, but in no case has my study been able to confirm it, except perhaps for the city wall.

(b) Secondly, the book of Jeremiah is shown to have some reliable statements about external events. (This goes against the views of Robert Carroll who was a member of this Seminar.) It has not been possible to draw conclusions about much of the data relating to internal events of the Judaean court or the interpersonal relations which have such a prominent place in the book, though the broad outline of the court infighting and politics, Jeremiah's reliance on a network of supporters and relatives, and the ambivalent attitude of Zedekiah fit the general situation.

(c) Other books present a less credible picture. Ezekiel may have some additional information about Nebuchadnezzar's activities that are so far unrecorded in native records. Yet his statements ('prophecies) are sometimes contradictory (that Nebuchadnezzar would conquer Tyre) or incredible (that Nebuchadnezzar would conquer and so desolate Egypt that it would remain uninhabited for 40 years). Similarly, Daniel seems to draw its information from a (mis)reading of earlier biblical books and from legendary material so far removed from its original historical context as to be unusable for historical purposes.

4. Where the biblical material seems to have some reliable material, some statements are more likely to be usable than others. Where the statements of 2 Kings and Jeremiah are shown to be confirmed by external sources, this is usually when they relate to a straightforward description of events or actions where the biblical author is unlikely to have had a particular motive for mentioning the events. Thus, names, dates, the 'political' actions of kings, and similar things are most likely to be reliable. When 'theological' or 'religious' issues become a consideration (e.g. where a king is 'righteous' or 'wicked'), however, invention and distortion for ideological reasons is more likely to have taken place.

5. The compiler of 2 Kings (the 'Deuteronomistic Historian'?) is likely to have had a documentary source or sources of some sort. The type of reliable information attested for 2 Kings is the sort that might come from a source very much like the *Babylonian Chronicles*. Each entry would be short and factual, with little embellishment or comment, though occasional miscellaneous information might have been present. Such a source might have been a court chronicle, a temple chronicle, or something similar. This would allow the writer to obtain information on the age of the king at accession, the length of reign, the name of his mother, the main deeds, even including such information as a special tax

placed on the 'people of the land' by the king. But the elaboration of this information, especially as it relates to theological matters would probably have been the creation of the author/compiler.

6. The same may be true of Jeremiah, but the source of this writer's information looks to be of a different sort. Most of what we find would seem to be best explained by the use of a personal writing ('biography'? diary?) of someone associated with Jeremiah himself. The references to Nebuchadnezzar look to be those of someone contemporary or nearly contemporary with the events. The description of the actions of Jeremiah are seen from a quite personal point of view but look to be different from the source(s) of the prophecies. Although one could explain it all as coming from Baruch who acted as Jeremiah's scribe, one would have to ask about the significance of the Baruch seal impression. If it is genuine (and there are many who question this) and to be associated with the Baruch of Jeremiah, it suggests an individual high in the royal bureaucracy. One would then have to ask whether a high court official, as Baruch seems to have been, would be an amanuensis to Jeremiah.

Some of the above six points mentioned here are likely to be broad principles about use of the biblical text, but we need to be careful about too much generalization: other historical periods (and biblical texts) might show a different pattern. More work needs to be done to test out these principles in other areas.

BIBLIOGRAPHY

Albertz, Rainer
    1994   *A History of Israelite Religion in the Old Testament Period*. I. *From the Beginnings to the End of the Monarchy*; II. *From the Exile to the Maccabees* (London: SCM Press).
Avigad, Nahman
    1978   'Baruch the Scribe and Jerahmeel the King's Son', *IEJ* 28: 52-56.
    1986   *Hebrew Bullae from the Time of Jeremiah: Remnants of a Burnt Archive* (Jerusalem: Israel Exploration Society).
Avigad, Nahman, revised and completed by Benjamin Sass
    1997   *Corpus of West Semitic Stamp Seals* (Jerusalem: Israel Academy of Sciences and Humanities/Israel Exploration Society).
Barkay, Gabriel
    1993   'A Bulla of Ishmael, the King's Son', *BASOR* 290-91: 109-14.
Becking, Bob
    1993   'Baalis, the King of the Ammonites: An Epigraphical Note on Jeremiah 40.14', *JSS* 38: 15-24.
    1997   'Inscribed Seals as Evidence for Biblical Israel? Jeremiah 40.7–41.15 *Par Exemple*', in Grabbe (ed.) 1997: 65-83.
Bordreuil, Pierre, Felice Israel and Dennis Pardee
    1996   'Deux ostraca paléo-hébreux de la Collection Sh. Moussaïeff', *Semitica* 46: 49-76.
    1998   'King's Command and Widow's Plea: Two New Hebrew Ostraca of the Biblical Period', *NEA* 61: 2-13.

Borger, Rykle
 1967 *Die Inschriften Esarhaddons Königs von Assyrien* (*AfO* Beiheft, 9; Osnabrück: Biblio Verlage, 2nd edn).
Bright, John
 1959 *A History of Israel* (Philadelphia: Westminster Press).
 1980 *A History of Israel* (Philadelphia: Westminster Press, 3rd edn).
Broshi, Magen
 1974 'The Expansion of Jerusalem in the Reigns of Hezekiah and Manasseh', *IEJ* 24: 21-26.
Cahill, Jane M.
 2003 'Jerusalem at the Time of the United Monarchy: The Archaeological Evidence', in Vaughn and Killebrew (eds.) 2003: 13-80.
Carroll, Robert P.
 1981 *From Chaos to Covenant* (London: SCM Press).
 1986 *Jeremiah: A Commentary* (OTL; London: SCM Press).
 1997 'Madonna of Silences: Clio and the Bible', in Grabbe (ed.) 1997: 84-103.
Claburn, W.E.
 1973 'The Fiscal Basis of Josiah's Reforms', *JBL* 92: 11-22.
Cogan, Mordechai [Morton]
 1974 *Imperialism and Religion: Assyria, Judah and Israel in the Eighth and Seventh Centuries B.C.E.* (SBLMS, 19; Missoula, MT: Society of Biblical Literature).
 1993 'Judah Under Assyrian Hegemony: A Re-examination of Imperialism and Religion', *JBL* 112: 403-14.
Cohen, Rudolf
 1981 'Excavations at Kadesh-barnea 1976–1978', *BA* 44: 93-107.
 1997 'Qadesh-barnea', in Meyers (ed.) 1997: IV, 365-67.
Cohen, Rudolph, and Yigal Yisrael
 1995 'The Iron Age Fortresses at 'En Ḥaṣeva', *BA* 58: 223-35.
Coogan, Michael D., J. Cheryl Exum and Lawrence E. Stager (eds.)
 1994 *Scripture and Other Artifacts: Essays on the Bible and Archaeology in Honor of Philip J. King* (Louisville, KY: Westminster/John Knox Press).
Elat, Moshe
 1975 'The Political Status of the Kingdom of Judah within the Assyrian Empire in the 7th Century B.C.E.', in Yohanan Aharoni, *Investigations at Lachish: The Sanctuary and the Residency (Lachish V)* (Tel Aviv University, Publications of the Institute of Archaeology, 4; Tel Aviv: Gateway Publishers): 61-70.
Eph'al, Israel, and Joseph Naveh
 1998 'Remarks on the Recently Published Moussaieff Ostraca', *IEJ* 48: 269-73.
Fantalkin, Alexander
 2001 'Meẓad Ḥashavyahu: Its Material Culture and Historical Background', *TA* 28: 1-165.
Finkelstein, Israel
 1988–89 'The Land of Ephraim Survey 1980–1987: Preliminary Report', *TA* 15-16: 117-83.
 1994 'The Archaeology of the Days of Manasseh', in Coogan, Exum and Stager (eds.) 1994: 169-87.
 2003 'The Rise of Jerusalem and Judah: The Missing Link', in Vaughn and Killebrew (eds.) 2003: 81-101.
Finkelstein, Israel, and Neil Asher Silberman
 2001 *The Bible Unearthed: Archaeology's New Vision of Ancient Israel and the Origin of its Sacred Texts* (New York: Free Press).

Garfinkel, Yosef
    1990   'The *Eliakim Na'ar Yokan* Seal Impressions: Sixty Years of Confusion in Biblical Archaeological Research', *BA* 53: 74-79.

Geva, Hillel
    2003   'Western Jerusalem at the End of the First Temple Period in Light of the Excavations in the Jewish Quarter', in Vaughn and Killebrew (eds.) 2003: 183-208.

Gogel, Sandra Landis
    1998   *A Grammar of Epigraphic Hebrew* (Society of Biblical Literature Resources for Biblical Study, 23; Atlanta: Scholars Press).

Grabbe, Lester L.
    1987   'Fundamentalism and Scholarship: The Case of Daniel', in B.P. Thompson (ed.), *Scripture: Method and Meaning: Essays Presented to Anthony Tyrrell Hanson for his Seventieth Birthday* (Hull: Hull University Press): 133-52.
    1997   'Are Historians of Ancient Palestine Fellow Creatures—Or Different Animals?', in Grabbe (ed.) 1997: 19-36.
    1998   '"The Exile" under the Theodolite: Historiography as Triangulation', in Lester L. Grabbe (ed.), *Leading Captivity Captive: 'The Exile' as History and Ideology* (JSOTSup, 278; ESHM, 2; Sheffield Academic Press): 80-100.
    2001   'Jewish Historiography and Scripture in the Hellenistic Period', in Lester L. Grabbe (ed.), *Did Moses Speak Attic? Jewish Historiography and Scripture in the Hellenistic Period* (JSOTSup, 317; ESHM, 3; Sheffield Academic Press): 129-55.
    forthcoming   '"The Lying Pin of the Scribes": Jeremiah and History'.

Grabbe, Lester L. (ed.)
    1997   *Can a 'History of Israel' Be Written?* (JSOTSup, 245; ESHM, 1; Sheffield: Sheffield Academic Press).
    2003   *'Like a Bird in a Cage': The Invasion of Sennacherib in 701 BCE* (JSOTSup, 363; ESHM, 4; London and New York: Sheffield Academic Press).

Grayson, A.K.
    1975   *Assyrian and Babylonian Chronicles* (Texts from Cuneiform Sources, 5; Locust Valley, NY: J.J. Augustin).
    1991a   'Chapter 23. Assyria: Sennacherib and Esarhaddon (704–669 B.C.)', in *CAH*: III/2, 103-41.
    1991b   'Chapter 24. Assyria 668–635 B.C.: The Reign of Ashurbanipal', in *CAH*: III/2, 142-61.

Greenberg, Raphael
    1993   'Beit Mirsim, Tell', in *NEAEHL*: I, 177-80.

Griffith, F.L. (ed.)
    1909   *Catalogue of the Demotic Papyri in the John Rylands Library* (3 vols.; Manchester: Manchester University Press).

Gross, Walter (ed.)
    1995   *Jeremia und die 'deuteronomistische Bewegung'* (BBB, 98; Beltz: Athenäum).

Hendel, Ronald S.
    1996   'The Date of the Siloam Inscription: A Rejoinder to Rogerson and Davies', *BA* 59: 233-47.

Herr, Larry G.
    1985   'The Servant of Baalis', *BA* 48: 169-72.

Herzog, Ze'ev
    2001   'The Date of the Temple of Arad: Reassessment of the Stratigraphy and the Implications for the History of Religion in Judah', in Mazar (ed.) 2001: 156-78.

James, T.G.H.
    1991   'Chapter 35. Egypt: The Twenty-Fifth and Twenty-Sixth Dynasties', in *CAH*: III/2, 677-747.

Keel, Othmar, and Christoph Uehlinger
    1998   *Gods, Goddesses, and Images of God in Ancient Israel* (trans. Thomas H. Trapp; Minneapolis: Fortress Press; Edinburgh: T. & T. Clark); ET of *Göttinnen, Götter und Gottessymbole: Neue Erkenntnisse zur Religionsgeschichte Kanaans und Israels aufgrund bislang unerschlossener ikonographischer Quellen* (Quaestiones Disputatae, 134; Freiburg: Herder, 4th expanded edn, 1998).

Killebrew, Ann E.
    2003   'Biblical Jerusalem: An Archaeological Assessment', in Vaughn and Killebrew (eds.) 2003: 329-45.

Kletter, Raz
    1999   'Pots and Polities: Material Remains of Late Iron Age Judah in Relation to its Political Borders', *BASOR* 314: 19-54.

Knauf, Ernest Axel
    2001a   'History, Archaeology, and the Bible', *TZ* 57: 262-68.
    2001b   'Hezekiah or Manasseh? A Reconsideration of the Siloam Tunnel and Inscription', *TA* 28: 281-87.

Kuhrt, Amélie
    1995   *The Ancient Near East c. 3000–300 BC, I–II* (Routledge History of the Ancient World; London and New York: Routledge).

Lipschits, Oded
    2003   'Demographic Changes in Judah between the Seventh and the Fifth Centuries B.C.E.', in Oded Lipschits and Joseph Blenkinsopp (eds.), *Judah and the Judeans in the Neo-Babylonian Period* (Winona Lake, IN: Eisenbrauns): 323-76.

Lohfink, Norbert
    1995   'Gab es eine deuteronomistische Bewegung?', in Gross (ed.) 1995: 313-82.

Long, Burke O.
    1982   'Social Dimensions of Prophetic Conflict', in Robert C. Culley and Thomas W. Overholt (eds.), *Anthropological Perspectives on Old Testament Prophecy* (Semeia, 21; Chico, CA: Society of Biblical Literature): 31-53.

Manor, Dale W., and Gary A. Heron
    1992   'Arad', in *ABD*: I, 331-36.

Mazar, Amihai
    1993   *Archaeology of the Land of the Bible 10,000–586 B.C.E.* (New York: Doubleday; Cambridge: Lutterworth Press).
    1994   'The Northern Shephelah in the Iron Age: Some Issues in Biblical History and Archaeology', in Coogan, Exum and Stager (eds.) 1994: 247-67.

Mazar, Amihai (ed.)
    2001   *Studies in the Archaeology of the Iron Age in Israel and Jordan* (JSOTSup, 331; Sheffield: Sheffield Academic Press).

McKane, William
    1996   *A Critical and Exegetical Commentary on Jeremiah. II. Commentary on Jeremiah XXVI–LII* (ICC; Edinburgh: T. & T. Clark).

McKay, John W.
    1973   *Religion in Judah under the Assyrians 732–609 BC* (Studies in Biblical Theology, Second Series, 26; London: SCM Press).

Meyers, Eric M. (ed.)
    1997   *The Oxford Encyclopedia of Archaeology in the Near East* (5 vols.; Oxford and New York: Oxford University Press).

Miller, J. Maxwell, and John H. Hayes
    1986   *A History of Ancient Israel and Judah* (Minneapolis: Fortress Press; London: SCM Press).

Mowinckel, Sigmund
    1914   *Zur Komposition des Buches Jeremia* (Kristiania: Jacob Dybwad).

Mykytiuk, Lawrence J.
    2004   *Identifying Biblical Persons in Northwest Semitic Inscriptions of 1200–539 B.C.E.* (SBL Academia Biblica, 12; Atlanta: Society of Biblical Literature).

Na'aman, Nadav
    1991   'The Kingdom of Judah under Josiah', *TA* 18: 3-71 (for a revision and update, see the contribution to the present volume, pp. 189-247).
    1995   'The Debated Historicity of Hezekiah's Reform in the Light of Historical and Archaeological Research', *ZAW* 107: 179-95.
    2001   'An Assyrian Residence at Ramat Raḥel?', *TA* 28: 260-80.

Niehr, Herbert
    1995   'Die Reform des Joschija: Methodische, historische und religionsgeschichtliche Aspekte', in Gross (ed.) 1995: 33-55.

Norin, Stig
    1998   'The Age of the Siloam Inscription and Hezekiah's Tunnel', *VT* 48: 37-48.

Oates, J.
    1991   'Chapter 25. The Fall of Assyria (635-609 B.C.)', in *CAD*: III/2, 162-93.

Ofer, Avi
    2001   'The Monarchic Period in the Judaean Highland: A Spatial Overview', in Mazar (ed.) 2001: 14-37.

Reich, Ronny, and Eli Shukron
    2003   'The Urban Development of Jerusalem in the Late Eighth Century B.C.E.', in Vaughn and Killebrew (eds.) 2003: 209-18.

Rogerson, John, and Philip R. Davies
    1996   'Was the Siloam Tunnel Built by Hezekiah?', *BA* 59: 138-49.

Rollston, Christopher A.
    2003   'Pillaged Antiquities, Northwest Semitic Forgeries, and Protocols for Laboratory Tests', *Maarav* 10: 135-94.

Sass, Benjamin
    1993   'The Pre-Exilic Hebrew Seals: Iconism vs. Aniconism', in Sass and Uehlinger (eds.) 1993: 194-256.

Sass, Benjamin, and Christoph Uehlinger (eds.)
    1993   *Studies in the Iconography of Northwest Semitic Inscribed Seals: Proceedings of a Symposium Held in Fribourg on April 17–20, 1991* (OBO, 125; Fribourg: University Press; Göttingen: Vandenhoeck & Ruprecht).

Shiloh, Yigal
    1986   'A Group of Hebrew Bullae from the City of David', *IEJ* 36: 16-38.

Shiloh, Yigal, and David Tarler
    1986   'Bullae from the City of David: A Hoard of Seal Impressions from the Israelite Period', *BA* 49: 196-209.

Shoham, Yair
    1994   'A Group of Hebrew Bullae from Yigal Shiloh's Excavations in the City of David', in Hillel Geva (ed.), *Ancient Jerusalem Revealed* (Jerusalem: Israel Exploration Society; Washington, DC: Biblical Archaeology Society): 55-61.

2000 'Hebrew Bullae', in D.T. Ariel (ed.), *Excavations in the City of David* (Qedem, 41: Jerusalem: Institute of Archaeology, Hebrew University): IV, 29-57.
Spieckermann, Hermann
    1982 *Juda unter Assur in der Sargonidenzeit* (FRLANT, 129; Göttingen: Vandenhoeck & Ruprecht).
Steiner, Margreet
    2001 'Jerusalem in the Tenth and Seventh Centuries BCE: From Administrative Town to Commercial City', in Mazar (ed.) 2001: 280-88.
    2003a 'Expanding Borders: The Development of Jerusalem in the Iron Age', in Thomas L. Thompson, with the collaboration of Salma Khadra Jayyusi (ed.), *Jerusalem in Ancient History and Tradition* (JSOTSup, 381; CIS, 13; London and New York: T&T Clark International): 68-79.
    2003b 'The Evidence from Kenyon's Excavations in Jerusalem: A Response Essay', in Vaughn and Killebrew (eds.) 2003: 347-63.
Stern, Ephraim
    1994 'The Eastern Border of the Kingdom of Judah in its Last Days', in Coogan, Exum and Stager (eds.) 1994: 399-409.
    2001 *Archaeology of the Land of the Bible.* II. *The Assyrian, Babylonian, and Persian Periods (732–332 B.C.E.)* (The Anchor Bible Reference Library; New York: Doubleday).
Stern, Ephraim (ed.)
    1992 *The New Encyclopedia of Archaeological Excavations in the Holy Land* (4 vols.; New York: Simon & Schuster; Jerusalem: Israel Exploration Society).
Tatum, Lynn
    1991 'King Manasseh and the Royal Fortress at Ḥorvat 'Usa', *BA* 54: 136-45.
    2003 'Jerusalem in Conflict: The Evidence for the Seventh-Century B.C.E. Religious Struggle over Jerusalem', in Vaughn and Killebrew (eds.) 2003: 291-306.
Uehlinger, Christoph
    1993 'Northwest Semitic Inscribed Seals, Iconography and Syro-Palestinian Religions of Iron Age II: Some Afterthoughts and Conclusions', in Sass and Uehlinger (eds.) 1993: 257-88.
    1995 'Gab es eine joschijanische Kultreform? Plädoyer für ein begründetes Minimum', in Gross (ed.) 1995: 57-89 (for a revision and update in English, see the contribution to the present volume, pp. 279-316).
    2003 'Clio in a World of Pictures—Another Look at the Lachish Reliefs from Sennacherib's Southwest Palace at Nineveh', in Grabbe (ed.) 2003: 221-305.
Ussishkin, David
    1976 'Royal Judean Storage Jars and Private Seal Impressions', *BASOR* 223: 6-11.
    1977 'The Destruction of Lachish by Sennacherib and the Dating of the Royal Judean Storage Jars', *TA* 4: 28-60.
    1988 'The Date of the Judaean Shrine at Arad', *IEJ* 38: 142-57.
    1995 'The Rectangular Fortress at Kadesh-Barnea', *IEJ* 45: 118-27.
    1997 'Lachish', in Meyers (ed.) 1997: III, 317-23.
Vaughn, Andrew G.
    1999a *Theology, History, and Archaeology in the Chronicler's Account of Hezekiah* (Archaeology and Biblical Studies, 4; Atlanta: Scholars Press).
    1999b 'Palaeographic Dating of Judaean Seals and Its Significance for Biblical Research', *BASOR* 313: 43-64.

Vaughn, Andrew G., and Ann E. Killebrew (eds.)
    2003   *Jerusalem in Bible and Archaeology: The First Temple Period* (SBLSymS, 18; Atlanta: Society of Biblical Literature).

Weidner, Ernst F.
    1939   'Jojachin, König von Juda, in babylonischen Keilschrifttexten', in *Mélanges Syriens offerts a Monsieur Rene Dussaud par ses amis et ses élèves* (2 vols.; Paris: Geuthner): II, 923-35.

KING JOSIAH IN THE CLIMAX OF THE DEUTERONOMIC HISTORY
(2 KINGS 22–23) AND THE PRE-DEUTERONOMIC DOCUMENT
OF A CULT REFORM AT THE PLACE OF RESIDENCE (23.4-15*):
CRITICISM OF SOURCES, RECONSTRUCTION OF LITERARY PRE-STAGES
AND THE THEOLOGY OF HISTORY IN 2 KINGS 22–23*

Christof Hardmeier

The question of the sources of 2 Kings 22–23 and their value for the Josianic reform and the origin of Deuteronomy is one of the evergreens of Old Testament studies.[1] Even today we are far from a reliable consensus concerning the answer to this question. The range of propositions reaches from a basic scepticism concerning the possibility of finding a pre-Deuteronomic source from Josianic times at all in 2 Kings 22–23,[2] through a number of contradictory literary critical reconstructions[3] to R. Albertz's supposition that the passage contains reliable memories generally speaking, but that the source text is only from early exilic times. Albertz, however, does not make plausible the function and linguistic shape of the supposed 'basic narrative' as such.[4]

1. *Methodological Aspects of the Literary Historical Reconstruction of Pre-Stages*

The problems inherent in this multitude of propositions are in my view mainly of a methodological nature. Therefore, some methodological considerations will be mentioned before the literary-historical analysis of 2 Kings 22–23. The problem of methods on the one hand touches basic questions of the possibility of reconstructing literary historical pre-stages. For reasons of the theory of text and communication, however, it is not enough to ascertain these pre-stages in the reconstruction of literary pre-stages, that is, in Deuteronomic (Dtr) major textual contexts, by subtracting only those parts of the text that are considered 'breaches'

---

* Translated by Anja-Marleen Krause.
1. Cf. the research report of Preuss 1982: 1-19; 1993, on 2 Kgs 22–23 in particular pp. 246-50, as well as Lohfink 1991a.
2. Cf., e.g., Hoffmann 1980: 264-70.
3. Cf., e.g., Spieckermann 1982: 30-160; Levin 1984; Lohfink 1991b; Koch 1992. Further, see the instructive summary in Albertz 1996: 308-309, especially nn. 7 and 8.
4. Thus Albertz first quotes H.-D. Hoffmann as his main authority for the reliability of the remembered content of 2 Kgs 22–23 (Albertz 1996: 308 n. 7) and argues for an 'older source in 22.2-11, 12-23.4*, 20b-23', that, 'however, (is) from early exilic times' because of 'the closeness to the Jeremiah-narratives' (1996: 309 n. 8).

or 'tensions'. In this, methodological differentiations are necessary and in the case of 2 Kings 22–23 can perhaps lead to reliable results concerning literary history, as this paper intends to show. On the other hand, the source value of archaeological evidence is not unequivocal at all. The archaeological evidence is only in exceptional cases able to support detailed textual statements; primarily and in the face of today's available material it is possible to draw a fairly accurate picture of the socio-historical world of experience for major periods of time, such as the age of Josiah, which the texts themselves always have referred to.[5] Generally one has to observe that the correlation between literary-historically reconstructed units of text, available to us as sources, and the socio-historical contexts of experience that can be inferred from archaeological evidence is very complex. This indirectly conveyed and multi-dimensional relationship has to be considered carefully in the debate on the historicity of the Josianic reform and on the source value of 2 Kings 22–23.

1.1. *The 'Minimal Approach' and the Controversy between H. Niehr and C. Uehlinger*
The most definite questioning of the Old Testament text's source value today is suggested from a branch of research that, under the name of the 'minimal approach', primarily or even exclusively depends on archaeological evidence as the primary source for the reconstruction of the religious, cultural and social history of Israel. On this basis H. Niehr tried to prove the picture of the Josianic reform as a Dtr 'fiction of a late pre-exilic reform and purification of the cult', which is supposed to have had—source-historically speaking—its only indication in 2 Kgs 23.8a. According to Niehr, 'a cult reform by Josiah, as it is reported in 2 Kings 22–23', cannot be 'historically proved; it even has to be qualified as historically unlikely'.[6]

More important for our question than this unilateral and rather simplistic position is C. Uehlinger's criticism of H. Niehr's approach,[7] especially since Uehlinger's results can be fully confirmed by the following reconstruction of a Josianic catalogue of measures in 2 Kgs 23.4-15* (cf. Appendix 2 below, p. 160) which lists some measures for removing and purifying the resident cult in Jerusalem. Because my reconstruction here is orientated towards literary-critical criteria only and operates analytically independent of archaeological evidence, Uehlinger's methodological criticism of Niehr is of specific importance in so far as the complementariness and mutual stimulation of both approaches of historical reconstruction become visible.

---

5. Cf., on principle, Hardmeier 1996: 9-12. On the reconstruction of the socio-historical everyday world in the late age of the kings, see Niemann 1993 and Kessler 1992. On the reconstruction of the cult-political and religious-historical circumstances of Josiah's time, cf. especially Niemann 1993: 224-45, as well as Uehlinger 1995: 57-89.

6. Niehr 1995, all quotations p. 51; on the reference to Levin 1984 (Niehr 1995: 39-40), on the methodological starting points of the 'minimal approach' (Niehr 1995: 34-37), and on the debate also Hardmeier 1996: 10-11.

7. Uehlinger 1995: 57-89.

On the one hand Uehlinger warns of an inappropriate *argumentum e silentio* that threatens to undermine somewhat the methodological minimalism which he shares with Niehr: 'even as "methodological minimalists" [we should] not take the historical work too easily: measures of cult reform under King Josiah cannot simply be considered to be out of the question because the primary sources do not say anything about them explicitly', especially since new archaeological evidence can easily bring such arguments to nothing.[8] On the other hand, Uehlinger does not rule out the source value of Old Testament textual witnesses *a limine*.[9] But he views the main danger as a 'sub-Deuteronomistic writing of history' which is 'particularly acute' in the case of the Josianic reform, if 2 Kings 22–23 is used as a source—in whatever way. Therefore, Uehlinger pleads for a religious-historical reconstruction of the Josianic reform of cult that primarily rests upon archaeological witnesses of the *histoire conjoncturelle* and that 'should not allow its agenda to be prescribed by the [literary] secondary sources'.[10]

Against the background of this later debate of methods, the following approach will not try to avoid the danger of sub-Deuteronomism (identified by C. Uehlinger) by the greatest possible distance or abstinence from the literary sources, but will take this danger seriously, even to make it the methodological basis of a literary-historical criticism of sources which allows the historical value of sources and indications of Old Testament literary witnesses to be made accessible in a new and reliable way.

1.2. *Coherence-Oriented Reconstruction of Literary Pre-Stages from the Angle of Later Stages*

One has to take for granted primarily a Dtr composition of 2 Kings 22–23, and that means a late and to some extent a reliable stage of formation. Only when, first, the specific peculiarity of this Dtr retrospective of the age of Josiah is grasped and depicted can the peculiarity of a catalogue of measures of cultic purification perhaps be worked out, and only when the (late) Dtr final shape of the text has been sufficiently clarified can we identify such a catalogue that has been incorporated into the Dtr outline of the text of 2 Kings 22–23 in case it can be differentiated significantly from its surroundings as a pre-stage.[11]

---

8. Uehlinger 1995: 63-64. Noteworthy also is the conceptual precision of the temporal type that archaeological evidence can primarily document, namely the *histoire conjoncturelle*, which, unlike the event history according to F. Braudel (cf. Uehlinger 1995: 62 nn. 19 and 23) refers to historical time contexts of a larger continuity: in other words, to the socio-historical circumstances of groups, societies and their institutions that are prone to a sudden change only under catastrophic conditions.

9. However, Uehlinger carefully points to remaining 'insecurities' and 'discretionary decisions' that have always to 'be passed' (1995: 73 n. 76), while he even grants the 'history of tradition' a historical moment of truth under certain circumstances: 'Whoever thinks that a historian only has to work with reconstructed basic layers acts as if there exists no history of tradition' (1995: 73). The possible source value of later, Dtr notes for the Josianic reform, Uehlinger would only consider refuted 'if there were plausible arguments that and why a certain measure would have been composed by a later, Dtr or post-Dtr editor' while 'vice versa there [should] exist plausible arguments if literary secondary texts are declared to be historically reliable' (1995: 73 n. 76).

10. All quotations from Uehlinger 1995: 61; on *histoire conjoncturelle* see n. 8 above.

11. As a more exact analysis of the Dtr stages of formation will show, within this main formation there are also late and post-Dtr reshapings visible, which, however, do not substantially touch on the

Methodologically one has, on the one hand, to show for both stages the textual coherence and uniformity as a discursive unity. On the other hand, its function within the socio-historical world of experience, which the pre-stage (as well as the final text) must have referred to, has to be made convincing. Literary pre-stages in particular are only reconstructable on condition that they—as written units of discourse—first of all played a describable role sufficiently relevant to be recorded, and secondly that—because of their relevance—they were preserved beyond the time of their use, so that the later Deuteronomists of the exile were able to go back to those writings. Such pre-stages therefore must be literary units that can be described even today according to their linguistic shape as well as determined according to their primary function. The determination of coherence and function has primarily to be oriented towards text-immanent and literary-historical criteria, while the results of the *histoire conjoncturelle*, inferred from archaeological evidence, serve as empirical control. They operate as a text-external authority which makes the plausibility of a socio-cultural determination of function verifiable. Methodologically, the literary-historical reconstruction thus has to proceed as a supplement to the approach of archaeological reconstruction without immediately relating individual literary findings to individual archaeological findings.

1.3. *The Base of Context and the Inductive Proceeding in 2 Kings 22–23.*

From these methodological reflections my procedure for reconstructing pre-stages in the shape of a Josianic catalogue of measures for cult purification and cult removal is derived. We start from the later or final shape of the Dtr account in 2 Kgs 22.1–23.30 which refers to Josiah's reign. This subunit of DtrH—framed by the stereotypical 'regnal resumé' of 2 Kgs 22.1 and 23.28-30—will count as the widest frame of text for whose delimitation there is no doubt.[12] Even if one does not share my thesis of a 'pre-Dtr work of annals from the age of Zedekiah',[13] it is indisputable that the frame created by 2 Kgs 22.1 and 23.28-30, stems from a pre-Dtr context which formally surrounds the account of Josiah in 22.2–23.27 and which in 23.29 even seems to contradict the Dtr promise of 22.20.[14] Thus, concerning the analysis of coherence and the determination of function of the final shape of the Dtr account of Josiah and his age, one can start from 2 Kgs 22.2–23.27 as a sufficient contextual base.

---

general architecture of the Dtr primary formation of DtrH. Because the primary aim of the present study is the reconstruction of a *pre*-Dtr catalogue of Josiah's measures of cult reform, the following investigation will concentrate on this Dtr primary formation which has incorporated this pre-stage into 2 Kgs 22–23 as a source text. Therefore, we will do without a more exact identification of late or post-Dtr reshapings on the basis of a systematic investigation of its reference connections here, without touching the conclusiveness of the reconstruction of a pre-Dtr pre-stage. To mention them briefly must be sufficient here.

    12.   Cf., among others, Hoffmann 1980: 33-38, as well as Hardmeier 1990b: 167, 179.
    13.   On the positive reception, see Schoors 1998: 20.
    14.   On this often mentioned—even if only apparent—contradiction, note the subtly differentiated considerations of Hoffmann 1980: 181-89 as well as n. 53 below.

For the following analysis of the text some major aspects should be mentioned. The approach is to a great extent inductive and formally pragmatic.[15] It is primarily oriented towards text signals which guide the process of reading and of reception and which constitute the horizon of ideas that is built up through the text, sequence by sequence.[16] Therefore, one has to grasp first the scenic and discursive logic, the intention of the account and the style of the Dtr formation and reshaping (cf. Appendix 1, p. 159) under the primary supposition of a synchronic arrangement. Only then, in case this recording of the main shape should indicate parts of the text older or younger—that is, late or post-Dtr additions—should one ask diachronically about the general shape, logic, function and stylistic peculiarity of these older pre-stages or their younger formations. A reconstruction of pre-stages is particularly conclusive, first of all, when this older stages prove to be a coherent textual unit in itself and, secondly, when the Dtr reshapings stand out from this older text like a younger re-painting.[17] In the process the observations naturally condition each other mutually. In the following, however, only the most important results can be shown to establish my thesis.

In order to include the coherence-creating function and thus the whole of the description of Josiah and his age, we start with the evaluative pre- and post-notes in 22.2 and 23.25-27 which narratologically express the aim and the function of this account.[18] These evaluative notes themselves stand out as a frame against the reports about Josiah's deeds which begins with the temporal marker in 22.3 and finishes with the same marker of time in 23.23.[19] Thus, the analysis of the coherence of these accounts and the determination of their function are guided by the framing notes of evaluation in 22.2 and 23.25-27, which as meta-narrative notes make explicit the Dtr horizon of intention *immanent* in the text. First, I shall qualify these notes in their external relations to DtrH in Section 2 of this paper, where it will be shown how far 2 Kings 22–23 shapes the climax of the epochal construction of history in DtrH, particularly via the intention of these frames. Then, against this background, in Section 3 we shall look at the single accounts of Josiah's exemplary deeds in 2 Kgs 22.3–23.24 in their function of pointing to the evaluative framing notes. The final section of this study, Section 4, concentrates on the literary-historical reconstruction of a pre-Dtr catalogue of Josiah's measures of cult reform in the style of annals.

---

15. On the formal pragmatic understanding of sense, which can also be used for reconstructing a way of understanding texts in so far as texts are always the material substratum of communication acts, however fashioned, cf. Habermas 1982: 196-203 (199) and recently Hardmeier 2003b and 2004.
16. Cf. Hardmeier 1990a: 23-32 as well as 1978: 142-48; 2003b: 57-59; 2004: 98-102, 110-16.
17. See the text of 2 Kgs 23.4-15 within its later context in Appendix 1. On the limitation of the analysis to the Dtr primary formation, see n. 11 above.
18. On the evaluation as a functional part of narratives or reports, see Hardmeier 1990a: 38-45 and the literature discussed there, as well as 2003b: 67-68; 2004: 193-200.
19. On the post-Dtr character of 2 Kgs 23.24a and on v. 24b as a postscript to v. 23, see below Sections 3.2.1 and 3.2.2; thus also stylistically there is a correspondence in the seamless connections of temporally oriented inner reports and evaluative frame remarks that determine the listening or reading directions of these reports.

2. *Josiah's Idealized Changing his Ways (2 Kings 22.2 and 23.25) and Yhwh's Inevitable Wrath (23.26-27) as the Climax of DtrH*

From 2 Kgs 22.2 as well as 23.25 it is evident that the accounts thus framed should be read as a depiction of Josiah's unique example of rule and kingship. Therefore, all partial accounts start with the king as protagonist (see 22.3, 11; 23.1, 4, 21). Thus, according to genre terminology it is appropriate to call these accounts Josiah's *res gestae*. Looking closer, 22.2 and 23.25 specify the unique excellence of the king with respect to the time and to its quality. Thus, they imbed Josiah's uniqueness into the general horizon of DtrH.

With respect to time, after 23.25 Josiah's uniqueness extends to the whole age of the kings and thus points to the exilic perspective that looks back on this whole period: there was no king in Israel or Judah 'like him', neither before nor after him.[20] Accordingly, in 22.2 there is a hint at 'David's way', the founder of the dynasty, 'in' which Josiah had moved completely (בכל) and without deviating to the left or to the right (v. 2b). This very predicate and its uniqueness has not been attributed to any other king since the foundation of the dynasty and there is a hint at the 'way' that David (according to 1 Kgs 2.3-4) recommended (even if in vain) to Solomon before his death.[21] More important are the qualitative aspects where the hints of the frames point to Josiah's uniqueness and state more precisely the hermeneutic focus through which the accounts of 22.3–23.24 should be read. According to 2 Kgs 23.25, Josiah's uniqueness consists of his unique *changing of his ways*, on the one hand, that he carried through according to the *whole* of Moses' torah (בכל תורה משה), on the other hand.[22] Both aspects have to be looked at in more detail.

2.1. *Josiah's Uniqueness (2 Kings 22.2 and 23.25) in the Dtr Construction of History Since the Time of Moses and Joshua*

In order to estimate the impact of the reference to Moses' torah, we should sketch some basic lines of the Dtr construction of history, though these can merely be outlined in this paper.

When DtrH is read synchronically, 'Moses' whole torah' must refer to 'this torah' (Deut. 1.5) which Moses performs according to Deut. 1.6–30.20 at the beginning of the Dtr history of Israel in Moab before crossing the Jordan.[23] Then

---

20. On the related formula of uniqueness in 2 Kgs 18.5, cf. n. 22 below.

21. See also 1 Kgs 9.4 and, on the whole of Josiah's idealization, Hoffmann 1980: 204-207, 250-52 and 269, while the 'writing of the history of the cult' and its unique climax in 2 Kgs 22–23 can be considered as a central but not as the all-embracing general topic, neither of the Dtr description of Josiah nor of the whole of DtrH. On the examples for the ideal following of directions without wavering 'to the right or to the left', see n. 27 below.

22. *This* qualitatively highest predicate of an all-embracing 'changing the way' in accordance with the torah is situated on a very different level than the uniqueness of the trust in Yhwh that 2 Kgs 18.5 ascribed to Hezekiah. It is therefore not in competition with this but goes far beyond Hezekiah's trust in Yhwh, which in the Dtr view he had proved in the siege situation of 701 according to 2 Kgs 18.9–19.37.

23. This historical flashback in Deut. 1.6–3.29 is not an historical introduction to inform the readers, but already part of the torah speech which is located in 3.29 speech-immanently at Beth-Peor.

'this torah' is written down by Moses after its performance according to Deut. 31.9, and is preserved as a document next to the Ark according to 31.24-26. Moreover, it should be read publicly every seven years according to 31.10-13.

The impact of the note of uniqueness in 2 Kgs 23.25, however, becomes fully clear when one follows the future fate of the torah in the course of the DtrH. Because contrary to the opening perspective of Deuteronomy 31, the public reading of the torah took place only once, and that was through Joshua according to Josh. 8.34. But from then on the text becomes rather quiet about this instruction. In 2 Kgs 23.2b there is the next and only further hint that Josiah read publicly the whole of the torah book, found in the temple.[24]

This gap in history, originating from the fact that the torah had not been read from Joshua to Josiah,[25] corresponds with the fate of the Ark next to which the torah writing was kept (Deut. 31.24, 26). The torah book must have reached

---

In this Moses refers to common experiences so far made in taking possession of the land (according to 1.19-46 first failed and from 2.16 successful in the country east of the Jordan), in order to provide Joshua (3.21-22; cf. 31.7-8) and the people (cf. 3.22 and 31.2-6 and esp. also 9.1-6 and 9.23) with the necessary object lesson for the immediate takeover of the country in the west.

24. The different names for the 'book found' in 2 Kgs 22–23 do not give rise to diachronic text operations. They are conditioned by the matter and witness to a careful usage of language that differentiates the various aspects of the book and its contents with relation to the context. (1) ספר התורה in 22.8 documents for the readership of DtrH the identity with the torah scripture, written down in Deut. 31 and preserved with the Ark (cf. Deut. 31.26 and also Josh. 1.8 and 8.34 next to ספר תורת משה in 8.31; 23.6; [24.26;] 2 Kgs 14.6), while according to the Dtr commentary of the law of the kings (Deut. 17.18-20*), the king should read in it continually (v. 19), which Josiah was the first and only one (apart from David in 1 Kgs 2.2-4) to do (2 Kgs 22.10b, 11, 16bβ). (2) The term תורת משה in the evaluative note of 23.25 is situated on the level of the global historical perspective of DtrH and names the whole of Moses' Dtr speech of Deut. 1.6–30.20 (cf. also Josh. 8.31-32; 23.6; 1 Kgs 2.3; and 2 Kgs 14.6). (3) Contrary to this, ספר הברית in 2 Kgs 23.2 and 23.21 captures in the specific context a particular aspect of the contents of the book found, namely the new entering into of the covenant (2 Kgs 23.3) that Moses had already performed with the second desert generation (from Deut. 2.16 on, cf. 3.29; 4.4; 5.2-3) like a model (Deut. 5.2-3; 26.16-19; 27.9-10; 29.9-14). Before he has instructed the people on the basic relationship to Yhwh and the conditions of renewing the Horeb covenant, he has recalled this primary covenant especially in 4.9-14 and in more detail in 5.4-31. Accordingly, before the new entrance into the covenant (reported in 2 Kgs 23.3) Josiah also reads aloud to the people, word for word, the entire 'book of the covenant' previously found in the temple as the Torah of Moses (v. 2b).

25. Between Deut. 31.10 and 2 Kgs 23.2-3 there exists an explainable tension as to the date of the feast on which the whole torah should be read. According to Deut. 31.10, the reading of the torah occurs at seven-year intervals at the Feast of Booths. According to 2 Kgs 23.21, on the other hand, one has to presume that the reading described in 23.2b coincides with the Passover festival that according to v. 21 had not been celebrated centrally in the shape of Deut. 16.1-7 since the age of the judges, that is, after Joshua. The instruction of Deut. 31.10-13, however, has in mind a regular permanent remembrance of the whole wording of the covenant over the generations, while in 2 Kgs 23.1-3 the Yhwh-covenant as such is renewed, as was the case before only at the beginning of Israel's history in Moab. The recalling of the basic relationship between Yhwh and his people, however, belongs to the Passover festival at which exactly this original relationship of election and freedom from Egypt is remembered (Deut. 16.1; 7.6-11), so that it is consequent that the Josianic renewal of the covenant—to which the performance of the torah as in Moab indispensably belongs—in the Dtr perspective also takes place at Passover.

Jerusalem with the Ark and found attention through David in his exhortation to Solomon (1 Kgs 2.3), but with the completion of the temple at the latest, the book was not with the Ark anymore. For, on the one hand, 1 Kgs 8.9 mentions expressly only the tablets of the commandments from Horeb as the contents of the Ark (cf. Deut. 10.5) when it was transferred to the completed temple. On the other hand, and within the Dtr construction of history, Moses' torah book could only be found again in the course of the temple refurbishment (2 Kgs 22.3-8) if this book was lost on the construction site before the completion of the temple.

These observations give rise to the supposition that Josiah's idealization in 2 Kings 22–23 is not at all limited to viewing him as the king of kings since David, or as the cult reformer *par excellence* who puts all predecessors in the shade.[26] Rather, after Moses in Moab and Joshua during the acquisition of the land, Josiah is the first and only one in the whole of the DtrH who fully understood the Dtr torah of Deuteronomy 1–30 and who consequently put it into practice as a whole. This general supposition will be verified by going through the individual *res gestae*.

Another aspect of Josiah's uniqueness can be found in the *formula of perfection* in 2 Kgs 22.2b which describes the ideal attitude in all ways of life. As shown above, this verse not only hints at Josiah's following 'David's way', as it is described in 1 Kgs 2.3-4 as a recommendation to Solomon the throne successor, rather the perfection of his obedience is underlined in 2 Kgs 22.2bβ by the predicate which, within DtrH, is only used for the exact following of the commandments of the torah: ולא סר ימין ושמאול. This predicate only appears in Moses' performance of the torah and in two instructions from the book of Joshua,[27] so that in 2 Kgs 22.2b (also in this respect concerning the whole DtrH horizon) Josiah is fashioned to be the only one who really understood and realized Moses' torah, particularly in the sense of the Dtr laws of the kings (see esp. Deut. 17.18-20), if one disregards Joshua.

A last aspect of the incomparable perfection is the *changing of ways* that Josiah performed through his unique following of the torah according to 2 Kgs 23.25. This change did not only take place 'with all his heart and all his soul' but also בכל מאד, recorded in this threefold wording only in one other place in the whole Hebrew Bible, that is the commandment of love in Deut. 6.5 where this elementary commandment together with שמע ישראל in 6.4 opens up the general teaching of the relation between Yhwh and his people.[28]

---

26. So the painstaking monograph of H.-D. Hoffman which is always worth reading. However, cf. n. 21 above.

27. Next to Deut. 17.11, which deals with the following of particular judicial expert instructions (= pre-Dtr model?), cf. Deut. 5.32; 17.20 (Dtr law of the kings!); 28.14, as well as Josh. 1.7 and 23.6.

28. Cf. the topic heading in 6.1 which introduces the מצוה (already revealed at Horeb, 5.31) that reaches to 26.19 as teaching about the covenant. From 12.1 on the teaching of חקים and משפטים (until 26.15) is subordinated to it as a material part of this teaching of the Yhwh relationship. The double formulation 'with all your heart/with all your soul', qualifying the intended relationship to Yhwh, appears in Deuteronomy only (and derivatively in Chronicles) and most often refers either to the love of or loyalty to Yhwh (Deut. 6.5; 10.12; 11.13; 13.4; 30.6; Josh. 22.5), to the return to him (Deut. 30.2, 10; 1 Kgs 8.48; 2 Kgs 23.25; Jer. 24.7, cf. Deut. 4.29), or to the keeping of his commandments

2.2. The Inevitability of Yhwh's Wrath (2 Kings 23.26-27) in Contrast to Josiah's Example of Changing his Ways as the Climax of DtrH

Apart from its uniqueness, Josiah's change emphasized in 23.25 is also central in view of the construction of the climax in DtrH. For already the Dtr torah-speech of Moses envisages a changing of the ways in the distant future, with the exile in mind (Deut. 30.1-9), after blessings and curses have come about and Israel—scattered among the nations—will have reflected on changing its way (v. 1). For this distant future Moses looks ahead to a mutual turning of Yhwh and his people, by Yhwh's turning anew to the Israelites who have changed (v. 2): on the one hand, in the change of the fate of their exile (v. 3-5) and, on the other hand, in the circumcision of their hearts (v. 6) as also promised in the closely related words of JerD in Jer. 31.31-34 (cf. 30.3) and 32.37-41.[29]

Additionally, Deut. 30.1-10 makes clear that the Moses Torah at the beginning of Israel's history looks beyond the end of the entire DtrH and—in the shape of an original utopia—thus speaks about the formative situation of this epoch work of theological history.[30] Only in this situation, when all effects of blessing and especially of the curses of Deuteronomy 28 (cf. 30.1) will have come about, does Deut. 30.2-13 promise a new turning of Yhwh towards his people and vice versa, when the people—because of their change (השיב אל לב, v. 1b)—will live and practise the relationship of love and respect for Yhwh taught in Deuteronomy 5–26, 'with all its heart and all its soul'.[31]

Opposed to this, the notes of evaluation of 2 Kgs 22.2 and 23.25—and, as will be shown, also his *res gestae* as such—portray Josiah as a model of changing his ways and of complete practising of the torah as a forerunner in the sense of

in one's life (Deut. 26.16; 1 Kgs 2.4; 2 Kgs 23.3; cf. Deut. 30.2); otherwise compare Josh. 23.14 and Jer. 32.41 as well as Stipp 1998: 73-74.

29. Within the scope of this paper, we can refer only peripherally to the close relation of JerD (the Deuteronomic revision of Jeremiah) to Deuteronomy, to which W. Thiel has already drawn attention and with which (not only) 2 Kgs 22–23 is pervaded in many ways; see below Sections 3.1.5 and 3.2.5 as well as nn. 32-34, 37, 51-53, 57, 67-68, 73-74 and 90.

30. Within the scope of this paper I cannot refer to further references, mainly from Deut. 4.25 on, which are, however, to be considered as late or post-Dtr (among other methodological presuppositions, see also Knapp 1987: from p. 34 on).

31. Cf. especially 30.2, 8 and 10 where the general denominator of loyalty and obedience to Yhwh with שמע בקל יהוה and the corresponding realizations in the change of ways (v. 2) and the practising of the commandments (vv. 8, 10) are suggested as an expression of the relationship of love and respect ('with all your heart/with all your soul', vv. 2b, 10b, cf. 6b! and 6.4-5). The global character of the leading term שמע בקל יהוה is also evident from Deut. 5.25. There the people delegate to Moses the further 'listening to Yhwh's voice' with the consequence that Yhwh—accepting the suggestion (5.28-29)—then reveals to Moses the whole teaching of the relationship and the incorporated commandments which he has to teach to the people (5.31) and which he subsequently teaches to the people from 6.1 on, though in Moab. Accordingly we find the phrase also in Deut. 27.10; 28.1, 14 as a leading term for the all-embracing loyalty and obedience to Yhwh. The final speech in Deut. 30 refers to this term congruently in its outlook. A decisive difference from the expectation of JerD in Jer. 30–31 and 32 is that Jer. 31.31-34 considers a *new* covenant while Deut. 30 takes into consideration the full, repeated realization of the Horeb covenant, already renewed in Moab, when the people will have experienced the effects of blessing and especially of the curses in the history of their failed relationship with Yhwh and will have had time to come to their senses.

Deut. 30.1-3, even though according to 2 Kgs 25 the finale of the fateful history conditioned by curses, is still to come. Thus 2 Kgs 22.1–23.25 is the climax of the whole of DtrH from Deuteronomy 1 to 2 Kings 25, which is confirmed in 2 Kgs 23.26-27. Even though Josiah is the only one who—in the whole of history since the completion of the acquisition of the land under Joshua—fully understood Moses' torah of Deuteronomy 1–30 'with all his heart, with all his soul' and is the only one who practised it 'with all his power' according to Deut. 17.18-20, Yhwh's wrath (ultimately brought on by Manasseh's apostasy) has *not* yet changed according to 2 Kgs 23.26.

The dialectical logic of this climax is evident. What the one who is the best king in history so far did not manage even in the ideal practising of Moses' torah —namely, to avert Yhwh's wrath in time[32]—can only mean for the exiled readers and listeners, who had lived and suffered the most bitter effects of this wrath to the end,[33] now to seize the opportunity of practising the torah with the possibility of receiving blessings according to Deut. 30.1-10. For the reality of this original torah by Moses has drastically verified itself already through the catastrophe of 587 as a consequence of the curse arising from the failing relationship with Yhwh which was not in accordance with the torah.[34] Moreover, practising of the torah 'with all your heart and all your soul'—instructed through history and thus bringing Israel to its senses—in the renewed relation to Yhwh leads to the expectation of blessings. For this true-to-life faithfulness to the torah Josiah stands in 2 Kings 22–23 as a prototypical model and forerunner in the historical past.

In this historical-theological logic of the climax of 2 Kings 22–23 Josiah is not only singled out for his faithfulness to the torah and as a renewer of the covenant. In addition, the notes of evaluation in 22.2 stress his uniqueness as a *king* (in the sense of the Dtr law of kings) who even outdoes David. This is also of epochal relevance to the history of cult and dynasty. For the reflective quotation in 2 Kgs 23.27 revokes David's promise of 2 Sam. 7.11b-16 in so far as the house which David's successor will build for Yhwh ('for my name', v. 13), that is, the Jerusalem temple, will be the victim of Yhwh's wrath.[35] Eternal existence is guaranteed only to the 'house' in the sense of dynasty (2 Sam. 7.16), so that also against this background the final note of DtrH in 2 Kgs 25.27-30, which gives an account of the pardoning of Josiah's grandson Jehoiachin, becomes a clear promise.

If one takes into account that the torah in the Dtr reconstruction of history must have got lost on the construction site even before the completion of the temple and was only found again under Josiah, then the whole time of the first temple is considered in the Dtr construction of history as a period of torah oblivion or distance from the torah—a period that reaches its deserved end in the

32. Cf. 2 Kgs 22.13b with vv. 17, 19aα_1, 20a and 23.26.
33. Cf. here, besides Lam. 1 and 2, especially Jer. 44.6, 22-23.
34. See Jer. 44.2 as well as vv. 6 and 22-23.
35. Cf. 2 Kgs 23.27b$\beta\gamma$ where the Dtr idea of the temple of Deut. 12.5 (and *passim*) as well as 2 Sam. 7.13 is taken up, in the sense that the temple can be merely the place where Yhwh's name is called upon.

destruction of the temple, described in 2 Kings 25 at full length, thus fully corresponding to the reflective quotation of 2 Kgs 23.27. In correspondence with the perspective of JerD of Jeremiah 7 and 26, and against R. Albertz, the temple is thus not an inevitable means of salvation.[36] The temple even puts the torah so much into the background during this time that for the future neither a descendant of David nor a type of the temple builder Solomon is expected but a king like Josiah who—even in a time without a temple—realizes the Dtr torah in the first place. Thereby not only the kingdom but possibly also a new temple (which is not excluded *a limine*) would have to submit to the all-encompassing Dtr torah and its directions (esp. in Deut. 12–16) according to the example of Josiah's reform of the cult, as the Dtr writing of history portrays it to be ideal in his *res gestae*. However, the future expectation of DtrH is clearly not (or not yet) connected with the rebuilding of the temple. Moreover, the only physical continuation of pre-exilic ideas of salvation is seen in the continuation of David's dynasty, shining out with the pardon of Jehoiachin.

But this physical continuation will only lead to a new beginning if the new Davidide remembers his history just as his people (Deut. 30.1-10) and takes the ideal Davidide Josiah, who was faithful to the torah, as his model.[37] Just as the original torah speech by Moses in Deuteronomy 1–30 develops the exilic utopia of a covenant people, loyal to Yhwh and learning from its history, so at the end of this history 2 Kings 22–23 shows the ideal type of a torah-faithful king in Josiah, who becomes a model for future Davidides like Moses' torah which is a model for the new covenant people. Both future-oriented ideal types are verified in DtrH as to their reality and their real historical demonstration: on the one hand, through the negative effects that occurred through disregard and oblivion to Moses' torah in the past and, on the other hand, through the prototype of the torah-faithful Davidide Josiah who, as the anti-type of his antecedents (and followers!), was still unable to avert Yhwh's wrath that resulted historically in the catastrophe of 587. A closer look at Josiah's *res gestae* confirm these aspects in detail.

3. *Shape and Structuring of the* Res Gestae *Account in 2 Kings 22.3–23.24: 'Discovery Report' and 'Reform Report'*

The general structuring of 2 Kgs 22.3–23.24 is uncontested and can be sketched by the three following points. First of all, the narrative is not a narratological unit but consists of several episodes illuminating Josiah's various deeds strung together, that is, his *res gestae*. This account corresponds with other 'fillings' of

---

36. Albertz already (1989) counts the temple (in addition to the Davidic kingdom) to belong to the gifts of salvation set by Yhwh (see pp. 42-43) and assumes in a later study (1997: 319-38)—depending on H.-D. Hoffmann—behind the Dtr depiction of the Josianic reform in 2 Kgs 22–23 'the cultic option' of the 'authors of DtrH...for the future' (p. 328). But in this he exaggerates the positive temple orientation of DtrH to a great extent; he does not consider 2 Kgs 23.27 and misjudges the fundamental torah orientation of DtrH. On the further debate with Albertz, see n. 57 below.

37. Similarly Jer. 23.1-8.

the so-called king's frame; for instance, in 2 Kgs 18.3-8 (Hezekiah) where only in 18.9-10*, 18.13–19.37* does a 'narrative' as a unit with climatic tension and solution begin.[38] The reports in 2 Kings 22 and 23 only state Josiah's 'deeds' and measures, while in 22.3-20 a certain dramatization is visible, but without developing a climax and final conclusion as in 2 Kgs 18.9-10*, 18.13–19.37*. These episodic accounts are to be called *res gestae*.[39]

Accordingly, two parts of the report are usually differentiated. A so-called 'discovery report' of 2 Kgs 22.3-20 is followed by the 'reform report' of 23.1-24. There is only an internal object-logical connection between both of them, not a connective narratological one, and both illustrate Josiah's uniqueness. Both start with an activity of the king, who already is mentioned as a model in the evaluation of 2 Kgs 23.25. Correspondingly, the opening phrases (וי)שלח המלך of 22.3b and 23.1 are also constructed formally in a parallel way. The ring structure of the dating in 22.3/23.23 + 24b confirms the two-part division. Only in this ring of dating does the full characterization of Josiah as המלך יאשיהו (with the attributive ל) appear: on the one hand, in the opening of the first report which starts with sending Shaphan (22.3), and, on the other hand, in the ending of the second report (23.23) which in 23.1 begins with the calling of the people's representatives (the 'elders').[40] The homogeneity and complementariness of these two parts of the report in the narrative shaping of the frame is obvious.

Thirdly, both reports contain narrative elements and show an internal structuring. Only the first narrative shows a bit of a dramatic internal structure and can be considered as a narrative in the closer sense, while the 'reform report' is merely stating character. For in all parts of the episodes in the next structuring level below, the king appears to be the promoter who commands various measures, as becomes clear from the identical opening phrases ויצו המלך in 22.11-12; 23.4, 21. But the introduction of these directions in 22.12 with a preceding marker of time in v. 11—as opposed to the mere stating openings in 23.4 and 21—hints at a 'dramatic' shaping which reflects the time-flow of the narrated episodes itself and indicates their temporal state of dependence.

3.1. *Shape, Structuring and Source Value of the So-Called 'Discovery Report' (2 Kings 22.3-20)*

The narratological structure of the first narrative witnessing to Josiah's good example (2 Kgs 22.3-20) revolves around the axis of v. 11, that is, around the temporal marker that divides the account of 2 Kgs 22.3-20 into two parts:

---

38. A debate on the various genres and functions of narrating cannot be held here. With regard to 'narration' in the narrower sense, here the type of narrative accounts is meant that operates with the so-called contrast relation and shaping of climax (cf. here Hardmeier 1990a: 38-45; 2004: 193-200 and there the references to the theoretical works of W. Labov and U.M. Quasthoff. Contrary to this, I understand 'reports' to be narrative accounts of events that are descriptively stated and that do so without the formation of dramatic or climatic tensions (see also 1990a: 106-107).

39. See the introduction to Section 2.1, above.

40. Outside the ring, this marker appears in 2 Kgs 23.29; cf. the style of marking the milieu-related narratives of 2 Kgs 18–19; Jer. 36; 37–40, as well as Hardmeier 1990a: 118, 136, 204-205 n. 82, 307 and 454.

(22.11) ויהי כשמע המלך את־דברי ספר התורה ויקרע את־בגדיו

That the king has 'heard' and reacts thunderstruck (clothes being torn), is emphasized in the flow of the narrative and becomes the motive for further measures. Temporal markers that are designed in relation to events ('when he heard the words...') are very important narratological means to structure the narrated time and to provide it with scenic relief. They have a macrostructural function by relating special events like the oral reception of the book, found by coincidence in v. 10b, to the following scene (vv. 12-20) in a temporally marked way.[41] Noteworthy are also the renominalizations of המלך in v. 11 and again in v. 12 which are to be considered as a further means of stressing and giving a profile to persons and objects in their representation. The division into two parts, marked through v. 11, is also confirmed by the fact that both parts conclude with a report to the king (22.9aβ, 10 and v. 20b) from the envoys sent out in vv. 3 and 12-13.

3.1.1. *The first part (2 Kings 22.3-10): from the order to pay the wages to the torah book becoming known—a narrative of unexpected coincidence.* This first part shows Josiah in vv. 3-7 first of all as an exemplary king who puts into practice Joash's temple reform that followed the revolution against Athaliah (2 Kgs 11–12). The order given to Shaphan in 22.4-7 is worded in a mostly parallel manner to 2 Kgs 12.11b-14, even when the distribution of roles is considered: it is also the scribe in 2 Kgs 12.11b who is supposed to calculate the offering. Against the horizon of DtrH an intended analogy becomes visible between the child-king Josiah after the counter-revolt against Amon's murderers and the child-king Joash who is brought up by the priest Jehoiada after the bloody palace revolution: Josiah probably also started his reign under the guardianship of the priest's son Eliakim ben Hilkiah.[42] Whether this parallel is historical with regard to the retrospective of Joash can remain open in this context. In any case on the level of the historical construction of DtrH this opening 'proves' an exemplary measure of governing by Josiah, who had 'learnt' from the few positive models of David's dynasty from the beginning.[43]

---

41. In the previous investigations on 2 Kgs 22, this frame-setting marker of time has never—as far as I can see—been noted. Most exegetes maintain the structural caesura in v. 12 and are oriented towards ויצו המלך and the parallels in 23.4 and 21 (cf. Koch 1992: 81; Lohfink 1991b: 211; or Albertz 1996: 309 n. 8). However, the main emphasis of 22.3-20, which lies in Josiah's exemplary listening to and understanding of the torah, is thereby misjudged already from the analytical starting point.

42. Cf. Isa. 22.20-22. On the rebellion against Manasseh's successor Amon, who became victim to his own employees at the court (עבדים), see 2 Kgs 21.23-24 and Crüsemann 1997: 248-51. On the interim reign of the Hilkiades according to Isa. 22.20-22, see Hardmeier 1990a: 443-46. On the parallels of 2 Kgs 12 and 22, see Hoffmann 1980: 192-97, whose thesis of dependency, however, I do not share.

43. On the context, see Hoffmann 1980: 124. Hoffmann does not give further reasons why the financing of the construction work on the temple should be an early post-exilic topic. There are no compelling reasons. This could just as well be a prototypical backwards projection of the measures of reform in Josiah's time, however, from Dtr perspective too.

The second part of the episode in vv. 8-10 deals with the way 'the' torah book which was found accidentally in the course of the refurbishment of the temple is revealed. Step by step its content becomes known: At first the scribe Shaphan reads it. Then follows the report to the king who had sent Shaphan (vv. 9-10). Again through direct speech in v. 10aβ the circumstances of finding the book are especially emphasized, just like in v. 8aβ. Direct speeches are a special narrative means which put the performance of the speech itself—instead of a paraphrase of the contents—onto the stage of the narrated world. According to G. Genette, direct speech is the 'most mimetic' form of narrating and signifies the highest degree of importance.[44]

The logic of the scenic order in this first part is governed by coincidence and contingency. Despite very different original intentions of the king, in the end 'the' book is found and becomes familiar to him. The report on the distribution of offerings in v. 9 concludes sufficiently the plot introduced in v. 3: an order is given which is concluded by the report on its execution. The surprising moment, however, is the excessive contingency, namely the finding of the book that is also emphasized in the direct speeches in vv. 8aβ and 10aβ respectively.[45] That it is 'the' book—a well-known book, of which the narrator has the priest Hilkiah speak—alludes to the readers' and listeners' knowledge from DtrH. It is the torah which Moses wrote down after his performance (Deut. 31.9) and had preserved next to the Ark as ספר התורה (31.26). But according to 1 Kgs 8.9 and from a Dtr perspective, Moses' torah must have got lost before or during its transfer from the City of David to the Jerusalem temple at the latest, because only the stone tablets of Deut. 10.5 are mentioned with the Ark. Thus this first part of the scene obviously does not tell of the book's discovery but of the surprising coincidence by which the book became known. As a consequence the second part begins in v. 11 with emphasis on the book's coming to the king's special attention.

3.1.2. The second part (2 Kings 22.11-20): Josiah's exemplary understanding of the rediscovered torah and the prophetic ascertainment of its interpretation. The second part of the so-called 'discovery report' in 22.11-20 does not—unlike the first part—actually deal with the finding of the book. The naming of the whole documentary narrative as the 'discovery report' is thus misleading and should be avoided. What stands in the foreground—as the temporal marker and the king's reaction of horror show in v. 11—is how Josiah immediately understands correctly the message of the book found by coincidence and that he is deeply impressed and draws the appropriate conclusions for action from it from 2 Kgs 23.1 on. This leading topic of the ability to listen and to act accordingly determines the whole second episode.

---

44. Direct speech within narrative accounts draws the highest degree of attention to itself and is a special, even extreme form of emphasis (Genette 1994: 123), because it presents speech acts to the audience of readers and listeners of a narrative, just like in real time in a speech theatre and skips the difference between narrated time and time of narrating, see also Hardmeier 2003b: 71-75; 2004: 212-13.

45. On this motive of contingency in the narratological formation of structure, see, for example, also the narration of Saul's anointing in 1 Sam. 9–10.

According to vv. 12-13, Josiah sends a delegation of the Jerusalem governing aristocracy to interrogate the prophets (דרש את יהוה). In the group there are the high priest Hilkiah, the scribe Shaphan and his son Ahikam as well as a certain Achbor and Asaiah a client of the king (עבד המלך). The delegation addresses the prophetess Huldah (v. 14) who gives a complex answer to the enquiry 'about the matters of this book that has been found' (v. 13aβ). Then the delegation reports to the king the prophetess' message (v. 20b)—formally parallel to the report in the conclusion of the first major episode in vv. 9aβ, 10. The scenic styling of this enquiring part is shaped according to the same model of narrative as the oracle inquiry of Isaiah in 2 Kgs 19.2-7.[46]

Decisive in sending the delegation (vv. 12-13) is, however, not only the task of enquiring of Yhwh that is emphasized by direct speech. Even more important is the reason for this task:

(22.13b) כי־גדולה חמת יהוה אשר־היא נצתה בנו על אשר לא־שמעו
אבתינו על־דברי הספר הזה לעשות ככל־הכתוב עלינו

It shows that from the narrative perspective of this delegating episode Josiah understood at once much, if not all, of what is decisive about the matter of this book and its message. On the one hand, he understood that this book is to be grasped as a torah speech to make it topical. For Moses himself continually refers to the *here and now* of his performance of the torah before the second generation in Moab sitting before him (from Deut. 2.16 on; see 3.29 and 4.4)—even when referring back to the events and experiences of the past at Horeb and on the way to Moab (see esp. Deut. 5.2-3). Correspondingly, it does not only say in 2 Kgs 22.13bα that Yhwh's wrath is inflamed today 'against *us*', but also in v. 13bγ that in this book everything 'is written' 'about *us*', that is, with regard to the peculiarity of every present.

Further, Josiah understood that Yhwh's obviously threatening wrath had its reason in the lack of willingness and ability of the fathers to listen, since they did not follow the directions of the book by doing them (לעשות). Thus the narrator implicitly portrays Josiah as a listening and very understanding reader of the book who grasped the general message of the book at once, which is that the future preservation of a blessed life or the avoidance of Yhwh's wrath lies in the practising of the directives of Moses' torah while not following brings curses and wrath. Deuteronomy 9.7-24 in particular teaches how all kinds of apostasies have roused Yhwh's wrath since Horeb[47] and how Moses has already tried to avert this wrath prototypically through doing away with the original cult sacrilege at Horeb itself (Deut. 9.12, 16 and v. 21).[48]

---

46. Cf. here Sections 3.1.3 and 3.1.5, as well as n. 49.

47. Cf. especially the historical-theological paradigm of wrath in Deut. 9.7-24 with the summary frame phrase ממרים היתם עם־יהוה, which in v. 7 (למן־היום אשר יצאת מארץ מצרים) and in v. 24 (מיום דעתי אתכם) continues, and in 9.23 also includes the disregard of Yhwh in Kadesh-Barnea of Deut. 1.19-46 (cf. 1.26b and 43b with 9.23b).

48. That 2 Kgs 22.13b alludes especially to this paradigm of Deut. 9.7-24 becomes particularly clear with the fact that in 9.8-17 the apostasy of the molten calf is central already at Horeb itself, which Moses then removes with a prototypical original cult reform (9.21). Moses' cult reform

Against this background, thirdly, the need to enquire of the prophetess becomes clearer (2 Kgs 22.13a). The enquiry does not refer to how to interpret the rediscovered book nor how to understand it in general. Moreover, Josiah's enquiry is precisely focussed on how the immediately comprehended threat of wrath will affect himself as well as the people and Judah (v. 13aα). The prophetess Huldah is consulted, in the sense of Deut. 18.17-18 and in analogy to Jer. 37.3-10, to give an expert opinion in the concrete situation.[49]

3.1.3. *Huldah's oracle in 2 Kings 22.15-20*. In exact correspondence with the task of 2 Kgs 22.13a, Huldah interprets the king's insights for the present situation. In the first part (vv. 16-17) the prophetess answers the regal request 'for the sake of the people and of all of Judah'. Then in the second part, in vv. 18-20, the request is answered 'for my sake', that is, for the king's own sake. The complex interlocking of levels of communication in all of Huldah's oracle (vv. 15-20) not only reminds us of the oracle of 2 Kgs 19.5-7, but also of the one in Jer. 37.5-9; this connection, however, cannot be discussed in detail here. The structuring levels shown in the diagram opposite make the complex text of the oracle transparent.

In the first part of 2 Kgs 22.16-17 Huldah, on the one hand, confirms Josiah's assessment that Yhwh's wrath really will fall upon Judah (cf. v. 13bα with v. 17b). Josiah was able to gather this assessment in his reading of the torah (v. 16bβ) from the warnings, for example, of Deut. 6.14-15 or 28.15-68, as well as from the paradigm of wrath of 9.7-24.[50] According to Huldah's interpretation of the situation, the serious overall content of the torah book (v. 16bα, cf. vv. 10b and 13aβ.bγ) will fall upon 'this place and its inhabitants' in the shape of a

---

measures thus show, as an original model in condensed form, completely the features of Josiah's purification of the cult of 2 Kgs 23.4-15, as becomes especially clear in Deut. 9.21b. It is particularly in the brook at Horeb, into which Moses throws the dust of the destroyed cult figure (and which is missing in the later Sinai-pericope in Exod. 32.20 or is being transformed into the bitter water), that the brook of Kidron of 2 Kgs 23.12bβ (cf. v. 6a) is prototypically mapped, to which Josiah has the remains of the destroyed cult objects removed. Thus Josiah's purification of the cult (2 Kgs 23.4-15) in the horizon of the Dtr construction of history becomes a copy of Moses' removal of the bull pedestal of cast metal (see also already Hoffmann 1980: 312, and below, Section 3.2.5). After Josiah has read the torah by taking to heart Deut. 9.7-24 he realizes the extent of Yhwh's wrath (2 Kgs 22.13b) and, even if in vain (2 Kgs 23.26-27), sets about to assuage this wrath through an all-embracing programme of cult purification like Moses in Deut. 9.21 and other passages.

49. Deut. 18.17-18 only mentions one future prophet in the singular, and it seems to be the case that this prophet will be Jeremiah in the way that he is portrayed by JerD in the book of Jeremiah (note especially the antitypic of Jeremiah and Hananiah in Jer. 27–28, the criteria of false prophets in Jer. 28.16 and also Deut. 13.6 in connection with 18.20-22). But since Jeremiah was *historically* not yet active in Josiah's age in spite of Jer. 1.2 and 36.2 (see, among others, Levin 1981: 428-40), the Dtr construction of history lifts the otherwise completely unknown Huldah into the office of a prophet, while her oracle corresponds in structure and language in a well-known way with the phraseology of JerD (cf. Thiel 1981: 94) and is close to the consultation model of Jer. 37.3-9 and 2 Kgs 19.2-7.

50. Cf. the reference of Deut. 31.21 to the paradigm of wrath of 9.7-24. Deut. 31.21 makes explicit for the readership of DtrH the main function of preserving the torah next to the Ark. It would be a witness warning of the notorious stubbornness of the people and of its effects. This warning Josiah had already grasped in all its consequences when reading the torah.

catastrophe (רעה, 16aβ). On the other hand, the reason is not only the 'disobedience of the fathers', as Josiah had concluded in accordance with the torah (13bβ), but also the present disobedience to the first commandment (Deut. 5.7) especially by the inhabitants of Jerusalem who against the warnings of Deut. 6.14-15 served foreign gods (2 Kgs 22.17aα). The correspondences between the consequences that Josiah already draws from reading the book in v. 13 and Huldah's answer in vv. 16-17 are in a relationship of the general—to be anticipated from the Dtr torah—and the particular, the interpretation of which the prophetess undertakes in the present situation, while completely speaking the language of JerD.[51] Within the account of Josiah's *res gestae*, this answer corresponds exactly with the evaluation in Yhwh's autoreflection in 2 Kgs 23.26.

```
                              K5   K4   K3   K2   K1
                                        ותאמר אליהם (15)
                               כה־אמר יהוה אלהי ישראל
                           אמרו לאיש אשר־שלח אתכם אלי
                                        (16) כה אמר יהוה
                          הנני מביא רעה אל־המקום הזה ועל־ישביו
                          את כל־דברי הספר אשר קרא מלך יהודה:
                     (17) תחת אשר עזבוני ויקטרו לאלהים אחרים
                             למען הכעיסני בכל מעשה ידיהם
                             ונצתה חמתי במקום הזה ולא תכבה:
                 (18) ואל־מלך יהודה השלח אתכם לדרש את־יהוה כה תאמרו אליו
                               כה־אמר יהוה אלהי ישראל
                                   הדברים אשר שמעת
                        (19) יען רך־לבבך ותכנע מפני יהוה בשמעך
                               אשר דברתי על־המקום הזה
                             ועל־ישביו להיות לשמה ולקללה
                              ותקרע את־בגדיך ותבכה לפני
                                     וגם אנכי שמעתי
                                          נאם־יהוה
                     (20) לכן הנני אספך על־אבתיך ונאספת אל־קברתיך בשלום
                        ולא־תראינה עיניך בכל הרעה אשר־אני מביא על־המקום הזה
                                        וישיבו את־המלך דבר:
```

The second part of Huldah's oracle (vv. 18-20a) refers back to Josiah's affective reaction in v. 11b. Huldah speaks of Josiah's exemplary listening, his consternation and thus indirectly also his personal change; these are the praiseworthy aspects emphasized in the first part of the evaluation in 23.25. Yhwh's personal address to Josiah is therefore gradated from the first part in vv. 15b-17, which covers the interrogation for the sake of the city, the people and all of Judah (2 Kgs 22.13aα), and answers the interrogation בעדי ('for my sake', v. 13aα). In this the anacoluthon of v. 18bβ takes up Josiah's special readiness to listen, which is temporally stressed already in v. 11a: 'Concerning the words/matters

---

51. On הנני מביא רעה אל המקום הזה ועל־ישביו, see Jer. 19.3 and Stipp 1998: 23; on לאלהים אחרים ויקטרו, Jer. 1.16; 19.4; 44.8 and Stipp 1998: 119; on למען הכעיסני בכל מעשה ידיהם, Jer. 25.7; 44.8 and Stipp 1998: 69. On the depiction of Huldah as a Deuterojeremian prophetess, see below, Section 3.1.5.

that you heard'. In the face of this highly compressed descriptive style, the words and matters 'heard' included Josiah's ad-hoc interpretation of v. 13 as well as Huldah's situative interpretation (v. 16) that Josiah 'has heard' already immediately on the occasion of reporting the first half of the oracle. For especially v. 19aα$_2$ carries on Huldah's situative interpretation of v. 16aβ by specifying the forthcoming disaster as the curses of Deut. 28.15-68 coming into effect—again in similarity to Deuterojeremian phraseology.[52] Verse 19aβ makes clear that it is about the *whole* process of Josiah's contrition from the first hearing of the words and the non-verbal reaction of horror until the reaction to Huldah's interpretation (v. 19aα). This all-embracing 'listening' of Josiah leads to Yhwh's corresponding listening to Josiah (v. 19b). The latter's integral change initiates the mutual communication with Yhwh. It results in a word of salvation (v. 20a), introduced with לכן, that personally promises to Josiah a peaceful and honourable burial and that spares him having to observe the disaster threatened in v. 16aβ.[53]

The elaborate structure of Huldah's oracle is also shown in the ring structure arranged through the parallel openings of the future oracle in vv. 16aβ and 20a with הנני + pt. and with the announcement of disaster of v. 16aβ being taken up directly in v. 20aβγ again. Further, the oracle specifically and precisely refers to the task in 22.13a, as the directions to the delegation in v. 15 and v. 18 on the third and second level of communication respectively show. When taking into account the complex relations of imbedding, 22.15b is to be considered as a subordinate part of Yhwh's speech. This first Yhwh-speech is already introduced by the broad messenger formula (+ אלהי ישראל, v. 15aβ) and includes the delegation as addressees, too, in correspondence with the message of disaster that refers to the people as a whole. Therefore, the first person in אלי of v. 15bβ refers to Yhwh and not to Huldah, since Josiah has sent the delegation directly to Yhwh (v. 13a). Further, the king, who has ordered the consultation, is mentioned in Yhwh's perspective only as איש אשר שלח אתכם אלי, regardless of his regal function, because the fate of the people is at the centre of concern, and in the wording of the oracle itself (v. 16bβ) the king is only mentioned in the third person because the delegation is the immediate addressee of this first part of the oracle. Contrary to this, v. 18a is definitely a speech that Huldah directs towards the delegation on the second level of communication by speaking of Yhwh in the third person and naming the king explicitly as giving commands. For to him the second part of the oracle is rather explicitly directed (like the first one in v. 15aβ it is also introduced by the broad messenger formula in v. 18bα).

---

52. On להיות לשמה ולקללה, cf. Jer. 44.12, 22 and Stipp 1998: 158-59.
53. This motive not only takes into account 2 Kgs 23.30, but also there does not have to be a contradiction assumed here (Hoffmann 1980: 181-89 as well as n. 14 above). This motive clearly also points to the discussion about a possible dishonourable death which Jeremiah announces to King Jehoiakim (Jer. 22.13-19); this announcement, however, did not come true. Therefore, Zedekiah was especially pained by this sorrow (cf. Jer. 38.19-23 and 34.4-5 because of 36.30). Huldah scatters this 'sorrow' preventively like Jeremiah (34.4), who tries to dispel it from Zedekiah (also Hardmeier 1990a: 460).

3.1.4. *On the function of the first documentary narrative (2 Kings 22.3-20) in the overall context of 2 Kings 22–23*. From the explanations so far the function of the first documentary narrative (2 Kgs 22.3-20) within the whole section on Josiah should have become clear. The narrative on the one hand documents the ideal obedience of the king and on the other hand clarifies his personal fate in the face of the curses that result in an imminent catastrophe. Particularly through the temporal marker of Josiah's excellent readiness and ability to listen in v. 11a, a certain dramatic quality enters the story. This is taken up in the anacoluthon of v. 18bβ and in the recapitulation of Josiah's deep consternation in v. 19a that leads to Yhwh's readiness to listen in v. 19b. Yhwh's corresponding listening culminates in the personal 'oracle of salvation' on behalf of Josiah (v. 20a) in dialectical contrast to the oracle of disaster (vv. 15-17).

This narratively developed contrast in 22.3-20 corresponds exactly with the dialectic shaping of the climax in the evaluating part of 23.25 and 26-27. On the one hand, Josiah changed his way completely and in accordance with the whole Moses torah (23.25), which is prepared for through the exemplary listening and understanding of the book found (22.11-20) and which becomes practised from 23.1 on; Josiah, however, already becomes active (22.3-7) in the sense of the reform of Jehoiada and Joash (2 Kgs 12). Yhwh corresponds to this excellence of listening and changing his way in the personal 'oracle of salvation' (22.20a). On the other hand, with this oracle the historical theological contradiction—between the disaster that will befall Judah and Jerusalem inevitably and Josiah's blameless and torah-faithful attitude that spares him the disaster (which exactly corresponds with the historical-theological reflection in 23.26-27)—is resolved at the same time. Yhwh 'responded' to Josiah personally (22.19b) after he had 'heard' and understood Yhwh's instruction. But Josiah's initiative to change was not able to avert Yhwh's wrath against Jerusalem and its inhabitants (v. 17; cf. שוב in 23.25 and 26 with the reciprocal 'listening' in 22.19). For the curses were above the level of the individual and increased over the generations so that they weighed too heavily for Josiah to have been able to break them through his excellent faithfulness to the torah. This consequence is drawn by the self-reflective direct speech in 23.27.

3.1.5. *On the source value and the transmission of the first documentary narrative (2 Kings 22.3-20): a historical-theological construct of DtrH*. As mostly assumed in research today, the first documentary narrative is not based at all on historical events of the year 622. Also, in its synchronic homogeneity there are no hints at an older imbedded document of that time. It is a Dtr construct through and through, shaped from an exilic retrospective. In the climax of the Dtr presentation of the kings' age, Josiah is fashioned as a unique, ideal king of an epoch which otherwise is hopelessly characterized by the increasing sins from Jeroboam to Manasseh (23.26b) and runs towards the catastrophe of 587. In the whole DtrH, Josiah is the first and only—but also the last—king who lives in full accordance with the Dtr instruction in Deut. 17.18-20. Thus, he becomes the prototype of that future king who is quietly alluded to in the open ending of DtrH in 2 Kgs 25.27-30. As ideal king for the late exilic period during which expectancies of return sprouted, and just as in JerD a change of fate was expected (Deut. 30.1-10),[54] Josiah takes over the role of the forerunner (2 Kgs 22–23) who tried early but in vain to prepare the way for this change in following the torah in an exemplary manner.

In view of the possible transmission of this documentary narrative, it is possible to show that the account in 2 Kgs 22.3-20 follows the narrative conventions in more than one way, patterns of argument and topoi of controversial literature that have developed in the controversies about the uprising against Nebuchadnezzar after 594; this, however, has to be left to another essay.[55] Also from this point of view regarding genre, 2 Kgs 22.3-20 is a historical-typological construct, completely shaped by exilic Deuteronomism. Presumably the models and traditions of the typologies characterising the attitude of the last kings of Judah from the time of Zedekiah—designed in Jer. 21.11–22.30* + 23.5-6 and Jeremiah 36* and further developed by JerD—constitute the background of the documenting narrative of 2 Kgs 22.3-20.[56] That is why it is the case that Huldah completely speaks the language of JerD in her announcements of disaster in 2 Kgs 22.16-17, 19. Presumably one has to consider JerD and DtrH—unlike R. Albertz—as synchronic Dtr complementary formations after 547/539 that developed in close correspondence to each other, with only small differences in linguistic usage and theology of history. In a complementary manner both are outlining the possibilities of a change of fate and a new beginning in the country, and both show more or less royalistic tendencies.[57]

Concerning the question of literary pre-stages, we can conclude that there is no historical primary document in any of the accounts in 2 Kgs 22.3-20. The historical memory—as such presumably correct—that in Josiah's age there was introduced some kind of reform constitution in the shape of a pre-exilic Deuteronomy, is preserved in 2 Kings 22 from a Dtr retrospective.

54. Besides Deut. 30.3, see primarily Jer. 29.14; 30.3; 31.23; 32.44, as well as Stipp 1998: 130.
55. See, e.g., Jer. 36; 37.1–40.6, esp. 37.3-10 and 2 Kgs 18–19* as well as n. 40 above on the typical style of characterization X המלך in this narrative literature designed to be read aloud.
56. On the relationship of Jer. 36 and 2 Kgs 22, see the basic work of Lohfink 1978, even if his hypothesis should be corrected in more than one way and has to be considered anew in view of 2 Kgs 18–19 (cf. Hardmeier 1990a: 436-37).
57. For a closer analysis, see below, Section 3.2.5. As stated in n. 36 above, Albertz (1997) exaggerates on the one hand the positive temple orientation of DtrH, and on the other hand he diagnoses the position of JerD to be presumably critical of the king particularly, through a problematic exegesis of Jer. 22.29 (p. 327). By these indices, Albertz sees the reason for the 'grave differences in the tendency' of both works (p. 325), which he then puts down to contrary interests of different bearer groups in late exilic and early post-exilic times (pp. 330-33). As opposed to this, one has to consider the innumerable connections and counterparts as well as the common aims of both works in their parallel direction towards a (new) taking of the land or a return to the land, towards a new/renewed covenant and life in accordance with the torah, having learnt from the history of catastrophe and having realized the failures of the fathers and moving into the future by listening to Yhwh's voice. It is basically a *medial* difference that differentiates DtrH as an epochal work of history from the guidelines of orientation accompanying the present and topical recall that appears in the book of Jeremiah in the form of taking up and interpreting the Jeremiah tradition anew.

3.2. Outline, Structure and Diachronic Structure of the 'Reform Report' (2 Kings 23.1-24)

3.2.1. *The ring structure of 2 Kings 23.1-3 and 21-23, 24b around the catalogue of measures of cult purification in 23.4-20 and its source value.* Unlike the unsuitably named 'discovery report' for the first part of Josiah's *res gestae*, the account of Josiah's various measures of reform in 2 Kgs 23.1-24 can quite rightly be called 'reform report'. The reported measures and particularly the feast of Passover, celebrated centrally for the first time (2 Kgs 23.22-23), document a Dtr stage of the account that Josiah indeed put into practice major instructions from the newly discovered torah book. In this respect they continue the first documenting narrative. The aim of this torah-true realization is formulated in 2 Kgs 23.24b:

למען הקים את־דברי התורה הכתבים על־הספר
אשר מצא חלקיהו הכהן בית יהוה

Josiah 'brings' the words of the rediscovered torah almost literally 'up' (קום hiphil). The final sentence concludes the ring structure of 23.1-3 and 21-23 and refers to the whole 'reform report'. Just as Josiah understood at once the threatening historical-theological implications of the discovered torah (22.11-13), he realizes in 23.2-24* in the same year all of the major ritual requirements necessary in order to implement its content (דברי התורה) and—like the original cult reformer Moses (Deut. 9.21)—the possibility of soothing Yhwh's wrath.

Because of the openings in 23.1, 4 and 21, there exists a clear structure to the Dtr account. Stylistically one has to consider in these openings the renominalizations with the naming of the function המלך that can otherwise be found only in 23.2-3 following the *wyktb*-forms or in the final *ktb*-X sentences at the endings of the half-verses of 23.12a and 13b. The first opening in 23.1 initiates an assembly of the people to renew the covenant according to the model of the Dtr torah of Deuteronomy 5–30 (cf. esp. 5.2-3 and 29.9-14). In this—corresponding to Deut. 31.11-12—the full content of the newly found 'book of covenant' (כל דברי הברית)[58] is read (2 Kgs 23.2b), and 2 Kgs 23.3 reports the new entrance into the covenant that Moses performed with the second generation in Moab (Deut. 27.9-10; 29.9-14).[59] With the third opening the central celebration of Passover is directed according to Deuteronomy 16 with recourse to the 'book of covenant' read aloud to the people (2 Kgs 23.21). The Passover festival is the only possible yearly feast to be taken into account for a first and unique renewal of the covenant, because on this occasion Yhwh's election and first proof of love of Israel through the exodus from Egypt is remembered (cf. Deut. 7.6-8 with 26.17-19 and 16.1b, 3b). This feast of remembrance of the first—that is, the main—commandment, with which the renewal of the covenant through reading the torah as an instruction of the covenant is connected (2 Kgs 23.3), has to be differentiated from the reading of Moses' torah at the Feast of the Tabernacles

---

58. On the term 'book of covenant' in 2 Kgs 23.2-3, see above n. 24.
59. With regard to the Dtr stage of Deuteronomy and the renewal of the covenant at Horeb as a model, an investigation of its own is underway. See to this now Hardmeier 2000, 2003a.

every seven years (Deut. 31.10-13) since it is thought to be a *remembrance* of the covenant for the time *after* the renewal of the covenant (as also in Moab; cf. above n. 25).

From a linguistic as well as object-thematic point of view, 2 Kgs 23.1-3 and 21-23 + 24b thus constitute a frame around the third measure that is commanded by Josiah, namely the purification of the cult or 'cult reform' in 23.4-20 + 24a. This frame is mainly about a new cultic structuring of time and refers to the initial celebration of the centralized feast of Passover which is connected with the unique renewal of the covenant in 23.1-3. In recounting these measures the text exhibits no documentary pre-stages that could be viewed as primary sources for a celebration of Passover with covenant renewal under Josiah in the year 622. How far these measures are not only Dtr shaped but are also a retrospective construction based on historical facts or relate to historically reliable memory cannot be decided from the texts in 2 Kings 23, and judgment will basically depend on a literary-historical clarification of possible pre-stages of the Dtr stage of Deuteronomy. Only the report in 2 Kgs 23.4-20 + 24a is diachronically more complex within 2 Kgs 22.3–23.27, which gives rise to the presumption of a primary source in the background. The report, on the one hand, deals with measures of purification and removal of diverse ritual installations; on the other hand, with the removal of cult staff. It thus does not refer to the temporal aspect of celebrations or of the covenant renewal but to the spatial-material and personal aspect of ritual objects and cult staff. The structure of the paragraph, obviously quite heterogeneous, enforces the supposition of diachronic reshaping. The most obvious caesura is in 23.16. After the enumeration of various measures of purification or removal of cultic installations from 23.4 on, an episodal description reports on Josiah's additional measures of cult reform in the territory of the former Northern Kingdom. In order to grasp the literary-historical diachrony in 2 Kgs 23.4-20, 24a, one has to start with this second part.

3.2.2. *The second part of the 'reform report': 2 Kings 23.16-18, 19-20, 24a as a late-Dtr reshaping with a universal Israelite extension*. The three partial texts 2 Kgs 23.16-18, 19-20, 24a constitute an inner connection and are characterized by a stylistic homogeneity as a synchronic reshaping level that extends through the Dtr main text. First of all, 2 Kgs 23.16-18 is a report about fulfilling the story of 1 Kings 13 (cf. 13.32 with 2 Kgs 23.16b). Stylistically, the text speaks only of יאשיהו (v. 16a) without adding המלך like the rest of the text. It is merely a narrative account in the usual *wyktb*-style without *wktb*-forms. Further more, 2 Kgs 23.19-20 also belongs to this stage of reshaping. For, like vv. 16-18, v. 19aβ also speaks only of יאשיהו and in v. 19b turns into a narrative account, just as v. 16 after v. 15. In v. 20b even a return to Jerusalem by Josiah is reported while his going to Bethel in v. 15 is only presupposed but not narrated. There is a difference in the genre of the text. A non-narrative text of enumerations as far as v. 15 is opposed to a narrative report from vv. 16 to 19—this hints at a diachronic relationship. Concerning the contents, a reform of the Southern Kingdom (cf. בערי יהודה in v. 5aβ) is parallelized with an analogous reform in the former

Northern Kingdom (cf. בערי שמרון in v. 19aα₁) with an all-Israelite intention. In both cases the topic is the Dtr stereotype of abolishing or not abolishing the במות which 'the kings of Judah' or 'Israel' (v. 19aα₂) had 'made' or their ritual staff which they had 'given' (v. 5, cf. v. 20a). True, v. 19 does take up the style of v. 15 with וגם to begin a further paragraph, but then turns into an episodic account in v. 19b as already in v. 16.

On the other hand, 2 Kgs 23.15 is very reasonable as the ending of a Dtr catalogue of measures for ritual reform between Jerusalem and Bethel, since Bethel is mentioned already as a place at the beginning of this catalogue (23.4bβ) to which the ashes of the burnt ritual equipment from the Jerusalem temple were taken. 2 Kings 23.15 concludes this ring. The catalogue of measures starts with the removing of cult objects which represent other gods (23.6). In this the Asherah of the Jerusalem temple is the first cultic object that fell victim to this special measure (23.6), while the removal of the Asherah of Bethel (23.15) concludes the enumeration as the last measure and thus forms a closer ring within 23.6-15 without making a continuation through 23.16-20 necessary.[60] On the contrary, the episodal narrative unit of vv. 16-20 hangs in the air—topologically speaking—without the indirect localization of Josiah in Bethel in v. 15. Thus, 2 Kgs 23.16-20 is unthinkable without its older context of 23.4-15 and thus appears to be a secondary late-Dtr reshaping of the Dtr reform report of vv. 4-15 itself.

Finally, the peculiarities of 2 Kgs 23.19-20 are also relevant for 2 Kgs 23.24a which must belong to the same stage of later reshaping. Together with 23.19-20, 2 Kgs 23.24a presumably frames the older account of the Passover festival (23.21-23 + 24b). The syntax and stylistics of 23.24a largely correspond with 23.19a. In both partial texts there is an inverted verbal sentence, introduced with וגם and with a final *ktb*-form and יאשיהו as the subject. The reform content of 23.24a (removal of magic and mantic practices) belongs to the late-Dtr standard.[61] The text stage described (23.16-20, 24a) thus shows a high stylistic and

---

60. However, the text relations in v. 15 are correspondingly complex. If one takes the resumption of the beginning of v. 15 in 15aβ, with וגם as a hint that at least parts of v. 15aα originate in later expansions that made this repeated uptaking necessary in the first place, and if one considers within v. 15aα the syntactically difficult position of הבמה with the twofold explanatory relative clauses, then there remains for the measure of the cult removal from Bethel a definitely shorter sentence which in its structure completely coincides with 23.12 and 13 and which makes a resumption with וגם superfluous (as also in v. 12 and v. 13). But then in comparison with vv. 12 and 13, which themselves mention razed altar installations at the beginnings of the sentences, the question arises if the first גם at the beginning of v. 15 does not contradict the naked enumerative style of the catalogue of measures and has to be ascribed to the stylistic homogeneity of the later reshaping (from v. 16 on) which considers the reform in the former Northern Kingdom analogous to the Southern. Similar to v. 12 or v. 13 the primary-Dtr pre-stage for the late Dtr link would then have been phrased as follows: את־המזבח אשר בבית אל אשר עשה ירבעם בן־נבט נתץ ושרף אשרה (2 Kgs 23.15*).

The second אשר-clause has to be ascribed to the primary-Dtr transformation (cf. below, Section 3.2.4, point 6). Concerning the altar that Jeroboam built, see 1 Kgs 12.33. A close diachronic analysis of 2 Kgs 23.15 is of course possible (a) only in connection with 23.16-20, 24a, and (b) only in correspondence with the analysis of 1 Kgs 12–13. This analysis, however, cannot be done here.

61. Cf. Hoffmann 1980: 232.

object-thematic homogeneity which characterizes it clearly as a Dtr (maybe even in contrast with 23.21-23 as late-Dtr) partial text which shows no pre-stages.[62] In vv. 21-24 the phenomenon of attraction and mutual interlocking is visible as G. Braulik (among others) described it for Deut. 22.1-12.[63]

3.2.3. The textual situation in the first part of the account of measures in 2 Kings 23.4-15. The account of measures in 2 Kgs 23.4-15 consists of the following paragraphs that are not narratively or episodically structured through a sequence of scenes but determined by a object logic:

1. 2 Kgs 23.4-5 deals with the removal of ritual objects of the various other gods from the temple (v. 4) and with the removal of the staff of cults foreign to Yhwh (כמרים).
2. 2 Kgs 23.6-7 states as the first special measure the removal of the Asherah and of the workplaces of her ritual staff.
3. 2 Kgs 23.8-10 on the one hand refers to the further fate of priests named in v. 5aα as כמרים and their 'high places'. In spite of the change in terminology (כהנים/כמרים), the characteristics of their activity (קטר) and their geographic area (ערי יהודה) in comparison with v. 5aβ and aα, clearly show that on the Dtr level of the final shape in 23.8a, 9 the same group of priests must be meant. On the other hand and in contrast to this, vv. 8b and 10 introduce further actions: the removal of the gateway altars (v. 8b) and the Tophet (v. 10).
4. 2 Kgs 23.11 mentions the removal of the sun cult.
5. 2 Kgs 23.12-15a describes the removal of various altars and 'high places', while the note on the destruction of the Asherah of Bethel in 23.15b concludes the ring of the whole enumeration in 23.6-15.

Within these paragraphs determined by object logic there can be observed several examples of bumpiness ('tensions') in stylistic and subject respect which have to be explained (since they have often been named in research) and which provoke the question of a possible, Dtr-reshaped pre-stage of text:

1. According to v. 4a the king instructs the high priest Hilkiah and further temple staff to purify the temple. From the point of view of syntax and style, this giving of instruction corresponds to the narrative account of the Dtr frame in 22.12 and 23.21 (cf. also 22.3b). But from 2 Kgs 23.4b the king himself is suddenly the only subject of the measures of cult purification, as becomes obvious from the singular forms.[64]

---

62. Here no final decision will be made between Dtr and late or post-Dtr stages of reshaping, which would only be possible in the horizon of DtrH's general outline and its undoubted later reshapings. In 2 Kgs 23.16-20, 24 only a *relatively* later stage of reshaping is visible, the synchronic linking-up of which (in any case with 1 Kgs 12–13!) cannot be further investigated in this context.

63. Braulik 1988: 247-50.

64. Of course one could theoretically also presume that Hilkiah is meant as the responsible person and as *pars pro toto* of the executors. However, this supposition ultimately fails in the face of the explicit mention of the king as subject of the further measures of cult removal in 23.12 and 13. But especially the later interpretation of 23.16-20, 24a presupposes that it was Josiah who destroyed

2. Only 23.4aα₂ speaks of היכל; otherwise it always says בית [יהוה] when mentioning the temple (cf. 23.6, 7, 11 and within the narrative parts 22.3-20).
3. Only in 23.5aα does one encounter the infrequent expression כמרים for priests of foreign gods (cf. Hos. 10.5 and Zeph. 1.4 only) that are taken up in v. 8a with the usual term כהנים ('from the cities of Judah', cf. 5aβ!).
4. The paragraph 23.8-10 deviates in v. 8a and especially in v. 9 in its given shape from the object-logical style of the account that has fully dealt with the removal of cult objects. Contrary to this, these verses are designed narratively and report on the further fate of the ritual staff dismissed (v. 5).
5. In 23.11-15 the overloaded style of attributive sentences (mostly אשר-sentences) attracts attention. On the one hand, the ascriptions of the ritual installations to earlier kings who had brought these installations into being (אשר עשה/נתן/בנה) occur in larger numbers: the kings of Judah/Israel (5aα₂,11aα₂,12aα, cf. 19aα₂), Manasseh (12aβ), Solomon (13aα₂) and Jeroboam (15aα₂). On the other hand overloaded localization remarks are found especially in vv. 11a and 13a.

In trying to reconstruct a pre-Dtr text of the Josianic cult reform from 2 Kgs 23.4-15, one often but too fast considered criteria external to the text in order to prove the probability or improbability of one or the other measure. The following elaboration of a Dtr reshaping profile in 2 Kgs 23.15 (Section 3.2.4) and of a basic pre-stage of it (Section 4) is the result of an inductive methodical procedure that is primarily based on text-immanent criteria and in a permanent feedback following a twofold question. On the one hand, we ask alternately for the possible interests of the account that gives coherence, by which is guided either a possible Dtr reshaping and/or a presumably reshaped pre-stage over all of the partial text of 23.4-15. Complementarily, on the other hand, the linguistic items and manner, in which these different interests of the presentation take shape, are to be identified. This is done in consideration of the observable tensions in the text in which the literary-historical process of reshaping shows and can be proved. A high degree of evidence is reached if it is possible to name convincing intentions of the account for the presumed reshaping as well as for the supposed pre-stage, and to prove in detail their different linguistic markedness as a literary process of reworking the text. In the following, we first of all have to show and justify the Dtr profile of reshaping.

---

the altar of Bethel (v. 15). Yet then also the removal of the ashes of the burnt cult objects to Bethel in 23.4 already presupposes the king as subject. If one adds that the whole paragraph is not structured chronologically sequentially, but according to object-logical criteria, one can rely on two facts in the presumed historical reality. On the one hand, 2 Kgs 23.4, 15 implies only one visit to Bethel; on the other hand, Josiah of course did not performed the whole reform of the cult alone and with his own hands, even if these measures in the catalogue are attributed to him as the person who is finally responsible for them.

3.2.4. *The Dtr reshaping in 2 Kings 23.4-15 in its object-thematic and stylistic individuality: the 'great cult reform'*. With the following observations and considerations it can plausibly be argued that a Dtr reshaping in 2 Kgs 23.4-15 generalizes an older catalogue of measures and extends it as a Josianic measure of reform with respect to the territory and history of the epoch. It is possible to show that a pre-stage, which contains a 'minor' cult reform (cf. Section 4), is transformed into a 'major' reform by adding interpretations of text, a reform which removes Jeroboam and Manasseh's 'sin' once and for all, generalizing this 'sin' about the cult of the high places and the practice of burning incense, and charging with it all of the priests in every territory of Judah and the former northern empire. In order to understand this process of literary reshaping in the context, we refer to the reproduction of the text in Appendix 1.

1. In order to be able to integrate a object-oriented catalogue of measures (pre-stage) into the narratively sequential frame of Josiah's *res gestae* (22.3–23.24), this catalogue—which was presumably kept in an enumerating and not in a narrative *wktb*-style[65]—was narratively reshaped and thus assimilated to its context. This narrative assimilation becomes clearest in the opening in 23.4a which is formulated on the analogy with 22.12 and 23.21. Correspondingly there are further narratively sequential passages in 23.5aβ,[66] 8a, 9, 12bα (and dominantly in 16-20, 24a). In the course of this assimilation presumably also the openings of the object-oriented pre-stage parts in 23.6, 8, 11, as well as partly the continuations such as those in vv. 4b, 6-7, 14aβ, b, 15b were transformed from the enumerative *wktb*-style into *wyktb*-narratives, while in the middle and final parts of these paragraphs the enumerative style of the pre-stage was kept (cf. vv. 4bβ, 5aα, 8b, 10a, 12bβ and the end of v. 15b).

2. The reshaping shows a special interest in the 'high places' and the 'priests of the high places' in Judah (5aβ, 8a, 9, on the late-Dtr reworking also in Israel, cf. 23.19-20). Contrary to this, the pre-stage is limited to the removal of the priests characterized as כמרים (23.5aα) who—limited to Jerusalem and its surroundings—served the foreign cults of the Assyrian lords (in the Jerusalem temple, 23.4b, 5*) and their diplomatic representatives (on the Mount of Olives, 23.13a). The starting point for the Dtr generalization of a countrywide 'cult of the high places' presumably lies in the pre-stage in 23.8b, while the abolishing of altars in the area of the gate listed there could possibly have referred to

---

65. Cf. also Section 4.1.3 below. On the view of the Hebrew tense system and the 'and'-syndesis held here, cf. Hardmeier 1993: 56-58; 2003b: 70-71, 106-107; 2004: 299-302. In enumerative texts (e.g. Jer. 22.15b) that do not constitute a narrative sequence but list events that are according to the perspective of the speaker in no temporal sequential context, the ו remains limited to its basic additive function of connecting, *without* signalling the additional semantic moment of an irreversible sequence. Accordingly we do not find an inversion of the aspect of the *ktb*-form here. It represents the perfective aspect of events that according to the perspective of the speaker are described as concluded events (cf. Hardmeier 1978: 181-85 and esp. 368-69 n. 181 as well as 1990a: 97 n. 21, further 2003b: 96-98; 2004: 129-30).

66. It is to be read as a plural.

one specific altar at the city gate as it is localized in v. 8bα₂β (cf. the *BHS* critical apparatus).

3. Also the generalization and concentration of all cult sins into the incense offering (קטר), about which Huldah accuses the inhabitants of Jerusalem generally of (22.17aα) and which correspond with the JerD general denominator of all worship of foreign gods,[67] has its starting point in the pre-stage in 2 Kgs 23.5b. There, however, this practice of the cult is limited concretely to the named cults as well as to the non-Israelite foreign priesthood (כמרים) who alone practised it (המקטרים). The Dtr reshaping, though, ascribes also this practice to the priests of the high places 'in the towns' of Judah[68] (23.5aβ, 8aβ) and thus projects the exilic criticism of the cult of Jeremiah 44 already back to the situation of Josiah's time. Next to the general transference of blame to illegitimate Yhwh-priests, one also has to consider the generalized territorial extension towards the Judaean landscape ('from Geba to Beersheba', 23.8aγ).

4. Against this background the introduction in 2 Kgs 23.4a has the function of ennobling Hilkiah, plus the priests of the new part of the city and the keepers of the thresholds as a reform priesthood, and withdrawing them from the general verdict in vv. 5aβ and 8aβ. There exists no further motive within 2 Kings 22–23 (apart from the reference to 22.4-10), for mentioning this group of priests in the opening part of the cult reform measures, which are then performed by the king alone.

5. The Dtr incrimination of the cult of the high places is visible also in the corresponding reshaping in v. 15 that possibly consists of three stages. Presumably in the same late-Dtr stage as 23.19-20, the abolition of the 'high place' at Bethel is put next to the destruction of the altar in the pre-stage, while the destruction of the altar itself in the Dtr primary reshaping (1 Kgs 12.33) is extended through the first relative sentence in 23.15aα₂.[69] The late-Dtr secondary reshaping would have been intended to generalize further the criticism of the cult towards 'Israel' by ending the limitation to Judah in 23.8a (inspired by Jer. 44) and being particularly interested in the בתי במות in the former northern empire (23.19a) which also play a special role in the reshaping of 1 Kgs 12–13 (cf. 1 Kgs 12.31). But this tendency to geographical extension can already be seen in the Dtr primary formation that extends the cults of foreign priests in the Jerusalem surroundings (cf. 23.5aγ, b and 13-14*) to the activities of the Judaean 'priests of high places' from the 'towns of Judah' (23.5aβ, 8a).

6. The Dtr tendency of generalizing and expanding with respect to the cultic installations (cult of the high places), the cult staff (priesthood of the Judaean countryside) and cult practice (incense offerings) corresponds

---

67. Cf., in general, Jer. 44 (especially v. 21!) on the one hand, and 1 Kgs 12.33; 13.2 on the other hand, as well as the passages in Stipp 1998: 119.
68. Cf. on the JerD stereotype of the 'towns of Judah', Stipp 1998: 56-57.
69. Cf. n. 60 above.

with a historical epochalization. This is shown in the conspicuous relative sentences that ascribe to earlier kings of Israel and Judah the establishment of abolished cultic installations and that from a text-stylistic perspective contribute decisively to the overloading of the catalogue of measures with attributives. With the stereotype formulation אשר עשה/נתן/בנה in vv. 5aα_2, 11aα_2, 12aα (cf. v. 19aα_2) 'the kings of Judah/Israel', Manasseh (v. 12aβ), Solomon (v. 13aα_2) and Jeroboam I (v. 15aα_2) are made responsible for the establishment of the abolished cults. With these Dtr post-interpretations the Josianic reform receives an epochal historical dimension that corresponds with the general outline of DtrH. Josiah removes once and for all the 'sins' of Solomon, Jeroboam and especially of Manasseh in the sense of DtrH. Therefore, in the Dtr notes of all the kings after Josiah there are missing any hints at the cult of the high places or at the 'sins' of earlier kings. For it was the exemplary Josiah who in the Dtr construction of history had had them all removed as the only material and infrastructural prerequisites of *these* sins forever.[70]

7. Also the individual measure of 23.12aα_2 (Manasseh's altar, 21.5b), the specifications of the Tophet cult (23.10b; cf. 21.6aα) and the explanation of the foreign cults on the Mount of Olives (23.13a$\alpha_2\beta$; cf. 1 Kgs 11.5-8) are to be counted within this generalizing reshaping (cf. also 23.24a with 2 Kgs 21.6$\alpha\beta$) in order to emphasize the removal of Manasseh's 'sin' (23.26b!).

8. As already with the 'priests of the high places' from the 'towns of Judah' (23.5a, 8a, cf. 23.19a), a tendency of revision that extends through the spatial horizons is also shown in the local specifications that, because of the temporal distance of the Dtr reworking, explain various localities to an exilic audience. For this audience the geography of the Jerusalem city gate was not known in detail any more, while the pre-stage partly shows an insider's intimate perspective. The term בית יהוה instead of היכל, corresponding to the style of the frame narrative has already been mentioned. Reference to the temple should be additionally dispensable in 23.6aα, 7aα, 11aα, 12aβ. The same applies to the hint at Jerusalem in 23.13aα_1 that explains in advance what is mentioned in the second relative clause in aα_2 for those who still knew the place. In any case, the further reference to Jerusalem in v. 9 is due to the Dtr reshaping.

This investigation of the Dtr reshaping in 2 Kgs 23.4-15 is of particular importance for the reconstruction of pre-stages. All interpretative remarks can also be linguistically identified to the extent that missing them out of the text would not leave an incoherent textual torso, but what would become visible would be a

---

70. This explanation withdraws the block models that claim a pre-exile DtrH (the thesis of F.M. Cross), their major clue being essentially seen in the judgments of the kings that changed after Josiah (without 'high places' or 'sins' of earlier kings). On further reasons for the refutation of the block model, cf. also Hardmeier 1990b: 180-84.

catalogue of measures of the 'minor' reform which can be described as an integrated text of annals in what follows. In this the subtracted textual passages, temporal transformations and interpretative additions witness to a gentle manner of literary reshaping; the Deuteronomists did not perform any major surgery on the pre-stage.

3.2.5. The 'major' cult reform in 2 Kings 23.4-15 within the frame of the climax of DtrH and its closeness to Jeremiah 44: a hint at the JerD bearer group of DtrH. The contents profile of the Dtr reshaping further makes clear how much the portrayal of Josiah in 23.4-15 as the cult reformer is also in the line of the climax formation and the late-exilic message of DtrH. In its closeness to Jeremiah 44 it allows conclusions about the milieu of the JerD people who created the DtrH. In the Dtr interpretation Josiah has already ideally removed altogether the infrastructure of the incense offerings to the foreign gods of heaven: the places of cult as well as the cultically infected priesthood of the country 'high places' (2 Kgs 23.5aβ, 8a) which is nevertheless historically a *vaticinium ex eventu* after 587. We know this because this cult practice and the worship of the gods of heaven existed until the time of those that were addressed also by the exilic 'Jeremiah' as a generation still hopelessly stubborn in their heart (Jer. 44.20-23).

However, Jer. 44.28 shows a little group of refugees from that generation who would escape the disaster in Egypt and return to Judah, and to those could also have belonged Baruch and the other followers of Jeremiah and descendants of Shaphan (Jer. 45.5). This little group, which was competent in writing and literacy, is the bearer group of the major formation of the book of Jeremiah (Jer. 45.1) that on the one hand, like Jeremiah, criticizes the attitudes of its contemporaries—which is leading to catastrophe—up to the exilic present.[71] On the other hand, for precisely this reason this group directs all its hope for the future towards a return of the Babylonian Golah[72] (Jer. 24.4-7) and towards a new Davidide (Jer. 23.5-8) who, like Josiah (Jer. 22.15b), will do 'right and justice' (Jer. 23.5b).

Against this background it is quite reasonable to presume the same bearer group—competent in writing and literacy—behind the Dtr construction of history of Deuteronomy 1–2 Kings 25, since at its climax Josiah is also idealized as a unique king who has realized all of Moses' torah. What these disciples and followers of Jeremiah learnt from the great prophet with respect to judging situations and orientation towards the future, within the all-embracing relationship to Yhwh, is documented, on the one hand, in the book of Jeremiah. By doing so, they interpreted the spirit of Jeremiah's words and witness towards their own situation and future by commenting on and reworking them. In view of this

---

71. Cf. Jer. 44.22-23 (ביום הזה [twice]!), and on the key phrase of רע מעלליםbesides Jer. 44.22 cf. the occurrences in Jer. 4.4; 21.12; 23.2, 22; 25.5 and 26.3 as well as Stipp 1998: 122.

72. In particular, the counterpoint of the programmatic vision of the basket of figs in Jer. 24.8-10 makes it clear in v. 8bβ that the JerD perspective sets itself explicitly apart from the Egyptian Golah; cf. also Jer. 29.10-15 and the contrastive formation in vv. 16-20 as well as Jer. 30.1-3; 31.27-34 and 32.36-44 in the antitypical contrast to 32.26-35.

practice of theological reflection and appropriation for the present situation, which Jeremiah always related to historical experiences and actual political challenges,[73] it was for the Jeremians of the second generation, on the other hand, only a small step to an historical-theological general concept of the DtrH. In its general outline this concept is surprisingly close to the historical-theological argumentation of Jeremiah 2–6 and transposes this model in a large scale into an epoch-embracing vision of the historical past, which can only be mentioned briefly here.[74] Just as Jeremiah 2, first, looks back to the forgetting of Yhwh and the disloyalty to the covenant in the opportunistic seesawing of politics since the Assyrian epoch (esp. Jer. 2.7-13, 18-19, 32, 36), DtrH looks back to the *whole* historical past and its failure since taking possession of the land (cf. *in nuce* Jer. 2.7). And as Jer. 2.2-3, 5-7a, 32, secondly, confronts the beneficial beginnings of an ideal covenant relationship between Yhwh and the people with this disastrous history of forgetting Yhwh, DtrH programmatically starts with Moses' torah teaching and the ideal performative renewal of the covenant in Moab. Thirdly, this confrontation in both outlines serves the parenetic aim, according to Jer. 6.8, to give a warning admonishment through seeing the failure of this history and to recognize the main reason for this failure in the failed relationship to Yhwh. While Jeremiah 2–6 thus still aims concretely at stopping Zedekiah's politics of uprising, which is unfaithfulness to Yhwh, and at averting Yhwh's manifest

---

73. Cf. especially Jer. 2–6 and also the following footnote, as well as Hardmeier 1996; 1998: 308-42.

74. In the history of the beginning the DtrH develops in Deut. 1–30 this ideal relationship as torah teaching of Moses in Moab which results in the symbolic performative renewal of the Horeb covenant (Deut. 27.9-10 and 29.9-14, cf. the declaration in 26.17-19 and the proclamation of making it present in 5.2-3). In the complete work will be shown how the forgetting of this primary relationship as a forgetting of the torah results in the catastrophe of 587 which was the consequence of Yhwh's wrath (2 Kgs 23.26). This historical-theological model is anticipated *in nuce* in the argumentations of Jer. 2(–6), as becomes especially clear in Jer. 2.2-3, 6, 7a, 32. Not only do we find prefigured here the concept of the עם קדוש (cf. Jer. 2.3 with Deut. 7.6 and 26.19) as well as the idea of a primary intimate covenant relationship, which in Jeremiah is still thought to be primarily a marital covenant relationship (cf. Jer. 2.2, 32), while the DtrH rather thinks of the relationship of a vassal treaty (cf. also the term of the עם סגלה [Deut. 7.6 and 26.18] in which the election of Israel in Egypt [cf. Deut. 7.7-8 and Jer. 2.6, 7a] is expressed in the metaphoric of political-military capture). Also the beginning historical perspective of the gift of the land (cf. esp. Deut. 8.7-10 as well as, among others, 6.10 and 7.1) with the following disregard is already prefigured in Jer. 2.6-7. Most importantly, however, the argumentation of Jer. 2 works with the basic reproach of a primary forgetfulness (cf. Jer. 2.2, 32) which became manifest in the disastrous covenant-political opportunism (2.36-37 cf. vv. 18-19) and its outcome in Nebuchadnezzar's punishment on Jerusalem (from 4.5 on) shown as a consequence of Yhwh's wrath (cf. 2.35; 4.8). This argumentation in Jer. 6.8 serves the aim (cf. 4.14, 18) of learning the lesson by recalling past experiences that had resulted in self-destruction (cf. Hardmeier 1998: 328-31). Accordingly, Moses' torah develops an insistent behavioural pedagogy of practical re-calling which permanently and from generation to generation recalls the unconditional covenant relationship to Yhwh, the constancy of being related to him and its potential danger to all matters of life. On this pedagogy of constant remembering, cf. among others, Deut. 4.9-10; 6.6-9, 10-15; especially 8.7-18; also 9.7-24, as well as the exhortations to remembrance in the commandment parenesis of 5.15; 15.15; 16.12; 24.18, 22, and here also Hardmeier 1992: 133-52. Further see especially 2003a, for this kind of wisdom and remembering pedagogy.

wrath, DtrH sees in correspondence with Jer. 31.31-34 (cf. 32.38-40) a future in a new faithful loyalty to the covenant (Deut. 31), expecting the return of the Golah and a new beginning together.

Accordingly, this bearer group expresses the following message by reshaping 2 Kgs 23.4-15 on a large scale and especially against the background of its criticism of the ongoing incense offerings and of the current worship of the gods of heaven in Jeremiah 44: just as Josiah, in following Moses at Horeb (Deut. 9.21), already brought a radical end to the worship of foreign gods—at least with respect to the infrastructure—without, however, having been able to avert Yhwh's wrath (2 Kgs 23.26!), the Babylonian Golah and the expected Davidide from Jehoiachin's descendants shall in future follow Josiah's example in order to soothe Yhwh's wrath which continued during the exilic period and to prepare a new beginning through removing the offending cults of the foreign gods (Jer. 44).[75]

4. *Structure and Peculiarity of the Pre-Dtr Catalogue of Cult Reform Measures in 2 Kings 23.4-15*: The 'Minor' Cult Reform*

Leaving aside the above-mentioned Dtr reshapings in 2 Kgs 23.4-15, there remains a catalogue of concrete measures that concern the purification and removal of particular cultic installations adverse to Yhwh in Jerusalem and its closer surroundings. This catalogue of measures—which could not be invented— is itself characterized by a quite homogeneous thematic and stylistic coherence, as the tabular presentation of this pre-stage in the Appendix 2 shows. Apart from one change in word order in 23.4 and the change of verse order in v. 12bβ after v. 11, which can easily to be accounted for, it follows fully the word sequence of the reshaped text.

4.1. *The Integral Coherence of the Pre-Dtr Pre-Stage*
4.1.1. *The thematic coherence: purification and removal of foreign cults at the king's residence of Jerusalem and its close vicinity.* The whole catalogue deals with the removal of cultic instruments, places or installations of cult as well as with the removal of cult staff within or in the immediate vicinity of Jerusalem. These are cultic media that were established for the cults of Baal and Asherah and of the astral gods. While the gods of heaven presumably refer to Assyrian influences that are constrained with the closing down of the corresponding cults, the removal of the cults of Baal and especially of Asherah seems to be connected with a purification of the Yhwh cult itself. This domestic measure was at the heart of the cult, on the one hand, according to the contemporary prohibition in Deut. 16.21-22, but on the other hand the cult object had spread further than the Jerusalem residence cult (cf. the note in 2 Kgs 23.15b that the Asherah of Bethel

---

75. Cf. here especially the historical-theological argumentation of Jer. 44.2-6 and 7-10 that v. 6 also shows the effects of Yhwh' wrath up to the present (כיום הזה!; cf. also v. 2 and 10 as well as on the close relation of Jer. 44 with 2 Kgs 22–23 also above nn. 33-34, 67 and below n. 90).

was also removed). Beyond this, the worship of 'Yhwh and his Asherah' is proved also outside of Jerusalem for the eighth century.[76]

1. In 23.4-5 the removal of the instruments and the removal of the cult staff that served all the cults of foreign gods in and around Jerusalem is mentioned as the first measure. In 23.4 there are *the instruments within the Jerusalem temple* that were installed for the foreign cults. 2 Kings 23.5 is about the *foreign priests* (כמרים) that were serving these cults (cf. perhaps also 23.13-14).

2. These general measures in 23.4-5 are followed by a number of measures in detail (23.6-7) that are directed against particular *material symbols* and *architectural infrastructures* of the cults mentioned in 23.4aβ, γ, 5b.

   23.6-10* is broadly about the removal of the infrastructure of the cult of Asherah (and Baal). Verse 6 notes the removal of the cult figure, v. 7 names the destruction of installations in which the cult of the Asherah was practised (houses of the cult prostitutes).[77] Verse 8b mentions the 'high places' that presumably refer to the single instance of altars in the niche of the gate,[78] and v. 10 names the profanation of the places for the offering of children (Tophet) that are to be viewed in a loose connection with the cult of Asherah (and Baal). Maybe the term 'high place' stems from this catalogue of measures which in Dtr thinking becomes used as a generalized term for all institutions of the cult of foreign gods.

   2 Kings 23.11-12 deals with the removal of the infrastructure to the cults of the sun and the stars that are mentioned summarily in vv. 4aγ and 5b. The account of v. 11* + 12bβ follows v. 6 closely. Just as the instruments of cult in 23.4 and the material cult symbol of the Asherah in v. 6, the figurative representatives of the astral gods in v. 11 are burnt (horses and sun vehicle), while in all cases the brook of Kidron is mentioned as the place or intermediate stop (v. 4) of the destruction. Next to the removal of these cult media (horses and sun vehicle) in v. 11aα₁, b, in v. 12a* the roof altars that the king (parallel to vv. 8b and 10) destroyed as a further measure are mentioned (v. 12a*).[79] In this way the catalogue

---

76. For proof, cf. Keel and Uehlinger 1998: 237-82 (255-64). We cannot formulate a religious-historical identification and explanation of the single objects and cult practices here, especially since the given evidence within the literary-historically reconstructed pre-stage of a Josianic text of annals generally coincides with the religious-historical evidence ascertained by Uehlinger 1995: 70-81.

77. Cf. the corresponding prohibition in Deut. 23.18, and on the prohibition of sacrificing children, 18.10a, which corresponds with the profanation of the Tophet cult in 2 Kgs 23.10.

78. Cf. above, Section 3.2.4 (point 2) and the references in Albertz 1996: 308 n. 2.

79. Because the plural suffix of עצרם in v. 12bβ can only refer to the burnt cult objects (v. 11; cf. also the mostly parallel syntax in v. 6), v. 12a breaks up the connection of vv. 11 and 12bβ possibly also in order to interlink with the following enumeration of altar installations, the removal of which is enumerated in vv. 13-15a. Whether this interlinking has taken place only in the course of the Dtr reshaping (cf. the compensating narrative element in v. 12bα), or whether it already existed in the pre-stage, cannot be decided. In the tabular depiction in Appendix 2, the transposition is marked with the siglum '!'.

of measures both linguistically and stylistically creates a transition to its third part that deals with the removal of altars in the close vicinity of Jerusalem.

3. 2 Kings 23.13-15* deals with the removal of cultic institutions against a wider geographic horizon in the closer (Mount of Olives, vv. 13-14) and farther (Bethel, v. 15) surroundings of Jerusalem. Both measures already close the polydimensional ring structure of the pre-Dtr catalogue that also persists in the final Dtr shape of the text (cf. 3.2.1). Thus also with respect to the linguistic and textual shaping it confirms the compactness and coherence of the pre-stage. The removal of the Asherah of Bethel in v. 15b at the end of the catalogue corresponds with the same measure in Jerusalem first mentioned in v. 6. Thus, Josiah implicitly finds himself at the same place where he had just brought the ashes of the destroyed cult instruments (v. 4bβ). Verse 5 and vv. 13-14 form an inner ring in so far as the foreign priesthood, dismissed in v. 5*, presumably did not serve at the Jerusalem temple but more likely in the cults on the Mount of Olives (vv. 13-14), where already 1 Kgs 11.5-8 places the cults of the 'diplomatic deputies' in the time of Solomon.[80]

4.1.2. The threefold nature of the catalogue of measures (23.4-5, 6-12, 13-15) according to object-thematic and topographic aspects. As already visible in the aforementioned ring structures, the measures and their execution show a great thematic closeness. In addition, the threefold catalogue is also structured systematically with respect to topography. While the first and second part in 23.4-5 and 6-12 is limited to the cultic installations within the city of Jerusalem, the third part (vv. 13-15) is extended to the closer and farther surroundings of Jerusalem. The first part is generally directed towards all cults of foreign gods and concentrates on cultic instruments and the foreign cult staff. It does not deal with altars or other immobile installations of foreign cults. The second part—coming from 23.4-5—consequently considers both central cults of foreign gods in detail: the one of Asherah and Baal in vv. 6-10 and the other of the astral gods in vv. 11-12. Besides the destruction of mobile material symbols of the cult, this part also mentions the profanation or removal of immobile installations (houses of the cult prostitutes, altars in gates, Tophet and roof altars). As far as they are mobile cult symbols, they are burnt just like the instruments from the Jerusalem temple (23.4b) and are connected with the brook of Kidron as the place of their removal. The third part (13-15) concentrates on the immobile cult installations outside of Jerusalem and mentions Asherah as a figurative cult object only at the end.

4.1.3. The terminological consistency as well as linguistic and stylistic homogeneity and peculiarity of the catalogue of measures. The measures of removal are phrased very homogeneously in terminology as becomes clear from the

---

80. Accordingly, the Dtr reshaping in 2 Kgs 23.13 ascribes the establishing of this cult to Solomon.

inventory of verbs of action: יצא (hiphil, vv. 4, 6), שרף (vv. 4, 6, 11), שבת (hiphil, vv. 5, 11), שלך (vv. 6, 12), נתץ (vv. 7, 8, 12, 15) and טמא (piel, vv. 10, 13). Further, the given details of the places where the various cult installations were situated and removed are very special and presuppose an intimate knowledge of the Jerusalem topography and local places. This evidence hints at a historically decisive precondition for writing this catalogue of measures. It witnesses to an authorship that very naturally took for granted this intimate knowledge in potential readers, too; that means if these were annalistic records, the potential readers were supposed to be able to handle these details of topography and places also in a more distant future. This is a sure indication of the fact that this catalogue of measures was written before 587 when people naturally presupposed the continuity of the city of Jerusalem and its architectural infrastructure. Unlike the 'major' cult reform of the Dtr reshaping, the geographic horizon of all measures of reform—with the exception of the altar(!) of Bethel[81]—also remains limited to Jerusalem, which means fully limited to the Davidide king's residence with its residential cult.

Further, one has to point to the stylistic homogeneity of the reconstructed pre-stage. It is characterized by the style of annalistic records. The *enumerating wktb-* and *w-X-ktb*-style is dominant. It does not narratively/consecutively give a *re*count of an irreversible connection of events, but like a catalogue it *ac*counts by enumerating single measures additively or according to systematic viewpoints without creating a narrative tension.[82] We find this style for example in the argumentation of Jer. 22.15b but also in the annalistic enumeration of regal measures such as in 2 Kgs 14.7 or 18.4. The material for comparison is rare, since there are no other major catalogues of measures and since they can always also be phrased semi-narratively. But in 2 Kgs 14.7 and 18.4 there are the precise text openings for such catalogues that are also easily thinkable for the opening of the pre-stage in 2 Kgs 23.4. The Dtr reshaping in v. 4a simply had to replace the former introduction in v. 4a (...הוציא הוא[ו]) through the infinitive construct form with ל in order to continue from its newly created opening of the textual extract with להוציא.[83]

The syntactic stereotypes and the partly unique usage of language are remarkable, too. With respect to syntax, we find in 23.4-11 a stereotype sequence of *measure, object of the measure* and *place* of the object or the carrying out of the measure, while the mobile objects include a additional note on the place where the ashes were deposited. In v. 11b there is a change of style visible in the sequence until the end of v. 15. In simple *w-X-ktb* sentences the object is at the beginning of the sentence, followed by a detail of place and the measure carried out at the end. Only 23.14*, 15b with *wktb*-openings follow the syntactic pattern

---

81. Because the destruction of the *altar* of Bethel (implied in 23.15*) can be neither verified nor falsified archaeologically, and because a possible measure of destruction of the cult presupposes the destruction of neither the shrine nor even the whole place, this final verse of the catalogue does not record processes that would have to be at all excluded for archaeological reasons from Josiah's time.

82. Cf. also above, Section 3.2.4 (point 1).

83. On this style of report and notes, see Hardmeier 1990a: 97.

of the first part. The diction often shows unique expressions or expressions deviating from the Dtr diction that sometimes also originate in uninventible and therefore authentic facts:
1. The term היכל in v. 4 for the temple deviates from the Dtr usage of language (בית יהוה) and also seldom occurs.
2. מסבים in v. 5 is unique in comparison to סביבים/ות, often used for 'surroundings' (otherwise, only 1 Kgs 6.29 and Cant. 1.12).[84]
3. We can further note the seldom-used but factual-conditioned term כמרים in v. 5 for the priests of foreign cults (cf. still Hos. 10.5 and Zeph. 1.4).
4. The term מזלות for fate-determining signs of the zodiac in v. 5 is a *hapax legomenon*.

Taking all these observations together, there can hardly be any doubt that an annalistic document forms the basis and pre-stage of the 'major' Dtr account of cult reform in 2 Kgs 23.4-15. This document contained a number of measures of purification of the Yhwh cult in the Jerusalem temple as well as of the destruction of illegitimate cults at the king's residence in Jerusalem and in Bethel which —as has been accounted for in 4.2—were carried through under King Josiah. This pre-stage is not a hypothetical construct or text torso but has been shown to be a homogeneous textual unit of its own that, moreover, easily stands out from its later reshaping context; we can speak of a literary primary source for Josiah's politics of cult. The fact that the 'minor' reform that this primary source documents widely coincides with the results on the range and direction of the Josianic cult reform, fundamentally derived from archaeological and religious historical evidence, underlines the validity of the literary historical reconstruction. This can only be sketched out roughly in the following section.

4.2. *The Cultural and Religious Historical Plausibility of the Reconstructed Pre-Stage for Josiah's Age and its Literary Sociological Place*

The reconstructed catalogue of measures easily fits into Josiah's reign. On the one hand, he opposes the Assyrian cult practices (worship of the astral gods: 23.4-6, 11-12) that had been established in the age of vassalage (since Manasseh at the latest) at the king's residence in Jerusalem. On the other hand, the catalogue deals with Canaanite infiltrations of the Yhwh cult which had been strongly criticized as Baalism since Elijah and Hosea and which had been expressed by rituals connected with Asherahs and stone pillars (23.6, 14, 15) as well as in cult prostitution (23.7) and the Tophet cult (23.10). These cult practices were opposed in the pre-exilic Deuteronomy (16.21-22; 18.10; 23.18-19) in the same way as they were destroyed or removed according to the Josianic catalogue of measures in 2 Kgs 23.4-15*. Behind the measure in 23.13 one can presume the closing down of the foreign cults of neighbouring nations on the Mount of Olives while the service of the foreign cult staff of these 'diplomatic deputies' was stopped (23.5). With respect to this, the Dtr reshaping in 23.13 remembers an accurate fact in the light of 1 Kgs 11.5-8.

---

84. Cf. also Stipp 1998: 57.

158					Good Kings and Bad Kings

In addition, all measures that C. Uehlinger considers as the critical minimum for a conceivable 'Josianic reform' solely because of the archaeological evidence and religious historical considerations, are also the main components of the literary-historically reconstructed catalogue of measures.[85] In respect of topography the measures are limited to the king's residence shrine in Jerusalem and the close vicinity, with the exception of Bethel—where only the altar was destroyed and the Asherah was removed according to the pre-stage of 23.15*—so that there is no need to presuppose a 'major' countrywide cult reform. Further, the reconstructed pre-stage, also with respect to the literary sociological aspects, easily follows the model of annalistic reports[86] that can certainly be presupposed for the Jerusalem court (as well as for the northern empire).[87]

This literary-historical evidence is particularly significant since it seamlessly coincides with H.M. Niemann's results concerning the range of cult organizing measures of the Judaic monarchy that were achieved mostly without considering Old Testament reports. According to Niemann, the Davidides even under Josiah had 'not yet exercised any considerable influence or dominance over the local cults of the country' 'apart from a legitimating theology of dynasty and residence in Jerusalem' with a 'corresponding residential cult for the southern kingdom'.[88] Only 'with and through Josiah', according to Niemann, can a 'clear sign of effort be recognized…to assign the Davidide residential cult a central role countrywide' (1995: 224-25). With these results exactly coincide the measures documented in the pre-stage, namely, purification of the residential cult by removal of the cultic installations foreign to Yhwh in Jerusalem and its vicinity with a clear statement 23.4-5, 11-12) and the neighbouring nations of the region (cf. 1 Kgs 11.4-8*[89] and 2 Kgs 23.4-5, 13-14).

85. Cf. the explanations of Uehlinger (1995) on the 'horse(s) and wagons of the sun god' (1995: 74-77), on the foreign priests and roof altars (1995: 77-81) and on the Asherah cult (1995: 81-83). For the historical proofs of the cult media, which are mentioned in the reconstructed catalogue of measures, see also Albertz 1996: 307-308 nn. 1-4 and 6.
86. Especially above in Section 4.1.3.
87. Cf. the references to the ספר דברי הימים—that is, some thing like a diary of important events of the kings of Judah and Israel. They are often to be found in the ויתר-formula of the king's frame (e.g. 2 Kgs 23.28); cf. also Hardmeier 1990b: esp. 178-79.
88. Niemann (1992: 234) in debate with Ahlström; see further pp. 224-27 and n. 207; also n. 209: 'It is fitting that Josiah's measures on the one hand effectively reached only the vicinity of Jerusalem and that on the other hand after Josiah…the "cult of high places" persisted and furthermore innumerable places and objects of the house and local cult remained in use' especially outside Jerusalem.
89. 1 Kgs 11.4-8 is also Dtr transformed. The typical generalization of 11.8 exactly corresponds to the Dtr standard reproach of burning incense offerings with the phrase קטר לאלהים, which besides the JerD passages appears, on the one hand, especially in Jer. 44 (eight times alone with the mentioning of the deity) and, on the other hand, significantly in the textual network of 2 Kgs 22–23 (22.17; 23.5, 8) and the corresponding passages of 1 Kgs 12.33 and 13.2 (otherwise in the books of the kings only in 2 Kgs 16.4 and 17.11 besides Hos. 2.15; 4.13; Isa. 65.3, 7 and in passages in Chronicles; see Stipp 1998: 119). That in 1 Kgs 11.8 especially the women of foreign countries (as in Jer. 44 basically the women of Judah) are reproached (cf. 44.25), is on the one hand a further hint for the Dtr standardization and generalization that was applied to this practice of offerings in the exilic Deuteronomism in the measure of Deut. 7.3-4 as a perfect example of apostasy that offended Yhwh.

All of these reasons on very different levels argue that the reconstructed catalogue of measures of cult purification and removal in 2 Kgs 23.4-15* is a document of primary source material which, as an excerpt from the annals (2 Kgs 23.28b), witnesses to a 'minor' reform of the cult during Josiah's reign. Against the scepticism of the 'minimal approach', it is therefore quite possible to reconstruct primary sources even from the traditional literature of the Hebrew Bible if we approach with care this literature in an inductive way and with reasonable methods which are appropriate to the text material for reconstructing literary historical pre-stages, as well as to the material remains of those times.

APPENDIX 1

The <u>Deuteronomic Reshaping</u> of the Josianic Catalogue of Reform Measures in 2 Kings 23.4-15

(4) <u>ויצו המלך</u> את־חלקיהו הכהן הגדול ואת־כהני המשנה ואת־שמרי הסף [הוא] <u>להוציא</u> מהיכל יהוה את כל־הכלים העשוים לבעל ולאשרה ולכל צבא השמים וישרפם מחוץ לירושלם בשדמות קדרון ונשא את־עפרם בית־אל:
(5) והשבית את־הכמרים <u>אשר</u> נתנו מלכי יהודה ויקטר בבמות בערי יהודה ומסבי ירושלם <u>ואת</u>־המקטרים לבעל לשמש ולירח ולמזלות ולכל צבא השמים:
(6) ויצא את־האשרה <u>מבית יהוה</u> מחוץ לירושלם אל־נחל קדרון וישרף אתה בנחל קדרון וידק לעפר וישלך את־עפרה על־קבר בני העם:
(7) ויתץ את־בתי הקדשים <u>אשר בבית יהוה</u> אשר הנשים ארגות שם בתים לאשרה:
(8) <u>ויבא את־</u>כל־הכהנים מערי יהודה וטמא את־הבמות אשר קטרו־שמה הכהנים מגבע עד־באר שבע ונתץ את־במות השערים אשר־פתח שער יהושע שר־העיר אשר־על־שמאול איש בשער העיר: (9) <u>אך</u> לא יעלו כהני הבמות אל־מזבח יהוה בירושלם כי אם־אכלו מצות בתוך אחיהם: (10) וטמא את־התפת אשר בני בני־הנם לבלתי להעביר איש את־בנו ואת־בתו באש למלך:
(11) וישבת את־הסוסים <u>אשר</u> נתנו מלכי יהודה לשמש מבא בית־יהוה אל־לשכת נתן־מלך הסריס אשר בפרורים ואת־מרכבות השמש שרף באש:
(12) <u>את</u>־המזבחות אשר על־הגג עלית אחז <u>אשר־עשו מלכי יהודה</u> ואת־המזבחות אשר־עשה מנשה בשתי חצרות בית־יהוה נתץ המלך <u>וירץ משם</u> וחשליך את־עפרם אל־נחל קדרון: (13) ואת־הבמות <u>אשר</u> על־פני ירושלם אשר מימין להר־המשחית <u>אשר</u> בנה שלמה מלך־ישראל לעשתרת שקץ צידנים ולכמוש שקץ מואב ולמלכם תועבת בני־עמון טמא המלך:
(14) ושבר את־המצבות ויכרת את־האשרים ימלא את־מקומם עצמות אדם:
(15) <u>וגם את</u>־המזבח אשר בבית־אל <u>הבמה אשר עשה ירבעם בן־נבט</u> אשר החטיא את־ישראל גם את־המזבח ההוא ואת־הבמה נתץ <u>וישרף</u> את־הבמה הדק לעפר ושרף אשרה:

On the other hand, the significant interrelation of Jer. 44; 1 Kgs 11.4-8, and 2 Kgs 22–23 refers to the common intellectual root of this generalization. It was probably invented by the Dtr interpreters of the Josianic catalogue of measures in 2 Kgs 23.8a and 5aβ on the base of v. 5b and in connection with 23.13-14 inserted into 1 Kgs 11.8. Moreover, these exegetes seem to belong to the same bearer group who also in Jer. 44 strongly criticizes this further practice of adoration toward the astral deities (see also above, Section 3.2.5).

APPENDIX 2

The Pre-Dtr Catalogue of Josianic Cult Reform Measures (2 Kings 23.4-15)

Measure	Place of the Objects/the Measures	Object	Measure	Reference
	(1) מבית יהוה	את כל־הכלים (2)	הוציא {והוֹצֵא}	23.4
	מחוץ לירושלם בשדמות קדרון	לבעל לאשרה		
	:בית־אל	suffix		
	מבית יהוה	הפברים	נאם	
		האשרה	הוֹשְׁבַּת	23.5
		הרכב השמש		
	מחוץ לירושלם אל־נחל קדרון	את האשרה	השריף	23.6
	בנחל קדרון	אתה		
		את בתי הקדשים	נתץ	23.7
		את הבמות	טמא	23.8b
		את הבמות השערים	נתץ	23.10
		את הסוסים	השבית	23.11
שלף באש		משכת ההבמה		
נתן לקדרון		את המזבחות	שרף	23.12bβ!
	את־המזבחות אשר על־הגג עלית אחז	את המזבחות		23.12abα!
	ואת המזבחות אשר־עשה מנשה בשתי חצרות בית־יהוה			
שבר אבנים		את המצבות		23.13
כרת		את האשרים		23.14
	את־הבמה אשר בבית־אל	המזבח		23.15
		הבמה	שרף	

BIBLIOGRAPHY

Albertz, Rainer
  1989   'Die Intentionen und die Träger des Deuteronomistischen Geschichtswerks', in Rainer Albertz, Friedemann Golka and Jürgen Kegler (eds.), *Schöpfung und Befreiung: Für Claus Westermann zum 80. Geburtstag* (Stuttgart: Calwer Verlag): 37-53.
  1996   *Religionsgeschichte Israels in alttestamentlicher Zeit.* I. *Von den Anfängen bis zum Ende der Königszeit* (ATD Ergänzungsreihe, 8/1; Göttingen: Vandenhoeck & Ruprecht, 2nd edn).
  1997   'Wer waren die Deuteronomisten? Das historische Rätsel einer literarischen Hypothese', *EvT* 57: 319-38.
Braulik, Georg
  1988   'Die Abfolge der Gesetze in Deuteronomium 12–26 und der Dekalog', in *idem*, *Studien zur Theologie des Deuteronomiums* (SBAB, 2; Stuttgart: Katholisches Bibelwerk): 231-55.
Crüsemann, Frank
  1997   *Die Tora: Theologie und Sozialgeschichte des alttestamentlichen Gesetzes* (Munich: Chr. Kaiser Verlag; Gütersloh: Gütersloher Verlagshaus, 2nd edn).
Genette, Gérard
  1994   *Die Erzählung* (Munich: Wilhelm Fink Verlag).
Gross, Walter (ed.)
  1995   *Jeremia und die 'deuteronomistische Bewegung'* (BBB, 98; Weinheim: Beltz Athenäum).
Habermas, Jürgen
  1982   *Theorie des kommunikativen Handelns.* I. *Handlungsrationalität und gesellschaftliche Rationalisierung* (Frankfurt: Suhrkamp Verlag, 2nd edn).
Hardmeier, Christof
  1978   *Texttheorie und biblische Exegese: Zur rhetorischen Funktion der Trauermetaphorik in der Prophetie* (BEvT, 79; Munich: Chr. Kaiser Verlag).
  1990a   *Prophetie im Streit vor dem Untergang Judas: Erzählkommunikative Studien zur Entstehungssituation der Jesaja- und Jeremiaerzählungen in II Reg 18–20 und Jer 37–40* (BZAW, 187; Berlin and New York: W. de Gruyter).
  1990b   'Umrisse eines vordeuteronomistischen Annalenwerks der Zidkijazeit: Zu den Möglichkeiten computergestützter Textanalyse', *VT* 40: 165-84.
  1992   'Die Erinnerung an die Knechtschaft in Ägypten: Sozialanthropologische Aspekte des Erinnerns in der hebräischen Bibel', in Frank Crüsemann, Christof Hardmeier and Rainer Kessler (eds.), *Was ist der Mensch...? Beiträge zur Anthropologie des Alten Testaments: Hans Walter Wolff zum 80. Geburtstag* (Munich: Chr. Kaiser Verlag): 133-52.
  1993   'Probleme der Textsyntax, der Redeeinbettung und der Abschnittgliederung in Jer 32 mit ihren kompositionsgeschichtlichen Konsequenzen', in Hubert Irsigler (ed.), *Syntax und Text: Beiträge zur 22. Internationalen Ökumenischen Hebräisch-Dozenten-Konferenz 1993 in Bamberg* (ATSAT, 40; Sankt Ottilien: Verlag Erzabtei Sankt Otilien): 49-79.
  1996   'Geschichte und Erfahrung in Jer 2–6: Zur theologischen Notwendigkeit einer geschichts- und erfahrungsbezogenen Exegese und ihrer methodischen Neuorientierung', *EvT* 56: 3-29.
  1998   'Zeitverständnis und Geschichtssinn in der Hebräischen Bibel: Geschichtstheologie und Gegenwartserhellung bei Jeremia', in Jörn Rüsen, Michael Gottlob and Achim Mittag (eds), *Die Vielfalt der Kulturen: Erinnerung, Geschichte, Identität 4* (STW, 1405; Frankfurt: Suhrkamp Verlag): 308-42.

2000 'Das Schᵉma' Jisra'el in Dtn 6,4 im Rahmen der Beziehungstheologie der deuteronomistischen Tora', in Erhard Blum (ed.), *Mincha: Festgabe für Rolf Rendtorff zum 75. Geburtstag* (Neukirchen–Vluyn: Neukirchener Verlag): 61-92.

2003a 'Die Weisheit der Tora (Dtn 4,5-8): Respekt und Loyalität gegenüber JHWH allein und die Befolgung der Gebote—ein performatives Lehren und Lernen', in Christof Hardmeier, Rainer Kessler and Andreas Ruwe (eds.), *Freiheit und Recht: Frank Crüsemann zum 65. Geburtstag* (Gütersloh: Gütersloher Verlagshaus): 224-54.

2003b *Textwelten der Bibel entdecken: Grundlagen und Verfahren einer textpragmatischen Literaturwissenschaft der Bibel: Band 1/1* (Textpragmatische Studien zur Literatur- und Kulturgeschichte der Hebräischen Bibel, 1/1; Gütersloh: Gütersloher Verlagshaus).

2004 *Textwelten der Bibel entdecken: Grundlagen und Verfahren einer textpragmatischen Literaturwissenschaft der Bibel: Band 1/2* (Textpragmatische Studien zur Literatur- und Kulturgeschichte der Hebräischen Bibel, 1/2; Gütersloh: Gütersloher Verlagshaus).

Hoffmann, Hans-Detlef
 1980 *Reform und Reformen. Untersuchungen zu einem Grundthema der deuteronomistischen Geschichtsschreibung* (ATANT, 66; Zürich: Theologischer Verlag).

Keel, Othmar, and Christoph Uehlinger
 1998 *Göttinnen, Götter und Gottessymbole. Neue Erkenntnisse zur Religionsgeschichte Kanaans und Israels aufgrund bislang unerschlossener ikonographischer Quellen* (QD, 134; Freiburg: Herder, 4th edn).

Kessler, Rainer
 1992 *Staat und Gesellschaft im vorexilischen Juda vom 8. Jahrhundert bis zum Exil* (VTSup, 47; Leiden: E.J. Brill).

Knapp, Dietrich
 1987 *Deuteronomium. IV. Literarische Analyse und theologische Interpretation* (GTA, 35; Göttingen: Vandenhoeck & Ruprecht).

Koch, Klaus
 1992 'Gefüge und Herkunft des Berichts über die Kultreformen des Königs Josia', in Jutta Hausmann and Hans-Jürgen Zobel (eds), *Alttestamentlicher Glaube und Biblische Theologie: Festschrift für Horst Dietrich Preuß zum 65. Geburtstag* (Stuttgart: W. Kohlhammer): 80-92.

Levin, Christoph
 1981 'Noch einmal: Die Anfänge des Propheten Jeremia', *VT* 31: 428-40.
 1984 'Joschija im deuteronomistischen Geschichtswerk', *ZAW* 96: 351-71.

Lohfink, Norbert
 1978 'Die Gattung der "Historischen Kurzgeschichte" in den letzten Jahren von Juda und in der Zeit des Babylonischen Exils', *ZAW* 90: 319-47.
 1991a 'Zur neueren Diskussion über II Kön 22–23', in Lohfink 1991c: 179-207.
 1991b 'Die Kultreform Joschijas von Juda. 2 Kön 22-23 als religionsgeschichtliche Quelle', in Lohfink 1991c: 209-27.
 1991c *Studien zum Deuteronomium und zur deuteronomistischen Literatur*, II (Stuttgarter biblische Aufsatzbande, 12; Stuttgart: Katholisches Bibelwerk).

Niehr, Herbert
 1995 'Die Reform des Joschija', in Gross (ed.) 1995: 33-56.

Niemann, Hermann Michael
 1993 *Herrschaft, Königtum und Staat: Skizzen zur soziokulturellen Entwicklung im monarchischen Israel* (FAT, 6; Tübingen: J.C.B. Mohr [Paul Siebeck]).

Preuss, Horst Dieter
    1982   *Deuteronomium* (EdF, 164; Darmstadt: Wissenschaftliche Buchgesellschaft).
    1993   'Zum deuteronomistischen Geschichtswerk', *Theologische Rundschau* 58: 229-64, 341-95.

Schoors, Antoon
    1998   *Die Königreiche Israel und Juda im 8. und 7. Jahrhundert v. Chr.: Die assyrische Krise* (BE, 5; Stuttgart/Berlin/Köln: W. Kohlhammer).

Spieckermann, Hermann
    1982   *Juda unter Assur in der Sargonidenzeit* (FRLANT, 129; Göttingen: Vandenhoeck & Ruprecht).

Stipp, Hermann-Josef
    1998   *Deuterojeremianische Konkordanz* (ATSAT, 63; Sankt Ottilien: Verlag Erzabtei Sankt Otilien).

Thiel, Winfried
    1981   *Die deuteronomistische Redaktion von Jeremia 26–45: Mit einer Gesamtbeurteilung der deuteronomistischen Redaktion des Buches Jeremia* (WMANT, 52; Neukirchen–Vluyn: Neukirchener Verlag).

Uehlinger, Christoph
    1995   'Gab es eine joschijanische Kultreform?', in Gross (ed.) 1995: 57-90.

The Glorious Days of Manasseh

Ernst Axel Knauf

It is the Bible that connects our culture and our present to that other culture in the distant past—in another country at another time—in which King Manasseh and his contemporaries flourished. A historical treatment needs to regard both (a) what really happened (as far as we are able to perceive it) in this foreign world some 2650 years ago; and (b) how the memory of what had happened was preserved—or contorted—by the tradition which is part of our world.

My methodological introduction will be brief. As always, I work 'from history to tradition and interpretation' when reconstructing a past real world. I will take my data from wherever I can find them. In the case of literary 'sources',[1] data retrieval will include the separation between facteme and factoids. A facteme I define as the minimal information which is either true or false in the real world, while a factoid (following the late lamented R.P. Carroll) is information which was created in the mental process of formulating and transmitting the narrative, or wrongly placed in terms of time or space. An example will help to clarify: 'On the evening of Valmy, Goethe said to Field-Marshal Blücher: "On this very day a new chapter of world history commenced, and you will be able to say you were present when it happened"'. This apocryphal story contains four factoids and one facteme: (1) Goethe was present at the cannonade of Valmy (true); (2) Blücher was also present (false); (3) Blücher was already a field-marshal in 1792 (false); (4) Goethe spoke to Blücher (false: impossible because of [2]); (5) what Goethe wrote 30 years after Valmy, claiming to have said on the evening of the event, is not corroborated by any of the numerous people he actually spoke to on this very day, most of them prolific writers of letters and diaries. The distinction between factemes and factoids will more frequently be made implicitly rather than explicitly.

---

1. I deem the term most inappropriate at the present stage of historical scholarship—are data from archaeology, geography and social anthropology 'sources'? Does the very term 'source' not represent a remnant from the time when writing history meant rewriting the narratives of our antique colleagues? I prefer to retrieve data from written material as well as from any other remnant of the past.

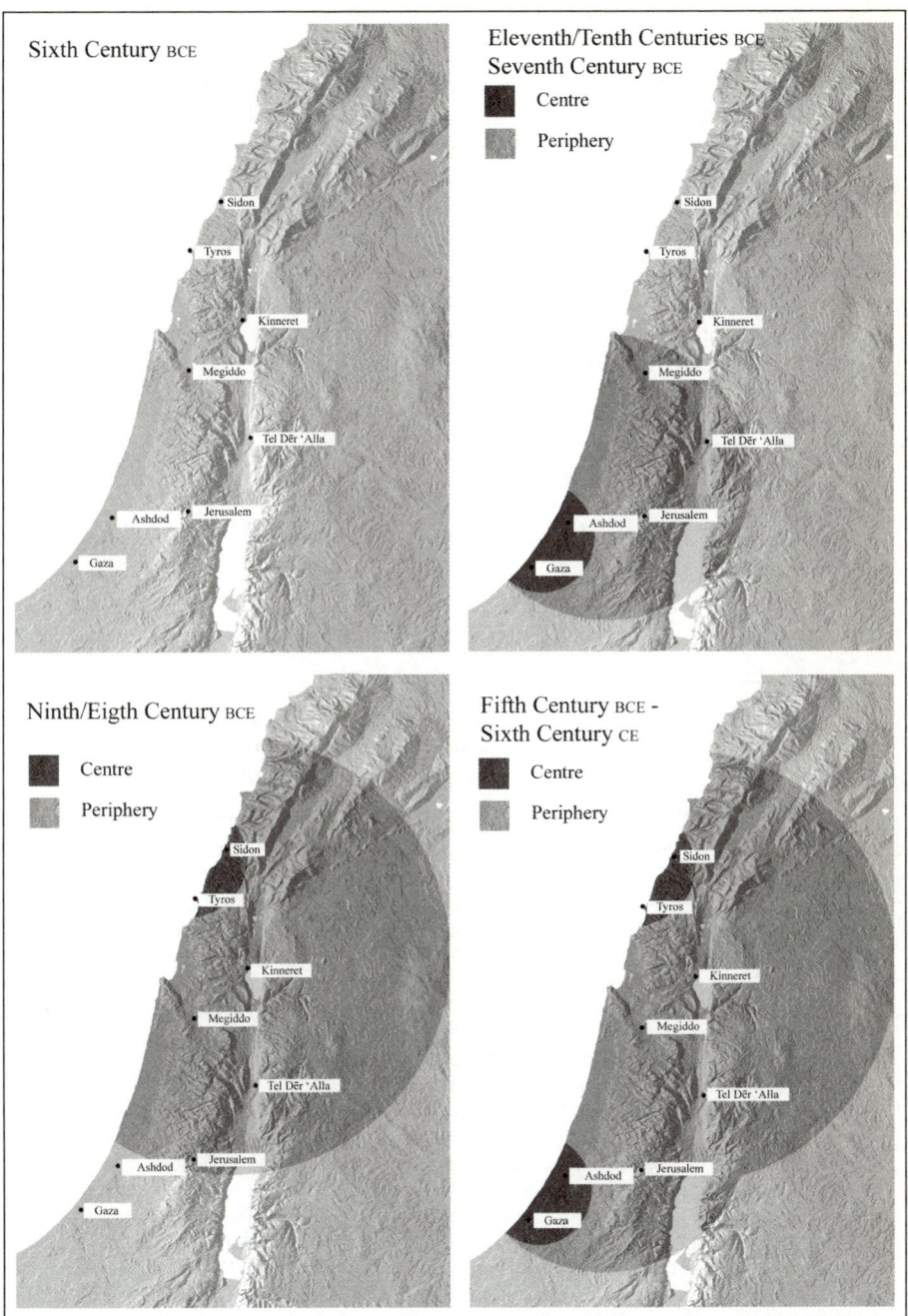

Figure 1. *The Four Spatial Distributions of Socio-Economic Cores and Peripheries in Israel/Palestine in the Course of the First Millennium* BCE

$$1. f(-7) = f(-10)?^2$$

The macrohistorical structure of the seventh century BCE was a partial recast of the tenth century. In the eleventh and tenth centuries, Philistia represented the core area of the Palestinian economic system, with the concomitant and well-known results for Philistia's Judaean periphery. In the ninth and eighth centuries, Phoenicia outclassed Philistia and gave rise to the secondary states of Omride Israel and Aram-Damascus, Judah becoming the periphery's periphery.[3] In the seventh century, relations between Assyria and Phoenicia were strained, to say the least, resulting in Assyria's development of Philistia as a hub in international trade[4] and economic decline in northern Israel and southern Syria. The urban development of Ekron tells the story well (Table 1):

Table 1. *Growth and Decline of Philistine Cities and Jerusalem (in ha/hectares), Twelfth–Sixteenth Centuries* BCE

century	Ashdod	Ekron	Gath	Jerusalem
-12	7	20	4	2?
-11	7	24	6-12?	2-3?
-10	1	24	12-16?	3-5?
-9	7	4	24-40	5-8?
-8	30	4	1	8-16?
-7	15[5]	24	1	40-50
-6	15	0	1	0-1

Ekron behaves as expected, whereas Jerusalem (probably) grew even in the period of Ekron's decline. The sub-system of the mountains might have profited from the plain's decline; but the picture is more complicated than that, as soon as we regard the other two Philistian cities on which we have data (in the case of Gath, still preliminary).[6]

---

2. *f* is a function or a family of functions which gives the approximate socio-political core-periphery distribution in the Southern Levant according to centuries; (-7), for example, stands for the seventh century BCE.

3. E.A. Knauf, 'Jerusalem in the Late Bronze and Early Iron Periods—A Proposal', *TA* 27 (2000), pp. 75-90; idem, 'Israel, II. Geschichte 1. Allgemein und biblisch', in H.-D. Betz *et al.* (eds.), *Die Religion in Geschichte und Gegenwart* (Tübingen: J.C.B. Mohr, 2001), VI, pp. 284-93, and, in the same volume, 'Israel und seine Nachbarn in Syrien-Palästina', pp. 311-13; I. Finkelstein, 'The Rise of Jerusalem and Judah: the Missing Link', *Levant* 32 (2001), pp. 105-15.

4. S. Gitin, 'The Neo-Assyrian Empire and its Western Periphery: The Levant, with a Focus on Philistine Ekron', in S. Parpola and R.M. Whiting (eds.), *Assyria 1995: Proceedings of the 10th Anniversary Symposium of the Neo-Assyrian Text Corpus Project Helsinki, September 7–11, 1995* (Helsinki: Helsinki University Press, 1997), pp. 77-103.

5. Ashdod-Yam was the successor of Ashdod which lay waste in the seventh and sixth centuries.

6. I. Finkelstein and L. Singer-Avitz, 'Ashdod Revisited', *TA* 28 (2001), pp. 231-59; C.S. Ehrlich, 'Die Suche nach Gat und die neuen Ausgrabungen auf Tell eṣ-Ṣāfî', in U. Hübner and E.A. Knauf (eds.), *Kein Land für sich allein. Studien zum Kulturkontakt in Kanaan, Israel/Palästina und Ebirnâri für Manfred Weippert zum 65 Geburtstag* (OBO, 186; Freiburg: Universitätsverlag; Göttingen: Vandenhoeck & Ruprecht, 2002), pp. 56-69, and, in the same volume, H.M. Niemann, 'Nachbarn und Gegner, Konkurrenten und Verwandte Judas: Die Philister zwischen Geographie und Ökonomie, Geschichte und Theologie', pp. 70-91. For Jerusalem in the sixth century, cf. O. Lipschits, 'Demographic Changes in Judah between the Seventh and Fifth Centuries B.C.E', in O. Lipschits and

Was the rise of Jerusalem due to alliances with Gath that were to the disadvantage of Ekron in the tenth and early ninth centuries, with Hazael to the disadvantage of Gath in the second half of the ninth century, and with Ashdod in the eighth century? In the seventh century, it is evident that Jerusalem benefited from Assyrian rule much more than Ekron did. Enter Manasseh.

Before we allow him to enter the stage, however, a brief glance at demography and the distribution of wealth is in order. To estimate the welfare of non-monetary societies, various 'data of indirect approach' are available. In Iron I Giloh, the average household had to use its food-processing pottery (cooking pots) also for food consumption (bowls and craters), simply because they did not own any specialized household ware for the latter purpose. At Tel 'Ira VII (an indisputably Manassean site), the picture has completely changed:[7]

Table 2. *Percentages of Household Pottery according to Function*

Ware	Giloh 11th century	Tel 'Ira VII B	Tel 'Ira VII E	Tel 'Ira VII E L. 572
storage	50.3%	23%	16%	33%
food-processing	26.6%	7%	12%	2%
food-consumption	21.2%	65%	66%	63%
lamps	–	5%	6%	2%

So, the ordinary populace lived a much better life under Manasseh than in the eleventh and tenth centuries (Tel 'Ira was not a rich settlement—the jewelry is predominantly made of bronze[8]), but of course they could not know this. What they could see was that inequality in the distribution of wealth became much more pronounced than had been the case in their fathers' generation. For a rough estimate of the inequality factor q one could use the obvious correlation between the distribution of settlement sizes within a given territory and the distribution of wealth within these settlements. In Iron I Judah, the smallest settlements covered 0.5 ha (or less), and no settlement exceeded 5 ha.[9] So the expected inequality coefficient would be $q = f(10)$.[10] In Manassean Judah, the smallest settlements still ranged around 0.5 ha, but the largest, Jerusalem, reached 50 ha; $q = f(100)$. The growing social inequality results, of course, not from decadence and moral corruption, as the united social romantics of all ages would have it, but from population growth: Manasseh's Judah had c. 100,000 inhabitants, tenth-century Judah less than 10,000. In today's world, q is c. $f(500,000)$: the poorest inhabitants of this world make less than US$ 2 a day, the richest easily 1,000,000.

J. Blenkinsopp (eds.), *Judah and the Judaeans in the Neo-Babylonian Period* (Winona Lake, IN: Eisenbrauns, 2003), pp. 323-76.

7. I. Finkelstein, *The Archaeology of the Israelite Settlement* (Jerusalem: Magnes Press, 1988), pp. 192-93.

8. Thirteen pieces as opposed to six pieces made of silver.

9. I. Finkelstein, 'The Great Transformation: the "Conquest" of the Highland Frontiers and the Rise of Territorial States', in T.E. Levy (ed.), *The Archaeology of Society in the Holy Land* (New York: Facts on File, 1995), pp. 349-65 (356 fig. 3). There are no sites > 5 ha south of Shechem.

10. The coefficient q is not only determined by the distribution of individual wealth, nor is it necessarily proportional to the distribution of wealth; f, thus, is probably not linear.

2. King Manasseh in all his Glory—
As a Faithful Servant of Assyria

Between 674 and 671,[11] Esarhaddon built a new armoury at Nineveh (Nin A V 40-VI 1; translations are by the present author if not stated otherwise):

> (47)... The inhabitants of the countries, which my bow had acquired, I let them carry pickaxes and baskets, (49) and they made bricks... (54) I called up the kings of Hatti (Syria) and the Transeuphrates: Ba'al, King of Tyre; Manasseh (¹me-na-si-i), King of Juda (ᵘʳᵘIa-ù-di); (56) Qausgabr, King of Edom; Muṣur, King of Moab; (57) Ṣil(l)bēl, King of Gaza; Mit(t)inti, King of Ascalon; (58) Ikausu/Achis, King of Ekron; (59) Milk'asapa, King of Byblos; (60) Mattan-Ba'al, King of Arwad; (61) Abi-Ba'al, King of Shamshimoron; (62) Pada'el, King of Bet-'Ammon; and Aḫi-Milk, King of Ashdod; (63) (altogether) 12 kings from the littoral; ... (71) ... (altogether) 10 kings from Cyprus (72) in midst the ocean; in sum 22 kings from coastal Syria (73) and from in midst the ocean—and, on my command, they had (74) strong beams, high posts... (75) of cedar-wood and cypress-wood, a product of Amanus and Lebanon, (76) which had grown stronger and higher for a long time, [follow various kinds of stone] (82) carried, for the benefit of my palace, in toils and labours, (VI 1) to Niniveh, my residence.

So deportees from newly conquered countries did the construction work, whereas the Syrian and Cypriote vassals mustered corvée to quarry stones, cut wood and drag the materials to Niniveh. Thus, Judaeans from the time of Manasseh got to see the world—Niniveh, if a detachment of Judaeans went all the way, or at least Lebanon, if the Judaean contribution was restricted to wood-cutting and northern (or sea-faring) vassals took over from there. One should perhaps not over-interpret the determinative URU ('city') in front of 'Judah' (all the kingdoms in this list are called 'cities'), but it matches the demographic situation under Manasseh, when 12–15% of the Judaean populace lived in the capital.[12] Athaliah, Uzziah or Hezekiah might have started to transform the tribal state of Judah into a 'city state' with a rural *hinterland*, but it was Manasseh who completed the process.

Were Judaean troops also involved in the capture of Arzâ (Tell Jemme) in 679/8, the unsuccessful invasion of Egypt in 673, and in the Egyptian campaigns of 671 and 669? Esarhaddon does not tell, but Ashurbanipal[13] does:

> The Captain-General, the governors, and the kings of Transeuphrates altogether, with their troops and ships, the loyal kings of Egypt with their troops and ships, I added them to my previous forces and dispatched them to drive Taharka from Egypt and Cush. (Prism E 10,13-21; First Egyptian Campaign)

---

11. Cf. Nin. A V 26-33 with ABC 14, 21f.; the Egyptian campaign of 671 is not yet mentioned in Nin. A. Sigla for Esarhaddon's inscriptions according to R. Borger, *Die Inschriften Asarhaddons, Königs von Assyrien* (*AfO* Beih., 9; Graz: Weidner, 1956).

12. I. Finkelstein and N.A. Silberman, *The Bible Unearthed* (New York: Free Press, 2001), pp. 243-45; B. Halpern, 'Jerusalem and the Lineages in the Seventh Century BCE: Kingship and the Rise of Individual Moral Liability', in B. Halpern and W. Hobson (eds.), *Law and Ideology in Monarchic Israel* (JSOTSup, 124; Sheffield: JSOT Press, 1991), pp. 11-107.

13. See, for the texts, R. Borger, *Beiträge zum Inschriftenwerk Assurbanipals* (Wiesbaden: Otto Harrassowitz, 1996).

(II 37) In the course of my campaign, (38) Ba'al, King of Tyre; (39) Manasseh, King of Judah; (40) Qausgabr, King of Edom; (41) Muṣur, King of Moab; (42) Ṣil(l)bēl, King of Gaza; (43) Mit(t)inti, King of Ascalon; (44) Ikausu/Achis, King of Ekron; (45) Milk'asapa, King of Byblos; (46) Yakinlû, King of Arwad; (47) Abi-Ba'al, King of Shamshimoron; (48) Amminadab, King of Bet-'Ammon; (49) Aḥi-Milk, King of Ashdod; [(50)-(59) follow the kings of Cyprus] (60) altogether 22 kings from the littoral, (61) from in midst of the ocean and from the continent, (62) my loyal servants, (63f.) brought me their heavy tribute and kissed my feet. (65) The same kings with their troops and ships (66f.) I made at land and at sea beat the track together with my troops. (Prism C, First Egyptian Campaign).

There is no evidence from the Assyrian texts—which does not mean that there is no evidence at all—that the Judaean Negev was affected by the Shamash-shum-ukin troubles and the 'Arab rebellion' 652–648, nor are there any indications that Manasseh ever wavered in his loyalty.[14] The stalemate between Assyria and Egypt from 701 to 670 made Philistia a disputed zone and a possible field of battle—and Jerusalem its flanking position.[15] Between 701 and 670, Assyria had every reason to invest in the growth and fortification of Jerusalem.

The archaeological evidence corroborates the image of Manasseh as presented in the Assyrian annals. Manasseh left Assyrianizing monumental architecture, and his kingdom did not only prosper from its integration into the Assyrian world economy, it actually survived on the basis of this integration.

The Siloam tunnel, usually attributed by 'goodkingitis' to Hezekiah,[16] was without military value; it was supposed to serve as a spectacular piece of waterworks (of Assyrian inspiration) within a royal garden (of Assyrian inspiration) which was, however, never completed.[17] The Assyrianizing character of the

---

14. When Ashurbanipal states that Shamashshumukin made Gutium, Amuru (i.e. the West) and Ethiopia the enemies of Assyria (Prism A III103-105), he does not state more than is obvious: the civil war endangered Assyria's hold on its more distant vassals. It is safe to assume that opposition to Assyria in Amurru was restricted to parties against which action was taken: Palaetyrus, Akko and the Arabs.

15. Cf. E.A. Knauf, '701: Sennacherib at the Berezina', in L.L. Grabbe (ed.), *'Like a Bird in a Cage': The Invasion of Sennacherib in 701 BCE* (JSOTSup, 363; ESHM, 4; London and New York: Sheffield Academic Press, 2003), pp. 141-49.

16. 'Goodkingitis' is an intellectual disability which affects predominantly biblical scholars trying to do history and results in heaping attributions of great achievements on 'good kings' to the detriment of 'bad kings' (a distinction which is also a symptom of the affliction). The character of this mental disease is aptly diagnosed by W.C. Sellar and R.J. Yeatman, *1066 and All That: A Memorable History of England, Comprising all the Parts you can Remember, Including 103 Good Things, 5 Bad Kings and 2 Genuine Dates* (London: Methuen, 1999 [originally published 1930]). For its impact on Iron Age Palestinian history, cf., already, I. Finkelstein, 'The Archaeology of the Days of Manasseh', in M.D. Coogan, J.C. Exum and L.E. Stager (eds.), *Scripture and Other Artefacts: Essays in Bible and Archaeology in Honor of Philipp J. King* (Atlanta: Scholars Press, 1994), pp. 169-87.

17. Cf. D. Ussishkin, 'The Water Systems of Jerusalem during Hezekiah's Reign', in M. Weippert and S. Timm (eds.), *Meilenstein* (Festgabe für Herbert Donner; Ägypten und Altes Testament, 30; Wiesbaden: Otto Harrassowitz, 1995), pp. 289-307; for more Assyrian parallels, cf. D.T. Ariel and A. De Groot, 'The Iron Age Extramural Occupation at the City of David and Additional Observations on the Siloam Channel', in D.T. Ariel (ed.), *City of David. V. Extramural Areas* (Qedem, 40; Jerusalem: Institute of Archaeology, 2000), pp. 155-69 (166).

project suggests a date under Manasseh rather than under any of his predecessors.[18] The re-dating of the Siloam inscription to the time of Manasseh is supported by palaeography: it is inconceivable that cursive letter forms (by themselves an indication of a sharp increase of writing on 'paper' and thus, of a newly flourishing bureaucracy) in a monumental inscription predate their appearance on private seals.[19] The fact that the Siloam inscription was never completed (and other surfaces prepared for inscriptions and/or reliefs left completely blank) indicates that the royal park project was abandoned (the Siloam inscription only gives the *narratio*, probably drawn from the royal annals; the *incipit* which should have named the commissioning king and his god[s] was never added). The abandonment of the project might be due to the *coup d'état* of 640, which brought Manasseh's disloyal opposition into power. It may, however, also indicate economic decline which might have commenced in this part of the empire shortly after 650 as a consequence of the civil war and resulting unrest along the periphery.

Ramat Raḥel VA was an Assyrianizing palace built by Jerusalemite craftsman under the supervision, probably, of Phoenician architects in the first half of the seventh century, preceded by a smaller structure destroyed in 701 (VA), but indicative of a royal estate. Na'aman assumes the palace was built for the Assyrian 'governor' (rather: *qēpu*) stationed in Manassean Judah.[20] The latter assumption is not wholly convincing: the normal position of the Assyrian representative would have been at the royal court wherever the king and his entourage abode. I suggest regarding Ramat Raḥel VA as another *pardes*, or royal park and garden, or 'conspicuous luxury consumption'. It is a pleasant, well-aired place (especially in summer) with a commanding view over Jerusalem as far as the Mount of Olives. The quality of craftsmanship displayed at Ramat Raḥel and lacking, as Na'aman astutely observes, at other Judaean sites of the same period only attests to the widening gap in power, wealth and prestige between the upper class (with the king at its top) and the 'ordinary citizen'. At the end of the same century, the king of Ammon had a similar 'royal estate' on the doorsteps of his capital.[21]

The territorial losses of 701 were compensated for by increased trade activities, notably along the east–west axis. These activities are well attested at Tel Beersheba II,[22] most probably destroyed in the early years of Manasseh.[23]

18. E.A. Knauf, 'Hezekiah or Manasseh? A Reconsideration of the Siloam Tunnel and Inscription', *TA* 28 (2001), pp. 281-87.
19. A.G. Vaughn, 'Palaeographic Dating of Judaean Seals and Its Significance for Biblical Research', *BASOR* 313 (1999), pp. 43-64 (58-59). My thanks to Benjamin Sass for drawing my attention to this reference.
20. N. Na'aman, 'An Assyrian Residence at Ramat Raḥel?', *TA* 28 (2001), pp. 260-80.
21. As attested by the Siran bottle inscription. For Sennacherib's pronounced interest in 'gardening', and thus setting an example for his western vassals as did, later, Louis XIV's Versailles for the petty princes of Germany, cf. E. Frahm, *Einleitung in die Sanherib-Inschriften* (*AfO* Beih., 26, Vienna: Institut für Orientalistik, 1997), pp. 275-78.
22. L. Singer-Avitz, 'Beersheba—A Gateway Community in Southern Arabian Long Distance Trade in the Eighth Century B.C.E.', *TA* 26 (1999), pp. 3-74.
23. E.A. Knauf, 'Who Destroyed Beersheba II?', in Hübner and Knauf (eds.), *Kein Land für sich allein*, pp. 181-95.

Tel Beersheba was replaced by Tel 'Ira VII, four times as large as Tel Beersheba was, and relocated to the northwest (which might indicate from where the threat against Judah's desert outposts originated). East–west trade is also evidenced for 'Ira VII,[24] though it seems that 'profits' were increasingly absorbed by the royal administration resulting in less of them remaining on-site.

It was the loss of the Shephelah, a prime agricultural area, which necessitated some colonization in the Negev.[25] The Judaean mountains are not suited for large-scale production of cereals. They have, however, a certain horticultural potential. In all probability it was from there that the olives came which were processed at Ekron in large quantities. Cash-crops now dominating the Judaean economy must have resulted in latifundialization and the marginalization of independent farmers: the olive oil factories of Ekron clearly did not sign contracts with hundreds of subsistence farmers. Another agricultural product that Judah might have produced in large quantities for export to Philistia might have been cattle.[26] One day, the age structure of the animals consumed in seventh century Ekron should tell that story.

EXCURSUS

Manassean Jerusalem

According to Ariel and De Groot,[27] the size of Jerusalem decreased from Hezekiah to Manasseh. The opposite should be expected—so either the present reconstruction of the reign of Manasseh is wrong, or else the traditional Iron Age chronology for Jerusalem is.

Table 3. *Stratigraphy and Chronology*

Stratum	City of David Chronology	Low Chronology
15—Iron I	12th–11th centuries	11th–10th centuries
14—Iron II	10th century	9th century
13—Iron II	9th century	8th century
12—Iron II	8th century	first half 7th century
11—Iron II	7th century	second half 7th century
10—Iron II	second half 7th century–586	late 7th/early 6th century

A basic problem of the 'City of David' stratigraphy is that it is a 'virtual stratigraphy'. Since there is no profile connecting all areas, and because of the well-known problems of the site, 'strata' are reconstructed on the basis of the material culture assigned to the periods in question. This looks basically like the good old 'locus to stratum' approach which failed so gloriously at Megiddo. It also means that ceramic find dating—once the eighth through sixth centuries corpora from Lachish, Tel Beersheba and Arad are available—can only be done for area strata

24. By Edomite (or imitated Edomite) and Cypro-Phoenician (or imitated Cypro-Phoenician) pottery.

25. I. Beit-Arieh (ed.), *Tel 'Ira* (Tel Aviv: Institute of Archaeology, 1999), pp. 1-3. It is possible that Manasseh was already compensated for the loss of the Shephelah with Benjamin, which formed part of the Judaean cultural and political sphere at the end of the seventh century (cf. R. Kletter, 'Pots and Politics: Material Remains of Late Iron Age Judah in Relation to its Political Borders', *BASOR* 314 [1999], pp. 19-54), and stayed with Yehud throughout the Neo-Babylonian and Persian periods.

26. Possibly indicated by deforestation in the vicinity of Tel 'Ira when the agricultural activities of the seventh century set in, cf. A. Horowitz, 'Pollen Analysis', in Beith-Arieh (ed.), *Tel 'Ira*, p. 114.

27. Ariel and De Groot, 'The Iron Age Extramural Occupation' (note well that this occupation cannot be called 'extramural' anymore, cf. n. 28).

or even loci with abundant pottery. According to the Low Chronology, the abandonment of the Eastern Suburb[28] should be dated to c. 650 or later and would indicate the emerging and economic troubles of the late seventh century. There is a military argument in favour of this revision: the lower city wall, dominated by the slopes of Silwan would have been completely useless against Assyrian archery[29]—so its construction in '701' would have been a waste of resources. But it might have given the inhabitants of the eastern suburb a sense of protection (nurturing a sense of protection among his subjects is one of the most imperative tasks of an oriental king), and it would actually have protected them against bandits, Bedouins and raids by Judah's Transjordanian neighbours. The lower city wall was probably built by Manasseh and abandoned in the second half of the seventh century. That Jerusalem played a role in the east–west trade from the seventh century onwards is attested by a group of ancient North Arabian or Early Greek pottery incisions from Stratum 10 (or the surface).[30]

For the reconstruction of Judah's religion in the days of Manasseh, sufficient iconographic evidence is available. Family religion favoured the Goddess, attested by hundreds of 'pillar figurines' (Judaeans, at least Judaean women, continued their preference for the Goddess well into the reign of Josiah).[31] The Assyrian 'Lord of the West', Sin of Harran, together with other astral powers, is represented on Judaean seals from the seventh century to the same extent as everywhere else in contemporary Transeuphratesia.[32] Yhwh was not yet regarded as creator of heaven and earth, because an ostracon from seventh-century Jerusalem mentions Elqone'arṣ, according to the orthography a name and not an apposition.[33] The temple of Arad was probably constructed under Uzziah or Hezekiah (Stratum X) and continued to be used in the early seventh century (Stratum IX); it was dismantled at the end of Stratum IX, or in the course of founding Stratum VIII (Manasseh).[34]

---

28. I cannot see that the evidence presented in *City of David* V justifies the assumption that this suburb originated prior to the eighth century.

29. The problem is also stated by Ariel and De Groot, 'The Iron Age Extramural Occupation', p. 161. Cf., for the lower city wall now, R. Reich and E. Shukron, 'The Excavations at the Gihon Spring and Warren's Shaft System in the City of David', in H. Geva (ed.), *Ancient Jerusalem Revealed* (Jerusalem: Israel Exploration Society, exp. edn, 2000), pp. 327-39 (338). My thanks to G. Barkay for a tour of the water system in the course of which I had the privilege to stand on the foundations of Manasseh's city wall and raise my eyes to the slope of Silwan.

30. M. Höfner, 'Remarks on Potsherds with Incised South Arabian Letters', in D.T. Ariel (ed.), *City of David*. VI. *Inscriptions* (Qedem, 41; Jerusalem: Institute of Archaeology, 2000), pp. 26-28; B. Sass, 'Arabs and Greeks in Late First Temple Jerusalem', *PEQ* 122 (1990), pp. 59-61.

31. *GGG* §§ 190-95; Kletter, 'Pots and Polities'.

32. *GGG* fig. 297a; 305c; 306a and b; 316, 317 a and b; 319; T. Staubli, 'Sin von Harran und seine Verbreitung im Westen', in *idem* (ed.), *Werbung für die Götter* (Freiburg: Universitätsverlag, 2003), pp. 65-89.

33. For the same reason, the reconstruction *ziqnē hā'arṣ* is impossible; *pace* J. Renz and W. Röllig, *Handbuch der althebräischen Epigraphik* (3 vols.; Darmstadt: Wissenschaftliche Buchgesellschaft, 1995), I, pp. 197-98 (Jer[8].30); their dating (late eighth century) is probably too high, based on the pseudo-historical traditional date for the Siloam inscription. As opposed to their edition, there is neither a word-divider (agreed) nor a spatium between the *nun* and the *aleph* (controversial), cf. Renz and Röllig, *Handbuch*, III, Taf. XIX.2.

34. The absolute dates are mine. For the stratigraphy, see Z. Herzog, 'The Date of the Temple at Arad: Reassessment of the Stratigraphy and the Implications for the History of Religion in Judah', in

Manasseh was a loyal vassal of the Assyrian king. Under his leadership, the Kingdom of Judah did not only survive its severe losses of 701, it more than compensated for them and prospered. As a result, social differences within Judah became more pronounced. Politically, economically and culturally, Judah was well integrated into the Assyrian world. If a good king is a king who brings as much peace, security and prosperity to his people as his times allow, than Manasseh was one of the two best kings Judah ever had (the other one was Herod the Great). At the end of his reign, Judah might already have been affected by the commencing decline of the Assyrian world.

3. *Biblical Literature from the Days of Manasseh?*

Before we have a look at the representation of Manasseh in biblical literature, let me indulge in some speculations concerning biblical literature possibly deriving from the reign of Manasseh. Since David, Solomon, Hezekiah and Josiah have lots of such literature attributed to them (mostly misattributions due to more recent research), it would be highly unfair to leave Manasseh without any. Historical readings—or readings informed by historical knowledge—of biblical literature never provide hard evidence, but the game is too much fun not to be played.

Deuteronomy 32.8-9* (following the LXX and Qumran) clearly predates Yhwh's rise to supreme power in heaven which presumably took place under Josiah.[35] It reads: 'When Elyon allotted the peoples in fief (נחל causative[36]) | when he distributed the earthlings (בני אדם) || he fixed the territories of the hosts (עמים[37]) | according to the number of the sons of El. || Thus it came to be that Yhwh's share is his levy | Jacob the estate of his fief.' This fine piece of polytheistic theology (= polytheology?) is preserved in the Bible because after Josiah, the 'Supreme Being' was identified with Yhwh. This is, however, hardly the

---

A. Mazar (ed.), *Studies in the Archaeology of the Iron Age in Israel and Jordan* (JSOTSup, 331; Sheffield: Sheffield Academic Press, 2001), pp. 156-78. Herzog attributes Arad IX and thus, the dismantling of the altar, to the reign of Hezekiah. A detailed analysis of the pottery corpora of Arad X–VIII in comparison with Tel Beersheba II, Lachish III and Tel 'Ira VII will decide the question, one day. See further below, Appendix III.

35. M.Weippert, 'Synkretismus und Monotheismus. Religionsinterne Konfliktbewältigung im Alten Israel', in J. Assmann and D. Harth (eds.), *Kultur und Konflikt* (Edition Suhrkamp, NF, 612; Frankfurt: Suhrkamp, 1990), pp. 146-47. Regardless of the date of the final composition of Deut. 32.1-43, the fragment v. 8-9 must have been conceived prior to Josiah, under whom Yhwh, in all probability, became the 'supreme god'; Ps. 82 and L.K. Handy, 'A Realignment in Heaven: An Investigation into the Ideology of the Josianic Reform' (PhD dissertation, University of Chicago, 1987), pp. 333-56 (it is, however, an exaggeration to call the supreme deity of this psalm 'a single god'); on the other hand, 'Jacob' for 'Israel' in a Jerusalemite tradition indicates a date after Hezekiah; cf. E.A. Knauf, 'Stämme Israels', in E. Fahlbusch (ed.), *Evangelisches Kirchen-Lexikon* (5 vols.; Göttingen: Vandenhoeck & Ruprecht, 3rd edn, 1986–97), IV, pp. 479-83.

36. Cf. Ugaritic *nḥlt* ('fief'), Sabaic *nḥl* ('grant lease', causative 'hire out').

37. For עם ('levy', militia'), see Th.Willi, 'Kirche als Gottesvolk? Überlegungen zu einem Verständnis von Kirche im Kontext alttestamentlich-frühjüdischer Konzeptionen von Gottesvolk, Gebot und Gottesreich', *TZ* 49 (1993), pp. 289-310 (291-92).

original meaning, because according to v. 9, as a son of El (= 'Elyon), Yhwh would always have been his own father or son. This notion is much too Christian for the seventh century BCE. Even if this theology was already formulated under Hezekiah (the *terminus a quo*), it adopted a new meaning under Manasseh, wholly in accordance with Assyrian theology. The Assyrians did not demand their vassals to join the cult of Ashur (what these joined instead, and entirely of their own free will was, according to overwhelming iconographic evidence, the veneration of Sin of Harran, regarded by everybody—including the Assyrians—as the 'Lord of the West'); but they attributed to the local deities the status of 'sons (or daughters) of Ashur'.[38] Deuteronomy 32.8 does not mention the proper name of the 'supreme god'—but nobody in his or her right mind in Manassean Judah could or would have doubted that the epithet refers to Ashur (the opposite would have amounted to high treason).

If Deuteronomy 32.8-9* preserves the official Judaean theology of Manasseh's court, Isaiah 6–8* formulates the opposite: the voice of the opposition (every society always has its mavericks who are not, or not completely, sensible in the common way). That there was a Judaean opposition to Manasseh and his politics can be deduced from several circumstantial facts: given the speed and the degree of rapid social and economic change in the first half of the seventh century, it would be a surprise indeed if no one had raised his or her voice against it; given that the opposition came to power in 640 (and, to judge from its program or, at least, from the results of its politics, did the exact opposite of what Manasseh would have done), it is reasonable to assume that it crystallized some time before. The first edition of the book of Isaiah makes use of a pro-Assyrian collection of prophetic utterances (at least one of them by a female prophet) from the year 734, most probably used by Manasseh's government to justify its own pro-Assyrian politics. With the introduction (Isa. 6.1-10) to the first edition of (the Book of) Isaiah, this intention is turned around: what the prophet(s) of 734 said was intended to be misunderstood by the 'people of unclean lips', that is, the majority. In addition, it is now Yhwh who sits on the throne, that is, who assumes the position of the supreme god.[39]

Judaean participation in, at least, Ashurbanipal's first campaign into Egypt might well be reflected in Isa. 18.1-6; 19.1-17, although Persian campaigns of the fourth century (with the support of Judaean mercenaries) cannot be ruled out as the referent.[40] Cush (18.1-6) points, however, specifically to the seventh century.

38. Cf. B.N. Porter, 'What the Assyrians Thought the Babylonians Thought about the Relative Status of Nabû and Marduk in the Late Assyrian Period', in Parpola and Whiting (eds.), *Assyria 1995*, pp. 253-60 (258), and, in the same volume, G. Frame, 'The God Aššur in Babylonia', pp. 55-64 (63-64 n. 50).

39. Cf. E.A. Knauf, 'Vom Prophetinnenwort zum Prophetenbuch: Jesaja 8,3f im Kontext von Jesaja 6,1-8,16', *lectio difficilior. European Electronic Journal for Feminist Exegesis* 2/2000 <www.lectio.unibe.ch>, partially following U. Becker, *Jesaja—von der Botschaft zum Buch* (FRLANT, 178; Göttingen: Vandenhoeck & Ruprecht, 1997). For the text, see below, Appendix I.

40. J. Blenkinsopp, *Isaiah 1–39* (AB, 19; New York: Doubleday, 2000), p. 314; O. Kaiser, *Der Prophet Jesaja Kapitel 13–39* (ATD, 18; Göttingen: Vandenhoeck & Ruprecht, 1976), pp. 75-97.

As far as the redactional history of Isaiah is concerned, the Egyptian material pre-dating 586 was probably incorporated by the 'Hezekiah edition' from the times of Zedekiah.[41]

4. *Manasseh in Biblical Literature*

The statements contained in the biblical narratives will be broken down according to the following classification: true (and corroborated by contemporary documents)—most probably true (but not corroborated by documentary evidence)—not completely untrue (but badly in need of critical interpretation in the light of the documents)—impossible to evaluate—utter ideological nonsense.

(a) *Kings*
The following statement is undoubtedly true:
- Manasseh was the successor of Hezekiah (2 Kgs 20.21).

The following statements are most probably true:
- He was also the son of Hezekiah (2 Kgs 20.21).
- He was 12 years old at the beginning of his reign (21.1)—which would imply that the government during the early years of the king, and his 'higher education', were in the hands of high-ranking officials which, according to the circumstances immediately after 701, could only have belonged to the pro-Assyrian faction among Jerusalem's politicians.
- He ruled for 55 years, and in Jerusalem (21.1).
- His mother was called Hephzibah (21.1).
- He was buried in his royal garden (21.18).
- He was succeeded by Amon, who was also his son (21.18).
- His son followed the pro-Assyrian politics (and the trend towards acculturation to Assyria) of his father (21.20-22).

The following statements might not be completely untrue:
- He made an Asherah (21.3).
- He venerated the Host of Heaven (21.3).
- He built altars for the Host of Heaven in the Temple (21.5; 23.12).
- He used the contemporary means of divination (21.6).
- He spilt some, not necessarily streams of not necessarily innocent blood (21.16).
- In brief, he 'seduced' Judah (21.9, 11, 16), that is, he promoted or allowed religious attitudes regarded as heretical by the Deuteronomists of the sixth and the following centuries.

---

41. C. Hardmeier, *Prophetie im Streit vor dem Untergang* (BZAW, 187; Berlin: W. de Gruyter, 1990); Becker, *Jesaja*, pp. 47-59, 200-12. The Hezekiah redaction also made use of a collection of prophecies concerning '701' (Isa. 28–31*) which must have been transmitted independently of the collection '734' (Isa. 7-8*) and the early edition(s) of the book (Isa. 6–8*; 9*).

Both the veneration of the Goddess and of the astral deities like Sin of Harran are iconographically well attested for seventh-century Judah. How much need there was for 'royal seduction' to do so, we cannot know. The deuteronomistic authors probably attributed as much royal interference in cultic affairs to Manasseh as Josiah practiced, or as they thought or wished that Josiah would have practiced. Most probably, the king gave nothing more than a 'bad example'. It is, however, not inconceivable that the state now increasingly interfered in religious matters, also on the local level, outside Jerusalem (see further *infra*, Appendix III). That his politics encountered opposition is most likely; that he dealt with his most outspoken opponents in the way deemed appropriate in his period can be surmised. The 'innocence' of his victims is a moot question: your terrorist is my resistance fighter, and vice versa. From a legitimistic (and royalist) point of view, the innocence of Manasseh's victims can well be doubted.

The following statements cannot possibly be evaluated:
- He sacrificed (or cremated?) one of his sons (21.6). Cremation of an infant dead of natural causes might have been interpreted by Manasseh's detractors as 'child sacrifice'. On the other hand, child sacrifice was one of the standard accusations brought forward by antique (not just Judaean) 'anti-Canaanism'. The cliché might as well be added to Manasseh's sins without any *fundamentum in re*.
- Manasseh restored the high-places destroyed by Hezekiah (21.3)—but did Hezekiah destroy any?[42]
- He built altars for Baal (21.3)—but the divine name or epithet 'Baal' does not figure prominently in the documentation for the seventh century, if at all; it became a *passe-partout* for any 'illegitimate' male deity in the deuteronomistic tradition. So it remains unclear which deity is meant, if any specific deity is meant at all.

The following statements are utter ideological nonsense:
- Manasseh did not keep the Torah of Moses (21.2-8, esp. v. 8)—well, he couldn't, it wasn't written and published yet.
- Jerusalem was destroyed in 586 because of Manasseh's sins (21.10-16; 23.26-27; 24.3-4, Jer. 15.4). This is ridiculous: had all of Manasseh's successors kept to his politics, Jerusalem would most certainly not have been destroyed (and there would be no Bible today). The 'bad king' Manasseh is made the scapegoat for the catastrophe brought about by the 'good king' Josiah and his ideological heirs.

(b) *Chronicles*
2 Chronicles 33.1-10 is a rewrite of 2 Kgs 21.1-9 (now more than one son 'goes through the fire'). But then Manasseh was deported by an Assyrian army to Babylonia(!), repented, returned, made sure that no other god than Yhwh was adored on the high-places, and built a wall 'west of the Gihon' to include the Ophel (33.14).

---

42. For the evidence from Tel Beersheba, cf. Knauf, 'Who Destroyed?', p. 183 n. 7; on Arad, above with n. 34.

Although Assyrian armies had plenty of opportunity to pick up Manasseh on their way to Egypt, it is impossibly to see why, in the best of Assyria's interest, they should have done so. At least in 668, the opposite was the case: Manasseh's troops joined the Assyrians invading Egypt. Turning a 'bad king' into a 'good king', the Chroniclers prove themselves the better historians (in comparison to the Deuteronomists). The historical reasoning behind the project is impeccable: a king who ruled for 55 years cannot have been completely bad. The Chronicler, as opposed to many of his colleagues, contemporary as well as modern, evidently knew how to read numbers. In exculpating Manasseh from the burden to have caused the fall of Jerusalem, and in attributing this mischief to the combined deeds and misdeeds of Judah's kings (2 Chron. 36.15-16) he proves himself again a better historian than the compilers of Samuel–Kings.

The statement on Manasseh's building activities in the Kidron Valley (2 Chron. 33.14) is, surprisingly, true according to recent archaeological evidence.[43] So the Chronicler possibly had one piece of source material (or local tradition?) which he used in reshaping Manasseh from a 'bad king' to a 'bad king turned good king'. Whoever argues that these building activities are misattributed to Manasseh, and should be attributed to Hezekiah, argues against all historical and critical logic (achievements attributed to 'good kings' are not necessarily theirs, achievements attributed to 'minor figures' probably are).

(c) *Solomon*

The Solomon of 1 Kings 1–11 is a composite figure, combining features derived from the activities of various Israelite and Judaean kings:[44] Ahab ruled from Dan to Beersheba with every Israelite or Judaean sitting contently under his vine and his fig tree (1 Kgs 5.5). Athaliah built the palace of Jerusalem (1 Kgs 3.1; 9.15).[45] Jehoshaphat ventured into Phoenician–Arabian trade (1 Kgs 9.26-28; 22.49-50). Jeroboam II fortified Hazor, Gezer and Megiddo (1 Kgs 9.15). Manasshe sent wood-cutters into Lebanon (1 Kgs 5.13-14), and built the wall around the Ophel (1 Kgs 3.1; 9.15).

It is impossible to write a biography of King Manasseh. The king's name is a *chiffre* for the Judaean *classe politique* of the first half of the seventh century. With every newly found seal impression, stratum or inscription from this period, it becomes increasingly possible to write a history of Judah in the days of Manasseh.

43. See above, with n. 28.
44. Cf. for the differences between the biblical Solomon and the Judaean king of the tenth century answering to the same name, preliminarily E.A. Knauf, 'King Solomon's Copper Supply', in E. Lipiński (ed.), *Phoenicia and the Bible* (Studia Phoenicia, 11; Leuven: Peters), 1991), pp. 167-86; *idem*, 'Le roi est mort, vive le roi! A Biblical Argument for the Historicity of Solomon', in L.K. Handy (ed.), *The Age of Solomon: Scholarship at the Turn of the Millennium* (SHCANE, 11; Leiden: E.J. Brill, 1997), pp. 81-95; *idem*, 'Solomon at Megiddo?', in J.A. Dearman and M.P. Graham (eds.), *The Land that I Will Show You: Essays on the History and Archaeology of the Ancient Near East in Honour of J. Maxwell Miller* (JSOTSup, 343; Sheffield: Sheffield Academic Press, 2001), pp. 119-34.
45. Cf. I. Finkelstein, 'The Rise of Jerusalem and Judah: The Missing Link', *Levant* 32 (2001), pp. 105-15.

An evaluation of the rule of Manasseh (and his leading administrators) can only be preliminary. Clearly he brought survival to most, and prosperity to some Judaeans. Could he have mitigated the social cleavages opening up in Judaean society which later provided the Deuteronomists and their disastrous politics with a power base? The question might already over-estimate the relative importance of internal politics on the general development; the loss of prestige of the Manassean elite due to the breakdown of Assyrian rule in southern Syria after 640 might have been more decisive, and the true party names might easily have been 'Assyrianists' vs. 'Egyptianists' rather than 'Internationalists' vs. 'Nationalists'. It is remarkable, though, that the idea of 'social justice' by redistribution seems to originate only in societies beyond the level of frequent exposure to subsistence crises.[46] The traditional behaviour in the face of that problem was a *tirage* among the population in times of scarcity: the first class to be fed was the productive adults; the second class, the children (the adults' social insurance); the last class, the post-productive adults.[47] If ideas of 'social justice' are imported by a subsistence–insecure society, and groups of 'exploiters' (who, incidentally, are always also the distributors of basic goods) are eliminated, immediate famine is the result.[48] Ironically, by leading Judah out of a subsistence economy with ever-looming crisis, the Manassean elites nourished the revolutionaries, both physically and mentally, who were to oust them from power in 640.

Appendix I

The First Edition of the 'Book of Isaiah' from the Times of Manasseh

In what follows, the source used by the editor/author, the collection of various prophecies concerning '734', is given in italics. It is assumed that early Judaean prophetic literature looked like Assyrian prophetic literature: in a first redactional stage, reports of individual prophetic utterances to the court; in a second redactional stage, collections of prophecies concerning a decisive (and disputed) event to legitimize the present royal family and/or its politics.[49]

---

46. Western and central Europe's last subsistence crisis dates back to 1817 and is thoroughly forgotten. Globally and according to the *longue durée*, nineteenth- and twentieth-century Europe is a very rare exception rather than the rule in world history.

47. Still to be observed in rural Africa in the 1950s. Today, the international aid industry becomes sooner or later active in such cases, and reduces the local level of productivity further. Under circumstances like these, which had also been the rule for Israel and Judah well into the eighth century, the fifth commandment really means: 'Feed your retirees well in order to be fed in turn by your offspring—if you can afford it without doing damage to your offspring and yourself'.

48. As it was observed in Ethiopia immediately after the revolution in the 1970s, and can be observed in southern Africa in the first decade of the twenty-first century.

49. Cf. S. Parpola, *Assyrian Prophecies* (SAA, 9; Helsinki: Helsinki University Press, 1997), pp. XLVIII-LII; M. Nissinen, *References to Prophecy in Neo-Assyrian Sources* (SAAS, 7; Helsinki: The Neo-Assyrian Text Corpus Project, 1998), p. 164.

Isa. 2.1 The word/thing that Isaiah son of Amoz saw concerning Judah and Jerusalem,
6.1a in the year that King Uzziah died.
6.1b I saw the Lord sitting on a throne, high and lofty;
6.1c and the hem of his robe filled the temple.
6.2a Seraphs were in attendance above him;[50]
6.2b each had six wings:[51]
6.2c with two they covered their faces,
6.2d and with two they covered their feet,
6.2e and with two they flew.
6.3a And after[52] one called to another
6.3b and said:
6.3c 'Holy, holy, holy is the LORD[53] of hosts;
6.3d the whole earth is full of his glory'
6.4a the pivots on the thresholds shook at the voices of those who had called,
6.4b and the house filled with smoke.[54]
6.5a And I said:
6.5b 'Woe is me!
6.5c I am lost,
6.5d for I am a man of unclean lips,
6.5d and I live among a people of unclean lips;[55]
6.5e yet my eyes have seen the King, the LORD of hosts!'
6.6a Then one of the seraphs flew to me,
6.6b holding a live coal from the altar.[56]
6.7a The seraph touched my mouth with it
6.7b and said:
6.7c 'Now that this has touched your lips,
6.7d your guilt has departed
6.7e and your sin is blotted out'.
6.8a Then I heard the voice of the LORD saying,
6.8b 'Whom shall I send,
6.8c and who will go for us?'
6.8d And I said,
6.8e 'Me here, send me!'
6.9a And he said,
6.9b 'Go say to this people:
6.9c "Keep listening,

50. Most probably, there was a row of seraphim adorning the frieze of the *debir*, resulting from Uzziah's refurbishing of the temple (in the Egyptian style of the time) after the earthquake damage mentioned in Amos 9.1; cf. E.A. Knauf, 'Review of W. Zwickel, *Der salomonische Tempel* (Kulturgeschichte der antiken Welt, Bd. 83; Mainz, 1999)', *Theologische Literaturzeitung* 126 (2001), pp. 160-61.
51. For four-winged seraphs in the 'official' iconography of Judah, cf. *GGG* fig. 274b-d; for a good photograph of a seraph-seal impression, cf. Ariel (ed.), *City of David*, VI, p. 83 Plate 4. The Yhwh of the opposition has the mightier seraphs than the Yhwh of the king!
52. The *qatal*-x prepares for the *wayiqtol* of 6.4a
53. The *'adonay* of 6.1b, characterized as the supreme god, is now identified by his name—which is neither El nor Ashur, as most of the editor's contemporaneans would have expected.
54. A theophany of the god within his home—even where he is present, he needs to appear.
55. The editor characterizes the silent majority of his days; it is highly doubtful whether an active prophet of the eighth century would have expressed this kind of self-esteem.
56. 'That had been taken with a pair of tongs' (6.6c) is a gloss by someone who had forgotten that seraphs were fiery beings, originally (he probably imagined them anthropomorphically).

6.9d but do not comprehend;
6.9e keep looking,
6.9f but do not understand".
6.10a Make the mind of this people dull,[57]
6.10b and stop their ears,
6.10c and shut their eyes,
6.10d so that they may not look with their eyes,
6.10e and listen with their ears,
6.10f and comprehend with their minds,
6.10g and might turn
6.10h and be healed.'

7.1a In the days of Ahaz son of Jotham son of Uzziah, king of Judah,
7.1b King Rezin of Aram and King Pekah son of Remaliah of Israel went up to attack Jerusalem,
7.1c but could not mount an attack against it.
7.2a When the house of David heard
7.2b that Aram had allied itself with Ephraim,
7.2c the heart of Ahaz and the heart of his people shook as the trees of the forest shake before the wind.
7.3a Then the LORD said…[58]
7.4d *Do not fear,*
7.4e *and do not let your heart be faint because of these two smouldering stumps of fire-brands,…*[59]
7.5 *Because Aram—Ephraim and the son of Remaliah—has plotted evil against you, saying,*
7.6a *Let us go up against Judah*
7.6b *and cut off Jerusalem*
7.6c *and conquer it for ourselves*
7.6d *and make the son of Tabeel king in it;*
7.7a *therefore thus says the LORD God:*
7.7b *It shall not stand,*
7.7c *and it shall not come to pass.*

[A second oracle]
7.14b *{É} Look, the young woman is with child*
7.14c *and shall bear a son,*
7.14d *and shall name him Immanuel.*
7.15 *He shall eat curds and honey*[60] *by the time he knows how to refuse the evil and choose the good.*
7.16a *For before the child knows how to refuse the evil and choose the good,*
7.16b *the land before whose two kings you are in dread will be deserted.*

8.1a Then the LORD said to me,
8.1b Take a large tablet

57. Such an intention on the part of a god has long irritated commentators rightly. The editor wants to say—in all modesty, of course—that he (and his comrades) were the first to understand the 'true' intention of the commonly known (at least in their circles) sayings of '734'.

58. The location of the following dialogue is drawn from the Rabshakeh-encounter and thus belongs to the last pre-exilic redaction of the book.

59. 'Because of the fierce anger of Rezin and Aram and the son of Remaliah' is another gloss—the Hebrew is as bad as the logic of the phrase.

60. That is, the standard of living of the king's entourage will not decrease within the next three years; don't worry—be happy.

8.1c and write on it in common characters,
8.1d 'Belonging to Maher-shalal-hash-baz',
8.2a and have it attested for me by reliable witnesses, the priest Uriah and Zechariah son of Jeberechiah.[61]
8.3a And I went to the prophetess,
8.3b and she conceived
8.3c and bore a son.
8.3d *Then the* LORD *said to me,*
8.3e *Name him Maher-shalal-hash-baz;*
8.4a *for before the child knows how to call 'My father' or 'My mother',*
8.4b *the wealth of Damascus and the spoil of Samaria will be carried away by the king of Assyria.*[62]

8.11a For the LORD spoke thus to me while his hand was strong upon me,
8.11b and warned me not to walk in the way of this people,[63] saying:
8.12a Do not call conspiracy all
8.12b that this people calls conspiracy,
8.12c and do not fear what it fears,[64]
8.12d or be in dread.
8.13a But the LORD of hosts, him you shall regard as holy;
8.13b let him be your fear,
8.13c and let him be your dread.
8.14   He will become a sanctuary, a stone one strikes against; for both houses of Israel he will become a rock one stumbles over—a trap and a snare for the inhabitants of Jerusalem.
8.15a And many among them shall stumble;
8.15b they shall fall
8.15c and be broken;
8.15d they shall be snared
8.15e and taken.

8.16a Bind up the testimony,
8.16b seal the teaching among my disciples.[65]

Appendix II

A Mid-Seventh-Century Reading of Psalm 48

What do we do whenever we read a text historically? In the worst case, we ask whether the story 'actually happened' as told—a very naive and stupid question, because stories never happened or happen—they are just told and retold. The

---

61. According to 2 Kgs 16.10-16, Uriah was a Jerusalemite priest who refurbished the altar according to the wishes of Ahaz—surely not a person of high esteem among the Deuteronomists. Zechariah might have been Ahaz' father-in-law (2 Kgs 18.2). The names might identify two families from among Manasseh's disloyal opposition who sponsored the first edition of Isaiah—and protected its editor.
62. As in 7.14, the mother should have given the name. The two oracles share the same content: the Israelite–Aramaean threat will be over before three years have passed, and Ashur will be victorious.
63. The people of 'unclean lips', 6.5d.
64. Because they see and hear and can't comprehend, remember?
65. The last paragraph and the colophon of the first edition of Isaiah leaves little doubt that this is conspirative literature.

more sophisticated ask whether there is an 'historical core' to the story—which can hardly ever be isolated from the story itself (much too many possibly cores, for example), especially not with the instruments of the literary critic (because historical and literary studies are different fields of research; you don't buy your donuts from a pharmacy, either). The core of the story might be identified from the known history of the time, and then—and here the literary critic comes in— you show how the core could have been narratively developed into the story as it is. Or you ask how this or that feature from the story, if taken as a fact, combines with the other known facts from the period and region in question. Or you try to date the story—the story as written or even the story told behind the story written[66]—by isolating all features from it which indicate its date and then look for a time which matches them (there can easily be more than one, provided you know enough history).

Here I will try another approach. How would a pro-Assyrian (pro-Manasseh) citizen of Jerusalem have read (or heard) Psalm 48 around 650 BCE? How would he have filled the 'gaps' in the literary text[67]? It is presupposed that parts of Psalm 48 existed c. 650 BCE. This is indeed likely, but does not apply to 48.10-12 (an addition within the framework of the Bene Korah collection) and 48.15b (in my opinion, the redactional catchline for Ps. 49 to set in).[68]

Our supposed reader is well-versed in history, mythology and geography— otherwise, he/she wouldn't be able to understand a thing. The holy mountain of Yhwh, Zion, is in Yhwh's city (v. 2)—very much the same way as Ashur's holy mountain was in the city of Ashur. Now he/she might ask whose holy mountain is the 'joy of all the earth' (v. 3a)—Yhwh's, Ashur's, or both?—or she/he might settle for the reading '(Jerusalem) is the joy of all the land (of Judah)'. People in the countryside might have objected to such a reading, but our supposed reader is a Jerusalemite, and would certainly agree. He/she knows that Jerusalem is not situated 'in the far north' (NRSV), so she/he will read 'remote Zaphon', the Canaanite Mount Olympus; which, on the other hand, is not a—and therefore, nobody's—city. So the character (and heritage) of Zaphon is claimed for the Zion, which is impertinent, but our Jerusalemite would agree again: did his/her century not see the demise of Phoenicia, at least its exclusion from the Syro-Palestinian markets? Did Jerusalem not turn, during the last decades and well within human memory, from a miserable agglomeration of huts into a splendid

---

66. One can do even that; cf. E.A. Knauf, 'Towards an Archaeology of the Hexateuch', in K. Schmid et al. (eds.), *Abschied vom Jahwisten* (BZAW, 315; Berlin: W. de Gruyter, 2002), pp. 275-94; idem, 'The Queens' Story: Bathshebah, Maacah and Athaliah and the "Historia" of Early Kings', *lectio difficilior. European Electronic Journal for Feminist Exegesis* 2/2000 <www.lectio.unibe.ch>.

67. How a prominent contemporary theologian fills them is attested by, for example, E. Zenger in F.-L. Hossfeld and E. Zenger, *Die Psalmen* (Die neue Echter Bibel. Altes Testament, 29; Würzburg: Echter Verlag, 1993), pp. 294-99 (I take this commentary as an example, because it is excellent). Zenger reads Ps. 48 monotheistically, with a missionary aim and a deep anti-Assyrian attitude. This reading is perfect on the level of the final context—be it Psalms or the Tanakh. But it fills in the 'gaps' in a way not necessitated by the text itself, as the 'historical' reading will show.

68. Cf. Zenger (in Hossfeld and Zenger, *Die Psalmen*) for details and arguments.

city, rivalling Sidon and Tyre? And who is the 'Great King' (presupposing our reader also knows a bit of Aramaic or even Assyrian, because in Hebrew, *melek rab* would mean 'plenty king',[69] but of course it stands for Akkadian *sharru rabbu*)? Readers of the Bible, of course, will never think in this connection of anyone else but Yhwh. In the seventh century, however, there was no Bible, and the easiest reading is the obvious: the Akkadian/Aramaic *calque* refers to the Assyrian king. So the present splendour of Jerusalem, outsplendouring for once the cities of the coast, is due to the double patronage of the city by (a) Yhwh and (b) the Assyrian Great King.

As we have seen, the claim of v. 3a is not necessarily universal. With Zaphon, Yhwh claims the heritage of Baal/Hadad, not yet/yet not(?) the role of El: the Yhwh of Psalm 48* leaves room for other gods beside himself, among them, for example, Ashur.

The historical narrative of vv. 5-8 would have been quite transparent to our reader. He/she would not have thought of a mythic *völkersturm* (because, in all likelihood, she/he would never have heard of such a thing), nor of 701, because then, Judaeans were dealing with a single king who never came up to the city in person, and anyway, are we loyal pro-Assyrian Judaean citizens of 650 BCE really concerned about that slight misunderstanding in our long-established relation with Ashur (of mutual benefit) that occurred at the end of Hezekiah's reign? But he/she might have thought of the events of 734 (a memory also kept alive by royal Judaean propaganda), when two kings—Aram and Israel—came to Jerusalem, saw, and went back home again. Psalm 48.5-7 is probably not a bad narrative of what really happened in 734. In this context, the enigmatic v. 8 starts to make sense; 'like an east wind used to shatter the Tarshish ships' is nonsense: an east wind is exactly what the Phoenician sailors needed to get to Tarshish.[70] The 'east wind' shattering the proud Phoenicians was the Assyrian king, whether they were behind the Israelite–Aramean coalition of 734 or not. Due to him, Mt Zion could claim the heritage of Zaphon...

Now the transition between the historical narrative of vv. 5-8 and the prosperity of Jerusalem as present proof of Yhwh's might is also clear: what started in 734, Judaean loyalty to Assyria, has paid well. Jerusalem is filled with the city-residencies (ארמנות—not royal palaces nor 'citadels', but buildings of substance) of the rich, and Manasseh just built new walls around it... It is safe to assume that the intended reader of Psalm 48* did not come from the slums that—most probably—also existed in seventh-century Jerusalem.

The intended reader of Psalm 48 is a pro-Assyrian member of the Judaean upper-class with a residency in Manassean Jerusalem. It stands to reason that the text was produced by the royal department of public information, and exactly for that audience.

---

69. In the Isaiah legends Isa. 36–39, the title is translated: 'the Great King (*melek gadol*), the King of Ashur'. Is this another indication that the Isaiah legends postdate the time of Manasseh?

70. I doubt that events from the ninth century as mentioned in 1 Kgs 22.48 were of such an impact on the public mind as to become proverbial.

Appendix III

The Centralization of Cults in Judah, and the 'Law of Cultic Centralization', Deuteronomy 12

Archaeological evidence for the cancellation of local cults comes from Beersheba and Arad. An altar used in Beersheba IV (or III) was dismantled, with re-use of its stones, in Beersheba III or II.[71] A temple was constructed in Arad X, and intentionally (and carefully) razed at the end of Arad IX.[72] Z. Herzog, with many others,[73] links this evidence to Hezekiah's reform,[74] which biblical scholars tend to regard as fictitious, and with good reasons.[75] The reverend care with which the altars and stelae were buried at Arad—and not vandalized, as one would expect from reading 2 Kgs 18.4; 2 Chron. 31.1—contradicts rather than confirms the biblical account.

'715', Herzog's date for the end of Arad IX, derived from the Bible, does not hold water; the probable dates for Arad X and IX have to be calculated on the basis of the archaeological evidence. L. Singer-Avitz[76] has firmly established the following relative chronology:

Table 4. *Comparative Stratigraphy of Southern Judaean Sites according to Singer-Avitz*

Period	Arad	Beersheba	Tel 'Ira	Lachish
Iron IIB	X	III	VII	III
	IX	III	VII	III
	VIII	II	VII	III
Iron IIC	VII	—	VI	II
	VI	—	VI	II

71. Knauf, 'Who Destroyed', p. 182 n. 7.

72. Z. Herzog, 'The Fortress Mound at Tel Arad: An Interim Report', *TA* 29 (2002), pp. 3-109 (32-40).

73. R. Albertz, 'Jahwe allein! Israels Weg zum Monotheismus und dessen theologische Bedeutung', in *idem* (ed.), *Geschichte und Theologie. Studien zur Exegese des Alten Testaments und zur Religionsgeschichte Israels* (BZAW, 326; Berlin: W. de Gruyter, 2003), pp. 359-82 (366 n. 31), who is dependent on outdated archaeological information (cancellation of the Beersheba and Arad cults in the eighth or seventh centuries), jumps to the conclusion that they attest either Hezekiah's or Josiah's reform, as if nobody else ruled in Judah between 800 and 601 BCE—another severe case of 'goodkingitis' which could have been avoided by a simple calculation: if the cancellation of the Arad temple could not be dated more precisely than to a span of 200 years (which is no longer the case), then, according to the length of reigns, it could be attributed to Manasseh with a probability of 27.5%, to Josiah with 15.5%, and to Hezekiah with 14.5%.

74. Herzog, 'The Fortress Mound', pp. 65-67, taking 2 Chron. 31.1 as historical, which it clearly is not: Hezekiah had no chance to destroy temples in Manasseh and Ephraim. From a purely archaeological point of view, it is evident that nobody destroyed the temple of Bethel between 734 and 520 BCE. Cf. 'Bethel', in RGG^4, pp. 1315-16; *idem*, 'Bethel: The Israelite Impact on Judaean Language and Literature', in O. Lipschits and M. Oeming (eds.), *Judah and the Judaeans in the Achaemenid Period* (Winona Lake, IN: Eisenbrauns, forthcoming).

75. Cf. L.K. Handy, 'Hezekiah's Unlikely Reform', *ZAW* 100 (1988), pp. 101-11.

76. L. Singer-Avitz, 'Arad: The Iron Age Pottery Assemblages', *TA* 29 (2002), pp. 110-214 (182).

The historical interpretation of the comparative table has to take into account (1) that there is a considerable gap at Lachish between the destruction of Lachish III and the foundation of Lachish II, which in all probability does not exist at the other sites; (2) that Sennacherib did not operate in the Negev so that no destruction of Negev sites can be firmly dated to 701;[77] (3) that Tel 'Ira VII is the successor of Beersheba II as the central administrative centre in the Negev; and (4) that the destructions of Arad VII and VI are extremely close to each other, the commanding officer of the place being, in both cases, Eliashib. It is perfectly possible that both destructions took place in the course of the Edomite war of 601–598;[78] if one assumes that the Edomite occupation of the Judaean south had to wait until 586, Arad VI might have been rebuilt after 598. Furthermore, that the 'Lachish III' pottery horizon ends at Lachish in 701 (because the town was destroyed by Sennacherib) does not imply that every other place with Lachish III pottery was destroyed in the same year. It is perfectly possible (though not probable) that Arad X–VIII predate 701; it is equally possible (and equally improbable) that all three Arad strata date after 701. It is likely that Arad X predates Lachish III, that Arad IX is roughly contemporary with Lachish III (but not destroyed in 701 and thus, extending into the first decennium of the seventh century), and that Arad VIII postdates Lachish III. The most plausible reconstruction of the whole system then runs as follows:

Table 5. *Comparative Stratigraphy of Southern Judaean Sites as Proposed by the Present Author*

Period	Arad	Beersheba	Tel 'Ira	Lachish	Pottery horizon
2nd half 8th century	X	III		III	Lachish III
700	IX	III		III (701)	
700–680	VIII	II		—gap—	
680–650	—gap—	—gap—	VII		
650–625	VII or gap	—	VI	—gap—	Lachish II
625–600	VII (601–598)	—	VI (601–598)	II	
600–586	VI (598 or 588/6)	—	—	II (587/6)	

Arad IX was not, as far as the available reports go, violently destroyed, but was restructured to make way for what looks like a *suq*, a commercial district.[79] In the course of this reconstruction, which falls into the early years of Manasseh,[80] the temple was reverently buried.

As far as the archaeological data go, there is some evidence for the abandonment of some local/rural sanctuaries only for the time of Manasseh. The sanctuary

---

77. Knauf, 'Who Destroyed?', pp. 184-90; *idem*, '701'.
78. Cf. 2 Kgs 24.1-12 and Ps. 60, and cf. further Knauf, 'Psalm xl und Psalm cviii', *VT* 50 (2000), pp. 55-65.
79. Cf. Herzog, 'The Fortress Mound', pp. 38-39, fig. 16.
80. In accordance with the Assyrian seal of fig. 35.2, TA 29.82, dating to the time of Sennacherib (705–681). The probability that it was produced prior to 701 is 16.7%, the probability that it reached Arad prior to 701 is considerably less. In other words: the probability that the seal was deposited at Arad after 701 is definitely higher than 83.3%, and most probably higher than 90%.

of Bethel, of much more importance, was not destroyed, neither by the Assyrians, nor Manasseh, nor Josiah.[81] But Bethel was an Israelite temple, even if it was politically incorporated into Judah in the course of the seventh, or the second half of the seventh century. That there was some, not complete, cultic centralization under Manasseh agrees well with his politics, or the socio-economic development in his day. In a situation when 15–20% of the population of Judah was concentrated in the capital, the countryside was much devalued. It also agrees well with the Assyrianizing fashion of the time: Ashur, after all, also had only one temple in the world. So, if the temple of Arad X and IX had been a temple of Yhwh (what we do not know, but all assume), it now had to go. If, however, Yhwh was venerated at Bethel under the name of 'Bethel',[82] there was no reason to cancel this sanctuary.

An Assyrian background of the law in Deuteronomy 12 is quite probable.[83] It is another question, however, what this law in a seventh-century context intended. If it meant, from the very beginning, that there can be only one legitimate temple of Yhwh in the world, then why did Jews build temples in *Al Yahudu* in Babylonia[84] or in Elephantine[85] at a time when the temple of Jerusalem was admittedly destroyed, but the temple of Bethel perfectly functioning,[86] and continue to use a temple of Yahô in Idumea (at Lachish or at Mareshah) well after 515, and why did the authorities of both Samaria and Jerusalem allow the restoration of the Elephantine temple in 407/6? Either Deuteronomy 12 did not yet exist at all (which is rather improbable), or it was understood differently from its perception in, for example, Jn 4.20, where Jews and Samaritans agree that there should be one, and only one, temple of Yhwh, but disagree concerning its location. By the time of John 4, however, the book of Kings was part of the biblical canon for most (not all) of the Jews, and it is Kings—and Kings only—which identifies *hammaqōm ʾašēr yîbḥar yhwh lāśūm ʾet šᵉmo šām* with Jerusalem,[87] and

---

81. Cf. above, n. 73.

82. The divine name 'Bethel' is attested, possibly, Gen. 35.7 (as Gen. 33.20, either a construct chain 'El of Bethel', or a divine name with an apposition 'El, that is, Bethel', or a nominal sentence 'El is Bethel'; and certainly, if polemically, by Jer. 48.13.

83. Cf., e.g., E. Otto, 'Die Ursprünge der Bundestheologie im Alten Testament und im Alten Orient', *Zeitschrift für Altorientalische und Biblische Rechtsgeschichte* 4 (1998), pp. 1-84; H.U. Steymans, *Deuteronomium 28 und die adê zur Thronfolgeregelung Asarhaddons* (OBO, 145; Freiburg: Universitätsverlag; Göttingen: Vandenhoeck & Ruprecht, 1995).

84. Mentioned, as rumour has it, in a cuneiform archive from Iraq, illegally excavated and exported and on the market for quite a time.

85. The temple of Elephantine was most probably founded by Judaeans and/or Benjaminites who migrated to Egypt in the course of the sixth century (586–525) for economic reasons; cf. for the history of Elephantine, E.A. Knauf, 'Elephantine und das vorbiblische Judentum', in R.G. Kratz (ed.), *Religion und Religionskontakte im Zeitalter der Achämeniden. Sechs Jahre Arbeitsgemeinschaft zur Erforschung der altorientalisch-hellenistischen Religionsgeschichte des 1. Jahrtausends in Göttingen* (VWGTh, 22; Munich: Chr. Kaiser Verlag, 2002), pp. 165-74.

86. As presupposed by Ezek. 33.25.

87. 1 Kgs 8.16, 44, 48; 11.13, 32, 36; 14.21; 2 Kgs 21.7; 23.27. It is the intention of 2 Kgs 22–23 to present its interpretation of Deut. 12 as 'original', and it is this very intention which casts further

denounces the establishment of the Bethel cult as 'the sin of Jeroboam'. Previously, nobody (except for the circle which composed and transmitted Kings) seems to have understood Deuteronomy 12 as referring to a single place, and this is grammatically feasible. The *māqōm* of a potential sanctuary is partially determined by the relative clause and therefore, has the definite article.[88] Whether Yhwh's election pertains to only one place, or several in succession,[89] or to several at one and the same time, the text does not say.

> Determination in Hebrew can be partial or total, without any difference on the level of its morphosyntactical expression. The determination of the father and the mother whom a man will leave on the occasion of his marriage (Gen. 2.24) is total, there exists only one of each kind (at least biologically). The determination of *'bd* as in שמע עבד ירבעם is partial, it does not imply that Jeroboam II had only one minister.[90] The determinative power exercised by a relative clause is partial in most cases. Genesis 44.17 *hā'îš 'ªšer nimṣā' haggābîa' bᵉyādō hū' yihyeh lî* does not imply that Joseph knows already the culprit's name by the time of speaking; if two of the suspects had split the booty among them, he would even refer to two men. In Num. 22.35 *haddābār 'ªdabbēr 'ēlêkā* does not mean that Yhwh knows already what he will tell Balaam to say. It simply means: 'Only tell what I will say'. In the same vein Deuteronomy 12* means: 'You shall have a cult of Yhwh only at such places as he chooses to have a cult at'.

Originally, then, Deuteronomy 12* was not a law on cultic centralization, it was a law of cultic legitimacy. Only those sanctuaries are henceforward legitimate, of which the deity him- or herself has indicated that she/he intends to inhabit them. And, of course, such legitimacy was easier to prove in the case of a royal sanctuary at Jerusalem, or even for Bethel with its school and archive, than for tiny Arad, where people at the end of Arad IX might still have remembered who built it and why 40 or 50 years before... For an Assyrian, such a law would have stated the obvious: only a deity could establish ways and means to approach it.[91] For Judah in the seventh century, it was an Asyrianizing innovation. Deuteronomy 12.8—'You shall not do as we were wont to do until now'—might not just refer, within the textual world of the Bible, to the altars of the patriarchs or other cultic installations mentioned previous to Deuteronomy 11. It might refer to an established Israelite[92] and Judaean practice prior to the seventh century, not only

---

doubts on the historicity of 2 Kgs 22–23; cf. already Ch. Levin, 'Joschija im deuteronomistischen Geschichtswerk', *ZAW* 96 (1984), pp. 351-71; for a more positive position, but only just slightly more, see Ch. Uehlinger, 'Gab es eine joschijanische Kultreform? Plädoyer für ein begründetes Minimum', in W. Gross (ed.), *Jeremia und die 'deuteronomistische Bewegung'* (BBB, 98; Weinheim: Athenäum, 1994), pp. 57-89.

88. Note that the antecedent of *'ªšer* is nearly always determined.

89. Shiloh (Josh. 18.1; 1 Sam. 1.3) is never denounced as illegitimate, and even in the case of Jerusalem, the election can be revoked (2 Kgs 23.27).

90. It is quite entertaining to watch the famous grammarian E. Kautzsch ('Ein althebräisches Siegel vom Tell el-Mutessellim', *MNDPV* 10 [1904], pp. 1-14 [5-7]) miss the point.

91. Cf. A. Berlejung, *Die Theologie der Bilder* (OBO, 162; Freiburg: Universitätsverlag; Göttingen: Vandenhoeck & Ruprecht, 1998); V. Hurowitz, *I Have Built You an Exalted House* (JSOTSup, 115; Sheffield: Sheffield Academic Press, 1992).

92. Note, however, that the temple of Succoth took care to post publicly a text which proved that the gods used to visit the place, and that the conviction that a god was present at Dan lasted well into the second century BCE.

referred to in biblical texts,[93] but also archaeologically at Kuntillet 'Ajrûd and Arad.[94]

In sum: cultic centralization set in, under Assyrian influence, during the reign of Manasseh. The standard interpretation of Deuteronomy 12, denouncing each and every temple of YHWH with the exception of his temple at Jerusalem, was elaborated, at the earliest, during the exile by the Babylonian Golah, or in the early restoration period, out of competition between the Golah and the *'am ha-'aretz* and their sanctuaries, Jerusalem and Bethel. The law was later, after the fourth century, turned against the Samaritan temple on Mt Gerizim. But this interpretation of Deuteronomy 12 was not yet commonly accepted in Samaria, Judaea and Idumaea in the fifth and fourth centuries. The first who presupposes it by putting it into practice was John Hyrcanus in 108 (or 114–111) BCE, when he destroyed the Gerizim temple.

---

93. Judg. 17.1-6 might be intended as polemical, but what about 1 Kgs 8.12-13, where the king and temple-builder blatantly contradicts Yhwh's intention?

94. For the temple at Arad, see above; for Kuntillet 'Ajrûd, cf. M. Bernett and O. Keel, *Mond, Stier und Kult am Stadttor* (OBO, 161; Freiburg: Universitätsverlag; Göttingen: Vandenhoeck & Ruprecht, 1998), pp. 60-61.

JOSIAH AND THE KINGDOM OF JUDAH*

Nadav Na'aman

Introduction

King Josiah acceded to the throne of Judah following the murder of Amon (who had reigned only briefly) by his courtiers. The court rebellion was quickly suppressed; following the execution of the conspirators, Josiah, the young son of the late ruler, was crowned at the tender age of eight (2 Kgs 21.23-24; 22.1). It may be assumed that during the first years of his reign, the young king was supported by his mother and by those circles which had ensured his accession, and that he assumed full authority only upon reaching maturity. He reigned for 31 year (639–609 BCE), and was killed at Megiddo by Pharaoh Necho II of Egypt.

Whereas Josiah's accession to the throne, as well as his death and the crowning of his heir, Jehoahaz (2 Kgs 23.29-30; 2 Chron. 35.20-24; 36.1), are described in considerable detail, our information on his foreign policy, his relations with neighbouring countries and with the great powers then struggling for hegemony throughout the fertile crescent, is drawn entirely from non-biblical sources. Assyria is not mentioned at all in the book of Kings following Sennacherib's campaign against Judah during Hezekiah's reign, in 701 BCE; nor did Egypt take part in the chain of events before the episode of Josiah's death. None of Judah's near neighbours, in fact, is mentioned in the description of Josiah's time. That description focusses on the restoration of the Temple and the discovery of the 'Book of the Law', as well as on the reform enacted by Josiah throughout his kingdom; the passages in question include little on the extent of his kingdom and/or his activities during his reign (2 Kgs 23.8a, 15, 19-20; 2 Chron. 34.6). This difficulty is aggravated by the total lack of details concerning the state of affairs in Judah between Sennacherib's campaign in 701 and Josiah's coronation in 639 BCE. It should be remembered that Sennacherib's campaign was a disastrous event for the kingdom bringing about the destruction of dozens of its cities and the deportation of many thousands of its inhabitants. Vast districts were grievously damaged; their resettlement was a slow and gradual process. Many of the refugees certainly fled to the capital, Jerusalem—which, since the eighth century, had become a metropolis immeasurably larger (in both area and population) than any other city in Judah. The campaign greatly increased the degree of

---

* This is a slightly revised version of Na'aman 1991a. One section (4) of the original article was dropped (Na'man 1991a: 16-22), the text was slightly revised, and some updated references were inserted in square brackets.

subjugation to Assyria, as well as of Assyrian involvement in the internal affairs of the kingdom, and gave rise to significant 'foreign' influences in the spheres of cult and culture. Sennacherib's campaign represented an historical turning point of the utmost significance to the Kingdom of Judah, following which the kingdom underwent a series of profound demographic, social, economic, and cultural changes. The paucity of information on the six decades between Sennacherib's campaign and Josiah's accession, and on the latter king's activities, present a difficulty when attempting to sketch the outline and contemporary history of Josiah's kingdom.

The limited nature of the source material has not prevented scholars from investigating the period of Josiah's rule, due to its crucial importance in the history of the Jewish people. It is commonly accepted that 'the Book of the Law' (2 Kgs 22.8, 11)—otherwise known as 'the Book of the Covenant' (23.2, 21)— was written in the seventh century BCE, perhaps even during Josiah's early reign, and that its composition gave rise to a comprehensive cultic reform throughout the kingdom, and to the initial widespread influence and literary activity of the Deuteronomistic school. The years of Josiah's reign constitute an important starting point for the study of developments in Jewish religion, cult, law, and literature, and have therefore gained the attention of a considerable number of scholars, starting in the earliest days of biblical research. The scarcity of biblical data invited a wide variety of opinions concerning the extent of the kingdom, its internal structure, economy, etc. Some scholars have concluded that Josiah's kingdom consisted mainly of the area between the Beersheba Valley and Bethel; others, by contrast, have suggested that Josiah attempted to restore the kingdom of David in all its glory, and that he controlled much of the Cisjordanian areas.

In the framework of this introduction, let me emphasize the importance of the archaeological findings to the discussion of Josiah's kingdom, and the vast progress made in this field since the early 1970s. It was the new excavations and surveys conducted throughout the area of the Kingdom of Judah which first pointed out the destructive consequences of Sennacherib's campaign and the many changes which occurred in the kingdom during the seventh century BCE. The considerable progress made in archaeological research is reflected in the discussion of the *lmlk* seal impressions. For many years it was widely accepted to date these impressions to the seventh century, and specifically to Josiah's day. For that reason, archaeologists tended to date the layers of settlement in which such impressions were unearthed to the seventh century, and to use their distribution as a basis for determining the extent of Josiah's kingdom. However, recent studies have indicated that the jars bearing the *lmlk* seal impressions were manufactured in the late eighth century BCE, and that their production and distribution are apparently related to the preparations for Sennacherib's campaign against Judah. These conclusions led to the redating of levels in many sites in Judah, and eliminated the basis for the assumption that any direct connection might have existed between the *lmlk* jars and Josiah's kingdom. These stratigraphic conclusions also provided additional clarification of the relationships between the Kingdom of Judah and its near neighbours in the area of material culture. It appears that, in the eighth century BCE, the borders of Judah were largely closed, and contacts with neighbouring states to the east and west were limited; on the other hand, in the seventh century, following the *pax Assyriaca*, the borders were opened, and the available evidence of material culture attests to manifold contacts with various regions within the Assyrian empire (Zimhoni 1990: 47-49). Thus, recent archaeological research has provided us with new data pertinent to the study of this period—data which were not at the disposal of those scholars who discussed Josiah's kingdom in the past—enabling a re-evaluation of the written sources. It appears that, by re-integration of all these sources, we may now suggest a fairly new picture of Josiah's kingdom—including its territorial extent, population, economic power, and international status—a picture based on firmer foundations than previous reconstructions.

It is not my intention to deal here with all the aspects of Josiah's kingdom. Religious and cultic matters within the kingdom, as well as the development of the Deuteronomistic school and its effect on the reform, require extensive discussions which have no place within the present work. Hopefully, the conclusions reached in this study will provide a sounder basis for the study of these central issues; primarily, however, my intention is to review Josiah's kingdom and its contemporary history in a new historical perspective, and thus to attempt to make an additional contribution to the study of the last hundred years of the Kingdom of Judah.

I. *Josiah's Kingdom and the Town Lists of Judah and Benjamin*

1. *Previous Discussions of the Town Lists*

Much of the research on the town lists in the book of Joshua is founded on A. Alt's basic work, 'Judas Gaue unter Josia' (Alt 1925). In that article, Alt proposed the separation of the town lists from the system of borders, and the independent discussion of each of these two groups. While dating the system of tribal allotments at the end of the period of the Judges, he felt that the town lists of the southern tribes (Josh. 15.21-62; 18.21-28; 19.2-8, 40-46) more properly belonged to King Josiah's time. In his opinion, there had originally existed a single list encompassing all the towns within the Kingdom of Judah; a later editor had divided that list into four parts and assigned each section to the tribe within whose inheritance it was geographically located. Due to inattention on the part of that editor, certain place names are mentioned twice, as belonging to two different tribes (Zorah and Eshtaol appear within the inheritances of Dan and Judah; Kiriath-jearim and Beth-arabah, within the allotments of Judah and Benjamin). The towns of Simeon are also mentioned in the town list of Judah; the two lists appear to have a common source. Alt considered the internal division of the list into sections, separated by a count of towns in each section, as reflecting the array of districts—twelve in all—within the Kingdom of Judah (Alt 1925: 105-106). He also attempted to ascertain the course of development of each district by examining its affinity to the patterns of settlement existing in Late Bronze Age Canaan, and the settlement in the mountain regions during the Iron Age I. The array of ten districts first developed after the division of the kingdom; the conquered districts of Bethel and Ekron (the inheritance of Dan) were added during Josiah's reign. Some of the districts persisted into the Persian period, and served as administrative districts of the province of Yehud.

The article by Cross and Wright (1956), published some thirty years later, constitutes an additional milestone in the study of the town lists. Cross and Wright maintained that the town list of Dan matches the gap left between the borders of neighbouring tribes (Judah, Benjamin, Ephraim). This list includes a passage comprising a border description, and thus belongs to the 'mixed' lists, in which border descriptions were appended to town lists. The appearance of Zorah and Eshtaol in both the town list of Judah and the inheritance of Dan also indicates that those towns do not belong to the same boundary system. In view of the above, Cross and Wright reached the conclusion that the town list of Dan should be considered as part of the array of tribal allotments, and detached from the town list of the other southern tribes (Judah, Simeon, Benjamin). The scope of towns reviewed in those three lists corresponds to the area of the Kingdom of Judah; the lists themselves were originally included in a document written in King Jehoshaphat's day, describing the division of the kingdom into twelve districts. By contrast to Alt, who appended the wilderness district of Judah (Josh. 15.61-62) to the eastern district of Benjamin (Josh. 18.21-24), Cross and Wright distinguished between the two, classifying them as neighbouring districts. In this manner, they also reached a total of twelve districts for the kingdom.

Cross and Wright's statement that the town list of Dan should be detached from the other southern town lists has been generally accepted by scholars.[1] Several scholars have later tended to consider it as independent of the boundary system (B. Mazar 1960; Strange 1966; Aharoni 1979: 311-13; Galil 1985; Kallai 1986: 361-71). I have attempted to show that Cross and Wright's conclusions are correct, and that there are weighty reasons in favour of appending that list to the system of tribal allotments (Na'aman 1986a: 75-117).

An article by Kallai, published two years after Cross and Wright's study, raises an exceptional hypothesis: the division of the southern towns into four separate lists, each of which belonging to a different period in the history of Israel (Kallai-Kleinmann 1958; Kallai 1986: 372-404). The principal justification given for this division is that of the duplications in the town lists, which would never have occurred in a single, orderly system of records. In view of this consideration, Kallai believes the town list of Simeon to have been drawn up during the reign of King David; that of Dan, under King Solomon; that of Benjamin, under King Abijah; and that of Judah, under King Hezekiah.

The separation of the town lists of Dan and Simeon from the other town lists is accepted by many scholars; moreover, the differences of opinion regarding their extent and dates are not my concern in the framework of this article. How-

---

1. Auld (1980: 52-67) claimed that the lists of towns and tribal allotments of the ten tribes west of the Jordan were composed at the same time, in the seventh century BCE. Auld, however, contented himself with a textual discussion, and did not deal with any of the topographical or geographical–historical problems related to those lists.

ever, the definition of the town list of Benjamin as an independent section in its own right, reflecting a special historical situation, changes the entire picture. If this is the case, we may no longer speak of one ancient document, which includes all the towns in the kingdom; but rather, of documents of varying origin and date, assembled and compiled by a later editor.

The date specified by Kallai for the town list of Benjamin (Josh. 18.21-28) is puzzling. In another work published at about the same time, Kallai reconstructed the extent of the borders of Josiah's kingdom, set its northern border (in the first stage of that king's expansionist activity) at Geba-Ephraim, north of Bethel and Ophrah, and claimed that this border became stable in the late First Temple period (Kallai 1960: 74-78). This northern border is identical in every detail to the northern border of the town list of Benjamin, as traced by Kallai in his first article (see Kallai 1986: 398-404 and map no. 2). It is difficult to understand why Kallai ascribed the town list to Abijah (it is doubtful whether that king had undertaken a campaign to the Bethel area, as related in 2 Chron. 13 [Klein 1983], and he certainly did not annex it to his territory), and not to Josiah, as his own discussion (and Alt's basic work) would seem to warrant.

Another of Kallai's innovations is his ordering of the Shephelah sections listed in Josh. 15.33-44. Alt (1925: 105-106, 117) and later Noth (1953: 91, 95-96; also Cross and Wright 1956: 213, 217-19) believed that the three Shephelah sections were listed in order from north to south. By contrast, Kallai claimed that the third and fourth sections were located alongside each other on the north–south axis: the third (Josh. 15.37-41) in the lower Shephelah to the west, and the fourth (Josh. 15.42-44) in the higher Shephelah to the east (Kallai-Kleinmann 1958: 155-56; Kallai 1986: 379-86). Both these proposals have additional adherents, and will be further discussed below.

Additional studies of the southern town lists, published since the early 1960s, have primarily addressed the problem of identification of individual towns—a significant factor in the analysis of the lists. (See recently de Vos 2002, with earlier literature in pp. 340-60.) The dating of the lists has remained controversial; the arguments advanced by these studies have not changed the situation, nor enabled a decisive settlement of the question. Scholars are generally agreed upon two basic assumptions: that the lists reflect the original documents from whence they were extracted; and that, in their present form, they portray the administrative districts of the kingdom. This concept was expanded upon in the works of Galil, who divided all the sections appearing in the hills of Judah, the Shephelah of Judah, and the northernmost Shephelah (in the inheritance of Dan) into small sub-districts, each of which included several settlements and functioned as an administrative section (Galil 1984, 1985, 1987).

Notwithstanding the great number of discussions of the southern town lists, several of the basic problems have not yet been solved, and a number of central questions are still the subjects of dispute. It now seems possible to discuss these questions yet again; to present arguments not yet advanced in prior publications; and, by means of these arguments, to reach a better understanding of the lists. The problems which I intend to address are as follows:

1. Do the town lists of Judah and Benjamin constitute two lists dating from different times, or were they originally part of a single list?
2. Does the internal division of these lists really reflect the administrative system of the Kingdom of Judah?
3. To which period should the town lists of Judah and Benjamin be dated?

The answers to these questions are complex and call for balanced, multi-faceted discussion. It seems, nevertheless, that such a discussion can reach clear conclusions concerning the dating, composition, and nature of the town lists, thus enabling a better use of the lists in historical research.

2. *The Town Lists of Judah and Benjamin and the System of Tribal Allotments*
Two towns are mentioned twice in the town lists of Judah and Benjamin: Beth-arabah (Josh. 15.61; 18.22) and Kiriath-jearim (Josh. 15.60; 18.28). Some scholars have claimed that this duplication exists only in one instance—that of Beth-arabah—and that the second instance actually refers to two separate settlements: Kiriath-jearim in Judah (Josh. 15.60), and Gibeath-kiriath-jearim in Benjamin (Josh. 18.28) (Mazar [Maisler] 1947: 319; Aharoni 1959: 228-29; 1979: 350-51, 356; Kallai 1960: 34-35 n. 82; 1986: 134-35, 400 n. 152, 403; B. Mazar 1976: 271; Galil 1984: 222). This question should be investigated before discussing the affinity between the two groups of towns.

The argument in favour of distinction between the two settlements is based on the fragmented passage of Josh. 18.28, whose original Hebrew reads *gb't qryt 'rym 'rb' 'śrh wḥṣryhn* and is translated in the RSV as 'Gibeah and Kiriath-jearim—fourteen cities with their villages'. Scholars have postulated that the document originally read *gb't qryt <y'rym> 'rym...* and was subsequently miscopied. Corroboration for this claim is found in the mention of 'Gibeah' in the account of the Ark of the Covenant, which was halted at Kiriath-jearim and brought up from that town by David (1 Sam. 7.1; 2 Sam. 6.3). This hypothesis, however, engenders great difficulty. In the tradition concerning the Ark of the Covenant, the names of Kiriath-jearim and Gibeah have obviously been interchanged (compare 2 Sam. 6.2-3). It appears that 'Gibeah' (literally, '[the] hill') was the name used for the cultic site in Kiriath-jearim, where the Ark of the Covenant was placed—in accordance with the custom by which cultic sites in ancient Israel were given distinct names (Na'aman 1987a: 19-21). The Gibeah mentioned in the Ark of the Covenant cycle has nothing to do with the Gibeah cited in the town list of Benjamin. Moreover, the versions of the LXX of Josh. 18.28 read: *wgb't wqryt y'rym 'rym...* (in the A and Luciani manuscripts), or: *wqryt wgb't y'rym 'rym...* (in the B manuscript). The hypothetical existence of a settlement called 'Gibeath-kiriath-jearim' has not been corroborated by any ancient source. As this name is not mentioned in the Bible, and especially as tripartite place names are extremely rare in the toponomy of Palestine, this possibility should be viewed as dubious. It thus seems best to assume (as do most scholars) that the original document mentioned two places—Gibeah and Kiriath-jearim (Steuernagel 1900: 224-25; Holmes 1914: 68; Albright 1924: 32; Noth 1953: 108). In discussing the affinity between the town lists of Judah and

Benjamin, the duplication of the names Beth-arabah and Kiriath-jearim should he clarified.

In my opinion, the reason for these duplications lies in the efforts made by the author of the book of Joshua to adapt the town lists to the border between Judah and Benjamin as it appears in the description of the tribal allotments. In the latter system, Beth-arabah was included within the inheritance of Judah, Jerusalem was considered part of Benjamin, and Kiriath-jearim was part of Judah. On the other hand, the Jericho area, including Beth-arabah and Hoglah to the south, became part of the Northern Kingdom until its collapse. Jerusalem, as the capital of the Kingdom of Judah, gradually grew in size and importance. During the eighth and seventh centuries BCE, it expanded considerably, becoming the largest city in the kingdom; at its zenith, its area and population were many times larger than those of any other city. Metropolitan Jerusalem, with its surrounding agricultural areas, must have encompassed vast areas of the tribal inheritances of both Judah and Benjamin. By contrast, Kiriath-jearim, which appears in the system of tribal allotments as a sort of salient at the northern edge of the inheritance of Judah, formed a ramified network of connections with neighbouring towns to the north, until it was eventually considered as part of Benjamin; for this reason, it appears alongside the towns of Benjamin in lists composed at the time (Josh. 9.17b;[2] 18.28; Ezra 2.25; Neh. 7.29). When the author of the book of Joshua attempted to integrate the document containing the town lists into his work, he encountered a series of discrepancies between the system of tribal allotments and the situation prevailing in his own day. In an effort to make the ancient border conform to the later array of settlements, the author apparently reworked the town list in the following manner:

1. Beth-arabah and Hoglah, which, as stated above, belonged to the Northern Kingdom, were listed in the document among the eastern towns of Benjamin. In order to adapt the phrasing of the document to the ancient border, he added Beth-arabah to the town list of Judah, thus creating the duplication mentioned above.
2. Jerusalem was added to the town list of Benjamin, in accordance with the ancient border, although, at the time the town list was composed, the city was already totally detached from the ancient district of Benjamin.
3. Kiriath-jearim was listed in the document among the western towns of Benjamin. In an attempt to adapt the town list to the ancient border, the author appended Kiriath-jearim to Rabbah, its southern neighbour in the hill country, thus creating a miniature 'district' comprising only two towns, which scholars have found so difficult to explain.[3] Thus, the town

---

2. It appears to me that this later reality is reflected in Josh. 9.17b ('Now their cities were Gibeon, Chephirah, Beeroth, and Kiriath-jearim'), and that this half-verse was stuck into the tale of the Gibeonites at a later date, apparently in the post-exilic period. The fact that very little pottery from the Iron Age I was found at Khirbet Kefireh, the site of Chephirah, despite the painstaking survey conducted there, is discussed by Vriezen (1975).

3. A number of scholars have solved the problem of the tiny two-town section by attaching it to the western section of the towns of Benjamin (Alt 1925: 105-106; Noth 1953: 91, 99; Cross and

of Kiriath-jearim appears twice: once in Benjamin, to which it belonged in the author's day, and once in Judah, to which it had belonged in former times.

The effort to adapt the area of Judah as defined in the system of tribal allotments to the town list also elucidates the appearance of Philistine cities (Josh. 15.45-47) among the towns of Judah—a fact which some scholars have had difficulty in explaining, and have attempted to relate to special historical circumstances. The author of the system of tribal allotments appended the Philistine coast to the area of Judah (though, in reality, it was never a part of Judah), as part of an overall trend to expand and glorify his tribe (Na'aman 1986a: 62-66). The town list of Judah in the original document did not, of course, include the Philistine cities. For the sake of congruence between the two systems, the author of the book of Joshua also appended the Philistine cities to the town list of Judah.

It is not impossible that the attachment of Kedesh to the cities of the south (Josh. 15.23)—assuming that town is to be identified with Kadesh-barnea—was added in order to adapt the southern border of the inheritance of Judah to the town list. (For additional discussion of the status of Kadesh-barnea, see Part II Section 2, below.)

Another—by no means coincidental—similarity between the boundary system (and the traditions of conquest as set forth in the Book of Joshua) and the town list lies in the appearance of archaic appellations beside the names of some towns: 'Kerioth-hezron (that is, Hazor)' (Josh. 15.25); 'Kiriath-sannah (that is, Debir)' (Josh. 15.49) (Orlinsky 1939); 'Kiriath-arba (that is, Hebron)' (Josh. 15.54); 'Kiriath-baal (that is, Kiriath-jearim)' (Josh. 15.60); 'Ephrathah (that is, Bethlehem)' (LXX, following Josh. 15.59, in a district omitted in the Hebrew);[4] 'Jebus (that is, Jerusalem)' (18.28). We cannot assume that these archaic appellations appeared in the original document (or, more correctly, administrative list) from which the author of the book of Joshua obtained the town names. The additional appellations are to be ascribed to the author of the book of Joshua, who attempted to reconcile the town list with descriptions appearing in the system of tribal allotments, thus instilling in the former an odour of antiquity.

Finally, let us consider the different attitudes evidenced by the author toward the tribes of Judah and Ephraim. While the inheritance of Judah is reflected in its

---

Wright 1956: 213, 221-22; Galil 1984: 219-21). By contrast, other scholars have included the two towns in the framework of a separate, independent district (Aharoni 1979: 346-55; Kallai 1986: 394-95 and map no. 2; but compare Kallai 1971: 251). The attempt to identify Rabbah within the northern Shephelah is dubious, as is the addition of areas in the Shephelah to the framework of the mountain districts (Aharoni 1969: 137-41; 1979: 346-55; Galil 1984: 219-23). The town lists make a clear and sharp distinction between the mountain districts and those of the Shephelah, and there is no justification for the formation of an artificial district including both mountain and Shephelah towns. Rabbah is to be sought in the mountain district, not far from Kiriath-jearim. In this connection, let me recall the B manuscript of the LXX mentioning the town of Sotheba, which may be identified with Suba, southeast of Kiriath-jearim (Kallai 1986: 392-95).

4. For the reconstruction of the missing section in Josh. 15.60, see Hollenberg 1881: 99-100; Steuernagel 1900: 214; Noth 1953: 99; Kallai 1986: 392-93.

complete and unabridged dimensions, in accordance with its description in the system of tribal allotments, the author does not follow the same policy with that of Ephraim, and does not 'correct' reality by concealing the encroachment upon its territory by the northern towns of Benjamin.[5] This preferential attitude toward the tribe of Judah is also reflected in additional descriptions in the book of Joshua (see Na'aman 1986a: 62-66), thus indicating the tendentiousness of its author.

Generally speaking, it seems that the author's tendentiousness and 'literary' considerations played an important role in the formulation of the town lists of Judah and Benjamin as they now stand. The lists are not exact copies of administrative documents incorporated word for word into the book of Joshua, as Kallai assumed in his proposal to separate them and assign them different dates.[6] Moreover, the practice of reworking ancient documents is familiar to us from the analysis of other lists in the book of Joshua and other books of the Bible; the town lists discussed here are not the only topographical documents to have undergone reworking in view of literary and theological considerations.[7]

Given the above conclusions, we may again examine the affinity between the town lists of Judah and Benjamin. As it seems, we have to reject the assumption that, at the time of composition of the original lists, the ancient division still existed between the two main sections comprising the kingdom (Judah and Benjamin), and that later administrative town lists were drawn up on that basis. This assumption constitutes the basis for Kallai's hypothesis that the lists of Judah and Benjamin should be separated and assigned to different periods. The very assumption that the author had in his possession a separate list of towns within the area of ancient Judah, at least two hundred years after the establishment of the kingdom and the merging of Judah and Benjamin, seems far from plausible. The separation between the two sections is artificial, and was implemented by the author of the book. Apparently, there had originally existed a single town list

---

5. Auld (1980: 87 n. 50) examined the possibility that the border of the tribal allotment of Benjamin described in Josh. 18.12-14 is secondary to the town list of Benjamin. This is not the appropriate framework for a detailed discussion of this original proposition. It should, however, be emphasized that the problem of incompatibility between the northern border of the tribal allotment of Benjamin and the scope of the town list is not solved in this way: if the town list was indeed at the disposal of the author who traced the border of Benjamin, why is there no compatibility between the two? Concerning the theory that the southern border of the tribal allotment of Benjamin is no more than an adaptation of the northern border of that of Judah, see Schmitt 1980: 39-42; Na'aman 1986a: 102-104.

6. One of Kallai's basic hypotheses, reflected in all his works, is that documents which served the administration of the kingdom were reproduced in the Bible word for word, with no attempt at modification or adaptation to suit the author's tendencies. This approach is also reflected in his discussions of the town lists in the book of Joshua (Kallai-Kleinmann 1958; Kallai 1986: 346-48). This basic hypothesis (which Kallai shares with other scholars) is criticized by Auld (1980: 37-42). It is important to stress that a simplistic approach of this type is not at all appropriate to a discussion of the biblical material, and that it is impossible to deal with the geographical lists in the Bible without considering the tendencies of their authors. To illustrate the great importance of discussion of these tendencies, see Na'aman 1986a: 55-58, 64-66, 84-91, 116-17, 174-76, 216-36, 244-51.

7. See the works cited in the previous note, as well as the following additional examples: Auld 1975; Williamson 1979, 1981; Na'aman 1986b: 5-11.

covering the entire Kingdom of Judah, and the author, who ascribed that list to Joshua's time—a period governed (according to his description) by tribal regime—was responsible for dividing it between the tribal allotments of Judah and Benjamin. Any discussion of the original town lists should be based on the combination of both lists: Josh. 15.21-62 and 18.21-28.

3. *The Districts of the Kingdom of Judah and the Town Lists*

Garfinkel presented arguments against the concept that the town lists reflect the administrative districts of the Kingdom of Judah (Garfinkel 1987). He argued that administrative procedure as reflected in documents discovered at Arad, Horvat 'Uza, Lachish, and Tel Beersheba is not in line with the commonly held interpretation of the system of districts. In a detailed rebuttal, Galil (1984, 1985, 1987) attempted to defend both the accepted concept regarding the affinity of the town lists to the administrative districts of the kingdom, and his own concept, which goes so far as to hold that the town lists actually reflect sub-sections within the framework of those districts. It should be stated that the paucity of documents discovered to date throughout Judah, their fragmented nature, their incomplete preservation and deciphering, and their brief and concise phrasing, all preclude any definitive observations concerning the *modus operandi* of the administrative system then in force. A few of the settlements mentioned in the Arad archive were possibly located in the hill country (Maon; concerning the others, see nn. 17-18, below); nevertheless, there is no way to determine their administrative status in the period during which the document was written, nor their historical situation at the time (as it may be claimed that they reflect an exceptional state of affairs). This is also the situation regarding the reference to the men of Moladah, *rntn* (or *rptn*) and Makkedah in the Horvat 'Uza ostracon, and Azekah, Lachish and Beth-achzib in the Lachish ostraca. Garfinkel is correct in stating that the tiny sub-districts reconstructed by Galil are nowhere reflected in the administrative documents from the First Temple period. In any event, the division into 'mini-districts' is not supported by any evidence from the administration of neighbouring countries or from the Bible; it is entirely the result of an artificial process of re-grouping based on the town lists in the book of Joshua. Internal groupings may be created in any list drawn up in any kind of geographical order, without constituting evidence of the status of those groups within the administration of the kingdom.[8] The few documents discovered to date in excavations do not enable us to determine the then existing array of districts within the Kingdom of Judah; we must, accordingly, seek other means of handling this complex problem.

It seems to me that the key to this problem may be found by examining the status of Jerusalem in the framework of the town lists. As stated above, Jerusalem expanded considerably during the eighth century BCE, and became a metropolis occupying some 600 dunams and housing thousands of residents—several times larger than the area and population of any other city in the kingdom. Jerusalem

---

8. For criticism (with which I wholeheartedly agree) of Garfinkel 1987, see Eph'al and Naveh 1988.

was located in the centre of a sort of district, which encompassed the capital and its periphery, including the agricultural areas of the city's residents, as well as satellite settlements directly connected to Jerusalem proper (Barkay 1985: 399-401). A similar situation prevailed in every metropolis of the ancient Near East. The city's exceptional, singular status in the framework of the kingdom is indicated by the phrase 'Judah and Jerusalem'. Furthermore, in the array of districts in force in the post-exilic period—an array parallel in some respects to the town lists of Judah and Benjamin (Alt 1925: 115-16; Aharoni 1956: 152-55; Kallai 1960: 92-94)—Jerusalem is included as an independent region (Neh. 3.9, 12). The special status of Jerusalem in the Kingdom of Judah is not reflected in the town lists; this fact cannot be reconciled with the hypothesis defining them as lists of the districts of the Judahite kingdom.

An additional difficulty encountered by that hypothesis becomes evident when we consider the location of the central cities in the southern areas of the Judean hill country.[9] Hebron is situated near the eastern edge of the area within which it is mentioned; by contrast, Debir lies on the northern border of the area within which it is included, while its two near neighbours, Arab and Dumah, are listed one 'district' to the north. Galil correctly noted that the internal division of the hill country does not list the information at our disposal concerning the places of residence of the main families occupying the hill country (Galil 1984: 210-11, 213-16, 224). This is obvious in the case of the sons of Caleb, whose families dwelt in three different 'districts'; even Hebron itself, the most important Calebite city, is detached from its 'descendants' (Jorkeam, Maon, and Beth-zur; see 1 Chron. 2.44-45), which are listed in separate 'districts'. The family of Othniel also resided in two different 'districts'. The present order of the town lists in Joshua 15 is not based on any genitive principle. Yet the discrepancy ostensibly existing between the main families of the Judean hill country and the town lists results entirely from the hypothesis that the division of those lists reflects districts within the kingdom. A different explanation for the division of the town lists into groups of towns may resolve this discrepancy.

A special problem is posed by the settlement of Zior, mentioned in the framework of 'district VI' (Josh. 15.54). The site, which has preserved its name, Si'ir, is located one 'district' to the north, and pottery from the Iron Age II was found there (Kochavi 1972: 21, 54, site 100; Galil 1984: 212; Kallai 1986: 389). In view of its location, some scholars have rejected the identification of Si'ir with Zior, claiming that it is irreconcilable with the identification of other sites listed in the same 'district', and that the similarity between the names is purely coincidental (Noth 1953: 97-98; Kochavi 1972: 21, 54; Galil 1984: 212). Admittedly, acceptance of this identification creates a conspicuous deviation in the descriptions of the settlements in the Judean hill country, as these are usually grouped in well-defined geographical areas. Nevertheless, this identification should not be rejected out of hand; its acceptance would constitute additional evidence that the internal division in the hill country does not reflect a system of districts.

---

9. See the maps published in Kochavi 1972: 22; Aharoni 1979: 346; Kallai 1986: map no. 2

In view of this discussion, it may be hypothesized that the town lists were based on an administrative document listing the settlements of the kingdom, in accordance with a division into broad geographical-administrative territories. The town list in Joshua 15 features the headings *bngbh* ('in the Negev', Josh. 15.21), *bšplh* ('in the Shephelah', 15.33), *bhr* ('in the hill country', 15.48), *bmdbr* ('in the wilderness', 15.61); that in Joshua 18 is headed 'of the tribe of Benjamin' (Josh. 18.21). It should be noted that the conquest descriptions in Joshua, written by the Deuteronomist during a period not distant from that of the lists discussed here, frequently mention a similar geographical division prevailing in Judah (10.40; 11.2, 16; 12.8; see also Deut. 1.7). Even more striking is the fact that Jeremiah, a contemporary of our list as well as of the Deuteronomist, makes use of the same division as that appearing in our list in describing the entire Kingdom of Judah: Jer. 17.26—'And people shall come from the cities of Judah and the places round about Jerusalem, from the land of Benjamin, from the Shephelah, from the hill country, and from the Negev…'; Jer. 32.44—'in the cities of the hill country, in the cities of the Shephelah, and in the cities of the Negev…'; Jer. 33.13—'in the cities of the hill country, in the cities of the Shephelah, and in the cities of the Negev, in the land of Benjamin, the places about Jerusalem, and in the cities of Judah…' It may be postulated that this division into broad geographical territories (Negev, hill country, Shephelah, Jerusalem and vicinity, Benjamin) reflects the administrative division of the Kingdom of Judah, and that this was the external framework for the preparation of the original document on which our town lists are based.

One may further ask whether the numerical totals of towns accompanying the list were also copied from the original document, or were added up by the later author. On the one hand, it may be shown that some contradictions exist between the totals given and the number of towns actually listed—a fact which may attest to the originality of the numerical totals. On the other hand, we know of cases in which the sum total was secondarily added to an existing list of towns.[10] Scholars have ascertained that the division of the broad territories into sub-sections generally corresponds to the natural topography; this may reinforce the hypothesis that the totals of towns comprised an integral part of the original document. Nonetheless, it may just as easily be claimed that these totals were added by the later author, who was familiar with the topography of the kingdom; if this is the case, that author, while breaking down the list into separate groups, could have simply recorded the total number of places listed in each group. In any event, even if the numerical totals were drawn from the original document, this does not prove the existence of administrative sub-districts; the figures may merely have been technically recorded as sub-totals, as part of the grand total of towns in the list.

In closing, we may state that the division of the town lists of Judah and Benjamin into sub-groups does not reflect the administrative division of the

---

10. See Noth 1953: 93. For the attempt to reconcile the contradiction between the total number of Negeb towns (36 in all) and the summation (15.32) 'in all, 29 cities, with their villages', see Talmon 1965. For the secondary nature of the summations in the list of Levitical cities, see Na'aman 1986a: 209, 214.

kingdom; nor is it certain that these groups of towns constituted administrative sub-districts within the kingdom. The broad geographical areas apparently corresponded to the districts of the kingdom and constituted distinct organisational–administrative units; they included Benjamin, Jerusalem, the Judean hill country, the Shephelah, the Negev, and possibly the Wilderness. It appears to me that, at the time of Sennacherib's campaign, when it became necessary to organise a supply system for times of war and siege, the kingdom was organised on a slightly different basis, and divided into four 'districts': three in the hill country and one in the Shephelah (Yadin 1961; Aharoni 1962: 53-56; 1979: 398-99; Na'aman 1986b: 14-17). It may be postulated that the division into districts had been initiated a short while after the emergence of the Kingdom of Judah, when it became necessary to adapt administrative procedure to the newly established kingdom, and was maintained throughout the First Temple period.

4. *The Dating of the Town Lists*
In his seminal study of the southern town lists in Joshua, Alt proposed that they be dated to Josiah's reign (Alt 1925: 106-12). He argued that the town list of Benjamin includes Bethel, Ophrah, and Jericho—towns which had been controlled by Israel up to its conquest by Assyria, and did not pass into Judah until Josiah's day. Alt even explained that the town list of Dan reflects the westward expansion of the Kingdom of Judah at that time, and that the mention of Lod, Hadid, and Ono in the lists of the 'Returning Captives' (the 'Gola List') indicates that those places belonged to Judah in the last stages of the kingdom's existence —in view of the assumption that the exiles returned to the places from which they had been exiled by the Babylonians. This date has been accepted by other, principally German, scholars (Proksch 1928: 45-46; Noth 1953: 13-14; 1960: 273-74; Welten 1969: 93-102; Soggin 1984: 245). The present writer has raised additional arguments in its favour (Na'aman 1986a: 229-30; 1986b: 18 n. 6).

On the other hand, some scholars have dated the list to an earlier time. Cross and Wright (1956: 212-26) dated it to Jehoshaphat's reign. Mazar initially supported this date; however, following his excavations at En-gedi, he apparently changed his opinion and began to favour a later date.[11] Aharoni also assumed that the initial division into districts was accomplished under Jehoshaphat, but that the list in its present form (except for Josh. 18.21-24) reflects the situation in Uzziah's reign (Aharoni 1959: 239-46; 1979: 268-72). Schunck dated the list to Uzziah's time, but considered the lists in Josh. 18.21-24 and 19.41-46 as supplements from Josiah's reign (Schunck 1962: 141-45 n. 18; 1963: 153-68). Kallai dated the town list of Benjamin to Abijah's reign, and ascribed that of Judah to the reign of Hezekiah (Kallai 1960: 24-26, 33-34; 1986: 372-77); his view was accepted by Galil (1984: 223; 1985: 12; 1987: 55, 60).

---

11. Mazar initially distinguished between the town list of Judah, which he ascribed to Jehoshaphat's reign, and that of Benjamin, which he ascribed to Josiah's day (Mazar [Maisler] 1944: 74 n. 9; 1950: 718). He later viewed both town lists as having been composed under Jehoshaphat (1958: 566). After directing the Tel Goren (En-gedi) excavations, he again changed his opinion concerning the dating of these lists (1967: 223).

As observed above, the separation of the town lists of Judah and Benjamin into two distinct periods does not withstand the test of criticism. The date proposed by Kallai for the town list of Judah is principally based on the omission of Beth-shemesh, Timnah, and Aijalon—towns which the Philistines conquered from Ahaz (2 Chron. 28.18); on the other hand, Hezekiah conquered Philistia (2 Kgs 18.8), which Kallai believes explains the inclusion of the Philistine towns in the town list of Judah (Josh. 15.45-47). It seems, however, that these arguments can be easily disproved. A significant number of *lmlk* seal impressions were uncovered in the excavations of both Beth-shemesh and Timnah (Tel Batash), indicating that these towns belonged to the Kingdom of Judah on the eve of Sennacherib's campaign (Na'aman 1986a: 11-17). Nor is there any basis for the assumption that Hezekiah annexed the Philistine towns mentioned in Josh. 15.45-47, as his entire intention was to form an alliance headed by him and in cooperation with Egypt, not to conquer or annex. Moreover, as suggested above (see Section 2), the addition of the Philistine towns to the list was implemented by the author of the book, and they did not appear in the original document.

The arguments raised in favour of dating the town list to the ninth or eighth century BCE are not convincing, and it now seems appropriate to focus the discussion on the most likely alternative datings: the second half of the eighth century, or the second half of the seventh century. Significantly, during the two hundred years after the establishment of the Kingdom of Judah (the late tenth century BCE) there was continuity of settlement and material culture in the kingdom, with no destruction or disruption of culture. Thus, we are unable to make a detailed study of the situation prevailing in Uzziah's reign, as, with the exception of several verses in 2 Chronicles (26.6-15) whose reliability is doubted by some scholars,[12] almost nothing is known of his time, and there is no way of isolating archaeological findings from his period. This continuity of settlement was interrupted by Sennacherib's campaign in 701 BCE, when many cities were destroyed, causing a significant break in the history of the Kingdom of Judah for the first time since its establishment. The cultural characteristics of Judah in the seventh century, and their geographical distribution, differ considerably from those in the eighth century. The choice of the 'Hezekiah or Josiah' alternative (or rather, the second half of the eighth or the second half of the seventh century BCE) is the most fruitful for discussion, as their reigns are also covered by considerable documentation, in addition to archaeological findings. Obviously, dating the list in the eighth or seventh century will require us to re-examine the rulers who reigned at that time, in an attempt to determine whose rule is more appropriate to the dating of the town list.

Following are a number of points to be considered in analysing the proposed alternatives:[13]

---

12. For the reliability of the descriptions of Uzziah's reign in Chronicles, see Welten 1973: 153-63, with earlier literature; Knauf 1985: 116-19, 122.

13. I will not compare here the lists of Judah and Benjamin to the genealogies appearing in Chronicles, nor to additional lists appearing in those books and ascribed to the period of the monarchy, as they have no direct relevance to the issue under discussion.

(1) The Benjamin district (Josh. 18) includes the town of Avvim (v. 23)—a settlement named for a group of immigrants brought in from Avva (a town located on the border between Elam and Babylon; see 2 Kgs 17.24, 31; 18.34; 19.13) and settled in the Bethel district by King Sargon II of Assyria in approximately 708 BCE.[14] If this assumption is correct, the town list dates, at the earliest, to Hezekiah's reign, several years before Sennacherib's campaign to Judah.

(2) The appearance of Bethel, Ophrah, and Jericho in the town list—as observed by Alt (1925: 109-10; see also Klein 1983)—is only appropriate to Josiah's time. Since the foundation of the Kingdom of Israel, these cities were located in its territory; after the Assyrian conquest, they were annexed to the Assyrian province of Samaria. Only after the Assyrian retreat was Josiah able to expand northward, to conquer Bethel and annex it, as well as other nearby cities (e.g. Jericho), to his kingdom. The town of Geba mentioned in this group (Josh. 18.24) is Geba of Benjamin, which, being located near the northern border of the Kingdom of Judah since its establishment, had protected the vital eastern route running from Baal-hazor through Ophrah to Jerusalem. Thanks to its important strategic status, Geba was fortified, along with Mizpah, by Asa (1 Kgs 15.22); in the description of Josiah's reforms (2 Kgs 23.8), it is mentioned (in the phrase 'from Geba to Beersheba') as denoting the northern border of the kingdom. The latter passage explicitly relates to the reform implemented in 'the cities of Judah', and the author clearly differentiates between this early reform and the reform later implemented in Bethel (2 Kgs 23.15-18). Accordingly, it seems to me that there is no basis for the suggested location of Geba as far north as et-Tell in the hill country of Ephraim, nor for setting the border of the kingdom that far north.[15] The northern border of the Benjamin district (Josh. 18.21-28) should be set along the Bethel–Ophrah line; this deviates northward from the traditional border of the Kingdom of Judah, which, from Asa's time to the beginning of Josiah's rule, had been set along the line Geba–Mizpah.

(3) Conspicuously absent from the town list of Benjamin are many cities mentioned in Isaiah (10.28-32). The only towns common to both lists are Ramah, Geba, and Gibeah (= Gibeah of Saul; for determination of the phrasing in Josh. 18.28, see Section 2, above); missing are Aiath, Migron, Michmash, Maabara ('the Pass'), Bat-gallim ('Daughter of Gallim'), Laishah, Anathoth, Madmannah, Gebim, and Nob (admittedly, some of these are not towns, but toponyms located along the route). Kallai noted that a group of places in Benjamin was missing from the town list, and suggested that an entire district had been omitted from the

---

14. Na'aman 1986a: 229-30 n. 47; Na'aman and Zadok 1988: 45-46. It is possible that the name 'Ophni' (Josh. 18.24) is that of a settlement named for a group of exiles brought in from some distant place bearing that name. No suitable identification has as yet been suggested for this toponym (Noth 1953: 108; Schunck 1962: 152-53; Kuschke 1965: 108-109; Kallai 1972).

15. Mazar (Maisler) 1941, 1954; Smirin 1952: 91; Liver 1958: 420; Kallai 1960: 75-76; 1986: 400-401 and map no. 2; Cogan and Tadmor 1988: 286. Aharoni distinguished between the Geba mentioned in Josh. 18.24, which he identified with Geba (Ephraim) (1959: 232-33; 1976: 12), and the Geba mentioned in 2 Kgs 23.8, which he identified with Geba (Benjamin) (1979: 404). See Aharoni 1985. Demsky proposed the identification of the Geba mentioned in 2 Kgs 23.8 with Gibeon (Demsky 1973: 30-31).

list (Kallai 1960: 33; 1986: 399-400 map no. 2). By refraining from identifying Geba (Josh. 18.24) with Geba of Benjamin, or Gibeah (Josh. 18.28) with Gibeah of Saul, Kallai artificially expanded the 'missing area'. In fact, what is missing is not a 'district', but simply a group of towns, notably Michmash, Anathoth, and Alemeth, all located northeast of Jerusalem. Possibly, this group was initially listed after Gibeath (v. 28), and was mistakenly omitted. The original text may be restored thus: 'Gibeah <of Saul...> and Kirjath-jearim' (Na'aman 1986a: 229 n. 45). The absence of this group of towns from Josh. 18.21-28 prevents us from determining whether any correspondence exists between the town list of Benjamin and the group of places mentioned in Isa. 10.28-32, or whether the two lists belong to different periods; the latter supposition would allow for the possibility that some of the towns mentioned in the prophecy were destroyed in Sennacherib's campaign and not inhabited at the time of composition of the town list.

(4) There is a considerable difference between the Shephelah town list in Joshua 15 and that cited in Micah (1.10-16), which reflects the period of Sennacherib's campaign to Judah. The only towns common to both lists are Zenan, Lachish, Achzib, Mareshah, and Adullam. On the other hand, the towns of Gath, Beth-leaphrah (or 'Aphrah), Shaphir, 'Eriah ('Nakedness'), Maroth, and Moresheth-gath are missing from the list in Joshua 15. (For the toponyms in Mic. 1.10-16, see Na'aman 1995.) It is hard to avoid the conclusion that the two lists belong to different periods of time, and that some of the places destroyed in Sennacherib's campaign were not inhabited at the time of composition of the town list.

(5) The lack of correspondence between the Shephelah town list and the state of affairs in that area during Hezekiah's rule is also evident when comparing the list to the distribution of *lmlk* seal impressions. The storage jars bearing these impressions were manufactured in a central royal pottery, sent to various districts of the kingdom to be filled with agricultural produce, and then brought to the towns as reserve rations for use in time of war and siege (Na'aman 1986b: 15-17; see Mommsen, Perlman and Yellin 1984; Garfinkel 1988: 70; Eshel 1989 [also Vaughn 1999; Kletter 2002]). Their distribution reflects both the preparations for siege and the array of settlements in the Kingdom of Judah under Hezekiah, immediately prior to Sennacherib's campaign. Fairly large numbers of *lmlk*-impressed handles were found in Gezer (37), Tel 'Erani (15), Tel Batash (11), Tell es-Ṣâfi (6), and Tel Miqne-Ekron (3); all of the above (except, possibly, Tel 'Erani) are located west of the area included in the list of Shephelah towns in Joshua 15. There is also a conspicuous degree of discrepancy on the northern border; the northern cities (Bethel and Ophrah) are not included in the logistical array of the *lmlk* jars. (For an updated list of the *lmlk* seal impressions, see Vaughn 1999.)

(6) Among the other towns which may be linked with Hezekiah's day, the name of *mmšt*—one of the four towns whose names appear in the *lmlk* seal impressions—is conspicuously absent from our list. I proposed that the list of 'cities for defence' mentioned in 2 Chron. 11.6-10 be detached from Rehoboam to whom it is ascribed, and linked to the preparations made by Hezekiah to meet

the Assyrian attack in 701 BCE (Na'aman 1986b: 5-11). The towns appearing in this list, but missing from the town list of Judah, include Adoraim in the hill country and Aijalon and Gath in the Shephelah. Acceptance of this suggested date would provide additional confirmation that the number and distribution of the towns of Judah in Hezekiah's day differ from those reflected in our town list.

(7) The genealogical lists in 1 Chron. 4.21-23 mention the following places in the Shephelah: Lecah, Mareshah, Beth-ashbea, Cozeba, Lahem(?), Netaim, Gederah. The proposals for the identification of Lecah with Lachish and Lahem with Lahemas (Yeivin 1962; Demsky 1966: 213 n. 15; Galil 1987: 64) are unsupported and should be rejected. The town list includes Mareshah, Cozeba-Achzib, and Gederah, which appear in the genealogical lists, while the remaining places, Lecah, Beth-ashbea, Lahem(?), Netaim, are unknown. The mention of 'the house of linen workers' (v. 21) and 'the potters...' who 'dwelt there with the king for his work' (v. 23) indicate that these lists date from the time of the monarchy, and may refer to royal potteries and workshops established in the region by the kings of Judah during that kingdom's great expansion in the eighth century BCE (Demsky 1966; Aharoni 1968: 168-69 n. 29; Lemaire 1977: 136-37 n. 123; Mommsen, Perlman and Yellin 1984: 111-12). If this conclusion is correct, it provides additional testimony to the striking difference in urbanisation patterns in the Shephelah between the town list and the lists reflecting settlement in the eighth century.

(8) Let me now consider the correspondence between the town list and the state of settlement in Judah in the seventh century, beginning with the testimony on the marriages of the kings of Judah. Manasseh married a woman from Jotbah (2 Kgs 21.19); Amon married a woman from Bozkath (22.1); Josiah married women from Libnah (23.31; 24.18) and Rumah (23.36); Jehoiakim married a woman from Jerusalem (24.8). One of these women, then, came from the capital, and two of the others from the Shephelah (Bozkath and Libnah). The origin of the remaining two is disputed. Some scholars have proposed that they came from towns in the Galilee, and their marriages to kings of Judah reflected a policy of intentional efforts on the part of those kings to achieve rapprochement with the Galilean population (Smirin 1952: 56; Aharoni 1957: 132; Broshi 1958; Yeivin 1960: 254-55; Liver 1968; Cogan 1974: 91). Such a policy, however, was by no means appropriate to Manasseh, a vassal to Assyria throughout his reign; moreover, it is doubtful whether Rumah and Jotbah in the Valley of Beth-netophah could have been settled in the seventh century. Both towns were destroyed in the campaign of Tiglath-pileser III in 733–32 BCE and their population exiled (Tadmor 1967), and there is no evidence of the town having been resettled by exiles from other places. The archaeological survey attests to a significant decrease in settlement in the Lower Galilee in the seventh century, as a direct result of the Assyrian campaign and the subsequent Assyrian policy in that area (Gal 1988–89). Accordingly, the assumption that the kings of Judah married women from that distant and desolate area is difficult to accept. Ginsberg (1950: 350) has proposed an emendation reading 'Juttah' (for 'Jotbah') and 'Dumah' (for 'Rumah'), enabling the location of both these places in the southern Judean

hill country. Given the many *resh–daleth* substitutions in the Bible, the emendation 'Dumah' appears possible (though certainly not compulsory), and may refer to the Dumah mentioned in the town list (15.52). The emendation 'Juttah', however, is not corroborated by any other ancient version, and should be rejected. Thus, those scholars who sought to locate it outside Judah, possibly on the Idumaean border, may well be correct; the Idumaean location would be appropriate to Manasseh's rule and to the *pax Assyriaca*.[16]

(9) Both 2 Kings and the town list in Joshua mention Geba and Beersheba (2 Kgs 23.8), Bethel (23.17), and Mizpah (25.23, 25). Both the book of Jeremiah and the town lists mention Tekoa and Beth-haccerem (Jer. 6.1), Kiriath-jearim (26.20), Gibeon (28.1; 41.12, 16); Ramah (31.14), Lachish and Azekah (34.7), Mizpah (chs. 40–41), and Bethlehem (41.17). Moreover, I have already discussed the similarity between the names of the regions in the town list and in Jeremiah (Section 3, above). Anathoth, Jeremiah's home town, is missing from the town list; following Kallai, I have suggested that Anathoth, and other towns, were inadvertently omitted from the town list of Benjamin (paragraph 3, above). Also missing from the town list are Netophah, home of Seraiah and the sons of Ephai (2 Kgs 25.23; Jer. 40.8); and Nehalim, which—as some scholars have postulated—may have been the home town of Shemaiah of 'Nehelam' (Jer. 29.24-32) (Kochavi 1972: 28 Site 32; Galil 1984: 218 n. 64). It should be noted that additional towns, mentioned in lists ascribed to David's time (Harod, Hushah, Atroth-beth-joab), are missing from the town list pertaining to the Bethlehem area ('district IX'). Was this group of towns omitted from the list, as in the case of the town list of Benjamin? This assumption, of course, is by no means compulsory; the absence of Netophah (and, perhaps, of Nehalim) may also result from the fact that the town list is not complete, and that individual places were omitted (see below).

(10) Let me now compare the town list with a number of seventh-century inscriptions found in excavations in various towns in Judah.

Ostraca of the Arad archive[17] mention Beersheba, Yanum,[18] Kinah, Arad, Maon, Hazar-susah, and Baalath,[19] all of which appear in the town list. On the other hand, Ramath-negeb—which appears in an Arad ostracon, in the town list of Simeon (Josh. 19.8), and in the list of towns to which David sent the spoils of Amalek (1 Sam. 30.27)—is missing from the Negev town list in Joshua 15.

---

16. Montgomery 1951: 521; Gray 1970: 711; McKay 1973: 23-25; Williamson 1982: 390, 395. It should also be remembered that a place named Arumah was located close to Shechem (Judg. 9.41), and that the root *rwm* is quite common in ancient Palestinian toponyms (Isserlin 1957: 141-43).

17. For publication of the inscriptions from Arad, see Lemaire 1977: 145-235; Aharoni 1981 [also Renz 1997: 290-306, 347-403, with earlier literature in p. 367]. Three place names mentioned by Aharoni (*'nym, zp, ygwr*) have been left out, as the transliteration of their names cannot be ascertained (see notes by Aharoni and Lemaire to inscriptions 17, 25, 42).

18. There can be no certainty that the word *ynm* indeed denotes a place-name. See the literature cited in Aharoni 1981: inscription 19.

19. Lemaire (1977: 216-17) read inscription No. 60 (ll. 1-2) as *kprh hb'lty*—that is, a certain person originating from Baalath. However, his suggested rendering is quite uncertain.

Inscriptions from Lachish[20] mention Achzib, Azekah, Lachish, and perhaps also Ashan (Ussishkin 1978: 83-84), all of which appear in the town list. On the other hand, Beth-harapid, if this is in fact a name of a town (see Lemaire 1977: 110-12), does not appear in the town list.

A Ḥorvat 'Uza ostracon (Beit-Arieh 1986–87) mentions Moladah and Makkedah, both of which appear in the town list; on the other hand, *rptn* is not mentioned.

A considerable degree of correspondence seems to exist between the seventh-century epigraphic findings and the town list. However, a few individual towns (Ramath-negeb, *rptn*, and perhaps also Beth-harapid) do not appear in the list, and this problem should be examined before summing up the chronological details.

(11) Turning to the archaeological excavations and surveys conducted in Judah, we see that the large number of settlements mentioned in the town list exceeds the number of contemporary sites discovered by archaeological research. A good example of this trend is provided by the Negev district, for which the list mentions 35 towns, a number greater than that of the sites discovered in the area over many years. Accordingly, it may be assumed that the list also included a number of small sites inhabited by several households each. This situation makes it difficult to discuss the archaeological findings. Let me illustrate this difficulty by means of the excavations in various Shephelah sites. Several large sites in this area (Beth-shemesh, Tell 'Aiṭûn, Tell Beit Mirsim) revealed no pottery from the seventh century BCE (Ussishkin 1974: 118-20; Aharoni and Aharoni 1976; Aharoni 1982: 261-64; Ayalon 1985; Zimhoni 1985). Are we to conclude that these places were not included in the list (on the assumption that the list indeed belongs to that period)? Could these places have been inhabited by a few individual families and thus included in the list, but not discerned in archaeological investigations, as their material remains are located near the surface of the mound, making them extremely difficult to trace?

This example illustrates how careful one has to be to avoid reaching negative conclusions on the basis of archaeological findings; and, as observed above, all the archaeological arguments raised thus far concerning the dating of the town lists were based on the absence of layers of settlement from certain periods at sites supposedly belonging to those periods. Nor should we forget that a prerequisite for any historical interpretation of archaeological findings is the certain identification of the site(s) under discussion. Thus, for example, there is no real historical basis for the archaeological discussions concerning Tell el-Far'ah in the south, as its identification with Sharuhen/Shilhim is not well founded, and it was apparently located outside the borders of the Kingdom of Judah (Na'aman 1980: 147-48). Given those limitations, it may be stated that stratigraphic evidence from the sites cannot provide a definitive dating of the town lists, and that, at best, such evidence may serve as auxiliary tools, alongside the historical evidence and the distribution of special findings (*lmlk* seal impressions, or 'rosette' jar handles).

---

20. The Lachish inscriptions are quoted according to Lemaire 1977: 83-143.

The Tel Goren (En-gedi) excavations showed that the settlement here was established in the seventh century BCE; this, at first glance, supposedly constituted evidence that the town list did not date from before that period.[21] However, surveys conducted around En-gedi have shown that the oasis was also settled in the eighth century, therefore the Tel Goren findings cannot be used to settle this issue (Aharoni 1979: 351). None of the pottery found at Ramat Raḥel dates from before the eighth century; if the identification of that site with Beth-haccerem is correct, this information—like the En-gedi findings—may be used to set an upper limit to the list (Aharoni 1956: 152-55; 1979: 351). A similar situation is reflected in the Aroer excavations: the findings indicate that the site was established in the eighth century, perhaps even in the second half of that century (Biran and Cohen 1981: 270-73); the identification of Aroer with Adadah (i.e. Ararah, by *resh–daleth* substitution), a town appearing in the town list, enables the setting of an upper limit to the list. Finally, let me mention Ḥorvat 'Uza, a site on the southeastern border of the Kingdom of Judah, which some scholars have identified with Kinah, a town appearing in the town list and in an Arad document (Lemaire 1973: 18-22; Mittmann 1977: 234-35; Na'aman 1980: 145). The excavations here revealed no pottery dating to before the seventh century (Beit-Arieh 1986; Beck 1986 [also Beit-Arieh and Cresson 1991]). If we accept the proposed identification, this will constitute the first evidence that the town list does not date from before the seventh century BCE.

Noteworthy also is the enormous difference between the number of settlements found in the recent surveys of the Shephelah and the number of settlements in the town list: 92 settlements have been discovered in the incomplete survey conducted so far (Broshi and Finkelstein 1990: 12), whereas the overall number mentioned in Josh. 15.33-44 is 40. The discrepancy in numbers is another indication that the town list should not be dated to the eighth century BCE.

(12) Of the many seventh-century archaeological finds unearthed in the Judean hill country, it is important to examine the distribution of one particular type of artifact, the 'rosette' seal impression. These impressions appear on the handles of a jar type which developed from jars bearing *lmlk* seal impressions. Neutron activation analysis of two jars bearing rosette impressions found in Jerusalem and Tel Batash (Timnah) showed that both jars were manufactured in the Shephelah, probably at the same pottery centre which manufactured the *lmlk* jars (Mommsen, Perlman and Yellin 1984: 106-107). Were the rosette jars manufactured by a royal authority, as were those inscribed *lmlk*? Scholarly opinions differ: some believe the rosette to have been a royal symbol (Albright in Mendelsohn 1940: 21 n. 51; Barkay 1978: 213 n. 27; Aharoni 1979: 400); others, the trade-mark of a group of potters (Mendelsohn 1940: 20-21; Welten 1969: 32-33; Cross 1969: 22b [see recently Cahill 1995: 231-46]). In any event, given the striking discrepancy between the distribution of the jars marked *lmlk* and the town list (see paragraph 5, above), it is especially interesting to examine the affinity between the distribution of rosette jars and the town list.

21. See n. 11, above.

Following is a list of the sites in which rosette-stamped jar handles were found, arranged by districts (see Welten 1969: 191; Barkay 1978: 212-13 nn. 16-22; 1985: 416-18 and n. 11; A. Mazar 1985: 317; Nadelman 1989: 132) [for an updated list of the rosette seal impressions, see Cahill 1995: 244-46; Kletter 1999: 34-37; for a distribution map, see Cahill 1995: 245]:

Benjamin:	Tell en-Naṣbeh, Tell el-Ful, Gibeon.
Jerusalem area:	Jerusalem, Ramat Raḥel.
Judean hill country:	Manaḥat, er-Ras, Nebi Daniel, Beth-zur.
Negev:	Tel Malhata, Arad, Tel 'Ira.
Wilderness:	En-gedi.
Shephelah:	Lachish, Azekah, Socoh, Tell Bornât, Tell el-Beidah, Tel 'Erani.
West of Judah's northwestern border:	Gezer, Tel Batash, Tel Miqne-Ekron.

It may be stated that the distribution of rosette-stamped jar handles corresponds, to a great extent, to that of the town list, as all the districts in the kingdom are represented. The towns in the list of rosette seal impressions correspond more closely to the distribution of rosette jars than to the distribution of jars bearing *lmlk* seal impressions. However, it should be borne in mind that the number of *lmlk* jar handles found to date (about 1716; Vaughn 1999: 185-97) is some 6.9 times greater than the number of rosette jar handles (about 250; Cahill 1995), and that, for this reason, any comparison should be cautiously undertaken.[22] Moreover, the majority of the rosette jar handles were found in Jerusalem and Ramat Raḥel, only about a quarter were found in the Shephelah, and the central Judean mountains and the Negev are almost negligible (Kletter 1999: 37). A better understanding of the distribution patterns of the *lmlk* and rosette seal impressions depends on comprehension of their function in the administration and economy of the Kingdom of Judah in the eighth and seventh centuries BCE respectively.

Both jar types are well represented in the Benjamin district; not a single specimen of either type has been found to date in the southern hill country of Ephraim (except for one *lmlk* jar handle from Bethel; see Eshel 1989). In the west, however, there is a nearly complete correspondence between the town list and the distribution of rosette jars, in contrast to the *lmlk* jars. The three exceptions in the Shephelah are Tel Miqne-Ekron, Tel Batash (Timnah) and Gezer, which are not included in the town list, although rosette jars were found there. In the seventh century, Timnah was apparently part of the kingdom of Ekron (see Part II Section 1, below); the presence of rosette jars at sites located outside the borders of the Kingdom of Judah constitutes an obvious exception. Could this possibly result from the proximity of Timnah and Gezer to the place where the jars were manufactured, and/or their close economic connections with the Shephelah towns of Judah at the time?

---

22. *Lmlk* seal impressions were frequently stamped on several handles of the same jar (see Ussishkin 1976), whereas rosette seal impressions were stamped on two handles at most (A. Mazar 1985: 317 and n. 44). This factor should be taken into account when attempting to compute the total number of jars bearing impressions.

In summary, the information at our disposal reveals that there is little correspondence between the names and distribution of the towns in the list, on one hand, and the state of affairs prevailing in eighth-century Judah (especially in Hezekiah's day), on the other. This information also indicates the great degree of destruction and desolation which befell the Kingdom of Judah following Sennacherib's campaign; clear testimony, from both documents and archaeological findings, attests to the fact that many settlements were not inhabited in the kingdom's later stages of existence.

The inclusion of the Jericho and Bethel areas in the town list also weighs the dating question in favour of Josiah's day, as Alt claimed. The great majority of towns existing in the seventh and early sixth centuries BCE, and mentioned in the Bible or in epigraphic documents, also appear in the town list of Joshua. Conspicuous is the absence of Beth-shemesh, located on the western border of Judah, which was apparently not inhabited in the seventh century BCE. Among the other towns not mentioned in the town list are Netophah, Ramath-negeb, *rptn*, and perhaps also Nehalim and Beth-harapid. We thus see that individual towns in the kingdom may, for one reason or another, have been omitted from the list. Notable among the above mentioned omissions is Ramath-negeb, mentioned in an Arad ostracon, in a list seemingly dating from David's day (1 Sam. 30.27) and in the town list of Simeon; if this town is to be identified with Tel 'Ira, as some scholars have proposed, it was both inhabited and fortified in the late eighth and seventh centuries BCE.[23] The distribution of rosette jars—which date from the seventh century BCE—corresponds to the scope of the town list, providing additional corroboration of my conclusion as to its proper dating.

II. *The Kingdom of Josiah and his Political Status*

1. *The Geopolitical Background and Date of the Assyrian Retreat from Palestine*
Josiah is usually considered as a strong and independent ruler, who was active for many years in the vacuum formed by the Assyrian retreat from Palestine, and succeeded in considerably expanding the borders of his kingdom. This view has many variants, concerning such points as the date of release from Assyrian bondage; the number and distribution of towns conquered by Josiah and annexed to his kingdom; and his relations with Egypt. My conclusions regarding the limited borders of the Kingdom of Judah under Josiah are of extreme importance in evaluating his achievements; these conclusions clash with many generally accepted conventions pertinent to the history of his reign.

I will now turn to examine the sources relevant to Josiah's time and activity, in order to determine how they may be integrated with the conclusions obtained from analysis of the town list. I will first examine the date of the Assyrian retreat from Palestine. Some scholars have claimed that the Assyrian domination of

---

23. For the excavations at Tel 'Ira, see Beit-Arieh 1985; Biran 1985 [see recently Beit-Arieh (ed.) 1999]. For the identification of the site, see Lemaire 1973: 21-22; Na'aman 1980: 146, with earlier literature in n. 48.

Palestine collapsed several years before the death of Ashurbanipal in 631 BCE, and that, at the time of Josiah's rise to power, the Assyrian presence had become so weak as to be scarcely noticeable, enabling Josiah to operate for many years in the vacuum thus created (Ginsberg 1950: 351-53 and n. 19; Smirin 1952: 13-14, 31-32, 57-58, 62-63; Cross and Freedman 1953; Noth 1960: 272-73; Cogan 1974: 71; Malamat 1974: 270-71; Spalinger 1978a: 49-51; Eph'al 1979: 281-82; Spieckermann 1982: 37; Miller and Hayes 1986: 381-85; Halpern 1987: 97). According to those scholars, the premature Assyrian retreat from Palestine was occasioned by pressure on the part of northern tribes, especially the Scythians—whose campaigns, according to Herodotus, reached as far as the Egyptian border—as well as by the erosion of Assyria's own power following the protracted wars against Babylonia, Elam, and the Arabs in 652–645 BCE. Thus Eph'al claimed that the Gezer cuneiform tablet dated to 651 BCE, from which the name of the eponym then in office is lacking, indicates 'serious breakdowns in communication and control in Palestine and perhaps in other parts of the western region of the Assyrian empire'. According to his view, the revolt of the towns Ushu and Akko in c. 644, and Manasseh's revolt as described in 2 Chron. 33.11, indicate that Assyrian control of the West began to wane in the early second half of the seventh century, and 'seems to have declined rapidly thenceforward and to have ended within a few years' (Eph'al 1979: 281-82). However, in a document from Gezer, written in 649 BCE, the name of the eponym then in office appears; we may therefore state that, even if there had been a brief lapse in communications in 651, following the revolt of Shamash-shum-ukin in Babylonia, it was rapidly remedied. Revolts along the coast of Lebanon recurred frequently under Sennacherib, Esarhaddon, and Ashurbanipal; the revolt of Ushu and Akko, which was suppressed by Ashurbanipal, was no exception. The account of Manasseh's revolt conceals a good deal more than it reveals (to the point that many scholars believe that no such revolt took place);[24] even if it did happen, it was quickly overcome and the rebel ruler exiled, a fact which certainly does not indicate any Assyrian weakness.

Cogan claimed that the omission of any reference to Assyria in the account of the murder of Amon, king of Judah (2 Kgs 21.23-24), indicates that by that time (640 BCE) Judah had already begun to free itself of the Assyrian yoke (Cogan 1974: 70-71). Yet the Assyrians are not mentioned throughout the description of the reigns of Manasseh, Amon, and Josiah; thus, by the same reasoning, the continuity of the book of Kings should lead readers to conclude that Judah had freed itself of the Assyrian yoke as early as Hezekiah's day (see below). The author of the book, in describing Amon's murder, focused on the ascension of a descendant of the House of David to the throne, and did not go into detail regarding the background of the deed. The Assyrians may have supported the measures enacted by those circles who placed the heir of the ancient dynasty of Judah on the throne; as their own interests were, in any event, not damaged by this development, they

---

24. Wellhausen 1899: 206-207; North 1974: 383-86; Spieckermann 1982: 35-37. For a survey of scholarly opinions concerning the reliability of the description of Manasseh's exile and return, see Cogan 1974: 67 n. 15; Williamson 1982: 391-93.

may have preferred not to intervene. On the other hand, the Assyrians may have intervened, and the author of the book of Kings may have ignored this, since he described the progression of events without reference to the Assyrian presence.

Faced with these scholarly claims, we must nonetheless emphasize that during the decade from 650 to 640 BCE, the Assyrians were still assiduously active in the defence and development of the southwestern provinces. Evidence to that effect may be found in Ezra 4.9-10: following the campaigns against Babylonia (652–648 BCE) and Elam (647–646), Ashurbanipal exiled residents of those remote areas and resettled them in the province of Samaria. In addition, once Ashurbanipal was no longer occupied with the wars in the southern and eastern regions of his empire, he launched a campaign against the Arabs dwelling on the edge of the Syro-Arabian desert, striking them down in numbers, and thus protecting the border areas of Syria and Palestine (Eph'al 1982: 157-64). A year later (c. 644 BCE), the Assyrian army again played a major role in the area, suppressing the revolt which had broken out in the province of Tyre.[25] Thus it may be seen that during the decade 650–640 BCE, the Assyrians were still active in the Syro-Palestinian arena, suppressing elements which endangered their rule, and ensuring security and prosperity throughout the region.

The last of Ashurbanipal's annals was written in 639 BCE. From that time until the appearance of the Babylonian chronicles describing the revolt in Babylonia in 626–623 BCE, we have no 'historical' documents enabling the reconstruction of the history of the Assyrian empire. The Babylonian documents inform us that the years 647–627 BCE were years of peace and economic growth, characterised by continuous and uninterrupted Assyrian rule in Babylonia (Brinkman 1984: 105-11). In 609–607 BCE, when all the major cities of Assyria had already fallen into his hands, King Nabopolassar of Babylonia launched campaigns into districts south of the kingdom of Urartu; this leads us to conclude that, throughout its existence, the Assyrian empire maintained control of its northern districts, up to its border with Urartu (Wiseman 1961: 19-20, 45-46, 62-65). Are we to assume that a different state of affairs prevailed on its southwestern front, and that Assyria had previously withdrawn from that front? The answer to this question is related to two central problems which have been extensively discussed in research to date: the evaluation of Herodotus' testimony concerning the Scythian invasion of Syria and Palestine, and the date of the Egyptian expansion north of the Sinai peninsula.

Herodotus describes the Scythians as having played a major role in the chain of events throughout Western Asia in the second half of the seventh century BCE. He states (1.103-106) that, following their victories over the Cymmerians and the Medes, the Scythians continued southward into Egypt; when they reached Syria

---

25. Oppenheim 1969: 300b; Katzenstein 1973: 293-94; Oded 1974: 42 n. 55; Eph'al 1982: 157; Elayi 1983: 56. The excavations at Tell Kisan unearthed a fragment of a Neo-Assyrian cuneiform tablet listing an allotment of food rations to various persons whose names are not preserved. As the Akko Plain was annexed by the Assyrians only in the last years of Esarhaddon's reign, it may be assumed that those mentioned in the tablet were exiles brought there by Ashurbanipal (Sigrist 1982; cf. Spycket 1973).

and Palestine, 'Psammetichus king of Egypt met them and persuaded them with gifts and prayers to come no further'. On their way back, some of them robbed the temple of 'Divine Aphrodite'; the Scythians then 'ruled in Asia for twenty-eight years', until their defeat by the Medes under Cyaxares.[26]

Although a great deal of ink has been expended on the subject of the Scythian invasion and their protracted control of Asia, this issue remains obscure and puzzling. Among the Indo-Iranian groups mentioned in seventh-century Assyrian documents, the Scythians may be identified with the Ishguzans, whose leader Protothyes has been identified with Partatua, a contemporary of Esarhaddon, king of Assyria (681–669 BCE).[27] Partatua's son Madyes would thus be the Scythian ruler who vanquished the Cymmerians and the Medes and ruled Asia. However, the reign of Esarhaddon (in whose time Protothyes ruled) and that of Cyaxares (in whose time Madyes was active) are separated by more than fifty years, a fact which makes it difficult to integrate the two sources from a chronological standpoint. Moreover, during the reign of Esarhaddon's heir Ashurbanipal, the Ishguzans had no role in the chain of events. Thus the Assyrian sources do not help to clear up the historical picture drawn by Herodotus.[28]

The fantastic description of a huge Scythian campaign, which reached as far as the Egyptian border, and yet, within a short time, retreated and disappeared into the north, leaving no impression on the region through which its vast forces supposedly passed, is hardly plausible.[29] The overall form of the account bears some resemblance to the description of the 'Hyksos' invasion given by Manetho (Josephus, *Contra Apion* 1.14); in that passage, the Hyksos were also described as having come 'from the eastern lands' to Egypt, and, following a protracted period of rule, having retreated into Syria. It should be remembered that invasions by such nomad groups always leave a distinctive mark, for they not only overthrow the ruling power in the area, but generate widespread havoc and destruction. Neither such an Assyrian defeat nor its disastrous consequences are attested to in either documents or material culture; accordingly, those scholars who cast doubt on Herodotus' tale of the Scythian invasion of Syria and Palestine

---

26. The quotations are cited from the edition in the Loeb Classical Library (1946).

27. For the problem of the affinity between the Scythians and Ishguzans (and the biblical Ashkenaz), see Wilke 1913: 230-32; Loewenstamm 1950; Cazelles 1967: 29-30; Kammenhuber 1976–80, with earlier literature.

28. For attempts to date the Scythian activities and to reconstruct their course, see Labat 1961; Cavaignac 1961; Cogan and Tadmor 1977: 80-81 n. 26; Spalinger 1978a; 1978b: 406-409; Millard 1979.

29. Many scholars have considered the Scythian invasion of the Philistine coast to be a historical event, and some have even attempted to date that event and to integrate it into a historical context (Malamat 1951: 154-59; Rowley 1962–63: 206-12, with earlier literature on p. 211 n. 3; Spalinger 1978a; Millard 1979; Miller and Hayes 1986: 390). Cazelles (1967) proposed that the Scythians mentioned in Herodotus be considered as a garrison sent by the Assyrians to Ashdod, to stand against the Egyptian invasion of the Philistine coast. This garrison held out for 29 years (638–609 BCE), until repulsed by Pharaoh Necho II. In this way, Cazelles distinguished between the Scythians acting from the lands north of the Assyrian empire and their brethren who assisted Assyria in its struggle against Egypt.

appear to have been right (Wilke 1913: 225-33; Hyatt 1940: 501-502; Avi-Yonah 1962: 123-27; Otzen 1964: 92-95; Vaggione 1973; Cogan and Tadmor 1988: 301 n. 35). Possibly the Scythians played a certain role in the struggles between the large Indo-Iranian nomad groups then present north and northwest of the Assyrian empire, and perhaps even in the crystallisation of the kingdom of Media.[30] Nonetheless, no ancient Near Eastern documents now in our possession can confirm this hypothesis; our evaluation of Herodotus' descriptions is largely based on an overall evaluation of the reliability of the information appearing in his writings on Western Asia.[31]

Generally speaking, it seems that no one managed to oust Assyria from Syria and Palestine before Ashurbanipal's death in 631 BCE and the outbreak of the revolt in Babylonia in 626 BCE.[32] It seems that the revolt which arose in Assyria following the accession of Ashur-etel-ilani in 631 BCE was no more than an episode, no different from similar rebellions following the rise of various rulers in Assyria (e.g. Tiglath-pileser III, Sargon II, and Esarhaddon) during the eighth and seventh centuries. The great crisis in the Assyrian empire did not begin until after the outbreak of the revolt in Babylonia (which Assyria—despite repeated attempts—did not manage to crush between 626 and 623 BCE), and reached its zenith following the outbreak of the civil war between Sin-shar-ishkun and one of his generals in 623 BCE (Na'aman 1991b: 262-64). It is no coincidence that Josiah's cultic reform began in the following year, 622 BCE, in the eighteenth year of the king's reign (2 Kgs 22.3; 23.23), as only at that point did he feel sufficiently secure to carry out a comprehensive purge throughout the kingdom, eradicating 'foreign' cults and concentrating worship of the God of Israel in the Temple in Jerusalem. Although the Chronicler's account (2 Chron. 34.3) ostensibly indicates that the reform had begun in the twelfth year of Josiah's reign, the entire description of that reform in 2 Chronicles 34 does not seem plausible. Moreover, the specified date was artificially created, in view of the special doctrine of retribution held by the author of the book: being a righteous king, Josiah would have had to demonstrate his devotion to the God of Israel immediately on attaining maturity and independence at the age of twenty, as otherwise he could have been accused of tolerating idolatry in his kingdom and capital until the age of twenty-six (the eighteenth year of his reign).[33]

---

30. See the articles cited in nn. 27-28, above. Concerning the role of Assyria in the formation of the Median Kingdom, see S.C. Brown 1986.

31. For the problem of the historical reliability of the information on Mesopotamia and Egypt given in Herodotus, see, e.g., de Meulenaere 1951; H. Lewy 1952; Baumgartner 1959; Africa 1963; Otzen 1964: 50-51, including a listing of additional literature in n. 28; T.S. Brown 1965; Wilson 1970; Lloyd 1975; Armayor 1978; Diakonoff 1985: 149-99; Zawadzki 1988: 64-98, with earlier literature; Fehling 1989.

32. For a cautious and considered discussion of the problem of the Assyrian retreat from Palestine, see Barth 1977: 242-50; Nelson 1983: 177-84; Cogan and Tadmor 1988: 291-93.

33. Gressmann 1924: 313-16; Rudolph 1955: 321; Mosis 1973: 195-200; Cogan 1980: 169-70. A number of scholars have adopted the chronology given by the author of Chronicles as the cornerstone of their own works (Oestreicher 1923: 60-65; Proksch 1928: 20-27; Smirin 1952: 58-65; Cross and Freedman 1953; Liver 1958: 418-20; Jepsen 1959: 104-108; Nicholson 1967: 7-14; Aharoni 1979: 401-404).

Last to be discussed is the Egyptian factor. We know that Pharaoh Psammetichus I ascended the throne of Egypt with the support of Assyria, which assisted him in thwarting the attempted retaking of Egypt by the rulers of the Nubian (Twenty-Fifth) Dynasty and took pains to maintain his senior status among the Delta princes (Kitchen 1973: 391-406; Spalinger 1974a: 316-26; 1974b: 322-25; 1976). In 656 BCE, Psammetichus I managed to unite all of Egypt under his rule, and to dethrone his competitors among the Delta princes. Neither Egyptian nor classical sources attest to any rivalry between Assyria and Egypt (Kitchen 1973: 399-400, 455-61; Spalinger 1976: 133-42; 1982). Only once is Egypt even mentioned in the later Assyrian sources: King Gyges of Lydia is accused of having 'sent his troops to aid Tushamilki/Pishamilki, king of Egypt, who had thrown off my yoke' (Cogan and Tadmor 1977: 79-80). The said military support is no more than a dispatch of mercenaries from Lydia to Egypt, which is in line with Herodotus' report (II.152) that Psammetichus I enlisted the aid of Ionian and Carian mercenaries, and with the mention in Jeremiah (46.9) of 'men of Lud' in the Egyptian army. The beginning of hostilities between Gyges and Assyria should, it seems, be dated in the mid-650s (Cogan and Tadmor 1977: 78-79 n. 25, 84; Spalinger 1978b)—which is apparently when Psammetichus I freed himself from the Assyrian yoke. The Assyrian, Egyptian, and Greek sources tell us nothing about hostile relationships between Assyria and Egypt; it appears that the Assyrian retreat took place following the conclusion of an agreement with Psammetichus I, Assyria's protégé-turned-ally (Gyles 1959: 20-23; Spalinger 1978a: 51; 1978b: 402-403).

The next testimony which has come down to us concerning the relations between Assyria and Egypt is from a later period: in 616 BCE, the Egyptian army was sent to the aid of king Sin-shar-ishkun of Assyria, then at war with the Babylonian army (Wiseman 1961: 11-13, 44, 54-55). Two questions now arise: When did the Egyptians enter Asia, and when had Egypt become so close to Assyria as to be willing to send its army to assist its sorely beset ally? These questions have no unambiguous answers. As it seems, the Egyptian entry into Asia was not a forcible conquest, but part of an Assyrian retreat by agreement, with Egypt (gradually or rapidly) taking the place of Assyria in the vacated areas. It appears that the alliance between the two powers became especially close during the reign of Sin-shar-ishkun, after he had crushed the rebellion of his general (end of year 623 BCE), and he was willing to pay a heavy territorial price in the west in order to overcome the severe danger facing him and his kingdom in the south and east.[34] The renewed alliance between Assyria and Egypt may thus have been concluded in the late 620s; this, in turn, would mean that only then did Assyria retreat from (and Egypt enter) the territories beyond the Euphrates (for Jer. 2.18, see Holladay 1981: 64).

Herodotus states that Psammetichus I besieged Ashdod (Azotus) for 29 years before finally taking the city (II.157). Tadmor attempted to interpret this passage

---

34. Na'aman 1991b: 257-67; see also Borger 1965; Zawadzki 1988, with earlier literature. Noteworthy is a document that includes a sort of declaration of war by a Babylonian king (possibly Nabopolassar) against an Assyrian king (possibly Sin-shar-ishkun) (Gerardi 1986: 30-38).

as meaning that the siege took place, and the city fell, in 635 BCE, the twenty-ninth year of Psammetichus I's reign. He then went on to conclude that Assyria had retreated from the coast of Philistia even before 635 BCE (Tadmor 1966: 101-102; Miller and Hayes 1986: 383-84; Cogan and Tadmor 1988: 300). This assumption, however, is not compatible with the meaning of Herodotus' statement ('Of all the cities, that Azotus, to the best of our knowledge, held out the longest time in the face of the siege'[35]); those scholars who linked the 29 years mentioned in this context with Herodotus' former comment (I.106) on the 28 years of Scythian rule in Asia (Wilke 1913: 229; de Meulenaere 1951: 30-33; Gyles 1959: 22-23; Cazelles 1967: 24-27, 38-39, 44) appear to have been correct. It seems that the '29 years of siege' grew out of chronological speculation on Herodotus' part: according to his calculations, the siege began when Psammetichus I set out to meet the Scythians on the coast of Philistia and persuaded them to retreat (I.105), and ended immediately after the Scythian defeat by the Medes 28 years later, putting an end to their rule in Asia. It seems that this is not a date enabling exact chronological dating. Apparently, Herodotus merely wished to state that Ashdod was conquered after the Scythian defeat by Cyaxares—that is, in the late seventh century BCE.

To conclude, it seems that no element endangered the Assyrian control of Syria and Palestine prior to the death of Ashurbanipal and the outbreak of the revolt in Babylonia, in the 620s, and that Assyrian rule continued until that time in Palestine as well. While Egypt may have attained a foothold on the Philistine coast in some prior period, this cannot be effectively proven. Nor do we know whether Egypt was forced to conquer some of the places evacuated by Assyria, as there may well have been resistance (like that of Ashdod) or even revolts at the critical stage of the change of sovereignty. In principle, the Assyrian retreat was implemented in coordination with Egypt, which could, from all possible standpoints, be considered as a sort of 'successor state' for the territories vacated by Assyria.[36] It may thus be concluded that Josiah was a vassal of Assyria during the first half of his reign, and that, even after freeing himself from the Assyrian yoke, he became (at least nominally) a vassal of Egypt. Yet Egypt was tied up with obligations at that time, both because it had to ensure its control of the coast and maritime transportation routes which had fallen into its hands, and because of its commitment to assist Assyria in return for the territories which it had obtained west of the Euphrates.[37] Nor should we forget the pattern of Egyptian rule dating from the period of the New Kingdom, when the main emphasis was placed on control of the valley districts and the coast, whereas the mountain areas were considered of secondary importance. This state of affairs gave Josiah considerable freedom of action in the internal regions of the country, and there can be no doubt that he exploited this freedom to gather strength, to unify and

35. See n. 26, above.
36. See the literature cited above, and Na'aman 1987b: 11-12. For the term 'successor state', taken from international law, see Malamat 1982: 195, with earlier literature in n. 17.
37. Miller and Hayes (1986: 383-85, 388-90) came to the conclusion that Judah was under Egyptian dominance and probably an Egyptian vassal throughout Josiah's reign.

crystallise his kingdom (the cultic reform played a major role in these trends), and, to a certain extent, even to expand his borders.

In my opinion, the kingdom's subjugation to Assyria during the first half of Josiah's reign, and the formal subordination to Egypt during the second half, explain the way in which the author of the book of Kings presented the relationship of the Kingdom of Judah to Assyria and Egypt. According to the description in that book, Judah freed itself from the Assyrian yoke following Sennacherib's campaign, and did not become an Egyptian vassal until after Josiah's death. This extraordinary presentation, so different from the historical reality of the seventh century BCE, is (among other motives) intended to mask the fact that Josiah, the ruler of unparalleled loyalty to God and his precepts (2 Kgs 23.25), was subordinate to foreign rulers for most of his days—a subordination perceived in the Deuteronomistic outlook as unfitting the righteous king.[38] By selecting only specific material, the author was able to present a different picture of the past, thus portraying Josiah as having acted independently of foreign dictates throughout his rule, and having been capable of implementing the necessary reforms without the intervention of a foreign element (for a comprehensive discussion of this subject, see the summary in Part II Section 5, below).

2. *The Extent of Josiah's Expansion in the East and North*
In beginning my discussion of the extent of Josiah's conquests, we should make the distinction between the kingdom proper and the conquered areas outside its borders. Although it is impossible to state with any certainty the original purpose of the document in which the town lists were recorded and from which the author of Joshua drew the data for his composition, it may be assumed that it was used by the administration of the kingdom as a basis for the obligations and charges imposed by the king on his subjects. The town lists of Judah and Benjamin, then, reflect the area which was subordinate to the regular administration of the kingdom. Included in this area was the Kingdom of Judah in its old borders, 'from Geba to Beersheba' (2 Kgs 23.8), plus a number of additional cities (including Jericho, Zemaraim, Bethel, Ophrah) which were conquered and appended to its territory.

We shall attempt below to determine which additional areas Josiah conquered up to his death in 609 BCE. This question is one of profound controversy among scholars, and various solutions have been proposed. In the following discussion, we shall deal separately with each front.

In an article never published but quoted by others, Alt proposed that Josiah expanded into Transjordan, and that his territorial claims on the districts of Israel in that area are reflected in the town lists of Gad and Reuben (Num. 32; Josh. 13). This gave rise to hostility between Jehoiakim son of Josiah and the kingdoms of Moab and Ammon (2 Kgs 24.2) (Alt in Proksch 1928: 47-48). Noth hypothesized that Josiah attempted to expand into Transjordan, and that the thirteenth district

---

38. For the associative affinity between the sins of Ahaz and Judah's subjugation to Assyria in his day (a subjugation viewed as punishment for his sins), see Ackroyd 1968: 25-26; Tadmor and Cogan 1979: 498-99, 506-508.

of Josiah's kingdom included a series of towns whose list is now submerged in Joshua 13 (vv. 17b-20, 27aα) (Noth 1935: 252-55; 1944: 48-57). Ginsberg, on the other hand, suggested that Josiah conquered districts of Transjordan and, in the process, clashed with the Ammonites (see Bardtke 1936: 250-51; Ginsberg 1950: 362-63; Aharoni 1979: 404). However, none of these hypotheses have any solid textual basis; in fact, they are nothing more than bold reconstructions.[39]

Based on the existence of Galilean town lists in Joshua 19, Alt assumed that Josiah realized his claim on areas of the kingdom of Israel, conquered Galilee (in which there still remained a significant Israelite population), and annexed it to his territory (Alt 1927). From the absence of town lists pertaining to Samaria, he concluded that Josiah skipped that area deliberately—apparently in view of the considerable non-Israelite population there—and contented himself with the destruction and annexation of Bethel. This hypothesis has not been supported even by Alt's own students, and is of no real validity.[40]

Most scholars agree that, following the Assyrian retreat, Josiah conquered all of the Samarian hill country; some even believe that he included that area within his cultic reform (see, e.g., Smirin 1952: 63-64; Milgrom 1971: 26-27; Malamat 1974: 271). This assumption is based on the text of 2 Kgs 23.19, 'And all the shrines also of the high places that were in the cities of Samaria, which kings of Israel had made, provoking the Lord to anger, Josiah removed; he did to them according to what he had done at Bethel'. It seems, however, that vv. 19-20 (or, more correctly, the entire section, from v. 16 to v. 20) are a later expansion, written by an author who edited the description of the destruction of the altar at Bethel (vv. 16-17a) (Welten 1969: 163 n. 21; Ogden 1978: 31-33; Spieckermann 1982: 116-19, 427-28; Rofé 1982: 145-46). It may be assumed that Josiah could then act without hindrance throughout the province of Samaria, which, following its annexation and reorganisation and the 'two way' mass deportations by the Assyrians, had lost a great deal of its former national identity, and, after the Assyrian retreat, no longer had the strength and internal cohesion to compete with him. Possibly, he tried to uproot the Assyrian cult in that province—a cult which was practiced throughout the Assyrian provinces and constituted a vital factor in their unification into a single, well-formed group.[41] Yet we must cast doubt upon the assumption that he carried out in Samaria a reform similar to that implemented in Judah and Jerusalem, in whose wake all the local centres of cult were cancelled. Unfortunately, we do not know which sources the author had at his disposal when composing the description in vv. 19-20: whether he developed and expanded the tale of reform at Bethel without benefit of additional sources, or based his narrative on additional written material covering Josiah's reign.

The problem of the scope of Josiah's action and the extent of his presence in the area involves two further questions: (1) Did he also expand his influence

39. For criticism of these hypotheses, see Smirin 1952: 90; Liver 1958: 420-21; Kallai 1986: 413-14.

40. Proksch (1928: 46-47) supported this hypothesis; Noth (1935: 215-30), however, rejected it. See Kallai 1986: 405-10.

41. For the role played by Assyrian cult in the formation of the provinces, see Cogan 1974: 49-55.

into Galilee? (2) What were the circumstances which led him to his death at Megiddo? The second question will be covered in a separate section; the first will be discussed here.

Many scholars have used the text of 2 Chron. 34.6-7, 33 as a basis for arguing that Josiah's expansion extended into Galilee, and that that area was even included in his cultic reform (see Smirin 1952: 90; Cross and Freedman 1953: 57-58; Liver 1958: 421; Noth 1960: 274, 278; Kallai 1960: 75-76; Aharoni 1979: 309-310). This is the origin of the radical view which holds that Josiah had concrete claim to the entire territory of the kingdom of Israel, and that he attempted to reinstate the great kingdom of David, in theory and in practice, throughout the territory of Israel, up to its remotest borders (Proksch 1928: 48; Ginsberg 1950: 362; Smirin 1952: 63, 97; Cross and Freedman 1953: 56; Noth 1960: 274; Otzen 1964: 62-123; Aharoni 1979: 310; Clements 1984: 96). To illustrate this, let me quote Cross' work:

> He (Josiah) attempted to restore the kingdom or empire of David in all detail. The cultus was centralized according to the ancient law of the sanctuary, and Passover was celebrated as it had not been 'since the days of the Judges'. The story of the renewal of the covenant and the resurrection of the Davidic empire by the reincorporation of the North is told at a length not given to the labors of other approved kings after David (Cross 1973: 283; see von Rad 1958: 89).

These reconstructions, however, are built on shaky foundations and the presentation of a cultic reform which encompassed all of the Cisjordanian areas is mainly the result of the deliberately tendentious description given by the author of Chronicles, in light of his special perception of the last period in the history of the kingdoms of Judah and Israel, from Hezekiah's day to the destruction of the kingdom (Williamson 1977: 119-31; Japhet 1977: 254-55, 282-84). While the content of Chronicles is indicative of its author's unique historiography, we must not use this material as the basis for a description of Josiah's rule. It is, of course, possible that the fall of Assyria may have aroused hopes and longings for a return to the glorious past; nonetheless, hopes and longings are often incompatible with historical reality, and there are no grounds for the assumption that Josiah attempted to conquer the entire North and to impose his reforms throughout the territory of Palestine.

In summary, it is definitely possible that Josiah expanded in the Samarian hill country, although the information on this is not sufficiently clear and there is no way to determine the actual extent of his activity in the area. On the other hand, his expansion certainly ran no further north than the central hill country, and there is no basis for the hypothesis that either Galilee or the Jezreel Valley was also included within the boundaries of his kingdom.

3. *The Extent of Josiah's Expansion in the West and his Relations with Egypt*
In light of the assumption that the town list of Dan (Josh. 19.41-46) belongs to the original town list document, Alt assumed that Josiah conquered and annexed the northern Shephelah area, as far south as Joppa (Alt 1925: 109-11, 115). For hundreds of years this area had been controlled by foreign kingdoms; when Josiah

acquired sufficient strength, he conquered it, as well as the neighbouring kingdom of Ekron [for the territory of Ekron in the seventh century, see Na'aman 1998: 223-25]. Alt found corroboration for this theory in the list of those returning from Babylonia (Ezra 2.33; Neh. 7.37), which mentions men from Lod, Hadid, and Ono. In his opinion, those settlements were included within the borders of the Kingdom of Judah from the time of their conquest by Josiah and up to the destruction of the kingdom; their inhabitants were then exiled by the Babylonians (Alt 1925: 110-11).

The assumption that the town list of Dan reflects Josiah's expansion to the west has not been accepted by most scholars (see above); nevertheless, several scholars have considered the list of those returning from Babylonia as attesting to the westward expansion of the kingdom (Smirin 1952: 97; Liver 1958: 420; Kallai 1960: 77; Barth 1977: 256-59). This view celebrated its victory with the discovery of the Meṣad Ḥashavyahu fortress in northern Philistia, near Yavneh-Yam (for the excavations of the site, see Naveh 1977: 862-63; Reich 1989). Found there were ostraca whose text, written in the Hebrew alphabet, is in a language close to Biblical Hebrew and includes a number of Yahwistic names (Hoshaʻyahu, Ḥashavyahu, ʻObadyahu). In light of the above, it has been assumed that Meṣad Ḥashavyahu was built by Josiah during his takeover of the coastline south of Joppa; these findings have been presented as conclusive proof of the argument that Josiah conquered vast areas in the northern Shephelah, down to the coast itself.[42]

Was Meṣad Ḥashavyahu indeed built by the king of Judah? It seems to me that the data must be interpreted in a manner different from previous interpretations. First, we must emphasize that the plan of the fortress is unparalleled by any other fortress excavated to date in Judah, and that its roots must apparently be sought elsewhere. Typical Eastern Greek pottery, originating in the eastern Greek islands and in Asia Minor, was discovered on the site in large quantities, indicating the presence of mercenaries of western origin. By contrast, only a few sherds of this type of pottery have been found to date in other excavations in Judah (Tel Kabri is an exception).[43] There is no evidence of western mercenaries having served in the army of Judah during this period, and the assumption that Josiah enlisted such mercenaries into his army is largely based on interpretation of the findings at Meṣad Ḥashavyahu.[44] On the other hand, there is clear evidence that mercenar-

---

42. Naveh 1960: 136-39; 1977: 863; Tadmor 1966: 102; Strange 1966: 134-39; Welten 1969: 66, 100-102; Malamat 1974: 272, 277; Barth 1977: 257-59; Aharoni 1979: 312, 403; Spieckermann 1982: 145. Miller and Hayes (1986: 389), on the other hand, suggested that Greek and Judahite contingents were stationed by the Egyptians at Meṣad Ḥashavyahu and were employed to guard the coast south of Joppa. For a similar suggestion, see Na'aman 1987b: 12-14.

43. For the distribution of Eastern Greek pottery in Palestine, see E. Stern 1982: 283-86; Biran 1985: 27. [For recent publications and discussions, seeWaldbaum 1994, 1997; Waldbaum and Magness 1997; Niemeier 2001: 19-24.]

44. Frequently mentioned in the Arad ostraca are the Kittim. Aharoni (1981: 12-13) regarded them as 'Greek or Cypriot mercenaries serving in the Judahite army, perhaps especially in garrisons of the more remote fortresses'. He further noted the Eastern Greek pottery found at Meṣad Ḥashavyahu, suggesting that 'here was a garrison of Greek mercenaries working for Josiah'. This

ies from Asia Minor served in the Egyptian army, and even occupied fortresses built within Egypt. In the annals of Ashurbanipal, King Gyges of Lydia is accused of having sent his army to the assistance of King Psammetichus I of Egypt (cf. Jer. 46.9); this evidence is contemporary (mid-seventh century) with the service of mercenaries from western Anatolia in the Egyptian army (Cogan and Tadmor 1977: 79-80; Spalinger 1978b). Herodotus (II.152) states that Psammetichus I took control of Egypt with the aid of Ionian and Carian mercenaries. In another place (II.30), Herodotus mentions three border fortresses staffed with Greek mercenaries during Psammetichus I's reign: Elephantine on the Nubian border, Daphnae (Tahpanhes) on the Arabian border, and Marea on the Libyan border. Excavations at Tell Defenneh have revealed clear ceramic evidence, including locally manufactured Eastern Greek pottery, attesting to the settlement of mercenaries from Asia Minor; also discovered, in the foundation layer, were cartouches of Psammetichus I, indicating the date of establishment of the site (Petrie 1888; Boardman 1980: 133-34; Oren 1984: 12-13, 37-38). The site of Migdol, called Stratopeda by Herodotus (II.152), close to the Pelusian arm of the Nile, has been excavated, revealing Eastern Greek pottery alongside Phoenician and Palestinian pottery (Oren 1984). In the opinion of the excavator, the non-Egyptian pottery (Eastern Greek, Phoenician, and Palestinian) had been brought there by foreign mercenaries settled on the site.[45]

In this context, let me also quote the words of Jeremiah (44.1; 46.14) regarding the settlement of Jews in Migdol, Tahpanhes, and Memphis. This evidence is in line with the evidence from Elephantine regarding the settlement of Jewish mercenaries there (Porten 1968: 3-27), and with additional evidence of Phoenicians having served as mercenaries and garrisons in Egypt (Katzenstein 1978; Oren 1984: 36). It may be stated that, in the days of the Twenty-Sixth Dynasty, starting in the reign of Psammetichus I, mercenaries from Asia Minor, Phoenicia, and Judah served in the Egyptian army, took part in campaigns, and even dwelt in fortresses built by the Egyptians (de Meulenaere 1951: 22-43; Kienitz 1953: 35-47; Otzen 1964: 51-62; Spalinger 1976: 137-38, 145-46 nn. 30-43; Oren 1984: 30-38).

In view of the above, the Meṣad Ḥashavyahu findings should be re-examined. [See recently Fantalkin 2001; Niemeier 2002.] I have already pointed out that mercenaries of western origin were posted on the site, and that the findings there included ostraca bearing Yahwistic names; however, another ostracon found at Meṣad Ḥashavyahu bears an obviously Phoenician name (with the theophoric element of 'Ba'al') unknown in Judah in the seventh century BCE (Naveh 1962: 30-31; Lemaire 1977: 268-69). It thus appears that the fortress was built by the Egyptians, perhaps according to an Egyptian plan (therefore its plan is alien by comparison to that of fortresses in Judah), and was staffed by mercenaries of mixed origin—Greek, Phoenician, and Judahite—similar to the situation which

hypothesis had already been raised by Aharoni in the original publication of the ostraca (1966: 4-5 and n. 9).

45. [For a recent discussion of the Greek mercenaries in the Orient, see Niemeier 2001: 16-19, with earlier literature; 2002.]

prevailed in other sites at the time of the Saitic (Twenty-Sixth) Dynasty in Egypt. It seems that, following their takeover of Palestine after the Assyrian retreat, the Egyptians felt a need to ensure the route running from the Philistine coast to the port of Joppa and the north, and for this reason they built a fortress near the border of Philistia and populated it with foreign garrisons.

At this point, we should inquire: What was the background for the service of Judahites in the fortress, and in the fields of a nearby place called Ḥaṣar Asam; and what is the situation reflected by the letter of complaint found on the site? In order to answer these questions, let me first examine the manner in which the Egyptians ran their administrative centres in the conquered lands.

The best source available for the study of this problem is the Amarna archive, which admittedly reflects a period hundreds of years before the Saitic Dynasty. The Amarna documents indicate that the Egyptians relied, to a great extent, on their vassals in Canaan to manage their administrative centres (Helck 1971: 246-55; Na'aman 1981: 177-81, 184-85; 1982: 195-212, 241-51; Hachmann 1982). They were required to serve as garrisons in the cities, guarding their walls, gates, and installations; to plough and reap the fields adjoining those cities; and to repair the damages caused to them. Enlisted to work the land were workers from nearby or even distant kingdoms, and the responsibility for performance of that work was imposed on the rulers of those kingdoms (Na'aman 1988).

The picture reflected in the Amarna letters is well in line with the Meṣad Ḥashavyahu findings; the presence of a garrison from Judah in the fortress, and of corvée workers in the adjoining fields (see below), are best explained in light of the assumption that Judah was then subject to Egypt. If this is so, we may attempt to reconstruct the situation reflected in the letter of complaint as follows.[46] The group of reapers, including the complainant, was working in Ḥaṣar Asam near the fortress. Each worker had to reap a certain quota of land during the period allotted for the work, and then to store the harvested grain. As the complainant did not complete his quota in time, he was punished by having his garment taken away by his superior, Hashaʻyahu. As scholars have shown, this punishment is suitable for corvée workers, who were not paid for their labour, but not for paid workers, tenant farmers, or sharecroppers, who could be punished by reducing their salary or share in the harvest (Amusin and Heltzer 1964: 154-57; Talmon 1964; Pardee 1978: 55-57). After some time, when his garment had not been returned to him, the punished worker complained to the officer of the fortress. The latter was certainly appointed by the king of Judah and in charge of all the recruits—both military personnel and corvée workers—serving in that area; we have seen that the Amarna documents also indicate that the responsibility for implementation of works was imposed upon the Canaanite rulers. Thus, the officer was able to order Hoshaʻyahu to restore the complainant's garment to him.[47]

---

46. For the interpretation of the Meṣad Ḥashavyahu ostracon, see Naveh 1960: 129-39; Lemaire 1977: 259-69, including a listing of additional literature on pp. 259-60; Sasson 1978, 1984; Pardee 1978, 1980; Suzuki 1982; Weippert 1990. [See recently Kleer and Kröger 1992; Dobbs-Allsopp 1994; Hübner 1997.]

47. For the term $śr$ ('officer'), see Rütersworden 1985.

The exact date of the Meṣad Ḥashavyahu ostraca is unknown, nor can we determine whether they belong to Josiah's day (and thus indicate his subordination to Psammetichus I), or to those of his sons Jehoahaz or Jehoiakim, both of whom were vassals to Necho II. The desertion of the fortress by the mercenaries may be dated at 604 BCE, the year in which Nebuchadnezzar launched a campaign to the Philistine coast, thrust out the Egyptians, and destroyed Ashkelon (Wiseman 1961: 28, 47, 68-69 ll. 18-20; Malamat 1975: 130-31). [See recently Fantalkin 2001: 128-36; contra Niemeier 2002.]

The subordination of Judah to Egypt is also indicated by the findings at Arad. In a series of ostraca, the Arad fortress commander Elyashib is ordered to transfer large quantities of supplies to members of a group referred to as Kittim (ktym). Aharoni noted that the reference is to Greek or Cypriot mercenaries, but interpreted this as evidence that such mercenaries served in the Judahite army.[48] It is, however, more likely that these were mercenaries in the Egyptian or Babylonian army, and that the king of Judah, then subordinate to either Egypt or Babylonia, was obligated to transfer supplies to these units, which were surely en route through the Beersheba Valley, or encamped in fortresses along the roads (Miller and Hayes 1986: 389, 417). It is difficult to determine the extent of the Kittim units, in view of the uncertainty concerning the quantities of bread and wine consumed by one soldier in one day, as well as the exact volume of the measuring units mentioned in the documents (bath, homer, etc.); nevertheless, these units apparently consisted of several tens of soldiers each.[49] The transfer of supplies to the mercenaries of Egypt or Babylonia was implemented by the Arad fortress commander, and certainly by other local commanders, and was a considerable burden on the kingdom. [For the Kittim, see Dion 1992.]

The findings from the fortress at Kadesh-barnea may also indicate the service of Judahites in a local garrison. The fortress, constructed in the late eighth or seventh century, is rectangular in shape; its casemate walls rest on massive underground offset/inset foundation walls (Dothan 1965: 134-43 [also Ussishkin 1995]; contra Cohen 1981, 1983). In my opinion, Egyptian control of the site during the last phase of the fortress' existence is hinted at by the presence of ostraca in hieratic writing, bearing various figures (from 1 to 10,000) and dimension units commonly in use in the area at the time (Lemaire and Vernus 1980, 1983). These may have been used by pupils of Semitic origin, for practice in the Egyptian method of record-keeping then in force; this would explain the few Semitic words appearing on the ostraca. Some of the pottery vessels discovered

---

48. See the literature cited in n. 44, above; Lemaire 1977: 159-61, 229-30, 233. For the Kittim (Kittiyim) in the Bible, see Loewenstamm 1962, with earlier literature.

49. Lemaire 1977: 229-30; Aharoni 1981: 15-16, 144-45. Lemaire (1977: 159-60) considered the possibility that the Kittim were merchants of Greek origin, but preferred the hypothesis that they were Greek mercenaries. Rainey suggested that the Kittim were convoy leaders from the town of Kition in Cyprus, and were therefore Phoenicians and not Greeks. Their supplies were provided in the framework of the duties imposed on the Kingdom of Judah as vassal to the Neo-Babylonian Empire then controlling the area (Rainey 1986: 25; see Herzog et al. 1984: 31). Notwithstanding the above, the hypothesis of dozens of convoy leaders marching along the Beersheba Valley under the protection of the Neo-Babylonian Empire seems unlikely.

on site were made by hand ('Negevite' pottery), and others on a potters' wheel; the latter resemble vessels from Judah and coastal sites. Some examples of coloured 'Idumaean' pottery, originating in southern Transjordan, were also found (Cohen 1983: 12; E. Mazar 1985: 264). Additional ostraca discovered at the site are written in alphabetic writing. Admittedly, only after complete publication of the material will it be possible to formulate a considered opinion of the cultural relations between the site and the neighbouring kingdoms during that period. Nevertheless, as a 'working hypothesis', I would like to propose that the building of the casemate fortress with wide offset/inset foundation walls at Kadesh-barnea was initiated by the Assyrians, and that the last phase of this fortress was controlled by the Egyptians. It was staffed by garrisons from the vassal kingdoms, or perhaps by Semitic mercenaries from the surrounding kingdoms.

Why, in any event, did Josiah go no further westward than the edges of the northern Shephelah, and refrain from penetrating the biblical inheritance of Dan? An unequivocal answer to this question has been given by archaeological research. Excavations at Tel Miqne (Ekron) have shown that a very large town, over 200 dunams in area, flourished there during the seventh century, and that its economy was principally based on the production of olive oil (Gitin 1989 [also 1997]). The sudden growth of Ekron, following a period of decline which had lasted some 200–250 years—since the destruction of the Iron I city in about the mid-tenth century BCE—indubitably resulted from Sennacherib's campaign to Judah. Following that campaign, most of the Shephelah towns were razed, and a considerable portion of their inhabitants exiled to Assyria. This state of affairs permitted Ekron to take the place of its stronger neighbour to the east, to exploit some of its agricultural territories, to expand its area and population, and to develop its economy. Judah's obvious weakness along its western border following Sennacherib's campaign, no less than Ekron's rise to power, prevented Josiah from expanding westward. It should be remembered that Egypt had always had interests on the Philistine coast, and that any strike against one of the more important Philistine kingdoms was considered a direct strike against Egyptian interests. This was the reason for the destruction of Philistine cities, Egypt's protégés, by the Babylonians during their conquest of the area. The territory of Judah in the northern Shephelah, as reflected in the town list in Joshua, included only Zorah and Eshtaol: to the west extended the territory of the Kingdom of Ekron, with Timnah (Tel Batash), and certainly also all of the biblical inheritance of Dan, included therein.[50]

How can we explain the appearance of residents of Lod, Hadid, and Ono in the list of those returning from Babylonia? As we recall, Alt proposed that those places were included in the Kingdom of Judah on the eve of the Babylonian conquest, following which their inhabitants were exiled, a proposal supported by additional scholars. Are we indeed to assume that every place mentioned in the list of those returning from Babylonia belonged to the Kingdom of Judah in the last years of the First Temple?

---

50. For the role of Tel Batash in the border system of the seventh century, see Na'aman 1987b: 14 n. 21.

In order to clarify this problem, let me (briefly) examine the tribal genealogies of Benjamin (Rudolph 1955: 77-79; Kallai 1960: 38-40; Williamson 1982: 84-85). Mentioned in those lists is Elpaal, who built Ono and Lod (1 Chron. 8.12); also mentioned are Beriah and Shema, 'heads of fathers' houses of the inhabitants of Aijalon' (8.13). Noteworthy is the appearance of Beriah in the genealogies of Benjamin. The family of Beriah was originally an important Ephrathite family (7.23). Following the fall of the Northern Kingdom, as families from Benjamin migrated westward and settled in Aijalon, formerly an Ephrathite city, they mingled with families there, including that of Beriah. The latter family was thus listed in the tribal genealogies of Benjamin.

It seems to me that this migration of the Benjaminite families to Aijalon, Lod, and Ono belongs to the period of the *pax Assyriaca* in the seventh century BCE, when borders were opened and relations strengthened between the various districts in and around the empire.[51] During that period, groups left Benjamin and wandered outside the borders of the Kingdom of Judah, to settle in areas which promised them a better living. During the Babylonian conquest, residents of those places, as well as members of many other groups in the area, may have been exiled in circumstances unknown to us.[52] Their Benjaminite origin may have caused them to strengthen their relations with the Judahite exiles in Babylonia; during the post-exilic period, they came back to their places of origin in Palestine.

One may likewise assume that the lists of those 'who came up out of the captivity' in Ezra 2 and Nehemiah 7 in fact combine those who returned (listed by family association) and those who had remained in the land (listed by their place of residence) (Galling 1951: 157; Japhet 1983: 114; Williamson 1987a: 31). The inhabitants of Lod, Hadid, and Ono lived outside the confines of Judah in the pre-exilic and post-exilic periods, but nevertheless were considered as Israelites by the author of the books of Ezra and Nehemiah due to their Benjaminite origin. [See Lipschits 1997.]

In my opinion, the lists of those returning from Babylonia cannot provide a solid basis for determining the extent of the Kingdom of Judah in its last years. Thus, for example, there is no way to ascertain whether Bethel remained within the borders of Judah after the Babylonian conquest, or was returned to the Babylonian province of Samaria. Only a careful examination of all the sources enables

---

51. Dating the westward migration of the Benjaminites in Josiah's period is in line with the dates proposed by Rudolph (1955: 77) and Kallai (1960: 40). Concerning the *pax Assyriaca* and its effects on economics and settlement, see Na'aman 1987b: 8-15.

52. A fitting example of a deportation whose background remains obscure is given by Josephus, quoting the third-century Chaldean historian Berossus (*Ant.* 10.232; *Contra Apion* 1.136-37). Following Nebuchadnezzar's defeat of the Egyptians at Carchemish in 605 BCE, 'the prisoners—Jews, Phoenicians, Syrians, and those of Egyptian nationality' were conducted to Babylonia (M. Stern 1976: 58). For a discussion of this passage and its historical background, see Katzenstein 1973: 306-307, with earlier literature; Malamat 1975: 130; Miller and Hayes 1986: 389. The settling of exiled groups belonging to various nations in Babylonia during the sixth and fifth centuries BCE is indicated by the documents unearthed in the excavations; however, only in a very few instances have actual historical sources for deportations been preserved.

us to attempt to determine which places were included within the territory of Judah on the eve of the Babylonian deportations at the beginning of the sixth century BCE, and what was the territorial affinity between them and the places mentioned in the list of those returning from Babylonia.

4. *The Circumstances Leading to Josiah's Death*
In the discussions of the relationship between the Kingdom of Judah and Egypt, an important role is occupied by the death of Josiah near Megiddo in 609 BCE. A great deal of literature has been written on this subject, with the main difference of opinion centring on the question whether to give credence to the version related in 2 Chron. 35.20-24, despite its drastic deviation from that given in 2 Kgs 23.29-30 (Spieckermann 1982: 138-53; Višaticki 1987: 121-28; Begg 1987; Williamson 1987b; Cogan and Tadmor 1988: 300-302). In 609 BCE Pharaoh Necho II (610–595 BCE) launched a campaign to northern Syria, in an effort to assist his ally Ashur-uballiṭ II, who was sorely beset by the Babylonians and Medes and about to lose his last foothold in western Mesopotamia. Many scholars tend to accept the hypothesis that, on his way north with his army, Necho II passed through Palestine and encountered Josiah near Megiddo. In this context, let me pose a question not hitherto sufficiently discussed: Why did the Pharaoh and his army have to pass through Palestine on their way to northern Syria? Why did Necho II not adopt the tactics of the Egyptian kings at the time of the New Kingdom, who often sailed as far as the Lebanese coast and launched campaigns from there, via the Nahr el-Kebir (Eleutheros), to the Orontes?[53] In this way, Necho II could have gone by sea to the Lebanese coast and set out from there on foot, by way of his military base at Riblah on the Orontes, to northern Syria, shortening the travel time and refraining from exhausting his forces in a gruelling forced march from the Egyptian border to the battlefield near the Euphrates.

In this context we note that Egypt controlled Phoenicia during the years prior to the campaign of 609 BCE. Indicative of Egypt's control of the Lebanese coast at that time is a stele dated to Psammetichus I's fifty-second year (612 BCE), which records the burial of an Apis and mentions the tax paid by the Phoenician kings to Egypt and the appointment of an Egyptian inspector over them (Freedy and Redford 1970: 477; Spalinger 1977: 228-29; 1978a: 55 n. 27). A stele of Psammetichus I was discovered in Arwad; a fragment of an inscription, perhaps dating from that king's reign, was found in Tyre; and a stele of Necho II was found in Sidon (Otzen 1964: 90-91; Katzenstein 1973: 299 n. 24, 313 n. 100). The Nebuchadnezzar inscription from Wādi Brisa mentions 'the evil enemy', undoubtedly the King of Egypt, who controlled the mountains of Lebanon until his eviction by the Babylonian ruler.[54]

---

53. Alt 1950; Helck 1971: 137-56; Na'aman 1986a: 131. Several scholars have assumed that, on previous campaigns, the Egyptians conveyed their forces to Syria by sea (Smirin 1952: 100; Liver 1958: 421; Yoyotte 1960: 372, 375). For the development of marine transportation under the Twenty-Sixth Dynasty, see de Meulenaere 1951: 60-63; Gyles 1959: 29-30; Spalinger 1978c: 20-21, with earlier literature.

54. For a translation of the inscription, see Oppenheim 1955: 307. For a discussion of it, see Spalinger 1977: 227-29, with earlier literature in nn. 18-19. It should be emphasized that Egypt

It appears to me that the reason why Necho II chose to travel via Palestine lies in the transfer of power which had taken place in Egypt not long before. Psammetichus I had died between July and September of 610 BCE, and 609 was the second regnal year of his successor, Necho II (Freedy and Redford 1970: 474 nn. 47-48). Helck has pointed out that Egyptian officials customarily took an oath of fealty to the reigning Pharaoh; when the king died, the oath became invalid, and the officials had to swear an oath to his successor. In view of this fact, Helck raised the hypothesis that during the period of the New Kingdom the Canaanite kings also had to swear fealty to every new ruler, and gave this as the explanation for campaigns made by several Egyptian kings to Canaan in the first year of their rule (Helck 1971: 247; see Lorton 1974: *passim*; Redford 1985: 7 n. 2).[55] Necho II apparently came to Palestine in 609 BCE for that very reason: to administer an oath of fealty to his vassals, whose previous oath had become invalid on his father's death. There is, then, no need to assume that the entire Egyptian army passed through Palestine on the way north; it is even probable that Necho II reached Palestine by sea on his way to the Lebanese coast, and stopped there only briefly. Moreover, one may wonder whether he did not take the opportunity to enlist an army from among his vassals and append them to the Egyptian expeditionary force on its way north. It should be remembered that, at various times during the time of the New Kingdom, auxiliary forces were enlisted from among the vassals, in order to assist the Egyptian army in its wars (Na'aman 1981: 180-81 n. 46). This may also have been the case in 609 BCE: Necho's vassals may have been ordered to dispatch army units to assist in the northward campaign.

It is against this background that we should re-examine the biblical description of the events of 609 BCE. Let me first cite the passage from 2 Kgs 23.29: 'In his days Pharaoh Necho king of Egypt went up to the king of Assyria to the river Euphrates. King Josiah went to meet him; and Pharaoh Necho slew him at Megiddo, when he saw him.' The verse opens with the word *bymyw* ('in his days')—a typical editorial opening formula which introduces a chronistic account (cf. 1 Kgs 16.34; 2 Kgs 8.20; 24.1) (Montgomery 1934: 49; Spieckermann 1982: 139; Cogan and Tadmor 1988: 96, 291). The account that follows does not give the slightest hint of a battle. It is therefore possible that Josiah reported to the Egyptian ruler, his lord, at Megiddo, to swear an oath of fealty to him, and that, in the critical situation of the new ruler's impending first campaign to the north, Josiah was suspected or accused of disloyalty and slain on the spot.[56]

---

controlled the coast of Lebanon at the time, and that this was not merely a case of trade relations, as was assumed by Katzenstein (1973: 298-304). See also Otzen 1964: 78-95.

55. For a different opinion, see Morschauser 1988.

56. Some scholars, rejecting the version given in Chronicles and viewing it as a sort of later interpretation arising from an attempt to fill in the gaps in Kings, have proposed various reconstructions for the account of Josiah's death. According to one supposition, Josiah was executed because his responses did not satisfy the Egyptian ruler before whom he was brought to trial (Welch 1925; Boehmer 1933: 203); another hypothesis states that Josiah controlled Megiddo, but, by some unknown means, fell into Necho's hands and was put to death (Noth 1960: 278-79); or Josiah may have controlled Megiddo, set out to greet Necho as he passed through the town, and was thus caught and killed (Pfeifer 1969: 305-306); or the two rulers may have met as allies, in an attempt to reach a

Immediately afterward, Necho II continued on his northward campaign, and Jehoahaz son of Josiah was crowned in Judah (2 Kgs 23.30). Nevertheless, although he failed in his campaign against Babylonia and was forced to retreat from Mesopotamia,[57] Necho II was still in absolute control of Judah: he was able to arrest the Judahite ruler who appeared before him in Riblah in order to swear an oath of fealty and obtain Necho's permission to rule in Judah, to crown another ruler (Jehoiakim) according to his own choice, and to impose a heavy tax on the kingdom (2 Kgs 23.31-35). During the implementation of these measures, Necho II remained in Riblah in Syria, and, to the best of my knowledge, required no military means in order to impose his will. This is enough to confirm the conclusion that, as early as Josiah's day, Judah was at least formally subordinate to Egypt, and that the slaying of Josiah was intended to intimidate the Judahites into abiding by the Egyptian ruler's instructions.

Did Josiah perhaps try to change the status quo and rebel against Egypt? Did he take advantage of the transfer of power and of the crucial situation of 609 BCE in order to attack the new ruler when he passed through Palestine? This is the conjecture made by several scholars, who rejected the evidence given in Kings and preferred the detailed account in 2 Chron. 35.20-24.[58] I will not analyse this problematic account, the wide range of opinions expressed concerning it, or the complex historiographic problems which it raises.[59] It seems to me that the entire description is no more than a far-ranging, speculative interpretation given by the author of Chronicles to the brief and unenlightening description in Kings in an attempt to adapt it to his own special doctrine of retribution, while integrating descriptions of the deaths of two rulers—Ahab, king of Israel (1 Kgs 22.29-36),

---

mutual understanding, but Necho traitorously slew Josiah in the course of that meeting (Nelson 1983: 186-89). A few scholars have discussed this incident without suggesting solutions of their own (Frost 1968: 376; Miller and Hayes 1986: 402; Cogan and Tadmor 1988: 301).

57. For the Egyptian campaign against Haran in 609 BCE, see Wiseman 1961: 18-19, 45, 62-63 ll. 66-69; Grayson 1975: 96 ll. 66-69. In the course of that campaign, a large Egyptian army crossed the Euphrates and set out for Haran. On the way, it conquered a town occupied by a Babylonian garrison (this, in my opinion, is the correct completion of l. 67), and encamped opposite Haran. Line 69 reads: 'Until the month of Elul they did battle against the city but achieved nothing. [They turned (?) and] withdrew' (*mim-ma ul il-[qu-ú issuḫūma*(?) *ana arki-šu]-nu iḫḫisu*). Wiseman's and Grayson's translation for the end of the line ('they did not withdraw') is mistaken. We must rather adopt the reconstructions suggested by J. Lewy (1925: 76-77 l. 69) and Landsberger and Bauer (1926: 88 and n. 2).

58. For the theological interpretation of the war and its consequences, see Augustin 1988.

59. Williamson (1987b) attempted to prove that the author of Chronicles had at his disposal an independent source, in addition to the book of Kings, from which to drew his description. The main reason for this claim was the order of writing used to describe this incident in Chronicles, which differs from that in Kings, whereas, in other descriptions, the order of writing in the two books is more or less the same. It may be, however, that a later editor intervened, changing the order of writing in Kings after that book had been used as a source by the author of Chronicles; or that the latter author had at his disposal a different version of Kings, in which the incidents were recorded in inverse order (for this problem, see Lemke 1965). The argument proposing the existence of an independent source which antedated Chronicles obviously does not prove the reliability of that hypothetical source; in my opinion, the evidence cited by Williamson seems hardly sufficient to confirm his hypothesis concerning the existence of a source of this type.

and Ahaziah, king of Judah (2 Kgs 9.27-28)—which he found in his source, the book of Kings (Welch 1925: 255; Welten 1969: 164-66).

It is important to emphasize that the assumption of a battle near Megiddo raises a number of difficulties. Why would the ruler of a small kingdom choose to fight the ruler of a great power in battle on an open field, in circumstances giving the larger, stronger army all possible advantages?[60] Why would he make a stand in a place so far from his kingdom, which did not provide him with any advantage at all?[61] Furthermore, if Josiah was such a strong ruler as to dare to report for battle on an open field against the king of Egypt, why did his kingdom surrender unconditionally so soon after his death, enabling Necho II to assume absolute control? Why did king Jehoahaz of Judah not trust his fortresses and his army, in those districts where the Egyptian army was obviously weak and where he could have enjoyed a significant advantage over his rival—especially as the king of Egypt had just failed in his campaign and was hard pressed by the Babylonians? Why did he report, of his own will, to distant Riblah, even though he could easily have guessed the king of Egypt's reaction (cf. Jer. 22.10-12)?

In view of these considerations, it seems preferable to adopt the brief, untendentious testimony in the book of Kings, rather than the detailed and colourful description in the book of Chronicles, and to assume that Necho II slew Josiah when he appeared before him, perhaps to swear an oath of fealty. The background for this deed is unknown, and any possible hypothesis in this regard (dissatisfaction at the independence shown by the king of Judah and evidenced by his reforms; his activity in Samaria, outside the borders of his kingdom; his refusal to send an army to assist the king of Egypt in his campaign) will remain unproven.[62]

5. *Summary: Josiah in Historiography and in Historical Reality*
The picture of Josiah's reign, as reflected in this discussion, is far removed from the description of those years as reflected in the book of Kings, and no less distant from the sketch of his period presented in modern historiography.

---

60. On reporting for battle in an open field, see Eph'al 1983: 91-94.

61. Some doubt should be cast upon the multi-level 'structure' erected by Malamat (1973), in his effort to explain why Josiah reported for battle, of all places, in distant Megiddo. His reconstruction is founded on the assumption that the king of Judah launched a surprise attack on the Egyptian army which was then headed northward, toward the Euphrates (1973: 274-78). Nonetheless, those accepting the testimony in 2 Chron. 35.20-24 cannot simultaneously accept this hypothesis: according to the Chronicler's description, negotiations initially took place between the parties, and only after that did the two armies take up positions opposite each other and commence the battle, in the course of which Josiah was killed by the Egyptian archers (just as Ahab had been killed, in a similar situation, by the Aramean archers). The assumption of a surprise attack and of springing 'an ambush on his enemy in the Plain of Megiddo...before the Egyptian army could deploy on the plain or find protection within Megiddo' (1973: 277) has no basis in the Chronicler's description of the event.

62. Based on 2 Kgs 23.29, Yoyotte (1960: 380) assumed that Necho II's campaign in late 609 BCE was directed against Assyria, Egypt's long-time ally, and that Ashur-Uballiṭ II, last king of Assyria, was killed during that campaign. It is, of course, possible that Necho II decided to get rid of the Assyrian king, who had lost all his lands and was no longer useful, and therefore put him to death. There is, however, certainly no reason to assume that Assyria, rather than Babylonia, was the prime target for the Egyptian campaign

By utter contrast to historical reality, the author of the book of Kings presented Hezekiah's revolt against Assyria as an impressive success, and the Assyrian campaign into Judah as having ended in the failure and retreat of the Assyrian ruler, following the dramatic intervention of the God of Israel. In order to reinforce this picture of the revolt as a success, the author omitted any mention of Assyria from that point on: anyone reading the history of Manasseh, Amon, and Josiah in the book of Kings, and finding there no hint of the Assyrian domination, would have to conclude—in view of the internal sequence of events of the book of Kings—that Judah fell under the yoke of Assyria in the reign of Ahaz and was freed during that of Hezekiah. In this way, the author of the book of Kings avoided having to describe the external reality in Josiah's day—a reality in which Judah was subjugated to one great power for many years, and, following the retreat of that power, became subordinate (at least nominally) to another; a reality far out of line with the image of the righteous king. Instead, the author concentrated on internal affairs, and described in great detail the implementation of the reforms, by which all foreign cults were eradicated, leaving only the sacred worship of the God of Israel, centred in the Temple in Jerusalem. Not until the account of Josiah's death, and even then with deliberate brevity, did the author make any further reference to Judah's foreign affairs; from that point on, the great powers and external politics assume a central role in his work. According to the description in the book of Kings, Judah became subjugated to Egypt during the reign of a sinful king (Jehoahaz), just as it had become subjugated to Assyria under another sinful king (Ahaz), and had won its liberty under a righteous king (Hezekiah). Nor should we marvel that all of the last kings of Judah, who were dominated by foreign powers (first Egypt, then Babylonia), were described in the book of Kings as having done 'what was evil in the sight of the Lord', a phrase which may not represent the actual state of affairs in their time.

The gaps in the book of Kings have been filled in by the works of various scholars; the manifold nuances of these works have repeatedly been pointed out in the course of this discussion. Many scholars have assumed that Josiah freed his kingdom from the Assyrian yoke in the early stages of his reign, enjoyed many years of independent rule, and expanded his kingdom over vast areas. A few have gone so far as to assume that he controlled most of the Israelite territory, and even to ascribe to him the tendency to restore David's kingdom to its former glory.

By contrast, I have attempted to show that Josiah was subjugated to Assyria throughout the first portion of his reign, and that, following the Assyrian retreat, Egypt entered the scene and took over Assyria's territories and, to a not insignificant extent, its status. The idea of rival pro-Assyrian and pro-Egyptian factions operating in Judah in Josiah's time seems, in my opinion, to be divorced from reality and based on an erroneous analogy with the state of affairs at a later period, when Babylonia and Egypt were struggling for control of Palestine.[63] In

---

63. Malamat 1953; 1973: 271; 1975: 125-26; Milgrom 1955: 65-67; Cazelles 1967: 92. For a critique of the concept of 'pro-Assyrian' or 'anti-Assyrian' policy as implemented by the kings of Judah (Manasseh, Amon, and Josiah), see Nelson 1983: 177-83.

Josiah's time, Assyria and Egypt were allies, not rivals. Accordingly, it might be possible to speak of nationalist circles calling for political daring, as against more conservative circles which, in light of the lessons learned from Sennacherib's campaign, advocated compromise with the great powers and restraint from measures which might endanger the well-being of the kingdom; yet it is certainly not correct to speak of opposite Assyrian and Egyptian orientations.

We do not know whether or not Egypt gained a foothold on the coast of Philistia even before the Assyrian retreat from Palestine. In any case, the main change in the state of affairs in the area took place only after Assyria failed in its efforts to suppress the Babylonian revolt, which began in 626 BCE, and after the outbreak of civil war in 623 BCE. Following these developments, Assyria retreated from *Ebir nāri* ('Beyond the River'), and turned those territories over to Egypt in exchange for military aid. In subsequent years, Egypt occupied itself with reinforcing its status in the evacuated regions and with military assistance to Assyria; therefore, Judah enjoyed a considerable measure of independence, despite being formally subordinate to Egypt.

Josiah took advantage of this situation to implement comprehensive reforms in his kingdom, focused on the extirpation of 'foreign' cults and the concentration of worship in the Temple in Jerusalem; in this, he was assisted by the awakening of nationalist consciousness in extensive circles throughout the kingdom, although other, oppositionist circles no doubt did all in their power to prevent the implementation of the reforms. Some time later, Josiah expanded northward; he captured Bethel, the cult centre which had been Jerusalem's great rival throughout the days of the Kingdom of Judah, destroyed the site of worship, and annexed the area to his kingdom. He may also have extended his rule into Samaria, outside the range of Egypt's immediate political interests, in which there was no well-formed body to assume control and concentrate independent power following the Assyrian retreat. The extent of Josiah's activity in the former Assyrian province of Samaria is not known; however, he surely did not dare to annex the entire region, in view of the expected Egyptian response to such a deed, and because of the great difficulties foreseen in attempting to assimilate its population into his kingdom. Throughout their history Israel and Judah were two different kingdoms, and following its conquest Samaria became an Assyrian province; its annexation would have been regarded as an act of aggression and the assimilation of its vast population was probably beyond the power of the small Kingdom of Judah.

Josiah was unable to expand westward, due to the danger of conflict with Egypt, as well as the growth and strengthening of his neighbour Ekron, which became a sort of buffer state between the coastal area and the Kingdom of Judah.

The extent of the Kingdom of Judah in Josiah's time is reflected in the town lists of Judah and Benjamin in the book of Joshua. These lists, their meaning and date, constitute a starting point for the discussions in the second part of this study. The information at our disposal on the period of Josiah's reign, drawn from the descriptions in the books of Kings and Chronicles, is surprisingly limited, and does not enable us to determine the extent of his kingdom, let alone its strength and economic power. The dating of the town lists in Josiah's time, and the integration of the date with the archaeological data on the extent of settlement, strength, and deployment in Judah in the seventh century BCE, provide the foothold so vital to our discussion.

The combination of textual and archaeological information enables us to state that, in all matters related to the extent of its borders, its strength of settlement and economic power, Josiah's kingdom was considerably weaker than the kingdom which had existed in the eighth century BCE. The destructive results of Sennacherib's campaign remained evident even in the last years of Josiah's reign, almost a century after the end of the campaign. Indeed, no few sites which had been destroyed in 701 BCE and their inhabitants exiled were still unsettled. The period of *pax Assyriaca* enabled Judah to recover gradually, restore some of its settlements, and strengthen its economy (Na'aman 1987b: 9-15). But not only Judah enjoyed a period of tranquillity and prosperity at this time; so did its eastern and western neighbours, whose expansion was to exert considerable influence on Judah's fate in the last stages of its existence.

Josiah enjoyed a protracted period of peace throughout his rule; following the Assyrian retreat, he took energetic action toward the stabilization of his kingdom, and perhaps also toward its northward expansion. There can be no doubt that these actions were accompanied by a burst of popular enthusiasm and the awakening of nationalist ambitions, along with hopes for expansion and prosperity. In reality, however, things were different: Egypt strengthened its presence in the region, and Josiah's activity within his kingdom and beyond its northern border irritated the great power. The details of the occurrences cannot be precisely reconstructed, nor can we state why Necho II decided to rid himself of Josiah when the latter appeared before him at Megiddo. In any event, Josiah's death cooled the recently awakened hopes, and Egyptian intervention in the internal affairs of the Judahite kingdom became an established fact.

Would it have been possible to expect great things of Josiah, had he not been killed before his time? We cannot reconstruct historical events which did not actually take place; any discussion of what might have been is necessarily hypothetical. It can, however, be seen that the hopes of great expansion and glory could not have been realized in the conditions prevailing in the late seventh century. Within a few short years, Babylonia was to take the place of Assyria and Egypt as the ruling power in the area, and attempts by the kings of Judah to demonstrate an independent policy led Judah directly into destruction and exile. It seems that many scholars were deceived by the false similarity between Josiah's reign and the biblical description of the days of the United Monarchy. By placing emphasis on the hopes and longings based on the assumed distant past, they managed to reconstruct a concrete reality in which those hopes and longings were achieved in fact. It is important to remember that the period in which Josiah lived and acted was different in every characteristic from that of his forefathers, as his hands were constantly tied and his ability to realize his ambitions was limited. Accordingly, there is no basis to compare the achievements attained in his day with the earlier reality.

My historical conclusions are in line with the lack of descriptive material concerning conquests and expansions in Palestine under Josiah—a lack which has puzzled and perplexed many scholars, and has engendered many and varied explanations. Even the argument in favour of a 'conspiracy of silence', supposedly formed about Josiah's death, seems unfounded to me (Frost 1968). Those reading the enthusiastic, pro-Josiah description in the book of Kings will naturally be surprised at the fate of the righteous king; those presenting an historic picture which emphasizes Josiah's great achievements by contrast to the weakness of his successors will be no less surprised by the near-absence of any reflection of his death in the words of scribes and prophets active at the time.[64] Indeed, the above mentioned 'conspiracy of silence' argument is primarily based on the assumption that the king's death was a fateful event in the history of the Kingdom of Judah, and one which cast the kingdom from the topmost heights into the lowest depths. The presentation here of a different historical picture casts this 'silence' of his contemporaries in a different light. The grief at the king's sudden death was certainly heavy, and the feeling of immediate crisis was surely no less acute. Nevertheless, it is doubtful whether this episode drastically altered the course of events; and anyone observing the event from a slightly later perspective might not even have perceived it as fateful. It appears that the impression made on contemporaries by the slaying of Josiah was less profound than assumed by modern scholars, and, for that reason, was so sparingly mentioned in works dating from after Josiah's time.

The author of the book of Kings emphasized the scope of Josiah's actions in the fields of religion and cult, which won him an unprecedentedly favourable evaluation (probably awarded by a later editor):[65] 'Before him there was no king like him, who turned to the Lord with all his heart and with all his soul and with all his might, according to all the law of Moses; nor did any like him arise after him' (2 Kgs 23.25). Studying the history of Josiah from an overall historical perspective, it seems that this evaluation is acceptable; even though his modest political and territorial achievements were wiped out by his death, his actions in the areas of religion and cult remained engraved in the hearts of his supporters from among the members of the Deuteronomistic school for generations, and exerted considerable influence on the development of Judaism during the Babylonian exile and the post-exilic period.

BIBLIOGRAPHY

Ackroyd, P.R.
    1968   'Historians and Prophets', *Svensk Exegetisk Årsbok* 33: 18-54.
Africa, T.W.
    1963   'Herodotus and Diodorus on Egypt', *JNES* 22: 254-58.

---

64. Compare the history of Josiah and his heirs as presented in detailed articles by Malamat (1973, 1975, 1988).

65. The paragraph in 2 Kgs 23.25-27 belongs to a later stratum of Deuteronomistic historiography. See (from various viewpoints): Seeligmann 1969–74: 279-80; Cross 1973: 285-87; Spieckermann 1982: 43-46, with earlier literature.

Aharoni, M., and Y. Aharoni
    1976   'The Stratification of Judahite Sites in the 8th and 7th Centuries BCE', *BASOR* 224: 73-90.

Aharoni, Y.
    1956   'Excavations at Ramat Rahel, 1954: Preliminary Report', *IEJ* 6: 102-11, 137-55.
    1957   *The Settlement of the Israelite Tribes in Upper Galilee* (Jerusalem: Hebrew University [Hebrew]).
    1959   'The Province List of Judah', *VT* 9: 225-46.
    1962   *Excavations at Ramat Rahel, Seasons 1959 and 1960* (Serie Archaeologica, 2; Rome: Centro di Studi Semitici).
    1966   'Hebrew Ostraca from Tel Arad', *IEJ* 16: 1-7.
    1968   'Trial Excavation in the "Solar Shrine" at Lachish: Preliminary Report', *IEJ* 18: 157-69.
    1969   'Rubute and Ginti-kirmil', *VT* 19: 137-45.
    1976   'The Solomonic Districts', *TA* 3: 5-15.
    1979   *The Land of the Bible: A Historical Geography* (Philadelphia: Westminster Press, 2nd edn).
    1981   *Arad Inscriptions* (Judean Desert Studies; Jerusalem: Bialik Institute and Israel Exploration Society).
    1982   *The Archaeology of the Land of Israel* (Philadelphia: Westminster Press).
    1985   'From Geba to Beer-sheba', in B.Z. Luria (ed.), *Studies in the Book of Kings* (Jerusalem: The Israel Society for Biblical Research): 321-30 (Hebrew).

Albright, W.F.
    1924   *Excavations and Results at Tell el-Fûl (Gibeah of Saul)* (AASOR, 4; New Haven: American Schools of Oriental Research).

Alt, A.
    1925   'Judas Gaue unter Josia', *PJb* 21: 100-16 (reprinted in Alt 1953: 276-88).
    1927   'Eine galiläische Ortsliste in Jos. 19', *ZAW* 45: 59-81.
    1950   'Das Stützpunktsystem der Pharaonen an der phönikischen Küste und im syrischen Binnenland', *ZDPV* 68: 97-133 (reprinted in Alt 1959: 107-40).
    1953   *Kleine Schriften zur Geschichte des Volkes Israel*, II (Munich: Beck).
    1959   *Kleine Schriften zur Geschichte des Volkes Israel*, III (Munich: Beck).

Amusin, J.D., and M.L. Heltzer
    1964   'The Inscription from Meṣad Ḥashavyahu: Complaint of a Reaper of the Seventh Century B.C.', *IEJ* 14: 148-57.

Armayor, O.K.
    1978   'Did Herodotus Ever Go to Egypt?', *JARCE* 15: 59-73.

Augustin, M.
    1988   'The Literary Form of the "Constructed War Chronicle with Theological Interpretation" in the Books of Chronicles', *Proceedings of the Ninth World Congress of Jewish Studies. Panel Sessions: Bible Studies and Ancient Near East* (Jerusalem: Magnes Press): 133-40.

Auld, A.G.
    1975   'Judges 1 and History: A Reconsideration', *VT* 25: 261-85.
    1980   *Joshua, Moses and the Land: Tetrateuch–Pentateuch–Hexateuch in a Generation Since 1938* (Edinburgh: T. & T. Clark).

Avi-Yonah, M.
    1962   'Scythopolis', *IEJ* 12: 123-34.

Ayalon, E.
> 1985 'Trial Excavation of Two Iron Age Strata at Tel 'Eton', *TA* 12: 54-62.

Bardtke, H.
> 1936 'Jeremia der Fremdvölkerprophet', *ZAW* 54: 240-62.

Barkay, G.
> 1978 'A Group of Iron Age Scale Weights', *IEJ* 28: 209-17.
> 1985 'Northern and Western Jerusalem in the End of the Iron Age' (PhD Thesis, Tel Aviv University [Hebrew]).

Barth, H.
> 1977 *Die jesaja-Worte in der Josiazeit* (WMANT, 48; Neukirchen–Vluyn: Neukirchener Verlag).

Baumgartner, W.
> 1959 'Herodots Babylonische and Assyrische Nachrichten', in *idem, Zum Alten Testament und seiner Umwelt: Ausgewählte Aufsätze* (Leiden: E.J. Brill): 282-331.

Beck, P.
> 1986 'A Bulla from Ḥorvat 'Uzza', *Qadmoniot* 19: 40-41 (Hebrew).

Begg, C.T.
> 1987 'The Death of Josiah in Chronicles: Another View', *VT* 37: 1-8.

Beit-Arieh, I.
> 1985 'Tel 'Ira—A Fortified City of the Kingdom of Judah', *Qadmoniot* 18: 17-25 (Hebrew).
> 1986 'Ḥorvat 'Uzza—A Border Fortress in the Eastern Negev', *Qadmoniot* 19: 31-40 (Hebrew).
> 1986–87 'The Ostracon of Ahiqam from Ḥorvat 'Uza', *TA* 13-14: 32-38.

Beit-Arieh, I. (ed.)
> 1999 *Tel 'Ira: A Stronghold in the Biblical Negev* (Sonia and Marco Nadler Institute of Archaeology, Tel Aviv University, Monograph Series, 15; Tel Aviv: Emery and Claire Yass Publications in Archaeology).

Beit-Arieh, I., and B.C. Cresson
> 1991 'Horvat ᶜUza: A Fortified Outpost on the Eastern Negev Border', *BA* 54: 126-35.

Biran, A.
> 1985 'Tel 'Ira', *Qadmoniot* 18: 25-28 (Hebrew).

Biran, A., and R. Cohen
> 1981 'Aroer in the Negev', *ErIs* 15: 250-71 (Hebrew).

Boardman, J.
> 1980 *The Greeks Overseas: Their Early Colonies and Trade* (New York: Thames & Hudson, rev. edn).

Boehmer, J.
> 1933 'König Josias Tod', *Archiv für Religionswissenschaft* 30: 199-203.

Borger, R.
> 1965 'Der Aufstieg des neubabylonischen Reiches', *JCS* 19: 59-78.

Brinkman, J.A.
> 1984 *Prelude to Empire: Babylonian Society and Politics, 747–627 B.C.* (Occasional Publications of the Babylonian Fund, 7; Philadelphia: University Museum).

Broshi, M.
> 1958 'Jotbah', in *Encyclopaedia Biblica*, III (Jerusalem: Bialik Institute): 672 (Hebrew).

Broshi, M., and I. Finkelstein
> 1990 'The Population of Palestine in 734 BCE', *Cathedra* 58: 3-24 (Hebrew).

Brown, S.C.
    1986   'Media and Secondary State Formation in the Neo-Assyrian Zagros: An Anthropological Approach to an Assyriological Problem', *JCS* 38: 107-19.

Brown, T.S.
    1965   'Herodotus Speculates about Egypt', *American Journal of Philology* 86: 60-76.

Cahill, J.M.
    1995   'Rosette Stamp Seal Impressions from Ancient Judah', *IEJ* 45: 230-52.

Cavaignac, E.
    1961   'À propos du début de l'histoire des Médes', *Journal Asiatique* 249: 153-62.

Cazelles, H.
    1967   'Sophonie, Jérémie, et les Scythes en Palestine', *RB* 74: 24-44.

Clements, R.E.
    1984   *Isaiah and the Deliverance of Jerusalem: A Study of the Interpretation of Prophecy in the Old Testament* (JSOTSup, 13; Sheffield: JSOT Press).

Cogan, M.
    1974   *Imperialism and Religion: Assyria, Judah and Israel in the Eighth and Seventh Centuries B.C.E.* (SBLMS, 19; Missoula, MT: Scholars Press).
    1980   'Tendentious Chronology in the Book of Chronicles', *Zion* 45: 165-72 (Hebrew).

Cogan, M., and H. Tadmor
    1977   'Gyges and Ashurbanipal: A Study in Literary Transmission', *Or* 46: 65-85.
    1988   *II Kings: A New Translation with Introduction and Notes* (AB, 11; Garden City, NY: Doubleday).

Cohen, R.
    1981   'The Excavations at Kadesh-Barnea (1976–1978)', *BA* 44: 93-104.
    1983   'Excavations at Kadesh-Barnea, 1976–1982', *Qadmoniot* 16: 2-14 (Hebrew).

Cross, F.M.
    1969   'Judean Stamps', *ErIs* 9: 20*-27*.
    1973   *Canaanite Myth and Hebrew Epic: Essays in the History of the Religion of Israel* (Cambridge, MA: Harvard University Press).

Cross, F.M., and D.N. Freedman
    1953   'Josiah's Revolt against Assyria', *JNES* 12: 56-58.

Cross, F.M., and G.E. Wright
    1956   'The Boundary and Province Lists of the Kingdom of Judah', *JBL* 75: 202-26.

Demsky, A.
    1966   'The Houses of Achzib: A Critical Note on Micah 1: 14b', *IEJ* 16: 211-15.
    1973   'Geba, Gibeah, and Gibeon—An Historico-Geographic Riddle', *BASOR* 212: 26-31.

Diakonoff, I.M.
    1985   'Media', in I. Gershevitch (ed.), *The Cambridge History of Iran*. II. *The Median and Achaemenian Periods* (Cambridge: Cambridge University Press): 36-148.

Dion, P.-E.
    1992   'Les KTYM de Tel Arad: Grecs ou Phéniciens?', *RB* 99: 70-97.

Dobbs-Allsopp, F.W.
    1994   'The Genre of the Meṣad Ḥashavyahu Ostracon', *BASOR* 295: 49-55.

Dothan, M.
    1965   'The Fortress at Kadesh-Barnea', *IEJ* 15: 134-51.

Elayi, J.
    1983   'Les cités phéniciennes et l'empire assyrien à l'époque d'Assurbanipal', *RA* 77: 45-58.

Eph'al, I.
    1979   'Assyrian Dominion in Palestine', in A. Malamat (ed.), *The Age of the Monarchies: Political History* (The World History of the Jewish People; Jerusalem: Massada): 276-89, 364-68.
    1982   *The Ancient Arabs: Nomads on the Borders of the Fertile Crescent 9th–5th Centuries B.C.* (Jerusalem: E.J. Brill).
    1983   'On Warfare and Military Control in the Ancient Near Eastern Empires: A Research Outline', in H. Tadmor and M. Weinfeld (eds.), *History, Historiography and Interpretation* (Jerusalem: Magnes Press): 88-106.

Eph'al, I., and J. Naveh
    1988   'The Use of Epigraphical Sources for the Study of Biblical History', *Zion* 53: 211-13 (Hebrew).

Eshel, H.
    1989   'A *lmlk* Stamp from Bethel', *IEJ* 39: 60-62.

Fantalkin, A.
    2001   'Meẓad Ḥashavyahu: Its Material Culture and Historical Background', *TA* 28: 3-165.

Fehling, D.
    1989   *Herodotus and His 'Sources'* (Arca, 21; Leeds: Cairns).

Freedy, K.S., and D.B. Redford
    1970   'The Dates in Ezekiel in Relation to Biblical, Babylonian and Egyptian Sources', *JAOS* 90: 462-85.

Frost, S.B.
    1968   'The Death of Josiah: A Conspiracy of Silence', *JBL* 87: 369-82.

Gal, Z.
    1988–89   'The Lower Galilee in the Iron Age II: Analysis of Survey Material and Its Historical Interpretation', *TA* 15-16: 56-64.

Galil, G.
    1984   'The Administrative Districts of the Judean Hill Area', *Zion* 49: 205-24 (Hebrew).
    1985   'The Land of Dan', *Tarbiz* 54: 1-19 (Hebrew).
    1987   'The Administrative Division of the Shephelah', *Shnaton: An Annual for Biblical and Ancient Near Eastern Studies* 9: 55-71 (Hebrew).

Galling, K.
    1951   'The "Gola-List" according to Ezra 2/Nehemiah 7', *JBL* 70: 149-58.

Garfinkel, Y.
    1987   'The City-List, Epigraphic Evidence and the Administrative Division of the Kingdom of Judah', *Zion* 52: 489-94 (Hebrew).
    1988   '2 Chron. 11.5-10 Fortified Cities List and the *lmlk* Stamps—Reply to Nadav Na'aman', *BASOR* 271: 69-73.

Gerardi, P.
    1986   'Declaring War in Mesopotamia', *AfO* 33: 30-38.

Ginsberg, H.L.
    1950   'Judah and the Transjordan States from 734 to 582 B.C.E.', in S. Lieberman (ed.), *Alexander Marx Jubilee Volume* (New York: The Jewish Theological Seminary of America): 347-68.

Gitin, S.
    1989   'Tel Miqne-Ekron: A Type-Site for the Inner Coastal Plain in the Iron Age II Period', in S. Gitin and W.G. Dever (eds.), *Recent Excavations in Israel: Studies in Iron Age Archaeology* (AASOR, 49; Winona Lake, IN: Eisenbrauns): 23-58.

1997 'The Neo-Assyrian Empire and its Western Periphery: The Levant, with a Focus on Philistine Ekron', in S. Parpola and R.M. Whiting (eds.), *Assyria 1995: Proceedings of the 10th Anniversary Symposium of the Neo-Assyrian Text Corpus Project* (Helsinki: Neo-Assyrian Text Corpus Project): 77-103.

Gray, J.
1970 *I & II Kings: A Commentary* (OTL; London: SCM Press).

Grayson, A.K.
1975 *Assyrian and Babylonian Chronicles* (Locust Valley: J.J. Augustin).

Gressmann, H.
1924 'Josia and das Deuteronomium', *ZAW* 42: 313-37.

Gyles, M.F.
1959 *Pharaonic Policies and Administration, 663–323 B.C.* (Chapel Hill: The University of North Carolina Press).

Hachmann, R.
1982 'Die ägyptische Verwaltung in Syrien während der Amarnazeit', *ZDPV* 98: 17-49.

Halpern, B.
1987 '"Brisker Pipes than Poetry": The Development of Israelite Monotheism', in J. Neusner, B.A. Levine and E.S. Frerichs (eds.), *Judaic Perspectives on Ancient Israel* (Philadelphia: Fortress Press): 77-115.

Helck, W.
1971 *Die Beziehungen Ägyptens zu Vorderasien im 3. and 2. Jahrtausend v. Chron.* (Wiesbaden: Otto Harrassowitz).

Herzog, Z., M. Aharoni, A.F. Rainey and S. Moshkovitz
1984 'The Israelite Fortress at Arad', *BASOR* 254: 1-34.

Holladay, W.L.
1981 'A Coherent Chronology of Jeremiah's Early Career', in P.-M. Bogaert (ed.), *Le Livre de Jérémie. Le Prophète et son milieu; les oracles et leur transmission* (Bibliotheca Ephemeridum Theologicarum Lovaniensium, 54; Leuven: Peeters): 58-73.

Hollenberg, J.
1881 'Zur Textkritik des Büches Josua und des Büches der Richter', *ZAW* 1: 97-105.

Holmes, S.
1914 *Joshua, the Hebrew and Greek Texts* (Cambridge: Cambridge University Press).

Hübner, U.
1997 'Bemerkungen zum Pfandrecht: Das Judäischen Ostrakon von Meṣad Ḥašavyāhu, alttestamentliches und griechisches Pfandrecht sowie ein Graffito aus Marissa', *UF* 29: 215-25.

Hyatt, J.P.
1940 'The Peril from the North in Jeremiah', *JBL* 59: 499-513.

Isserlin, B.S.J.
1957 'Israelite and Pre-Israelite Place-Names in Palestine: A Historical and Geographical Sketch', *PEQ* 89: 133-44.

Japhet, S.
1977 *The Ideology of the Book of Chronicles and Its Place in Biblical Thought* (Jerusalem: Bialik Institute [Hebrew]).
1983 'People and Land in the Restoration Period', in G. Strecker (ed.), *Das Land Israel in biblischer Zeit* (Göttingen: Vandenhoeck & Ruprecht): 103-25.

Jepsen, A.
1959 'Die Reform des Josia', in J. Herrmann (ed.), *Festschrift Friedrich Baumgärtel zum 70. Geburtstag* (Erlangen: Universitasbund Erlangen): 97-108.

Kallai, Z.
1960 *The Northern Boundaries of Judah from the Settlement of the Tribes until the Beginning of the Hasmonean Period* (Jerusalem: Magnes Press [Hebrew]).
1971 'The Kingdom of Rehoboam', *ErIs* 10: 245-54 (Hebrew).
1972 'Ophni', in *Encyclopaedia Biblica*, VI (Jerusalem: Bialik Institute): 321-22 (Hebrew).
1986 *Historical Geography of the Bible. The Tribal Territories of Israel* (Jerusalem: Magnes Press; Leiden: E.J. Brill).

Kallai-Kleinmann, Z.
1958 'The Town Lists of Judah, Simeon, Benjamin and Dan', *VT* 8: 134-60.

Kammenhuber, A.
1976–80 'Kimmerier', *Reallexikon der Assyriologie* V: 594-96.

Katzenstein, H.J.
1973 *The History of Tyre, from the Beginning of the Second Millennium B.C.E. until the Fall of the Neo-Babylonian Empire in 538 B.C.E.* (Jerusalem: Shocken Institute for Jewish Research).
1978 'The Camp of the Tyrians at Memphis', *ErIs* 14: 161-64 (Hebrew).

Kienitz, F.K.
1953 *Die politische Geschichte Ägyptens vom 7. bis zum 4. Jahrhundert vor der Zeitwende* (Berlin: Akademie Verlag).

Kitchen, K.A.
1973 *The Third Intermediate Period in Egypt (1100–650 B. C.)* (Warminster: Aris & Phillips).

Kleer, M., and M. Kröger
1992 'Das gepfändete Gewand', *BN* 61: 38-50.

Klein, R.W.
1983 'Abijah's Campaign Against the North (II Chron. 13)—What Were the Chronicler's Sources?', *ZAW* 95: 210-17.

Kletter, R.
1999 'Pots and Polities: Material Remains of Late Iron Age Judah in Relation to the Political Borders', *BASOR* 314: 19-54.
2002 'Temptation to Identify: Jerusalem, *mmšt*, and the *lmlk* Jar Stamps', *ZDPV* 118: 136-49.

Knauf, E.A.
1985 'Mu'näer and Mëuniter', *Die Welt des Orients* 16: 114-22.

Kochavi, M.
1972 'The Land of Judah', in M. Kochavi (ed.), *Judaea, Samaria, and the Golan: Archaeological Survey 1967–1968* (Jerusalem: Carta): 17-89 (Hebrew).

Kuschke, A.
1965 'Historisch-topographische Beiträge zum Buche Josua', in H. Graf Reventlow (ed.), *Gottes Wort and Gottes Land, Festschrift für H.H. Hertzberg* (Göttingen: Vandenhoeck & Ruprecht): 90-109.

Labat, R.
1961 'Kaštariti, Phraorte et les débuts de l'histoire Mède', *Journal Asiatique* 249: 1-12.

Landsberger, B., and T. Bauer
1926 'Zu neuveröffentlichten Geschichtsquellen der Zeit von Asarhaddon bis Nabonid', *ZA* 37: 61-98.

Lemaire, A.
1973 'L'ostracon "Ramat Negeb" et la topographie historique du Negeb', *Semitica* 23: 11-26.
1977 *Inscriptions Hébraïques*. I. *Les Ostraca* (Paris: Cerf).

Lemaire, A., and P. Vernus
 1980 'Les ostraca paléo-hébreux de Qadesh-Barnéa', *Or* 49: 341-45.
 1983 'L'ostracon paléo-hébreu N° 6 de Tell Qudeirat (Qadesh-Barnéa)', in M. Görg (ed.), *Fontes atque Pontes. Eine Festgabe für Hellmut Brunner* (Wiesbaden: Otto Harrassowitz): 302-26.

Lemke, W.E.
 1965 'The Synoptic Problem of the Chronicler's History', *HTR* 58: 349-63.

Lewy, H.
 1952 'Nitokris-Naqî'a', *JNES* 11: 264-86.

Lewy, J.
 1925 *Forschungen zur alten Geschichte Vorderasiens* (Mitteilungen der Vorderasiatischen Gesellschaft, 29/2; Leipzig: J.C. Hinrichs).

Lipschits, O.
 1997 'The Origins of the Jewish Population of Modi'in and Its Vicinity', *Cathedra* 85: 7-32 (Hebrew).

Liver, J.
 1958 'Josiah', in *Encyclopaedia Biblica*, III (Jerusalem: Bialik Institute): 417-24 (Hebrew).
 1968 'Manasseh', in *Encyclopaedia Biblica*, V (Jerusalem: Bialik Institute): 41-45 (Hebrew).

Lloyd, A.B.
 1975 *Herodotus Book II: Introduction* (Leiden: E.J. Brill).

Loewenstamm, S.E.
 1950 'Ashkenaz', in *Encyclopaedia Biblica*, I (Jerusalem: Bialik Institute): 762-63 (Hebrew).
 1962 'Kittim', in *Encyclopaedia Biblica*, IV (Jerusalem: Bialik Institute): 394-98 (Hebrew).

Lorton, D.
 1974 *The Juridical Terminology of International Relations in Egyptian Texts through Dynasty XVIII* (Baltimore and London: The Johns Hopkins University Press).

Malamat, A.
 1951 'The Historical Setting of Two Biblical Prophecies on the Nations', *IEJ* 1: 149-59.
 1953 'The Historical Background of the Assassination of Amon King of Judah', *IEJ* 3: 26-29.
 1974 'Josiah's Bid for Armageddon', *Journal of the Ancient Near Eastern Society of Columbia University* 5 (T.H. Gaster Festschrift): 267-79.
 1975 'The Twilight of Judah in the Egyptian-Babylonian Maelstrom', in G.W. Anderson *et al.* (eds.), *Congress Volume, Edinburgh 1974* (VTSup, 28: Leiden: E.J. Brill): 123-45.
 1982 'A Political Look at the Kingdom of David and Solomon and Its Relations with Egypt', in T. Ishida (ed.), *Studies in the Period of David and Solomon and Other Essays* (Tokyo: Yamakawa-Shuppansha): 189-204.
 1988 'The Kingdom of Judah between Egypt and Babylon: A Small State within a Great Power Confrontation', in W. Classen (ed.), *Text and Context: Old Testament and Semitic Studies for F.C. Fensham* (JSOTSup, 48; Sheffield: Sheffield Academic Press): 117-29.

Mazar, A.
 1985 'Between Judah and Philistia: Timnah (Tel Batash) in the Iron Age II', *ErIs* 18: 300-24 (Hebrew).

Mazar (Maisler), B.
    1941   'Topographical Studies 1: From Geva to Beer-sheba', *Bulletin of the Jewish Palestine Exploration Society* 8: 35-37 (Hebrew).
    1944   'Topographical Studies III: The Hill of God', *Bulletin of the Jewish Palestine Exploration Society* 10: 73-75 (Hebrew).
    1947   'Kiriath-arba which is Hebron', in Y.F. Baer, I. Gutman and M. Schwabe (eds.), *Dinaburg Jubilee Volume: Studies Presented to Ben-Zion Dinaburg* (Jerusalem: Kiryat Sepher): 310-25 (Hebrew).
    1950   'Eretz Israel', in *Encyclopaedia Biblica*, I (Jerusalem: Bialik Institute): 667-741 (Hebrew).
Mazar, B.
    1954   'Geba', in *Encyclopaedia Biblica*, II (Jerusalem: Bialik Institute): 412 (Hebrew).
    1958   'Jehoshaphat Son of Asa', in *Encyclopaedia Biblica*, III (Jerusalem: Bialik Institute): 565-70 (Hebrew).
    1960   'The Cities of the Territory of Dan', *IEJ* 10: 65-77.
    1967   'En-Gedi', in D.W. Thomas (ed.), *Archaeology and Old Testament Study* (Oxford: Clarendon Press): 223-30.
    1976   'Kiriath-jearim', in *Encyclopaedia Biblica*, VII (Jerusalem: Bialik Institute): 270-73 (Hebrew).
Mazar, E.
    1985   'Edomite Pottery at the End of the Iron Age', *IEJ* 35: 253-69.
McKay, J.
    1973   *Religion in Judah under the Assyrians 732–609 B.C.* (SBT, Second Series, 26; London: SCM Press).
Mendelsohn, I.
    1940   'Guilds in Ancient Palestine', *BASOR* 70: 17-21.
Meulenaere, H. de.
    1951   *Herodotus over de 26ste Dynastie* (II, 147- III, 15) (Bibliothèque du Muséon, 27; Leuven: Leuvense Universitaire Uitgaven).
Milgrom, J.
    1955   'The Date of Jeremiah, Chapter 2', *JNES* 14: 65-69.
    1971   'Did Josiah Take Over Megiddo?', *Beth Mikra* 16: 23-27 (Hebrew).
Millard, A.R.
    1979   'The Scythian Problem', in J. Ruffle *et al.* (eds.), *Glimpses of Ancient Egypt: Studies in Honour of H.W. Fairman* (Warminster: Aris & Phillips): 119-22.
Miller, J.M., and J.H. Hayes
    1986   *A History of Ancient Israel and Judah* (Philadelphia: Westminster Press).
Mittmann, S.
    1977   'Ri. 1,16f and das Siedlungsgebiet der kenitischen Sippe Hobab', *ZDPV* 93: 213-35.
Mommsen, H., I. Perlman and J. Yellin
    1984   'The Provenience of the *lmlk* Jars', *IEJ* 34: 89-113.
Montgomery, J.A.
    1934   'Archival Data in the Book of Kings', *JBL* 53: 46-52.
    1951   *A Critical and Exegetical Commentary on the Books of Kings* (ICC; Edinburgh: T. & T. Clark).
Morschauser, S.N.
    1988   'The End of the *Sdf(3)-Tr(yt)* "Oath"', *JARCE* 25: 93-103.

Mosis, R.
    1973   *Untersuchungen zur Theologie des chronistischen Geschichtswerkes* (Freiburger theologiche Studien, 92; Freiburg: Herder).

Na'aman, N.
    1980   'The Inheritance of the Sons of Simeon', *ZDPV* 96: 136-52.
    1981   'Economic Aspects of the Egyptian Occupation of Canaan', *IEJ* 31: 172-85.
    1982   'Palestine in the Canaanite Period: The Middle and the Late Bronze Ages', in I. Eph'al (ed.), *The History of Eretz Israel*, I (Jerusalem: Keter and Yad Izhak Ben-Zvi): 131-275 (Hebrew).
    1986a   *Borders and Districts in Biblical Historiography: Seven Studies in Biblical Geographical Lists* (Jerusalem Biblical Studies, 4; Jerusalem: Simor).
    1986b   'Hezekiah's Fortified Cities and the *LMLK* Stamps', *BASOR* 261: 5-21.
    1987a   'Beth-aven, Bethel and Early Israelite Sanctuaries', *ZDPV* 103: 13-21.
    1987b   'The Negev in the Last Century of the Kingdom of Judah', *Cathedra* 42: 3-15 (Hebrew).
    1988   'Pharaonic Lands in the Jezreel Valley in the Late Bronze Age', in M. Heltzer and E. Lipiński (eds.), *Society and Economy in the Eastern Mediterranean (c. 1500–1000 B.C.)* (Orientalia Lovaniensia Analecta, 23; Leuven: Departement Oriëntalistiek): 177-85.
    1991a   'The Kingdom of Judah under Josiah', *TA* 18: 3-71.
    1991b   'Chronology and History in the Late Assyrian Empire (631–619 B.C.)', *ZA* 81: 243-67.
    1995   '"The House-of-No-Shade Shall Take Away Its Tax from You" (Micah I 11)', *VT* 45: 516-27.
    1998   'Two Notes on the History of Ashkelon and Ekron in the Late Eighth–Seventh Centuries B.C.E.', *TA* 25: 219-27.

Na'aman, N., and R. Zadok
    1988   'Sargon II's Deportations to Israel and Philistia (716–708 B.C.)', *JCS* 40: 36-46.

Nadelman, Y.
    1989   'Hebrew Inscriptions, Seal Impressions and Markings of the Iron Age II', in E. Mazar and B. Mazar (eds.), *Excavations in the South of the Temple Mount* (Qedem, 29; Jerusalem: The Hebrew University of Jerusalem): 128-37.

Naveh, J.
    1960   'A Hebrew Letter from the Seventh Century B.C.', *IEJ* 10: 129-39.
    1962   'More Hebrew Inscriptions from Meṣad Ḥashavyahu', *IEJ* 12: 27-32.
    1977   'Meṣad Ḥashavyahu', in M. Avi-Yonah (ed.), *Encyclopedia of Archaeological Excavations in the Holy Land*, III (Jerusalem: Israel Exploration Society & Carta): 852-63.

Nelson, R.
    1983   'Realpolitik in Judah (687–609 BCE)', in W.W. Hallo, J.C. Moyer and L.G. Perdue (eds.), *Scriptures in Context. II. More Essays on the Comparative Method* (Winona Lake, IN: Eisenbrauns): 177-89.

Nicholson, E.W.
    1967   *Deuteronomy and Tradition* (Philadelphia: Fortress Press).

Niemeier, W.-D.
    2001   'Archaic Greeks in the Orient: Textual and Archaeological Evidence', *BASOR* 322: 11-32.
    2002   'Greek Mercenaries at Tel Kabri and Other Sites in the Levant', *TA* 29: 328-31.

North, R.
    1974   'Does Archaeology Prove Chronicles Sources?', in H.N. Bream, R. Heim and C. Moore (eds.), *A Light unto My Path: Old Testament Studies in Honor of Jacob M. Myers* (Philadelphia: Temple University Press): 375-401.
Noth, M.
    1935   'Studien zu den historisch-geographischen Dokumenten des Josuabuches', *ZDPV* 58: 185-255 (reprinted in *Aufsätze zur biblischen Landes- und Altertumskunde*, I [Neukirchen–Vluyn: Neukirchener Verlag, 1971]: 229-80).
    1944   'Israelitische Stämme zwischen Ammon und Moab', *ZAW* 60: 11-57 (reprinted in *Aufsätze zur biblischen Landes- und Altertumskunde*, I [Neukirchen–Vluyn: Neukirchener Verlag, 1971]: 391-433).
    1953   *Das Buch Josua* (Tübingen: J.C.B. Mohr, 2nd edn).
    1960   *The History of Israel* (London: A. & C. Black).
Oded, B.
    1974   'The Relation between the City-States of Phoenicia and Assyria in the Reigns of Esarhaddon and Ashurbanipal', in *idem*, *Studies in the History of the Jewish People and the Land of Israel*, III (Haifa: University of Haifa): 31-42 (Hebrew).
Oestreicher, T.
    1923   *Das deuteronomische Grundgesetz* (Beiträge zur Förderung christlicher Theologie, 27/4; Gütersloh: Bertelsmann).
Ogden, G.S.
    1978   'The Northern Extent of Josiah's Reforms', *Australian Biblical Review* 26: 26-34.
Oppenheim, A.L.
    1969   'Babylonian and Assyrian Historical Texts', *ANET*: 265-317.
Oren, E.D.
    1984   'Migdol: A New Fortress on the Edge of the Eastern Nile Delta', *BASOR* 256: 7-44.
Orlinsky, H.M.
    1939   'The Supposed Qiryat-Sannah of Joshua 15 49', *JBL* 58: 255-61.
Otzen, B.
    1964   *Studien über Deuterosacharja* (Copenhagen: Munksgaard).
Pardee, D.
    1978   'The Judicial Plea from Meṣad Ḥashavyahu (Yabneh-Yam): A New Philological Study', *Maarav* 1: 33-66.
    1980   'A Brief Note on Meṣad Ḥashavyahu Ostracon, l. 12: *W'ML*'', *BASOR* 239: 47-48.
Petrie, W.M.F.
    1888   *Tanis. Part II: Nebesheh (Am) and Defenneh (Tahpanhes)* (London: Trübner).
Pfeifer, G.
    1969   'Die Begegnung zwischen Pharao Necho und König Josia bei Megiddo', *Mitteilungen des Instituts für Orientforschung* 15: 297-307.
Porten, B.
    1968   *Archives from Elephantine: The Life of an Ancient Jewish Military Colony* (Berkeley and Los Angeles: University of California Press).
Proksch, O.
    1928   'König Josia', in *Festgabe für Theodor Zahn* (Leipzig: A. Deichert): 19-53.
Rad, G. von
    1958   *Theologie des Alten Testaments*, I (Munich: Chr. Kaiser Verlag).
Rainey, A.F.
    1986   'Arad in the Latter Days of the Judean Monarchy', *Cathedra* 42: 16-25 (Hebrew).

Redford, D.B.
 1985 'Sais and the Kushite Invasions of the Eighth Century B.C.', *JARCE* 22: 5-15.
Reich, R.
 1989 'The Third Season of Excavations at Meṣad Ḥashavyahu', *ErIs* 20: 228-32 (Hebrew).
Renz, J.
 1997 *Die althebräischen Inschriften*. Part 1. *Text und Kommentar*, in J. Renz and W. Röllig, *Handbuch der althebräischen Epigraphik*, I (5 vols., Darmstadt: Wissenschaftliche Buchgesellschaft).
Rofé, A.
 1982 *The Prophetical Stories: The Narratives about the Prophets in the Hebrew Bible: Their Literary Types and History* (Jerusalem: Magnes Press [Hebrew]).
Rowley, H.H.
 1962–63 'The Early Prophecies of Jeremiah in their Setting', *BJRL* 45: 198-234.
Rudolph, W.
 1955 *Chronikbücher* (HAT, I/21; Tübingen: J.C.B. Mohr).
Rüterswörden, U.
 1985 *Die Beamten der israelitischen Königszeit. Eine Studie zu śr und vergleichbaren Begriffen* (Stuttgart: W. Kohlhammer).
Sasson, V.
 1978 'An Unrecognized Juridical Term in the Yabneh-Yam Lawsuit and in an Unnoticed Biblical Parallel', *BASOR* 232: 57-63.
 1984 'A Matter to be Put Right: The Yabneh-Yam Case Continued', *JNSL* 12: 115-20.
Schmitt, G.
 1980 'Bet-Awen', in R. Cohen and G. Schmitt, *Drei Studien zur Archäologie und Topographie Altisraels* (Wiesbaden: Ludwig Reichert): 33-76.
Schunck, K.D.
 1962 'Bemerkungen zur Ortsliste von Benjamin (Jos. 18,21-28)', *ZDPV* 78: 143-58.
 1963 *Benjamin: Untersuchungen zur Entstehung und Geschichte eines israelitischen Stammes* (BZAW, 86; Berlin: Alfred Töpelmann).
Seeligmann, I.L.
 1969–74 *From Historical Reality to Historiographic Conception in the Bible. P'raqim*, II (Jerusalem: Shocken Institute for Jewish Research): 273-313 (Hebrew).
Sigrist, R.M.
 1982 'Une tablette cuneiforme de Tell Keisan', *IEJ* 32: 32-35.
Smirin, S.
 1952 *Josiah and His Age* (Jerusalem: Bialik Institute [Hebrew]).
Soggin, J.A.
 1984 *A History of Israel: from the beginnings to the Bar Kochba Revolt, AD 135* (London: SCM Press).
Spalinger, A.
 1974a 'Esarhaddon and Egypt: An Analysis of the First Invasion of Egypt', *Or* 43: 295-326.
 1974b 'Assurbanipal and Egypt: A Source Study', *JAOS* 94: 316-28.
 1976 'Psammetichus, King of Egypt: I', *JARCE* 13: 133-47.
 1977 'Egypt and Babylonia: A Survey (c. 620 B.C.–550 B.C.)', *Studien zur Altägyptischen Kultur* 5: 221-44.
 1978a 'Psammetichus, King of Egypt: II', *JARCE* 15: 49-57.
 1978b 'The Date of the Death of Gyges and its Historical Implications', *JAOS* 98: 400-409.

1978c	'The Concept of the Monarchy during the Saite Epoch—An Essay of Synthesis', *Or* 47: 12-36.
1982	'Psammetichus I', in W. Helck and W. Westendorf (eds.), *Lexikon der Ägyptologie*, IV (Wiesbaden: Otto Harrassowitz): 1164-69.

Spieckermann, H.
1982   *Juda unter Assur in der Sargonidenzeit* (FRLANT, 129; Göttingen: Vandenhoeck & Ruprecht).

Spycket, A.
1973   'Le culte de Dieu-Lune à Tell Keisan', *RB* 80: 384-95.

Stern, E.
1982   *The Material Culture of the Land of the Bible in the Persian Period 538–332 B.C.* (Warminster: Aris & Philips).

Stern, M.
1976   *Greek and Latin Authors on Jews and Judaism*. I. *From Herodotus to Plutarch* (Jerusalem: Israel Academy of Arts and Sciences).

Steuernagel, C.
1900   *Übersetzung and Erklärung der Bücher Deuteronomium and Josua und Allgemeine Einleitung in den Hexateuch* (HAT; Göttingen: Vandenhoeck & Ruprecht).

Strange, J.
1966   'The Inheritance of Dan', *Studia Theologica* 20: 120-39.

Suzuki, Y.
1982   'A Hebrew Ostracon from Meṣad Ḥashavyahu: A Form-Critical Reinvestigation', *Annual of the Japanese Biblical Institute* 8: 3-49.

Tadmor, H.
1966	'Philistia under Assyrian Rule', *BA* 29: 86-103.
1967	'The Conquest of Galilee by Tiglath Pileser III, King of Assyria', in H.Z. Hirschberg (ed.), *All the Land of Naphtali* (The Twenty-Fourth Archaeological Convention October 1966; Jerusalem: Israel Exploration Society): 62-67 (Hebrew).

Tadmor, H., and M. Cogan
1979   'Ahaz and Tiglath-Pileser in the Book of Kings: Historiographic Considerations', *Biblica* 60: 491-508.

Talmon, S.
1964	'The New Hebrew Letter from the Seventh Century B.C. in Historical Perspective', *BASOR* 176: 29-38.
1965	'The Town Lists of Simeon', *IEJ* 15: 235-41.

Ussishkin, D.
1974	'Tombs from the Israelite Period at Tel 'Eton', *TA* 1: 109-27.
1976	'Royal Judean Storage Jars and Private Seal Impressions', *BASOR* 223: 1-13.
1978	'Excavations at Tel Lachish—1973–1977', *TA* 5: 1-97.
1995	'The Rectangular Fortress at Kadesh-barnea', *IEJ* 45: 118-27.

Vaggione, R.P.
1973   'Over All Asia? The Extent of the Scythian Domination in Herodotus', *JBL* 92: 523-30.

Vaughn, A.G.
1999   *Theology, History, and Archaeology in the Chronicler's Account of Hezekiah* (Atlanta: Scholars Press).

Višaticki, K.
1987   *Die Reform des Josija and die religiöse Heterodoxie in Israel* (Dissertationen theologische Reihe, 21; St Ottilien: EOS Verlag).

Vos, J.C. de
  2002 'Das Los Judas. Über Entstehung und Ziele der Landbeschreibung in Josua 15' (PhD dissertation; Rijksuniversiteit, Groningen).
Vriezen, K.J.H.
  1975 'Ḥirbert Kefīre—eine Oberflächenuntersuchung', *ZDPV* 91: 135-58.
Waldbaum, J.C.
  1994 'Early Greek Contacts with the Southern Levant, ca. 1000–600 B.C.: The Eastern Perspective', *BASOR* 293: 53-66.
  1997 'Greek in the East or Greeks and the East? Problems in the Definition and Recognition of Presence', *BASOR* 305: 1-17.
Waldbaum, J.C., and J. Magness
  1997 'The Chronology of Early Greek Pottery: New Evidence from Seventh-Century B.C. Destruction Level in Israel', *AJA* 101: 23-40.
Weippert, M.
  1990 'Die Petition eines Erntearbeiters aus Meṣad Ḥašavyāhū und die Syntax althebräischer erzählender Prosa', in E. Blum, C. Macholz and E.W. Stegemann (eds.), *Die Hebräische Bibel und ihre zweifache Nachgeschichte. Festschrift für Rolf Rendtorff* (Neukirchen–Vluyn: Neukirchener Verlag): 449-66.
Welch, A.C.
  1925 'The Death of Josiah', *ZAW* 43: 255-60.
Wellhausen, J.
  1899 *Prolegomena zur Geschichte Israels* (Berlin: Georg Reimer, 5th edn).
Welten, P.
  1969 *Die Königs-Stempel. Ein Beitrag zur Militärpolitik Judas unter Hiskia und Josia* (Abhandlungen des Deutschen Palästinavereins; Wiesbaden: Otto Harrassowitz).
  1973 *Geschichte and Geschichtsdarstellung in den Chronikbüchern* (WMANT, 42; Neukirchen–Vluyn: Neukirchener Verlag).
Wilke, F.
  1913 'Das Skythenproblem im Jeremiabuch', in A. Alt *et al.* (eds.), *Alttestamentliche Studien Rudolf Kittel zum 60. Geburtstag dargebracht* (BWANT, 13; Leipzig: J.C. Hinrichs): 222-54.
Williamson, H.G.M.
  1977 *Israel in the Books of Chronicles* (Cambridge: Cambridge University Press).
  1979 'Sources and Redaction in the Chronicler's Genealogy of Judah', *JBL* 98: 351-69.
  1981 '"We Are Yours, O David": The Setting and Purpose of I Chronicles xii 1-23', *OTS* 21: 164-76.
  1982 *1 and 2 Chronicles* (NCBC; Grand Rapids: Eerdmans; London: Marshall, Morgan & Scott).
  1987a *Ezra and Nehemiah* (Old Testament Guides; Sheffield: JSOT Press).
  1987b 'Reliving the Death of Josiah: A Reply to C.T. Begg', *VT* 37: 9-15.
Wilson, J.A.
  1970 *Herodotus in Egypt* (Leiden: E.J. Brill).
Wiseman, D.J.
  1961 *Chronicles of Chaldean Kings (626–556 B.C.) in the British Museum* (London: British Museum).
Yadin, Y.
  1961 'The Fourfold Division of Judah', *BASOR* 163: 6-11.
Yeivin, S.
  1960 *Studies in the History of Israel and His Country* (Tel Aviv: M. Newman [Hebrew]).

	1962	'Lecah', in *Encyclopaedia Biblica*, IV (Jerusalem: Bialik Institute): 503-504 (Hebrew).
Yoyotte, J.		
	1960	'Néchao', in *Dictionnaire de la Bible*, Supplement, VI (Paris: Letouzey et Ane): 363-93.
Zawadzki, S.		
	1988	*The Fall of Assyria and Median–Babylonian Relations in Light of the Nabopolassar Chronicle* (Poznan: Adam Mickiewicz University Press).
Zimhoni, O.		
	1985	'The Iron Age Pottery of Tel 'Eton and Its Relation to the Lachish, Tell Beit Mirsim and Arad Assemblages', *TA* 12: 63-90.
	1990	'Two Ceramic Assemblages from Lachish Levels III and II', *TA* 17: 3-52.

THE BLACKBALLING OF MANASSEH

Francesca Stavrakopoulou

As is well known, King Manasseh of Judah is repeatedly and personally held responsible for the destruction of Judah and the exile of the people in the book of Kings (2 Kgs 21.11-15; 23.26-27; 24.3-4), despite having lived and died several generations before the catastrophe. In contrast to his portrayal in Kings, recent historical reconstructions of the period of Manasseh's reign have emphasized that Manasseh was probably one of Judah's most successful monarchs. It was under the direction of Manasseh that the kingdom not only recovered from the devastation wrought by Assyria in c. 701 BCE, but positively flourished: Judah was transformed from an economically decimated city-state into a prospering and enlarged kingdom (Halpern 1991; Finkelstein 1994; Ben Zvi 1996; Finkelstein and Silberman 2001). Yet curiously there remains a reluctance to abandon the conventional imaging of Manasseh as a villainous and wicked monarch.

Though it is widely recognized that the account of Manasseh's reign in 2 Kgs 21.1-18 is theologically heavily stylized, many remain convinced that it harbours, to a greater or lesser extent, reliable information about the historical Manasseh and the period of his reign. In general terms, this conviction is probably founded upon the persistent assumption of the basic historicity of the biblical texts. More specifically, the repeated insistence in the book of Kings that it is Manasseh, rather than a later king,[1] who is personally responsible for incurring the destruction of Judah, appears to suggest that the historical Manasseh earned himself a reputation as a particularly wicked or idolatrous monarch, and was therefore a most suitable villain for the book of Kings.[2] Further compounding the presumed historicity of the negative portrayal of Manasseh is the Chronicler's appraisal of his reign (2 Chron. 33.1-20), in which the idolatrous king is taken captive to Babylon where he repents of his wickedness, is restored to his throne and subsequently purges the temple cult. This material is usually held to be theologically

---

1. The capture and exile of Jehoahaz (2 Kgs 23.33-34), Jehoiachin (24.12-15), Zedekiah (24.20; 25.6-7) and Jehoiakim's rebellion against Babylon (24.1) would all offer the writer of Kings the theological scope to hold a later monarch responsible for the exile; indeed, placing the blame upon one of Josiah's successors, rather than Manasseh, would possibly ease some of the theological tensions between Josiah's reform and the irrevocable nature of the Babylonian conquest.

2. It should be noted that other reasons for the fall of Judah are briefly offered in Kings: in 2 Kgs 23.32 and 23.37 the Davidic monarchy as a whole appears to be blamed, whereas in 24.19-20 Jehoiakim and Zedekiah seem to be responsible. However, neither of these explanations receives the thorough-going attention ascribed to the 'Manasseh alone' theory.

crafted, rather than historically reliable, for the figure of Manasseh seems to function as a symbol of the punished, repentant, restored and newly blessed community for whom the Chronicler is writing (Mosis 1973: 192-94; Williamson 1982: 389-90; Schniedewind 1991: 451-55).[3] Therefore the negative tradition which the Chronicler shares with Kings tends to be imbued with a greater degree of historical credibility. Consequently, historical reconstructions of this period tend to accept uncritically the negative biblical portrayal of Manasseh (as noted by Ahlström 1982: 75; Evans 1992: 497). However, it is not necessary to accept this picture of Manasseh in order to account for his biblical vilification. Rather, a closer consideration of the ideological dynamics of Kings may offer a more cogent explanation.

Manasseh is vilified as a means of accounting theologically for the fall and exile of Judah. In this sense, he serves an important ideological purpose in Kings, for Manasseh functions as a scapegoat, distancing Judah from direct responsibility for the catastrophe (Lasine 1993).This is made explicit in the oracle of judgment against Jerusalem and Judah (2 Kgs 21.10-15) which accounts for the coming destruction with the words, 'Because King Manasseh of Judah has committed these abominations...' (v. 11; cf. 23.26-27; 24.3-4). Given that the Kings Writer[4] accuses other monarchs of religious malpractice, vilifying Manasseh necessarily entails presenting him as committing more cult crimes than any other king: he rebuilds the *bamoth* (v. 3), sets up altars to Baal (v. 3), worships the Host of Heaven (vv. 3, 5), makes an *asherah* (v. 3), sets an image of the *asherah* in the temple (v. 7), passes his son over in fire (v. 6) and personally participates in various divinatory practices (v. 6). Manasseh's culpability is compounded by the departure of Assyria from the story during Hezekiah's reign, thereby presenting his crimes as his own innovations, rather than as symbols of imperial vassalage (Sweeney 2001: 54; Barrick 2002: 6). Moreover, the assertions that Manasseh led the people to do evil (v. 9), caused Judah to sin with his idols (vv. 11, 16), and shed so much innocent blood that Jerusalem was filled from end to end (v. 16), emphasize his personal villainy, encouraging further the distancing of Judah from direct responsibility for the exile.[5]

This blackballing of Manasseh is constructed upon two ideological premises pervading Kings. The first is that cultic mispractice is the behaviour of the foreign nations, behaviour which is outlawed because it is alien to 'correct' YHWH-worship (e.g. 1 Kgs 11.1-13) and prompts divine punishment in the form of expulsion from the land (1 Kgs 14.24; 2 Kgs 16.3). This notion, which is strongly

---

3. For discussions favouring the basic historicity of the Chronicler's distinctive material concerning Manasseh, see Tatum 1991; Japhet 1993: 1003-1004; Cogan 1998: 253-54; Kelly 2002.

4. Given the variety of theories concerning the so-called Deuteronomistic History and its composition, the terms 'Deuteronomist(s)' and 'Deuteronomistic' have become so overloaded with interpretative definitions as to be rendered unhelpful to this discussion. Thus for the sake of clarity, the label 'Kings Writer' will be employed to refer to the author of Kings.

5. Lasine (1993: 182) makes the interesting suggestion that the vagueness of the accusation in 21.16 allows the 'innocent' readers of Kings to find among Manasseh's victims their own 'innocent' ancestors.

reminiscent of that in Deuteronomy (9.4-6; 12.29-31; 18.9-12), is not unexpectedly given a heavy emphasis in the extensive narrative describing and accounting for the fall and exile of the Northern Kingdom (2 Kgs 17): the Kings Writer insists that YHWH destroyed the Kingdom of Israel as a punishment for following the cult practices of the foreign nations: 'This occurred because the people of Israel sinned against YHWH their God...they worshipped other gods and walked in the customs of the nations whom YHWH drove out before the Sons of Israel' (vv. 7-8a; cf. 11, 15). It is thus by means of a series of comparisons with the foreign nations that Manasseh's fate as the destroyer of his kingdom is set out: in the preface to the catalogue of Manasseh's cult crimes the king's behaviour is likened to that of the foreign nations whom YHWH expelled from the land (v. 2). This comparison is intensified at the end of the cult crime list with the statement that Manasseh misled the people to do *more* evil than these nations (v. 9), an accusation which is itself worsened in the subsequent charge that Manasseh committed crimes more wicked than even the Amorites, a people cast out of the land before the Israelites (v. 11) and associated elsewhere with idolatry (1 Kgs 21.26; cf. Josh. 24.15, 18). Thus the Judahite exile is explained as the direct result of Manasseh's 'foreign' cult practices.

However, because other monarchs are depicted as tolerating or participating in foreign cult practices, the Kings Writer must emphasize that it is specifically the cultic mispractices of Manasseh which will lead to exile. As observed above, one of the ways in which this is achieved is by presenting Manasseh as the worst of all royal cultic offenders. For example, whereas previous monarchs had simply tolerated the *bamoth*, Manasseh encourages illegitimate worship by rebuilding the *bamoth* Hezekiah had destroyed (2 Kgs 21.3). Similarly, though Ahaz passed his son over in the fire—probably a biblical euphemism for a type of child sacrifice—Manasseh additionally participates in a variety of divinatory practices associated with this rite (2 Kgs 21.6; cf. 17.17; Deut. 18.10-11). Furthermore, Manasseh is accused of worshipping the Host of Heaven and setting up altars to them in the Temple complex (2 Kgs 21.3, 5; cf. 23.56), which in Kings is a unique royal crime, elsewhere levelled only at the inhabitants of the Northern Kingdom.[6] In these ways then, the extreme 'foreignness' of Manasseh's behaviour, a necessary element of his vilification, is repeatedly brought into focus.

The second ideological premise governing the blackballing of Manasseh is the extensive theological denigration of the Northern Kingdom throughout Kings. Though this denigration is evident in the theologically negative appraisal of nearly every Northern king (Cross 1973: 274-89; Brettler 1995: 112-34; Ash 1998; Sweeney 2001: 77-92),[7] it is in the account of the fall and exile of the Kingdom of Israel in 2 Kings 17 that it finds its most polemical expression. In this chapter, the Israelite kings and their subjects are not only predictably depicted as

---

6. Outside of Kings, worship of the Host of Heaven is associated with the Judahite kings in Jer. 8.1-2; 19.13; cf. Deut. 4.19; 17.3; Zeph. 1.5.

7. Only two Northern kings do not receive a formulaic theological appraisal: Elah, who is portrayed as a drunkard (1 Kgs 16.8-10) and Shallum, who is presented as a short-lived political usurper (2 Kgs 15.10, 13-15).

behaving like the foreign nations, but they are accused of despising YHWH's statutes, covenant and prophetic warnings and becoming false by following false idols (v. 15). In this chapter the Kings Writer justifies his trenchant anti-Northern stance by appealing to his story of the Northern people's rejection of the Davidic monarchy and the Jerusalem cult in favour of the kingship of Jeroboam ben Nebat and his illegitimate YHWH-cults at Bethel and Dan (1 Kgs 12–13). According to the Kings Writer, this initial religious crime, subsequently perpetuated by successive generations, had two significant results: it fixed the idolatrous character and tendency of the people and their kings, leading inevitably to their exile (2 Kgs 17.21-23; cf. v. 16), and it established the 'separateness' of Israel and Judah, as is made clear in 1 Kgs 12.19, 20b: 'So Israel has been in rebellion against the House of David to this day... There was no one who followed the House of David, except the tribe of Judah alone.' The notion of the 'separateness' of Israel and Judah heightens the anti-Northern tone of Kings further, and unsurprisingly occurs in the account of the exile of the North, employing language recalling that of 1 Kgs 12.20: 'YHWH was very angry with Israel and removed them out of his sight; none was left but the tribe of Judah alone' (2 Kgs 17.18). The emphasis upon the separateness of Israel and Judah distances Judah from Israel, and in combination with the pervading association of Israel with the religious practices of the nations, it implicitly characterizes the Northern Kingdom as 'foreign'. This polemic reaches its most remarkable expression in 2 Kgs 17.19-20, in which it is claimed that Israel has not only caused its own exile, but is even responsible for Judah's sins, and by implication, Judah's exile: 'Judah also did not keep the commandments of YHWH their God but walked in the customs that Israel had introduced. YHWH rejected all the descendants of Israel; he punished them and gave them into the hand of the plunderers, until he had banished them from his presence.' In this way, Judah is again distanced not only from Israel, but to a certain extent Judah is distanced from responsibility for its own fate.

In the light of these observations, it is thus unsurprising that Manasseh's cult crimes virtually mirror those of the Northern Kingdom (Dietrich 1972: 45; Schniedewind 1993: 657; Barrick 2002: 95). It is perhaps equally unsurprising that the disastrous fates of the kingdoms and their capital cities are paralleled so explicitly in the account of Manasseh's reign (21.11-15). But what is significant, however, is that Manasseh is explicitly compared with the arch-idolater of the Kingdom of Israel, Ahab, in v. 3 (cf. v. 13). Furthermore, elsewhere Ahab is compared with the Amorites (1 Kgs 21.26) just as Manasseh is (Steck 1968: 39-40; Schniedewind 1993: 654-55). On the basis of these verses, Manasseh is often described as 'Judah's Ahab' (Hobbs 1985: 311; Long 1991: 250; Smelik 1992: 132) and this comparison is thought to function on several levels (Smelik 1992: 132; Lasine 1993: 167-70; Schniedewind 1993; Sweeney 2001: 49-54). But it would appear that its primary purpose is to characterize further Manasseh as an idolater of unprecedented proportions, for his cult crimes are worse than those of Ahab: whereas Ahab erects an altar to Baal in a Baal temple and makes an *asherah* (1 Kgs 16.32-33), Manasseh goes further by setting up more than one altar to Baal, making an *asherah* and setting an image of the *asherah* in YHWH's temple (2 Kgs 21.3, 7-8; van Keulen 1996: 125). Similarly, and as noted above, though Ahab's religious crimes are simply likened to those of the Amorites (1 Kgs 21.26), Manasseh's cultic mispractices are claimed to be worse than those of the Amorites (2 Kgs 21.11); again, though Ahab worships idols (1 Kgs 21.26), Manasseh goes further in causing Judah to sin with his idols (2 Kgs 21.11).

The close analogy between Manasseh and the Northern Kingdom is heightened further by the implicit comparison of Manasseh with Jeroboam ben Nebat who, like Manasseh, is blamed for the eventual destruction of his kingdom (1 Kgs 14.16; 2 Kgs 17.21-23). In these texts Jeroboam is accused of causing the people to sin, a crime presented as the pervading inheritance of Jeroboam's successors by means of its formulaic application to all but three Northern kings.[8] It is thus significant that this accusation is also levelled at Manasseh (2 Kgs 21.9, 11), particularly in view of the fact that he is the only Southern king to be charged with this crime (Nelson 1987: 247-49; van Keulen 1996: 147-50). In his close alignment with the Northern Kingdom, and in particular with the worst of the Northern kings, Manasseh is therefore presented as a 'southern scoundrel dressed in northern colours' (Auld 1994: 85).

It would thus appear that the Kings Writer scapegoats Manasseh in order to distance Judah from direct responsibility for the exile. This is effected in two ways: first, his religious behaviour is portrayed as that of the foreign nations; second, Manasseh is explicitly and implicitly characterized as a Northern type of king. Yet the question remains: Why is it specifically Manasseh who carries the blame for the exile, rather than another king?

On a literary level, the majority of commentators correlate Manasseh's vilification with the heroic portrayal of Josiah, arguing that Manasseh's idolatry functions as a foil to his grandson's aggressive piety (Sweeney 2001: 62, 175; Lowery 1991: 185; Cogan and Tadmor 1988: 271). A possible merit of this suggestion is that the length of Manasseh's reign allows for the speculation that such a long period of idolatry was impossible to remedy within Josiah's shorter reign. However, given that this is not made explicit in Kings, and it would appear to contradict the notion that royal obedience to YHWH's statutes and commandments could prolong a monarch's life (1 Kgs 3.4), the suggestion that Manasseh acts as a foil to Josiah is unpersuasive.[9] Consequently, and as noted above, most scholars account for the vilification of Manasseh by accepting uncritically the negative presentation of Manasseh in Kings and attributing it with a considerable degree of historical reliability. As such, Manasseh is widely assumed to be an historical

---

8. The exceptions are Ahab, Shallum, and Hoshea. Shallum is portrayed as a political usurper who reigns for only a month before he is assassinated (2 Kgs 15.10-15), perhaps accounting for the absence of this standard critique. Ahab probably escapes this standard critique because his role as the ultimate Northern idolater renders this formulaic expression impotent (1 Kgs 16.31-33). Furthermore, he is held personally responsible for his own sin (21.20-22; 22.38). As the last reigning king of Israel, Hoshea is explicitly distanced from the evil of his predecessors in order to emphasize that it is the sin of Jeroboam I that caused the collapse of the kingdom (2 Kgs 17.2; cf. 7-8). For an analysis of this formula, see Mullen 1987.

9. Indeed, if any monarch were an appropriate foil to Josiah, Amon would be a more suitable candidate, particularly given that his reign is ended with his assassination (*pace* M. Smith 1975: 14).

villain—in spite of archaeological evidence for his clear success as a monarch—and thus a most natural scapegoat for the Kings Writer.

Yet having considered the ideological dynamics of Kings, it may be that a more persuasive explanation for Manasseh's vilification emerges. This explanation centres upon his name. The name Manasseh is popularly held to mean 'he who causes to forget' (de Geus 1992: 494; Wenham 1994: 397-98), as Gen. 41.51, Josephus (*Ant.* 2.6.1) and rabbinic literature (*b. Sanh.* 102b) would suggest. This has prompted some commentators to point to the theological significance of the name of the king who 'makes (the people) forget' the law of Moses (Johnstone 1997: II, 223) or the reforms of Hezekiah (Jarick 2002: 59). But in the light of the denigration of the Kingdom of Israel in the book of Kings, it is perhaps more than coincidental that the arch-villain of the story bears an unambiguously Northern name; indeed, Manasseh is the only biblical king to share his name with a Northern tribal-territory (cf. 1 Kgs 4.13). This factor may have singled Manasseh out as a 'quasi-northerner' in the eyes of the Kings Writer, thereby sealing his fate as a villain.[10] In his explicit portrayal of Manasseh as a typically rebellious, Northern type of king committing the same foreign cult crimes as the Northern Kingdom, the Kings Writer exploits Manasseh's Northern name in order to hold him personally responsible for the destruction of Judah, perhaps even complementing the assertion that Judah was disobedient and subsequently exiled because they followed the foreign customs which Israel introduced (17.19-20). In itemizing Manasseh's cult crimes and repeatedly blaming the king for the resulting exile, the Kings Writer thus poses a simple but powerful rhetorical question: What more could Judah have expected from a quasi-northern king? In this way, then, the Kings Writer is able to distance Judah from direct responsibility for the Babylonian catastrophe, claiming instead that '*because* King Manasseh of Judah has committed these abhorrent practices...' the kingdom will fall (21.11; 23.26-27; 24.3-4). Therefore rather than accepting the negative portrayal of Manasseh in Kings as an historical memory, it is entirely possible that Manasseh is both vilified and blamed for the fall and exile of his kingdom because he bears a Northern name.[11]

The blackballing of Manasseh in Kings casts a long shadow. This may be considered somewhat surprising given the Chronicler's portrayal of Manasseh as a paradigmatic repentant and cult reformer (2 Chron. 33.12-20). But the Chronicler's theological rehabilitation of Manasseh is necessarily and wholly dependent upon his initial portrayal of the king as an arch-idolater. Indeed, Manasseh's cult crimes are worsened in the Chronicler's account by means of their pluralization (Williamson 1982: 390).[12] Manasseh is also blamed for the Babylonian conquest

---

10. The Kings Writer may even intimate the connection of the name of the idolatrous king and the Northern tribe in the description of King Manasseh placing the image of the *asherah* in the place chosen by YHWH 'out of all the tribes of Israel' (21.7).

11. The potential historical significance and implications of Manasseh's name, which is confirmed by Assyrian sources, are discussed in Stavrakopoulou 2004: 102-106, 116-19.

12. For a detailed discussion of the Chronicler's portrayal of Manasseh, see Stavrakopoulou 2004: 46-59.

and exile of Judah in the book of Jeremiah, in which YHWH vows that he will make the people of Judah 'a horror to all the kingdoms of the earth because of what Manasseh son of Hezekiah, king of Judah did in Jerusalem' (15.4). As Carroll observed (1986: 321), the blaming of Manasseh in Jeremiah is unexpected, for it is usually the generation of the Babylonian invasion and destruction which is held responsible for the exile in this book. Though this brief and imprecise reference to Manasseh's culpability may suggest that further elaboration was unnecessary because his crimes were so well known, the vague generalization concerning 'what Manasseh did in Jerusalem' is probably a reflection of the close literary and ideological affinities between Jeremiah and Kings. Yet this fleeting reference curiously remains the only other mention of Manasseh outside Kings and Chronicles.

Given that he is the longest reigning of all Israelite and Judahite monarchs, it is curious that Manasseh is not mentioned, nor even alluded to, anywhere else in the Hebrew Bible.[13] He is not even referred to in the frequent chronological superscriptions included within prophetic books, prompting ancient Jewish and modern speculations (Rehm 1982: 210; Amaru 1983; Cogan 1998: 255; Soggin 1999: 269) that Manasseh persecuted and slaughtered his prophetic opponents, a speculation probably based upon 2 Kgs 21.16. Moreover, if Manasseh were as notorious as Kings, Chronicles and Jer. 15.4 insist, or even if he were taken captive as the Chronicler suggests, it would not be unreasonable to expect to find further comments about Manasseh and the events of his reign in the Hebrew Bible. This remarkable textual silence is suggestive of the exclusion, or even censorship, of Manasseh from the biblical texts (Nielson 1967: 103). When this consideration is set alongside the denigration of Manasseh in Kings, 2 Chron. 33.1-10 and Jer. 15.4, the possibility emerges that traces of 'anti-Manasseh polemic' exist within the Hebrew Bible. This possibility is further suggested by the portrayals of other biblical Manassehs.

Though there are very few biblical characters named Manasseh, a brief overview of those who do bear the name suggests that the name may harbour polemical undertones. The name Manasseh occurs twice in a list of returned exiles who are censured by Ezra for marrying foreign women (Ezra 10.30, 33; cf. 1 Esd. 9.31, 33). In view of the seemingly intentional association of Manasseh with 'foreignness' in Kings, it is perhaps unsurprising that this name should appear in this context. But given the fleeting nature of these references, little more of any significance can be discerned. However, the portrayal of the eponymous ancestor of the tribe of Manasseh offers itself as a more interesting example. As a reflection of the biblical presentation of Manasseh as the firstborn of Joseph and the elder brother of Ephraim (Gen. 41.50-52; 48.14, 18; Josh. 17.1), the name Manasseh tends to precede the name Ephraim (e.g. Gen. 46.20; 48.1; Num. 26.28-34; Josh. 14.4; 16.4). However, in several texts this order is frequently reversed (e.g. Gen. 48.5, 8-22; Num. 1.10, 32-35; 2.20; Deut. 34.2; Judg. 12.4).

---

13. *Pace* Oded (1977: 452), who suggests that Zeph. 1.4-6 and 3.1-4 allude to Manasseh's crimes, and Dietrich (1994: 463-90; 2001: 262) who holds that Nahum and Habakkuk make tangible to their readers prophetic resistance to Manasseh's policies.

Though the usurpation of the elder brother by the younger brother is a common biblical motif (Fox 1996), de Geus (1976: 79-80; 1992: 494) argues that the reversal of the names of Manasseh and Ephraim in Josh. 16–17 may attest to their secondary and deliberate emendation. This is probably to be related to the status-reversal of Manasseh and Ephraim in the story of their blessing by their grandfather Jacob in Gen. 48.8-20. This text describes how Ephraim came to receive the blessing of the firstborn which should have been Manasseh's by right of birth; as such it is often regarded as an aetiology reflecting the historical supremacy of Ephraim as the dominant northern territory (Alt 1913; Noth 1958: 58; de Geus 1992: 494), or, less frequently, the cultic superiority of Ephraimite Bethel over Manassite Shechem in the premonarchic period (Kingsbury 1967). But recent demographic and archaeological studies appear to confirm earlier proposals that the geographical area identified with the biblical territory of Manasseh developed more rapidly and remained more prosperous and powerful than that of Ephraim (Lemaire 1978, 1985; Finkelstein 1988; Zertal 1991, 1994, 2001; Thompson 1992: 221-39), thereby indicating that the territory identified as Manassite in biblical tradition was in historical terms probably the dominant territory in the north. Thus the biblical relegation of Manasseh in favour of Ephraim is not easily explained by the claim that Ephraim became the superior region. Rather, the subordination of the tribal-territory of Manasseh within the biblical texts is perhaps better considered an indication of an anti-Manasseh polemic in the Hebrew Bible.

Biblical commentators have long been aware of the polemical use of the name Manasseh in the Masoretic text of Judg. 18.30 (Moore 1958: 400-402; Tov 1992: 57). This occurs in the story of the corrupt Levite Jonathan, who leaves his Judahite home to serve as a priest in the idolatrous cult set up by Micah and taken over by the tribe of Dan (Judg. 17–18). A brief genealogical note in 18.30 appears originally to have traced Jonathan's ancestry back to Moses. However, a slightly raised נ has been employed to alter the name 'Moses' (משה) into the name 'Manasseh' (מנשה). The suggestion of this alteration is supported by the Septuagint and other Versions, which preserve the reading 'Moses', and the early provenance of the alteration is attested in its rabbinic discussion (*b. Bat.* 109b). It is widely assumed that the name of Moses has been deliberately distorted into that of Manasseh in order to disassociate Moses from the apostate priest Jonathan and the idolatrous cult he served. It is also widely assumed that the Manasseh who is grafted into the genealogy of Jonathan is intended to be understood as King Manasseh of Judah (in spite of its anachronistic implications) given his biblical fondness for idolatry. This is further suggested by the use of the term פסל to describe the idol in Judg. 18.30, a term which the Kings Writer employs uniquely of King Manasseh's cult image in 2 Kgs 21.7 and which also occurs in 2 Chron. 33.7.

However, in building upon a passing observation by Moore (1958: 400-402) Weitzman (1999) has associated this text with a post-biblical Manasseh who is significantly also vilified in terms of his correlation with the North. Weitzman constructs a plausible case in arguing that the Manasseh superimposed in Judg.

18.30 was not originally intended to be understood as King Manasseh, but a later Manasseh described by Josephus as a priestly Jewish defector and the first high priest of the Samaritan temple (*Ant.* 11.302-12). This Manasseh is said to be the brother of the high priest of Jerusalem and the husband of the daughter of the Samaritan governor Sanballat.[14] In the face of stern opposition to his marriage from the Jerusalemite elders, Manasseh flees to the North with his wife to become the first high priest of the new Samaritan temple. Weitzman (1999: 451-52) argues cogently that Josephus's Manasseh bears such a striking resemblance to the apostate Jonathan in Judges 17–18, that it is probably his name which is grafted into the genealogy of Judg. 18.30. Accordingly, the apostate Jewish priest of the Samaritan temple is discredited by means of his association with an apostate biblical priest.

In the light of the preceding discussion, it is certainly significant that another Manasseh is portrayed as participating within the supposedly deviant cult of the apostate North. Moreover, there is evidence to suggest that the name Manasseh has been deliberately applied to this figure. Josephus's story of Manasseh the Samaritan high priest is probably an expanded form of the fleeting tradition found in Neh. 13.28 (Grabbe 1987: 237-38; cf. Cross 1975, 1966) in which the biblical writer alludes to the marriage of a daughter of the Samaritan governor Sanballat to an unnamed member of the high priestly family in Jerusalem, who is expelled from the city because of his foreign marriage. It is likely that the anonymous son-in-law of Sanballat in the tradition reflected in this biblical text has acquired the name of the idolatrous king and territory called Manasseh as an indicator of his religious villainy (Grabbe 1987: 238). The interrelation of the ancient textual emendation apparent in Judg. 18.30 with the traditions exhibited in Josephus and Neh. 13.28 hinges upon the name Manasseh and its negative connotations; as such these texts attest to the polemical usage of the name, and are suggestive of the existence of an 'anti-Manasseh polemic' within certain biblical and post-biblical traditions.[15]

The apparent disparity between archaeological studies emphasizing Manasseh's successful kingship and his conventional imaging as an idolatrous villain derives from the assumed historicity of his negative portrayal in the book of Kings. However, this discussion has presented biblical material signalling that Manasseh's characterization in Kings is perhaps better understood as an ideological construct than an historical memory. His vilification in Kings is prompted by his name: in sharing a name associated with the Northern Kingdom, Manasseh is singled out as a religious deviant in the eyes of the Kings Writer. As a result, his

---

14. On the identification and correlation of this and other Samaritan figures named Sanballat throughout this period, see the discussions in Grabbe 1992: 112-14; Widengren 1977: 506-509 and Cross 1975, 1966.

15. It ought to be noted that not all post-biblical traditions concerning King Manasseh are wholly negative (e.g. Josephus's account of Manasseh's reign [*Ant.* 10.37-46] and the apocryphal *Prayer of Manasseh*); however, like the Chronicler's portrayal of Manasseh (2 Chron. 33.1-20), these texts necessarily depend upon the continued potency of the popular imaging of Manasseh as the ultimate sinner. See further Stavrakopoulou 2004: 121-39.

fate as a scapegoat is sealed, for in blaming Manasseh for the exile, Judah is effectively distanced from direct responsibility for its fate. However, the anti-Northern polemic facilitating his vilification in Kings seems to have encouraged an anti-Manasseh polemic in other biblical and post-biblical traditions.

One final observation remains: King Manasseh has continued to be vilified in modern times. Despite the re-evaluation and general rejection of perceived Assyrian religious influence in Judah (McKay 1973; Cogan 1974, 1993; *contra* Spieckermann 1982), and the emerging consensus that Judahite religion differed very little from that of the surrounding cultures (e.g. Edelman [ed.] 1995; M.S. Smith 2002), many commentators continue to blame Manasseh for the introduction or promotion of supposedly 'foreign' elements in the Judahite cult, such as Mesopotamian necromancy (Schmidt 1994: 292) and the worship of Ishtar as the Queen of Heaven (Houtman 1999: 678; cf. Weinfeld 1972: 149; Rose 1975: 213-68). Though Lowery (1991: 169-70) describes Manasseh's cultic policy as a return to Judah's traditional values (cf. Ahlström 1982: 75-81), he nevertheless asserts that Manasseh's royal religion was a syncretistic cult enhanced by Assyrian beliefs and practices. Milgrom (2000: 1386) adopts wholeheartedly the biblical portrayal of Manasseh as an arch-idolater:

> the difference in the state-endorsed religion of Judah between the eighth and the seventh century is largely summarized by a single word—rather, by a single person: Manasseh. By force majeure (2 Kgs 21.16), he reintroduced idolatry into Jerusalem and Judah, completely undoing the reform of his father, Hezekiah (2 Kgs 21.3), and, even succeeding the previous status quo, he installed idols in the Temple courtyards and in the sanctuary itself (2 Kgs 21.5, 7; 23.4-7).

Even those who recognize the severe distortions of the biblical portrayal of Manasseh credit the charges levelled against him with a degree of historicity, as the following quotation from van Keulen illustrates:

> in view of the extreme bias of the Manasseh account [in the book of Kings], the assessment of its value as a historical source must be negative. Yet, some notes in the account may have preserved historically reliable information, and it seems that the picture drawn of Manasseh as a king who introduced foreign cult in Judean religion is basically correct. (1994: 212)

All of these views are probably founded upon a persistent belief in the historical credibility of the biblical account of Manasseh's reign. Yet some commentators have accused Manasseh of cult crimes of which he is not even accused in the Hebrew Bible, such as the destruction of the ark of the covenant (Haran 1963; 1978: 276-88) and the conversion of temple buildings into workshops dedicated to Asherah (Bird 1997: 73).

It is particularly striking that Manasseh's personal and intentional villainy is frequently assumed by many commentators: Cogan and Tadmor (1988: 273) state that a motivating factor in Manasseh's religious policies was his personal rejection of Hezekiah's piety (cf. McKay 1973: 26-27; Cogan 1974: 113); similarly, Wiseman (1993: 290) claims that Manasseh's sin in reversing his father's policies was his own decision. Indeed, for some scholars, there is no excusing Manasseh at all: 'In the case of Solomon and Ahab, tolerance of polytheism was probably motivated by the same political conditions which led to their marriages with foreign princesses. In the case of Manasseh, the polytheism may have been the king's personal idiosyncracy' (Tigay 1986: 39).[16]

What is to be made of this tendency within modern scholarship to vilify Manasseh? On one level, there has been until recent years a general lack of scholarly interest in Manasseh and his reign, resulting in the persistence of biblically based, traditional portrayals of Manasseh in most modern histories of ancient Israel. This may reflect in part the oddly limited amount of biblical material relating to Manasseh, but can also be explained by the scholarly preoccupation with the heroes, rather than villains, of the biblical story, most notably David, Hezekiah and Josiah. On another level, it may be that the historicizing of the biblical portrayal of Manasseh provides scholars with their own villain to bear responsibility for features of Judahite history and religion that are difficult to explain or unpalatable for modern tastes. One example of this is the frequent accusation, based on 2 Kgs 21.16, that Manasseh persecuted and executed prophets of Yahweh, thereby accounting for the surprising lack of references to Manasseh and his reign in the prophetic literature (e.g. Rehm 1982: 210; Cogan 1998: 255). Another example is the common claim that Manasseh promoted child sacrifice so that it reached its zenith during his reign (e.g. Levine 1989: 260; Anderson and Freedman 2000: 532; Milgrom 2000: 1589), an accusation seeking to offer a partial rationale for an unpleasant practice that sits uneasily with modern sensibilities.

Locating these observations within the broader context of the historical reconstruction of ancient Israel and Judah, it would appear that there remains a tendency to accept relatively uncritically the biblical version of events, particularly that describing the monarchic period.[17] The Hebrew Bible offers itself as a window into the past, yet the possibility that the glass is distorted is often overlooked. The notion that the biblical writers could misrepresent their culture's past, whether intentionally or unintentionally, can be frustrating for a modern historian. So for some the uncertainties of historical reconstruction can be circumvented to a certain extent by the assumption of the basic historical reliability of the biblical texts. Yet the biblical portrayal of the past is often coloured by the ideological concerns of the biblical writers, and as such must be handled with cautious and critical rigour by modern historians.

This discussion is tentatively offered as an illustration of this preferable approach. The biblical portrayal of Manasseh as a villain has for a long time been widely adopted within modern scholarship, although it may be that this king's vilification was originally prompted by nothing more than his name. Despite

---

16. This comment also raises the interesting issue of the biblical blaming of foreign women for supposedly illegitimate religious practices, a notion that is often historicized within modern scholarship. In the case of Manasseh, McKay (1973: 24-25, 95) has argued unconvincingly that the 'Garden of Uzza' (2 Kgs 21.18, 26) was a cult place dedicated to an Arabian god and built for Manasseh's wife Meshullemeth.

17. This is perhaps due in part to the verification of several monarchs' names and the general periods of their reigns in Assyrian and Babylonian texts, and the persistent supposition that the book of Kings is to a certain extent based upon royal annals of some sort.

recent historical reconstructions suggesting that Manasseh was one of Judah's most successful kings, his vilification within scholarship has persisted, possibly because he has proved a most convenient scapegoat for modern commentators who share the biblical predilection for blaming Manasseh for introducing or promoting a variety of supposedly illegitimate or unpleasant practices. Yet in blaming the Manasseh of history for these 'crimes', modern scholarship has all too frequently perpetuated the blackballing of Manasseh.

BIBLIOGRAPHY

Ahlström, G.W.
    1982   *Royal Administration and National Religion in Ancient Palestine* (SHANE, 1; Leiden: E.J. Brill).

Alt, A.
    1913   'Israels Gaue unter Salomo', *Beiträge zur Wissenschaft vom Alten Testament* 13: 1-39.

Amaru, B.H.
    1983   'The Killing of the Prophets: Unravelling a Midrash', *HUCA* 54: 153-80.

Anderson, F.I., and D.N. Freedman
    2000   *Micah: A New Translation with Introduction and Commentary* (AB, 24E; New York: Doubleday).

Ash, P.S.
    1998   'Jeroboam I and the Deuteronomistic Historian's Ideology of the Founder', *CBQ* 60: 16-24.

Auld, A.G.
    1994   *Kings without Privilege: David and Moses in the Story of the Bible's Kings* (Edinburgh: T. & T. Clark).

Barrick, W.B.
    2002   *The King and the Cemeteries: Toward a New Understanding of Josiah's Reform* (VTSup, 88; Leiden: E.J. Brill).

Ben Zvi, E.
    1996   'Prelude to a Reconstruction of the *Historical* Manassic Judah', *BN* 81: 31-44.
    1991   'The Account of the Reign of Manasseh in II Reg 21, 1-18 and the Redactional History of the Book of Kings', *ZAW* 103: 355-74.

Bird, P.A.
    1997   'The End of the Male Cult Prostitute: A Literary-Historical and Sociological Analysis of Hebrew *Qādēš–Qĕdēšîm*', in J.A. Emerton (ed.), *Congress Volume, Cambridge 1995* (VTSup, 66; Leiden: E.J. Brill): 37-80.

Brettler, M.Z
    1995   *The Creation of History in Ancient Israel* (London: Routledge).

Carroll, R.P.
    1986   *Jeremiah: A Commentary* (London: SCM Press).

Cogan, M.
    1974   *Imperialism and Religion* (SBLMS, 19; Missoula, MT: SBL and Scholars Press).
    1993   'Judah under Assyrian Hegemony: A Reexamination of *Imperialism and Religion*', *JBL* 112: 403-14.
    1998   'Into Exile: From the Assyrian Conquest of Israel to the Fall of Babylon', in M.D. Coogan (ed.), *The Oxford History of the Biblical World* (Oxford: Oxford University Press): 242-75.

Cogan, M., and H. Tadmor
    1988   *II Kings: A New Translation with Introduction and Commentary* (AB,11; New York: Doubleday).
Cross, F.M.
    1966   'Aspects of Samaritan and Jewish History in Late Persian and Hellenistic Times', *HTR* 59: 201-11.
    1973   *Canaanite Myth and Hebrew Epic: Essays in the History of the Religion of Israel* (Cambridge, MA: Harvard University Press).
    1975   'A Reconstruction of the Judean Restoration', *JBL* 94: 4-18.
Day, J.
    2000   'The Religion of Israel', in A.D.H. Mayes (ed.), *Text in Context* (Oxford: Oxford University Press): 428-53.
Dietrich, W.
    1972   *Prophetie und Geschichte: Eine redaktionsgeschichtliche Untersuchung zum deuteronomistischen Geschichtswerk* (FRLANT, 108; Göttingen: Vandenhoeck & Ruprecht).
    2001   '1 and 2 Kings', in J. Barton and J. Muddiman (eds.), *The Oxford Bible Commentary* (Oxford: Oxford University Press): 232-66.
Edelman, D.V. (ed.)
    1995   *The Triumph of Elohim: From Yahwisms to Judaisms* (CBET, 13; Kampen: Kok Pharos).
Evans, C.D.
    1992   'Manasseh, King of Judah', in *ABD*, IV: 496-99.
Finkelstein, I.
    1988   *The Archaeology of the Israelite Settlement* (Jerusalem: Israel Exploration Society).
    1994   'The Archaeology of the Days of Manasseh', in M.D. Coogan, J.C. Exum and L.E. Stager (eds.), *Scripture and Other Artifacts: Essays on the Bible and Archaeology in Honor of Philip J. King* (Louisville, KY: Westminster/John Knox Press): 169-87.
Finkelstein, I., and N.A. Silberman
    2001   *The Bible Unearthed: Archaeology's New Vision of Ancient Israel and the Origin of Its Sacred Texts* (New York: Free Press).
Fox, E.
    1996   'Stalking the Younger Brother: Some Models for Understanding a Biblical Motif', *JSOT* 60: 45-68.
Geus, C.H.J. de
    1976   *The Tribes of Israel* (Amsterdam: Assen).
    1992   'Manasseh (Place)', in *ABD*, IV: 494-96.
Grabbe, L.L.
    1987   'Josephus and the Reconstruction of the Judean Restoration', *JBL* 106: 231-46.
    1992   *Judaism from Cyrus to Hadrian* (London: SCM Press).
Halpern, B.
    1991   'Jerusalem and the Lineages in the Seventh Century BCE: Kingship and the Rise of Individual Moral Liability', in B. Halpern and D.B. Hobson (eds.), *Law and Ideology in Monarchic Israel* (JSOTSup, 124; Sheffield: JSOT Press): 11-107.
Haran, M.
    1963   'The Disappearance of the Ark', *IEJ* 13: 46-58.
    1978   *Temples and Temple-Service in Ancient Israel* (Oxford: Clarendon Press).

Hayes, J.H., and J.M. Miller (eds.)
    1977   *Israelite and Judaean History* (London: SCM Press).

Hobbs, T.R.
    1985   *2 Kings* (WBC, 13; Waco, TX: Word Books).

Houtman, C.
    1999   'Queen of Heaven', in K. van der Toorn, B. Becking and P.W. van der Horst (eds.), *Dictionary of Deities and Demons* (Leiden: E.J. Brill, 2nd rev. edn): 678-80.

Japhet, S.
    1993   *I & II Chronicles: A Commentary* (London: SCM Press).

Jarick, J.
    2002   *1 Chronicles* (Readings: A New Biblical Commentary; Sheffield: Sheffield Academic Press).

Johnstone, W.
    1997   *1 and 2 Chronicles* (JSOTSup, 253, 254; 2 vols.; Sheffield: Sheffield Academic Press).

Kelly, B.E.
    2002   'Manasseh in the Books of Kings and Chronicles (2 Kings 21.1-18; 2 Chron 33.1-20)', in V.P. Long, D.W. Baker and G.J. Wenham (eds.), *Windows into Old Testament History: Evidence, Argument, and the Crisis of 'Biblical Israel'* (Grand Rapids: Eerdmans): 131-46.

Keulen, P.S.F. van
    1996   *Manasseh Through the Eyes of the Deuteronomists: The Manasseh Account (2 Kings 21.1-18) and the Final Chapters of the Deuteronomistic History* (OTS, 38; Leiden: E.J. Brill).

Kingsbury, E.C.
    1967   'He Set Ephraim before Manasseh', *HUCA* 38: 129-36.

Lasine, S.
    1993   'Manasseh as Villain and Scapegoat', in J.C. Exum and D.J.A. Clines (eds.), *The New Literary Criticism and the Hebrew Bible* (JSOTSup, 143; Sheffield: JSOT Press): 163-83.

Lemaire, A.
    1978   'Les Bene Jacob', *RB* 85: 321-37.
    1985   'La haute Mesopotamie et l'origene de Bene Jacob', *VT* 34: 95-101.

Levine, B.A.
    1989   *Leviticus* (JPSTC, 3; New York: Jewish Publication Society).

Long, B.O.
    1991   *2 Kings* (FOTL, 10; Grand Rapids: Eerdmans).

Lowery, R.H.
    1991   *The Reforming Kings: Cults and Society in First Temple Judah* (JSOTSup, 120; Sheffield: JSOT Press).

McKay, J.W.
    1973   *Religion in Judah under the Assyrians, 732–609 BC* (SBT, 26; London: SCM Press).

Milgrom, J.
    2000   *Leviticus 17–22: A New Translation with Introduction and Commentary* (AB, 3A; New York: Doubleday).

Moore, G.F.
    1958   *Critical and Exegetical Commentary on Judges* (Edinburgh: T. & T. Clark, 2nd edn [first edn 1876]).

Mosis, R.
    1973   *Untersuchungen zur Theologie des chronistischen Geschichtwerkes* (Freiburg: Herder).
Mullen, T.E.
    1987   'The Sins of Jeroboam: A Redactional Assessment', *CBQ* 49: 212-32.
Nelson, R.D.
    1987   *First and Second Kings* (Atlanta: John Knox Press).
Nielsen, E.
    1967   'Political Conditions and Cultural Developments in Israel and Judah during the Reign of Manasseh', in *The Fourth World Congress of Jewish Studies, Papers, I* (Jerusalem: Magnes Press): 103-106.
Noth, M.
    1958   *The History of Israel* (trans. S. Godman; London: A. & C. Black).
Oded, B.
    1977   'Judah and the Exile', in Hayes and Miller (eds.) 1977: 435-88.
Rainey, A.F.
    1993   'Manasseh, King of Judah, in the Whirlpool of the Seventh Century BCE', in A.F. Rainey (ed.), *'Kinattutu ša dārâti': Raphael Kutscher Memorial Volume* (Tel Aviv Occasional Publications, 1; Tel Aviv: Tel Aviv University Press): 147-64.
Rehm, M.
    1982   *Das zweite Buch der Könige. Ein Kommentar* (Würzburg: Echter Verlag).
Rose, M.
    1975   *Der Ausschiesslichkeitsanspruch Jahwes: Deuteronomische Schultheologie und die Volksfrömmigkeit in der späten Königszeit* (BWANT, 106; Berlin: W. de Gruyter).
Schmidt, B.B.
    1994   *Israel's Beneficent Dead: Ancestor Cult and Necromancy in Ancient Israelite Religion and Tradition* (FAT, 11; Tübingen: J.C.B. Mohr).
Schniedewind, W.M.
    1991   'The Source Citations of Manasseh: King Manasseh in History and Homily', *VT* 41: 450-61.
    1993   'History and Interpretation: The Religion of Ahab and Manasseh in the Book of Kings', *CBQ* 55: 649-61.
Smelik, K.A.D.
    1992   'The Portrayal of King Manasseh: A Literary Analysis of II Kings xxi and II Chronicles xxxiii', in *idem, Converting the Past: Studies in Ancient Israelite and Moabite Historiography* (OTS, 28; Leiden: E.J. Brill): 129-89.
Smith, M.
    1975   'The Veracity of Ezekiel, the Sins of Manasseh, and Jeremiah 44.18', *ZAW* 87: 11-16.
Smith, M.S.
    2002   *The Early History of God: Yahweh and the Other Deities in Ancient Israel* (Grand Rapids: Eerdmans, 2nd edn).
Soggin, J.A.
    1999   *An Introduction to the History of Israel and Judah* (trans. J. Bowden; London: SCM Press, 3rd edn).
Spieckermann, H.
    1982   *Juda unter Assur in der Sargonidenzeit* (FRLANT, 129; Göttingen: Vandenhoeck & Ruprecht).

Stavrakopoulou, F.
    2004   *King Manasseh and Child Sacrifice: Biblical Distortions of Historical Realities* (BZAW, 338; Berlin and New York: W. de Gruyter).
Steck, O.
    1968   *Überlieferung und Zeitgeschichte in den Elia-Erzählungen* (WMANT, 26; Neukirchen–Vluyn: Neukirchener Verlag).
Sweeney, M.A.
    2001   *King Josiah of Judah: The Lost Messiah of Israel* (Oxford: Oxford University Press).
Tatum, L.
    1991   'King Manasseh and the Royal Fortress at Ḥorvat 'Uza', *BA* 54: 136-45.
Thompson, T.L.
    1992   *Early History of the Israelite People from the Written and Archaeological Sources* (SHANE, 4; Leiden: E.J. Brill).
Tigay, J.H.
    1986   *You Shall Have No Other Gods: Israelite Religion in the Light of Hebrew Inscriptions* (HSS, 31; Atlanta: Scholars Press).
Tov, E.
    1992   *Textual Criticism of the Hebrew Bible* (Philadelphia: Fortress Press).
Weinfeld, M.
    1972   'The Worship of Molech and the Queen of Heaven and Its Background', *UF* 4: 133-54.
Weitzman, S.
    1999   'Reopening the Case of the Suspiciously Suspended *Nun* in Judges 18.30', *CBQ* 61: 448-60.
Wenham, G.J.
    1994   *Genesis 16–50* (WBC, 2; Dallas: Word Books).
Widengren, G.
    1977   'The Persian Period', in Hayes and Miller (eds.) 1977: 489-538.
Williamson, H.G.M.
    1982   *1 and 2 Chronicles* (London: Marshall, Morgan & Scott).
Wiseman, D.J.
    1993   *1 and 2 Kings* (Tyndale Old Testament Commentaries; Leicester: Inter-Varsity Press).
Zertal, A.
    1994   '"To the Land of the Perizzites and the Giants": On the Israelite Settlement in the Hill-Country of Manasseh', in N. Na'aman and I. Finkelstein (eds.), *From Nomadism to Monarchy* (Washington: Biblical Archaeology Society): 37-70.
    2001   'The Heart of the Monarchy: Pattern of Settlement and Historical Considerations of the Israelite Kingdom of Samaria', in A. Mazar (ed.), *Studies in the Archaeology of the Iron Age in Israel and Jordan* (JSOTSup, 331; Sheffield: Sheffield Academic Press): 38-64.

KING MANASSEH OF JUDAH AND THE PROBLEM OF THEODICY
IN THE DEUTERONOMISTIC HISTORY*

Marvin A. Sweeney

I

The field of biblical studies is currently witnessing a crucial debate concerning the interpretation of the historical narratives of the Hebrew Bible. Since the nineteenth century, modern biblical interpreters have been fundamentally concerned with the question of history in their efforts to arrive at a viable understanding of the Hebrew Bible. Although the interpretation of all types of literature in the Hebrew Bible has been influenced by the modern preoccupation with history, the reading of the so-called 'historical books' has been especially affected by such concerns insofar as scholars have attempted to read the biblical books with an eye to recovering the actual historical events that are purportedly reported in these books. In their efforts to establish history as the ultimate criterion of theological truth, modern scholars tend to dismiss overtly theological writings, such as the books of Chronicles and Ezra–Nehemiah, and to focus instead on those works that provide the seemingly soundest basis for historical reconstruction, that is, the books of the so-called Deuteronomistic History (DtrH): Joshua, Judges, Samuel, and Kings.

But with the recognition over the past fifty years that the DtrH (and the Chronicler's work) itself has a theological agenda (or agendas), contemporary scholars have come to recognize that the DtrH likewise does not provide a fully objective base for the reconstruction of historical events.[1] One might observe, for example, that the account of the conquest of the land in Joshua displays a marked theological agenda in which Israel conquers the entire land of Canaan in return for its pledge to observe YHWH's commands, but the archeological record points to a very different process of sedentarization by semi-nomads entering the land from the east and intermittent conflict between the hill country and coastal plain.[2] Most recently, a group of revisionist scholars has made such observations the foundation for their proposal that it is all but impossible to reconstruct history on

---

* An earlier version of this paper was presented as the author's Presidential Address at the Society of Biblical Literature Pacific Coast Regional Meeting, St Mary's College of California, Moraga, CA, 25 March 2002.
 1. See Noth 1967. For a recent overview of discussion since Noth, see Römer and de Pury 1996.
 2. For a convenient overview of literary and archeological study of the book of Joshua, see Boling 1992. For more recent treatments of the book and the period it purports to represent, see Mazar 1990: 295-367; Fritz 1994; Rowlett 1996.

the basis of the biblical narratives (Lemche 1998; Thomson 1999; Davies 1992). They maintain that the Bible's historical narratives are the fictionalized inventions of the post-exilic Persian or Hellenistic Jewish communities that sought to justify their own existence by projecting their own community structures, religious practices, and theological perspectives back into prior history. Of course, their proposals are not entirely devoid of contemporary political agendas insofar as they project a pre-Jewish 'Palestinian' society as the basis for understanding the true nature of pre-exilic Israel. Despite the politicized nature of the debate, the claims of these 'revisionist' historians have reopened an old—and necessary—methodological debate concerning the interrelationship between history and literature. It is therefore incumbent upon us to re-examine the question to arrive at a full understanding of the issues at hand.

In order to undertake such re-examination, I would like to focus on the figure of King Manasseh of Judah in the DtrH. Although much attention has been paid to better-known figures, such as David, Solomon, or Josiah, in this debate, Manasseh is a particularly attractive object for such methodological reflection because of the combination of theological and historical concerns that the accounts of his reign present. On the one hand, the DtrH blames him alone for the destruction of Jerusalem and the Temple, because of his great sins, which prompted YHWH to renege on an earlier promise to David that his sons would sit upon the throne in Jerusalem forever.[3] It is striking that the Chronicler presents a very different account of his reign, that is, Manasseh repented from his sins after he was dragged in fetters to Babylon to stand before the Assyrian king. Although the Chronicler's account is likewise clearly designed to serve a theological agenda—indeed, the Chronicler blames Josiah for his own death and for Jerusalem's suffering—Manasseh's forced appearance before the Assyrian king in Babylon provides a potentially secure historical basis for explaining his idolatrous and murderous reign, that is, he was forced to appear in Babylon at the time that Assurbanipal put down a bloody revolt led by his own brother, Shamash Shum-ukin. When viewed in relation to the Babylonian revolt against Assyria, Manasseh's idolatry and bloody suppression of opposition emerge as parts of his effort to impress his Assyrian overlords that he was indeed a loyal vassal king.

In order to address the problem of the interrelationship between history and theology in the presentation of Manasseh's reign, specifically the theological issue of theodicy in the DtrH, I would like to proceed in three stages: (1) to re-examine the DtrH narrative concerning Manasseh in 2 Kgs 21.1-18 in an effort to point to the problems that it poses, specifically, its contention that the actions of one man, Manasseh, are responsible for the destruction of Jerusalem and the Temple; (2) to re-examine the Chronicler's account of Manasseh's reign in 2 Chron. 33.1-20 in an effort to establish both its theological agenda and its worth for historical reconstruction; and (3) to return to the DtrH narrative concerning Manasseh in an effort to assess the interrelationship between theology and history in the account of his reign. Specifically, I wish to ask why the DtrH

---

3. See Sweeney (2001: 52-63) for a recent overview of issues pertaining to the presentation of Manasseh in 2 Kgs 21 and a redaction-critical analysis of the chapter.

portrays YHWH's reneging on the eternal promise to the house of David insofar as YHWH's decision to destroy Jerusalem and Judah—easily the single most important event in ancient Judah's existence since Israel's foundation—is based upon the sins of one man, Manasseh. These considerations will point to the need to take account of both theological agendas and historical events in the interpretation of biblical literature, insofar as the two are closely interrelated, that is, historical events provide the basis for the development of theological perspective and theology provides the basis by which readers—whether ancient or modern—understand and reflect upon historical events.

II

The DtrH account of Manasseh's reign in 2 Kgs 21.1-18 presents Manasseh unequivocally as the worst monarch in the entire Davidic line. The litany of Manasseh's sins begins with the charge that he acted abominably like the nations that YHWH drove out from the land prior to Israel's settlement within it, and it continues with specific examples of such actions, including the building of high places, altars to Baal, and an asherah like that of Ahab; worship of the Host of Heaven and the building of altars dedicated to the worship of the Host of Heaven in the Temple itself; passing his son through fire and the practice of divination and soothsaying; and the placing of an asherah image in the Temple. Later charges in the narrative include the shedding of innocent blood throughout the entire extent of the city of Jerusalem and the general charge that Manasseh caused Judah to sin. The charges levelled against Manasseh are remarkable in that they place him in direct comparison to King Ahab of Israel, who, apart from Jeroboam ben Nebat, the purported founder of golden calf worship at the sanctuaries of Dan and Beth El, stands as the most sinful monarch of northern Israel according to the DtrH. The DtrH narrative takes care to compare Manasseh's building of an asherah to that built by Ahab, and YHWH's announcement of judgment against Jerusalem and Judah explicitly states that YHWH will apply the measuring line of Samaria and the measuring weight of the house of Ahab as the criteria by which judgment is determined. Overall, YHWH states the intention to wipe Jerusalem as one wipes and overturns a plate and to uproot the remnant of the people, that is, the remnant of Israel left in Jerusalem and Judah, so that they might be handed over to their enemies.

This narrative is remarkable for two basic reasons: (1) it applies the standards of judgment employed by the DtrH to justify the destruction of the northern kingdom of Israel to the impending destruction of Jerusalem and the southern kingdom of Judah, and (2) it holds one man, Manasseh, ultimately responsible for the destruction of the entire nation. Both of these features require sustained reflection.

By applying the standards of judgment employed against the Northern Kingdom of Israel to Jerusalem and Judah, the DtrH clearly attempts to justify the impending Babylonian destruction of Jerusalem and Judah as an act of divine righteousness that was prompted by the sins of the people in their failure to keep their covenant with YHWH. The recognition of such an agenda stands at the basis of all critical work on the DtrH from the time of Noth's initial work on the literary character and theological outlook of the DtrH. Because of tensions in the narrative, specifically a tendency to criticize the Northern Kingdom of Israel and to emphasize YHWH's promise to David of an eternal dynasty in Jerusalem, scholarly treatment tends to promote a redaction-critical understanding of this issue. An early edition of the DtrH was written in the late-seventh century BCE to point to the reign of the Davidic King Josiah of Judah as the culmination of Israel's history. In the view of the proposed seventh-century edition of the DtrH, Josiah's program of religious reform and national restoration would see the reunification of the twelve tribes of Israel following a lengthy period in which the northern tribes had revolted from the house of David and rejected YHWH at the instigation of its first king, Jeroboam ben Nebat, to engage in idolatrous worship at the sanctuaries at Dan and Beth El. As a result of such apostasy, the northern tribes had suffered punishment from YHWH when the Assyrian empire invaded and destroyed the Northern Kingdom.[4] Scholars persistently maintain that the Josian DtrH was intended to portray Josiah's reunification of the twelve tribes of Israel as the culmination of YHWH's promise to guarantee the security of the house of David forever. In the aftermath of the Babylonian destruction of Jerusalem and Judah, however, the Josian DtrH was updated to account for the later tragedy. Whereas the Josian DtrH had focussed on the sins of Jeroboam and the people of the Northern Kingdom of Israel, the exilic DtrH emphasized Manasseh's sins as the cause for YHWH's decision to punish Jerusalem and the people of Judah.

As long as the issue is viewed from such a diachronic, redaction-critical perspective, it is easily accepted, that is, the exilic edition of the DtrH merely updated the earlier Josian edition by adding accounts concerning the guilt and destruction of Jerusalem and Judah to the overall scenario of northern Israelite guilt and punishment. But when the issue is viewed from a synchronic literary perspective, a troublesome theological problem begins to emerge, namely, the DtrH narrative does not prepare the reader by signalling Jerusalem's guilt or by suggesting that Jerusalem might be subject to the same punishment as Israel. It does point to the wrongdoing of various Judean kings, most notably their tolerance for high places and other idolatrous religious installations and practices in both Jerusalem and Judah, but the narrative suggests only in the account of Solomon's reign the possibility that such actions might one day result in such severe divine punishment (1 Kgs 9.1-9). Indeed, the narrative stresses YHWH's fidelity to the relationship with Jerusalem and the house of David insofar as the account of Hezekiah's reign portrays YHWH's deliverance of Jerusalem and the healing of the king despite past wrongdoing when Hezekiah turns to YHWH in prayer in the face of enemy invasion and debilitating, terminal illness (2 Kgs 18–20).

This of course points to the second major issue in the DtrH presentation of the punishment of Jerusalem and Judah, that is, one man, King Manasseh of Judah, is ultimately held to be responsible for YHWH's decision to bring about the punishment. Perhaps this should not be surprising given the role that Jeroboam ben Nebat plays in the DtrH as the quintessential sinful monarch who sets the

---

4. Among others, see Sweeney 2001: 33-177; van Keulen 1996; Nelson 1981; Cross 1973.

pattern of sin for the entire Northern Kingdom throughout its history (see esp. Cross 1973). Indeed, every northern monarch is said to have followed in the sins of Jeroboam. Nevertheless, the narrative takes care to inform the reader that it is not the sins of one man or even a few that results in the destruction of the Northern Kingdom; it is the actions of the entire nation throughout the entire course of its history that results in the divine decision to destroy northern Israel (2 Kgs 17).

The focus on King Manasseh is all the more remarkable when viewed in relation to the divine promises to the house of David articulated throughout the DtrH. Although the references to the Davidic promise in Kings are qualified in the account of Solomon's reign with statements that YHWH will ensure the rule of the house of David provided that his sons observe YHWH's commandments, etc. (see 1 Kgs 2.4; 8.24-26; 9.4-5; cf. 8.13), the initial statement of the Davidic promise in 2 Samuel 7 is absolute:

> When your days are filled and you sleep with your fathers, I will establish your seed after you which goes forth from your loins, and I will establish his kingdom. He will build a house for my name, and I will establish the throne of his kingdom forever. I will be a father to him, and he will be a son to me. When he sins, I will smite him with the rod of men and the blows of human beings, but I will not remove my fidelity from him as I removed it from Saul, whom I removed before you. And your house and your kingdom shall be secure forever before you. Your throne shall be established forever. (2 Sam. 7.12-16)

Clearly, the foundational statement of the Davidic promise in 2 Samuel 7 does not envision the potential end of the Davidic line or even the removal of the Davidic king from Jerusalem, but the statements concerning the Davidic promise in the books of Kings and the account of YHWH's decision to destroy Jerusalem because of the sins of Manasseh envision precisely such a possibility. When viewed from a synchronic perspective, the absolute promise of 2 Samuel 7 becomes qualified by the perspectives stated in Kings. The Davidic promise is not an absolute promise at all, but a qualified promise in which the kings—or at least Manasseh—fail to abide by their responsibilities in their relationship with YHWH.

The tension in the narrative is quite clear, and it demands explanation. Does the narrative represent a struggle to reconcile theological perspective and historical experience? Indeed, does it represent a failed struggle to reconcile competing truth claims of divine promise to Jerusalem and the house of David and the reality of Babylonian destruction and exile? In order to begin to address this issue further, it is first necessary to examine the other account of Manasseh's reign in 2 Chron. 33.1-20.

III

The Chronicler's account of Manasseh's reign in 2 Chron. 33.1-20 is particularly noteworthy in that it differs so markedly from the Deuteronomistic account in its assessment of the king.[5] The Chronicler's narrative begins much like that of the

---

5. For treatment of the Chronicler's account of Manasseh, see especially Japhet 1993: 999-1014.

DtrH with an account of Manasseh's sins that differs from its counterpart in 2 Kings 21 only in textual details. The Chronicler begins once again with the charge that Manasseh committed abominations like the nations that were driven out by YHWH and that Manasseh rebuilt the high places that Hezekiah had torn down, as well as the altars to Baal and Asherah; he resumed worship of the Host of Heaven and built altars for them in the Temple courtyards; he passed his son through the fire in the Ben-Hinnom Valley; he supported divination and soothsaying; and he erected idols in the House of the Deity. The Chronicler later charges Manasseh with leading Jerusalem and Judah astray to do evil. Unlike the DtrH account, however, the Chronicler does not charge him with shedding innocent blood.

The point at which the Chronicler differs so markedly from the DtrH appears in vv. 10-17, which relate YHWH's sending the army officers of the Assyrian king to drag Manasseh, bound in fetters, to Babylon, presumably to appear before the Assyrian king. The Chronicler tells us nothing about the purpose of this action, but it does relate that this experience prompted Manasseh to repent, to pray to YHWH, and to recognize YHWH as the Deity, as well as his actions to reverse his many sins following his return to the city of Jerusalem. The ensuing account refers to Manasseh's building the outer wall of the City of David; his appointment of military officers throughout the fortified cities of Judah; his removal of foreign gods, their images, and their altars from Jerusalem; and his establishment of an altar to YHWH, his own sacrifices to YHWH at the altar, and his instructions to his people to serve YHWH. The segment concludes with the notice that people continued to sacrifice at the high places, but the Chronicler's narrative makes it clear that Manasseh did not instigate such practice.

Sincethe early work of Wellhausen, scholars have tended to dismiss the Chronicler's account of Manasseh's captivity and repentance as an attempt to reconcile Manasseh's lengthy reign with the Chronicler's own theological agenda (Wellhausen 1973: 206-207; Japhet 1993: 1001-1004). Having reigned for fifty-five years, Manasseh is easily the longest reigning monarch of the Davidic line, and yet the DtrH account of his reign identifies him as the most wicked monarch among them all. Given the Chronicler's understanding that wickedness must be punished and goodness rewarded, interpreters concluded that the Chronicler must have been faced with an irreconcilable set of facts in the DtrH narrative, and chose to change the narrative so that Manasseh's repentance would justify his lengthy reign. Little credence was given to the possibility that the Chronicler might have preserved a historical account.

Several presuppositions clearly underlie such a view. First, the Chronicler does not function fully as an author, but is instead a sort of redactor or editor who reworks the earlier account in Kings to suit the Chronicler's own theological agenda. Second, the account in Kings is by and large historically trustworthy whereas the account in Chronicles is not. Third, there could be no historical reason for Manasseh to be taken to Babylon to appear before the Assyrian king.

The reader might assume that Manasseh's actions following his repentance, particularly his fortification of Jerusalem and his appointment of military commanders throughout the fortified cities of Judah, would indicate an attempt by the monarch to assert his independence from foreign—specifically Assyrian—control. And yet it is striking that, when one considers ancient Near Eastern historical sources outside of the Bible, it becomes apparent that Manasseh's reign sees the high point of Assyria's imperial power and expansion throughout western Asia and northeastern Africa. Contrary to the biblical accounts of Sennacherib's invasion of Judah during the reign of Manasseh's father Hezekiah, Jerusalem and Judah were not miraculously delivered by YHWH's destruction of the Assyrian army. Not only did Sennacherib devastate the entire land of Judah, he seems to have forced Hezekiah to come to terms, although those terms seem to have allowed Hezekiah to remain on the throne in Jerusalem.[6] Although Sennacherib was apparently assassinated in 681 BCE, his successor, Esarhaddon was apparently able to conquer Egypt by 671 BCE. Esarhaddon's successor, Assurbanipal, was able to continue Assyria's dominance in the region, although he appears to have done so by means of a relationship with the emerging Twenty-Sixth or Saite Dynasty in which the Saite monarchs were given a relatively free hand to exercise control over Egypt.[7] Assyria was able to control the Syro-Israelite region for some time—as indicated by Assyria's extensive investment in olive oil production in the region—albeit in conjunction with their Saite Egyptian allies.[8] Assurbanipal was challenged in 652–648 BCE by a Babylonian revolt against his rule led by his own brother, Shamash Shum-ukin, but Assurbanipal brutally suppressed the revolt and killed his brother (Kuhrt 1998: II, 587-89). It was only after Assurbanipal's death at some point during the period 631–627 BCE that Assyria began to weaken in anticipation of its later collapse (Kuhrt 1998: II, 540-46), but this is well beyond the conclusion of Manasseh's reign in 642 BCE.

Archeological evidence in the land of Israel must also be considered insofar as it points to a period of relative peace and Assyrian control of the region. Assyria's extensive investment in olive oil production was noted above. Excavations at Tel Miqne, ancient Ekron, indicate that the city became a major center for the production of olive oil; the large number of olive presses in the city during the seventh century BCE indicates sufficient capacity to supply the needs of the entire Assyrian empire. Furthermore, the nineteen four-horned altars found at the site indicate that a substantial number of the people brought to work there were Israelite, presumably from the former Northern Kingdom of Israel and the Judean Shephelah, where Sennacherib had concentrated his attack (Gitin 1993). Indeed,

---

6. For treatments of the biblical texts and extra-biblical historical sources concerning Sennacherib's invasion, see Sweeney 1996: 454-88; Gallagher 1999.

7. Although many earlier interpreters held that Psamtek's reunification of Egypt entailed the expulsion of the Assyrian garrison, interpreters increasingly follow the lead of Spalinger, who argues that Necho I and his son Psamtek had concluded a treaty with Assurbanipal that insured them of Assyrian support as they secured their control over Egypt and reunified the country. See Spalinger 1974: 316-28 (323); 1976: 133-47 (140-42). See especially the discussions by A.K. Grayson on the reign of Assurbanipal and T.G.H. James on the rise of the Twenty-Sixth (Saite) Dynasty in Boardman *et al.* 1991: 142-61, 677-747. For other recent discussion of the rise of the Saite dynasty in Egypt and its relations with the Assyrian empires, see Kuhrt 1998: II, 499-501, 634-44; Redford 1992: 430-35.

8. For discussion of Assyria's role in olive oil production in the region, see Gitin 1989, 1993, *contra* Stager 1996.

settlement patterns in Judah suggest a shift away from the Shephelah, where the Assyrians would have consolidated their presence, and into the Judean hill country and Negev desert, especially in the vicinity of Beer Sheba (Finkelstein 1994). The seventh century BCE sees the building or fortification of a number of Negev sites, such as Tel Masos, Tel Mahata, Horvat 'Uza, Horvat Radom, Tel 'Ira, 'Aro'er, etc., apparently in an effort to protect the Negev trade routes and the southern borders of Judah. There are lingering questions concerning the interpretation of this building activity, however; namely: Was it carried out to serve Assyrian interests to control the region and to provide a secure basis for Assyrian expansion into Egypt or does it represent the assertion of Judean power and potential independence from Assyria?

Indeed, the Chronicler's account of Manasseh's being dragged in fetters to Babylon provides some basis for resolving the question. As noted above, Assurbanipal was in Babylon in 648 BCE to put down the revolt against his power led by his brother Shamash Shum-ukin. Although Assyrian records say nothing of the matter, it would make a great deal of sense for Assurbanipal to summon Manasseh to Babylon at this time to ascertain and guarantee his loyalty to the Assyrian empire.[9] Manasseh was after all the son of Hezekiah, who had revolted against Sennacherib some fifty years earlier. Key to Hezekiah's strategy of revolt was his alliance with the Babylonian prince, Merodach-baladan. An account of the diplomatic encounter between Hezekiah and Merodach's emissaries appears in Isaiah 39 and 2 Kgs 20.12-19, in which the prophet Isaiah condemns the alliance. The strategy seems to have called for a two-pronged revolt against Assyria from both the east and the west in which Merodach-baladan and Hezekiah would coordinate their efforts to split Assyrian power and to overcome the Assyrians from both ends of the empire (see esp. Brinkman 1964). The strategy failed however, when Sennacherib was able to move with sufficient speed to subdue Hezekiah in the west so that he could rush back to the east and subdue Merodach after having worked out his terms for Hezekiah. In such a situation, it makes a great deal of sense that Assurbanipal would suspect Manasseh of collusion with Shamash Shum-ukin. Of course, we may never know if the Babylonians had enlisted Judean support at this time, but later experience suggests that such an arrangement can not be dismissed lightly. Manasseh's grandson, Josiah, later died in 609 BCE in an effort to support the Babylonians in their war against Assyria by preventing the Egyptian army from moving north to Haran to support the Assyrians. Even after Josiah's death, pro-Babylonian elements in Jerusalem and Judah, including the family of Shaphan, Josiah's secretary, and the prophet Jeremiah, continued to call for alliance with Babylon as the means to ensure Judah's security (Wilcoxen 1977; Sweeney 2001: 208-33 [208-15]).

---

9. Cf. Williamson 1982: 288-95, who cites earlier literature. Williamson also raises the possibility that Manasseh was summoned in 672 BCE in order to safeguard the succession to the Assyrian throne from Esarhaddon to Assurbanipal. See the remarks by Bustenay Oded in Hayes and Miller (1977: 455-56) who notes that Manasseh's lenient treatment parallels that of several other rulers, such as the king of Tyre, Necho I, and Psamtek I.

Although not entirely conclusive, the historicity of the account of Manasseh's having been dragged in fetters to Babylon to appear before the Assyrian king enables us to make sense of the historical data. Assyria did continue to control Judah and the entire Syro-Israelite region, and Judah's expansion into the Negev would serve both Assyria's and Judah's interests insofar as Judah would assert control over Negev trade routes, both for its own economic and military welfare as well as for the welfare of its Assyrian overlords. Perhaps Manasseh's demonstration of loyalty to Assurbanipal won him an even greater measure of freedom to pursue Judah's own interests in the Negev, even under the suzerainty of Assyria. Such a model would not be unlike that of the Assyrian relationship with the Saite Egyptian dynasty, in which the Saites exercised great freedom in their control of Egypt—even while Egypt remained an Assyrian vassal/ally.[10] With such an understanding, Manasseh's actions as presented in 2 Chron. 33.1-20 become quite understandable, namely, Manasseh functioned as a loyal vassal to Assyria throughout his reign, and he may well have won greater freedom of action in the aftermath of the failed Babylonian revolt. The theological stamp of the Chronicler of course remains, namely, Manasseh repented to YHWH, and this enabled him to rebuild Judah and perhaps to eliminate some overt signs of his relationship to the Assyrians.

We might also note that Manasseh's repentance paves the way for the Chronicler's contention that Josiah is at least in part responsible for his own death and the subsequent fate of his nation. When Josiah marches his army to Megiddo to stop Pharaoh Necho from supporting the Assyrians, Necho tells him, 'What (conflict) is between us, O King of Judah? Not against you do I come today, but against the house of my enemy. And the Deity has commanded to hasten me. Stop! This is from the Deity, who is with me, so that he will not destroy you.' Of course, Josiah does not stop, and he is killed in the ensuing battle, which begins the process by which Jerusalem will ultimately meet its destruction in Chronicles. We might add that Cyrus emerges as YHWH's designated monarch at the end of the book (2 Chron. 36.22-23); the house of David appears no more.

We must now return to the implications of these observations for reading the DtrH account of Manasseh's reign.

IV

Our examination of the Chronicler's account of Manasseh's reign in 2 Chron. 33.1-20 indicates that there is a plausible historical basis for the main features of its contents, including his idolatrous actions, his transfer to Babylon, and his building and military activities. At the same time, it demonstrates the Chronicler's theological viewpoint insofar as it portrays Manasseh's repentance and return to the Deity as the basis for its later claim that Josiah bears responsibility for his own death and the later downfall of Jerusalem, Judah, and the house of David.

---

10. See n. 7 above; Kuhrt 1998: II, 499-501, 634-44; Redford 1992: 430-35.

Historically speaking, our examination of the Chronicler's account also provides some basis for understanding the historicity of the DtrH narrative, insofar as Manasseh's idolatrous and criminal actions appear to be those of a vassal monarch who attempts to quash opposition within his own kingdom and to demonstrate loyalty to a very threatening suzerain. Of course, it also points to a very clear theological stamp, insofar as Manasseh is charged with responsibility for the destruction of Jerusalem and its people. Indeed, Manasseh's shedding of blood throughout the entire city renders it impure from a Levitical perspective, and requires that the city be cleansed and purged of its impurity. Nevertheless, the question of the Deity's culpability in reneging on the promise to the house of David and in holding the entire nation responsible for the actions of one man remains.

Past interpretation has tended to overlook the issue of divine culpability in the destruction of Jerusalem in the DtrH. This is due in part to the same reasons noted above by which interpreters were able to accept the contention that Manasseh is responsible: (1) Manasseh's sins are read in relation to the sins of northern Israel and Judah, so that the theological justification for the destruction of Jerusalem is accepted by the reader; (2) the DtrH is the product of at least two writers, a Josian writer who promoted Josiah as the greatest of Israel's monarchs and an exilic writer who updated the history following Jerusalem's destruction (Sweeney 2001: 170-77). In such a scenario, the assignment of blame to Manasseh was necessary in light of Josiah's (and Hezekiah's) righteousness as well as in relation to historical reality. But both of these explanations side-step the issue. The first does not explain why a work that focuses on the collective identity of the people as the basis for its judgments of guilt and innocence can shift to blaming an individual for the suffering of an entire nation. The second ignores the synchronic plane by which the present form of the DtrH narrative is read.

Although some contend that the literary tension in the narrative indicates that there is no coherent DtrH (e.g. Rösel 1999), there have been attempts to address the tension posed by a synchronic reading of the narrative. Von Rad offers an explanation that does attempt to account for the synchronic literary form of the narrative, namely, Jehoiachin's release from prison at the end of the narrative is a sign of hope that the house of David will be restored to the throne in keeping with YHWH's promise (von Rad 1984; cf. 1962–65: I, 334-47). But one must note that Jehoiachin's release to eat at the table of the Babylonian king Evil-merodach mirrors David's treatment of Saul's only surviving heir, Mephibosheth. David's care of Mephibosheth hardly signalled the potential restoration of the Saulide line, especially since Mephibosheth publicly gave up his claims to his father's and grandfather's inheritance (2 Sam. 19.24-30). Indeed, once Solomon ascends the throne, the house of Saul never again poses a challenge to the house of David, and it never regains the throne. One might conclude much the same for the house of David; Jehoiachin's eating at the table of the Babylonian king marked the end of the Davidic monarchy, especially since YHWH had declared that Manasseh's actions warranted such drastic punishment.

Wolff (1975) holds out another possibility for a synchronic reading of the narrative, namely, the DtrH calls for repentance on the part of its readers, which in turn entails the possibility for the restoration of the people. Although such an agenda may well be ascribed to the DtrH, Wolff's proposal is rather one-sided in that it takes no account of the potential for divine culpability.

And yet the issue of divine culpability must be taken seriously. Whereas past approaches have overlooked or denied the possibility that the Deity reneged on the promise to the house of David and to Jerusalem, it seems that the issue stands at the center of the DtrH presentation of Israel's and Judah's history. Did YHWH renege on a promise? Based upon a synchronic reading of the DtrH narrative, it appears that this is precisely what YHWH did. Such a contention does not deny the responsibility assigned to the people throughout the DtrH narrative, but it highlights the role of YHWH in a manner that requires serious consideration of its role within the overall DtrH narrative.

As readers, we must remember that the present form of the DtrH addresses the question of the destruction of Jerusalem, Judah and Israel, and the exile of the people. Such destruction constitutes the absolute denial of the foundations of Israel's or more properly Judah's existence, that is, YHWH guaranteed the security of Jerusalem and the house of David. But of course, the Babylonian exile called these fundamental premises into question. How does a reader understand and respond to the DtrH presentation? One might conclude that the people had sinned, and therefore deserved the Babylonian exile as a righteous punishment brought about by the Deity. Certainly, the DtrH provides ample assertions of Israelite and Judean sin within a framework of divine reward for righteousness and punishment for wrongdoing, but this does not provide the full explanation for Jerusalem's downfall. One might conclude that the Babylonian gods had won, and that YHWH was no longer the omnipotent the Deity of Israel/Judah. Indeed, the Elijah narratives pose such a charge against Baal, when the prophets of Baal are unable to prompt Baal to consume the sacrifice on the altar. But the contention that YHWH may have lost against the Babylonian gods does not explain the need to write a history that emphasizes YHWH's continuing role in history beyond the destruction of Jerusalem and the Temple. Finally, contrary to the assertions of divine fidelity throughout the Bible, one might conclude that the Deity had simply reneged on the promise to secure Jerusalem and the house of David. Certainly, there was no lack of cases in the ancient Near Eastern world, particularly Mesopotamia, in which a god turned against or abandoned its own people. One might recall Tiamat's attempt to destroy her own children, the Annunaki's decision in the Atra-hasis flood story to inaugurate death, illness, and stillbirth as means to limit human population growth, or even their role in bringing about the flood itself.[11] Biblical examples likewise abound, for example, the expulsion of

---

11. Note that in both the Enuma Elish account of creation and the Atra-Hasis account of the flood, the gods turn against humankind. In the case of the Enuma Elish, the chief god Anu proposes to kill all of the lesser gods because their noise leaves him unable to sleep. Following his assassination, his wife, Tiamat, gathers an army of sea monsters to attack the gods. Following her defeat, human beings are created from the blood of her commander, Kingu, to serve the gods by building temples, canals,

Adam and Eve from the garden when it is not clear that Eve committed a sin (Gen. 3); the Deity's commission of Isaiah to ensure that the people do not see or hear lest they repent and avoid divine punishment (Isa. 6; see Sweeney 2000a); the Deity's affliction of Job and his children (see Fackenheim 1990); and the Deity's absence in the book of Esther at a time grave national danger (see Sweeney 2000b).

Perhaps it is time to recognize that the failure to resolve the issue of divine culpability in the DtrH is deliberate, because that is a primary issue with which the reader must grapple. History is written for reflection. On the one hand, it might be designed to provide answers, that is, Jerusalem was destroyed because of the sins of Manasseh, and Israel was destroyed because of the sins of its people. On the other, it might be designed to raise questions for reflection, namely: Did YHWH fail to maintain the promise to the house of David—and thus to the people of Israel/Judah/Jerusalem at large? Exilic and post-exilic Judah would have been faced with such questions in its attempts to come to grips with the disaster that the nation suffered and the prospects of attempts at restoration in the very new reality of Persian rule. For its own part, the DtrH provides the basis for consideration of both the past and the future. If true, such a contention places Wolff's (1975) understanding of the DtrH agenda as a call for repentance into a very different light. On the one hand, the people faced a need to learn from the mistakes of the past, insofar as the DtrH indicates a willingness by its writers and readers to assume responsibility for the past disaster and to build for a future in which such mistakes would not be repeated. But on the other hand, it points to the reality that YHWH may well have failed, insofar as a Babylonian and later a Persian monarch sat on the throne in the place of the now-defunct Davidic dynasty. Although tremendous efforts to identify YHWH with Cyrus appear in biblical literature that appears in the time following the Babylonian exile and the appearance of the DtrH, for example, the full form of the book of Isaiah; Chronicles; and Ezra–Nehemiah, the DtrH points to the possibility that YHWH failed. It thereby points to a potentially uncertain future, and it functions as an early example of the literature of theodicy, much like Job, Habakkuk, Esther, and even the Song of Songs. But as an early example of the literature of theodicy, it provides the basis for theological reflection at a time when the wounds of destruction and exile were very, very raw. Much like the present generation of Jewish thinkers which is actively engaged in coming grips with the theological problems posed by the Shoah or Holocaust—including the possibilities that the Deity is dead, impotent, or morally culpable,[12] so the DtrH represents an early attempt to come to grips with theological problems posed by the Babylonian exile.

---

etc. A similar situation occurs in the Atra-Hasis when the Annunaki class of gods propose to kill humankind by flood when their noise becomes too great. Humans are saved when Ea/Enki tells Atra-Hasis to build a sea vessel to escape the flood. In the aftermath of the flood, the gods impose death, disease, and stillbirth on human beings to keep their numbers down. For an edition of the Enuma Elish, see *ANET*: 60-72. For the Atra-Hasis, see Lambert and Millard 1969.

12. For a recent overview and analysis of this discussion, see Braiterman 1998.

V

By way of conclusion, I would like to stress the role that both historical and theological considerations must come into play in the reading of the historical literature of the Hebrew Bible. Indeed, the example of Manasseh, who singlehandedly led his entire nation to destruction in the eyes of the DtrH and who likely saved them from retaliation in the eyes of the Chronicler at the time of the Babylonian revolt, demonstrates the necessity for such a two-pronged approach. Both narratives appear to have their basis in history, and both certainly display the theological perspective by which the historical events of his reign are read. It seems, therefore, that we cannot go back to the days in which we uncritically and naively read biblical literature as a witness to history precisely as it is presented in the narrative, but neither can we naively and uncritically dismiss it as historical literature simply because it presents history according to its own theological and historiographical viewpoint.

BIBLIOGRAPHY

Boardman, John, *et al.*
    1991   *Cambridge Ancient History*, III/2 (Cambridge: Cambridge University Press).
Boling, Robert G.
    1992   'Joshua, Book of', in *ABD*, III: 1002-15.
Braiterman, Zachary
    1998   *(G-d) After Auschwitz: Tradition and Change in Post-Holocaust Jewish Thought* (Princeton, NJ: Princeton University Press).
Brinkman, J.A.
    1964   'Merodach-Baladan II', in *Studies Presented to A. Leo Oppenheim, June 7, 1964* (Chicago: Oriental Institute): 6-53.
Cross, Frank M., Jr
    1973   'The Themes of the Books of Kings and the Structure of the Deuteronomistic History', in idem, *Canaanite Myth and Hebrew Epic* (Cambridge, MA: Harvard University Press): 274-89.
Davies, Philip R.
    1992   *In Search of 'Ancient Israel'* (JSOTSup, 148; Sheffield: JSOT Press).
Fackenheim, Emil
    1990   *The Jewish Bible after the Holocaust: A Rereading* (Bloomington and Indianapolis: Indiana University Press).
Finkelstein, Israel
    1994   'The Archaeology of the Days of Manasseh', in M.D. Coogan, J.C. Exum and L.E. Stager (eds.), *Scripture and Other Artifacts: Essays on Bible and Archaeology in Honor of Philip J. King* (Louisville, KY: Westminster/John Knox Press): 169-87.
Fritz, Volkmar
    1994   *Das Buch Josua* (HAT, 1/7; Tübingen: J.C.B. Mohr [Paul Siebeck]).
Gallagher, William R.
    1999   *Sennacherib's Campaign to Judah: New Studies* (SHCANE, 18; Leiden: E.J. Brill).

Gitin, Seymour
    1989   'Tel Miqne-Ekron: A Type Site for the Inner Coastal Plain in the Iron Age II Period', in S. Gitin and W.G. Dever (eds.), *Recent Excavations in Israel: Studies in Iron Age Archaeology* (AASOR, 49; Winona Lake, IN: Eisenbrauns): 23-58.
    1993   'Seventh Century B.C.E. Cultic Elements at Ekron', in *Proceedings of the Second International Congress on Biblical Archaeology, June 1990* (Jerusalem: Israel Exploration Society): 248-58.

Hayes, John H., and J. Maxwell Miller (eds.)
    1977   *Israelite and Judaean History* (OTL; Philadelphia: Westminster Press).

Japhet, Sara
    1993   *I & II Chronicles: A Commentary* (OTL; Louisville, KY: Westminster/John Knox Press).

Keulen, Percy S.F. van
    1996   *Manasseh Through the Eyes of the Deuteronomists: The Manasseh Account (2 Kings 21.1-18) and the Final Chapters of the Deuteronomistic History* (OTS, 38; Leiden: E.J. Brill).

Kuhrt, Amélie
    1998   *The Ancient Near East c. 3000–330 BC* (2 vols.; London and New York: Routledge).

Lambert, W.G., and A.R. Millard
    1969   *Atra-Hasis: The Babylonian Story of the Flood* (Oxford: Clarendon Press).

Lemche, Niels Peter
    1998   *The Israelites in History and Tradition* (Louisville: Westminster/John Knox Press).

Mazar, Amihai
    1990   *Archaeology of the Land of the Bible (10,000–586 B.C.E.)* (New York: Doubleday).

Nelson, Richard D.
    1981   *The Double Redaction of the Deuteronomistic History* (JSOTSup, 18; Sheffield: JSOT Press).

Noth, Martin
    1967   *Überlieferungsgeschichtliche Studien. Die Sammelnden und Bearbeitenden Geschichtswerke im Alten Testament* (Darmstadt: Wissenschaftliche Buchgesellschaft, 3rd edn): 1-110.

Rad, Gerhard von
    1962–65   *Old Testament Theology* (trans. D.M.G. Stalker; New York: Harper & Row).
    1984   'The Deuteronomic Theology of History in I and II Kings', in *idem*, *The Problem of the Hexateuch and Other Essays* (trans. E.W. Trueman Dicken; London: SCM Press): 205-22.

Redford, Donald B.
    1992   *Egypt, Canaan, and Israel in Ancient Times* (Princeton, NJ: Princeton University Press).

Römer, Thomas, and Albert de Pury
    1996   'L'historiographie deutéronomiste (HD). Histoire de la recherche et enjeux du débat', in A. de Pury, T. Römer and J.-D. Macchi (eds.), *Israël construit son histoire. L'historiographie deutéronomiste à la lumière des recherches récentes* (Geneva: Labor et Fides): 9-120.

Rösel, Hartmut
    1999   *Von Josua bis Jojachin. Untersuchungen zu den deuteronomistischen Geschichtsbüchern des Alten Testaments* (VTSup, 75; Leiden: E.J. Brill).

Rowlett, Lori L.
    1996   *Joshua and the Rhetoric of Violence: A New Historicist Analysis* (JSOTSup, 226; Sheffield: Sheffield Academic Press).

Spalinger, Anthony
    1974   'Assurbanipal and Egypt: A Source Study', *JAOS* 94: 316-28.
    1976   'Psammetichus, King of Egypt I', *JARCE* 13: 133-47.

Stager, Lawrence
    1996   'Ashkelon and the Archaeology of Destruction: Kislev 604 B.C.E.', *ErIs* 25: 61*-74*.

Sweeney, Marvin A.
    1996   *Isaiah 1–39, with an Introduction to Prophetic Literature* (FOTL, 16; Grand Rapids and Cambridge: W.B. Eerdmans).
    2000a   'Isaiah and Theodicy after the Shoah', in T. Linafelt (ed.), *Strange Fire: Reading the Bible after the Holocaust* (Biblical Seminar, 7; Sheffield: Sheffield Academic Press): 208-19.
    2000b   'Absence of G-d and Human Responsibility in the Book of Esther', in W. Kim et al. (eds.), *Reading the Hebrew Bible for a New Millennium: Form, Concept, and Theological Perspective*. II. *Exegetical and Theological Studies* (Studies in Antiquity and Christianity; Harrisburg, PA: Trinity Press International): 264-75.
    2001   *King Josiah of Judah: The Lost Messiah of Israel* (Oxford and New York: Oxford University Press).

Thompson, Thomas L.
    1999   *The Mythic Past: Biblical Archaeology and the Myth of Israel* (New York: Basic Books).

Wellhausen, Julius
    1973   *Prolegomena to the History of Israel* (Gloucester, MA: Peter Smith).

Wilcoxen, Jay
    1977   'The Political Background of Jeremiah's Temple Sermon', in A.L. Merrill and T.W. Overholt (eds.), *Scripture in History and Theology* (Festschrift J.C. Rylaarsdam; Pittsburgh: Pickwick): 151-66.

Williamson, H.G.M.
    1982   *1 and 2 Chronicles* (New Century Bible; London: Marshall, Morgan, & Scott; Grand Rapids: Eerdmans).

Wolff, Hans Walter
    1975   'The Kerygma of the Deuteronomistic Historical Work', in W. Brueggemann and H.W. Wolff (eds.), *The Vitality of the Old Testament Traditions* (Atlanta: John Knox Press): 83-100.

WAS THERE A CULT REFORM UNDER KING JOSIAH?
THE CASE FOR A WELL-GROUNDED MINIMUM*

Christoph Uehlinger

Preliminary Remarks

The original version of the following article, which was published in German in 1995, originated as an invited response to a paper presented by Herbert Niehr at a conference on Jeremiah and Deuteronomism held in Frankfurt on the Main by Catholic biblical scholars (Gross [ed.] 1995).[1] Although the present version has been partly rewritten in order to stand as an autonomous study, it still follows the outlines of the original paper. As a rule, responses cannot address a topic in its full complexity, but concentrate instead on a limited number of issues. In the present instance, these include basic considerations on historical concepts and methodology, discussions of selected archaeological material whose interpretation may or may not elucidate our understanding of Josiah's reform, and an historical evaluation of selected aspects of the so-called 'reform notices' (*Reformnotizen*) preserved in 2 Kings 23. In spite of its peculiar character as a literary tradition preserved for religious purpose, the biblical text remains the most relevant source when we deal with 'Josiah's cult reform'—as long as no other, extrabiblical document closer to the time of Josiah refers to anything resembling measures of cultic realignment. 'Josiah's reform', regardless of whether exposed by 'maximalists' or 'minimalists', is essentially a scholarly construct built upon the biblical tradition; without that tradition no one would look out for a 'cult reform' when studying the archaeology of Judah of the Iron Age II C.

Ideally, therefore, the quest for the historical reality that may have given rise to the literary traditions about 'Josiah's reform'[2] should start with an independent examination of the biblical text and its own redactional history, as far as it can be reconstructed by historical-critical argument. Our first task would thus be to ascertain the text which is at the basis of our literary tradition.[3] Neither this nor the ensuing literary- and redaction-critical analysis can be accomplished

---

* Bruce Wallace (Emory University) is to be credited for the draft translation of the original German paper into English, and Lester Grabbe (University of Hull) for his unfailing editorial support.
 1. Cf. Niehr 1995; Uehlinger 1995.
 2. Note that I do not address the Chronicler's version of the story, which appears in 2 Chron. 34–35, nor later works of Jewish historiography.
 3. See now Schenker 2004: 34-84 for detailed comparisons of the Hebrew and Greek textual traditions.

here.⁴ As for the other side of the argument, selected evidence collected from the archaeological, epigraphical, and iconographical record, my presentation will summarize much that has been laid out in greater detail in a book co-authored in 1992 with O. Keel.⁵

What sense does it make to repeat an argument more than ten years after its inception? New material has surfaced since, and long-known material appears in another light as a result of renewed analysis.⁶ A mass of secondary literature on Josiah's reform published since 1994 has added to the multiplicity of views and the complexity of issues.⁷ While I have tried to take stock occasionally of new evidence and arguments, doing so systematically would have required me to write a completely different article. The fact that the original paper continues over the years to be referred to regularly in the secondary literature, however, may justify its updated translation here.

* * *

The question of the extent, meaning, purpose and main actors of King Josiah's cultic reform is discussed in Old Testament scholarship as a problem not only of biblical exegesis but also of Israelite and Judahite religious history. Almost 200 years ago, W.M.L. de Wette identified the 'Torah Scroll' (ספר־התורה, 2 Kgs 22.8, 11) or 'Scroll of the Covenant' (ספר־הברית, 23.2, 21), which according to 2 Kings 22 was found in the Jerusalem Temple in the eighteenth year of Josiah, with the original scroll of Deuteronomy.⁸ Ever since this identification, the reform itself has continued to be regarded as *the* key datum not only for Pentateuchal criticism but also for the religious history of pre-exilic Judah, as 'the event which, despite all uncertainties, is our firmest point of orientation' in the realm of the 'deuteronomistic phenomenon' (Lohfink 1987: 460).⁹ In recent years, however, the historicity of the reform and the reliability of our sources have been thoroughly called into question by a number of biblical scholars. Among the most radical critics, C. Levin has advocated a *Grundschicht* within 2 Kings 22–23, which, for a few verse fragments left to the historian, would reduce the cult

---

4. After the original version of this paper had been published, several authors, approaching the biblical tradition from a very different angle, arrived at conclusions which considerably overlap those defended here regarding reform measures that might be considered historical. Cf. Hardmeier 2000, a translated and revised version of appears in this volume, above pp. 123-63; Arneth 2001: 189-216.

5. *GGG*; *GGIG* (English translation of *GGG* 3rd edn). I shall refer to the English version (henceforth abbreviated *GGIG*) except for the 'Anhang' (*GGG* §§251-62), which was written for the German 4th edition and not yet available to the English translation.

6. Especially the shrine located in the Judahite fortress of Arad, for which see below, Section 2.1, but also finds from neighbouring areas which put evidence from Judah into proper perspective. The presence of first class forgeries among recently published glyptic and epigraphic material requires even more circumspection than before when critically considering unprovenanced data.

7. Cf., *inter alia*, Dever 1994; Rainey 1994; Einykel 1995 (for which see my review, Uehlinger 1997); Toloni 1998; Sweeney 2001: 40-51; Barrick 2002; Fried 2002; and studies mentioned above, n. 4.

8. But cf. Paul 1985.

9. Cf. Lohfink 1985; 1991a: 210.

reform to a mere fantasy.[10] Taking Levin's minimal *Grundschicht* as a starting-point for his own religio-historical evaluation, H. Niehr (1995) has equally minimalized the reform's extent and significance on the basis of a sharp distinction between so-called 'primary' and 'secondary sources'.[11] Others have argued the lack of independent archaeological evidence that could substantiate the claim of a significant cultic and/or administrative reform under King Josiah.[12]

As a result, what we thought to be a firm point of orientation only a decade ago has turned into a long series of question marks: Was there a cult reform at all during the reign of king Josiah, or should we understand the report of 2 Kings 22–23, a 'secondary source' at best, as merely a literary fiction? Was the reform—however its contours are to be sketched in detail—part of the *mainstream* history of seventh-century (or 'pre-exilic') Judahite state religion, or just a convenient invention of a small group of later ('exilic' or even 'post-exilic') Deuteronomists?[13] If there was a reform in the time of Josiah, did it include, as 2 Kings 23 contends, a complex set of cult-political measures carried out quite systematically beyond the Jerusalem Temple, with dramatic consequences for local sanctuaries (במות) all over Judah and even in regions that had formerly belonged to the Northern Kingdom (esp. Bethel)?[14] Or did it merely consist of the diversion to Jerusalem of taxes that had hitherto benefited some local shrines of the Judean countryside?[15] Should one, then, speak of an actual *cult* reform at all?[16] Was it not, rather, an economically and politically motivated effort to centralize and consolidate the power of the Judahite state administration in Jerusalem, without any genuinely religious aim and purpose, but merely related to religion in terms of cult-economy, undoubtedly a major preoccupation for a ancient Near Eastern state's policy and legitimacy? Admittedly, if an independent cult reform cannot be singled out (which is the main thesis advocated by H. Niehr[17]), it becomes more difficult for the historian to deal with specifically *religious* and *cult-related* aspects of Josiah's reform.[18]

10. Levin 1984.
11. For a more recent exposition of his methodological and material position, see Niehr 1999.
12. Most recently Fried 2002 (with references to earlier literature).
13. On the sociological contours of 'Deuteronomism', cf. Albertz 1992: 304-66, 390-97 (English translation Albertz 1994); and Lohfink 1995.
14. On this, see Lopasso 1999.
15. A thesis advocated long ago by Claburn 1973; cf. more recently, Zwickel 1999.
16. Cf. Hjelm 1999.
17. Cf. Niehr 1995: 51.
18. It will become clear in the following investigation that I do not aim at gathering indications of a cult reform driven by 'purely religious' interests, with no economic motives and consequences. To interpret Josiah's reform in such a way would result in a gross anachronism. The sacrificial and tithing system of ancient Judah must be understood in analogy to taxation in the realm of political economics, which conversely did not function independently from religion. The measures described or implied by Deuteronomy, for instance, liberalizing domestic meat consumption while at the same time diverting taxes to the central shrine, demonstrate how deeply political, economic and religious issues were interrelated in antiquity. Consequently, Niehr's conjecture that the set of measures described in 2 Kgs 23.8a (the removal of priests from the cities of Judah and the desecration of local shrines, which Niehr holds for the only historical kernel) could have been executed without any genuinely *religious* motivation is anachronistic and inadequate.

Niehr's objective was 'to investigate the parameters that must be considered in current research if one wants to find a basis for something else than mere assertions and declarations'.[19] In this article, I shall therefore address questions of method and terminology (Section 1) before discussing specific details of Josiah's reform (Sections 2-4).[20]

1. *Prerequisites*

1.1. *Primary and Secondary Sources*

In a ground-breaking and important essay on historiography and historical method,[21] E.A. Knauf has established the necessity of prioritizing so-called *primary sources* over *secondary sources*.[22] Following this distinction and according to the definitions given by Knauf, the Hebrew Bible contains only secondary (and tertiary, quarternary, etc.) sources. Indeed, every historian who works with biblical texts will concede with Knauf that 'we simply do not have the documents; all we can do is in some cases reasonably assume that we may have copies of copies' (Knauf 1991a: 47 n. 1). This material lack of original documents (and not the issue of the sources' reliability) is the decisive reason why we cannot speak of primary sources when addressing the Bible (Uehlinger 2001: 31-36). Another well-known fact also mentioned by Knauf, namely that biblical representations of history all belong to the class of texts 'that were produced after the events in an attempt to clarify for future generations how things were thought to have happened' (Knauf 1991a: 46), is of related significance but comparatively less distinctive. As a matter of fact, the same evaluation would apply to ancient Near Eastern royal inscriptions, that is, primary sources: they were not only designed as propaganda for the gods and for contemporary society but explicitly present themselves again and again as documents written in view of later generations. In the interest of distinctiveness, we should therefore concentrate on two *formal* criteria when defining the concept of primary sources, and do without qualifications regarding their content and credibility:

---

19. Quote translated from a private communication (19 July 1993) preceding the Frankfurt meeting mentioned in the preliminary remarks.

20. Secondary literature on the reform abounds; when preparing my paper, I consulted Lowery 1991: esp. 190-209; Laato 1992: esp. 37-68; Reuter 1993; cf. also Zwickel 1990: 210-33; Weinfeld 1991: 65-84; and literature refered to in the preceding and following notes.

21. See Knauf 1991a: esp. 46-47, 51, on 'primary' and 'secondary evidence', and cf. also Ahlström 1991.

22. The term 'source' is taken here in a broad, conventional sense (as in German *Quelle*) and does not imply the intention of preserving and communicating memory on behalf of original authors (as would be the case for a 'document'). While it may be useful to distinguish between 'data', 'remains', 'monuments' and 'documents' on the side of evidence, it is the historians who through inquiry and interpretation give any of them the character of a 'source'. I would not object to the concept of 'data' as long as it is not misconstrued in a positivistic sense, as if history could work on *bruta facta* without ever interpreting them. The English term 'evidence' is notoriously misleading, at least to a non-native speaker, but will also be deployed in the present discussion for the sake of convenience.

1. Primary sources are documents that can be *dated* on the material basis of *archaeological* criteria (context of the find, typical classification, style, palaeography, or the like) with relative accuracy (criterion of *being dateable*).
2. Primary sources originated during or shortly after[23] the reported events (criterion of *temporal proximity*).

In my view, the distinction between primary, secondary, tertiary sources, etc. does not imply an *a priori* judgment regarding *historical reliability*. Reliability does not automatically follow from temporal proximity. It can only be critically assessed by evaluating the function of a document, which (regardless of whether it is a text or a picture) is generally related to its *genre*, and by comparing it to other documents wherever available. Primary sources can offer tendentious, concocted history, while tertiary sources may well pass down historically reliable information. Still, it must be obvious to anyone that the difficulty of documenting the past grows with increasing temporal distance from the events that should be related. Hence, secondary and tertiary sources always suffer from a deficit of experience and relative lack of documentation when compared with primary sources, a deficit for which they usually seek to compensate through outside information that can no longer be verified by the author, and/or through recourse to an author's *own* experience. Belonging however to another period and context, the latter generally cannot make up the deficit. Increasing temporal distance from past events therefore leads to anachronisms, generally unintended but quite unavoidable; growing cultural distance produces analogous distortions. Hence, any historical reconstruction interested in matters of historicity must take the primary sources as its starting point.[24]

1.2. *Braudelian Times*

It has become fashionable in recent years for Bible scholars to refer to the work of the French historian Fernand Braudel[25] and his differentiation between *histoire*

---

23. Knauf's definition for primary sources, namely 'texts that were produced in the course of the events as they were happening' (1991a: 46), is in my opinion too narrow and would require knowledge about the exact circumstances of text production which remains exceptional even in well-documented instances (such as the redaction of Assyrian annals).

24. The terminology, of course, implies hierarchy and a value judgment—which is precisely its heuristic function. That the biblical texts should in an *historical* inquiry be examined as *secondary* sources only, whenever primary evidence is available, will irritate not a few exegetes. In this regard, the requirements of historical method contradict the theological *a priori* of the Bible's normative character as Scripture (most exegetes and 'biblical historians' are first of all trained as theologians). They also contradict the current practice in 'histories of Israel' of postulating a general reliability of biblical texts as a historical source only because it represents the *only* available source for much that is written in the Bible. From a methodological standpoint, the fact that a text may be our only available source does not prejudice its character and quality as a reliable source. Apart from that, many 'history of Israel' textbooks are almost blind to archaeology and iconography, which limits their use for historical research.

25. In addition to Braudel's classic *La Méditerranée et le monde méditerranéen à l'époque de Philippe II* (1990 [first published 1949]), one may refer to the essay 'Histoire et sciences sociales, la

événementielle and *histoire de la longue durée*. That this distinction was introduced into the fields of Palestinian archaeology and the 'history of Israel'[26] scarcely three decades ago is symptomatic of a field characterized by considerable lack or bias of methodological reflection (cf. M. Weippert 1993: 103).[27] As it happens, belated reception is often rather superficial, and fashionable scholarship trademarked by the redundant use of slogans and catchwords (in our case, *longue durée*) instead of actual theoretical refinement.[28]

It is ironic to note that H. Niehr's re-evaluation of Josiah's reform should reduce the chain of events to a minimum, a single event if any, and at the same time claim that scholars must consider the reform in a *longue durée* perspective. What reform should we consider at all, if the sources scarcely allow us to reconstruct its main features? How should we relate a few bits and pieces of event history (*histoire événementielle*) with the realm of actual *longue durée*? I doubt whether the *longue durée* provides the adequate background for dealing with an historical phenomenon like Josiah's reform. We better recall that Braudel not only distinguished between two kinds of history, the events and the *longue durée*; he also described an intermediate level, which is frequently overlooked in discussions of the history of Palestine/Israel: the *histoire conjoncturelle*.

For Braudel (1990: 13-14), each of his three levels of history relates to a particular kind or concept of time and historical awareness:

I. History by events (*histoire événementielle*) is most readily experienced by individuals and can be described in terms of individual time: this is 'traditional history, if one likes, the history not of the general human dimension, but of the individual dimension'. This level operates for any of us in our own biography; to Braudel—whose ultimate subject is the Mediterranean sea—it appears like 'a mere agitation of the surface'.

II. History as shaped by large collective destinies and a confluence of factors of change or 'conjunctures' (*histoire conjoncturelle*) is related to social time: 'a slowly rhythmical history; one would readily say, if the expression had not been deprived of its full meaning, a social history, that of groups and social movements'.

III. Long-term history (*histoire de la longue durée*), shaped by natural environment and geography, relates to geographical time: this is 'an almost motionless history, that of the human race in its relationship with the environment that surrounds it; a history that flows slowly, is transformed slowly, often creates constant, renewable patterns, cycles started anew without ceasing'.[29]

longue durée' (1958). H. and M. Weippert have accurately referred to A. Alt as a proponent of a *longue durée* approach *avant la lettre* (1991: 371).

26. Notably by Coote and Whitelam 1987: 8-9, 15-16, 21, etc.; H. and M. Weippert 1991: 369-81; Knauf 1991a: 42-44, and Ahlström 1993: 23-24, among others, also have recourse to Braudel.

27. Considering the generation-long debate on the status of archaeology for biblical history (W.F. Albright, M. Noth, R. de Vaux), it is more appropriate to speak of a bias rather than a lack of methodological reflection. Still, the debate evolved within an intellectual province of its own called 'biblical archaeology', a paradigm long dominated by theology-related preoccupations.

28. But see Brandfon 1987 for the rather complex state of the problem.

29. Such realities or 'structures' are normally beyond human reach, except when it comes to communication between places along roadways that generally follow rules imposed by topography.

There can be no doubt that the *histoire de la longue durée* would deserve more attention than it has received up to now in the realm of religious history, in Palestine as elsewhere. Among other benefits, a *longue durée* perspective could relativize not a few theological debates on exclusive or distinctive *propria* of biblical creeds and beliefs, a debate that is too often fed by confessional prejudices and historical ignorance. The most appropriate level for the religious history of Israel and Judah, however, and surely for the discussion of a topic such as Josiah's reform, is the *histoire conjoncturelle*. Throughout the short existence of Israel and Judah as states, their history was influenced by political developments in Egypt and Mesopotamia and by fluctuations between these major centres of power, prestige, and learning. While an event or chain of events such as Josiah's reform first represents a phenomenon on the level of the *histoire évenementielle* —regardless of whether one thinks of the reform as an historical fact or as a literary projection—the contextual conditions that would have prepared and shaped it, and perhaps also its consequences, certainly belong to the realm of the *histoire conjoncturelle*.

This intermediate level is also the favourite realm for archaeology, which in recent years has come to be considered the first and foremost 'data pool' for critical history-writing. It is archaeology that provides the primary data and allows us to analyse and interpret historical processes that lie between single events on the one hand (level I), and the structures of geography, whose changes count in millennia (level III), on the other. When dealing with a topic such as Josiah's reform, we should therefore concentrate on the *histoire conjoncturelle* (level II) and address the relevant archaeological record.

1.3. *Methodological Minimalism*

Knauf has described the concept of a 'minimalist approach' as an alternative to the 'maximalist approach' generally followed by textbooks on the 'history of Israel' (Knauf 1991b: 171), terms that have since become commonplace and are sometimes used with a rather polemical overtone. I suspect that between the maximalist approach ('everything in the sources that could not be proved wrong has to be accepted as historical', in the words of Knauf) and a minimalist approach *stricto sensu* ('everything which is not corroborated by evidence contemporary with the events to be reconstructed is dismissed') there remains a broad spectrum of 'third ways', or, at least, various possibilities to practise and adapt methodological minimalism to specific data.[30] Since I agree with Knauf that only primary sources, that is, dateable archaeological finds, should be the *starting-point* for a religious history of Israel and Judah,[31] I am inclined to follow some kind of minimalist approach. However, 'methodological minimalists' should not take their task too easily. Measures possibly taken under king Josiah in order to redesign the Judahite state cult cannot simply be dismissed because they are not explicitly mentioned as such in primary sources: such a conclusion would

---

30. The qualification, '*corroborated* by evidence contemporary with the events' obviously needs further argument.

31. See above, Section 1.1, and n. 24.

proceed from an *argumentum e silentio* which should be inadmissible for maximalists and minimalists alike. Arguments of that kind—seldom proved but regularly disproved by new archaeological data—should be avoided, whether in a minimalist or in any other approach. As a historical procedure, even a 'minimalist' approach should take stock of a maximum of available sources, however critically scrutinized.

The crucial question, then, is which kind of data or 'evidence' should be considered as primary sources when addressing a topic such as King Josiah's reform?

1.4. *Which are the Primary Sources to be Considered When Looking for Josiah's Reform?*
History of *religion*, as any other attempt at critical history writing, must start from the primary sources. Histories of the religion(s) of Israel and Judah that take the biblical texts as their starting-point always run the risk of projecting 'exilic' and 'post-exilic' agendas and concepts back into the two kingdoms' 'pre-exilic' history. Such is the case with many textbooks on the 'History of Israel'[32] when they address matters of religion. Their perspective has aptly been characterized as 'sub-deuteronomistic history-writing' by M. Weippert (1993: 73).[33] Considering the eminent place of 2 Kings 22–23 in the Deuteronomistic History, the risk of writing 'sub-deuteronomistic history' is particularly acute with our topic, Josiah's reform.

In order not to allow our agenda to be dictated by secondary or tertiary sources, we should broaden our focus beyond isolated features that might be related to some detail of the biblical scenario. When examining developments in Judahite religion during the seventh century, we should certainly address the finds that previous research has hypothetically correlated with Josiah's reform (see below, Section 2.1), and we should certainly consider cultic structures that a definition based on biblical texts would identify as *bamôt* shrines (Nakhai 2001: 161-200; Fried 2002 with divergent conclusions). But we must not limit our view to these. Otherwise, we would still be methodologically prejudiced and proceed within a more subtle variant of 'sub-deuteronomism'—or, for that matter, *e silentio* argument. On methodological grounds, one should preferably start from an overall picture of Judahite religion at the end of the Iron Age II C as it can be ascertained from a maximum of primary sources.[34] Comparing this picture with documented finds from earlier and later periods may allow us to formulate hypotheses about *conjunctures* and *developments* within Judahite religion from the eighth to the sixth century. Once these have been ascertained, we can examine whether one or several aspects or features might be related to Josiah's reform.

32. Many publications on the *religious* history of Israel and Judah could equally be characterized in this way; correspondingly, the boundary between religious history and theology often remains unclear in these works.

33. Even Ahlström's massive *History of Ancient Palestine* (1993) still follows these lines to a large extent, despite the programmatic beginning in the Palaeolithic period and numerous critical corrections of the biblical tradition.

34. See Holladay 1987; H. Weippert 1988; *GGG, GGIG*; and now Zevit 2001, especially Chapters 2–5.

* * *

Having clarified my methodological point of departure, the remaining parts of this paper will proceed in three steps: in Section 2, I shall first examine salient items from the primary documentation that are or have been thought to be directly relevant for interpreting the religious history of Judah during the seventh century BCE. Attention will then be drawn very selectively to a few archaeological finds which demonstrate that Yahwistic religion had indeed a *history* in seventh-century Judah and that *changes* are discernible during that period alongside aspects of continuity.[35] In Section 3, I shall turn to the biblical tradition and consider selected features of Josiah's reform as described in 2 Kings 23. The last section will address the problem of correlating archaeological data and biblical sources.

2. Selected Primary Evidence from Seventh/Sixth-Century Judah

2.1. *Finds of Questionable Evidence: The Arad Shrine and Other Cult Places*

Two finds that only a generation ago served as the principle archaeological evidence for Hezekiah's or Josiah's reform, or for both,[36] can no longer be used for that purpose: the disassembly of the great horned altar at Tell es-Seba' some time during the second half of the eighth century BCE,[37] and the (supposed) removal of the shrine of Arad in two stages during the Iron Age II C.[38] Tell es-Seba' must not retain us for long, since the relevant features are chronologically too far removed from Josiah's reform. Stones that had once belonged to a monumental, ashlar-built horned altar were found reused as constructional material in the wall of a pillared storehouse of Str. II and under the Str. II glacis. While the destruction of Str. II provides a *terminus ante quem*, which may be connected with the campaign of Sennacherib (701 BCE),[39] it is impossible to ascertain the date of the altar's disassembly, even less its date of construction, beyond a very general date during the second half of the eighth century BCE. While the dismantling of the original altar may well have occurred during the reign of Hezekiah, we do not even know whether it occurred in the town of Str. III or just preceding the construction of the Str. II public defenses. Hence it is impossible positively to ascribe the inferred event at Tell es-Seba' to a putative cult reform under Hezekiah.[40] In

---

35. I do not assert that such changes must automatically be ascribed to Josiah's reform. Strictly speaking, the reform—as Josiah himself—is not for the time being a subject of primary sources. For this reason, it was only mentioned in passing in *GGIG* (§215).

36. Cf. the reserved construal of both finds and their interpretation by Keel and Küchler 1982: 205-208, 227-33; Conrad 1979: 28-32; Laato 1992: 47-49; Rainey 1994.

37. For various summaries, cf. Holladay 1987: 255-56, 294 and n. 128; H. Weippert 1988: 623-24; Reuter 1993: 203-208; Zevit 2001: 171-74.

38. Cf. Holladay 1987: 256-57, 294 n. 128; H. Weippert 1988: 624; Reuter 1993: 193-202; Zevit 2001: 156-71, with both a presentation of the *communis opinio* and a detailed critique already informed by first sketches of Z. Herzog's revision (cf. above, p. 289).

39. Knauf considers a date during the reign of Manasseh (2002: 181-95).

40. See Na'aman 1995; 2002: esp. 593-95; Fried 2002: 447-48. Fom a different angle, Swanson 2002.

any case, Tell es-Seba' cannot contribute to the debate on Josiah's reform. Strictly speaking, we do not even now for sure whether the considerably smaller settlement of Str. I belonged to Josiah's kingdom.[41]

The situation is much more complicated at Tel Arad. Over the last two decades the archaeological interpretation of the finds has undergone fundamental revisions resulting from refined pottery analysis, various observations concerning the architectural remains, and a thorough reconsideration of the Iron Age stratigraphy. The following comments by Z. Herzog, who is entrusted with the final publication of the dig, are illuminating from a methodological point of view. Having defended Aharoni's interpretation of the site's history over many years against all sorts of scholarly criticism, Herzog thoroughly re-examined all the available documentation and arrived at conclusions that now depart quite radically from Aharoni's. According to Herzog, former interpretations of the archaeological evidence at Arad had suffered from relying too heavily on putative biblical parallels:

> A strong impact of the 'biblical archaeology' paradigm directed both Yohanan Aharoni and his crew members [among which Herzog himself] to look for a simplistic correlation between the archaeological data and biblical references. This method, now viewed as oversimplified, is considered a most disturbing and misleading approach... The present reassessment of the temple in Arad negates most of the correlations with the biblical account suggested in previous treatments of the site. (Herzog 2001: 158, 175)

Y. Aharoni's attempt to interpret the history of the Arad shrine in close correlation with 2 Kgs 18.4 and 23.8, the two texts relating cultic reforms under Kings Hezekiah and Josiah in the Judean countryside, did find many followers among scholars and tourists alike until recently. According to Aharoni, the earliest cult place had been established by local Kenites in the twelfth century BCE, and the temple's foundation went back to King Solomon. The building's ritual organization underwent two major modifications in Str. VIII and VI, which Aharoni dated to the late eighth and seventh centuries: first, the courtyard and sacrificial altar were suppressed and the area leveled out, a measure that Aharoni related to a cult reform under King Hezekiah;[42] second, the shrine itself was dismantled and built over in Str. VI by a casemate wall, which Aharoni dated to the time of Josiah. Defended by the Arad publication team over many years (Herzog *et al.* 1984), this interpretation had been repeatedly questioned by a number of scholars, among them D. Ussishkin (1988) who suggested that the shrine first came into existence with Str. VII, that is, as late as the seventh century, and remained in use until the early decades of the sixth century BCE, that is, well beyond the time of Josiah. According to Ussishkin, 'The dating of the shrine...means that its construction and destruction can hardly be related in any way to the religious reforms conducted in Judah by Hezekiah and Josiah' (1988: 156). Surprisingly,

---

41. Ostracon no. 3 from Arad Str. VI (early sixth century BCE) mentions Beersheba as a place in the jurisdiction of the administrator Elishab, who was stationed at Arad (*AHI* no. 2.003, lines 3-4). However, whether this and the biblical town should be sought at Tell es-Seba' or at Bir es-Seba', as suggested long ago by A. Alt, remains disputed.

42. For arguments against this, cf. the studies mentioned above, n. 40.

it has taken more than a decade until this theory met with substantial criticism. One suspects that it took so long because of the rather precarious state of stratigraphic documentation of the Arad excavations, which did not allow for an easy rebuttal.[43]

Starting from 1997, however, Z. Herzog has presented the long-awaited reinterpretation of the Arad 'evidence' in a series of articles and an expanded interim report.[44] According to the new scenario, the shrine was built together with the solid-walled fortress of Str. X in the mid-eighth century BCE. It remained in use during Str. IX, which Herzog dates to the second half of the eighth century, but did not exist longer than Str. IX. At some time towards the end of the eighth century, the shrine was dismantled and covered with a thick layer of earth that would have hidden any trace of the ancient sanctuary. According to Herzog, this measure affected the altar, the open courtyard and the actual shrine at one and the same time. It remains unclear to me whether the temple's cancellation should be attributed to the people stationed at the fortress at the end of Str. IX (Fried 2002: 447) or to those who designed the subsequent Str. VIII fortress, when secular (administrative) buildings were erected over the area, taking no notice of the former sanctuary buried underneath.[45] Following Herzog's reinterpretation, the shrine's cancellation should have occurred during the reign of Hezekiah, since either Str. IX or VIII may have destroyed by Sennacherib.[46]

Both Ussishkin and Herzog reduce the duration of the shrine's existence to merely two instead of Aharoni's four or five occupational strata. They diverge in their dating because they attribute the building to either Str. VII–VI (Ussishkin's late dating) or X–XI (Herzog's early dating). To the best of my understanding, this surprising contradiction is due to the precarious state of published documentation and to the relative paucity of clearly datable finds from the temple proper. The attribution of the shrine's two occupational phases to either Str. X–XI (VIII) or VII–VI ultimately rests on the absolute height of floor and wall levels rather than on a strictly stratigraphical argument.[47] Herzog's new theory is

43. Cf. Herzog 2001: 156-57; Na'aman 2003: 588-89.
44. Herzog 1997: 174-76; 2001; 2002: esp. 21-72.
45. Note that Na'aman (2003: 587-89) has criticized Herzog's division of walls and loci between Str. IX and VIII and thinks that the temple continued to be used during Str. VIII, albeit with a modified access to its cella. According to his view, 'the layers of earth that the members of the Arad publication team interpreted as a deliberate burial of the courtyard are the destruction level of Stratum VIII and the earth used for leveling the ground by the builders of Stratum VII', which Na'aman attributes to Manasseh (p. 592).
46. As already noted, Knauf prefers a date during the reign of Manasseh for the destruction of both Arad VIII and Beersheba II; cf. above, n. 39.
47. This has led to continuous debate on whether certain 'strata' should actually be regarded as such or rather as sub-phases within a given stratum; cf. Zimhoni 1985; Mazar and Netzer 1986; Ussishkin 1988, who all considered 'Strata' X–VIII and VII–VI as merely two distinct strata which they dated to the eighth-to-seventh centuries and to the early sixth century respectively. The reinterpretation of the remains by Herzog, who introduces a clear distinction between Str. IX and VIII, attributing features to Str. IX that were formerly considered belonging to Str. VIII, has prompted immediate criticism by N. Na'aman. Clearly it is difficult to speak in stratigraphical terms when no sections have been recorded.

supported by L. Singer-Avitz's refined pottery analysis (2002) and will probably outrule Ussishkin's late dating, although the shrine's status in Str. VIII remains to be clarified (see Na'aman 2003: 587-92).

Regardless of whether one follows Ussishkin's or Herzog's phasing and interpretation, however, it is impossible to relate the archaeological evidence to the biblical testimony about Josiah's reform. The shrine's cancellation is characterized by Herzog as an emphatically careful treatment of cultic paraphernalia within the building proper: two horned incense altars[48] and a massebah were all laid on their sides at their respective positions, a measure which seems to indicate an intention to preserve and not to destroy them. It is rarely noticed that the shrine has apparently produced rather meagre finds in terms of pottery and small objects, particularly with regard to Str. IX (Herzog 2002: 66).[49] The sanctuary could not have functioned with only a handful of jars and bowls,[50] and this may be another indication of the shrine's precautious cancellation by those who had run it for the Judahite state administration. While we cannot know the precise reasons of the cancellation, protective measures at a time when the southern border of Judah came under military pressure and Judahite defensive control could not be guaranteed anymore to provide the most reasonable scenario.[51] This may have occurred during the years of Hezekiah's revolt against Sennacherib, although other explanations are equally valid.[52] In Herzog's view, 'In any case, the careful burial of the symbolic objects expresses the desire or hope for a restoration of cultic activities in the future' (2002: 66).[53] This interpretation certainly does not fit the biblical report of a violent defilement of high places throughout the country—whether such a defilement took place under Hezekiah, or Josiah, or both. While we cannot exclude for the time being that the precautionary measures observed at Arad were taken during the reign of King Hezekiah, there is simply no common denominator between them and the flash notice in 2 Kgs 18.4—not even the abstract notion of 'reform'.[54] Interpreting the Arad evidence in terms of Hezekiah's reform therefore is an unnecessary hypothesis and looks like still another version of

48. For these, cf. Zwickel 1990: 116-17.
49. Interestingly enough, several Judahite pillar figurines were apparently found in the temple; cf. Kletter 1996: 63, 108 with fig. 35. To the best of my knowledge they had never been mentioned in earlier reports.
50. See Str. IX pottery published in Singer-Avitz 2002: figs. 30 and 33.10-14, all from the courtyard. Str. X finds including an (Assyrian) lion weight and two inscribed bowls are slightly more impressive, cf. Herzog 2002: 58.
51. But see Knauf's contribution to the present volume (above, pp. 164-88) for a rather imaginative alternative.
52. According to Knauf (see above, n. 39), eighth- and seventh-century destructions in the Negev should not be attributed to Sennacherib's campaign. Knauf would date the precautionary measures in the days of Manasseh, but I see no compelling evidence for this hypothesis.
53. As mentioned above (n. 45), Na'aman has raised doubts against this scenario. He thinks that the incense altars were deliberately used as part of a wall blocking the cella's east entrance, and that the entrance to the cella was then shifted south. This hypothesis raises a new difficulty: Why should the incense altars be taken out of function and used as building material for the wall the cella, if the latter—and according to Na'aman, the whole temple—continued to function as before?
54. *Pace* Herzog 2002: 66-67.

'biblical archaeology', an outdated scholarly procedure based upon doubtful methodology.

According to N. Na'aman, the decision not to rebuild the Arad shrine in the Str. VII fortress was part of a general pattern that can be observed at other abandoned cult places in Israel and Judah. He suggests

> that it was a royal decision not to restore the sacred sites, which reflected the efforts of rulers to centralize power in their hands and to strength [*sic*] their hold over the districts and towns of their kingdoms. Local shrines must have enjoyed prestige, achieved a certain degree of independence and competed with the royal court for economic gains. The king was considered responsible for their maintenance and restoration and had reasons for trying to reduce their number. (Na'aman 2002: 596)

However, such an explanation is not entirely satisfactory in the case of Arad. The Arad shrine of Str. X–XI (VIII) was *not* a 'local shrine' but had been founded by royal decision in a state garrison built for administrative and defensive purposes. The issue at stake is therefore a different one, and concerns a change within state religion. Under what conditions and for what reasons would a monarch refrain from repairing a state sanctuary? Various explanations are possible, among them the need to minimize the dispersal of economic resources. After a certain gap of occupation, the Str. VII fortress at Arad went on again collecting taxes from the area, but Yahweh, instead of being served immediately, would henceforth get his share in his Jerusalem temple only. Should we label this reaffectation of sacrificial dues from one place to another, from a provincial outpost to the capital city a religious 'reform'? The parallel with Deuteronomic cult centralization may be stunning on first sight, but it can also be thoroughly misleading. What Deuteronomy and 2 Kings 22–23 present as a divine commandment and a programmatic effort on behalf of an idealized king—paradigmatic literature, if anything—may well, in historical terms, reflect a process that took a generation or two in order to materialize. Consider Arad Str. VIII in ruins: Manasseh would first take hold again of the area and reinstall the taxation system. We do not know (*pace* Na'aman) whether it was he who built the Str. VII fortress already in the first half of the seventh century, or whether that fortress was rebuilt only later under Josiah. Who of Hezekiah, Manasseh or Josiah was responsible for the centralization of the Judahite state cult in Jerusalem? All three, each in his own way, and probably none of the three with an explicitly 'deuteronomistic' agenda in mind![55] What matters most in the perspective of critical medium-term history is not the individuals anyway, but the process which reflects the growing centrality of

---

55. At this point, I disagree with Na'aman who writes as a 'sub-Deuteronomist' when it comes to Josiah's reform. Note the following: 'By what means did the king and his followers justify their moves and explain to the elite and the populace the cultic reform that contradicted in many ways their ancestral traditions? Josiah must have cited the laws of the Book of Deuteronomy and claimed that his acts were the restoration of former glory... The work describing the history of Israel from the wandering in the wilderness to the time of Josiah (the Deuteronomistic History) was also written as part of the reform, and was composed in order to supply a solid historical basis for the act of reform' (2003: 173). This assessment can hardly be reconciled with the redactional complexity of the biblical sources.

Jerusalem in the religious and political administration of the Judahite kingdom. Arad Str. VII was a result of and a contribution to this process.

Arad and Tell es-Seba' have played the main roles in the scholarly discussions about cult reforms and archaeology because evidence from these two sites had been emphatically related to the biblical tradition by their excavator.[56] Other Israelite and Judahite sites and features had at best an occasional share in the debate. They have been recently surveyed by Lisbeth S. Fried, who concluded that 'there is no archaeological evidence consistent with the assumption that Josiah removed cult sites from the Iron Age II cities of Judah, Samaria, Megiddo, or the Negev... Neither the reforms of Josiah nor those of Hezekiah against the *bāmôt* should be considered historical' (Fried 2002: 460).[57] It thus seems that conventional ways of looking at the problem of archaeology and cult reforms have for the time being exhausted their potential.[58] It may be worthwhile to examine other avenues.

2.2. *Glyptic*

Representations of Assyrian deities are rare on seals from Iron Age II Palestine/Israel; they occur almost exclusively on imported material, mostly cylinder seals which must have belonged to Assyrian officials who occupied administrative functions in provincial outposts (*GGIG* §§168-71). Locally produced glyptic of the eighth and early seventh centuries shows however a stark tendency to portray astral symbolism, a tendency that is clearly related to growing Assyro-Aramean influence (*GGIG* §§172-88). Through this striking astral imagery, deities of the night with the moon god of Harran at their pinnacle entered the foreground in a way scarcely known before. This is all the more remarkable since astral imagery, to the best of my knowledge, has no continuation in sixth-century glyptic from Judah.

Several groups of Judahite seals and bullae have been published in recent years. They form a reference corpus of hundreds of documents. Most of them can be dated fairly precisely between the last third of the eighth and the first quarter of the sixth century, although we still lack criteria for a clear subdivision within the seventh century. Data known up to 1993 were collected by N. Avigad and

---

56. Y. Aharoni was highly esteemed among critical biblical scholars, particularly in Germany where the paradigms established by A. Alt and M. Noth long went unchallenged. He held a much more nuanced position than his opponent Y. Yadin in the debate on the so-called Israelite *Landnahme* and entertained close relations with a whole generation of German biblical scholars who studied in the 1960s and early 1970s, with some of them actively participating in Aharoni's digs in southern Judah and the Negev.

57. There is a strange hiatus between the fully documented discussion of archaeological evidence for Judahite cult places and the rather conservative treatment of biblical traditions about Hezekiah's and Josiah's reforms in Zevit's *Religions of Ancient Israel* (2001), where obvious tensions between the archaeological data and the biblical record do not seem to get an adequate treatment.

58. Note however that if 'archaeological evidence indicates only four cult sites among all the cities, towns, and villages of eighth-century Judah' (Fried 2002: 450), one is forced to conclude that this cannot reasonably represent the whole reality and that archaeology has still missed dozens of places where ancient Judahites practised their cults during the Iron Age.

B. Sass in their *Corpus of West Semitic Stamp Seals* (1997b [hereafter *WSS*]),[59] which includes excavated and unprovenanced material side by side. Since 1993, new catalogues of unprovenanced seals and sealings from the antiquities market and private collections appeared almost every year, most of them compiled by the same author-editor who has almost created a new genre.[60] At the very moment when 'biblical archaeology' is fading away, it is superseded by a new kind of 'biblical collectorship'. Both the pace of publication and the apparent competition engaged between several prestigious private collectors has created a somewhat uneasy situation for critical scholarship: Should we simply ignore material whose provenance cannot be ascertained, or should we with all due caution consider this material as a significant enlargement of our database? Is it possible and reasonable to look for procedures that take stock of the new material without however giving it undue weight in the scholarly argument? How can we minimize the risks of affecting historical research by fakes and forgeries? A reasonable way of dealing with the situation, in my opinion, is to practise one's research and build up one's theory in concentric circles: much as we deal with primary, secondary and tertiary sources, we should consider excavated material first, and it is certainly legitimate to consider it exclusively. Still, it is also legitimate to test it with additional material once we have established a working hypothesis, without however giving undue weight to material belonging to the second (unprovenanced objects with clear parallels in excavated material), third (unprovenanced objects without parallels) or fourth circle (doubtful material). Any opportunity to put unprovenanced material to the test of science (e.g. by thermoluminescence analysis) should be taken. And valid historical hypothesis should proceed, if at all, from the inner to the outer circles but *never* vice versa.

According to these principles, the group of 49 bullae excavated in a well-stratified context in Area G of Y. Shiloh's 'City of David' excavations in Jerusalem obviously occupies a first-rank position.[61] These bullae probably represent the remains of a family archive recording real estate transactions extending over two or three generations until the city's conflagration in 587 BCE.[62] Among the 40 or 41 individuals represented in the archive, only three used an uninscribed seal; they were probably people from elsewhere, since their seal designs are typical for the Shephelah (dove and twig impressed with a bone seal), the Philistine coast or Egypt (sphinx and scarab), and North Syria (a moon crescent of Harran impressed with a conical seal). In contrast, local seals display a conspicuous reservation towards iconic designs and merely use decorative features and space fillers. A twig or a star may occasionally serve as an additional identity marker—but what

---

59. Cf. my review, Uehlinger 1998.
60. See Deutsch and Heltzer 1994, 1995, 1997, 1999; Deutsch 1999, 2003a, 2003b; Deutsch and Lemaire 2003, all published by Archaeological Center Publications at in Tel Aviv-Jaffa. See further Lemaire 1999; Avigad, Heltzer and Lemaire 2000.
61. Shiloh 1986; Shiloh and Tarler 1986; Shoham 1994, 2000. *WSS* (pp. 167-68) provides a useful concordance.
62. Since only a few bullae show sealings from identical seals, the archive cannot result from regular business transactions.

kind of identity: family, club, or professional guild? Clearly enough, neither iconic design in general nor astral symbolism in particular were *en vogue* among the literate Jerusalemites represented in the 'House of the Bullae' archive.

A second group of 211 unprovenanced bullae ('Tell Beit Mirsim' or Jerusalem?) published by N. Avigad almost twenty years ago (1986) presents a rather different picture. First, there is a greater variety in decorative designs; second, a number of bullae display architectural and vegetal or floral motifs which can be related tentatively to temple and/or fertility symbolism (*GGIG* §208). One bulla even shows a worshipper. In neither of the two groups, however, would one find an anthropomorphic portrayal of a deity—neither Assyrian nor Syro-Palestinian—or such conspicuous astral symbols as the crescent moon or stars of earlier periods.[63] Some of the Avigad sealings clearly go back to late eighth- and early seventh-century seals. These, as other seals and sealings of earlier periods, are less uniform than the designs of the late seventh and early sixth centuries.[64] Two instances of an enthroned (lunar?) god depicted on Judahite seals[65] are especially noteworthy. A *dea nutrix* presenting her breasts is known on an eighth-century anepigraphical seal from Lachish (*GGIG* fig. 323).[66] Globally speaking, Israelite and Judahite glyptic of the eighth century were relatively open and receptive to anthropomorphic and theriomorphic representations (deities and genies, sphinxes, scarabs, uraei, etc.). During the seventh century, some Judahite workshops seem to have adopted at least occasionally the astral symbolism which was *en vogue* at that time,[67] while others developed remarkable skills in vegetal and floral decoration. In contrast, late pre-exilic seals and sealings are clearly reluctant to use anthropomorphic and theriomorphic representations and concentrate instead on calligraphy and geometric decorum. One may conclude from such comparisons that astral symbolism may have affected part of the earlier Judahite glyptic but was clearly not (no longer?) fashionable among the Jerusalem elite in c. 600 BCE.[68]

We should not draw hasty conclusions with regard to Josiah's reform. First of all, let us recall that the cult reform is reported in 2 Kings 23 as a series of events and thus typically belongs to the *histoire événementielle*; in contrast, the seals testify to developments on the level of *histoire conjoncturelle*. Moreover, only rarely can seals be dated so precisely that we could assign them, for instance, to the reign of Josiah but not of Jehoiakim, or vice versa. The sensitive handling of sources requires that we respect the limits of what they can tell. Still, when we

---

63. Cf. *GGIG* §§187-88 with §§206-207; Sass 1993: 239-40.

64. As a rule, Northwest Semitic inscribed stamp seals prefer worshippers to anthropomorphic portrayals of deities; cf. Ornan 1993; Uehlinger 1993: 262-65.

65. *GGIG* figs. 305c and 306a; Sass 1993: 232-34 Motif F6.

66. A frontally placed, nude female(?) figure flanked by two falcons appears on the seal of a certain Ahaz published by Deutsch and Lemaire 2003: no. 15.

67. Compare, e.g., Deutsch and Lemaire 2003: nos. 41, 45, 71, 84.

68. Differences are also notable when we compare Judahite glyptic of the seventh and sixth centuries with contemporaneous seals from Moab and Ammon. Eggler 2003 stresses the different iconographic profiles of inscribed vs. uninscribed seals from Moab. Still, astral symbolism is common to both categories.

consider the overall picture of Judahite glyptic from the eighth to the sixth centuries, we may discern a clear evolution of preferences characterized by the rarefaction of iconic and otherwise deity-related seal designs.

Another aspect of the problem has only recently come to my attention.[69] If one considers the evolution of the glyptic repertoires all over Palestine during the seventh century BCE, it is striking to see the strong impact of Twenty-Sixth-Dynasty Egypt from Philistia and the Beersheba area in the south, to the Jezreel plain, the Beth-Shean Valley, the Galilee and the coastal cities in the north, particularly during the long reign of Psammetichus I (664–610 BCE). To this, one should add Egyptian small finds of various kind, such as bronze statuary or even cultic vessels and utensils. Clearly Egypt was back in these areas during the second half of the century, following the retreat of the Assyrian administration, and entertained close economic, political and cultural ties with the region.[70] However, Judah did not completely participate in this broad general conjuncture. In comparison with lowland developments, Judahite glyptic shows an almost traditionalist character—traditionalist in the sense of clear focus on established local repertoire. Seal-cutting workshops in Jerusalem do not seem to have been even slightly affected by the resurgence of *Aegyptiaca* (of which a few items made their way to the Judahite capital). Considering the admittedly narrow evidence of sealings and a sherd from Ramat Raḥel displaying human figures, costume among the Judahite elite remained unchanged, that is, indebted to previous Assyro-Aramean fashion.[71] There are a few seals and sealings that are reminiscent of Egypt-related symbolism, some of which may have belonged to people with pro-Egyptian sympathies who undoubtedly had their place in Jerusalem, too. But on the whole, Judahite symbolism of the late seventh and early sixth centuries was remarkably parochial and rather conservative—a picture which fits rather nicely the general cultural profile of the reign of Josiah as we perceive it from the biblical record.

2.3. *Epigraphical Sources*

Epigraphical sources may yield more distinctive results than seals for our purpose, especially when they can be dated with more precision. If we limit ourselves to Hebrew inscriptions from the time of Hezekiah to the end of the monarchy, they seem to reflect a development that one may generally label as an expansion of Yahweh's divine authority, which *eo ipso* implies a transfer of authority from other deities or divine entities and thus their relative deprivation of power.[72]

---

69. See Uehlinger 2001: 61-71, with references to the primary sources.

70. Na'aman 1991 has clearly demonstrated that that no power vacuum existed in Palestine at the time of Josiah; cf. also Na'aman's article in the present volume (pp. 189-247).

71. On this and the influence of politics on vestimentary fashion among the elite, see Uehlinger 1996.

72. Texts in the book of Jeremiah suggest that in the course of the seventh century Yahweh was promoted to a creator god, but there are currently no clear primary sources to document this development; cf. H. Weippert 1981. A fragmentary inscription from Jerusalem (*AHI* no. 4.201) has been thought to refer to a deity *'lqn'rṣ* (H. Weippert 1981: 16; cf. *GGIG* §§180 and 200 for tentative pictorial correlations), but this seems doubtful in the light of the inscription's fuller treatment by Renz

Hebrew and particularly Judahite inscriptions make it probable that between c. 700 and 587 Yahweh took over specific functions as provider of blessing and salvation from 'his Asherah'. That several inscriptions on the pithoi from Kuntilet 'Ajrud contain blessings *lyhwh X wl'šrth* is well known and does not need to be commented on here, since the inscriptions dated c. 800 BCE are Israelite rather than Judahite. Suffice it to say that the blessings of Kuntilet 'Ajrud represent a standard epistolary greeting formula.[73] Roughly a century later, similar notions about blessing and salvation were expressed in a cave inscription near Khirbet el-Kom, apparently commissioned by a certain Uriah.[74] According to line 3, Yahweh had saved him 'from his adversaries "through" (or "for the sake of") his Asherah' (*wmṣryh l'šrth hwš'lh*). A slightly different reading has been suggested by A. Lemaire (1977), who believes that the syntagma *l'šrth*, which appears two more times below, was erroneously displaced and should be read in sequence with the preceding line, where he reconstructs a blessing that would parallel the formulae known from Kuntilet 'Ajrud: 'Blessed be/is Uriah through (or "on behalf of") Yahweh and through ("on behalf of") his Asherah'. Whether one follows Lemaire's suggestion or not, it is clear that the author of the inscription regarded Yahweh's Asherah as a major instance of salvation and/or blessing. In contrast, more recent greeting formulas found in letters from Arad (Str. VI) and Lachish (Str. II), that is, in contexts that are roughly contemporaneous with the above-mentioned bullae from Jerusalem, do not mention Asherah (anymore?).[75] While the primary sources do not explain to us the reasons behind this change, that it occurred in such a tradition-bound context as greeting and blessing is remarkable.[76] To put it squarely, something must have happened to Yahweh's Asherah between roughly 700 and 587 BCE.

The inscriptions on the two silver amulets from Ketef Hinnom in Jerusalem[77] are famed for their variations of the priestly blessing known through Num. 6.24-26. More interesting for our concern, they seem to count on the effectiveness of Yahweh even in the underworld, which would again imply a remarkable extension of Yahweh's power. The blessing of the second, smaller amulet directly addresses dead Oniyahu ([*'t*]*h brw*[*k'*]*nyhw*, II.1-2). The corresponding lines are missing from the larger amulet, but there would have been enough space for a similar formula. Amulet I reads, 'Indeed/for through him [Yahweh] is salvation;

1995: 198. The syntagma *yhwh 'lhy kl h'rṣ* in inscription A from Khirbet Beit Lei may emphatically designate Yahweh as 'God of the *whole* land' (*AHI* no. 15.005 = [!] 15.006), which would make equal sense in the face of an Assyrian attack or shortly after the exclusion of the Shephelah and the Negev following Sennacherib's campaign, rather than 'God of the whole earth' (*GGIG*, p. 312; Renz 1995: 246). A very different reading is defended by Zevit 2001: 417-27.

73. On this cf. *GGIG* §§134, 143; cf. Müller 1992: esp. 21-23, 35-37.

74. *AHI* no. 25.003; Renz 1995: 202-11; *GGIG* §141; cf. Zevit 2001: 359-70 (with a different interpretation of *'šrth*).

75. Cf. *GGIG* §209.

76. The authors of inscriptions B and C from Khirbet Beit Lei (*AHI* nos. 15.007 and 15.008; Renz 1995: 248-49; Zevit 2001: 426, 429) also apparently expect salvation from Yahweh only; however, their 'quick prayers' are not of the same genre.

77. Barkay 1992; *GGIG* §210.

indeed/for Yahweh brings light back to us' (*ky bw g'lh ky yhwh* [*y*]*šybnw* [*x²*] *'wr*, I.11-14).⁷⁸ Salvation through Yahweh is here metaphorized with the notion that Yahweh brings back light: this recalls the common Near Eastern concept of the sun-god who travels through the underworld during the night and literally 'brings back light' in the morning.

As O. Keel and I have argued elsewhere (1994), Yahweh originally came to Jerusalem as a typical storm god. As the patron deity of the Davidic dynasty, Yahweh increasingly took over aspects and functions of other deities, among them the former city god who had probably solar characteristics. From the end of the eighth century onwards, Yahweh himself was to a large extent perceived as a royal solar deity.⁷⁹ Another step in the integration of divine roles opened the way towards the netherworld, to which Yahweh had not been related before. The two amulets from Ketef Hinnom, originally made for living persons and not specifically for the dead,⁸⁰ document an advanced stage of this development. One could probably buy such amulets in the vicinity of the Jerusalem Temple, maybe choose from a repertoire of blessing formulae and have one's own name put on them. When their owners died, the amulets were placed with them in the grave. Once the idea developed that Yahweh could be active in the grave and netherworld and preserve the dead from evil, too, some sort of competition between the main deity of Jerusalem and other gods who were traditionally related to the netherworld (among them, *mlk*?) became inevitable.

If a cult reform ever took place under King Josiah, it must be plausibly situated within the religio-historical context implied by the afore-mentioned developments.

3. *Notes on Selected Reform Measures Mentioned in 2 Kings 23*⁸¹

Let us now turn to the 'secondary source' on Josiah's reform as preserved in 2 Kings 23—still our best 'source' for that matter. Scholars have long noted the differences in style and divergences in content which distinguish the so-called 'reform report' (*Reformbericht*, 2 Kgs 23.4-20) from the report on the scroll's discovery and ensuing covenant ceremony (2 Kgs 22.3–23.3, 21-24).⁸² The reform report never refers to the scroll found in ch. 22; conversely, that chapter contains only a single reference to inappropriate cultic behaviour (v. 17), which clearly stems from a late deuteronomistic hand and offers no motive for the

---

78. *AHI* no. 4.301]*šynmw* [] *kwr* follows the reading by Barkay; a look at the photo and drawing show its difficulty, cf. Yardeni 1991: 178-79 with fig. 1.

79. In an important investigation of the iconography of the Hebrew name-inscribed seals, B. Sass observed that in the realm of astral motifs, the solar symbolism was clearly dominant while portrayals of the moon and other stars appear only occasionally (1993: 238-40). This stands in sharp contrast to the glyptic of (Ammonite and) Moabite name seals (cf. above, n. 68) and must be connected with the different orientation of the respective state deities.

80. In I.8, *mškb* ('resting place') does not necessarily mean the grave; the word could just as well denote 'a place for the night'; cf. Beuken 1993: 1310-11.

81. For overviews of recent research, cf. Lohfink 1985; Preuss 1993: 246-50; Gieselmann 1994.

82. Cf. Hardmeier's article in the present volume (above, pp. 123-63).

particular reform efforts described in ch. 23.[83] Hence not only the correlation between the reform report and the book of Deuteronomy,[84] but the thematic and chronological relationship between the reform report and the 'scroll' are open to debate. In the present context of an approach aiming at critical minimalism, I shall limit my discussion to some selected features mentioned in the reform report.[85] Since my demonstration will be focused on particular measures and the quest for relevant primary sources, I shall use the term 'reform notices' (*Reformnotizen*) when addressing them individually. This terminology does not imply that I consider the 'reform report' as it stands a planless piece of atomized notices, but the literary analysis of the chapter as a whole is far beyond the subject of this study.[86]

3.1. *Centralization or Purification of the Cult? Literary Criticism and Critical Minimalism*

Even a superficial examination of the reform-notices allows one to distinguish two kinds of measures which are usually designated by the keywords 'centralization' vs. 'purification' of the cult. Centralization has received greater scholarly attention because it could be more easily correlated with Deuteronomic requirements (cf. Deut. 12). In contrast, the purification measures or purges mentioned in 2 Kings 23 are less easily related to Deuteronomic law.[87] Many authors, among

---

83. 2 Kgs 22.17, where the reasons are given for the disaster with which Yahweh threatens *Jerusalem*, concerns the *inhabitants of the city* who have fallen away from Yahweh: 'because *they* have left me and *offered incense to other deities*, in order to anger me through all the pitiful work of their hands'. Nothing in ch. 23 relates to this diagnosis. Only cults practised in the capital would have come into question, such as those mentioned in v. 5b, where *burning incense* for other deities is again mentioned. However, v. 5 is not concerned with the inhabitants of Jerusalem in general but with כמרים, a particular group of priests (see below, Section 3.3); not Yahweh, but 'Baal, the sun, the moon, the constellations and the entire host of heaven' are named as the addressees of their cult. On the basis of its phraseology, 22.17 belongs to the literary horizon of Jer. 1.16; 19.4 (קטר לאלהים אחרים with עזב את יהוה), 44.3, 5, 8, 15 (only קטר לאלהים אחרים) and 25.6, 7; 32.20; 44.8 respectively (for כעס את יהוה במעשה ידים; see also Deut. 31.29; 1 Kgs 16.17 (cf. Tagliacarne 1989: 129-30, 377-78). Like the first part of the Huldah oracle in general, the verse is directed at the capture and destruction of Jerusalem in 2 Kgs 25 and justifies this through the cultic offences named there. It should not be used as a historical source for cult practices observed in seventh-century Jerusalem.

84. Doubts about the correlation between the reform and Deuteronomy have been expressed time and again, for example by Ahlström 1993: 774-77. Tagliacarne's careful investigation concludes that 'the connections to Deuteronomy are conspicuously less than one would suppose from the literature'. Substantially more themes connect with Jeremiah.

85. More attention than usual should be paid to the fact that the Old Greek (OG) seems to have relied on a Hebrew *Vorlage* which considerably differed from the Masoretic text (MT). Schenker (2004: 34-74) has defended the priority of a pre- and proto-MT closer to OG than MT. Within the limits of this article, I shall comment on his arguments only as far as they concern the particular reform measures discussed below.

86. I may refer to Hardmeier's and Arneth's studies (above, n. 4) in addition to Lohfink 1987: 460-65; Sweeney 2001: 40-45.

87. Deuteronomy mentions neither כמרים priests and their burning incense for divine heavenly bodies (v. 5) nor a Tophet (v. 10); neither chariots nor horses of the sun-god (v. 11), and no roof altars (v. 12). These cult practices and their equipment could be subsumed under Deuteronomy's

them Niehr and Levin, think that cult centralization was the main if not the only purpose of Josiah's reform and that the various notices on purges were added by later deuteronomistic redactors. Others, in contrast, reconstruct a reform report which contains no reference to centralization.[88] As will be shown below, a number of purgative measures are more plausibly explained as late-seventh century features than cult centralization in Jerusalem, which, at least as far as state cult is concerned, did not require particular impetus at the time of Josiah. Provided Herzog's interpretation of Arad is correct, the lack of a new shrine in the fortress of Str. VII indicates that Jerusalem was at that time the uncontested centre of Judahite state religion, a situation which may well have prevailed since the very days of Manasseh.

Niehr assumes that the notices on purges are, on the whole, post-exilic additions and thus irrelevant to the religious policy of King Josiah. Such an extensive, deliberately self-imposed rejection of source material is amazing. Instead of providing an argument, Niehr simply refers to the authority of C. Levin, who is known for his rather radical literary-critical approach. In an essay published 20 years ago, Levin had tackled 2 Kings 22–23 and postulated a torso-like *Grundschicht* consisting of merely six verses (22.1-2; 23.8a, 25a [up to מלך], b, 28-30).[89] According to Levin, 'whoever believes he or she cannot do without additional Old Testament material [on Josiah's reform] does not write history but passes on legends'.[90] Levin's literary-critical impetuousness may be excused, since his reading of 2 Kings 22–23 disclosed to him a text 'of unprecedented corruption', indeed the '*cloaca maxima* of the Old Testament' (1984: 356-57 = 2003: 201-202). Such judgments may accommodate with radical minimalism, but they can hardly be regarded as unbiased.[91] Why should history of religion be based on such an eccentric viewpoint—especially since Levin shows little if any interest in actual historical questions and accordingly, primary sources? Whoever thinks that critical history writing should limit itself to the hypothetical reconstruction of putative 'original sources' embedded in secondary, tertiary or quaternary tradition, ignores the full heuristic potential of tradition and redaction history. Considering later, secondary texts as essentially unreliable is doubtful methodology. Even if a number of measures described in 2 Kings 23 may not belong to the *Grundschicht* of the text, it would not follow automatically that they must be irrelevant for the historical quest of Josiah's reform. Such a conclusion would require a reciprocal argument, namely that the assumption of a later,

---

generally formulated rejection of astral cults (Deut. 17.3), fire cults (18.10) or foreign cults in general, but in contrast to the reform-notices, they do not represent a *specific* problem in Deuteronomy.

88. Among others, Würthwein 1976: 415-18; Hollenstein 1977: 330-35; cf. Hardmeier's article in the present volume (pp. 123-63).

89. Levin 1984: 358-63 (= 2003: 205-208).

90. Levin 1984: 364 (= 2003: 209): 'Wer auf das übrige alttestamentliche Material nicht glaubt verzichten zu können, schreibt nicht Geschichte, sondern tradiert Legende'.

91. Let alone that, as every archaeologist knows, sewers and cesspools can be unimaginably rich in information about the daily life of an epoch. Synchronic analyses demonstrate 2 Kgs 22–23 is far less 'corrupt' than Levin thought; cf. Hoffmann 1980: 208-52; Tagliacarne 1989 and others.

deuteronomistic or post-deuteronomistic addition is intrinsically more plausible and provides a more coherent explanation within a later historical context.[92]

Within the limits of this article, we may cut down the historical problem to the following question: Does 2 Kings 23 list measures that are most plausibly understood against the background of the political and religious situation of Judah during the latter part of the seventh century BCE than at any other period?[93] At least two measures appear to be directed against cult practices or institutions whose introduction in Judah must have been originally connected with the Assyrian expansion and the accompanying reception of Assyro-Aramean traditions of astral cults: the removal of the horses and chariots of the sun-god (v. 11*) and the suppression of the כמרים priests (v. 5*). Both measures are reported in similar terminology (X את והשבית/וישבת).[94] The purged cult practices are said to have been 'introduced by the kings of Judah' (אשר נתנו מלכי יהודה).[95] Although this

---

92. Needless to say, good reasons must be available if literary, secondary texts are to be declared historically reliable. But the matter should not be considered closed without discussion.

93. Concerning the general political climate at the time of Josiah, we may again refer to Na'aman 1991, cf. also his article in the present volume (above, pp. 189-247).

94. The use of *waw* conjunctive + Perfect in the reform report (seven occurrences: vv. 4b, 5, 8b, 10, 12b, 14a, 15b) is an old crux that cannot be resolved here. Hoffmann (1980: 215-16) and Tagliacarne (1989: 171 n. 355) avoid the problem. A thorough discussion of all the evidence but no plausible solution is presented by Spieckermann 1982: 120-30. Spieckermann is criticized by M. Weippert (1990), who argues for a '(proto-) middle Hebraic crystal embedded in an old Hebraic text' and 'a reworking' of the relevant verses (p. 453) without following the consequences of this thesis in any detail. To postulate a common literary origin for all seven occurrences (Hollenstein 1977; Würthwein 1976: 414-15: post-Chr!) may be elegant but too simple because the corresponding passages vary starkly in content. W. Von Soden (1991) and K. Koch (1992) independently postulated a specific function, which they call 'habitative', for *waw* conjunctive + Perfect constructions. In contrast to simple narrative, this tense would characterize actions or events which are meant to have durable effects. While this suggestion allows for a more subtle perception of the text, it does not dispense us from literary-critical considerations. A new, detailed analysis is provided by Barrick (2002: 64-105), who concludes that three occurrences (vv. 5, 8b, 10) are 'intrusive in the larger context of the pericope', four (vv. 4b, 5, 10, 12b) should be seen as 'doublets or echoes of material in the "original" report', while two (vv. 12b, 14a) should be considered as 'editorial "fine-tuning"' (2002: 104). Regarding v. 5, however, its excision from the original report is argued by Barrick on the sole ground that the mention of 'the cities in Judah' in v. 5a do not fit a Jerusalem-based context (2002: 3). Barrick makes no attempt at diachronic analysis within v. 5. He can consider v. 5a a doublet of v. 8a + 9 because he does not differentiate between כמרים and כהנים priests (2002: 67-70; but see below, Section 3.3), while v. 5a is merely 'a doublet (of a sort) of v. aab' (2002: 72). I cannot find all this very convincing, particularly since in the final run, Barrick is left wondering from where the putatively late redactor could have taken his apparently quite specific knowledge and terminology (כמרים, מזלות): 'Presumably this information is not completely imaginary, but has some basis in the realities known to the author-compiler responsible for the items to be comprehensible to his intended audience' (2002: 105). While I cannot prove that the כמרים passage as understood in the following paragraph is original, I hope to show that seventh-century realities provide the most plausible background to v. 5*.

95. This is also said of the altars on the roof (of the Temple; v. 12* with עשה instead of נתן, because it deals with objects; so again in v. 19 for the high places of Samaria). Note that OG ascribes the installation of altars on the roofs [*sic*] to King Ahaz. Schenker (2004: 72-73) is among those who favour this reading.

last remark may go back to a late redactor,[96] the two measures thus glossed may well be considered to be historically reliable.

3.2. *The Horses and Chariots of the Sun(-God) (2 Kings 23.11)*

The removal of the horses and chariots of the sun is a measure that, in my opinion, can be traced back to Josiah with great probability.[97] The statement is so detailed that even Levin concedes that it could have 'a concrete cult practice in view' (1984: 361 n. 38 = 2003: 206)[98]—albeit not one dating to the seventh century.[99]

H. Spieckermann has not only rightly underscored the absence of deuteronomist phraseology in v. 11* (1982: 107) but also pointed out that the סרים, in whose chamber at the entrance to the Yahweh Temple the horses were supposed to have been stationed, bore not a religious but a civic title of Assyrian provenance, which led him to ask 'whether an apparent political functionary in the Temple might not have exercised some sort of surveillance in relation to the cult' (1982: 109). In any case, the man bore the title of an Assyrian government official, and he was not a priest. As for the horses, the Masoretic text does not consider them as inanimate votive statues or cult symbols but as living animals,[100] which explains why they had to be cared for by a civil official. The listing of horses and chariots next to each other suggests chariot horses.

Except for attributing the horses to the sun(-god), the laconic note in v. 11 does not allow one to specify their function with certainty. Spieckermann's interpretation (1982: 245-51) is based on a neo-Assyrian *tāmītu* ritual of the seventh century (*KAI* 218). In this ritual, a horse is carefully chosen through an oracular procedure by Adad and Shamash to serve with a divine chariot. This function gives the animal itself almost sacred status: 'Binding and loosing are given to you as to a god' (v. 6). The horse is believed capable of intercession: 'Concerning NN,... the governor (*šakkanaku*), speak good about him, speak up for him!' (vv. 7-8). To have the horse do this in the desired way, one must

---

96. The statement has a compensatory character. Lacking a clear reference in the previous chapters (a helpful table is provided by Hoffmann 1980: 253) or other sources, the historiographer is not in the position to ascribe the vile cult practice to a particular king.

97. *GGIG* §199; Taylor 1993: 176-82; and see now Arneth 2001: 196-201.

98. Cf. also Würthwein 1976: 417.

99. One should be aware, however, that the Masoretic and the Greek text (especially the Antiochene tradition) show considerable disagreement about the realia involved: According to the Antiochene text, Josiah '*burned* the horses *consecrated* to the sun by the kings of Judah...and he burned the chariot [*sg.*!] of the sun in fire *in the house/temple of Bethôn* (בית און), *which the kings of Israel had built as a high place for Baal and all the Host of Heaven*'. In other words, this text views the horses as votive statues, which could explain the emphasis on their locale, whereas the MT clearly thinks of *living* horses. And it reserves a separate treatment to the chariot which had to be moved to Beth On prior to its destruction. This text form is preferred by Schenker (2004: 67-72) although it requires considerable reconstructive efforts with limited support by Lucifer of Cagliari's Old Latin version. It seems preferable to consider it as a midrashic expansion and to retain the MT for the purpose of our historical inquiry.

100. Hence, the late-deuteronomistic glossator uses the verb נתן instead of עשה, as with the כמרים priests of v. 5 (see above, n. 95).

whisper an incantation in its left ear and offer him a sacrifice, 'as to the gods' (*kīma ilāni*, v. 11). Currently, this text is the only first-millennium witness for the cultic use of living chariot horses, beyond that of pulling divine chariots. Since it is methodologically difficult to fill out our sketchy knowledge about the 'horses of the sun' expelled by Josiah with a *tāmītu* from Assur, especially since no duplicate of this text is known from other cities, we cannot simply accept that the horses of the sun in Jerusalem also had an intercessory function (Spieckermann 1982: 252). But the Assyrian text gives at least a possible direction for further investigation.[101]

Both horses and chariots are assigned to the sun or sun-god in 2 Kgs 23.11. Spieckermann would like to identify this god with Assyro-Babylonian Shamash. A consideration of iconography might support this assertion. The connection between horse and sun-god has no tradition in Palestine itself but is typical of Assyria, especially during the late eighth and early seventh century (the time of Sargon and Sennacherib), when the horse was repeatedly represented as the symbolic animal of the sun-god (Seidl 1989: 234-35; Schroer 1987: 282-300). Furthermore, the all-knowing sun-god is known to have acted in the time of Sargon as a major deity addressed by the diviners, along with Adad, particularly for concerns of state security (Starr 1990). At the same time period, however, and indeed *only* under Sennacherib, are divination rituals before divine (albeit unharnassed) chariots represented on palace reliefs, a custom that was apparently felt to be obsolete at the time of Ashurbanipal.[102] Against this background, one might understand the horses and chariot of the sun-god supervised by a סרים (2 Kgs 23.11) as standard equipment for Assyrian divination practices which may have been introduced in the time of Sennacherib, presumably under King Hezekiah.[103]

From among the great Assyrian divinities, why should Shamash in particular be worshipped or be asked an oracle? The likely coincidence that the Jerusalem Temple was regarded as the residence of a solar deity may have favoured such a plausible arrangement (cf. also Ezek. 8.16). In the history of Near Eastern religions, we can observe time and again that the functions and roles of deities had a stronger local inertia than even their names, which could be combined, exchanged, grouped genealogically, and brought into line with political and economic shifts. Yahweh, the weather god, had taken the place of a local sun-god in Jerusalem during the tenth century, and during the reign of Hezekiah he was likely perceived as a solar king divine. Once Assyria distinguished itself as an irresistible power, what would be more logical than to install horses and a chariot in the temple of Jerusalem's solar deity in accordance with Assyrian custom? We

---

101. Cf. Weinfeld 1972: esp. 151 on horse donations during the neo-Assyrian era.
102. Cf. Pongratz-Leisten, Deller and Bleibtreu 1992. The standards, always portrayed in pairs, do not represent the sun-god but Adad and Nergal (or Ninurta) as patrons of the Assyrian military campaigns. In textually attested divination rituals, however, Adad and Shamash are consulted.
103. That the Assyrian sun-god had a chariot can be concluded indirectly from the epithets *rākib narkabti* ('chariot driver') and *mukīl appāti* ('rein-holder') of two subordinate gods attending Shamash; cf. Cogan 1974: 85 n. 106.

do not know whether this goes back to an Assyrian or a Judahite initiative.[104] Nor do we know whether and how Judahites mastered the techniques of horse divination or whether the horses only served as draught animals for the sun-god's processional chariot. At any rate, the perpetuation of this somewhat obsolete and rather expensive institution no longer sensible in the second half of Josiah's reign, when politics and religion were no longer conditioned by Assyria's symbol system.[105] The arrangement of Sîn-shar-ishkun with Psammetich I (around 625 BCE) had consecrated a territorial order firmly established during the preceding decade. From that time at the very latest, Judah was no longer a vassal state of Assyria but again part of an Egypt-ruled region.[106] However, in Egyptian symbolism as in local Jerusalem symbolism neither horses nor chariots had a place in the vicinity of the sun-god.

The measure thus mirrors an economically and politically conditioned reorientation of the cult practised at the royal shrine of Jerusalem. The burning of the chariots gives it considerable emphasis, but I do not think one should explain the event as an anti-Assyrian demonstration. Assyria was gone, and time was ripe to come back to local custom.

3.3. *The kêmārîm (2 Kings 23.5*)*

The priestly title כמרים is not attested in Israel/Judah before Hosea (10.5) and disappears from biblical vocabulary after Zephaniah (1.4). Hence, it was probably just as rare in Judah as it was typical for the seventh century. It is not originally Assyrian (akk. *kumru* is not attested in first-millennium cuneiform texts), but of North Syrian provenance (Spieckermann 1982: 85).[107] The title is attested in Aramaic on two funerary steles from seventh-century Neirab that were set up by priests of the moon god (*kmr šhr*).[108] Both inscriptions conjure punishment not only by the moon god, but also Shamash (only *KAI* 225), Nikkal, and Nusku upon him who would desecrate the graves. Nikkal is the bride, Nusku the son of the moon god. Thus, all the gods mentioned belong to the astral realm. Against this background and the strong astral symbolism documented in seventh-century

---

104. Religious pressure from Assyria is neither suggested by the text nor attested as a usual Assyrian practice; cf. *GGIG* §167 and Cogan (1993: 403-14) who concludes: 'No Assyrian text states or implies that conquered peoples were required to worship the gods of Assyria... But in the end, it was a new cultural and technological *koine*, Assyro-Aramean in derivation, that ultimately dominated the entire region' (pp. 412-13). In the case of Jerusalem's 'horses of the sun', one should probably think of a more or less 'voluntary accommodation to the institutions of the sovereign' (Würthwein 1976: 417) of the now uncontested superpower.

105. The fact that only a סרים, but no priest or oracle specialist, is mentioned, a man who bears the telling name נתנמלך, may indicate that the institution was no longer in practise anyway, now that Judah had no more contact with Assyria. I am sceptical whether this נתנמלך should be identified with the 'servant of the king' Nathan-melech whose seal was impressed on a recently published unprovenanced bulla. Cf. Deutsch 1999: 73-74 n. 9; McCarter 1999: 146.

106. Cf. above, Section 2.2.

107. Albertz (1992: 297, 308 n. 2) and Koch (1992: 84 n. 11) maintain that the כמרים were experts in astral divination. As far as I know, the only piece of evidence for this is the mention of the מצלות in 2 Kgs 23.5 (on which see Spieckermann 1982: 271-73).

108. *KAI* 225 and 226.

glyptic from Palestine (see above 2.2.), the association of the כמרים with astral cults in 2 Kgs 23.5 is thoroughly plausible.

Nonetheless, the verse in its present form is rather muddled. The use of the problematic *wĕ-qāṭal* should perhaps express the definitive elimination of the כמרים.[109] The sentence must have originally read:

והשית את הכמרים
(or אשר נתנו מלכי יהודה לקטר*)[110]
המקטרים
[...][111]לשמש ולירח ולמזלות ולכל צבא השמים

which would yield the following translation: 'He (Josiah) removed (permanently) the כמרים priests, who burned incense to the sun(-god), the moon(-god), the fixed stars/constellations, and the entire heavenly host'.

Levin, considering the entire v. 5 a mess of secondary or tertiary additions, simply takes the כמרים for 'priests not from Jerusalem', whom he identifies with the כהנים of vv. 8-9.[112] Practised on such premises, history of religion becomes superfluous. In contrast, we should maintain that the כמרים represent a *specific* priestly group whose cultic activities seem to have been exclusively directed towards astral deities, and whose existence in Judah and/or Jerusalem in the seventh century probably go back to Aramean influence.[113] Note that, if correctly reconstructed, our text concerns measures within Jerusalem, close to the temple or actually in the temple area (Spieckermann 1982: 84). Regardless of whether the dissolution[114] of the כמרים by Josiah was a success or whether they could

---

109. See above, n. 94. Unlike the regular priests (כהנים), 'The *hakumarīm* are removed completely, without mention of an "afterwards" regarding them (cf. v. 9a-b); in the estimation of Josiah (and the transmitter of the text), they thus represent a more wicked group' (Tagliacarne 1989: 179). A scholarly way of doing away with the כמרים is to prefer the OG and conjecture כהנים for the original text (Schenker 2004: 63-66).

110. The subordinate clause אשר נתנו מלכי יהודה is probably a late-deuteronomistic addition (see above, n. 96). The entire sentence from ויקטר through ירשלם is a continuation of the subordinate clause. The following ויקטר makes best sense if one applies it with RaDaQ to every single Judahite king *except* Josiah or to an unspecified subject ('each and everyone') who burned incense all over Judah and in the greater Jerusalem area, but it cannot then concern specifically the כמרים. To conjecture לקטר on the basis of Greek and Vulgate is a *lectio facilior* (Tagliacarne 1989: 169-70). Since המקטרים can hardly designate a profession, the participle must have originally specified the cultic activity of the כמרים.

111. The absence of a copula before לשמש reveals לבעל to be a later insertion (in view of Jer. 7.9; 11.13, 17; 32.29; cf. Tagliacarne 1989: 182; *pace* Arneth 2001: 201).

112. Levin 1984: 360 (= 2003: 205) with a thoughtless quote from Budde in n. 35: 'The כמרים are undoubtedly the same people as the כהנים of the high places from all the cities of Judah'. Similarly Barrick 2002: 67-70, but see above, n. 94.

113. A characteristic class of seventh-century stamp seals made of dark brown limestone show a new type of individuals, some of them lyre and double-flute players, worshipping astral symbols or cult symbols of astral deities. These seals have been found at various places in Palestine/Israel, including Jerusalem, but they are not specifically limited to Judah (cf. *GGIG* §176).

114. Not extermination, unless one prefers the Greek text with Schenker (2004: 66-67), who has the idolatrous priests burned as their Samarian colleagues of v. 20. השבית only implies the cessation of activity and permanent dissolution of the institution, *pace* Levin 1984: 360 (= 2003: 205).

hold on for a while (Zeph. 1.4!), they are absent from cultic law and the books of Jeremiah and Ezekiel, books that seem to have been most concerned with ritual matters during the 'exilic' and 'post-exilic' periods. Apparently, כמרים no longer practised in Judah after the exile. It is therefore scarcely conceivable that their dissolution by King Josiah was only an invention of a post-exilic redactor.

3.4. *Roof Altars (2 Kings 23.12*)*
Let us examine a third measure: the destruction of the altars that the kings of Judah had set up 'on the roof of the upper chamber of Ahaz'.[115] Again, it is probable that the narrator relies on outside information with a pre-deuteronomistic kernel. The roof altars may well belong to the context of seventh-century astral cult practices, since nocturnal worship addressed to the gods of the night and the stars of heaven fits very well a setting on the roofs. Unfortunately, however, no primary sources support this hypothesis. Offering sacrifices on the roofs does not seem to be an Assyrian or Aramean custom. Spieckermann's assertion that 'Assyrian influence is obvious' (1982: 109)[116] is surely overstated. A piece of evidence from the Ugaritic Kirtu epic (KTU 1.14 II 20-27, IV 3-8) is too remote to offer any help. Zephaniah 1.5 and Jer. 19.13 (cf. 32.29) mention incense offerings presented to the 'host of heaven' on the roofs of Jerusalem. The roof altars of 2 Kgs 23.12* must have served the same purpose. However, whereas in Zephaniah and Jeremiah private (household?) cult is envisioned, as shown by the plural הגגות ('roofs', 2 Kgs 23.12*) seems to presuppose cult practices in the precincts of the Temple.[117] The passages quoted from the books of Zephaniah and Jeremiah, which assume that worship on the roofs continued after Josiah's reform, therefore do not contradict the historicity of Josiah's measures, since they remained confined to the temple and, again, affected a *specific* cult practice, namely sacrifice.[118]

* * *

To sum up, the end of the seventh century, quite an 'axial age' in the history of the region, still offers the most plausible religious-historical background for the three reform measures discussed above, albeit with a different degree of certainty for each. We do not know if all three purges occurred at the same period of time. Obviously, 2 Kings 23 does present the reforms in a chronological order (Lohfink 1991a: 219-21). Still, a certain coherence may be discerned:

115. The 'upper chamber of Ahaz' (עלית אחז) is often considered a gloss by modern commentators. In contrast, the Antiochene Greek text speaks of 'the roof*s* of the upper chamber*s* of *King* Ahaz', cf. Schenker 2004: 72-75. According to Schenker, who again favours the Greek text, these upper chambers were probably meant to be situated within the temple compound.
116. R. Borger, Spieckermann's mentor and expert resource for Assyriological matters, would have pointed to roof altars if they were known from Assyrian texts.
117. Cf. n. 115.
118. Indeed, altars, not observatories, are the topic here, and thus it is doubtful whether 'a religious interpretation of astronomical phenomena' in the technical sense was the concern (*pace* Spieckermann 1982: 109; Lowery 1991: 205). Note that מזלות are mentioned, typically enough, in v. 5, but neither in v. 12 nor, for that matter, in Zeph. 1.5; Jer. 19.13; 32.29. Cf. Taylor 1993: 168-72.

1. All three purges are concerned with the elimination of practices that have lost their plausibility in view of the changed political climate with its new economic and cultural orientation and significantly lessened contacts with northern Syria and Assyria. Also, their upkeep costs (horses, a society of priests, roof-sacrifice) perhaps no longer stood in a realistic relationship to projected benefits and usefulness.
2. All three concentrated on the Jerusalem Temple, that is, on the royal shrine and the state cult, and did not affect cults outside of the capital, not even guild and family cults practised in the city. In this respect, their profile is, for example, clearly different from the desecration of the Tophet in the Valley of Hinnom (2 Kgs 23.10), whose historicity can be doubted in view of the continued polemic of much later times (Jer. 7.31-32; 19.5-6, 11-13; cf. 32.35; Ezek. 16.21; 20.26, 31; Lev. 18.21; 20.2-4).[119]
3. All three concern some kind of astral worship, which may be considered the hallmark of the seventh century, a period of strong Assyro-Aramean influence.[120]

Whether Josiah's purging of the Jerusalem state cult or royal shrine from rituals that had become obsolete should be called a 'religious reform' is debatable. A reform implies an agenda, but the actual motives behind those of Josiah's purges that can be historically substantiated are far from clear. The biblical sources present Josiah's reform as a 'new religious beginning' (Lohfink 1991a: 225), while modern scholars have sometimes construed it as a political-religious declaration of independence with anti-Assyrian tendencies.[121] Neither of these two rather far-reaching agendas seem to fit the more confined picture based on critical historical research.

4. Correlations between Primary and Secondary Sources?
On the Removal of the Jerusalem Asherah (2 Kings 23.6)

The observations presented thus far have sought entry into the religious history of Judah and Jerusalem from two sides. Looking back, I realize that to a large extent the two paths run off quite independently one from another. Methodologically, this has the advantage of avoiding biblicist or historicist short circuits. The last section has also demonstrated, however, that our picture of the religious history of Judah remains incomplete if we base ourselves exclusively on the

---

119. But cf. Dearman 1996.
120. Cf. *GGIG*, Chapter VIII (pp. 283-372); Barrick 2002: 159-64.
121. Cf. Lohfink 1987: 466-68; Ahlström 1993: Chapter 18; and most recently Arneth 2001: 208, 216. Two remarks are in order: first, the motives of the historical measures may have differed from those of the biblical reform report, a point acknowledged by Arneth who firmly postulates an anti-Assyrian tendency for the literary report only. Second, however, I can see no overtly anti-Assyrian stance in the report. Arneth himself seems to be hesitating on that matter, sliding from opposition against Assyria to one against 'Assyrian-influenced institutions' in his conclusions (p. 216). Asherah certainly cannot be counted among these.

archaeological primary sources. No serious historian should dismiss secondary sources on the sole argument that they cannot be confirmed with utter precision. On the other hand, we must of course endeavor to build only upon such secondary sources that plausibly fit the primary framework based on primary sources.

The correlation of primary and secondary sources is a notoriously difficult business that in many respects can only be practised as a fragile, hypothetical combination of circumstantial evidence. A catchword like *minimalist approach* does not help much. The *minimalist approach* becomes extremely *maximalist* when it approaches the sources with inappropriate expectations, just to drop them as soon as they do not respond to gross questions. Take my hypothesis that the removal of the horses and chariots of the sun-god from the precincts of the Temple did in fact happen under Josiah: to see these measures confirmed through primary sources would be extremely unlikely. What kind of sources should we expect? An ostracon with instructions for the Nathanmelek, a dated receipt from the royal stable master for having received a number of horses to be trained for military service? Chariot fittings with solar symbols in the Kidron Valley? There is no purpose in drawing up the agenda for forgers of 'biblical antiquities'. We can know so little about the past, that we should endeavor to interpret adequately what little we have.

Still, there is *one* correlation which may supplement the picture of Josiah's reform efforts as we have sketched them thus far. 2 Kings 23.6 reports that Josiah removed the Asherah from the Temple of Yahweh to the Kidron Valley, had it burned there and the dust thrown on the graves of the common people. Many consider this report, which doubtlessly responds to 2 Kgs 21.7, particularly suspect of deuteronomistic prejudice. Yet, consider the omission of *'šrth* in the later Judahite blessing formulae; consider that those of the Jerusalem elite who possessed seals appear to have placed no importance whatsoever to specific Asherah symbolism; consider the long- and medium-term transfer of divine roles and competences to Yahweh: you may then hesitate to hold Josiah's removal of Asherah from the Jerusalem Temple as a mere invention. As far as I can see, there are neither primary nor secondary sources that attest to the existence of Asherah in the Jerusalem Temple (be it as a cult symbol or as a statue of a goddess) after Josiah.[122] It may well be that the removal of personified 'evil' towards Shinar in Zechariah's sixth vision (Zech. 5.5-11) concerns the banning of a goddess, formerly worshipped 'in the entire land' (v. 6). But the text is enigmatic enough and does not provide evidence for a continued worship of Asherah in the pre-exilic temple of Jerusalem.[123]

Let us stop here, before removing ourselves too far from likelihood towards sheer possibility, which would go beyond the limits of sensible historical work. Still other reform efforts mentioned in 2 Kings 23 could well go back to the

---

122. A stamped terracotta relief applied on a sixth-century vessel from En-Gedi, portraying an enthroned man with a raised hand before a stylized tree (*GGIG* fig. 348), may come close to the idea of a royal Asherah cult. However, it can scarcely be correlated unambiguously with the Jerusalem Temple, and is probably a Phoenician product.

123. *GGIG* §227; Uehlinger 1994: 93-103.

historical Josiah, though the current lack of sources prevents us from evaluating these reforms with probability comparable to that offered in the cases above.[124]

5. Conclusion

The last thirty years or so of Old Testament scholarship has witnessed a strong general trend towards a late dating of biblical sources to the 'late pre-exilic', 'exilic' or 'post-exilic' period. At the same time, ever increasing weight has been placed on the importance of archaeological primary sources for the reconstruction of the history of Israel and Judah. Recently, archaeology has in turn come in the maelstrom of 'down-dating' with the important debate on I. Finkelstein's 'Low chronology' proposal. From the point of view of historiography and its methodological awareness, the trend towards the primary sources can only be welcomed. Nothing remains for exegetes interested in historical research but to take note of the new methodological hierarchy which implies the necessary subordination of non-archaeological, secondary documentation, including the biblical texts, to primary data.

A secondary effect of this development, however, could be the drifting apart of history and theology—a process obvious since the advent of post-modernism but engaged for the past two and a half centuries at least. Lessing's assertion, 'The accidental truths of history can never become the proof of necessary truths of reason', has become just as questionable today as the *a priori* of dialectical theology, that the truth of history stands in glaring contrast to the (deceptive) truth of myth, and that (salvation) history alone may be bear revelation. These are some of the deep roots of latent 'sub-deuteronomism' of most text books on the 'history of Israel', in addition to the unquestionably difficult state of the sources that makes it easier to write a 'history' that retells the Bible rather than to get involved with the more arduous business of archaeology.

The time of Josiah and his successors until the capture of Jerusalem and the destruction of the 'First' Temple represents an 'axial age', for the religious history of Judah just as much as for the history of Old Testament theology. Though highly stylized as a time of de-connection by the deuteronomistic historians, it is also an age that provides the necessary *link* between Old Testament theology and its ancient Judahite (and ultimately 'Canaanite') roots. In the interest both of historical and theological research, we should therefore neither overstrain this link with historicist or biblicist naiveté, nor simply leap over the gap with dismissively minimalist assumptions.

---

124. In contrast to Hollenstein (1976: 327-30) and Würthwein (1976: 417; but see 1984: 452-53, 456), I do not consider the destruction of the cult utensils in 2 Kgs 23.4 to be part of Josiah's historical measures. The controversy over the proper cult utensils occurred in the early post-exilic period, cf. Ackroyd 1972: 166-81. On a literary and ideological level, Josiah's destruction of all utensils used in foreign cults is the premise for the concept that only pure utensils were carried off to Babylon (2 Kgs 25.14; Jer. 27.18, 21-22, note the discrepancies between the MT and OG!). Those returning from exile could use this argument to legitimate their claims to control the Second Temple.

Bibliography

Ackroyd, Peter R.
    1972   'The Temple Vessels: A Continuity Theme', in G.W. Anderson *et al.* (eds.), *Studies in the Religion of Ancient Israel* (VTSup, 23; Leiden: E.J. Brill, 1972): 166-81.

Aharoni, Miriam
    1993   'Arad: The Israelite Citadels', in E. Stern (ed.), *New Encyclopaedia of Archaeological Excavations in the Holy Land* (4 vols.; Jerusalem: Israel Exploration Society): I, 82-87.

Ahlström, Gösta W.
    1991   'The Role of Archaeological and Literary Remains in Reconstructing Israel's History', in Edelman (ed.) 1991: 116-41.
    1993   *The History of Ancient Palestine from the Palaeoloithic Period to Alexander's Conquest* (JSOTSup, 146; Sheffield: Sheffield Academic Press).

Albertz, Rainer
    1992   *Religionsgeschichte Israels in alttestamentlicher Zeit* (Altes Testament Deutsch Ergänzungsbände = Grundrisse zum Alten Testament, 8; Göttingen: Vandenhoeck & Ruprecht).
    1994   *A History of Israelite Religion in the Old Testament Period: From the Beginnings to the End of the Monarchy* (OTL; Louisville, KY: Westminster/ John Knox Press).

Arneth, Martin
    2001   'Die antiassyrische Reform Josias von Juda. Überlegungen zur Komposition und Intention von 2 Reg 23,4-15', *Zeitschrift für Altorientalische und Biblische Rechtsgeschichte* 7: 189-216.

Avigad, Nahman
    1986   *Hebrew Bullae from the Time of Jeremiah: Remnants of a Burnt Archive* (Jerusalem: Israel Exploration Society).

Avigad, Nahman, Michael Heltzer and André Lemaire
    2000   *West Semitic Seals: Eighth–Sixth Centuries BCE* (The Reuben and Edith Hecht Museum Collection, vol. B; Haifa: Reuben and Edith Hecht Museum).

Avigad, Nahman, and Benjamin Sass
    1997a   *Corpus of West Semitic Seals* (Jerusalem: Israel Academy of Sciences and Humanities).
    1997b   *Corpus of West Semitic Stamp Seals* (Jerusalem: Israel Exploration Society).

Barkay, Gabriel
    1992   'The Priestly Benediction on Silver Plaques from Ketef Hinnom in Jerusalem', *TA* 19: 139-92.

Barrick, W. Boyd
    2002   *The King and the Cemeteries: Toward a New Understanding of Josiah's Reform* (VTSup, 88; Leiden: E.J. Brill).

Beuken, W.A.M.
    1993   'משכב', in J. Botterweck *et al.* (eds.), *Theologisches Wörterbuch zum Alten Testament*, VII (Stuttgart: W. Kohlhammer): 1306-18.

Brandfon, Frederick R.
    1987   'Kinship, Culture and "Longue Durée"', *JSOT* 39: 30-38.

Braudel, Fernand
    1990   *La Méditerranée et le monde méditerranéen à l'époque de Philippe II* (Paris: Armand Colin, 9th edn [first published 1949]).

    1958   'Histoire et sciences sociales, la longue durée', *Annales. Économies, Sociétés, Civilisations* 13: 725-53; reprinted in F. Braudel, *Écrits sur l'histoire*, I (Champs, 23; Paris: Flammarion, 1984): 44-61.

Claburn, W. Eugene
    1973   'The Fiscal Basis of Joasiah's Reforms', *JBL* 92: 11-22.

Cogan, Mordechai
    1974   *Imperialism and Religion: Assyria, Judah and Israel in the Eighth and Seventh Centuries B.C.E.* (SBLMS, 19; Missoula, MT: Scholars Press).
    1993   'Judah under Assyrian Hegemony: A Reexamination of Imperialism and Religion', *JBL* 112: 403-14.

Conrad, Diethelm
    1979   'Einige (archäologische) Miszellen zur Kultgeschichte Judas in der Königszeit', in A.H.J. Gunneweg and O. Kaiser (ed.), *Textgemäß. Aufsätze und Beiträge zur Hermeneutik des Alten Testaments* (Festschrift E. Würthwein; Göttingen: Vandenhoeck & Ruprecht): 28-32.

Coogan, M., J.C. Exum and L.E. Stager (eds.)
    1994   *Scripture and Other Artifacts: Essays on the Bible and Archaeology in Honor of Philip J. King* (Louisville, KY: Westminster/John Knox Press).

Coote, Robert B., and Keith W. Whitelam
    1987   *The Emergence of Early Israel in Historical Perspective* (SWBA, 5; Sheffield: Sheffield Academic Press).

Dearman, John A.
    1996   'The Tophet in Jerusalem: Archaeology and Cultural Profile', *JNSL* 22: 59-71.

Deutsch, Robert
    1999   *Messages from the Past: Hebrew Bullae from the Time of Isaiah Through the Destruction of the First Temple* (Tel Aviv-Jaffa: Archaeological Center Publications).
    2003a   *Biblical Period Hebrew Bullae: The Josef Chaim Kaufman Collection* (Tel Aviv-Jaffa: Archaeological Center Publications).
    2003b   'A Hoard of Fifty Hebrew Bullae from the Time of Hezekiah', in *idem* (ed.), *Shlomo: Studies in Epigraphy, Iconography, History and Archaeology in Honor of Shlomo Moussaieff* (Tel Aviv-Jaffa: Archaeological Center Publications): 45-98.

Deutsch, Robert, and Michael Heltzer
    1994   *Forty New [sic] Ancient West Semitic Inscriptions* (Tel Aviv-Jaffa: Archaeological Center Publications).
    1995   *New Epigraphic Evidence from the Biblical Period* (Tel Aviv-Jaffa: Archaeological Center Publications).
    1997   *Windows to the Past* (Tel Aviv-Jaffa: Archaeological Center Publications).
    1999   *West Semitic Epigraphic News of the 1st Millennium BCE.* With a contribution by Gabriel Barkay (Tel Aviv-Jaffa: Archaeological Center Publications).

Deutsch, Robert, and André Lemaire
    2003   *The Adoniram Collection of West Semitic Inscriptions* (Tel Aviv-Jaffa: Archaeological Center Publications).

Dever, William G.
    1994   'The Silence of the Text: An Archaeological Commentary on 2 Kings 23', in Coogan, Exum and Stager (eds.) 1994: 143-68.

Edelman, Diana V. (ed.)
    1991   *The Fabric of History: Text, Artifact and Israel's Past* (JSOTSup, 127; Sheffield: Sheffield Academic Press).

Eggler, Jürg
    2003   'Die eisen-II-zeitlichen Siegel und -abdrücke aus Grabungen in Moab', in F. Ninow (ed.), *Wort und Stein. Studien zur Theologie und Archäologie* (Beiträge zur Erforschung der antiken Moabitis [Ard el-Kerak], 4; Frankfurt: Peter Lang): 33-87.
Einykel, Erik
    1995   *The Reform of King Josiah and the Composition of the Deuteronomistic History* (OTS, 33; Leiden: E.J. Brill).
Fried, Lisbeth E.
    2002   'The High Places (*BĀMÔT*) and the Reforms of Hezekiah and Josiah: An Archaeological Investigation', *JAOS* 122: 437-65.
Gieselmann, Bernd
    1994   'Die sogenannte josianische Reform in der gegenwärtigen Forschung', *ZAW* 106: 223-42.
Gross, W. (ed.)
    1995   *Jeremia und die 'deuteronomistische Bewegung'* (BBB, 98; Weinheim: Beltz Athenäum).
Hardmeier, Christof
    2000   'König Joschija in der Klimax des DtrG (2Reg 22f.) und das vordtr Dokument einer Kultreform am Residenzort (23,4-15*). Quellenkritik, Vorstufenrekonstruktion und Geschichtstheologie in 2Reg 22f.', in R. Lux (ed.), *Erzählte Geschichte. Beiträge zur narrativen Kultur im alten Israel* (Biblisch-Theologische Studien, 40; Neukirchen–Vluyn: Neukirchener Verlag): 81-145.
Hardmeier, Christof (ed.)
    2001   *Steine—Bilder—Texte. Historische Evidenz außerbiblischer und biblischer Quellen* (Arbeiten zur Bibel und ihrer Geschichte, 5; Leipzig: Evangelische Verlagsanstalt).
Herzog, Ze'ev
    1997   'Arad: Iron Age Period', in E. Meyers (ed.), *The Oxford Encyclopedia of Archaeology in the Near East* (5 vols.; Oxford: Oxford University Press): I, 174-76.
    2001   'The Date of the Temple at Arad: Reassessment of the Stratigraphy and the Implications for the History of Religion in Judah', in A. Mazar (ed.), *Studies in the Archaeology of the Iron Age in Israel and Jordan* (JSOTSup, 331; Sheffield: Sheffield Academic Press): 156-78.
    2002   'The Fortress Mound at Tel Arad: An Interim Report', *TA* 29: 3-109.
Herzog, Ze'ev, Miriam Aharoni, Anson F. Rainey and Shmuel Moshkovitz
    1984   'The Israelite Fortress at Arad', *BASOR* 254: 1-34.
Hjelm, Ingrid
    1999   'Cult Centralization as a Device of Cult Control?', *SJOT* 13: 298-309.
Hoffmann, Hans-Detlef
    1980   *Reform und Reformen. Untersuchungen zu einem Grundthema der deuteronomistischen Geschichtsschreibung* (ATANT, 66; Zürich: TVZ).
Holladay, John S.
    1987   'Religion in Israel and Judah Under the Monarchy: An Explicitly Archaeological Approach', in Miller, Hanson and McBride (eds.) 1987: 249-99.
Hollenstein, Helmut
    1977   'Literarkritische Erwägungen zum Bericht über die Reformmaßnahmen Josias 2 Kön. xxiii 4ff'., *VT* 27: 321-36.
Keel, Othmar, and Max Küchler
    1982   *Orte und Landschaften der Bibel. Ein Handbuch und Studienreiseführer.* II. *Der Süden* (Zürich: Benziger; Göttingen: Vandenhoeck & Ruprecht).

Keel, Othmar, and Christoph Uehlinger
- 1992 *Göttinnen, Götter und Gottessymbole. Neue Erkenntnisse zur Religionsgeschichte Kanaans und Israels aufgrund bislang unerschlossener ikonographischer Quellen* (QD, 134; Freiburg: Herder [5th edn 2001]).
- 1994 'Jahwe und die Sonnengottheit von Jerusalem', in W. Dietrich and M. Klopfenstein (eds.), *Ein Gott allein? JHWH-Verehrung und biblischer Monotheismus im Kontext der israelitischen und altorientalischen Religionsgeschichte* (OBO, 139; Freiburg: Universitätsverlag; Göttingen: Vandenhoeck & Ruprecht): 269-306.

Kletter, Raz
- 1996 *Judaean Pillar-Figurines and the Archaeology of Asherah* (BAR International Series, 636; Oxford: Tempus Reparatum).

Knauf, Ernst Axel
- 1991a 'From History to Interpretation', in Edelman (ed.) 1991: 26-64.
- 1991b 'King Solomon's Copper Supply', in E. Lipiński (ed.), *Phoenicia and the Bible* (Studia Phoenicia, 11; Orientalia Lovaniensia Analecta, 44; Leuven: Peeters): 167-86.
- 2002 'Who Destroyed Beersheba II?', in U. Hübner and E.A. Knauf (eds.), *Kein Land für sich allein. Studien zum Kulturkintakt in Kanaan, Israel/Palästina und Ebirnâri für Manfred Weippert zum 65. Geburtstag* (OBO, 186; Freiburg: Universitätsverlag; Göttingen: Vandenhoeck & Ruprecht): 181-95.

Koch, Klaus
- 1992 'Gefüge und Herkunft des Berichts über die Kultreformen des Königs Josia. Zugleich ein Beitrag zur Bestimmung hebräischer "Tempora"', in J. Hausmann and H.-J. Zobel (eds.), *Alttestamentlicher Glaube und Biblische Theologie* (Festschrift H.D. Preuss; Stuttgart: W. Kohlhammer): 80-92.
- 1999 'Molek astral', in A. Lange, H. Lichtenberger and D. Römheld (eds.), *Mythos im Alten Testament und seiner Umwelt* (Festschrift H.-P. Müller; BZAW, 278; Berlin: W. de Gruyter): 29-50.

Laato, Antti
- 1992 *Josiah and David Redivivus: The Historical Josiah and the Messianic Expectations of Exilic and Postexilic Times* (ConBOT, 33; Stockholm: Almqvist & Wiksell).

Lemaire, André
- 1977 'Les inscriptions de Khirbet el-Qôm et l'Ashérah de Yhwh', *RB* 84 : 595-608.
- 1999 'New Palaeo-Hebrew Seals and Bullae', *ErIs* 26: 106*-15*.

Levin, Christoph
- 1984 'Joschija im deuteronomistischen Geschichtswerk', *ZAW* 96: 351-71; reprinted in C. Levin, *Fortschreibungen. Gesammelte Studien zum Alten Testament* (BZAW, 316; Berlin: W. de Gruyter, 2003): 198-216.

Lohfink, Norbert
- 1985 'Zur neueren Diskussion über 2 Kön 22–23', in *idem* (ed.) 1985: 24-48; reprinted in Lohfink 1991b: 179-207.
- 1987 'The Cult Reform of Josiah of Judah: 2 Kings 22–23 as a Source for the History of Israelite Religion', in Miller, Hanson and McBride (eds.) 1987: 459-75.
- 1991a 'Die Kultreform Joschijas von Juda. 2 Kön 22–23 als religionsgeschichtliche Quelle', in Lohfink 1991b: 209-27.
- 1991b *Studien zum Deuteronomium und zur deuteronomistischen Literatur II* (Stuttgarter Bibilische Aufsatz-Bände, 12; Stuttgart: Katholisches Bibelwerk).

1995 'Gab es eine deuteronomistische Bewegung?', in Gross (ed.) 1995: 313-82; reprinted in N. Lohfink, *Studien zum Deuteronomium und zur deuteronomistischen Literatur III* (Stuttgarter Bibilische Aufsatz-Bände, 20; Stuttgart: Katholisches Bibelwerk, 1996): 65-142.

Lohfink, Norbert (ed.)
1985 *Das Deuteronomium. Entstehung, Gestalt und Botschaft* (BETL, 68; Leuven: Peeters).

Lopasso, V.
1999 'La riforma di Giosia nel Nord', *BeO* 41: 29-40.

Lowery, Richard H.
1991 *The Reforming Kings: Cult and Society in First Temple Judah* (JSOTSup, 120; Sheffield: Sheffield Academic Press).

Mazar, Amihai, and Ehud Netzer
1986 'On the Israelite Fortress at Arad', *BASOR* 263: 87-91.

McCarter, P. Kyle
1999 'The Bulla of Nathan-Melech, the Servant of the King', in P.H. Williams and Th. Hiebert (eds.), *Realia Dei* (Festschrift E.F. Campbell; Scholars Press Homage Series, 23; Atlanta: Scholars Press): 142-53.

Miller, P.D., P.D. Hanson and S.D. McBride (eds.)
1987 *Ancient Israelite Religion* (Festschrift F.M. Cross; Philadelphia: Fortress Press).

Müller, Hans-Peter
1992 'Kolloquialsprache und Volksreligion in den Inschriften von Kuntillet 'Aǧrūd und Kirbet el-Qōm', *ZAH* 5: 15-51.

Na'aman, Nadav
1991 'The Kingdom of Judah under Josiah', *TA* 18: 3-71.
1995 'The Debated Historicity of Hezekiah's Reform in the Light of Historical and Archaeological Research', *ZAW* 107: 179-95.
1996 'The Dedicated Treasures Buildings within the House of Yhwh where Women Weave Coverings for Asherah (2 Kings 23,7)', *BN* 83: 17-18.
2002 'The Abandonment of Cult Places in the Kingdoms of Israel and Judah as Acts of Cult Reform', *UF* 34: 585-602.
2003 'The Distribution of Messages in the Kingdom of Judah in Light of the Lachish Ostraca', *VT* 53: 169-80.

Nakhai, Beth Alpert
2001 *Archaeology and the Religions of Canaan and Israel* (ASOR Books, 7; Boston, MA: American Schools of Oriental Research).

Niehr, Herbert
1995 'Die Reform des Joschija. Methodische, historische und religionsgeschichtliche Aspekte', in Gross (ed.) 1995: 33-55.
1999 'Auf dem Weg zu einer Religionsgeschichte Israels und Judas. Annäherungen an einen Problemkreis', in B. Janowski and M. Köckert (eds.), *Religionsgeschichte Israels. Formale und materiale Aspekte* (VWGTh, 15; Gütersloh: Gütersloher Verlagshaus): 57-78.

Ornan, Tallay
1993 'The Mesopotamian Influence on West Semitic Inscribed Seals: A Preference for the Depiction of Mortals', in Sass and Uehlinger (eds.) 1993: 52-73.

Paul, M.J.
1985 'Hilkiah and the Law (2 Kings 22) in the 17th and 18th Centuries: Some Influences on W.M.L. de Wette', in Lohfink (ed.) 1985: 9-12.

Pongratz-Leisten, Beate, Karlheinz Deller and Erika Bleibtreu
    1992   'Götterstreitwagen und Götterstandarten: Götter auf dem Feldzug und ihr Kult im Feldlager', *Baghdader Mitteilungen* 23: 291-356.

Preuss, Horst Dietrich
    1982   *Deuteronomium* (Erträge der Forschung, 164; Darmstadt: Wissenschaftliche Buchgesellschaft).
    1993   'Zum deuteronomistischen Geschichtswerk', *TRu* 58: 229-64.

Rainey, Anson F.
    1994   'Hezekiah's Reform and the Altars at Beersheba and Arad', in Coogan, Exum and Stager (eds.) 1994: 333-54.

Renz, Johannes
    1995   *Die althebräischen Inschriften*. I. *Text und Kommentar* (Handbuch der althebräischen Epigraphik, 1; Darmstadt: Wissenschaftliche Buchgesellschaft).
    2001   'Der Beitrag der althebräischen Epigraphik zur Exegese des Alten Testaments und zur Profan- und Religionsgeschichte Palästinas. Leistung und Grenzen, aufgezeigt am Beispiel der Inschriften des (ausgehenden) 7. Jahrhunderts vor Christus', in Hardmeier (ed.) 2001: 123-58.

Reuter, Eleonore
    1993   *Kultzentralisation. Zur Entstehung und Theologie von Dtn 12* (BBB, 87; Frankfurt: Hain).

Sass, Benjamin
    1993   'The Pre-Exilic Hebrew Seals: Iconism vs. Aniconism', in Sass and Uehlinger (eds.) 1993: 194-256.

Sass, Benjamin, and Christoph Uehlinger (eds.)
    1993   *Studies in the Iconography of Northwest Semitic Inscribed Seals* (OBO, 125; Fribourg: University Press; Göttingen: Vandenhoeck & Ruprecht).

Schenker, Adrian
    2004   *Älteste Textgeschichte der Königsbücher. Die hebräische Vorlage der ursprünglichen Septuaginta als älteste Textform der Königsbücher* (OBO, 199; Fribourg: Academic Press; Göttingen: Vandenhoeck & Ruprecht).

Schroer, Silvia
    1987   *In Israel gab es Bilder. Nachrichten von darstellender Kunst im Alten Testament* (OBO, 74; Freiburg: Universitätsverlag; Göttingen: Vandenhoeck & Ruprecht).

Seidl, Ursula
    1989   *Die babylonischen Kudurru-Reliefs. Symbole mesopotamischer Gottheiten* (OBO, 87; Freiburg: Universitätsverlag; Göttingen: Vandenhoeck & Ruprecht).

Shiloh, Yigal
    1986   'A Group of Hebrew Bullae from the City of David', *IEJ* 36: 16-38.

Shiloh, Yigal, and David Tarler
    1986   'Bullae from the City of David: A Hoard of Seal Impressions from the Israelite Period', *BA* 49: 196-209.

Shoham, Yair
    1994   'A Group of Hebrew Bullae from Yigal Shiloh's Excavations in the City of David', in H. Geva (ed.), *Ancient Jerusalem Revealed* (Jerusalem: Israel Exploration Society): 55-61.
    2000   'Hebrew Bullae', in D.T. Ariel (ed.), *Excavations in the City of David*. VI. *Inscriptions* (Qedem, 41; Jerusalem: Institute of Archaeology, Hebrew University): 29-57.

Singer-Avitz, Lily
    2002   'Arad: The Iron Age Pottery Assemblages', *TA* 29: 110-214.

Spieckermann, Hermann
    1982   *Juda unter Assur in der Sargonidenzeit* (FRLANT, 129; Göttingen: Vandenhoeck & Ruprecht).
Starr, Ivan
    1990   *Queries to the Sungod: Divination and Politics in Sargonid Assyria* (SAA, 4; Helsinki: Helsinki University Press).
Swanson, Kristin A.
    2002   'A Reassessment of Hezekiah's Reform in Light of Jar Handles and Iconographic Evidence', *CBQ* 64: 460-69.
Sweeney, Marvin A.
    2001   *King Josiah of Judah: The Lost Messiah of Israel* (New York and Oxford: Oxford University Press).
Tagliacarne, Pierfelice
    1989   *'Keiner war wie er'. Untersuchung zur Struktur von 2 Könige 22–23* (ATSAT, 31; St Ottilien: EOS).
Taylor, J. Glenn
    1993   *Yahweh and the Sun: Biblical and Archaeological Evidence for Sun Worship in Ancient Israel* (JSOTSup, 111; Sheffield: JSOT Press).
Toloni, G.
    1998   'Una strage di sacerdoti? Dalla storiografia alla storia in 2 Re 23,4b-5', *Estudios Bíblicos* 56: 41-60.
Uehlinger, Christoph
    1993   'Northwest Semitic Inscribed Seals, Iconography and Syro-Palestinian Religions of Iron Age II: Some Afterthoughts and Conclusions', in Sass and Uehlinger (eds.) 1993: 257-88.
    1994   'Die Frau im Efa (Sach 5,5-11): eine Programmvision von der Abschiebung der Göttin', *Bibel und Kirche* 49: 93-103.
    1995   'Gab es eine joschijanische Kultreform? Plädoyer für ein begründetes Minimum', in Gross (ed.) 1995: 57-89.
    1996   'Astralkultpriester und Fremdgekleidete, Kanaanvolk und Silberwäger. Zur Verknüpfung von Kult- und Sozialkritik in Zefanja 1', in W. Dietrich and M. Schwantes (ed.), *'Der Tag wird kommen'. Ein interkontextuelles Gespräch über das Buch des Propheten Zefanja* (Stuttgarter Bibel-Studien, 170; Stuttgart: Katholisches Bibelwerk): 49-83.
    1997   'Review of Eynikel 1996', *BO* 57: 144-51.
    1998   'Westsemitisch beschriftete Stempelsiegel: ein Corpus und neue Fragen', *Bib* 79: 103-19 (review of Avigad and Sass, *Corpus of West Semitic Seals*).
    2001   'Bildquellen und "Geschichte Israels": grundsätzliche Überlegungen und Fallbeispiele', in Hardmeier (ed.) 2001: 25-77.
Ussishkin, David
    1988   'The Date of the Judaean Shrine at Arad', *IEJ* 38: 142-57.
Von Soden, Wolfram
    1991   'Gab es bereits im vorexilischen Hebräisch Aramaismen in der Bildung und der Verwendung von Verbalformen?', *ZAH* 4: 32-45.
Weinfeld, Moshe
    1972   'The Worship of Molech and the Queen of Heaven and its Background', *UF* 4: 133-54.
    1991   *Deuteronomy 1–11* (AB, 5; Garden City, NY: Doubleday).
Weippert, Helga
    1981   *Schöpfer des Himmels und der Erde. Ein Beitrag zur Theologie des Jeremiabuches* (Stuttgarter Bibel-Studien, 102; Stuttgart: Katholisches Bibelwerk).

1988   *Palästina in vorhellenistischer Zeit* (Handbuch der Archäologie, Vorderasien II.1; Munich: Beck).

Weippert, Helga, and Manfred Weippert
1991   'Die Vorgeschichte Israels in neuem Licht', *TRu* 56: 341-90.

Weippert, Manfred
1990   'Die Petition eines Erntearbeiters aus *Mᵉṣad Ḥăšavyāhū* und die Syntax althebräischer erzählender Prosa', in E. Blum, C. Macholz and E.W. Stegemann (eds.), *Die Hebräische Bibel und ihre zweifache Nachgeschichte* (Festschrift R. Rendtorff; Neukirchen–Vluyn: Neukirchener Verlag): 449-66.
1993   'Geschichte Israels am Scheideweg', *TRu* 58: 71-103.

Whitelam, Keith
1986   'Recreating the History of Israel', *JSOT* 35: 45-70.

Würthwein, Ernst
1976   'Die joschijanische Reform und das Deuteronomium', *ZTK* 73: 395-423.
1984   *Die Bücher der Könige. I. 1. Kön. 17–2. Kön. 25* (ATD 11.2; Göttingen: Vandenhoeck & Ruprecht).

Yardeni, Ada
1991   'Remarks on the Priestly Blessing on Two Ancient Amulets from Jerusalem', *VT* 41: 176-85.

Zevit, Ziony
2001   *The Religions of Ancient Israel: A Synthesis of Parallactic Approaches* (London and New York: Continuum).

Zimhoni, Ora
1985   'The Iron Age Pottery of Tel 'Eton and its Relation to the Lachish, Tell Beit Mirsim and Arad Assemblages', *TA* 12: 63-90; reprinted in Zimhoni 1997: 179-210.
1990   'Two Ceramic Assemblages from Lachish Levels III and II', *Tel Aviv* 17: 3-52; reprinted in Zimhoni 1997: 211-62.
1997   *Studies in the Iron Age Pottery of Israel: Typological, Archaeological and Chronological Aspects* (Tel Aviv Occasional Publications, 2; Tel Aviv: Institute of Archaeology, 1997).

Zwickel, Wolfgang
1990   *Räucherkult und Räuchergeräte. Exegetische und archäologische Studien zum Räucheropfer im Alten Testament* (OBO, 97; Freiburg: Universitätsverlag; Göttingen: Vandenhoeck & Ruprecht).
1999   'Die Wirtschaftsreform des Hiskia und die Sozialkritik der Propheten', *EvT* 59: 356-77.

THE IMPORTANCE OF THE ARCHAEOLOGY OF THE SEVENTH CENTURY

David A. Warburton

Introduction

Jerusalem plays a significant role in the seventh century, both in terms of the archaeology and the biblical record, as even the widely differing interpretations of the archaeology implicitly agree. The traditional view argues that Judah and Israel were the 'dominant powers in Palestine during Iron Age II' (Mazar 1990: 531). Following an alternative approach, Finkelstein and Silberman stress the uneven development of the two kingdoms, but in detail they argue that the final state of Judah was the result of 'a long and gradual development over hundreds of years' (2001: 239). Most thus concur that the eclipse of Judah at the end of the seventh century terminated a period of formation and consolidation. Opinions may diverge over the 'chronology', but they converge on the idea that the archaeology of Judah and Jerusalem can be traced back several centuries, that it represents a substantial degree of continuity, and that the seventh century is merely a culmination.

These views differ distinctly from a global approach which lays more emphasis on the divergences between the Old Testament record and the Near Eastern sources. Archaeology in Palestine has revealed significant disparities between the records and the evidence. Certainly the evidence of a 'conquest' by Joshua is lacking, given, for example, the discrepancies between the evidence and the related story at, for instance, Jericho and Fara which indicate that these settlements were simply not occupied at the time. This is a characteristic problem with many of the texts, and encourages many to adopt a literary approach suggesting that the archaeological evidence is simply not relevant to the understanding of the Bible.

I would argue that a more nuanced image of the archaeology of the seventh century can be gained by contrasting it not only with the north, but also by drawing attention to assumptions about the preceding and following centuries. The following is an attempt at contrasting the actual archaeological material and the discussions of that material by archaeologists. It is not an attempt to present an alternative overview of the archaeology, but rather to draw attention to those points where the archaeological material can be interpreted in a different fashion than has generally been done. (It is assumed that the reader can develop an idea of the context from such sources as Ben-Tor 1992; Levy 1998; Weippert 1988;

NEAEHL; see also the survey offered by L.L. Grabbe in the present volume [pp. 78-122, above].)

I will argue that the archaeology of the seventh century is far from representative of continuity, but rather that it reflects a particular situation. It will be argued here that the archaeological evidence can be interpreted as indicating that Judah was a successor to—rather than contemporary with—Israel. Part of the argument will be based on the assumption that that the archaeological evidence is sufficient to assert that it need not necessarily be linked to a 'long and gradual development'. Finally, it will be suggested that this has implications for the interpretation of the biblical message as well as the narrative.

The Political Context

The eighth century brought an end to the Northern Kingdom of Israel, as this was incorporated into the Assyrian Empire, along with the coastal plain. From the mid-eighth century onwards, the largest and most important cities of the land were therefore those of the Assyrians: Samaria, Dan, Megiddo, Ashdod, Ekron, Ashkelon, etc. The history of Ekron is characteristic: after a brief *floruit* at the beginning of the Iron Age, the Philistine settlement at Ekron contracted significantly before reviving under the Assyrians. Under the Assyrians it became an industrial-scale producer of olive oil, and 'one of the largest Iron Age sites in Israel' (*NEAEHL*: 1051).

For the earlier period, the Mesha inscription demonstrates that Israel was hardly a dominant power before the advent of the Assyrians. Finkelstein and Silberman (2001) observe that the role of Judah before the Assyrian conquests was that of 'hinterland', and their interpretation is perhaps the most generous approach which could correspond to the archaeology. Combined with the material of the seventh century, this would mean than an approach suggesting that Israel and Judah were the dominant powers of Iron II must be modified, since the evidence implies that the Assyrians and/or Philistines must be accommodated and recognized as the major powers. Like the cities of Philistia, some of the Israelite cities may have flourished under Assyrian rule (e.g. Dan, Samaria), while some reveal mere traces of Assyrian presence (Hazor, Gezer). Aside from Jerusalem, those of Judah suffered. Lachish never recovered from the assault.

Rather than suggesting that 'Israel and Judah' were the 'dominant powers' of Iron II (*pace* Mazar), it would be more accurate to state that for a century (c. 850–750 BCE) Israel (alone) was 'a' power in a very crowded region, and that Assyria was the major power in Palestine for most of the seventh century.

Survey

The eighth century ended with the construction of a city-wall at Jerusalem, and the elaboration of a pre-existing water supply system. The new city wall and an additional gate cut through residential housing, possibly representing a reaction to the Assyrian assault. The reality and date of these fortifications can hardly be doubted, as Sennacherib himself records that Hezekiah was caught behind his own walls 'like a bird in a cage' (*ANET*: 288; cf. the essays in Grabbe [ed.] 2003). Although differing on details, the archaeological evidence, the Old Testament narrative (2 Kgs 18–19) and the Assyrian records (*ANET*: 288) agree that Jerusalem was a walled city with gates which was isolated but not conquered.

Attention has been directed at the details (where there are differences), whereas it is more significant that from the fall of the Northern Kingdom onwards, the divergence between the Old Testament versions and the Near Eastern versions is far smaller than the contrast between the records before that time. There is no agreement about the king responsible for the fall of Samaria (cf., e.g., 2 Kgs 17.3-6 vs. *ANET*: 284), whereas virtually all of the Assyrian kings from Sennacherib onwards are linked with events and times which correspond to those known from the Assyrian records. By contrast, prior to the fall of Samaria, there is little agreement, for example, where the Old Testament has Ahab combating the Arameans, Shalmaneser III identifies them as allies, and there is little evidence to imply an Aramean invasion during the reign of Ahab (*s.v.* 'Ahab', in *ABD*). This degree of confusion exceeds that present in later parts of the Old Testament narrative, and suggests a lack of familiarity with actual events and relationships in the period up to the fall of Samaria, when the situation changes radically.

The defences of seventh-century Jerusalem therefore reflect not only a radical transformation in the defences of Jerusalem, but also in the authenticity of the Old Testament historical perspective on Palestine in the Iron Age. The close links between these records should not, however, permit us to assume that either the Assyrian or the Old Testament records need be taken at face value, and that the archaeology should merely be employed to confirm any given approach.

The successful creation of the fortified state of Judah cannot be viewed in political-military terms alone. Given the Assyrian presence in the north and along the coast, the survival of the city of Jerusalem and the independent state lay in an accommodation with the Assyrians. Although the precise character of the independence might be debatable, it is evident that the seventh-century Assyrian advances into Egypt were at least partially based upon the certainty that there was no threat from the rear, and thus the policy of Assyrian neglect during the first half of the seventh century was not based merely on Assyrian weakness vis-à-vis Babylonia, but also on the acquiescence of Judah.

The final stages of the Assyrian conquest and domination have received adequate attention, as these tales are more or less identical in both the Old Testament narrative and the ancient Near Eastern sources, and these are reflected in the archaeological record. Rather than concentrating on this concord, we will pursue an alternative approach.

The evidence of the siege and destruction at Ramat Raḥel may have distracted attention away from some aspects of the palace there. It would appear that the palace built at Ramat Raḥel was strikingly similar to the royal enclosure at Samaria, both in plan and ornamentation (Mazar 1990: 424, 427).

For the present argument, it is extremely important that in the entry in the *NEAEHL*, the introduction states that the 'excavations carried out…have established that the first settlement was founded in the ninth or eighth century' (*NEAEHL*: 1261), whereas the summary of the stratigraphy indicates the earliest level to be eighth century in date (*NEAEHL*: 1263), confirmed by the excavator who believes that 'the first Iron Age buildings were erected' in the eighth century (*NEAEHL*: 1267). It is thus clear that there is no evidence of construction before the eighth century.

Barkay (1992: 319) remarks that the 'Proto-Aeolic' capitals from Jerusalem and Ramat Raḥel 'are typologically more developed' than the northern ones, and assumes that 'the difference in form may be of chronological rather than regional significance'. This typological deduction is also the logical conclusion to be drawn from the stratigraphic fact that the earlier military defences at Ramat Raḥel were destroyed by Sennacherib, and that the sealings found there confirm a date in the late eighth century. The palace there followed later. The similarity of the typology of the capitals in Jerusalem therefore also implies that the palace at Jerusalem may likewise have been built shortly after Samaria was destroyed. Although Shiloh (1985: 131) dates the earliest material in Jerusalem to the 'Israelite Period', he cautiously clarifies that by this he means 'eighth to seventh centuries', which is actually the era of the Kingdom of Judah, contemporary with or after the demise of Israel.

A different situation prevails at Tell en-Nasbeh where the fortifications look precocious if assigned to the ninth century (*NEAEHL*: 1101), although this does not prevent such speculation. Evidence for the date of the construction of the walls is 'lacking'. A similar difficulty prevails at Lachish Level IV where the date of the erection of the fortifications cannot be established (*NEAEHL*: 905).

The date of the destruction and abandonment of both Ramat Raḥel and Lachish could not be clearer, and thus the crushing impact of the Assyrian conquests is evident. This issue has, however, permitted the date of the construction of the foundations of the defences and urban establishments at Lachish, Ramat Raḥel and Tell en-Nasbeh to be neglected, on the assumption of they can be dated to before the eighth century, although superficially at least, the archaeological data cannot support this. Why?

Part of the confusion allegedly lies in the homogeneity of the archaeological record. 'The development of the pottery style in ninth- to seventh-century B.C.E. Judah was slow, and therefore difficult to trace in detail' (Mazar 1985: 54-55). Mazar assumes that the chronological obscurity of the record is at least partially attributable to the lack of destruction levels before the Assyrian and Neo-Babylonian invasions. Mazar (1990: 416) suggests that this lack of destruction levels means that pottery assemblages cannot be isolated, and therefore the development remains unclear. However, while (a) conceding that there does not appear to be much development, he (b) also neglects the fact that such destruction levels do exist. The excavators assume that several levels of the Israelite citadel at Arad were destroyed (six strata are assigned to the period between the twelfth and seventh centuries). Nevertheless, the sequence at Arad revealed very little change in the pottery during the Iron Age, 'contrary to what might have been expected' (*NEAEHL*: 84).

Mazar (1985: 54) suggests that, as a rule, 'the evolution of pottery vessels within individual geopolitical was a slow process'. This is apparently true of

Judah, as Mazar remarks, but this is perhaps remarkable rather than a mere intellectual challenge, since elsewhere in the region there were substantial changes in the pottery assemblages, exactly as one would expect. The decoration and types used by the Philistines between the twelfth and seventh centuries vary greatly (e.g. Mazar 1990: 533). This well-documented archaeological assemblage of the first half of the first millennium is therefore significant, as a chronological marker.

Equally importantly, 'Royal Stamped Jar handles...are overwhelmingly limited to "Judaean" sites' (Holladay 1998: 373), and 'all the types were used simultaneously during the reign of Hezekiah' (Mazar 1985: 47). That material which does differ and had previously been assigned to different eras (supporting the idea of continuity and depth in the archaeological record) can thus be dated to the end of the eighth century, while the rest of the material cannot be dated.

Of particular significance in this respect is the fact that foreign pottery types are prominent in the seventh-century assemblages of the south. This contrasts not only with the earlier period, but also with the evidence of international contacts in the material from the Northern Kingdom during the earlier period. Clearly the south became more 'international' and 'urban' after the demise of the Northern Kingdom. This can clearly be linked to the history of the kingdoms.

From an archaeological standpoint, however, the absence of imports before the seventh century is significant since the absence of the easily dated foreign imports means that any evidence for the dating is also absent; that is, there is no compelling evidence to argue in favour of dating the material to an earlier period. It is only speculation about the putative antecedants of the seventh-century material which allows the same material to be assigned an earlier age. This in turn allows the speculative date for the fortifications at Tell en-Nasbeh. This logic also allows the excavators to assume an earlier date for the construction of the fortifications at Lachish.

There are breaks in the archaeological record which deserve attention, such as those in the Iron Age sequence at Lachish. Significantly, the gap terminated with the construction of the defences of the major Judaean city of Lachish is dependent upon assumptions about the biblical narrative, and these interpretations have influenced the understanding of the pottery. We have noted that the timeframe for the pottery assemblages is based on the assumption of a Judaean state in the period from the ninth century onwards, and that this is based on the biblical narrative, and not on the evidence of changes in the archaeological material.

Significantly, 'the archaeological data are insufficient to date the foundation of' either Levels IV or V at Lachish (*NEAEHL*: 905). In fact, however, it can be argued that the archaeological evidence could allow one to date these levels to the eighth century, and that only the application of the biblical narrative would suggest that the archaeological evidence is 'insufficient'.

Many of the seal impressions found at Ramat Raḥel are identical to those found at Tell en-Nasbeh, where one of the most massive fortification walls erected in Palestine was also found (*NEAEHL*: 1098-102). Significantly, some of the best preserved 'four-room houses' typical of the Iron Age were erected at

Tell en-Nasbeh, and one of them clearly post-dates the abandonment of the wall, since it was built upon part of the abandoned gate structure. The only reasonable date for the abandonment of the wall would be the Neo-Babylonian conquest. Thus, this and perhaps other typical 'four-room houses' post-date the Neo-Babylonian conquest. On the other hand, however, the parallels with Ramat Raḥel imply dates in the seventh and eighth centuries, but not compellingly earlier.

The emphasis on the antiquity of the two kingdoms has also distracted attention away from the character of the archaeology of Palestine in the seventh century. Regardless of the evidence of the Northern Kingdom, the most important archaeological sites in Palestine after the Assyrian destruction of the Northern Kingdom were not those of Judah, but rather the Philistine cities of Ashdod, Ashkelon, and Ekron. During the seventh century, although partially Philistine, the Philistine identity was syncretistic with 'Assyrian, Egyptian, Israelite and Phoenician influences' evident in the archaeological assemblage (*NEAEHL*: 1058). In fact, the major cultural entity throughout the Iron Age was Philistine, and not Israelite. It is only by identifying the Philistine cities as archaeological sites, and then assuming the validity of the biblical account that the Philistine cities can be integrated into an 'Israelite' history of the Holy Land.

All are agreed that the archaeology of Judah before the late eighth century is quite obscure, and likewise that from this point onwards the archaeology is clear. If one were to consider the archaeological material of Judah itself alone, it would be dated to the seventh century and the end of the eighth. In view of the archaeological material, it would be more suitable to view Judah as a new and insignificant state which was peripheral to the Philistines in the seventh century.

Historical Context

We will have to jump back a bit to get an idea of the historical position of seventh-century Judah in the Near Eastern context. The formation of the Israelite state has been largely viewed in isolation, reflecting the biblical tradition that a group of refugees somehow coalesced and founded a state on the ruins of the Egyptian empire in Palestine. Finkelstein and Silberman (2001: 118) take an opposing view, suggesting that the Israelites were the same Canaanites who had always been there. On linguistic grounds, this can be disputed, and the material culture of that state has been compared to both Phoenician and the Aramean city-states, and the influences clearly came from here, rather than from Egypt or from Bronze Age Palestine. Although the Phoenician city-states were the successors of their Bronze Age predecessors, the Aramean states were new creations which emerged from the chaos at the collapse of the Bronze Age. The Near Eastern sources imply that the state of Israel was more closely allied with the Arameans than the Phoenicians; certainly Israel shared the fate of the Arameans rather than that of the Phoenicians. There is thus a case for arguing that this state was new, even if some elements of its culture can be traced back in time.

Although Bronze Age Canaan was dominated by Egypt, Assyria was decisive in the Iron Age. It is widely recognized that the expansion of Assyria was among the reasons for the end of the Bronze Age political structures, and at the beginning of the first millennium BCE the campaigns of Ashurnasirpal II and Shalmaneser III took the Assyrian armies beyond the Khabur and the Balikh, and then beyond the banks of the Euphrates.

Although this appears to be mere historical continuity, it is a striking development for Shalmaneser I, Tukulti-Ninurta I and Tiglath-Pileser I had led Assyrian armies to the Mediterranean coast of the Levant after the fall of the Hittite and Mitanni empires in the second millennium, a few centuries before.

At the end of the second millennium, the string of Assyrian forts stretching across the Assyrian corridor from Assur to the Euphrates was abandoned. The Assyrian records are silent on this point, but when the records resume—centuries later—the Assyrians are contending with new foes—small Hittite and Aramean kingdoms—rather than major empires. Neo-Babylonian sources indicate that during the reign of Tiglath-Pileser I's successor, Ashur-bel-kala, Arameans ransacked shrines in Babylonia. For centuries, the Assyrians were therefore pressed back from their eleventh-century conquests in northern Syria. The reign of Ashurnasirpal II gave new impetus to what had become a defensive war.

Their empire grew again as the war assumed an offensive character again, and the Assyrians slowly subdued their neighbours. As they transformed neighbouring vassals into provinces, they found new neighbours to pounce upon, and thus Tiglath-Pileser III, Shalmaneser V and Sargon II brought their forces into Palestine, eliminating Hazor, Dan and eventually Samaria. Sennacherib besieged Jerusalem and Lachish before withdrawing. Esarhaddon and Ashurbanipal added Egypt to their realm briefly, before the Assyrian power crumbled under the blows of the Medes and the Babylonians.

The Assyrians conquered Babylon several times during these centuries. Ultimately, however, making common cause with the Medes, Babylonian rulers were able to eliminate Assyria, and inherit the Assyrian Empire, more or less intact, after defeating the Egyptians who had intervened in favour of their Assyrian overlords.

The Archaeology as Historical Testimony

The significance of the relationship between the biblical account and the archaeological record of the seventh century can only be understood by comparison with the centuries preceding and following the seventh.

According to the biblical account, the incipient Israelite kingdom emerged from the debris of the collapse at the end of Bronze Age. All are agreed that regardless of what may one day be unearthed, the evidence for significant construction activity in Jerusalem at this period is lacking today. On the other hand, however, the history of the Northern Kingdom can be followed in the archaeological record at Samaria, Megiddo, Hazor, and Tel Dan, among other places.

This evidence in favour of the existence and importance of the Northern Kingdom must be contrasted with the lack of evidence for the Southern Kingdom, and particularly Jerusalem. Before the fortifications erected at the end of the eighth century and during the seventh century, the archaeology of Judah is not significant. With the exception of Jerusalem and Lachish, most of the sites are limited in size. Most are unfortified village settlements. The fortifications at Arad date to the period of the Southern Kingdom. There is no archaeological evidence which can unequivocally demonstrate that Lachish was fortified before the end of the Northern Kingdom, nor that the later city was more than a minor settlement before the destruction of Samaria.

The first traces of the transformed position of Jerusalem appear in the form of the walls dating to the reign of Hezekiah when Sennacherib besieged Jerusalem and Lachish. As is known, this state survived as a pocket in the Assyrian empire, and was ultimately destroyed by the Babylonians. The preceding notes were merely intended to stress that the archaeological record would imply that the seventh century is effectively the entire history of Judah, rather than merely the highpoint.

'Exile'

The Neo-Babylonian conquest led to the 'Exile', according to the biblical narrative. The author has stressed that from the end of the eighth century, the biblical record can be reconciled with the Near Eastern records and the archaeology. Debates about the history and archaeology of Israel have touched upon the 'Exile', and these issues also touch upon the significance of the archaeology of the seventh century. The significance of the 'Exile' of the king and his immediate retainers has been the major subject of debate. The symbolism of 'Exile' and 'Return' makes it appear almost too great to be fact, and this has led to the suggestion that it might not be. Archaeological sources have been used to buttress the case. Let us take (yet) another look.

Jeremiah (41.4-7) records that after the fall of Jerusalem, pilgrims from Shechem made their way to Jerusalem to make their offerings in the ruined temple. The mere existence of this procession should suffice to demonstrate that all Judah had not been deported, and that the land was not empty. Jeremiah (40) also reports that Gedaliyah, who had taken responsibility for Judah, attempted to persuade those remaining to return to their affairs.

This clearly meant that there must have been people in Shechem and Jerusalem as well as Mizpah after the beginning of the conquest. The record of the murder of Gedaliyah and of his companions and of the 'Exile' of the elite may portray only the fate of some members of the community. It could be contended that ordinary people remained in Judah and Israel during the period of the 'Exile'. By the same token it was clear that the presence of names with the Yahweh element in the Murashu archive (of Achaemenid date in Babylonia) confirm a community there after the end of the 'Exile', and the same applies to the communities at Elephantine and Delos (cf. the respective entries on 'Murashu', 'Elephantine', 'Delos', in *ABD*). Therefore, it is certain that Jewish communities remained in Babylonia, Egypt and Greece after the official end of the 'Exile'. Since it did not end, it could be argued that it did not begin either, and it therefore followed that it could be argued that the concept of an 'Exile' was a myth (cf. e.g., 'History of Israel, Post-Monarchic Period', in *ABD*). Part of this argument is based upon the archaeology. Biblical Archaeology was originally invented to provide scientific proof for the veracity of scripture. It signally failed to do this by revealing what could be interpreted as discrepancies between the Near Eastern sources and the Bible. The discrepancies between the biblical account and the ancient Near Eastern sources suggested that the two could not be reconciled, and Dever (1997: 317) concluded that biblical Archaeology 'had failed to achieve even its own limited agenda'. Archaeology proved disappointing to those of a Fundamentalist orientation, but those of a spiritual or literary inclination required no reassurance on the scientific veracity of the 'Exile' or any other aspect of the Bible. However, all were prepared to use archaeology to support a very different biblical agenda, namely to show that there was no 'Exile'. This literary approach to the Bible opened up a new approach to the interpretation of the archaeology by archaeologists.

Weippert (1988: 698) summarized her interpretation of the archaeological evidence thus:

> Freilich zeichnete sich schon in den Sechziger Jahren [des 20. Jhts. n. Chr.] ab, daß die babylonischen Zerstörungen an Orten nördlich von Jerusalem vorbeigegangen waren (Tell en-Nasbe, el-Gib, Bethel und Tell el-Ful) [...] Damit verwischte sich freilich die Zäsur zwischen der eisenzeitlichen und der babylonisch-persischen Kultur [...]
>
> Die Überwindung dieses Dilemmas verdankt man vor allem Ausgrabungen in nördlichen Küstenorten (Akko, Tell Kesan, Tell Abu Hawam, Tell es-Samak und Dor) [wo man] an Kleinfunden reiche Architekturschichten aus babylonisch-persischer Zeit entdeckt [...]
>
> Indeed, it emerged in the 60s [of the twentieth century] that the Babylonian destruction had bypassed the sites north of Jerusalem (Tell en-Nasbe, el-Jib, Bethel and Tell el-Ful) [...] Therefore, the distinction between the Iron Age and Babylonian–Persian cultural horizons became obscured [...]
>
> For the solution to this dilemma one is above all endebted to the excavations in the northern coastal regions (Akko, Tell Kesan, Tell Abu Hawam, Tell es-Samak and Dor) [where] architectural strata rich in small finds have been uncovered [...]

Although the statement seems to imply that there is no distinction between the material of the Achaemenid and Neo-Babylonian periods, it also seems to imply not only continuity, but also that the Neo-Babylonian destruction of the landscape was not complete. This opened the door to the prospect that archaeological evidence could demonstrate that the 'Exile' never took place, and that life continued in Palestine during the entire Neo-Babylonian period.

Barstad (1996: 47) extended the argument, assuming that it has 'actually been known for quite a while' that Judah was not completely destroyed. Citing the destructions at Beit Mirsim, Beth-Shemesh, Lachish and Ramat Raḥel, he went on to suggest that 'Several cities lying north of Jerusalem, in the traditional area of Benjamin, were not destroyed at all'. The following sentence is thus crucial:

> In contrast to sites excavated south of Jerusalem, these places in fact prospered in the later sixth century. (Barstad 1996: 48)

Since the 'Exile' presumably ended in the late sixth century and the Achaemenid support for the return of the exiles documented in the tale of the Old Testament, this sentence would appear to be important only if it could demonstrated that the sites prospered under Neo-Babylonian rule. Equally important here is the evidence from Lachish. Barstad explicitly assumes the destruction of Beth-Shemesh and Lachish, which has in fact been accepted, just as the Achaemenid residency at Lachish is a demonstration of that site's revival under Achaemenid administration.

In discussing the pottery from the exilic period at Gibeah (Tell el-Ful IIIB), N. Lapp (*NEAEHL*: 448) concluded that there were parallels at Bethel, Beth-Shemesh, Gibeon, Tell en-Nasbe, Samaria and Lachish. Lapp concludes however that Josiah's fortress at Gibeah was in fact destroyed during Nebuchadnezzer's 588–87 campaign, and that thereafter

> the Babylonians may have been unconcerned with the remainder of the town's inhabitants and allowed them to live in peace. (*NEAEHL*: 447)

It will be noted that this is not the implication of Weippert's suggestion, which was that the 'Babylonian destructions had missed' Gibeah. Barstad had concurred with Lapp in recognizing the destruction of the fortress, but suggested that this had preceded the growth of the town during the 'Exile'. In fact there is no hint of growth. Lachish was only resettled after the Achaemenid conquest of Babylon, as the site was deserted after the Neo-Babylonian conquest. In fact, the evidence from Tell Keisan suggests that whatever can be dated to this period is not representative of a major occupation (Briend and Humbert 1980: 131-56). The same applies to Beth-Shemesh (*NEAEHL*: 249-54). 'There is slight ceramic and stratigraphic evidence' at Tell Beit-Mirsim (*NEAEHL*: 180). The evidence of Tell en-Nasbeh cannot be used to argue occupation during the Neo-Babylonian period (after the death of Gedaliyah; cf. McCown 1947; Wampler 1947; *NEAEHL*: 1098-102).

None of these or any other sites suggest that there is any major building in Palestine which can be dated with certainty to the period of the 'Exile'. This contrasts substantially with the period before and after the 'Exile'. The land may not have been empty, but the elite was not in evidence.[1]

This conclusion applies to the material of the sixth century. There is some confusion in general since the usual system of dating applied to Palestinian archaeological sites places the 'Neo-Babylonian' together with the 'Achaemenid', and thus obscures two very different periods. At the same time, evidence of continued occupation of a site into the Neo-Babylonian period is not the same as demonstrating new elite construction activity during that period. This renders the search difficult, but a careful examination of the archaeological reports fails

---

1. Since this was written the issue has been treated at depth in Lipschits and Blenkinsopp 2003. The present writer continues to stress the element that there is a difference between archaeological remains possibly dating to this period and proof of significant construction activity during this period. The absence of significant construction contrasts substantially with the archaeological record of the Neo-Assyrian and Achaemenid periods, and this is important.

to indicate that any significant remains can be dated with certainty to the Neo-Babylonian period. This contrasts not only with the preceding age, but also with the Achaemenid period, where numerous major finds confirm settlement construction and occupation.

It is thus clear that the archaeological material confirms a gap between the Neo-Babylonian conquest and the Achaemenid period. This gap is present. The fact of the revival cannot deny the fact that exiles remained abroad, in Egypt, Babylonia and Greece. It is also clear that there was a consciousness of the difference between the community in Palestine and the Diaspora, as seen in the instructions concerning the temple at Elephantine (*ANET*: 492). By the same token, however, the existence of the Diaspora after the sixth century should not be permitted to eclipse the evidence which demonstrates beyond doubt that there was a Diaspora community which involved the worship of the god Yahweh outside of Palestine, and that this community looked to Jerusalem, and that the origins of this Diaspora can be traced back to the Neo-Babylonian period.

Summing Up

The only significant archaeological site which can be linked to the Neo-Babylonian period is Tell en-Nasbeh (*NEAEHL*: 1098-102), and there it is clear that (a) the defences were dismantled after the conquest, and (b) the site was abandoned near the start of the Neo-Babylonian period. Of singular importance for the archaeology of seventh-century Judah are the 'four-room houses', at least one of which at Tell en-Nasbeh post-dates the Neo-Babylonian conquest, since it was built over the abandoned gate. These facts remain true regardless of its identification as 'Mizpah'. Identifying the site with 'Mizpah' allows an historical context for the brief period of prosperity at the beginning of the Neo-Babylonian period, but this is not necessary.

This site is one of the few sources for a date for the architectural assemblage of Judah. This in turn is thus of manifold import for the argument in the first part of this paper, since it can accordingly be argued that the erection of the fortifications can be linked to the fall of Samaria. This argument is based upon the pottery and seal impressions from Ramat Raḥel. These are to be dated to this period, as I contended that the archaeological evidence must be interpreted as implying that fortifications and palace at Ramat Raḥel followed the Assyrian conquest of Samaria. Following the same logic of archaeological parallels and military defences, the archaeological material from Tell en-Nasbeh would imply that the fortifications there should be dated to the same period as Ramat Raḥel. The pottery of these fortifications can also be aligned with that at Arad, where there is no compelling archaeological evidence to indicate an earlier date.

Interpreting the evidence in this fashion, the author would be inclined to conclude that the fortifications and water-supply arrangements in Jerusalem took place during the eighth century. Such an interpretation would imply that the archaeological record in Judah reveals a transformation from the eighth century onwards. Prior to the eighth century, there is no compelling reason to view Judah as urban and politically organized. In the seventh century, these fortifications included the frontier defences at Arad and Tell en-Nasbeh, as well as a palace at Ramat Raḥel. Judah was clearly politically and militarily organized in the seventh century.

This must be contrasted with the state after 586 BCE. Despite suggestions to the contrary, there is virtually no evidence of a politically organized urban civilization in Palestine after 586. Jerusalem was clearly abandoned, as was Tell en-Nasbeh shortly thereafter. The evidence from Gibeah, Tell Keisan and Tell Beit Mirsim does not testify to any significant urban structures.

The evidence from the Achaemenid period onwards reveals a continuous pattern of flourishing culture.

Under the circumstances, the archaeology of the seventh century appears quite exceptional. I would also like to emphasize that the evidence of compatibility in the accounts in the Old Testament and in ancient Near Eastern sources also differs from the end of the eighth century onwards. From the siege of Jerusalem onwards, there is a close connection: the rulers and their activities are easy to correlate. Even more importantly, the archaeological record for Jerusalem simply does not demonstrate that Jerusalem was a significant city before the late eighth century. Extensive excavations have failed to reveal any significant structures from the early Iron Age in Jerusalem.

The pottery, the seals and the fortifications document a strong monarchical foundation after the destruction of Samaria. This corresponds to the biblical and archaeological records. However, this evidence of a strong monarchy in Judah during the seventh century conceals that there is, in fact, little trace of an 'alternative' monarchy in Judah during the period of the 'divided monarchy'. The 'royal' seal impressions can all be assigned to the period immediately after the fall of Samaria, as the defences of Jerusalem were prepared. Mazar (1985: 45) emphasizes that the 'Proto-Aeolic' capitals were used in both the north and the south. However, there is virtually no trace in the archaeological record of any significant royal construction in Judah before the fall of Samaria. Barkay (1992: 319) noted that the 'Proto-Aeolic' capitals from Jerusalem and Ramat Raḥel are probably later than those of the north. This would be the logical conclusion to be drawn from the fact that the palace there seems to have been constructed after the destruction of the military installation there. The similarity between this palace and the one at Samaria (Mazar 1990: 424-27) can thus be more than mere 'resemblance': the one was the successor of the other, and the earlier level at Ramat Raḥel cannot be assigned to a period much before the Assyrian destruction of the Northern Kingdom.

The evidence of the Northern Kingdom in the early stages of Iron II is also indisputable. The Near Eastern sources confirm that there was a kingdom in the region during the ninth and eighth centuries (Ashurbanipal, Shalmaneser, Tiglath-Pileser, Sargon). The material culture of this Northern Kingdom is clearly distinct from that of the Southern Kingdom (Mazar 1985: 55). However, it is difficult to distinguish any chronologically significant differences in the material culture of the Northern Kingdom. In fact there appears to be substantial 'continuity' (Barkay 1992: 305). It is virtually impossible to distinguish any element belonging to the tenth century, whereas the material culture of the eighth and ninth centuries is clearly identifiable. At the same time, the culture of this state—the Israelite state documented in the Near Eastern sources—appears to share features of a common culture across the Near East at this time. The ivories, the gates and the pottery are not exceptional. Exceptional is only the suggestion that certain elements be dated to the tenth century, for which there is no evidence.

Under ordinary circumstances, it would be logical to postulate that the archaeological material of the Northern Kingdom belongs to the ninth and eighth centuries, and that the archaeological material of the Southern Kingdom belongs to the eighth and seventh centuries. This would explain the apparent lack of development within the two cultural assemblages, and also the differences which distinguish them: they were chronologically and culturally distinct entities. At the same time, the continuity between the two—four-room houses, 'Proto-Aeolic' capitals—could be explained in terms of transfer, from north to south. The date and cause of this transfer can be assigned to the period of overlap. The campaigns of Tiglath-Pileser III and Sargon II eliminated the Northern Kingdom, leading to its displacement, with a new capital at Jerusalem.

It would appear, therefore, that a Northern Kingdom existed from some time in the ninth century, and that the capital of this kingdom, at Samaria, was destroyed by the Assyrians in the eighth. The capital was then moved to Jerusalem or Ramat Raḥel, and new defences erected to ward off the Assyrians. This new state flourished during the seventh century. This state was then in its turn destroyed by the Babylonians.

And, again, the archaeological evidence of the sixth century indicates that it is virtually impossible to establish any major construction activity, which can be indisputably assigned to the sixth century. There are occasional traces of occupation during the sixth century, but generally the evidence cannot be interpreted as implying a compelling argument in favour of a major occupation at any site in the Holy Land before the Achaemenid era. From the Achaemenid era onwards, the archaeological record and the biblical tales are in unison.

It therefore follows that some kind of 'Exile' ensued from the Neo-Babylonian conquest. The political elite certainly lost power and the urban character of the civilization was lost. At some point the Persians permitted the exiles to return, and some did (although others remained in Mesopotamia and Egypt). Upon their return, they had very clear memories of the last century of their independence, but very unclear memories of events before the fall of Samaria.

Following conventional wisdom, Mazar (1990: 531) simply assumes that Judah and Israel were the 'dominant powers in Palestine during Iron Age II'. Yet, Mazar (1990: 416) also remarks that the archaeology of Judah is obscure in the ninth and early eighth centuries, only becoming clear towards the end of the eighth.

Weippert (1998: 698) suggests that archaeological work has demonstrated continuity in the archaeological record through the Neo-Babylonian period. All are familiar with the excellent quality of the archaeological evidence from the

Achaemenid era (e.g. Stern 1982) onwards. In fact, however, there is very little in the way of significant archaeological remains which can be attributed with any certainty to the Neo-Babylonian period.

The implications of Mazar and Weippert's positions are that the archaeological evidence implies continuity of politically significant settlement in Israel and Judah from the ninth or tenth century onwards. Certainly, one can note the general tendency of increasingly settlement, culminating in denser and larger settlements towards the late eighth and seventh centuries, and the logical extrapolation that this was maintained in the following centuries would appear compelling. This approach would imply that the archaeological evidence from the seventh century is representative rather than unique.

Following the evidence, I would, however, suggest that the history of Jerusalem and Judah effectively begins in the late eighth century, and ends in the early sixth century. The concept of a 'united monarchy' and a 'divided monarchy' is not supported by the archaeological evidence. There has never been any evidence for significant construction in Jerusalem during the period of the 'united monarchy' or the 'divided monarchy'. Jerusalem and Ramat Rahel would represent successors to Samaria and the northern cities, rather than a parallel manifestation of political power and independence. We can thus conclude that Jerusalem was founded as a substitute capital after the fall of Samaria, and that it was surrounded by hostile powers. For most of the seventh century, the Assyrian domination and the Philistine culture were the most important features, and not Judah. After the Neo-Babylonian conquest, the cultural level of Palestine declined until the recovery of the Achaemenid period.

Facit

The archaeological material from Jerusalem in the seventh century should thus not be understood as merely illustrative of a single continuous development beginning in the tenth century and ending in the Roman conquest, but as a unique episode.

Despite the fact that the seventh century was its apogee, growth in Judah was restricted to peripheral regions, such as Arad, En-Gedi and Aroer. It is highly significant that such sites reveal no traces of occupation prior to the very latest era although mentioned only in reference to the earliest period of Israelite history in the Bible. The fortifications at Qumran likewise date to the same period, and thus the defensive line linking Tell en-Nasbeh, Qumran and Arad defines the settlement of Judah, temporally and spatially. The fall of Beth-Shemesh and Lachish eliminated the western defences, pressing Judah further into the hostile wastes.

While the eighth-century defences of Jerusalem are a striking confirmation of the preparations at this time, the fact that the wall cut through residential housing does not advocate that it be understood purely in terms of continuity. It is clear that the new approach was novel in terms of urban development. Equally significant is that the principal of the tunnels in the new contemporary water system bears a striking similarity to that known from Megiddo, roughly a century earlier. In the same way, the architecture of Ramat Raḥel bears a certain similarity to Samaria. As the Assyrian conquests meant that Megiddo and Samaria had been lost, the features are thus not only chronologically sequential, but also potentially, politically so, since there is no earlier evidence for the parallel existence of these northern and southern cities.

During the seventh century, Judah was not the dominant power, but rather it existed on the inhospitable margin of the major Philistine cities under Assyrian rule. Admittedly a number of early Hebrew inscriptions have been found in the Philistine cities—in fact more than in the alleged heartland. To this must be added the disappearance of the Philistines after the Neo-Babylonian conquest. One has the impression that the traditions which appeared in Palestine after the 'Exile' were at least partially based on the ideological vacuum created by the disappearance of the Philistines.

However, as a whole, the material culture of the Achaemenid period in Palestine is dominated by that of the traditional world of the Levant: Greek and Egyptian material is mixed with the Levantine tradition. During the Achaemenid period, there is very little evidence of any influence of the 'Israelite' tradition outside of the core region in Judah, and very little even here.

Following the majority, Finkelstein and Silberman (2001) assume that both the Northern and Southern Kingdoms worshipped the same god and shared the same customs. They also trace the identity of this community back through the centuries. First of all, there is, of course, no evidence for the claim that they worshiped the same god at the same time. Certainly the tale of the Old Testament does not suggest that the Northern Kingdom had any preference for worshiping a single god, and the archaeological record cannot support the claim to the worship of Yahweh in the south before the end of the eighth century.

Secondly, the archaeological evidence for common customs in the north and south is also open to debate. Mazar (1985: 55) notes that it 'is a simple task' to distinguish contemporaneous material from Judah and Israel, suggesting different traditions (even if one argues that they were not contemporaneous, but rather sequential, as the present author does). It is therefore striking that the Israelite and Philistine material at Beth-Shemesh and Timnah 'is indistinguishable' (Mazar 1990: 312). It is clear that the uniformity of the material means that conclusions about chronological and ethnic differences are actually strongly influenced by the archaeologist's interpretation of the history, rather than by the material, which is open to diverse interpretations.

In certain cases, however, the empirical evidence is of interest. In support of common shared customs, Finkelstein and Silberman (2001: 119) note that there are 'no pigs' in the early highland settlements. This is remarkable since the animal bones from, for example, Shiloh (theoretically a major cult center) imply a constant per cent of pig bones from the Middle Bronze Age through Iron II, with 2.3 per cent in Iron II (Grigson 1998: 255 Fig. 11, 260-62, 'pig' column). Aside from the slight increase in pig bones towards the end of the Iron age, there is no evidence of a significant change in eating habits after the end of the Neolithic.

There is clearly a difference between the proclaimed customs of the people in the south and the actual customs of those of the north, implying a different ethnic identity.

Although the first reference to 'Israel' in the Merneptah stele can be assigned to the very end of the Late Bronze Age (c. 1200 BCE), the linguistic evidence of the Amarna letters implies that the language spoken in Palestine during the first part of the second millennium BCE was not closely related to the biblical Hebrew of seventh-century Judah (Rainey 1996). The language they spoke bore a greater similarity to Ugaritic from further north. Likewise, the architecture and art of the early Northern Kingdom bears no relation to the preceding era in Palestine, but represents imports of Aramean, Neo-Hittite and Phoenician origin (Holladay 1998: 372). Like their neighbours in Syria, these newcomers from the north established a state in northern Palestine when the Egyptian empire fell apart. These newcomers revealed a new national identity similar to that of their neighbours, but they also continued to consume pork and worship a plethora of gods.

It is clear that the archaeological material reveals substantial differences between north and south. There is thus no reason to link the beliefs, customs and architectural expression of the seventh-century Southern Kingdom to the earlier Northern Kingdom and certainly not to any putative common forbears in the early Iron Age. We have argued that it is difficult to place a time depth of the archaeology of Judah allowing the associated archaeological assemblages to antedate the demise of the Northern Kingdom significantly.

This northern state of Israel did not differ significantly from the neighbouring societies with which it was allied in contests against the Assyrians. When this pagan state of Israel was eventually destroyed by the Assyrians, along with the other Aramean states, a vassal successor was established in the south, called Judah. Somehow this southern state claimed some form of independence, and established an historical link to the northern state by claiming a common political origin and a common religion. In fact, however, the Southern Kingdom was a creature of the Assyrians, with some very unique religious and social ideas. It had no independent history prior to the Assyrian conquests in the north. Its religion and customs can be recognized in the archaeology and the Old Testament narrative, but they do not antedate the Assyrians, and bear no relation to the customs of the northern state.

The archaeological history of the independent state of Judah would imply that this was politically insignificant and that it lasted little more than a century, ruling little more than a small region around Jerusalem. That this century happened to have been the seventh is just as important as the absence of evidence concerning any other period. Even during the seventh century, the major power was that which had antedated Judah.

Prior to the seventh century, the Philistines were the major power in southern Palestine, and their cities were only eclipsed with the Neo-Babylonian conquest. Curiously, the eclipse of Philistine culture took place at exactly the time the traditions of Israel crystallized, during the 'Exile'.

Based on the archaeological evidence, the Near Eastern sources, and the biblical narrative, I therefore conclude that the biblical narrative as presently preserved reflects a composition at a period when the memories of the Assyrians were relatively fresh, but the character and history of the Northern Kingdom unfamiliar to the authors.

The historical origins of Judah can thus be seen in the archaeology from the eighth century onwards, when the biblical account can be coherently linked to the Near Eastern records. Before this, neither the archaeology, nor the history can be linked. Judah can thus be understood as having adopted the Northern Kingdom as an ancestor, in order to secure an historical background, and to have re-written the history of that kingdom to accommodate a mythical common heritage. This was accomplished by postulating a period of a United Monarchy with Jerusalem as its capital. In the absence of an independent political identity, Judah was impelled to the development of a 'religious' identity, involving the unique worship of a single god, and this custom was ascribed to both the putative unified state and the northern state as well.

The Neo-Babylonian conquest and the 'Exile' can be seen in both the archaeology and the narrative. The century of 'Exile' allowed for the crystallization of the memories of the seventh century, and Jerusalem's claim to be the successor of the Northern Kingdom, as well as the southern, by asserting a common origin in a United Monarchy and a parallel history in a Divided Monarchy. This process depended upon denying the continuity of the national identity of the northern state as part of a local culture which can be traced back through to Bronze Age Palestine. This allowed the assertion of a specific identity along with a shared ideology, by means of which the state of Judah claimed to be a 'purer' form of the northern state. This depended upon assigning the two states the same ideology and a shared history. This in turn required a revision of history to accommodate a period when a state in Judaea and Samaria resisted the Philistines. In reality, of course, the northern state was at least partially Aramean in culture, and it was the southern state (which did not exist prior to the Assyrian conquests), which later contended with the Philistines, who were the most important power in Palestine during the apogee of the Judaean state.

Attitudes towards the Old Testament narrative have been employed to flesh out the archaeology of Palestine, with the result that virtually every interpretation of the archaeology is influenced by the respective author's attitude toward the text. Both those who rely upon the text and those who attempt to dismiss it miss crucial details of the archaeology as preserved.

While dismissing the general archaeological consensus that Israel and Judah were the major powers in Palestine during Iron II, Finkelstein and Silberman (2001: 240) still contend that 'continuity with the past…was Judah's most obvious characteristic in the early centuries of the Iron Age'.

The logic of this procedure was precisely the opposite of that applied to the early history of Israel by the traditional biblical archaeologists. In the first half of this paper, I have argued that assumptions about the reliability of the biblical record influenced the interpretation of the archaeology, and that these approaches failed to recognize the unique character of the archaeological evidence of the seventh century, as this evidence demonstrated that Judah lacked independent origins. In the second half of this paper, I have argued that assumptions about the unreliable character of the biblical narrative were extended to the period of the 'Exile'. In fact, however, a more balanced view will confirm that—regardless of the earlier inconsistencies—the archaeological record confirms the seventh-century state, and also the reality of the devastation following the Neo-Babylonian conquest. I merely draw to the attention of all concerned that the evidence of the seventh-century state also implies that this state was not only restricted to the seventh century, but also not closely related to the earlier northern state.

Therefore, in contrast to the concept of 'continuity', the archaeology of the seventh century represents a rupture with the past. Likewise, the archaeological consensus dismisses the 'Exile', whereas there is virtually no evidence of any major building in Palestine before the Achaemenid era. This in turn renders the archaeology of seventh-century Jerusalem even more significant, since the later reconstruction of pre-exilic history was based upon the return after the 'Exile'. Regardless of details, most approaches to the history and archaeology of the Holy Land follow the biblical narrative, placing that story at the center. In fact, the records suggest not only that Judah lacks time depth, but also that during the brief period of its existence Judah was peripheral to the Philistines. The key difference is that whereas the Philistines disappeared after the Neo-Babylonian conquests, the return after the 'Exile' permitted a different narrative to be established in which the Philistines were marginalized.

BIBLIOGRAPHY

Barkay, G.
    1992   'The Iron Age II–III', in Ben-Tor (ed.) 1992: 302-73.
Barstad, H.
    1996   *The Myth of the Empty Land* (Symbolae Osloenses Fasc. Suppl., 28; Oslo: Scandinavian University Press).
Ben-Tor, A. (ed.)
    1992   *The Archaeology of Ancient Israel* (New Haven and London: Yale and the Open University of Israel).
Briend, J., and J.-B. Humbert
    1980   *Tell Keisan: 1971–1976* (OBO, SA, 1; Fribourg: Éditions universitaires).
Dever, W.
    1997   'Biblical Archaeology', in E. Meyers (ed.), *Oxford Encyclopedia of Archaeology in the Near East* (5 vols.; New York: Oxford University Press): 315-19.
Dion, P.-E.
    1997   *Les Araméens à l'âge du fer: Histoire politique et structures sociales* (Études Bibliques, NS, 34; Paris: J. Gabalda).
Finkelstein, I., and N.A. Silberman
    2001   *The Bible Unearthed* (New York: Free Press).
Grabbe, L.L. (ed.)
    2003   *'Like a Bird in a Cage': The Invasion of Sennacherib in 701 BCE* (JSOTSup, 363; ESHM, 4; Sheffield: Sheffield Academic Press).

Grigson, C.
    1998   'Plough and Pasture in the Early Economy of the Southern Levant', in Levy (ed.) 1998: 245-68.
Holladay, J.S.
    1998   'The Kingdoms of Israel and Judah', in Levy (ed.) 1998: 368-98.
Lamon, R.S., and G.M. Shipton
    1939   *Megiddo I: Season of 1925–34. Strata I-V* (Oriental Institute Publications, 42: Chicago: University of Chicago Press).
Levy, T. (ed.)
    1998   *The Archaeology of Society in the Holy Land* (London: Leicester University Press).
Mazar, A.
    1985   'Archaeological Research on the Period of the Monarchy (Iron Age II)', in Shanks and Mazar (eds.) 1985: 43-57.
    1990   *Archaeology of the Land of Israel ca. 10,000–586 B.C.E.* (Anchor Bible Reference Library; New York: Doubleday).
McCown, Ch.
    1947   *Tell en-Nasbeh*. I. *Archaeological and Historical Results* (Berkeley and New Haven: Pacific School of Religion and American Schools of Oriental Research).
Lipschits, O., and J. Blenkinsopp
    2003   *Judah and the Judeans in the Neo-Babylonian Period* (Winona Lake, IN: Eisenbrauns).
Rainey, A.
    1996   *Canaanite in the Amarna Tablets: A Linguistic Analysis of the Mixed Dialect Used by the Scribes from Canaan* (Leiden: E.J. Brill).
Shanks, H., and B. Mazar (eds.)
    1985   *Recent Archaeology in the Land of Israel* (Washington and Jerusalem: Biblical Archaeology Society).
Shiloh, Y.
    1985   'Jerusalem—"The City Full of People"', in Shanks and Mazar 1985: 129-40.
Stern, E.
    1982   *Material Culture of the Land of the Bible in the Persian Period 538–332 B.C.* (Warminster: Aris & Phillips).
Wampler, J.C.
    1947   *Tell en-Nasbeh*. II. *The Pottery* (Berkeley and New Haven: Pacific School of Religion and American Schools of Oriental Research).
Weippert, H.
    1988   *Palästina in Vorhellenistischer Zeit* (Handbuch der Archäologie, Vorderasien, II/1; Munich: Beck).

Part III

CONCLUSIONS

REFLECTIONS ON THE DISCUSSION

Lester L. Grabbe

The summary which follows draws both on the papers printed in this volume and on the discussion in the meetings of the Seminar. Participants are indicated by their initials; however, in order to differentiate between points made in the papers and points arising in the discussion, the full surname is given when reference is to the individual papers and responses prepared for the Seminar.[1] Comments in the discussion itself are indicated by the use of only the initials.[2]

The ultimate aim of this volume, as all the others produced by the ESHM, is to ask about methodology in the task of writing history. This discussion will begin by looking at some of the individual issues that received more sustained discussion. It will then move to a more synthetic presentation about the implications of these and other examples for a coherent theory. The chapter will conclude, finally, by a brief summary of the views of individual participants on the methodological question. As will be clear, there is no consensus as such, but some views are more dominant than others. Above all, we have had a chance to air our views in a forum that listens to them seriously but critically.

Some of the Main Issues in the Discussion

Archaeology
We were all in agreement of the importance of the archaeology for the history of this period. Yet it is evident that there have been considerable differences of interpretation of the archaeology. The most far-reaching (re)interpretation is that of Warburton: he argues that the seventh century is not just the high point of Judah's history but *is* its history. Judah became a politically organized state and urban only in the late eighth century, a view supported by the archaeology at key sites (including Jerusalem) where clear evidence of earlier significant construction is lacking. Warburton argues that archaeology shows the existence of the

---

1. Neither M. Liverani nor H. Niehr were present for the discussion, though they are members of the Seminar. Nevertheless, they and also some other Seminar members have written studies that made points important to be taken account of in the debate and are thus referred to in this chapter: Niehr 1995 (see my summary of his paper on pp. 9-11, above); Liverani 2003 (also summarized above, pp. 6-9); Niemann 1993.
2. The following initials are used: RA, Rainer Albertz; BB, Bob Becking; EBZ, Ehud Ben Zvi; PRD, Philip R. Davies; LLG, Lester L. Grabbe; KJ, Knud Jeppesen; NN, Nadav Na'aman; TLT, Thomas L. Thompson.

Northern Kingdom in the ninth and eighth centuries (though not necessarily the tenth), but Judah did not become a politically organized entity until about the fall of Samaria or afterward. It then continued for a little over a century until the Neo-Babylonian destruction and the removal of the elite. This left a gap in major construction until the 'return' at the beginning of the Achaemenid period.

Although the argument that Judah only became a state in the eighth century will be seen by some as a radical position, it must be admitted that it is not at all new in a broad sense; on the contrary, it agrees with the earlier interpretation of such writers as D.W. Jamieson-Drake (1991) and H.M. Niemann (1993; see also Niehr 1995)—and it is a view gaining in popularity, though still vehemently opposed by some. This position does not suggest that Judah did not exist as such before the eighth century, but its position as a major organized state with Jerusalem as a capital city did not come about until the eighth century, though the invasion of Sennacherib in 701 BCE caused a major hiatus in Judah's development (Na'aman; Grabbe; cf. the essays in Grabbe [ed.] 2003). Yet this position of Warburton and others is hardly likely to go unchallenged from several points of view.

A part of Warburton's argument requires him to discuss the archaeology later than the seventh century: into the sixth century and even beyond. He seems to accept partially the arguments of H.M. Barstad (1996) that there was no 'empty land' during the mid-sixth century, but he still argues for a serious gap in occupation at the main sites. In this he seems to be supported by Liverani, who emphasizes the greatness of the destruction by the Babylonians and also notes that it was Babylonian policy to leave the conquered territory in a degraded sociocultural state (2003: 215-16). Similarly, the recent study of O. Lipschits (2003) argues for a small population during the rest of the Neo-Babylonian period, with Jerusalem uninhabited. Contrary to the seemingly more positive statements of Warburton that Judah recovered in the Persian period, however, Lipschits argues that the population of Judah in the Persian period was not greater than 30,000 at its largest. Judah remained a minor province in the Persian empire (Grabbe 2004), and was thus probably no more significant then than in the Assyrian empire of the seventh century.

Another area that could be considered as falling under the heading of archaeology is that of seals and iconography in general (Uehlinger; Grabbe; cf. also Niehr 1995: 34-37), seals being especially important. These seals show a potentially significant difference from earlier seals of the region: the astral imagery present in the late eighth and seventh centuries has disappeared by the time of the sixth-century seals (Uehlinger). In addition, the blessing and salvation functions provided by the 'Asherah' in earlier inscriptions had been absorbed by Yhwh by the time of the Arad and Lachish ostraca. Yhwh had also absorbed the functions of the sungod and the underworld. Thus, the archaeology—apart from the biblical text—suggests a change in religious orientation that needs to be taken account of.

It should be noted that arguments in the past for archaeological evidence of Josiah's reign, and especially his religious reform, should now be abandoned. Trying to make fine distinctions between the seventh-century finds is very subjective because there are no destruction layers between the invasions of Sennacherib and Nebuchadnezzar (Na'aman). This means that finds conventionally assigned to the reign of Josiah could actually come from Manasseh's, and vice versa (cf. Liverani 2003: 189). The two main points associated with the religious reforms were the altars at Arad and Beersheba, but interpreters are now sceptical that they demonstrate a religious reform (Knauf; Grabbe; Uehlinger; Niehr 1995: 35; Ussishkin 1988).

Manasseh
Sennacherib's attack devastated the central part of Judah. Most towns of any size were destroyed, much of the Shephelah seems to have been removed from Judaean control, and the population was considerably reduced (Finkelstein 1994). Only Jerusalem and the area to the north escaped major damage.[3] The question is where Judah would go from there. This is where a number of contributors argue that Manasseh provided the leadership that led to considerable recovery from quite a low situation, though this reality of trying to address a crisis and provide help to the nation was countered by theological prejudice. E.A. Knauf points out that in fact the Judaeans of Manasseh's reign were much better off because Judah was integrated into the Assyrian economy (though their *perception* might be that they were worse off). Knauf argues that the Siloam tunnel and the monumental building at Ramat Raḥel were prestige projects under Manasseh. Some biblical passages that apparently arose during Manasseh's time are actually positive toward the Assyrians (Isa. 6–8; Ps. 48), but editors of the biblical text were not interested in how Manasseh led the economic and physical recovery of the country. Their only concern was their concept of true religion, and in their eyes Manasseh was 'Judah's Ahab' who imported 'foreign' worship (Stavrakopoulou; Sweeney); indeed, a major reason for his vilification may be that he bears a northern name (Stavrakopoulou). His role in restoring Judahite society counted for nothing, but the astonishing situation is that the text—which normally blames the sins of the people for the nation's fall—holds Manasseh rather than the nation responsible for Judah's fall (Albertz; Knauf; Stavrakopoulou; Sweeney). This castigation and vilification has not been limited to the biblical text: modern scholars have gone even further and ascribed cult crimes to Manasseh beyond those in the Bible (Stavrakopoulou). Sweeney, however, notes the tension in the narrative of DtrH caused by the fact that Yhwh actually reneges on his promises.

On the question of whether the Chronicler knew anything more about Manasseh, opinion is divided. That the Chronicler had additional information on some of Manasseh's building activities (2 Chron. 33.14) is accepted by some (Knauf) and rejected by others,[4] but the main point of controversy concerns the alleged deportation to Babylon by 'the officers of the army belonging to the king of

---

3. Many scholars think that the destruction includes the main sites in the Negev, though Knauf argues against this (see the discussion and references in Grabbe [ed.] 2003: 14-18).
4. In an earlier article, E. Ben Zvi (1997) examined the matter in the context of the Chronicler's building reports and concluded that the Chronicler depicted building activity at those points in his narrative where Kings portrays new beginnings for Israel.

Assyria' (2 Chron. 33.11). This has often been argued in the past and is accepted as historical by Sweeney (perhaps because of Manasseh's expansion into the Negev); others consider it as possible (or 'not impossible') but problematic or unlikely (Grabbe), while others seem to reject it entirely (Knauf; cf. the silence in Liverani 2003: 165).

There seems to be general agreement, then, that Manasseh's reputation among biblical scholars needs a major rehaul. Yet there is still a question as to what extent we have sufficient data to characterize his reign. Knauf maintains that it is impossible to write a biography of Manasseh, but we can still say some things about him and especially about the history of Judah during his reign (see also Grabbe; Ben Zvi 1996). The one certain fact is that Manasseh succeeded Hezekiah as king. He also argues that some other statements are probably true: names of his parents, his age at his accession to the throne and the length of his reign, and the name of his son who succeeded him. Some statements, especially about his religious practices, are incapable of evaluation from the data available. Ideological nonsense are such statements as that Jerusalem fell because of his sins or that he did not keep the law of Moses (because it did not yet exist!), while 2 Chron. 33.1-20, alleging a deportation to Babylon, seems to be a rewriting of 2 Kings 21.

Josiah
Josiah's political aims. Josiah's reign is almost unique in the seventh century in having no attestation in Assyrian or Egyptian records. We have no confirmation of any of his activities or even of his existence. Considering the general reliability of the king lists in 1 and 2 Kings and also of the text of Kings for the seventh century (see below), there seems little question that Josiah existed; however, the main historical concern is how much of the biblical account we are justified in accepting as reliable.

Much of the interest in Josiah comes ultimately from a desire to learn more about the alleged cult reforms, but these have often been seen in the context of a wider political agenda. This is frequently expressed as Josiah's intent to make Judah into a 'greater Israel' or a renewal of the 'Davidic empire'. For example, M. Sweeney's recent study (2001) argues that Josiah wanted to restore a united kingdom of Israel with Jerusalem as its capital and the temple as its cult centre; however, this failed because of Josiah's death at Megiddo. A number of participants were willing to accept that Josiah wanted to expand Judah, but this was widely regarded as not having taken place (Na'aman; Grabbe; Hardmeier; Niehr 1995; Liverani 2003: 189-92). The idea that Josiah extended his rule as far as Megiddo and Meṣad Ḥashavyahu is probably to be rejected, unless it was only for a brief period.

An important insight has been provided by N. Na'aman: no power vacuum occurred as the Assyrians withdrew from the western regions of their empire following the death of Ashurbanipal. The Egyptians appear to have taken their place, by mutual agreement. This means that Josiah's freedom to manoeuvre was limited. This does not mean that a limited expansion and a religious reform could not have taken place, especially since the highlands had never been of major interest to Egypt. But any concerted attempt to take control of new territory was likely to have drawn Egyptian objections and intervention (Na'aman; cf. Davies; Niehr 1995). Albertz expresses some scepticism, since Isa. 8.23–9.6 suggests that the Assyrian withdrawal was seen as a great victory, but his main point is that Egyptian hegemony would not have prevented a cultic reform.[5]

Finally, the death of Josiah has been seen as a historical problem in recent decades. A number of contributors (Na'aman; Niehr 1995: 43) think that 2 Kgs 23.29-30 hides a mystery, partially covered over by 2 Chron. 35.20-24 which clearly states that Josiah sent an army against Necho. 2 Kings 23.29-30, on the other hand, says only that Josiah went 'to meet' Necho and was slain by him. This could mean not a military confrontation but the situation of a vassal who goes to do obeisance to his lord but is executed for treason. (The Egyptian army would not have marched overland to the Euphrates but would have been transported in ships.) If Josiah was disloyal, we do not know in what way he was. Liverani, however, points out that Josiah's forcing a military confrontation with Necho would have fitted Josiah's ideology (2003: 199-200). The Chronicler's account seems to take the view that Josiah was partially responsible for his own death (Sweeney).

Josiah's cultic reform. Although Josiah is alleged by the biblical text to have carried out a variety of activities, much of the accounts in 2 Kings and 2 Chronicles relates to his reforms. Once accepted as an explanation for a significant amount of the biblical literature, the reforms have become controversial in recent debate. The 'minimalist' argument is that the account in 2 Kings 22–23 is a late Deuteronomist invention, comparable to the 'reform' of Hezekiah and the 'Assyrian crisis' under Manasseh (Davies; Knauf; Niehr 1995). The literary account probably dates from no earlier than the exilic period or even as late as the fifth century (Davies). At most, one can say that Josiah profaned some altars as a part of his administrative centralization but without religious motives (Niehr 1995: 49). E.A. Knauf argues in Appendix III to his paper against 2 Kings 22–23 being based on a contemporary text. He notes that the 'one god/one sanctuary' ideal is not found in Deuteronomy 12. Its presence in 2 Kings 22–23 presupposes the rivalry between Bethel and Jerusalem in the period 520–445 BCE.

Two contributions here (Hardmeier, Uehlinger) rejected this complete scepticism but also argued that the reforms—though including religious intent—were restricted in extent and limited in geographical area; in addition, R. Albertz defends the traditional date for Deuteronomy and DtrH, thus arguing for their overall reliability for the general reform.[6] Hardmeier addresses in detail one of

---

5. Liverani (2003: 186-89) also emphasizes that the progressive imperial collapse after 640 BCE would have given a measure of freedom to the western vassal states, though he makes no specific reference to Na'aman's argument.

6. A recent discussion is also found in Albertz (2003: 271-302). N. Na'aman takes the position that 2 Kgs 22–23 is contemporary with the events described, apparently accepting the thesis (widely held in North America) that the first edition of DtrH dates from Josiah's time, though he provides no detailed discussion of the question.

the main concerns of those sceptical about the reform: to what extent can the account in 2 Kings be dated to Josiah's time? He argues (as does Uehlinger) that an original short list of measures has been greatly expanded by the DtrH editors. There is thus considerable agreement among contributors to this volume that much of 2 Kings 22–23 is to be assigned to later editors, but that does not mean rejecting any religious reform activities on Josiah's part. The evidence of seals and other considerations supports this interpretation of Josiah's accomplishments (Uehlinger).

As for the statement in 2 Chron. 34.3-7 that Josiah's reform began in his twelfth year (a dating that has been widely accepted), this is creative theology and not historical (Na'aman). Liverani's recent book (2003) seems to accept the account of finding the 'book of the law' but shows considerable scepticism toward many of the details: the book 'found', which encompasses conventional socio-juridical rules that had long been in the community, may have been written and planted there by Shaphan the scribe (Liverani 2003: 202). Nevertheless, it also contains genuine innovation, especially one god, one cult, and one cult site. The religious reform was primarily removing astral and other cults but also the reinterpretation of ancient Yahwistic customs (e.g. the pastoral festival of Passover was made a pilgrimage festival celebrating the exodus from Egypt). Josiah's early death meant that the reform lost momentum, though the historiographical scheme of the 'proto-Deuteronomist' served to structure the way Israel's history was portrayed in subsequent centuries.

In addition to the silence of the ancient Near Eastern sources, there are also some surprising gaps in the biblical text—at least, this is often alleged. It is often stated that Jeremiah and Zephaniah say nothing about Josiah's reforms (e.g. Ben Zvi; Davies; Niehr 1995: 50-51). Knauf would date those passages in Jeremiah that have been ascribed to the Josianic reform to the sixth century. This is clearly a moot point, with Albertz pointing to Jer. 3.22–4.2; 5.4-6; 8.7-8; 31.2-6. M. Sweeney adduces Jeremiah 2–4 and 30–31 (2001: 208-33) and Zephaniah (2001: 185-97; 2003), although he thinks the latter book was composed later and is generally read in relation to the Babylonian exile. If correct, these show knowledge of Josiah's reforms that had already taken place. Nevertheless, it does seem strange that at a time when the reforms were ostensibly in process, Jeremiah is completely silent on them. In addition, many of the prophetic texts supposedly mentioning Josiah are scholarly reconstructions (Ben Zvi). Various explanations have been given as to why this is, some more plausible than others, but it remains a problem (Ben Zvi). If the reform was a more modest one as argued by Uehlinger and Hardmeier, though, it might not have made such an impact on Jeremiah. Ben Zvi suggests that the books of Jeremiah and Zephaniah actually construct a negative image of late monarchic Judah and of its kings, including Josiah. Even if Josiah is referred to in passing, the impression of Josianic Judah is one of sin and rebellion. The prophetic books therefore construct and convey an image of the past that is different from that of Kings or Chronicles.

Implications for Writing History

The necessity of a debate over methodology is acknowledged by Sweeney, specifically over the relationship between the biblical literature and history. The theological perspective has to be recognized and taken account of: the narratives of both DtrH and Chronicles appear to have their basis in history but both also display a theological perspective. We can neither read biblical literature uncritically and naively as a witness to history as presented in the narrative nor dismiss it—naively and uncritically—simply because it presents history according to its own theological and historiographical viewpoint. Uehlinger comments on the 'sub-Deuteronomism' that has characterized too much writing about the history of Israel, in which the biblical text is only paraphrased and the archaeology slighted.

One of the points emphasized in a number of contributions (Uehlinger; Knauf; Grabbe; Niehr 1995) was the important distinction between 'primary' and 'secondary' sources. Primary sources are those demonstrably written at or near the time of the events they describe, whereas secondary sources are those further removed from the events. Not all members of the discussion were impressed by this distinction, since no rule of methodology is absolute: primary sources may contain false or distorted data and secondary sources may have been copied accurately from reliable sources. A primary source may also deliberately distort the truth. Nevertheless, historical reconstruction has to take into account the laws of probability: primary sources are more often and more likely to have usable historical data than secondary sources. This is why a number argue that primary sources should be given priority in historical reconstruction, where available.

This means that we normally begin with the primary sources and give most weight to them. This seems to be a working principle used in most or all the papers in this volume. The difficulty is that we do not possess primary sources for the entire period in question: for some potentially important events we have only secondary sources. Should we reject secondary sources as a matter of principle? Most historians think not. Uehlinger makes the point that no historian can reject the secondary sources when the primary are missing or inadequate. It is not a case of all or nothing but a critical discrimination between sources that takes account of all their characteristics, not just whether they are secondary or primary. This would include a secondary source that is often the only source we have, the biblical text. Of course, secondary sources—including the biblical text—are primary sources for the time when they were written, as has often been pointed out.

Where there seems to have been some confusion was over the term 'source'. Some wished to use other terms, such as 'data' or even 'evidence', and it was asked whether archaeology could be called a 'source'. This is not the first time or context in which such views have been voiced, but to my mind this is an unnecessary quibble, perhaps the result of a misunderstanding. The term 'source' is a neutral term serving nothing more than to designate where one gets the data to work with. A source can be written—inscription, literature, documents—or it can be unwritten—archaeology, social scientific studies, direct observation, measurements, experimentation. No historical work can be done without data or evidence or whatever term you use, but the data have to come from somewhere: our historical sources are simply those various places from which we obtain the data.

E.A. Knauf made a distinction between what he called a 'facteme' (the minimum information that is true or false in the real world) and 'factoid' (information created in the mental process of formulating and transmitting the narrative, which may be wrong in time and space). Among the discussants this distinction was somewhat controversial. It was suggested that there were only factoids or that with time a factoid become a facteme. One thought it was helpful by giving a context to a statement, but another thought it was not, because history had to be a narrative of data from the past. This is a view to which Knauf very much objects, arguing that this perspective makes no sense in his epistemology.

Several of the studies addressed the use of the biblical text for some aspects of the seventh century BCE (Albertz; Davies; Grabbe; Na'aman; Uehlinger). Some examples have already been discussed above. What becomes clear is that, relative to some other periods, we know a great deal about the seventh century: for some parts of it, we know almost year by year what was going on in Judah because of the availability of reliable primary sources (Grabbe). This gives probably the best opportunity so far in the Seminar discussions to evaluate the use of the biblical text for historical purposes. The archaeology also provides a great deal of data, though precise dating through this period is difficult (Na'aman; Liverani 2003: 189).

The ideological—theological, literary, social—aim of the biblical text is generally apparent. The various kings are presented and evaluated according to theological criteria that historians are likely to consider irrelevant. But that did not prevent most of the participants from arguing that usable data could nonetheless be obtained from such accounts. The fact is that a number of aspects of the various biblical accounts are corroborated in some way by primary sources. These seems to be more than coincidence. One can only conclude that *in some cases* and *for certain sorts of data* the biblical writings had worthwhile sources of information, whatever these were. What the sources were might be only a matter of speculation in most cases, but some can be guessed at with some degree of probability.

Several sections of the biblical account were analyzed and sources characterized in a general way (especially 2 Kgs 22–23 on which a variety of opinions was expressed). For DtrH (which serves as the backbone for any historical reconstruction that goes beyond the archaeology) the use of some sort of court chronicle has been eloquently argued for by Na'aman; Grabbe concurs that this is the best way to explain the reliable data that we seem to have in DtrH. The accurate historical references given in passing to provide a framework to Jeremiah are harder to explain. Some of them may well have been written near the actual time of Jeremiah, which suggests that some of the Jeremiah material was written down near the time of the actual events. But some references look like the addition of an editor, which would put their actual composition rather later. Thus, the writer would need to have had some sort of written account, but what that was is hard to say (cf. Grabbe forthcoming).

One of the most curious suggestions of A. Alt was that certain passages of Joshua reflect Judah under Josiah (Josh. 15.21-62; 18.21-28; 19.2-8, 40-46). Na'aman returns to this question and analyzes the passages in detail, arguing that the passages reflect the administrative situation only in the time of Josiah, not the tenth, ninth, or eighth centuries. A case is made that these lists were probably based on an administrative document listing settlements only by major geographical-administrative territories. This illustrates the complications in using the biblical text which, in this case, gives data for one period but ostensibly for another. Such examples may increase the scepticism of some, but the practice of saying one thing while pretending to say another is hardly new to literary critics. If George Orwell could write about barnyard animals but be commenting on the Stalinist system, why could the author/editor of Joshua not write about Josiah's reign while pretending to tell us about the situation centuries before? The important thing is not the general principle but the quality of the arguments used.

Both Grabbe and Knauf explicitly discussed in terms of relative probability what portions of the biblical narrative might be reliable. 'Probability' is of course a statistical term, whereas the data we have of the history of the ancient region of Palestine are not sufficient in most cases to attempt a proper statistical analysis. What we do instead is give a judgment of notional probability of various points in the narrative: which are more likely, which are less likely, which are unlikely. It is no different from what historians have long been doing, but an attempt to grade events in shades of grey rather than as either black (rejected) or white (accepted) seems desirable. As already noted, Liverani's study (2003) with its division into 'normal history' and 'invented history' seems to be a promising method of trying to come to grips with the different aspects of the biblical narrative. Like it or not, in a history of Israel (or ancient Palestine or southern Syria or whatever term one wishes to use) the biblical books have to be dealt with in some way, and one's way of dealing with them has to be justified methodologically.

The biblical text as a whole thus presents a mixed bag. Moving from the often-helpful accounts in DtrH and Jeremiah, we find the Chronicles account mainly derivative with an ideological interpretation. For the most part, it seems to be secondary and not at all reliable. Some feel the account of Manasseh's deportation to Babylon is based on credible information, but this is very controversial (see above). The Chronicler may know a bit about Manasseh's building activity that is not found in DtrH (Knauf), but he does not appear generally to have additional information (Grabbe; Knauf; cf. Liverani 2003: 165, 189). The writer of Daniel probably knew nothing about this period except what he read in Kings and Chronicles (Grabbe). His account of the taking of Jerusalem is impossible in the light of present data and seems to be a confused interpretation of the biblical statements on the question.

Although most of the participants were impressed that the biblical accounts were necessary and often important historical sources for this period, it would be going too far to say that there was a consensus. As always, participants present for the discussion were asked how they would summarize their approach to reconstructing or writing a history of this period. Here are their responses:

RA: We cannot trust DtrH concerning Manasseh. It is an open question whether there was a political vacuum after the Assyrians withdrew—I would like to know more. NN has given me encouragement about a Josianic reform. The Deuteronomistic History is exilic for the most part. There are no hints of a cult reform in post-exilic times. Only Deuteronomy 30 envisages the end of the exile, so a fifth-century dating of Deuteronomy seems to be ruled out.

BB: One chapter of 50 pages would be devoted to the seventh century, on the dissolution and decline of Judah. It would contain an analysis of all the sources, including the biblical text. Manasseh would be treated positively. A reform under Josiah would be accepted as taking place. The tragic process that led to the fall of Jerusalem would be dwelt on.

EBZ: We cannot accept the depiction of Manasseh or Manassic Judah in biblical sources (2 Kings, 2 Chronicles, Jeremiah) as historical. There was a slow but consistent recovery from Sennacherib's invasion and economic development. The so-called vacuum of hegemonic power in Josiah's days did not happen, nor did Josiah's territorial expansion, except to Bethel. As for the religious reform, something happened during his reign, but we do not know much about it. The account in 2 Kings (which is not from the Josianic period) refers to the finding of a book and suggests that such a book was close in some ways to Deuteronomy but refrains from identifying it with Deuteronomy, probably because the author of Kings did not and could not approve some sections of Deuteronomy (e.g. the law of the king and the law of the wayward city). Josiah is seen as a 'great guy'; the text tries to explain why.

PRD: Manasseh did what Assyria wanted. He possibly visited Mesopotamia, but there would have been no change of direction. Josiah did not expand Judah. A reform is attributed to him possibly because he was killed by an Egyptian king. Josiah may have conducted some sort of reform but, if so, it was not because of finding a book.

LLG: We must begin with the primary sources, especially archaeology, but cannot stop there: all sources must be analyzed and then used critically. In the case of the seventh century, the biblical text can often be tested, and 2 Kings is frequently seen to have good data. Yet in other instances, especially in literature such as Chronicles and Daniel, the account is very unreliable. The goal would be a total history that encompasses economy, society, culture, religion, administration, and political events.

KJ: Extra-biblical texts give the outline, so would need to begin there. We would then see how much of this also occurs in the biblical text. In general BB's approach is acceptable. Why do two kings exist in tension, a bad king and a good king?

NN: We would use all sources critically. The account in 2 Kings 22–23 was written in the time of Josiah and can be very much trusted. Its history of the seventh century was based on the personal knowledge of the author, though an exilic edition was produced by supplementation and correction. If the account was post-exilic, it would have been connected with Jehoiakim, not Manasseh. Josiah's reform is not mentioned in Jeremiah and Zephaniah because it was cut short.

TLT: The history of this period would be a short book of three chapters: (1) the economic impact of Assyrian rule (similar to EAK); (2) the cult and the changes made in the seventh and sixth centuries; (3) reception history, especially of the Assyrian texts into the biblical writings.

BIBLIOGRAPHY

Albertz, Rainer
    2003   *Israel in Exile: The History and Literature of the Sixth Century B.C.E.* (SBLSBL, 3; Atlanta: Society of Biblical Literature); ET of *Die Exilszeit: 6. Jahrhundert v. Chr.* (Biblische Enzyklopädie, 7; Stuttgart: W. Kohlhammer, 2001).

Barstad, Hans M.
    1996   *The Myth of the Empty Land: A Study in the History and Archaeology of Judah During the 'Exilic' Period* (Symbolae Osloenses, 28; Oslo and Cambridge, MA: Scandinavian University Press).

Ben Zvi, Ehud
    1996   'Prelude to a Reconstruction of the Historical Manassic Judah', *BN* 81: 31-44.
    1997   'The Chronicler as a Historian: Building Texts', in M. Patrick Graham, Kenneth G. Hoglund and Steven L. McKenzie (eds.), *The Chronicler as Historian* (JSOTSup, 238; Sheffield: Sheffield Academic Press): 132-49.

Finkelstein, Israel
    1994   'The Archaeology of the Days of Manasseh', in Michael D. Coogan, J. Cheryl Exum and Lawrence E. Stager (eds.), *Scripture and Other Artifacts: Essays on the Bible and Archaeology in Honor of Philip J. King* (Louisville, KY: Westminster/John Knox Press): 169-87.

Grabbe, Lester L.
    2004   *A History of the Jews and Judaism in the Second Temple Period 1: Yehud: A History of the Persian Province of Judah* (LSTS, 47; London and New York: T&T Clark International).
    forthcoming   '"The Lying Pen of the Scribe"? Jeremiah and History'.

Grabbe, Lester L. (ed.)
    2003   *'Like a Bird in a Cage': The Invasion of Sennacherib in 701 BCE* (JSOTSup, 363; = ESHM, 4; Sheffield: Sheffield Academic Press).

Jamieson-Drake, D.W.
    1991   *Scribes and Schools in Monarchic Judah: A Socio-Archeological Approach* (JSOTSup, 109; SWBA, 9; Sheffield: Almond Press).

Lipschits, Oded
    2003   'Demographic Changes in Judah between the Seventh and the Fifth Centuries B.C.E.', in Oded Lipschits and Joseph Blenkinsopp (eds.), *Judah and the Judeans in the Neo-Babylonian Period* (Winona Lake, IN: Eisenbrauns): 323-76.

Liverani, Mario
    2003   *Oltre la Bibbia: Storia antica di Israele* (Storia e Società; Rome: Editori Laterza).

Niehr, Herbert
    1995   'Die Reform des Joschija: Methodische, historische und religionsgeschichtliche Aspekte', in Walter Gross (ed.), *Jeremia und die 'deuteronomistische Bewegung'* (BBB, 98; Beltz: Athenäum): 33-55.

Niemann, Hermann Michael
    1993   *Herrschaft, Königtum und Staat: Skizzen zur soziokulturellen Entwicklung im monarchischen Israel* (FAT, 6; Tübingen: Mohr Siebeck).

Sweeney, Marvin
    2001   *King Josiah of Judah: The Lost Messiah of Israel* (Oxford: Oxford University Press).
    2003   *Zephaniah: A Commentary* (Hermeneia; Minneapolis: Fortress Press).

Ussishkin, David
    1988   'The Date of the Judaean Shrine at Arad', *IEJ* 38: 142-57.

INDEXES

INDEX OF REFERENCES

Old Testament
Genesis
2.24	187
3	275
33.20	186
35.7	186
41.50-52	254
41.51	253
43.14	38
44.17	187
46.20	254
48.1	254
48.5	254
48.8-22	254
48.8-20	255
48.14	254
48.18	254
49.1	39

Exodus
32	75
32.20	138

Leviticus
18.21	306
20.2-4	306

Numbers
1.10	254
1.32-35	254
2.20	254
6.24-26	296
22.35	187
24.14	39
26.28-34	254
32	217

Deuteronomy
Deut. 1–2 Kgs 25	151
1–30	130, 133, 152
1–3	39
1.1–4.40	70
1.6–30.20	129
1.6–3.29	128
1.7	200
1.19-46	129, 137
1.26b	137
1.43b	137
2.16	129, 137
3.21-22	129
3.22	129
3.23-28	39
3.29	39, 128, 129, 137
4–28	6
4	37, 39
4.1-40	39
4.3-4	39
4.4	129, 137
4.6	33
4.9-14	129
4.9	33
4.19	250
4.21-22	39
4.25-32	11, 39
4.25-28	39
4.25	131
4.29-31	37, 39, 40
4.29	40, 130
4.30	39, 40
4.44–30.20	40
4.44–11.32	70
5–30	143
5–26	131
5	39
5.2-3	129, 137, 143, 152
5.4-31	129
5.7	139
5.25	131
5.28-29	131
5.31	130, 131
5.32	130
6.1	130, 131
6.4-5	131
6.4	130
6.5	130
6.10	152
6.14-15	138, 139
6.14	32, 33
7.1	32, 72, 152
7.3-4	158
7.6-11	129
7.6-8	143
7.6	33, 152
7.7-8	152
7.7	33
7.14	33
7.16	33
7.17	32
7.22	32
8.7-10	152
8.20	32
9.1-6	129
9.1	32
9.4-6	250
9.4	32
9.5	32
9.7-24	137, 138

Deut. (cont.)		16.21-22	153, 157	26.18	152
9.7	137	17	35, 71	26.19	32, 33, 71,
9.8-17	137	17.3	250, 299		130, 152
9.12	137	17.4	71	27–34	70
9.16	137	17.8-13	35	27.9-10	129, 143,
9.21	137, 138,	17.9	35		152
	143, 153	17.11	130	27.10	131
9.21b	138	17.14-20	11, 34, 35,	28	131
9.23b	137		54	28.1	131
9.23	129	17.14-15	13, 73	28.10	33
9.24	137	17.14	32	28.14	130, 131
10.5	130, 136	17.16-20	13, 34	28.15-68	138, 140
10.12	130	17.16	35	28.36	13
10.15	33	17.16ab	999 35	28.37	33
10.16	40	17.18-20	129, 130,	28.61	30
11.13	130		141	28.64	33
11.23	32	17.19	32, 129	28.69–29.28	34
12–26	11, 13, 29,	17.20	130	29.9-14	129, 143,
	30, 32, 36,	18.9-12	250		152
	40, 70	18.9	32, 71	29.20	30
12–16	133	18.10-11	250	30	131, 348
12	17, 184,	18.10	157, 299	30.1-14	37, 38
	186-88,	18.10a	154	30.1-11	37, 40
	298, 343	18.14	32, 71	30.1-10	11, 39, 40,
12.1	70	18.17-18	138		131-33
12.2	32	18.18	59	30.1-9	131
12.5	132	18.20-22	138	30.1-3	132
12.8	187	19.1	32, 71	30.1	131
12.29-31	250	20	74	30.1b	131
12.29	32	20.1-9	35	30.2-13	131
12.30	32	20.1	7	30.2	39, 40,
13	55	20.15	32		130, 131
13.4	130	20.16	32, 71	30.2b	131
13.6	138	20.17	72	30.3-5	131
13.7-12	33	21.1-9	34	30.3	33, 142
13.8	33	21.10	129	30.5	40
14.2	33, 71	22.1-12	146	30.6	40, 130,
14.21	33	23.4	11		131
15.4	70	23.18-19	157	30.6b	131
15.6	32, 71	23.18	154	30.8	40, 131
16	143	24.12-17	7	30.10	40, 130,
16.1-7	129	24.16	33		131
16.1	129	26.15	130	30.10b	131
16.1b	143	26.16-19	34, 129	31.29	298
16.3b	143	26.16	131	31	129, 153
16.18–18.22	54	26.17-19	143, 152	31.2-6	129

31.7-8	129	15.25	196	*Judges*	
31.9-13	30	15.33-44	193, 208	3.1-6	37
31.9	129, 136	15.33	200	5.3	32
31.10-13	129, 144	15.37-41	193	5.5	32
31.11-12	143	15.42-44	193	9.41	206
31.21	138	15.45-47	196, 202	12.4	254
31.24-26	129	15.49	196	17–18	255, 256
31.24	30, 129	15.52	206	17.1-6	188
31.26	30, 129, 136	15.54	196, 199	17.6	37
		15.59	196	18.30	20, 255, 256
31.29	39	15.60	194, 196		
32.1-43	173	15.61-62	192	21.25	37
32.8-9	17, 173, 174	15.61	194		
		16–17	255	*1 Samuel*	
32.8	33, 174	16.4	254	1.3	187
32.9	174	17.1	254	7.1	194
32.49	71	18	65, 78, 200, 203	9–10	136
33	30			16–18	37
34	73	18.1	187	30.27	206, 210
34.2	254	18.12-14	197		
		18.21-28	18, 105, 191, 193, 198, 203, 204, 347	*2 Samuel*	
Joshua				2.9-10	30
1.1-11	37			3.12	30
1.7	130			3.21	30
1.8	129	18.21-24	192, 201	5.1-3	63
4.24	33	18.21	200	5.5	31
8.31-32	129	18.22	194	5.11	53
8.31	129	18.23	203	5.12	31
8.34	129	18.24	203, 204	6.3	194
9.17b	195	18.28	194-96, 203, 204	6.20-21	31
10.40	200			7	268
11.2	200	19	78, 218	7.1-17	37
11.16	200	19.2-8	18, 105, 191, 347	7.11b-16	132
12.8	200			7.12-16	268
13	217, 218	19.8	206	7.13	132
13.17b-20	218	19.40-46	18, 105, 191, 347	7.16	132
13.27a	218			8.15	31
14.4	254	19.41-46	201, 219	9	31
15	65, 78, 199, 200, 204	21.45-47	105	15.13	30
		22.5	130	16.15	30
		23.6	129, 130	16.18	30
15.21-62	18, 105, 191, 198, 347	23.14	131	17.4	30
		24.15	250	17.14	30
		24.18	250	17.15	30
15.21	200	24.26	129	17.24	30
15.23	105, 196			19.23	31

2 Sam. (cont.)		8.49	37	2 Kings	
19.24-30	273	8.53	33	4.2	157
19.42-44	30	8.55-61	37	8.20	227
23.1-7	37	8.60	33	8.49-50	38
		9.1-9	267	9.27-28	229
1 Kings		9.4-5	268	10.29	75
1–11	177	9.4	128	11–12	135
1.34	31	9.15	177	12–13	145
1.35	31	9.26-28	177	12	135, 141
2	131	11.1-13	249	12.11b	135
2.2-4	129	11.4-8	158, 159	12.33	145
2.3-4	128, 130	11.5-8	150, 157	14.6	55, 129
2.3	129, 130	11.8	158	14.7	156
2.4	131, 268	11.13	186	15.10-15	252
3.1	53, 177	11.32	186	15.10	250
3.4	252	11.36	186	15.13-15	250
4.1	31	11.42	31	15.22	203
4.13	253	12–2 Kgs 17	30	16.2	53
5.5	177	12–13	146, 149, 251	16.3	249
5.13-14	177			16.4	158
6.29	157	12	11, 31	16.10-16	181
8	37, 73	12.19	251	17	250, 268, 319
8.1	37	12.20	251		
8.9	37, 130, 136	12.20b	251	17.2	250, 252
		12.25–13.34	75	17.2-4	41
8.12-13	188	12.33	149	17.3-6	319
8.13	268	13	144	17.7-8	252
8.14-30	37	13.2	149	17.7-8a	250
8.16	37, 186	13.32	144	17.9	250
8.23	73	14.16	252	17.11	158, 250
8.24-26	268	14.20	186	17.15	250, 251
8.25	73	14.24	249	17.16	251
8.32	37	15.3	53	17.17	250
8.33-34	37	16.8-10	250	17.18	251
8.34	37	16.17	298	17.19-20	251, 253
8.36	37	16.31-33	252	17.21-23	251, 252
8.39	37	16.32-33	251	17.24-34a	36
8.43	33, 37	16.34	227	17.24	203
8.44-53	37	18.19	37	17.31	203
8.44-45	37	21.1-20	37	18–23	29
8.44	37, 186	21.20-22	252	18–20	101, 267
8.45	37	21.26	250-52	18–19	134, 142, 319
8.46-53	37	22.29-36	228		
8.46-50	38	22.38	252	18	68
8.48	37, 130, 186	22.48	183	18.2	181
		22.49-50	177	18.3-8	134
8.49-50	38	22.51	53	18.3	53

18.4	156, 184, 288, 290	21.11-15	248, 251	22.2–23.27	14, 126
		21.11	175, 249, 252, 253	22.2-11	123
18.5-6	41			22.2	14, 15, 53, 79, 127, 128, 131, 132
18.5	128	21.12	175		
18.8	202	21.13	251		
18.9–19.37	128	21.16	52, 79, 175, 249, 254, 257, 258		
18.9-10	41, 134			22.2b	128, 130
18.13–19.37	41, 134			22.3–23.27	144
18.13-16	101			22.3–23.24	127, 128, 133, 148
18.17–19.9	4	21.17	79		
18.34	203	21.18	79, 175, 258	22.3–23.3	68, 297
19.2-7	138			22.3-20	15, 134, 141, 142
19.5-7	138	21.19-26	79		
19.13	203	21.19	79, 205	22.3-10	15, 135
20.12-19	271	21.20-22	79, 175	22.3-8	130
20.20	83	21.23-26	79	22.3-7	79, 107, 135, 141
20.21	175	21.23-24	189, 211		
21–25	78	21.26	258	22.3	15, 127, 128, 134-36, 214
21	17, 265, 269, 342	21.26-27	176		
		22–23	9-11, 14, 22, 28, 30, 37, 43, 55, 68, 69, 76, 107, 111, 123-27, 130-33, 141, 142, 149, 153, 158, 159, 186, 187, 281, 286, 291, 299, 343, 344, 346, 348	22.3b	146
21.1-18	20, 78, 103, 248, 265, 266			22.4-14	93
				22.4-10	149
				22.4-7	135
21.1-9	176			22.8-10	79, 136
21.1	78, 175			22.8	27, 30, 190, 280
21.2-9	78				
21.2-8	176			22.8a	136
21.3	175, 176, 249-52, 257			22.9-10	136
				22.9	136
21.5	175, 249, 250, 257			22.9a	135, 137
				22.10	135, 137
21.5b	150			22.10a	136
21.6	150, 175, 176, 249, 250	22	22, 69, 134, 135, 142, 280, 297	22.10b	129, 135, 138
				22.11-20	15, 79, 136, 141
21.7-8	252			22.11-13	143
21.7	186, 249, 253, 255, 257, 307	22.1–23.30	79, 126	22.11-12	134
		22.1–23.25	132	22.11	27, 30, 128, 129, 135, 136, 141, 190, 280
		22.1-23	15		
21.8	176	22.1-3	49, 79		
21.9	175, 249, 252	22.1-2	10, 299		
		22.1	14, 49, 79, 126, 189, 205		
21.10-16	176			22.11a	139, 141
21.10-15	41, 79, 249			22.12–23.4	123

2 Kgs (cont.)

22.12-20	135		279, 281, 287, 294, 297-300, 305, 307	23.5-8	155
22.12-13	135, 137			23.5	16, 145, 147, 148, 154-60, 298, 300, 301, 303-305
22.12	134, 135, 146, 148	23.1-24	15, 134, 143		
22.13-14	159				
22.13	139, 140	23.1-3	129, 143, 144	23.5a	144, 146, 147-50, 151, 159, 300
22.13a	137-40				
22.13b	132, 137-39	23.1	128, 134, 136, 141, 143		
22.14-20	48				
22.14	137	23.2-24	143	23.5b	149, 154, 159, 298
22.15-20	56, 138	23.2-6	152		
22.15-17	141	23.2-3	129, 143	23.6-15	145, 146
22.15	140	23.2	129, 190	23.6-12	16, 155
22.15a	140	23.2b	129, 143	23.6-10	154, 155
22.15b	140	23.3	72, 129, 131, 143	23.6-7	146, 148, 154
22.16-20	15				
22.16-17	37, 138, 139, 142	23.4-20	15, 22, 68, 144, 297	23.6	22, 145, 147, 154-57, 159, 160, 301, 306, 307
22.16	140	23.4-15	14-16, 123, 124, 138, 145-48, 150, 151, 153, 157, 159, 160		
22.16a	139, 140				
22.16b	129, 138			23.6a	138
22.17	132, 141, 158, 297, 298			23.7-8	301
				23.7	147, 154, 156, 157, 159, 160
22.17a	139, 149				
22.17b	138	23.4-11	156		
22.18-20	138	23.4-7	79, 257	23.7a	150
22.18	140	23.4-6	157	23.8-10	146, 147
22.18a	140	23.4-5	15, 16, 146, 154, 155, 158	23.8-9	79, 304
22.18b	139-41			23.8	16, 156, 158, 159, 203, 206, 217, 288
22.19	141, 142				
22.19a	132, 140, 141	23.4	93, 128, 134, 135, 143, 144, 147, 153, 154, 156, 157, 160, 308		
22.19b	140, 141			23.8a	10, 124, 146-49, 151, 159, 189, 281, 299, 300
22.20	126				
22.20a	15, 132, 140, 141				
22.20b-23	123				
22.20b	135, 137	23.4a	146, 147, 148, 149, 154, 156	23.8b	146, 148, 149, 154, 160, 300
22.21-24	297				
22.21-23	81				
22.25	15	23.4b	145, 146, 148, 155, 300	23.9	146-48, 150, 159
23	49, 75, 134, 144,			23.9a-b	304

Index of References

23.10-14	79	23.15	37, 139,		127, 144,
23.10	146, 154,		144, 145,		145, 148
	156, 157,		147, 149,	23.24b	15, 134,
	159, 160,		155-60		143-45
	298, 300,	23.15a	145, 149,	23.25-27	14, 41, 79,
	306		150		127
23.10a	148	23.15b	148, 153,	23.25	15, 52,
23.11-15	147		155, 156,		128-31,
23.11-12	154, 155,		300		134, 139,
	157, 158	23.16-20	15, 145,		141, 217,
23.11	146, 147,		146, 148		233
	153, 154,	23.16-18	37, 144	23.25a	10, 299
	156, 159,	23.16-17a	218	23.25b	299
	160, 298,	23.16	139, 144,	23.26-27	56, 128,
	300-302		218		131, 132,
23.11a	147, 150,	23.16a	144		138, 141,
	154	23.16b	144		248, 249,
23.11b	139, 154,	23.17	206		253
	156	23.18-20a	139	23.26	132, 139,
23.12-15a	146	23.18	139		153
23.12	22, 103,	23.19-20	37, 63, 79,	23.26b	141, 150
	145, 156,		144, 145,	23.27	132, 133,
	159, 298,		148, 149,		186, 187
	300, 305		218	23.28-30	10, 14, 19,
23.12a	143, 147,	23.19	68, 139,		79, 81,
	150, 154,		144, 145,		113, 126,
	160		218, 300		299
23.12b	138, 148,	23.19a	144, 145,	23.28b	159
	153, 154,		147, 149,	23.29-30	53, 189,
	160, 300		150		226, 343
23.13-15a	154	23.19b	144, 145	23.29	7, 66, 134,
23.13-15	16, 155	23.20	304, 218		227, 229
23.13-14	149, 154,	23.20a	145	23.30	140, 228
	155, 158	23.20b	144	23.31-35	228
23.13	145, 155-	23.21-24	68, 146	23.31-34	79
	57, 159,	23.21-23	15, 79,	23.31	79, 205
	160		143-46	23.32	79, 248
23.13a	147, 148,	23.21	128, 129,	23.33-34	79, 248
	150		134, 135,	23.35–24.7	79
23.13b	143		143, 146,	23.35	79
23.14-15	37		148, 190	23.36	79, 2050
23.14	156, 157,	23.22-23	143	23.37	52, 79,
	159, 160	23.23	15, 127,		248
23.14a	148, 300		134, 214	23.56	250
23.14b	148	23.24	79, 146	24	5
23.15-18	79, 203	23.24a	15, 37,	24.17-25	80

2 Kgs (cont.)		26.6-15	202	36.22-23	272
24.1–25.21	80	28.18	202	34.29-32	79
24.1-12	185	29.3	4	34.33	79
24.1-2	79	31.1	184	35.1-19	79, 81
24.1	227, 248	32.19	32	35.20-27	79, 81, 113
24.2	217	33.1–35.27	79		
24.3-4	79, 176, 248, 249, 253	33.1-20	17, 20, 78, 248, 256, 265, 268, 272, 342	35.20-24	7, 19, 66
				35.25	55
				36.1-3	79
24.4	52			36.1-2	79
24.5-6	80	33.1-10	176, 254	36.1	189
24.6	113	33.1	78	36.3	79
24.7	80	33.2-9	78	36.4-8	79
24.8-17	80	33.7	255	36.4	79
24.8	80	33.10-17	6, 81, 103, 113, 269	36.6-7	5, 80, 81, 113
24.9	80				
24.10-17	80	33.10-13	78	36.6	108
24.10	5	33.11-13	5	36.8	80
24.12-15	248	33.11	211, 342	36.9-10	80
24.18–25.30	48	33.12-20	253	36.9	80
24.18	80, 205	33.14-17	78	36.10	80
24.19-20	80, 248	33.14	81, 111, 176, 341	36.11-21	80
24.20	248			36.11	80
25	132, 133, 298	33.15	101	36.12	80
		33.18	79	36.13-21	80
25.14	308	33.19	79	36.15-16	177
25.23	93, 111, 206	33.20	79		
		33.21-25	79	Ezra	
25.25	94, 206	33.21	79	2	225
25.27-30	37-39, 132, 142	33.22-23	79	2.2	32
		33.22	103	2.5	32
27.27b	132	33.24-25	79	2.25	195
		34–35	279	2.33	220
1 Chronicles		34.1-3	49	2.59	32
2.44-45	199	34.1	79	2.70	32
4.21-23	205	34.2	79	3.1	32
4.21	205	34.3-7	18, 79, 81, 107, 112, 344	3.3	33
4.23	205			3.8	49
6.13	93, 111			4.1-4	81
7.23	225	34.3	49	4.2	112
8.12	225	34.6-7	219	4.9-10	81, 112, 212
8.13	225	34.8-13	79		
9.11	93, 111	34.14-18	79	6.21	32, 33
		34.19-28	79	6.22	59
2 Chronicles		35.20-24	189, 226, 228, 229, 343	7.1	93, 111
11.6-10	204			9.1	32, 33
23.24-27	49			9.2	33

10	34	13.24a	31	6.3a	179
10.2	33	13.26	31, 33	6.3b	179
10.11	33	13.28	256	6.3c	179
10.30	254	13.30a	31	6.3d	179
10.33	254			6.4a	179
		Esther		6.4b	179
Nehemiah		2.6	108	6.5a	179
1.1–7.5a	31			6.5b	179
1.2	32	*Psalms*		6.5c	179
1.6	31	8	341	6.5d	179
1.11	38	48	17, 182,	6.6a	179
2.10	31		183	6.6b	179
2.16	32	48.2	182	6.7a	179
3.9	199	48.3a	182, 183	6.7b	179
3.12	199	48.5-8	183	6.7c	179
3.33	32	48.5-7	183	6.7d	179
3.34	32	48.10-12	182	6.7e	179
4.6	32	48.15b	182	6.8a	179
5	35	49	182	6.8b	179
5.1	32	60	185	6.8b	179
5.8	32, 33	89.4	34	6.8ca	179
5.9	33	89.20	34	6.8d	179
5.17	32, 33	106.46	38	6.8e	179
6.6-7	35			6.9a	179, 180
6.6	32, 33	*Song of Songs*		6.9b	179
6.16	33	1.12	157	6.9c	179
7	225			6.9d	180
7.7	32	*Isaiah*		6.9e	180
7.1b	31	2.1	179	6.10a	180
7.29	195	5.19	32	6.10b	180
7.37	220	5.24	32	6.10c	180
9.2	32	6–8	17, 174,	6.10d	180
9.24	33		175, 341	6.10e	180
9.30	33	6	275	6.10f	180
9.32	59	6.1-10	174	6.10g	180
10	34	6.1	179	6.10h	180
10.1	34	6.1a	179	7–8	175
10.28-32	203, 204	6.1b	179	7.1a	180
10.29	33	6.1c	179	7.1b	180
10.31	33	6.1d	179	7.1c	180
12.21-32	31	6.1e	179	7.2a	180
12.37-40	31	6.2a	179	7.2b	180
13.1-2	11, 33	6.2b	179	7.2c	180
13.4-31	31	6.2c	179	7.3a	180
13.18	31	6.2d	179	7.4d	180
13.23	32	6.2e	179	7.4e	180

8.30	172	24.22	152	31.27-34	151		
9.7-24	152	25.1-21	80	31.31-34	131, 153		
11.1-17	48	25.1	48, 80	31.31-33	40		
11.3-8	7	25.2-3	51	31.35-37	57		
11.13	304	25.3	48	32–35	39		
11.17	304	25.5	151	32	131		
15.4	19, 103, 176, 254	25.6	298	32.1-2	80		
		25.7	139, 298	32.20	298		
15.15	152	26	48, 133	32.26-35	151		
16.12	152	26.1	48	32.29	304, 305		
17.26	200	26.2	109	32.35	306		
19.3	139	26.3	151	32.36-44	151		
19.4	139, 298	26.20	206	32.37-44	40		
19.5-6	306	26.24	35	32.37-41	40, 131		
19.11-13	306	27.1-6	8	32.38-40	153		
19.13	250, 305	27.18	308	32.41	131		
21.11–22.30	142	27.20	108	32.44	142, 200		
21.12	151	27.21-22	308	33.13	200		
22.11	48	28	48	34.4-5	140		
22.10-12	229	28.1	206	34.4	140		
22.13-19	51, 53, 140	28.16	138	34.6-7	109, 112		
		28.18-19	51	34.7	80, 206		
22.13-17	12, 51-53	29.2	108	35	48		
22.13	52	29.10-15	151	35.1	48		
22.15	68	29.10-14	39	36	134, 142		
22.15b	148, 151, 156	29.10	39	36.1	48		
		29.14	142	36.2-3	51		
22.17	52	29.14a	39	36.2	48, 138		
22.18-19	5, 52, 80, 81, 108	29.14b	39	36.9-26	35		
		29.24-32	206	36.9	48		
22.18	48, 52	29.16-20	151	36.10	111		
22.19	12	30–31	4, 40, 57, 131, 344	36.12	92, 94, 111		
22.24	108						
22.28	108	30.1-3	151	36.26	94		
22.29	142	30.3	28, 131, 142	36.30	5, 140		
23.1-8	133			37–40	134		
23.1-7	34	30.5-31	57	37	48		
23.2	151	30.18-22	40	37.1–40.6	142		
23.5-8	151	30.24	39	37.1	48, 108		
23.5-6	142	31.2-6	11, 28, 43, 68, 344	37.3-10	138, 142		
23.5b	151			37.3-9	138		
23.22	151	31.10-14	40	37.5-9	138		
24.4-7	151	31.14	206	37.11	80		
24.7	130	31.15-22	28	38.14	36		
24.8-10	151	31.21-22	40	38.19-23	140		
24.8b	151	31.23-26	40	38.61	92		
24.18	152	31.23	142	39.1	80		

Jer. (cont.)		50.17-20	40	4.13	158
39.2	80	50.33-34	40	5.12-14	42
39.3	80	51.34-37	40	10.5	147, 157,
39.4-7	80	51.58	40		303
39.8-10	80	52	5, 48	14.2	40
40–43	48	52.1	80		
40–41	92, 206	52.3-4	80	*Amos*	
40	95, 324	52.5-7	80	9.1	179
40.8	206	52.8-11	80		
40.14	93, 111	52.12-14	80	*Micah*	
41.4-7	324	52.31	108	1.10-16	204
41.1	94	52.58-30	80	5.1-5	34
41.5	36				
41.12	206	*Lamentations*		*Habakkuk*	
41.16	206	1	132	1.6-10	7
41.17	206	2	132		
42.12	38	3.40	40	*Zephaniah*	
43.8-13	80			1.1	48
44	16, 149,	*Ezekiel*		1.4-10	59
	151, 153,	1.2	108	1.4-6	58, 59,
	158, 159	8.7-18	43		254
44.1	151, 221	8.12	43	1.4	147, 157,
44.2-6	153	8.16	22, 302		303, 305
44.2	132, 153	16.21	306	1.5	250, 305
44.3	298	20.26	306	1.6	59
44.5	151, 298	20.31	306	1.7	59
44.6	132, 153	26–27	80	1.8-9	59
44.7-10	153	26.7	80	1.9	59
44.8	139, 298	29–30	80	1.12	59
44.10	153	29.8-16	80	2.4-15	57
44.12	140	29.17-20	81		
44.15	298	30.20-26	81	*Haggai*	
44.18	68	33.25	186	1.7-11	36
44.20-23	151	34.23-24	34		
44.21	149	37.15-22	28	*Zechariah*	
44.22-23	132, 151	37.24-28	60	5.5-11	307
44.22	140, 151	37.24-25	34	5.6	307
44.25	158			9.9-10	34
44.28	151	*Daniel*			
44.30	80	1.1-7	5	*Malachi*	
45.1	48	1.1-2	5, 81	2.16	32
46–47	80	1.9	38		
46.2	48, 80	4	81	*1 Esdras*	
46.9	215, 221			9.31	254
46.14	221	*Hosea*		9.33	254
48.13	186	2.15	158		

Index of References 363

New Testament		100.486	93	Lachish Seal	
John		100.827	93	6	92
4.20	186				
		Arad Ostraca		Nabopolassar Chronicle	
Talmuds		1–18	66	2: 10	98
b. Bat.		1	91	2: 15	98
109b	255	2	91	2: 7	98
		4	91	3: 24	98
b. Meg.		5	91	3: 38	98
14b	64	7	91	3: 40	98
		8	91	3: 45	98
b. Sanh.		10	91	3: 50	98
102b	253	11	91		
		14	91	Nin A V	
Roman and Classical		17	91	26-33 with	
Josephus				ABC 14, 21f.	168
Antiquities		Babylonian Chronicle 5		40	168
2.6.1	253	Obverse: 5	99	47	168
10.11.1 §§220-26	99	Obverse: 1	99	49	168
10.37-46	256	Obverse: 10	99	54	168
10.232	225	Obverse: 15	99	56	168
11.302-12	256	Obverse: 20	99	57	168
		Reverse: 5	99	58	168
Against Apion		Reverse: 10	99	59	168
1.14	213			60	168
1.136-37	225	British Museum		61	168
		Text K 1295	98	62	168
Herodotus				63	168
1.103-106	212	CoS		71	168
I.105	216	III 132-33	90	72	168
I.106	216			73	168
II.152	215, 221	Cylinder C		74	168
II.157	215	i–ii	97	75	168
				76	168
Papyri and Inscriptions		KAI		82	168
AHI		218	301		
2.3 ll. 3-4	288	225	303	Nin A VI	
4.301	297	226	303	1	168
15.5	296				
15.6	296	KTU		Prism A	
15.7	296	1.14 II 20-27	305	i	96
15.8	296	1.14 IV 3-8	305		
4201	295			Prism B	
100.108	93	Lachish Letters		v	96
100.149	92	4	91, 109	iv	96
100.277	93				

Prism C II		48	169	Psammetichus	
37	169	49	169	Inscription	
38	169	50	169	II 95–96	100
39	169	59	169		
40	169	60	169	Rassam Cylinder	
41	169	62	169	i–ii	97
42	169	63f.	169		
43	169	65	169	TSSI	
44	169	66f.	169	2 text # 21	90
45	169				
46	169	Prism E			
47	169	10, 13-21	168		

INDEX OF AUTHORS

Ackroyd, P.R. 55, 217, 233, 308, 309
Africa, T.W. 214, 233
Aharoni, M. 207, 223, 234, 238, 288, 309, 311
Aharoni, Y. 192, 194, 196, 199, 201, 203, 205-208, 214, 218-20, 223, 234, 292
Ahlström, G.W. 42, 44, 66, 76, 249, 257, 259, 282, 286, 298, 306, 309
Albertz, R. 11, 27, 30, 35, 36, 38-40, 42, 44, 65, 68, 70, 74-76, 107, 116, 123, 133, 135, 142, 154, 158, 161, 184, 281, 303, 309, 343, 349
Albright, W.F. 194, 208, 234
Alt, A. 191, 195, 199, 201, 203, 217-20, 226, 234, 255, 259, 284, 288, 292
Amaru, B.H. 254, 259
Amusin, J.D. 222, 234
Anderson, F.I. 258, 259
Ariel, D.T. 169, 171, 172, 179
Armayor, O.K. 214, 234
Arneth, M. 301, 304, 306, 309
Ash, P.S. 250, 259
Augustin, M. 228, 234
Auld, A.G. 192, 197, 234, 252, 259
Avi-Yonah, M. 214, 234
Avigad, N. 92-94, 116, 293, 294, 309
Ayalon, E. 207, 235

Bardtke, H. 218, 235
Barkay, G. 83, 94, 116, 199, 208, 209, 235, 296, 309, 320, 328, 329, 334
Barrick, W.B. 249, 251, 259, 280, 300, 304, 306, 309
Barstad, H. 325, 334, 340, 349
Barth, H. 42, 44, 214, 220, 235
Bauer, T. 228, 239
Baumgartner, W. 214, 235
Beck, P. 208, 235

Becker, U. 174, 175
Becking, B. 93, 94, 116
Begg, C.T. 226, 235
Beit-Arieh, I. 171, 207, 208, 210, 235
Ben Zvi, E. 12, 47, 50, 54, 61, 62, 248, 259, 341, 342, 349
Ben-Tor, A. 317, 334
Berjelung, A. 187
Berlin, A. 50
Bernett, M. 188
Beuken, W.A.M. 297, 309
Biran, A. 208, 210, 220, 235
Bird, P.A. 259
Bleibtreu, E. 302, 314
Blenkinsopp, J. 31, 44, 59, 61, 75, 76, 174, 326, 335
Boardman, J. 221, 235, 276
Boehmer, J. 227, 235
Boling, R.G. 264, 276
Bordreuil, P. 91, 116
Borger, R. 95, 117, 168, 215, 235, 305
Braiterman, Z. 275, 276
Brandfon, F.R. 284, 309
Braudel, F. 283, 284, 309
Braulik, G. 146, 161
Brettler, M.Z. 250, 259
Briend, J. 326, 334
Bright, J. 102, 103, 117
Brinkman, J.A. 212, 235, 271, 276
Broshi, M. 83, 117, 205, 208, 235
Brown, S.C. 214, 236
Brown, T.S. 214, 236

Cahill, J.M. 117, 208, 209, 236
Carroll, R.P. 51, 109, 110, 117, 254, 259
Cavaignac, E. 213, 236
Cazelles, H. 213, 216, 230, 236
Christensen, C.F. 50, 57

Claburn, W.E. 105, 117, 281, 310
Clements, R.E. 57, 219, 236
Cogan, M. 102, 103, 117, 203, 205, 211, 213-18, 221, 226-28, 236, 245, 249, 252, 254, 257-60, 302, 303, 310
Cohen, R. 86, 117, 208, 223, 224, 235, 236
Conrad, D. 287, 310
Coogan, M.D. 117, 310
Cook, S.L. 47
Coote, M. 284, 310
Cowley, A. 36, 44
Cresson, B.C. 208, 235
Cross, F.M., Jr 66, 76, 192, 193, 195, 201, 208, 211, 214, 219, 233, 236, 250, 256, 260, 267, 268, 276
Crüsemann, F. 135, 161

Davies, G. 67, 76
Davies, P.R. 13, 28-32, 34, 35, 42, 44, 83, 107, 120, 276
Day, J. 260
De Groot, A. 169, 171, 172
Dearman, J.A. 310
Deller, K. 302, 314
Demsky, A. 203, 205, 236
Deutsch, R. 293, 294, 303, 310
Dever, W.G. 280, 310, 325
Diakonoff, I.M. 214, 236
Dietrich, W. 31, 44, 251, 254, 260
Dion, P.-E. 223, 236, 334
Dobbs-Allsopp, F.W. 222, 236
Dothan, M. 223, 236

Edelman, D.V. 257, 260, 310
Eggler, J. 294, 311
Ehrlich, C.S. 166
Einykel, E. 280, 311
Elat, M. 104, 117
Elayi, J. 212, 236
Eph'al, I. 91, 117, 198, 211, 212, 229, 237
Eshel, H. 204, 209, 237
Evans, C.D. 249, 260
Exum, J.C. 117, 310

Fackenheim, E. 275, 276
Fantalkin, A. 87, 105, 117, 221, 223, 237
Fehling, D. 214, 237
Finkelstein, I. 27, 28, 42-44, 63, 71, 76, 82, 84-87, 101-103, 106, 117, 166-69, 177, 208, 235, 248, 255, 260, 271, 276, 317, 318, 322, 331, 333, 334, 341, 349
Fox, E. 255, 260
Frahm, E. 170
Frame, G. 174
Freedman, D.N. 211, 214, 219, 236, 258, 259
Freedy, K.S. 227, 237
Fried, L.E. 280, 281, 286, 287, 289, 292, 311
Fritz, V. 276
Frost, S.B. 237

Gal, Z. 205, 237
Galil, G. 63, 192-94, 196, 198, 199, 201, 205, 206, 237
Gallagher, W.R. 270, 276
Galling, K. 225, 237
Garbini, G. 72, 76
Garfinkel, Y. 93, 117, 198, 204, 237
Geller, S.A. 33, 44, 73, 76
Genette, G. 136, 161
Gerardi, P. 215, 237
Geus, C.H.J. de 253, 255, 260
Geva, H. 82, 83, 118
Gieselmann, B. 297, 311
Ginsberg, H.L. 205, 211, 219, 237
Gitin, S. 166, 224, 237, 238, 270, 277
Gogel, S.L. 87, 90-93, 118
Grabbe, L.L. 4, 14, 24, 68, 77, 83, 101, 109, 111, 113, 114, 118, 256, 260, 318, 319, 334, 340, 341, 349
Gray, J. 206, 238
Grayson, A.K. 95, 118, 228, 238, 270
Greenberg, R. 85, 118
Gressmann, H. 214, 238
Griffith, F.L. 100, 118
Grigson, C. 331, 335
Gross, W. 24, 44, 118, 161, 279, 311

Gunneweg, A.H.J. 31, 44
Gyles, M.F. 215, 216, 238

Habermas, J. 127, 161
Hachmann, R. 222, 238
Halpern, B. 211, 238, 248, 260
Handy, L.K. 40, 41, 45, 173, 184
Hanson, P.D. 313
Haran, M. 257, 260
Hardmeier, C. 37, 41, 45, 111, 124, 126, 127, 134, 136, 140, 142, 143, 148, 150, 152, 156, 161, 162, 175, 280, 297, 299, 311
Hayes, J.H. 42, 45, 66, 77, 105, 120, 211, 213, 216, 220, 223, 225, 228, 241, 261, 271, 277
Helck, W. 222, 226, 227, 238
Heltzer, M. 43, 45, 222, 234, 293, 309, 310
Hendel, R.S. 118
Heron, G.A. 85, 119
Herr, L.G. 93, 118
Herzog, Z. 85, 118, 172, 184, 185, 223, 238, 287-90, 311
Hjelm, I. 281, 311
Hobbs, T.R. 251, 261
Höfner, M. 172
Hoffmann, H.-D. 123, 126, 128, 135, 138, 140, 145, 162, 299-301, 311
Holladay, J.S. 286, 287, 311, 321, 332, 335
Holladay, W.L. 52, 59, 215, 238
Hollenberg, J. 196, 238
Hollenstein, H. 299, 300, 308, 311
Holmes, S. 194, 238
Hölscher, G. 27, 34, 45, 69, 77
Horowitz, A. 171
Houtman, C. 257, 261
Hübner, U. 222, 238
Humbert, J.-B. 326, 334
Hurowitz, V. 187
Hyatt, J.P. 49, 214, 238

Israel, F. 91, 116
Isserlin, B.S.J. 206, 238

James, T.G.H. 110, 119, 270
Jamieson-Drake, D.W. 340, 349
Japhet, S. 219, 225, 238, 249, 261, 268, 269, 277
Jarick, J. 253, 261
Jepsen, A. 214, 238
Johnstone, W. 253, 261

Kaiser, O. 27, 43, 45, 65, 69, 77, 174
Kallai, Z. 192-94, 196, 197, 199, 201, 203, 204, 218-20, 225, 239
Kallai-Kleinmann, Z. 192, 197, 239
Kammenhuber, A. 213, 239
Karrer, C. 31, 45
Katzenstein, H.J. 212, 221, 226, 227, 239
Kautzsch, E. 187
Keel, O. 95, 119, 154, 162, 188, 287, 297, 311
Kellermann, U. 31, 45
Kelly, B.E. 249, 261
Kessler, R. 124, 162
Keulen, P.S.F. van 252, 257, 261, 267, 277
Kienitz, F.K. 221, 239
Killebrew, A.E. 82, 119, 122
Kingsbury, E.C. 255, 261
Kitchen, K.A. 215, 239
Kleer, M. 222, 239
Klein, R.W. 193, 203, 239
Kletter, R. 63, 87, 88, 105, 119, 171, 172, 204, 209, 239, 312
Kluger, R.A. 47
Knapp, D. 131, 162
Knauf, A. 15, 83, 84, 86, 89, 101, 107, 119, 166, 169, 170, 173, 174, 176, 177, 179, 182, 184-86, 202, 239, 282-85, 290, 312
Knoppers, G.N. 54
Koch, K. 123, 135, 162, 300, 303, 312
Kochavi, M. 199, 206, 239
Kröger, M. 222, 239
Küchler, M. 287, 311, 312
Kuhrt, A. 119, 270, 272, 277
Kuschke, A. 203, 239

Laato, A. 282, 287, 312
Labat, R. 213, 239
Lambert, W.G. 275, 277
Lamon, R.S. 335
Landsberger, B. 228, 239
Lasine, S. 249, 251, 261
Lemaire, A. 36, 45, 205-208, 210, 221-23, 239, 240, 255, 261, 293, 294, 296, 309, 310, 312
Lemche, N.P. 277
Lemke, W.E. 228, 240
Levin, C. 123, 124, 138, 162, 187, 281, 299, 301, 304, 312
Levine, B.A. 258, 261
Levy, T. 317, 335
Lewy, H. 214, 240
Lewy, J. 228, 240
Lipschits, O. 83, 85, 86, 119, 166, 225, 240, 326, 335, 340, 349
Liver, J. 203, 205, 214, 218-20, 226, 240
Liverani, M. 6, 24, 339, 341-44, 346, 349, 350
Lloyd, A.B. 214, 240
Loewenstamm, S.E. 213, 223, 240
Lohfink, N. 58, 70, 77, 107, 119, 123, 135, 142, 162, 280, 281, 297, 298, 305, 306, 312, 313
Long, B.O. 109, 119, 251, 261
Long, V.P. 4, 6, 24
Longman, T., III 4, 6, 24
Lopasso, V. 313
Lorton, D. 227, 240
Lowery, R.H. 252, 257, 261, 282, 305, 313

Magness, J. 220, 246
Malamat, A. 211, 213, 216, 218, 220, 223, 225, 229, 230, 233, 240
Manor, D.W. 85, 119
Mazar, A. 88, 119, 209, 240, 264, 289, 313, 317, 319, 321, 328, 329, 331, 335
Mazar, B. 192, 241, 335
Mazar (Maisler), B. 194, 201, 203, 241
Mazar, E. 224, 241
McBride, S.D. 313

McCarter, P.K. 303, 313
McCown, Ch. 326, 335
McKane, W. 51, 52, 110, 119
McKay, J.W. 102, 119, 206, 241, 257, 261
Mendelsohn, I. 208, 241
Meulenaere, H. de 214, 216, 221, 226, 241
Meyers, E.M. 120
Milgrom, J. 58, 218, 230, 241, 258, 261
Millard, A.R. 213, 241, 275, 277
Miller, J.M. 42, 45, 66, 77, 105, 120, 211, 213, 216, 220, 223, 225, 228, 241, 261, 271, 277
Miller, P.D. 313
Mittmann, S. 208, 241
Mommsen, H. 204, 205, 208, 241
Montgomery, J.A. 206, 227, 241
Moore, G.F. 255, 261
Morschauser, S.N. 227, 241
Moshkovitz, S. 223, 238, 288, 311
Mosis, R. 214, 242, 249, 262
Mowinckel, S. 45, 110, 120
Mullen, T.E. 252, 262
Müller, H.-P. 296, 313
Mykytiuk, L.J. 92, 94, 95, 120

Na'aman, N. 18, 29, 42, 45, 62, 63, 65-67, 77, 83, 86-89, 103, 105, 108, 120, 170, 189, 192, 194, 196, 197, 200-202, 204, 205, 207, 208, 210, 214, 215, 220, 222, 224-27, 232, 242, 287, 289-91, 295, 300, 313
Nadelman, Y. 209, 242
Nahman, A. 116
Nakhai, B.A. 286, 313
Naumann, Th. 31, 44
Naveh, J. 91, 117, 198, 220-22, 237, 242
Nelson, R.D. 34, 35, 39, 40, 45, 214, 228, 230, 242, 252, 262, 267, 277
Netzer, E. 289, 313
Nicholson, E.W. 214, 242
Niehr, H. 9, 24, 42, 45, 86, 107, 120, 124, 162, 279, 281, 313, 339-41, 343-45, 350

Index of Authors

Nielsen, E. 254, 262
Niemann, H.M. 124, 158, 162, 166, 339, 340, 350
Niemeier, W.-D. 220, 221, 223, 242
Nissinen, M. 178
Norin, S. 120
North, R. 211, 243
Noth, M. 37, 45, 193, 195, 196, 200, 201, 211, 218, 219, 227, 243, 255, 262, 264, 277, 292

Oates, J. 95, 120
Oded, B. 212, 243, 254, 262
Oestreicher, T. 214, 243
Ofer, A. 82, 84, 120
Ogden, G.S. 218, 243
Oppenheim, A.L. 212, 226, 243
Oren, E.D. 221, 243
Orlinsky, H.M. 196, 243
Ornan, T. 294, 313
Otto, E. 186
Otzen, B. 214, 221, 226, 227, 243

Pardee, D. 91, 116, 222, 243
Parpola, S. 178
Paul, M.J. 280, 313
Perdue, L.G. 48
Perlman, I. 204, 205, 208, 241
Person, R.F., Jr 37, 39, 45
Petrie, W.M.F. 221, 243
Pfeifer, G. 227, 243
Pongratz-Leisten, B. 302, 314
Porten, B. 221, 243
Porter, B.N. 174
Preuss, H.D. 123, 163, 297, 314
Proksch, O. 201, 214, 217-19, 243
Provan, I. 4, 6, 24
Pury, A. de 264, 277

Rad, G. von 219, 243, 273, 277
Rainey, A.F. 223, 238, 243, 262, 280, 287, 288, 311, 314, 332, 335
Redford, D.B. 226, 227, 237, 244, 270, 272, 277
Rehm, M. 254, 258, 262
Reich, R. 83, 120, 172, 220, 244
Reinmuth, T. 31, 46

Renz, J. 32, 46, 172, 206, 244, 295, 296, 314
Reuter, E. 282, 287, 314
Roberts, J.J. 49
Röllig, W. 32, 46, 172
Römer, T.C. 37, 38, 46, 264, 277
Rofé, A. 37, 46, 218, 244
Rogerson, J. 83, 120
Rollston, C.A. 92, 120
Rose, M. 257, 262
Rösel, H. 273, 277
Rowlett, L.L. 264, 278
Rowley, H.H. 48, 213, 244
Rudolph, W. 31, 46, 214, 225, 244
Rütersworden, U. 35, 46, 222, 244

Sass, B. 92-94, 116, 120, 293, 294, 297, 309, 314
Sasson, V. 222, 244
Schenker, A. 279, 298, 300, 304, 305, 314
Schmid, K. 39, 46
Schmidt, B.B. 257, 262
Schmitt, G. 197, 244
Schniedewind, W.M. 249, 251, 262
Schoors, A. 126, 163
Schroer, S. 302, 314
Schunck, K.D. 201, 203, 244
Seeligman, I.L. 233, 244
Seidl, U. 302, 314
Sellar, W.C. 169
Shanks, H. 335
Shiloh, Y. 92, 120, 293, 314, 335
Shipton, G.M. 335
Shoham, Y. 92, 120, 121, 293, 314
Shukron, E. 83, 120, 172
Sigrist, R.M. 212, 244
Silberman, N.A. 27, 28, 42-44, 63, 71, 76, 82, 86, 87, 101-103, 106, 117, 168, 248, 260, 317, 318, 322, 331, 333, 334
Singer-Avitz, L. 166, 170, 184, 290, 314
Smelik, K.A.D. 67, 77, 262
Smirin, S. 203, 205, 211, 214, 218-20, 226, 244
Smith, M. 252, 262
Smith, M.S. 257, 262

Isa. (cont.)		8.23–9.6	11, 57,	2.3	152
7.5	180		343	2.4–4.2	11, 42, 43
7.6a	180	8.23b–9.6	42	2.4	42
7.6b	180	9	175	2.5-7a	152
7.6c	180	10.16-19	61	2.6-7	152
7.6d	180	11.1–12.6	61	2.6	152
7.7a	180	11.1-5	34	2.7-13	152
7.7b	180	11.11-16	28	2.7	152
7.7c	180	14.24-27	61	2.7a	152
7.14b	180	17.12-14	61	2.14-18	42
7.14c	180	18.1-6	174	2.15	42
7.14d	180	19.1-17	174	2.16-18	42
7.15	180	19.22	40	2.16	42
7.16a	180	28–31	175	2.18-19	152
7.16b	180	28.23-29	61	2.18	215
7.17	11, 31	29.5-8	61	2.32	152
8.1a	180, 181	29.8	61	2.35	152
8.1b	180	30.11	32	2.36-37	42, 152
8.1d	181	30.12	32	2.36	152
8.2a	181	30.15	32	3.6-11	49, 50
8.3a	181	30.27-33	57, 61	3.6	48, 50
8.3b	181	31.1	32	3.12-13	50
8.3c	181	31.5	61	3.14-18	50
8.3d	181	31.8-9	61	3.19-25	50
8.3e	181	32.1-5	61	3.22–4.2	11, 43,
8.4a	181	32.15-20	61		344
8.4b	181	36–39	47, 183	4.3–6.30	11, 43
8.9-10	61	39	271	4.4	40, 151
8.11a	181	40.1-2	39	4.5	152
8.11b	181	65.3	158	4.8	152
8.12a	181	65.7	158	4.9-10	152
8.12b	181			4.14	152
8.12c	181	*Jeremiah*		4.18	152
8.12d	181	1–51	40	5.4-6	11, 43,
8.13a	181	1–45	39		344
8.13b	181	1.1-3	50	5.15	152
8.13c	181	1.2	48, 138	6.1	206
8.14	181	1.3	48	6.6-9	152
8.15a	181	1.4-10	58	6.10-15	152
8.15b	181	1.16	139, 298	7	133
8.15c	181	2–6	16, 43,	7.9	304
8.15d	181		152	7.31-32	306
8.15e	181	2–4	4, 344	8.1-2	250
8.16a	181	2	58, 152	8.7-18	152
8.16b	181	2.2-3	152	8.7-8	11, 43, 68,
8.17	31	2.2	152		344

Soggin, J.A. 201, 244, 254, 262
Spalinger, A. 211, 213, 215, 221, 226, 244, 245, 270, 278
Spieckermann, H. 103, 121, 123, 163, 211, 218, 220, 226, 227, 233, 245, 257, 262, 300-305, 315
Spycket, A. 212, 245
Stager, L.E. 117, 270, 278, 310
Starr, I. 302, 315
Staubli, T. 172
Stavrakopoulou, F. 19, 24, 253, 256, 263
Steck, O. 251, 263
Steiner, M. 82, 121
Stern, E. 82, 84, 86, 88, 102, 121, 220, 245, 330, 335
Stern, M. 225, 245
Steuernagel, C. 194, 196, 245
Steymans, H.U. 34, 46, 186
Stipp, H.-J. 131, 139, 140, 142, 149, 151, 157, 158, 163
Strange, J. 192, 220, 245
Suzuki, Y. 222, 245
Swanson, K.A. 287, 315
Sweeney, M. 3, 4, 20, 24, 49-51, 57, 58, 61, 65, 69, 77, 249-52, 263, 265, 267, 270, 271, 273, 275, 278, 280, 298, 315, 342, 344, 350

Tadmor, H. 203, 205, 213-17, 220, 221, 226-28, 236, 245, 252, 260
Tagliacarne, P. 299, 300, 304, 315
Talmon, S. 200, 245
Tarler, D. 92, 120, 293, 314
Tatum, L. 82, 121, 249, 263
Taylor, J.G. 301, 305, 315
Thiel, W. 138, 163
Thompson, T.L. 255, 263, 278
Tigay, J.H. 258, 263
Toloni, G. 280, 315
Tov, E. 37, 46, 255, 263

Uehlinger, C. 9, 21, 24, 43, 46, 84-86, 95, 107, 111, 119-21, 124, 125, 154, 158, 162, 163, 187, 279, 280, 282, 293-95, 307, 312, 314, 315

Ussishkin, D. 85, 86, 93, 121, 169, 207, 209, 223, 245, 288, 289, 315, 341, 350

Vaggione, R.P. 214, 245
Vaughn, A.G. 82, 88, 92, 94, 121, 170, 204, 209, 245
Veijola, T. 36, 46
Vermeylen, J. 57
Vernus, P. 240
Višaticki, K. 226, 246
Vlaardingerbroek, J. 49, 59
Von Soden, W. 300, 315
Vos, J.C. de 193, 246
Vriezen, K.J.H. 195, 246

Waldbaum, J.C. 220, 246
Wampler, J.C. 326, 335
Warburton, D. 23
Weidner, E.F. 100, 122
Weinfeld, M. 73, 77, 257, 263, 282, 302, 315
Weippert, H. 284, 286, 287, 295, 315, 317, 325, 329, 335
Weippert, M. 173, 222, 246, 284, 286, 300, 315
Weitzman, S. 255, 256, 263
Welch, A.C. 227, 229, 246
Wellhausen, J. 211, 246, 269, 278
Welten, P. 201, 202, 208, 209, 218, 220, 229, 246
Wenham, G.J. 253, 263
Whitelam, K.W. 284, 310, 315
Widengren, G. 256, 263
Wieder, A.A. 51
Wilcoxen, J. 271, 278
Wilke, F. 213, 214, 216, 246
Willi, Th. 173
Williams, D. 49
Williamson, H.G.M. 31, 46, 197, 206, 211, 219, 225, 226, 228, 246, 249, 253, 263, 271, 278
Wilson, J.A. 214, 246
Wiseman, D.J. 212, 215, 223, 228, 246, 257, 263
Wolff, H.W. 274, 275, 278
Wright, G.E. 192, 193, 196, 201, 236

Würthwein, E. 37, 46, 69, 75, 77, 299, 300, 308, 315

Yadin, Y. 201, 247, 292
Yardeni, A. 297, 315
Yeatman, R.J. 169
Yeivin, S. 205, 247
Yellin, J. 204, 205, 208, 241
Yisrael, Y. 86, 117
Yoyotte, J. 226, 229, 247

Zadok, R. 203, 242
Zawadzki, S. 214, 215, 247
Zenger, E. 182
Zertal, A. 255, 263
Zevit, Z. 286, 287, 292, 296, 315
Zimhoni, O. 191, 207, 247, 289, 315
Zwickel, W. 281, 282, 290, 315